Community Psychology

Foundations for Practice

Victoria C. Scott
University of South Carolina

Susan M. Wolfe
Susan Wolfe and Associates, LLC

Los Angeles | London | New Delhi
Singapore | Washington DC | Boston

Los Angeles | London | New Delhi
Singapore | Washington DC

FOR INFORMATION:

SAGE Publications, Inc.
2455 Teller Road
Thousand Oaks, California 91320
E-mail: order@sagepub.com

SAGE Publications Ltd.
1 Oliver's Yard
55 City Road
London EC1Y 1SP
United Kingdom

SAGE Publications India Pvt. Ltd.
B 1/I 1 Mohan Cooperative Industrial Area
Mathura Road, New Delhi 110 044
India

SAGE Publications Asia-Pacific Pte. Ltd.
3 Church Street
#10-04 Samsung Hub
Singapore 049483

Acquisitions Editor: Reid Hester
Editorial Assistant: Lucy Berbeo
Production Editor: Bennie Clark Allen
Copy Editor: Kris Bergstad
Typesetter: C&M Digitals (P) Ltd.
Proofreader: Sarah J. Duffy
Indexer: Julie Grayson
Cover Designer: Bryan Fishman
Marketing Manager: Shari Countryman

Copyright © 2015 by SAGE Publications, Inc.

Printed in the United States of America.

A catalog record of this book is available from the Library of Congress.

ISBN 978-1-4522-7868-1

This book is printed on acid-free paper.

14 15 16 17 18 10 9 8 7 6 5 4 3 2 1

Brief Contents

Contents

2   Guiding Principles and Competencies for Community Psychology Practice   35

Maurice J. Elias, William D. Neigher, and Sharon Johnson-Hakim

3   Understanding Ecological Systems   63

Stephen P. Stelzner and Richard M. Wielkiewicz

4 Effecting Social Change in Diverse Contexts: The Role of Cross-Cultural Competency

Kien S. Lee

7   Organizational and Community Capacity Building   189

Scotney Evans, Catherine Raymond, and Douglas D. Perkins

8   Community Organizing   220

Paul W. Speer and Brian D. Christens

9   Building and Strengthening Collaborative Community Partnerships   237

Judah J. Viola, Bradley D. Olson, Suzette Fromm Reed, Tiffeny R. Jimenez, and Christina M. Smith

10 Advocacy and Social Justice   262

Leonard A. Jason, Christopher R. Beasley, and Bronwyn A. Hunter

11　Planning, Implementing, and Developing Evidence-Based Interventions in the Context of Federally Funded Programs　290

Richard A. Jenkins

14   Community Psychology Education and Practice Careers in the 21st Century   379

Susan D. McMahon, Tiffeny R. Jimenez, Meg A. Bond, Susan M. Wolfe, and Allen W. Ratcliffe

15   A Vision for Community Psychology Practice   410

Bill Berkowitz and Victoria C. Scott

Foreword

One of the aspirations and motivational drives of community psychology, since its emergence as a distinct field, is that the historical dichotomy between research and practice could be reduced and perhaps even evaporated.

The nature of the work of community psychology is that every undertaking of inquiry includes premises about the practice steps taken or about to be taken given the unique life experiences, needs, and constraints affecting the collaborating citizens. The emerging point of view is: Attention and care must be expressed about the local conditions of informants and their need to be full partners in any community psychology expedition. These processes of creating a shared point of view for conceptions of research and practice have been evolving during the past 50 years.

This book illustrates that the field is in the midst of a new framing of scientific work to illustrate how research and practice together can in fact adapt to the needs and constraints of informants and participants. A long-standing notion for thinking about revising research methods is to enhance theoretical predictions or enhance the fidelity of research procedures. In contrast, practices are revised based on community needs, hopes, and aspirations for an improved life. The interdependence of research and practice now suggests that there are new opportunities to renew working relationships among community psychologists and citizens who are no longer subjects but co-participants.

The editors have served as our ambassadors and conveners of the positive contributions to be reported here.

The summaries of the various efforts of merging methods for practice and research presented in the book help to sort out the underlying points of view current in the field about the balance between a methodological focus and new forms of practice. In addition, these total contributions together with the two closing chapters are guideposts for the continuing evolution of the integration of research and practice in community psychology. Take a look.

In Chapter 1, Tom Wolff, Carolyn Swift, and Sharon Johnson-Hakim illustrate the difficulties in the past of realizing such challenging goals as the interdependence of research and practice. To some, making this shift so that practice is considered an equal partner and interdependent with research has been viewed as tedious, contentious, and uphill.

A Society for Community Research and Action (SCRA) committee proposed competencies for community psychologists that were accepted several years ago and have contributed to increased awareness of the interdependence between research and practice (SCRA, 2012). In my view, we are now seeing more evidence of at least parallel efforts, if not interdependence, between these previously contrasting traditions. For example, the recent presentation by Tebes, Thai, and Matlin (2014) on 21st-century science suggests we are making genuine progress! The presence of research teams rather than solo investigators could potentially be opportunities to share goals, with more occasions to examine the process of the work *and* activate the next integrated stages of the collaborations.

In Chapter 2, Maurice J. Elias, William D. Neigher, and Sharon Johnson-Hakim discuss the emerging process of developing competencies for community psychology practice. The chapter explicitly brings into focus the skills and competences that overlap practice and research, for example, professional roles that embrace both research skills (survey research methods) and practice skills (community organizing). Included in the chapter is reference to the work published in 1984 by Elias, Dalton, Franco, and Howe, who proposed suggestions where professional roles can contribute to the interdependence of practice and research. The 18 competences presented by the SCRA in 2012 in *The Community Psychologist* appear in Table 2.1 of Chapter 2 in this book.

In Chapter 3, Stephen P. Stelzner and Richard M. Wielkiewicz present an ecological perspective. This perspective holds promise to integrate research and practice in community psychology. By including examples, such as the physical relocation of an elementary school, they suggest concrete ways on how thinking ecologically can provide insights for solving community problems as well as suggest topics for further investigation. They appraise various proponents of ecological thinking and illuminate how these ideas are helpful in thinking about how to assess the potential of various collaborative styles between citizens and research investigators. Topics such as diversity in community leadership and community adaptations to externally influenced change are useful agendas to illustrate the process. In this chapter the authors provide a useful guide to ecological approaches by Barker, Bronfenbrenner, Trickett, myself, and others. These ideas and concepts are presented as useful guides to enable the practice or research to be interdependent with the local community.

Kien S. Lee in Chapter 4 presents a very revealing portrait of being a community psychologist who might not share demographic attributes with community members. Lee presents practical suggestions to reduce anxiety in the individual professional by not pressing hard to locate differences between the host community and the professional. This is done by articulating similarities between cultural groups in contrast to differences. This process note for the community psychologist is helpful to activate a listening and learning role in the early explorations for both community psychologists and citizens. Throughout the chapter there is wisdom for the unfolding of research and practice roles. A welcome addition!

Michael Morris in Chapter 5 contributes an informed, well-documented review of the ethical challenges community psychologists address in the day-to-day activities of professional work. He begins with an example of conducting an evaluation of an extended-day homework assistance program in a local school program in three elementary schools. The program had positive impact on the homework completion but did not lead to higher grades. The superintendent wants the researcher to downplay these latter results. With this situation, Morris gets down to brass tacks with ethical dilemmas. Topics include the development of competences in ethics, review of ethical topics in the community psychology literature, and definitions and strategies for developing ethical competence. There are practical suggestions such as keeping an "ethics journal" and using the SCRA listserv to raise issues and questions. The chapter summary includes discussion questions, key terms, readings, websites, and a self-exploration worksheet. An incisive and constructive challenge for the reader and the field.

In Chapter 6, Jomella Watson-Thompson, Vicki Collie-Akers, Nikki Keene Woods, Kaston D. Anderson-Carpenter, Marvia D. Jones, and Erica L. Taylor introduce us to participatory approaches for conducting community needs and resources assessments. The reports of increased knowledge that have been obtained can provide a consensus for continued community development. A priority is given to ethical dimensions (e.g., the essential topics of confidentiality, consent, and conflicts of interest). These dimensions point to whose interests are being served and who has the power to affect change. This chapter focuses upon the nitty-gritty of community practice. The chapter also presents a useful list of apt competences. The authors' strategies for developing ethical competence are very salient. The reader also may be stimulated by completing the Self-Exploration Worksheet.

Scotney Evans, Catherine Raymond, and Douglas D. Perkins introduce us to the topics of organizational and community capacity building in Chapter 7. Their particular focus is nonprofit organizations, especially salient for the work of community psychologists. This process involves enlarging collaborative skills with access to community resources in order to further their influence with others. It is a self-conscious program to elevate the position of influence of the community psychologist. Community organizing efforts to improve the organizations' influence and status become the goal. Networks, coalitions, and alliances are proposed as apt ways to create network and interorganizational structures. Investing in community capacity building is the emphasis.

Paul W. Speer and Brian D. Christens inform us about community organizing in Chapter 8. An opening exercise illustrates that a middle-aged homeowner files a third claim for repairs for his house as a result of three different environmental blows to his house. While community organizing is practiced by many community psychologists, the stories about the successes and struggles do not always reach the readers of professional journals. It is a method that has an earned history for those members of a community affected by imposed loss of dignity and loss of resources. Saul Alinsky and Paulo Freire are cited as pioneer advocates, along with Roger Barker and colleagues as a major influences with their many decades of research on social settings. In addition, listening and clarifying self-interests are cited as essential skills as well as intra- and interorganizational empowerment.

Judah J. Viola, Bradley D. Olson, Suzette Fromm Reed, Tiffeny R. Jimenez, and Christina M. Smith in Chapter 9 offer a very important discussion on building and strengthening collaborative partnerships. Their opening exercise focuses on a local museum. Using this brief description they present a case to illustrate shared power and collaboration in decision making. The details of their presentation not only enhance their own presentation, but reinforce that of many other chapters in the book. The chapter is an excellent orientation and rationale not only for doing community collaborative work, but also for being a community psychologist. The authors provide concrete examples, drawing the reader into the evolutionary process of their own work. Being model mentors, they provide advice and list other resources to provide support along the way of the community psychology expedition.

Leonard A. Jason, Christopher R. Beasley, and Bronwyn A. Hunter comment on the topics of advocacy and social justice in Chapter 10. This chapter provides a backbone rationale that underlies the premises presented earlier, including in Chapters 4, 6, 7, and 8. The chapter presents an elegant rationale for activist, public positions to help citizens address wrongs and create the possibility that justice can be achieved and preserved. The authors believe in earnest that Margaret Mead's dictum "Never doubt that a small group of thoughtful committed citizens can change the world; indeed it's the only thing that ever has" is still alive, vital, and does benefit people. Advocacy includes lobbying, which usually has a negative image, of those alliances with groups in power who wish to retain power. The authors cite the commandments of Mooney and Van-Dyke Brown as resources when lobbying is generated with values for fairness, decency, and integrity—a new take on the negative connotative meanings of lobbying. The chapter concludes with examples of two real-world uses of advocacy: chronic fatigue syndrome and addiction recovery.

Richard A. Jenkins presents in Chapter 11 evidence-based interventions (EBIs) via federally funded programs. The practice knowledge of stakeholders and stakeholders' needs has been a priority in building a grant proposal. The aspects of the planning process emerge as another significant component, especially the role of citizen advisory groups and how much the grant proposal has integrated their needs. Will the community groups have a key role in the continued work of the project throughout the tenure of the grant? Window dressing has been replaced by vital and substantial roles in the life of the grant. Addressing gaps in terms of unmet needs becomes a priority. With the above goals met, the strategic plan takes on more authenticity and impact. One of the positive benefits of the research process is expansion of local data archives, which, in turn, provide local communities with an increased capacity to establish their own monitoring organization. This is a major positive side effect of having a federal grant program.

David M. Fetterman in Chapter 12 presents a method that has been available for more than two decades. His ten principles are presented with clear recognition of the practice components in employing the empowerment evaluation approach. Among the ten principles, other topics integral to practice interests are community ownership, inclusion, democratic participation, community knowledge, and more. Three features of empowerment evaluation are noted as especially akin to the values of those who are invested in practice: inclusion, capacity building, and, of course, empowerment. The chapter includes a variety of resources for more information. There also is a brief example of a tobacco intervention in Arkansas.

Chapter 13, co-authored by Susan M. Wolfe, Louis G. Tornatzky, and Benjamin C. Graham, attends to two basic questions that require knowledge and insights: how knowledge is disseminated and how it achieves staying power. The authors extend the contributions of Rogers, Havelock, and Fairweather from years past. Concepts like implementation and diffusion become the focus. Constructs like gatekeepers are salient. The current work of Abe Wandersman and colleagues is featured, calling attention to the systems that support those who implement innovations along with other essential components. Jen Sandler's emphasis on structural constraints that reduce implementation become part of the effort. More scholars are cited to add clarity to the institutionalizing innovations. The chapter also includes topics on education for the roles of implementing innovation and draw upon classic work such as the Fairweather Community Lodge and Healthy Start. There are multiple resources cited throughout the text and websites. The chapter is a dossier of wisdom.

Chapter 14, co-authored by Susan D. McMahon, Tiffeny R. Jimenez, Meg A. Bond, Susan M. Wolfe, and Allen W. Ratcliffe, is an appraisal of careers in education and practice in the 21st century. The focus is on the challenges faced for careers in community psychology practice at the undergraduate, master's, and doctoral levels. The range of educational options described is international! Two groups within the field of community psychology—the SCRA Council of Educational Programs and the SCRA Practice Council—are stimulating more discussions and educating the field to be more aware of practice-oriented community psychology careers in local, state, and federal programs. Community psychologists more and more are being recognized for their practice skills and roles in such venues as health care, nonprofit agencies, education, all levels of government, community planning, criminal justice, foundations, research and development firms, business and technology, and academic settings. The chapter ends with strategies for locating careers. In future years the reader may see that careers for community psychologists are known in such venues as national and international relief organizations, cross-national movements, and idea incubation centers.

Chapter 15 presents a vision for community psychology practice by Bill Berkowitz and Victoria C. Scott. It is presented as the personal story of a community psychologist going back to his or her hometown after ten years and discovering and rediscovering qualities of places, people, and activities that enabled the community psychologist to do this work. In a neighborly, supportive way the writers model their practice skills and bring the reader along as a companion on their journey. The authors then critique their own path. Was it desirable, practical, feasible, and achievable? This journey is constructive, personable, and achievable. A refreshing, endearing, and motivating closure to the book.

It is my personal hope that these comments have encouraged you to begin your reading of this book. The contents are current, with advanced thinking embedded in them. The editors and authors have taken the request seriously to focus on the reader with respect and with a desire that you, the reader, will in turn contribute to the continued expeditions of community psychology with spirit, élan, and the commitment presented in these pages. I have enjoyed adding new understandings for myself as I read the chapters.

James G. Kelly

Seattle, WA

REFERENCES

Elias, M. J., Dalton, J. H., Franco, R., & Howe, G. W. (1984). Academic and nonacademic community psychologists: An analysis of divergence in settings, roles and values. *American Journal of Community Psychology, 12,* 281–302.

Society for Community Research and Action, Practice Council and Council on Education Programs. (2012). Draft: Competences for community psychology practice. *The Community Psychologist, 45*(4),8–14.

Tebes, J. K., Thai, N. D., & Matlin, S. L. (2014). Twenty-first century science as a relational process: From eureka! to team science and a place for community psychology. *American Journal of Community Psychology, 53,* 475–490.

Preface

Greetings! We are delighted to share this community psychology book with you. The idea for this book was born out of the Society for Community Research and Action (SCRA) Community Psychology Practice Council (CPPC). As the SCRA CPPC collaborated with the SCRA Council for Education Program (CEP) to define a set of competencies, the CPPC members recognized a need to elaborate on them and provide community psychology (CP) practitioners with a resource to facilitate their development. We were privileged to be entrusted with this task and are deeply grateful to the SCRA CPPC for its support and input as we developed the book proposal.

The aim of this book is to strengthen communities around the world by enhancing the capacity of community practitioners. Through this book, we hope to deepen the impact that community practitioners can have on their communities. We seek to do that by improving the knowledge, skills, and abilities of individuals such as you. There are three objectives associated with the book's aim. The first objective is to give readers a better understanding of the CP practice principles and competencies. The second is to describe ways in which competencies can be used to prevent or ameliorate community and social problems and issues. The third is to give readers a sense of how to develop the knowledge, skills, and abilities associated with each competency area. As you read our book, you will find that it is written through the lens of community psychology. We believe that CP has tremendous value to offer its practitioners because of its values and guiding principles.

CP Values and Guiding Principles

The SCRA, Division 27 of the American Psychological Association, is the professional association specifically dedicated to CP education, research, and practice. SCRA has developed a set of guiding principles for CP work. They can be found at http://www.scra27.org/who-we-are. These have been supplemented and elaborated on in a number of current CP textbooks (e.g., Kloos, Hill, Thomas, Wandersman, & Elias, 2011; Moritsugu, Wong, & Duffy, 2009). These values and guiding principles are ever-present and underlie each competency described in this book. They include:

- CP practitioners explicitly *attend to and respect diversity* among people and settings.

- Their work assumes a *systems perspective* whereby people are viewed within their social, cultural, economic, geographic, and historical contexts as a means of fully understanding competencies and problems.

- Change strategies target multiple levels and take an *ecological approach* to develop and support settings that promote competence and well-being.

- The focus of CP practice is often on *prevention and promotion of health and well-being*. The emphasis is on preventing illness and poor living conditions while promoting wellness rather than treatment.

- Rather than taking the typical top-down and "professionals know best" approach, CP practitioners actively collaborate with community members and allow community preferences and needs to guide the work *(empowerment)*.

- They encourage active participation by community members and work with them in partnership, forgoing the typical hierarchical helping relationship *(citizen participation)*. CP practitioners recognize that individuals and communities have unique insight into their own needs and have the capacity to be active participants in their own well-being.

- The field draws upon multi-sectoral, interdisciplinary partnerships and approaches that incorporate multiple perspectives. CP practitioners frequently partner with professionals from other disciplines (e.g., public health, education, social work) and a variety of community stakeholders.

- CP practitioners work to create a *sense of community* whereby community members experience a sense of belongingness.

- CP practice is *empirically grounded* whereby research is integrated into practice and the importance of data-informed decisions is emphasized.

- The approach is most frequently *strengths-based* with a focus on assets and resources rather the deficits.

- CP practice is grounded in *social justice* values, and the work of the practitioner may include advocacy for individual wellness and equality based on CP and social justice values. Research and action are undertaken to stimulate conditions that promote equitable resource distribution, equal opportunity, and to prevent exploitation.

- Finally, CP practice is *global* in nature. This discipline is not limited to the United States, and many CP practitioners work internationally. In saying this, we must emphasize that although these competencies may be applicable globally, they are based in the United States. In their *Global Journal of Community Psychology Practice (GJCPP)* article, Dzidic, Breen, and Bishop (2013) cautioned against taking the U.S.-derived CP competencies and transplanting them elsewhere. Other articles in this same *GJCPP* issue describe competencies specific to their countries, or the differential selection of competencies to emphasize based upon the specific needs and cultures of other countries (Carillo & Forden, 2013; Francescato & Zani, 2013). While many of the competencies, taken as a whole, are universal, the set of competencies may not fit in their entirety in other countries, or some may require adaptations to suit particular cultures.

The Audience for This Book

As was previously noted, one aim of this book is to serve as a text. Undergraduate students may utilize the book to learn more about what it would mean to be a CP practitioner and the various options available to them within the field. Understanding the competencies available may help them to select a graduate program that focuses on the type of training for the work they are interested in doing. For graduate study, this book may serve as the foundation for a course on CP practice by informing students about the range of competencies, what being competent looks like, and the application of the competencies in practice. Individual chapters may be utilized to supplement other materials on a class-by-class basis. An additional benefit for graduate students is the inclusion of information about career options and how to prepare for them.

Another audience is community psychology practitioners. Each chapter defines and describes a competency, including the associated knowledge, skills, and abilities. This book can be used as a reference book, or to refresh knowledge about a specific competency. CP practitioners may also find this book to be useful for expanding their knowledge, skills, and abilities with the resources provided in each chapter. A CP practitioner wrestling with a specific situation might find ideas or inspirations in the examples provided in each chapter.

Although the book is based upon CP practice competencies, our experience has shown that these competencies are relevant across a variety of other fields of practice. Thus, this book may also be of interest to faculty, students, and practitioners in other fields—including clinical, counseling, applied social, school, and organizational psychology; applied sociology; applied anthropology; social work; criminal justice; political science; hospital and public administration; public health; nursing; and community medicine. Individual chapters may even prove useful to other disciplines such as business, architecture, arts, or humanities.

Organization of Our CP Book

This book is organized into three primary sections. The first includes introductory chapters. Their purpose is to set the stage and give readers the context that underlies the remainder of the book. This section includes the Foreword by James G. Kelly; this Preface; Chapter 1: The History of Community Psychology Practice in the United States by Tom Wolff, Carolyn Swift, and Sharon Johnson-Hakim; and Chapter 2: Guiding Principles and Competencies for Community Psychology Practice by Maurice J. Elias, William D. Neigher, and Sharon Johnson-Hakim.

The second section describes each CP practice competency included in this volume.[1] Each chapter in this section includes definitions of the competencies and associated key terms; a description of the competency and the associated knowledge, skills, and abilities; information about how the competency can be developed; examples of the competency in action; and ancillary materials and resources.

The third section describes the options for education and training for CP practice and employment options and a vision for the future of CP practice.

Section I: Foundations of Practice

We are thrilled to share with you with a Foreword prepared by Jim Kelly, a gifted "father" of community psychology. His seminal ecological theories and subsequent writings have provided so much of the foundation for CP practice. His book *Becoming Ecological: An Expedition Into Community Psychology* (Kelly, 2006) is a must-read for every practitioner. It includes 13 of his publications from 1968 to 2002 with commentary that shows how each piece of work was influenced by various factors, especially personal experiences and historical context. The addition of four new essays provides additional insights directly relevant to practice and educating CP practitioners. Above all, throughout his career Kelly has demonstrated the value in combining an academic perspective and work with CP practice, and how both play an important role in helping the field of CP to grow its theory, research, and practice domains.

In Chapter 1, Wolff, Swift, and Johnson-Hakim provide the history of CP practice in the United States. In this chapter the reader is taken on a journey through time that provides the historical events that influenced the development of the field, the development of practice as a means of application of the developing theories and methods, the dynamics of the academic-practice relationship over time, and the relationship between practice and its settings. The chapter includes "spotlights" with first-person accounts from some of the pioneers in the field, which brings the materials to life.

Elias, Neigher, and Johnson-Hakim provide additional context in the second chapter. They describe what CP practitioners do and some of the settings they may practice in, the history of the definition of the competencies and their application, and a "value proposition" for CP practice that distinguishes CP from similar fields of study and practice. This chapter ultimately gives the readers a feel for why this is important and the value-added that CP training brings to organizations and communities.

Section II: Community Psychology Practice Competencies in Action

In this section of the book each set of authors describes a competency, including a conceptual definition; a description of the competency in practice; the associated knowledge, skills, and abilities; training, education, and experiences that enhance competency development; future directions for the competency; and examples of the application of the competency. This section of the book includes two sub-sections. The first three chapters in this section describe the foundational competencies that underlie all CP practice: "Understanding Ecological Systems" by Stephen P. Stelzner and Richard M. Wielkiewicz, "Effecting Social Change in Diverse Contexts: The Role of Cross-Cultural Competency" by Kien S. Lee, and "Professional Judgment and Ethics" by Michael Morris. All CP practitioners should have the requisite knowledge, skills, and abilities for these competencies.

In Chapter 3, Stelzner and Wielkiewicz provide a comprehensive conceptual definition that includes classic theories of Commoner, Bronfenbrenner, Barker, and Kelly as well as more recent applications of ecological perspectives. They also include information about developing competencies and the skills and abilities associated with utilizing an ecological approach, including personality, mindfulness, systemic thinking, listening skills, helping organizations to solve their own problems, facilitating communication, and cross-cultural competence. In Chapter 4, in contrast to the more common superficial treatment of this topic, Lee digs in and addresses related factors that include social identities and privilege and power. She provides some real-world examples that illustrate the points she makes throughout the chapter and challenges readers to think about this topic on a deeper level. Morris explores the ethical dimensions of community psychology practice in Chapter 5. He draws upon ethical standards from other professions to discuss ethical issues that are present across applied fields, such as evaluation and public health, and then describes how these issues may present somewhat differently in CP practice.

The remaining eight chapters in this section describe competencies that represent technical skills for CP practice. Most CP practitioners will receive training about and utilize a combination of these competencies, but not necessarily all of the competencies. The first two chapters in this section focus on community organization and capacity building. They are "Participatory Approaches for Conducting Community Needs and Resources Assessments" by Jomella Watson-Thompson, Vicki Collie-Akers, Nikki Keene Woods, Kaston D. Anderson-Carpenter, Marvia D. Jones, and Erica L. Taylor; and "Organizational and Community Capacity Building" by Scotney Evans, Catherine Raymond, and Douglas D. Perkins.

In Chapter 6 Watson-Thompson and her colleagues break down the tasks and skills for conducting needs and resources assessments and describe each step in detail—from identifying the purpose of the assessment through using the results for improvement. Their in-depth and specific treatment of this competency provides excellent guidance for anyone tasked with conducting a needs and resources assessment. In Chapter 7 Evans and colleagues discuss capacity building within the context of organizations and communities.

The next three chapters address competencies for community and social change. They are "Community Organizing" by Paul W. Speer and Brian D. Christens; "Building and Strengthening Collaborative Community Partnerships" by Judah J. Viola, Bradley D. Olson, Suzette Fromm Reed, Tiffeny R. Jimenez, and Christina M. Smith; and "Advocacy and Social Justice" by Leonard A. Jason, Christopher R. Beasley, and Bronwyn A. Hunter. These three chapters collectively provide a clear picture of the inherent complexities involved in engaging with communities to create social change.

In Chapter 8, Speer and Christens draw on the work of early community organizers and community psychologists such as Roger Barker, Saul Alinsky, Ira Iscoe, and Ken Heller as well as more current work by Marc Zimmerman, Ken Maton, and themselves and present the competencies required at multiple levels of analysis. Viola and colleagues present the various phases involved in building community collaborations and provide a detailed description of the knowledge, skills, and abilities associated with each phase in Chapter 9. In Chapter 10, Jason and colleagues expand on the two prior chapters and supplement them in their description of competencies required for advocacy and promoting social justice.

The final three chapters in this section discuss competencies for community program development. The chapters are "Planning, Implementing, and Developing Evidence-Based Interventions in the Context of Federally Funded Programs" by Richard A. Jenkins; "Empowerment Evaluation and Community Psychology: An Alignment of Values and Principles Designed to Improve the Human Condition" by David M. Fetterman; and "Dissemination and Sustainability: Changing the World and Making It Stick" by Susan M. Wolfe, Louis G. Tornatzky, and Benjamin C. Graham.

Jenkins provides detailed insight into the process of planning, implementing, and developing evidence-based interventions at the federal level in Chapter 11. This chapter takes us inside the box of the federal government to promote the reader's understanding of funding streams, the planning process, and implementation and describes the competencies necessary to navigate them. While nearly all CP practitioners receive training on evaluation methods in graduate school, in Chapter 12 Fetterman describes the empowerment evaluation model and the associated competencies, which is consistent with CP practice values and goals. His description includes discussion of the similarities between empowerment evaluation and community psychology and how the roles complement one another. In Chapter 13, Wolfe, Tornatzky, and Graham describe three different perspectives on dissemination and the knowledge, skills, and abilities associated with each, and then describe the competencies associated with promoting sustainability of programs and policies once they are disseminated and implemented.

Section III: Into the Future of Community Psychology Practice

The final two chapters in this volume are focused on looking toward the future for training CP practitioners, settings where the competencies may be utilized, and how the competencies may be applied to create a better world. They include "Community Psychology Education and Practice Careers in the 21st Century" by Susan D. McMahon, Tiffeny R. Jimenez, Meg A. Bond, Susan M. Wolfe, and Allen W. Ratcliffe; and "A Vision for Community Psychology Practice" by Bill Berkowitz and Victoria C. Scott.

In the first half of Chapter 14, McMahon and colleagues provide us with a description of the state of CP education. This includes undergraduate, master's level, and doctoral level education and a description of potential professional development sources and opportunities for early to late career CP practitioners. In the second half, the authors present a comprehensive list of potential employment settings and a description of the competencies associated with each. This chapter overall provides guidance for aspiring CP practitioners regarding training they may seek, as well as experienced CP practitioners who are making career changes. In Chapter 15, Berkowitz and Scott present a vision for what a community could look like in the future if it is designed according to CP practice principles. It gives us a taste of how the application of the competencies described in this book might lead to more vital and empowered communities with fully engaged members.

A Labor of Love Rooted in Great Hopes for Our Communities

While this book does not cover every competency associated with CP practice, it presents an overview of those most commonly employed in the field. The competencies range from the most basic ones that underlie all of CP practice to those utilized at the programmatic level, to the competencies associated with creating macro-level, long-term change and sustaining it. Overall, the co-editing of this volume was a labor of love. It provided us an opportunity to collaborate with an amazing group of exemplary CP practitioners. We are ever so grateful for their contributions to the book. As editors we had the opportunity to facilitate and grow with the development of each. Our hope is that those who read this volume find that it makes a valuable contribution to their own professional development.

Mostly, we are hopeful that this book will enable CP practitioners and other professionals who work in the communities to engage more effectively in the settings where they practice so as to achieve healthier, more vibrant communities—because we feel that for all CP practitioners, the work they do is a labor of love.

Susan M. Wolfe and Victoria C. Scott

NOTE

1. We have made an effort to include the core competencies most frequently utilized in practice. However, additional competencies have been and will continue to be added to the list. The competencies included in this book should not be considered to represent the competencies in their entirety.

REFERENCES

Carillo, A. M., & Forden, C. L. (2013). Community psychology practice competencies in Egypt: Challenges and opportunities. *Global Journal of Community Psychology Practice, 4*(4). Retrieved from http://gjcpp.org/

Dzidic, P., Breen, L. J., & Bishop, B. J. (2013). Are our competencies revealing our weaknesses? A critique of community psychology practice competencies. *Global Journal of Community Psychology Practice, 4*(4). Retrieved from http://www.gjcpp.org/

Francescato, D., & Zani, B. (2013). Community psychology practice competencies in undergraduate and graduate programs in Italy. *Global Journal of Community Psychology Practice, 4*(4). Retrieved from http://www.gjcpp.org/

Kelly, J. G. (2006). *Becoming ecological: An expedition into community psychology.* New York, NY: Oxford University Press.

Kloos, B., Hill, J., Thomas, E., Wandersman, A., & Elias, M. (2011). *Community psychology: Linking individuals and communities.* Belmont, CA: Wadsworth.

Moritsugu, J. G., Wong, F. Y., & Duffy, K. G. (2009). *Community psychology* (4th ed.). New York, NY: Pearson Higher Education.

About the Editors

Victoria C. Scott, PhD, MBA, is a community psychologist who has devoted her professional career to working with nonprofit organizations to optimize their performance through consultation, training, research, and evaluation. She is actively engaged with the Society for Community Research and Action, Division 27 of the American Psychological Association, which is a national organization devoted to strengthening communities around the world through theory, research, and action. Dr. Scott is especially passionate about improving the quality of health care and health care outcomes. She holds an academic appointment at the University of South Carolina, where she is both a clinical assistant professor in the Department of Neuropsychiatry and Behavior Science and director of research evaluation at the Office of Continuous Professional Development and Strategic Affairs. Dr. Scott is blissfully married to her best friend, C. Justin Scott, and mother of their beautiful daughter, Vienna.

Susan M. Wolfe, PhD, is a community and developmental psychologist with over 28 years of professional experience. She has worked across a variety of settings that include public hospitals, a community college district, a public school system, universities, research institutes, and the federal government. She has worked across topic areas such as domestic violence, homelessness, education, adolescent development, maternal-child health, technological innovation, children's mental health, nursing homes, and policy. She is currently CEO of Susan Wolfe and Associates, LLC, where she provides research, evaluation, capacity building, and coalition development services to nonprofit organizations, government, foundations, school districts, and public health organizations. She has a diploma from the Michigan College of Beauty Culture, a Bachelor of Science degree in clinical/community psychology from the University of Michigan-Flint, a Master of Arts degree and ABD in ecological psychology with a cognate in organizational psychology from Michigan State University, and a PhD in human development and communication sciences from the University of Texas at Dallas. She lives in Cedar Hill, Texas, with her husband, Charles Hipkins. Her family includes two sons, two stepsons, two daughters-in-law, a granddaughter, three grandsons, a Chihuahua, a Chiweenie, and two cats.

About the Contributors

 **Kaston D. Anderson-Carpenter,** MPH, MA, is a Board Certified Behavior Analyst (BCBA) and doctoral student in the Department of Applied Behavioral Science at the University of Kansas. He also serves as a Graduate Research Assistant in the KU Work Group for Community Health and Development. He holds master's degrees in public health and psychology from the University of Kansas and McNeese State University, respectively. His research interests are broadly centered on prevention and health promotion, with particular interests in addictive behaviors and disease prevention. In addition to research, Mr. Anderson-Carpenter consults with nonprofit organizations to provide assessment, planning, and evaluation for community-based initiatives.

 **Christopher R. Beasley** received his PhD in community psychology from DePaul University in 2013 and his MA in clinical psychology from Roosevelt University in 2010. He is currently a research associate at the DePaul University Center for Community Research. He examines social ecological processes related to community engagement. In particular, he has examined involvement in mutual-help addiction recovery groups and ways in which members support these groups and organizations. Dr. Beasley received an NIH NRSA predoctoral fellowship from the National Institute on Drug Addiction to examine factors related to such engagement. He is also interested in barriers to higher education for incarcerated and formerly incarcerated people. Dr. Beasley is the co-founder and president of the Returning Students Support Group, a mutual-help organization that assists people in their transition from prison to colleges.

 **Bill Berkowitz,** PhD, has created, directed, taught about, and written about community and neighborhood action efforts for more than 40 years. His four books and other scholarly publications deal with the skills, ideas, and personal qualities needed for effective community action. Bill is presently an emeritus professor of psychology at the University of Massachusetts Lowell and former coordinator of its graduate program in community social psychology. He has also been a founding team member, writer, and editor for the Community Tool Box (http://ctb.ku.edu), the largest single source of community development information now in existence. He has received his APA division's Community Practitioner award as well as its award for Distinguished Contributions to Community Practice. In his home community, Bill co-edited his neighborhood's newsletter for 15 years and has served in elected public office as a Town Meeting Member since the 1980s. His professional and personal interests continue to

focus on neighborhood and community development and the strengthening of resident participation in local community life.

 **Meg A. Bond,** PhD, is a professor of psychology and director of the Center for Women & Work at the University of Massachusetts Lowell. She is also a resident scholar at the Brandeis University Women's Studies Research Center. Her publications have addressed sexual harassment, collaboration among diverse constituencies, and empowerment issues of underrepresented groups in community and organizational settings. Her book, *Workplace Chemistry: Promoting Diversity through Organizational Change* (2007), chronicles a long-term organizational change project focused on issues of gender and race/ethnicity. Her ongoing research focuses on diversity-related workplace dynamics in community health centers. She is currently the lead editor for the comprehensive two-volume *Handbook of Community Psychology* to be published by APA. Meg is a former president of the Society for Community Research and Action (SCRA) and has received two career awards from SCRA—a Special Contributions Award (2001) and an Ethnic Minority Mentoring Award (2009). She has also served as chair of the APA Committee on Women, on the Executive Committee of the Society for the Psychological Study of Social Issues, and on the APA Board for the Advancement of Psychology in the Public Interest.

 **Brian D. Christens,** PhD, is an associate professor at the University of Wisconsin–Madison School of Human Ecology, where he teaches and collaborates with graduate students in the program in Civil Society & Community Research and teaches undergraduates in the Community & Nonprofit Leadership major. Brian works with community organizing groups through action research partnerships. For example, in recent years, he has been an academic partner for efforts to build strategic alignment between community organizing and other actors seeking to improve public health in Wisconsin. He has also worked with organizers, students, and local public health nurses to launch several youth organizing initiatives. His research examines the effects of organizing on participants and the effectiveness of community organizing efforts at achieving community and system-level changes.

 **Vicki Collie-Akers** holds a PhD in behavioral psychology from the University of Kansas, and a Master of Public Health with a concentration in behavioral science and health education from Saint Louis University. Her research is primarily focused on applying a community-based participatory research orientation to working with communities to understand how collaborative partnerships and coalitions can improve social determinants of health and equity and reduce disparities in health outcomes. Throughout her career, Dr. Collie-Akers has worked to promote health through research and practice, including assisting in research projects that studied coverage of prevention research in small market media, environmental assessments of walkability for children, mammography usage among African American women, and promoting involvement of neighborhood and faith-based organizations in a CDC-funded REACH 2010 project in Kansas City, Missouri. In her

position at the KU Work Group she directs several evaluation projects that support part-ners, such as the Medical Legal Partnership of Western Missouri, that are working to pro-mote health through their comprehensive initiatives. Additionally, she serves as principal investigator or co-investigator on several projects promoting health equity and reduction in health disparities in the Kansas City metropolitan area. Dr. Collie-Akers has provided consultation to a number of community initiatives on topics such as evaluation, logic model development, and sustainability. She has also been active in capacity building through trainings and webinars of individuals including public health practitioners and grassroots community representatives.

Maurice J. Elias is a professor in the Psychology Department at Rutgers University, a past president of the Society for Community Research and Action/Division of Community Psychology (27) of the American Psychological Association and a recipient of its Distinguished Contributions to Practice and Ethnic Minority Mentoring Awards, director of the Rutgers Social-Emotional Learning Lab and Rutgers's Collaborative Center for Community-Based Research and Service, a founding member of the Leadership Team for the Collaborative for Academic, Social, and Emotional Learning (www.CASEL.org), and a recent recipient of the Sanford McDonnell Award for Lifetime Achievement in Character Education. Among Dr. Elias's numerous books are ASCD's *Promoting Social and Emotional Learning: Guidelines for Educators, Social Decision Making/Social Problem Solving* (curricula for Grades K–8), *Bullying, Peer Harassment, and Victimization in the Schools: The Next Generation of Prevention* (2003), *The Educator's Guide to Emotional Intelligence and Academic Achievement: Social-Emotional Learning in the Classroom* (Corwin, 2006), *Urban Dreams: Stories of Hope, Character, and Resilience* (2008), the new e-book *Emotionally Intelligent Parenting*, and a book for young children: *Talking Treasure: Stories to Help Build Emotional Intelligence and Resilience in Young Children* (2012). He also writes a blog for educators and parents for the George Lucas Educational Foundation at www.edutopia.org.

With colleagues at the College of St. Elizabeth, he is developing an online credentialing program for Direct Instruction of Social-Emotional and Character Development programs in classroom, small-group, and afterschool settings, and for School-Focused Coordination of Social-Emotional and Character Development and School Culture and Climate.

Scotney Evans, PhD, is an associate professor in the Department of Educational and Psychological Studies in the School of Education and Human Development and the faculty master at Eaton Residential College. He directs the undergraduate major in human and social development and teaches in the master's program in community and social change. Dr. Evans is a community-engaged scholar researching and promoting the role of community-based human service organizations in the promotion of community well-being, social change, and social justice.

David M. Fetterman, PhD, is president and CEO of Fetterman & Associates, an international evaluation consulting firm. He has 25 years of experience at Stanford University, serving as a senior administrator, School of Education faculty member, and School of Medicine director of evaluation. David is the director of the Arkansas Evaluation Center and concurrently a professor at San Jose State University, the University of Charleston, and the University of Arkansas. He was a professor and research director at the California Institute of Integral Studies, principal research scientist at the American Institutes for Research, and a senior associate at RMC Research Corporation. David is a past president of the American Evaluation Association. He received both the Paul Lazarsfeld Award for Outstanding Contributions to Evaluation Theory and the Myrdal Award for Cumulative Contributions to Evaluation Practice. He also received the American Educational Research Association Research on Evaluation Distinguished Scholar Award. David is the founder of empowerment evaluation. He has published 16 books, including *Empowerment Evaluation in the Digital Villages: Hewlett-Packard's $15 Million Race Toward Social Justice; Empowerment Evaluation Principles in Practice* (with Wandersman); *Foundations of Empowerment Evaluation;* and *Empowerment Evaluation: Knowledge and Tools for Self-assessment and Accountability* (with Kaftarian & Wandersman).

Sharon Johnson-Hakim received her PhD in community psychology from Wichita State University in 2013. She is currently a postdoctoral fellow in applied community psychology at Atlantic Health System, in Morristown, New Jersey. Dr. Johnson-Hakim is interested in the relationship between the built environment and individual health-related behaviors. As a practitioner, she is committed to collaborative, community-based processes aimed at creating healthier contexts; her past projects, specifically focusing on community-wide food systems and the National School Lunch Program delivery, have seen success in increasing access to healthy, affordable, and culturally appropriate food. Dr. Johnson-Hakim has been active in the Society for Community Research and Action (APA Division 27) since 2008, and now serves as the co-chair of the SCRA Practice Council.

Bronwyn A. Hunter, PhD, is an NIH/NIDA T32 postdoctoral fellow at the Consultation Center, Yale University School of Medicine. She is a graduate of the Clinical Community Psychology program at DePaul University. Dr. Hunter's research program encompasses health and well-being among persons involved in the criminal justice system. As such, her research focuses on the relationship between state policies, perceived stigma, and coping strategies among formerly incarcerated individuals. She is specifically interested in policies and programs to support women involved in the criminal justice system. Dr. Hunter is also embedded in the community, where she works to build capacity for program evaluation and intervention development in community-based organizations.

Leonard A. Jason received his PhD in clinical psychology from the University of Rochester in 1975. He is currently a professor of psychology at DePaul University and the director of the Center for Community Research. This fall will be Jason's 40th year as a faculty member at DePaul University. He is a past director of clinical training for the clinical psychology doctoral program, past faculty sponsor of Psi Chi, and was one of the faculty members responsible for the creation of the human services concentration and community concentration within the psychology undergraduate program. Jason is a former president of the Division of Community Psychology of the American Psychological Association and a past editor of *The Community Psychologist*. Jason has served as the vice president of the International American Association of CFS/ME. He also served as the chair of the Research Subcommittee of the U.S. Chronic Fatigue Syndrome Advisory Committee, which makes recommendations to the Secretary of Health and Human Services. He has edited or written 23 books and has published over 600 articles and 75 book chapters on chronic fatigue syndrome; Oxford House recovery homes; the prevention of alcohol, tobacco, and other drug abuse; media interventions; and program evaluation. He has served on the editorial boards of ten psychological journals. He has received over $34 million in federal research grants.

Richard A. Jenkins, PhD, is a health scientist administrator in the Prevention Research Branch at the National Institute on Drug Abuse (NIDA), National Institutes of Health. Rich is a clinical-community psychologist whose current portfolio includes research related to HIV prevention and the development of new methodologies for prevention intervention research. Before coming to NIDA, he was involved in a variety of domestic and international projects related to HIV prevention, including preparations for HIV vaccine trials, investigations of the social and behavioral epidemiology of HIV exposure, and the design and evaluation of HIV prevention interventions. He also has conducted operational studies associated with early-stage HIV vaccine trials and community assessments of HIV risk among a variety of populations. Prior to his HIV work, Rich was involved in research related to coping with cancer and evaluating behavioral medicine interventions related to cancer treatment. He also was involved with community consultation and research related to mental health concerns in a variety of community settings.

Tiffeny R. Jimenez, PhD is an assistant professor at National Louis University and co-director of the doctoral program in community psychology. She has worked and written most on various community-based research projects spanning social justice issues, including coordinating a collaborative statewide cross-disability leadership training initiative, consulting on initiatives to change the culture of a university to be more supportive of women faculty in the STEM fields, and conducting a collaborative network system analysis with a community-wide systems change initiative across a tri-county area assisting in the development of a data-driven capacity-building process to increase the knowledge of community members for restructuring a local human services system. She is most passionate about creating more inclusive communities and socially just practices through organizational and community-level systems change, coalition development, addressing cross-cultural dynamics, and focusing on resource exchange sustainability. She is currently working with a national nonprofit organization that engages businesses in a process of becoming more socially responsible. She also currently serves on the Executive Committee of the Society for Community Research and Action (SCRA) and co-chairs a joint initiative of the SCRA Council of Education Programs and the Practice Council to strengthen graduate programs in community psychology research and action to better educate for community psychology practice careers. Tiffeny strives to excel in creating educational experiences for her students that overlay teaching, research, and community service that challenges the status quo and addresses the needs of diverse populations.

Marvia D. Jones, MPH, is a doctoral student at the University of Kansas in the Department of Applied Behavioral Sciences. She has earned a master's degree in public health and is pursuing a PhD in behavioral psychology. She serves as a graduate research assistant with the KU Work Group for Community Health and Development, where her interests include the application of behavioral approaches to reducing health inequities and addressing the social determinants of health.

James G. Kelly, PhD, is an emeritus professor at the University of Illinois at Chicago. He was a member of the Department of Psychology there from 1982 to 1999. Before that he was a member of the faculties of Ohio State University, University of Michigan, and University of Oregon. He has been active in the field since a doctoral student at the University of Texas from 1954 to 1958. He was a participant in the founding Swampscott Conference in 1965 and the first elected president of the APA Division of Community Psychology in 1968–1969. He has received several honors for his work in community psychology over the years: the Award for Distinguished Contributions to Community Psychology and Community Mental Health (1978–1979); American Psychological Association, Senior Career Award for Distinguished Contributions to Psychology in the Public Interest (1997); and the Seymour Sarason Award for Community Research and Action (2001). A sample of his contributions appears in *Becoming Ecological* (2006, Oxford University Press).

Kien S. Lee, PhD, vice president and principal associate of Community Science, specializes in issues affecting communities that are racially, ethnically, or culturally diverse. She brings more than 15 years of research and evaluation experience to this work, particularly in the integration of immigrants, strategies and programming for racial equity, the reduction of health disparities, and the development of cross-culturally competent organizations. Her knowledge of cross-cultural competency is derived from many research, evaluation, and implementation studies, among them the evaluation of The Colorado Trust's Equality in Health initiative intended to strengthen the capacity of nonprofits to be more responsive to the health needs of the diverse communities they serve; implementation of the Valuing Diversity Initiative, which assisted communities in bridging racial and ethnic relations, supported by the American Psychological Association and the W. K. Kellogg Foundation; and needs assessments of Montgomery and Howard counties' (Maryland) low-income and immigrant families. She is author of *The Importance of Culture in Evaluation* and *The Journey Continues: Ensuring a Cross-Culturally Competent Evaluation*, publications funded by The Colorado Trust, and is a recipient of the Society for Community Research and Action (Division 27 of the American Psychological Association) Award for Distinguished Contributions to Practice in Community Psychology in 2013.

 **Susan D. McMahon**, PhD, is a professor and department chair of psychology at DePaul University. Susan has been a leading contributor in conducting theory-based research and evaluations regarding violence and aggression, teacher victimization, classroom and school environment, stress and psychopathology, and individual and contextual factors that contribute to urban adolescent development. She has over 55 publications and a book, coauthored with Judah Viola, *Consulting and Evaluation With Nonprofit and Community-Based Organizations*; she has also given over 145 presentations. Susan has served in a variety of leadership roles at DePaul, as well as in the field of community psychology. For example, she served as university IRB chair and Community Psychology Doctoral Program director at DePaul for 6 years. She served in two national, elected leadership roles within Division 27 of the American Psychological Association (Society for Community Research and Action; SCRA), including chair of the Council of Education Programs and regional network coordinator. She is also a fellow in SCRA and received the Outstanding Educator Award from SCRA in 2012.

 **Michael Morris,** PhD, is professor of psychology at the University of New Haven, where he directs the Master's Program in Community Psychology. His research focuses on the ethical challenges encountered by program evaluators in their work, and he provides training in evaluation ethics to evaluators throughout the United States and abroad. In 1993 he published the first national study of ethical challenges among professional evaluators; the results of this research continue to be frequently cited in the field. Dr. Morris was the founding editor of the Ethical Challenges section of the *American Journal of Evaluation* and also served as the journal's associate editor from 2010 through 2013. His work has appeared in the *American Journal of Community Psychology*, the *Journal of Community Psychology*, *The Community Psychologist*, *Evaluation Review*, and *Evaluation and Program Planning*, in addition to the *American Journal of Evaluation*. His third book, *Evaluation Ethics for Best Practice: Cases and Commentaries*, was published in 2008. Previous books include *Poverty and Public Policy* (with John Williamson) and *Myths About the Powerless* (with Brinton Lykes, Ali Banuazizi, and Ramsay Liem).

William D. Neigher, PhD, is a community psychologist specializing in strategic planning, program development, and evaluation research. He has worked in these areas with the

United Nations, the U.S. Senate, Harvard University, the National Institute of Mental Health, the World Health Organization, Hoffman-LaRoche, and Memorial Sloan-Kettering Cancer Center. Dr. Neigher is vice president, system development, and chief strategy officer for the Atlantic Health System. Atlantic Health is ranked in the top 50 for both *U.S. News and World Report's* "Best Hospitals in America" and *Fortune Magazine's* "100 Best Companies in America to Work For." He is a fellow of the American Psychological Association and a past president of the Eastern Evaluation Research Society and the New Jersey Association of Mental Health Agencies. His publications include nearly 50 books, chapters, and journal articles, and he has been a member of the psychology faculty of The City University of New York and Rutgers University. In 2010 he received the Distinguished Contribution to Practice in Community Psychology award from the American Psychological Association's Division 27, the Society for Community Research and Action. He is most proud, however, of singing backup for Bennie Rabbit on an episode of *Sesame Street*.

Bradley D. Olson, PhD, is an assistant professor and co-directs the community psychology doctoral program at National Louis University. His research and advocacy efforts are focused on issues of human and civil rights, advocacy and activism, participatory action research, mixed quantitative and qualitative methodologies, ethics, and philosophy of science. He is a past president of Psychologists for Social Responsibility (www.psysr.org), co-founder of The Coalition for an Ethical Psychology (www.ethicalpsychology.org), president of the Society for the Study of Peace, Conflict, and Violence (Division 48 of the APA; www.peacepsych.org), and past chair of Divisions for Social Justice, a collaboration of 12 APA divisions.

Douglas D. Perkins, PhD, is professor of human and organizational development at Vanderbilt University, where he teaches in the the doctoral program in Community Research and Action, the MEd program in Community Development & Action, and the BS track in Community Leadership & Development. His collaborative research addresses youth, organizational, and community development, violence, crime, fear, social capital (participation, empowerment, neighboring, sense of community), and disorder in urban neighborhoods in America, Europe, China, and South Africa.

Allen W. Ratcliffe, PhD, has practiced community psychology in Tacoma-Pierce County, Washington, since 1975. He works on issues primarily associated with homelessness and mental health, as a volunteer consultant and advocate. He is not affiliated with an academic institution, and he practices currently as a volunteer member of the Tacoma Human Services Commission, the community Mental Health Advisory Board, and the HUD-mandated Homeless Continuum of Care Work Group. He collaborates widely among community leaders and service providers, seeking to knit together efforts and people working toward similar goals and outcomes.

 **Catherine Raymond,** PhD, has for more than 25 years assisted numerous organizations in arts and culture, education, environment, and human services to plan effectively for their organizational future as well as to plan, implement, and evaluate their programs. In addition to working with nonprofit clients, Catherine teaches program planning and evaluation at the University of Miami and nonprofit management at Florida International University. Catherine has a PhD in public affairs (with a focus on nonprofit capacity building) as well as an MS in adult education/human resource development.

 **Suzette Fromm Reed**, PhD, is an associate professor and founding director of the community psychology doctoral program at National Louis University (NLU) where she also works with master's and BA students on topics including but not limited to experimental psychology and research methods and mental health. She consults with community agencies on a variety of topics including obesity prevention, girl empowerment, violence prevention, scholastic achievement in nontraditional students, and other positive outcomes for youth and women. Suzette has written on these topical areas as well as published on the role of community psychologists outside of academia. Her research interests are varied, including examining how collective efficacy and social capital may play a role in buffering against child maltreatment, and how social marketing may be applied to this and similar topics. Currently, her research is primarily focused on health promotion through engaging communities in exercise and nutrition activities, female empowerment, and aging. Her recent presentations include serving as an expert panelist for Moving Forward: Re-Shaping Behavioral Health Services in the Chicago region hosted by the Health and Medicine Policy Research Group. Prior to NLU, she worked with nonprofit agencies at both the national and local levels on issues related to children and families. She has partnership experience both from an academic perspective as well as from the nonprofit side. For more information, see http://works.bepress.com/suzette_fromm_reed.

 **Christina M. Smith**, LCSW, is currently a doctoral student at National Louis University (NLU) and has more than 20 years of professional experience in the private and public human service field. In most recent years Ms. Smith has worked as an organizational consultant, providing executive and management coaching, program development, and evaluation and training to community-based organizations as well as state and local governmental agencies. Ms. Smith has also served on local community boards and advisory councils committed to social change and advocacy related to race, gender, class, and LGBT empowerment. One of her primary areas of research interest is examining the set of factors that explains how community-based organizations think about science and make decisions about whether and how to use science appropriately to explain and enhance their work.

Paul W. Speer, PhD, is a professor in the Department of Human and Organizational Development, Peabody College, at Vanderbilt University. His research is in the area of community organizing, participation, social power, and community change. Currently his work is focused on studying characteristics of organizations that support sustained civic engagement, network properties within organizations for developing strong participation, and the relationship between affordable housing and educational outcomes. He has published over 50 articles and chapters in a variety of journals, including the *American Journal of Community Psychology*, *Health Education & Behavior,* and the *American Journal of Public Health*. He currently teaches courses in action research, community development theory, and community organizing.

Stephen P. Stelzner, PhD, is a professor of psychology at the College of Saint Benedict and Saint John's University, two jointly operating academic institutions in central Minnesota. He obtained a PhD from the University of Illinois at Chicago in 1989. He teaches courses in introductory psychology, developmental psychology, community Psychology, and I/O psychology. His scholarly work has focused on using ecological principles to change social systems and the development of leadership processes that emphasize ethical and sustainable approaches for communities and organizations.

Carolyn Swift, PhD, was an early applied community psychologist. Graduating from the University of Kansas with a PhD in psychology, she joined APA's Division 27, then titled Community Psychology. She was the first applied community psychologist to serve on the Executive Committee of the Division. Across her career Carolyn has pioneered new professional roles in unconventional settings. Her first job was as a psychologist at a community mental health center in Kansas City, Kansas, hired to work with the city's mayor and police chief to develop (1) treatment programs for alcoholics, petty criminals, and jailed offenders; (2) training programs for police officers in their interactions with the public; and (3) recovery programs for delinquent young males. In cooperation with the police chief and career officers she created programs focusing on the needs of these populations as well as other programs (e.g., rape prevention) and funded them with grants she was awarded from a variety of resources. She succeeded in establishing a group home for young boys who'd run into trouble with the law, where they could attend school, work off their sentences, and have their arrest records expunged. Carolyn later moved to Columbus, Ohio, to work with a new experimental and cutting-edge interactive TV network (QUBE) with a goal of developing TV programs for children left home alone by their parents. Her final position was at Wellesley College, where she served as director of the Stone Center for Developmental Services and Studies, comprised of a Women's Research and Counseling Center, and the Jean Baker Miller Institute. She was elected and served as SCRA's president in 2006–2007.

Erica L. Taylor, BGS, is a graduate student at the University of Kansas in the Department of Applied Behavioral Science, with a specialty area in community health and development. Ms. Taylor is serving on the Community Youth Development and Prevention Team, within the Work Group for Community Health and Development at the University of Kansas. She earned her bachelor's degree in applied behavioral science from the University of Kansas, with a concentration in psychology. Her current graduate study research projects consist of violence prevention analysis, focusing on violence prevention efforts in Kansas City, Missouri. She also develops and evaluates positive youth engagement interventions in low-income neighborhoods in the Midwest, and she is interested in examining the implementation of community mobilization strategies and best practices in low-income urban neighborhoods.

Louis G. Tornatzky, PhD, was born and reared in Cleveland, Ohio, served in the United States Marine Corps, has a BA Cum Laude from Ohio State University, and a PhD from Stanford University. His research is focused on organizational aspects of social and technological innovation. He was a professor at Michigan State University; group leader in innovation processes research at the National Science Foundation; lab director at the Industrial Technology Institute in Ann Arbor; director of the Southern Technology Council; senior associate with Battelle Memorial Institute; senior scholar and VP for research at the Tomas Rivera Policy Institute; VP at Select University Technologies; and most recently department chair, professor, and co-director of the Center for Innovation & Entrepreneurship at California Polytechnic State University, San Luis Obispo. Dr. Tornatzky has authored over 150 books, journal articles, monographs, and papers on innovation. He has consulted with over 50 universities and regional technology organizations in the United States and abroad.

Judah J. Viola, PhD, is an assistant professor and co-director of the community psychology doctoral program at National Louis University in Chicago, Illinois. He also manages an independent consulting practice specializing in needs assessment, program evaluation, community building, and collaborative community research. Recent clients have included public school systems, museum and art institutions, social service agencies, and community development organizations. Judah's research and advocacy interests involve promoting healthy communities and increasing the civic engagement and prosocial behavior of individuals, and he studies a broad array of topics including urban education for students with disabilities, substance abuse aftercare, affordable housing, access to health care, access to healthy food, and youth obesity prevention. He is active in the Society for Community Research and Action and the Chicagoland Evaluation Association, a local affiliate of the American Evaluation Association, and serves on the Executive Committee of the Consortium to Lower Obesity in Chicago Children, a broad-based network of participants and organizations confronting the childhood obesity epidemic by promoting policies and environmental changes that support healthy and active lifestyles for children throughout the Chicago metropolitan area. Judah has written extensively on consulting and evaluation with community-based organizations including *Consulting and Evaluation With Nonprofit and Community-Based Organizations* (coauthored with S. D. McMahon). His most recent writing project is an upcoming book on the topic of diverse career paths in community psychology.

Jomella Watson-Thompson, PhD, is an assistant professor in the Department of Applied Behavioral Science and associate director for the Work Group for Community Health and Development at the University of Kansas. Through collaborative research, teaching, and service she examines the application of behavioral community psychology methods and interventions to improve how communities address issues related to community health and development. Dr. Watson-Thompson's research focuses on neighborhood development, positive youth development, and substance abuse and violence prevention. She supports community capacity-building efforts to address social determinants of health through community-based participatory research in urban neighborhoods and with disparate communities and groups. Her research has focused on the experimental analysis of the effects of community-based processes and interventions to promote change and improvement in community conditions and outcomes of concern. Dr. Watson-Thompson has extensive experience providing training, technical support, and evaluation for community and faith-based initiatives. She has coauthored articles on community capacity-building, youth development, and prevention. Dr. Watson-Thompson attained her BA in urban studies from Jackson State University in Jackson, Mississippi; a Master of Urban Planning, an MA in applied behavioral science, and a PhD in behavioral psychology, all from the University of Kansas.

Richard M. Wielkiewicz, PhD, is a professor of psychology at the College of Saint Benedict and Saint John's University, two jointly operating academic institutions in central Minnesota. He obtained a PhD from the University of Hawai'i in 1977. He teaches courses in statistics, research methods, principles of learning, and environmental or conservation psychology. His research interests are eclectic because they are often guided by topics that reflect the interests of students. However, since the early 1990s he has published consistently in the areas of leadership theory and measurement. He is passionate about environmental issues and has recently published an e-book titled *Sustainability and Psychology*.

Tom Wolff, PhD, is a community psychologist committed to issues of social justice and building healthy communities through collaborative solutions. A nationally recognized consultant on coalition building and community development, he has a lifetime of experience training and consulting with individuals, organizations, and communities across North America and around the globe. Tom has published numerous

resources to help communities solve their own problems. His most recent book is *The Power of Collaborative Solutions—Six Principles and Effective Tools for Building Healthy Communities,* published in 2010. His earlier writings on coalition building include *From the Ground Up: A Workbook on Coalition Building and Community Development* (with Gillian Kaye, 1997) and *The Spirit of the Coalition* (with Bill Berkowitz, 2000). He presently runs Tom Wolff & Associates (www.tomwolff.com) in Amherst, Massachusetts. Consulting clients include federal, state, and local government agencies; foundations; hospitals; nonprofit organizations; professional associations; and grassroots groups.

Nikki Keene Woods, PhD, is an assistant professor in the Department of Public Health Sciences at Wichita State University. She has earned master's degrees in behavioral science and public health, in addition to a PhD in behavioral psychology from the University of Kansas. She is a maternal, infant, and child health researcher and educator with an emphasis on addressing health disparities. Her work is community based and collaborative in nature, utilizing mixed methods to answer specific community health questions. Earlier research projects were community oriented and focused on behavior change at the population level and translational research in a clinical setting, including patient and provider behaviors and communication. She is currently active in local and state groups working to improve birth outcomes for infants and mothers in Kansas. Dr. Keene Woods has been a volunteer for several local and statewide efforts to improve birth outcomes for many years. Her experiences and knowledge are shared with students through undergraduate and graduate coursework and service-learning opportunities.

CHAPTER 1

The History of Community Psychology Practice in the United States

Tom Wolff, Carolyn Swift, and
Sharon Johnson-Hakim

INTRODUCTION

Community psychology practice encompasses all of the activities that bring the field's vision for a better world to life. Thus, we start this history of community psychology practice with a definition and vision of the field:

> The sub discipline of psychology that is concerned with understanding people in context of their communities, the prevention of the problems of living, the celebration of human diversity and the pursuit of social justice through social action. (Nelson & Prilleltensky, 2010, p. 23)

The vision for the field of community psychology as adopted by the Society for Community Research and Action (SCRA), the American professional association, is "to have a strong, global impact on enhancing well-being and promoting social justice for all people by fostering collaboration where there is division and empowerment where there is oppression." This wonderful, transformative definition and vision for community psychology demand not only the capacity to study issues but also to act to make the world a better place. From the earliest meetings giving birth to the field of community psychology at Swampscott, Massachusetts, the founders understood that community psychology would be a field encompassing academic theory, research, and field practice. This is how community psychology "walks the talk." Within the field, the role of practice has been to translate research, values, and principles into meaningful action; it is the means through which the field impacts communities and organizations around the world.

What Is Community Psychology Practice?

Although the field of community psychology was established in the 1960s, and community psychologists were involved in practice from the start, the first official definition of what it means to "practice" community psychology was not articulated until 2006, and was a result of work done by the Community Psychology Practice Council of SCRA to promote and support practitioners. The definition states that community psychology practice aims "to strengthen the capacity of communities to meet the needs of constituents and help them to realize their dreams in order to promote well-being, social justice, economic equity and self-determination through systems, organizational and/or individual change" (Julian, 2006, p. 68). Thus, community psychology practitioners are those who do community work as noted in the definition above and who have been trained as community psychologists.

In this chapter we will undertake to recount and understand the history of the development of community psychology practice. We do this by addressing four issues across two eras of the development of community psychology practice.

The first issue we address concerns the intersection of world events with the development of our field, called "Milestones of the Era." Community psychology grounds itself in the ecological approach, understanding individual behavior as connected to the context in which it occurs, therefore it is no surprise to look at the history of community psychology practice in any given era and see that it is deeply influenced by the events occurring in the world around it. In part this happens because the practitioners are tuned in to current issues and adapt their practice to emerging community and national issues. In part it happens because world and national events influence available funding for national, state, and local grants and practitioners are then engaged to address those issues. As we explore each time period we summarize the milestones of the era in the world: what was happening in the world, such as civil rights movements, wars, influential presidents, and policies or events, and how these external events and movements influenced the development of the field.

Second, we address community psychology practice as part of the developing field of community psychology, not only as a field of study, but also a field of application as well. The overriding questions being how to develop a community psychology practice that is clearly defined; skillful and based on established and accepted competencies; effective; acknowledged as a legitimate practice; visible to the public and to those in the field; and supported by peers and institutions. We address such questions as: What do community psychology practitioners do and what competencies are required to do the work at a professional level? This section is best thought of as the milestones of community psychology practice as it developed a life of its own within the field of community psychology.

The third issue discussed focuses on the dynamics of the relationships of the practitioners of community psychology and their academic colleagues. Throughout the history of community psychology there have been two parallel worlds of community psychologists: those who work in universities and those who work in applied settings. Historically, there has been tension between academic and applied community psychologists. Early on, the vital survival focus of the academic community psychologists was to gain acceptance within their psychology departments regarding the legitimacy of their research agendas. As a result, academic community psychologists were not always aligned in the pursuit of developing a practice. Over the last 30 years this rift has lessened through efforts on both sides. Although the split still exists, a focus on developing competencies for practice has helped the two groups work together and appreciate each other's role. The value of community psychology practice wherever it occurs, whether in a university setting or in a community setting, is that the practice allows for the manifestation of the community psychology vision. It enables community psychology to have an impact on the world, to reach out into communities, and it illustrates the capacity of community psychology to change the world.

The fourth and final issue we address is the relationship of community psychology practice to the work sites where people practice. What opportunities were created where community psychologists could actually practice community psychology? At the start of the field in the 1960s, as people were trained as community psychologists and went for their first job, if they were going into academia they had to go to a university psychology department and create a community psychology focus; similarly, practitioners had to go into the community and create community psychology positions. In the *Handbook of Community Psychology* in the chapter on "Practitioners' Perspectives" (Wolff, 1999), almost all the practitioners writing indicated that they had to create their own position and that indeed their organization did not know them as community psychologists. Over time this has evolved and we trace some of those changes. In exploring the dominant settings and forms of practice in the era we ask: Who are the people who identify as community psychology practitioners? What were they doing at this time? Where were they employed and what kind of skills did they bring to the jobs?

These critical issues will be supplemented with first person stories from prominent community psychology practitioners representing the dominant forms of practice. We hope that these Spotlights can help bring the history of community psychology practice to life and give readers a first person account of what it was like to work as a community psychology practitioner during different stages of the field's development by highlighting their work in a wide variety of applied settings.

The history of community psychology practice is presented as occurring in two separate eras in this chapter, chronologically from the 1960s to the 1990s and from the 1990s to the present. While community psychology is an international field, the history presented in this chapter focuses mainly on community psychology practice as it developed in the United States.

THE EARLY YEARS (1960–1990)

Milestones of the Era: Where Did We Start?

The Sixties

Community psychology practice emerged from the major events of the turbulent decade of the Sixties. Reviewing the events leading up to the Sixties paints a picture of social, political, and economic dissatisfaction building among key groups. Looking back on those events it is clear that the rumblings of discontent had been rising in various segments of American society for many decades. Here we note major events that led to the volatility and power of the Sixties and report some of the changes that resulted. Among these is the creation of the field of community psychology that began to establish itself in university psychology departments and community mental health centers (CMHCs) across the country.

The birth and development of community psychology practice was heavily influenced by what was happening in the broader world. The United States' involvement in the Vietnam War outraged the millions of American youth and their families whose lives were most directly affected. President John F. Kennedy's assassination in 1963 broadcast to the world that our ideals did not match our actions. The civil rights struggles in the South that had simmered beneath the surface since the Civil War burst forth and spread across the nation. Televised images of police beating and turning heavy hoses on peaceful Black and White protest marchers spilled from our television sets into our living rooms. Hundreds of college students from northern states rode buses south to join the campaign supporting African American citizens demonstrating for their right to vote. Martin Luther King Jr.'s March on Washington and his assassination in 1968 brought civil rights to the forefront of national attention.

A number of other major social issues emerged in the Sixties. For example, a drug culture flourished among the young. Women became more vocal in protesting the gender inequalities built into our system. The gay community in New York City, long persecuted by law enforcement, exploded when police raided the Stonewall Inn, a long-standing gay bar in New York City's Greenwich Village, forcing many of the patrons into patrol wagons and arresting them.

Community psychology was "born" of this conflicted culture, one that thirsted for greater justice, strove to be empowered, and valued diversity in thought and ways of life. As a field, community psychology distinguished itself from clinical psychology (the dominant form of psychological practice at the time) in a number of ways. First, the field treated problems and issues, both psychological and not, as having multiple layers of causation. This framework, the ecological model (Bronfenbrenner, 1979), encouraged community psychologists not to look at individual behavior without looking at the context in which it is occurring. Second, noting both the critical shortage of mental health professionals (Albee, 1959) and the differential care and access to care that mental health patients received based on ethnicity and income (Hollingshead & Redlich, 1958), community psychology focused on prevention; how to strengthen communities, social networks, families, and organizations to help individuals adapt and deal with the stresses of life in a healthy way. Third, rather than view individuals as passive recipients of treatment, community psychologists collaborate with those they are trying to help, and attempt to empower those individuals to realize the personal outcomes that they desire. By simply looking at these values, perspectives, and approaches, it is clear to see how the developing field drew on the social movements that were occurring around it.

The Seventies and Eighties

One early manifestation of community psychology principles was in the idea of community mental health, which was born in the era of President John F. Kennedy but came of age in the 1970s with CMHCs proliferating in every state in the nation. In part these CMHCs were created to provide the comprehensive services for the new emphasis on deinstitutionalizing the mentally ill. CMHCs also focused on early intervention, prevention, consultation, and community engagement, all of which are key community psychology principles. One of the required CMHC services was "consultation education and prevention" (CEP). Thus CMHCs hired directors and staff to carry out CEP activities and numerous community psychologists moved into those roles. One example of a community psychologist in a CMHC is John Morgan, whose career is discussed in the following

Spotlight. These services included consultation to community institutions such as schools and social service agencies, training of personnel in these systems, and systematic programming for targeted populations such as young children, the elderly, victims of sexual abuse, and others.

John Morgan

Trained as a clinical and child psychologist, John Morgan prides himself on taking a prevention-based approach to his work. The majority of his professional activities fall into two categories: ensuring that individuals have the coping skills and social support necessary to allow them to deal with "normal" stressors such as child rearing or divorce, and closely examining settings to make sure they are set up in a way that encourages health and well-being.

Fresh out of graduate school, John was hired as a staff psychologist by the community mental health center (CMHC) in Chesterfield County, Virginia, in 1976. At the time, CMHCs had been around for 7 or 8 years, and the CMHC in Chesterfield County was one of 40 centers in Virginia. John was immediately drawn to the orientation of the Chesterfield CMHC; it was embedded in the community not only with the intention of providing access to mental health services for underserved populations, but also to allow staff to actively partner with community organizations and residents to develop programs that strengthened the community-at-large.

As John reflects, for many community psychologists CMHCs offered a comfortable place to practice, a place where they could "give psychology away," a place that valued prevention and community input. John eventually moved into a consultation and evaluation role within the CMHC; there he was able to focus on designing and evaluating prevention-based programs for the community. He relied on his competencies in program management and implementation to successfully introduce prevention-oriented intervention into the community; an appreciation of the ecological model and person-environment fit led him to partnering with various community-based agencies. His advice for doing this: Find someone to champion your program in their setting.

From John's perspective, CMHCs represented not only a community resource, but also a "movement," a significant paradigm shift in how mental health services were approached and delivered. Unfortunately, the program was defunded at the national level before it met its true potential. For John, one of his lasting contributions is to the setting he worked in. Through his 30 years serving Chesterfield Mental Health Center he was able to influence the center so that its focus on prevention programming outlasted his tenure there.

John received the SCRA Award for Distinguished Contributions to Practice in Community Psychology in 1990. The lasting impact of John's work can be seen in the sustained, community-based prevention programming that is now a part of Virginia's state system. He currently works at Voices for Virginia's Children, tackling similar issues related to child and family well-being, but this time through a policy lens.

The 1970s and 1980s were also a time of consolidation in the field of mental health. CMHCs joined forces within a relatively new organization, the National Council of Community Mental Health Centers (NCCMHC). Open to all mental health professionals, this organization established a series of internal councils to address the variety of issues psychologists and social workers encountered.

One of the NCCMHC's internal councils was the Council on Prevention. It focused on developing consultation and education services, as these were defined by the National Institute of Mental Health (NIMH), in its efforts to address wellness and prevention issues. This Council developed standards for CEP services, disseminated useful resources, and designed trainings and conferences. These connections provided an important conduit to U.S. Congress members for easy contact when key legislation (such as bills focused on mental health prevention) was up for review. This was one of the first venues for the gathering of community psychology practitioners. Chapter authors Swift and Wolff were chairs of the Council on Prevention.

With the election of President Jimmy Carter the field gained a very strong advocate for prevention in mental health in the First Lady, Rosalyn Carter. Soon numerous states were appointing state-wide directors of mental health prevention, such as Betty Tableman in Michigan. As director of Prevention Services in Michigan, Betty Tableman believed in the importance of early nurturing and relationship development to an infant's social, emotional, and cognitive health. She was nationally recognized for her successful efforts in building a comprehensive system of mental health services for Michigan's children. At NIMH, Steve Goldston was a champion for prevention in mental health, supporting both academic and practitioner efforts. This provided great opportunities for both practitioners and academics in community psychology to develop and implement evidence-based models of prevention.

In 1981 Ronald Reagan was elected president of the United States and began to turn back the clock on progressive social programs, including CMHCs. The funding for these mental health services was transferred to state block grants, thus giving states the authority to set their own funding agenda and removing the influence of NIMH. State mental health departments mostly did not operate from a community mental health perspective but rather were tied up with their state hospital systems and issues of deinstitutionalization. Within one year of the Reagan funding shift, consultation education and prevention services mostly disappeared at CMHCs across the country.

In 1988 a group of community psychologists (Richard Price, Emory Cowen, Raymond Lorion, & Julia Ramos-McKay), working with the American Psychological Association (APA), edited a volume titled *14 Ounces of Prevention: A Casebook for Practitioners,* which provided 14 examples of high-quality evidence-based prevention programs such as David Olds's Prenatal/Early Infancy Program, David Weikart's High/Scope Perry Preschool Program, Myrna Shure and George Spivak's Interpersonal Cognitive Problem Solving work, Gilbert Botvin's Substance Abuse Prevention Through Life Skills Training, and Bernard Bloom's Separation and Divorce Program. This publication was followed by a Pew Charitable Trust–funded technical assistance program that funded conferences that were held across the country to disseminate these models to practitioners, academics, and funders (foundations and states). This was a successful joint venture of the academics who put the volume together and practitioners who led the dissemination effort; this process illustrated the interdependence of inquiry and intervention. Through this collaboration, these high-quality programs were made available in communities across the country, with the hope that they would be replicated.

Milestones in the World of Community Psychology

The Boston Conference on the Education of Psychologists for Community Mental Health in 1965 marked the birth of community psychology (Anderson et al., 1966). The meeting was held in Swampscott, Massachusetts, and became known as the Swampscott Conference. Psychologists working in field/applied settings comprised half the participants. Four of the six members of the committee who planned the conference and authored the conference report were applied, and two were academic members (Anderson et al., 1966).

The Swampscott Conference carved out the goals and issues that continue to guide the field of community psychology today. Reading the report almost four decades later elicits wonder at the prophetic counsel of the participants. The report's vision of the field as including the integration of applied and academic work is particularly prescient:

> In the development of social change settings, it was stressed that the dichotomy between the university and field stations needs to be overcome. There is, the Conference felt, a profound underlying convergence of interests between these institutions once the goal of social change research is accepted, since both settings are in need of theory, research skill, and community action skills and sanctions. It was urged that a variety of bridging positions between the two systems be developed so that eventually personnel could move between them with complete flexibility. (Anderson et al., 1966, p. 8)

Applied psychologists contributed to the subsequent formation of the American Psychological Association's Division of Community Psychology (Division 27) in 1967, and were consistently elected as officers to the division's Executive Committee for its first 8 years. They served as editors of the APA Division 27 Newsletter (now known as *The Community Psychologist*) for the first 6 years of its publication.

Applied/practice and academic community psychologists were roughly equally represented, in both conference leadership and participation, at the birth of community psychology. This balance shifted in the years after Swampscott. Applied community psychologist practitioners were a relatively silent group during the middle years of their official guild, the Division of Community Psychology. Although they are currently active participants in many aspects of the SCRA, this activity approaches a return to their previous visibility and influence, not a steady state across the 40 years of their discipline (Wolff & Swift, 2008).

Almost a decade after Swampscott the National Conference on Training in Community Psychology, an invitational conference, took place at the University of Texas in Austin. Funded primarily by NIMH, it was sponsored by APA's Division of Community Psychology. The major goal of the Austin conference was "to systematically examine the many questions and issues that have arisen with regard to appropriate models for doctoral training in Community Psychology" (Iscoe, Bloom, & Spielberger, 1977, p. xi). The Austin conference was long overdue, since many university community psychology programs had sprung up in the decade since Swampscott. And clearly the "blooming, buzzing" confusion over the content of such programs, their academic legitimacy, connection to field sites, and the supervision required for students placed in community internships, all determined that community psychology faculty command priority in conference attendance. Applied psychologists were relatively absent at the invitation-only Austin conference. A review of the official roster of 145 participants shows 111 (77%) were academics, 20 (14%) were applied, and 14 (10%) were in the Community Psychology Training Program at the University of Texas at Austin (Wolff & Swift, 2008).

The equity found at Swampscott in the number and influence of applied community psychologists was missing in Austin, and this was noted in several of the conference reports. One chapter in the proceedings, "Community-Based Community Psychologists," pointed out the issues raised by the relatively few applied psychologists present. Some were concerned that their applied colleagues were underrepresented. "Others stressed the irony of a field called Community Psychology attempting to plan its future with relatively little input or representation from those psychologists who work full time in community settings" (Slaikeu, 1977, p. 283).

During this period there were other conferences relevant to community psychology's development. The Vermont Conference on Primary Prevention was created by George Albee of the University of Vermont, a president of both SCRA and APA, and was held for seven consecutive summers at Burlington, Vermont. Here Albee brought together the cutting-edge thinkers, academics, practitioners, and politicians engaged in the world of prevention in mental health. Albee published a book following each conference. These publications are considered to be classical works for the field (Joffe, Albee, & Kelly, 1984).

The National Council of Community Mental Health Centers held national conferences annually that were occasions to educate psychologists in consultation and education services in CMHCs. National conferences played a vital role in keeping CMHC staff trained in the latest developments in the field of mental health and prevention, and in maintaining connections with the movers and shakers in this field.

SCRA Biennial Conferences began in 1987 in South Carolina. These were the first community psychology conferences run by SCRA that were not by invitation, thus giving practitioners a chance to participate and present.

Relationship Between Academic and Practice Community Psychologists

As community psychology developed as a field, the focus was almost solely on creating a legitimate academic field of research and scholarship that was respected within academia and the larger discipline of psychology. Thus it was not focused on defining, developing, or even attending to the growing community psychology practice that was emerging through new community psychology graduates who choose to work outside of academia, as well as through those existing practicing psychologists, drawn to the values and principles of community psychology, who adopted the community psychology identity in their community-based practice. However, there were champions of practice inside the academic environment; these professors not only engaged in community practice, but emphasized training for practice in their students. One example is Greg Meissen, whose story we share in the following Spotlight.

Greg Meissen

Greg Meissen is a professor at Wichita State University, in Wichita, Kansas. For over 25 years, in addition to teaching, conducting research, and advising graduate students, Greg ran a university-based nonprofit, the Self-Help Network, which served as a clearinghouse for self-help groups, connecting individuals to groups across the state. In addition, the Self-Help Network also engaged in systems-based research, looking not at what was going on inside these groups, but rather at how they started, why certain groups thrived, and the nature of their leadership.

The Self-Help Network grew exponentially in the early years; between 1985 and 1990 it was making between 10,000 and 15,000 referrals yearly as well as publishing a directory of self-help groups for public use. As director, Greg saw his role transform as he took on more policy-level and advocacy work. For example, through his work with the Self-Help Network he had established relationships with the Kansas chapter of the National Alliance for the Mentally Ill and consumer run organizations. One of the projects he worked on was getting family members and mental health consumers into the state advisory system on mental health, which was not an easy task.

The U.S. Surgeon General at the time, C. Everett Koop, MD, had brought national attention to self-help groups, recognizing them as important public health resources. This attention, combined with the managed care movement, which changed how individuals received health care, gave Greg and the Self-Help Network room to negotiate a relationship between the formal health system (doctors and insurance companies) and self-help groups within the state of Kansas. He was able to facilitate interchanges between these parties that eventually resulted in referral systems where doctors and insurance companies would use the Self-Help Network's resources to connect patients to local groups. This was a win-win as managed care agencies were looking for ways to cut down on health-care costs, and individuals were able to find their way more easily to self-help groups with the encouragement of their doctors.

For Greg, the competency he relied on the most during this time was collaboration. Successful collaboration with the state government, the health-care system, and others in the community allowed them to bring their work to scale. Additionally, the idea of collaborative partnerships fueled their research as well, with most of it being participatory. Greg describes what he and the Self-Help Network were doing as "adding vitamins to the water"; they were strengthening something that was already there and creating a structure that could be used to connect self-help groups to the larger community. As Greg reflects, "It wasn't that the individual groups didn't have the capacity to do that, it's that they were so focused internally, and they didn't see that as their role."

Greg is a founding member of the Community Psychology Practice Council and served as co-chair from 2005 to 2012, overseeing the process of the group becoming an official council of SCRA. In 2011 he received the SCRA Distinguished Contribution to Service Award. As a practitioner, Greg helped elevate the profile of self-help as a legitimate pathway to recovery, the impact of which can be seen today as self-help groups are more common, acceptable, and integrated into our formal health-care system than they were before.

While academic community psychologists struggled for recognition and legitimacy in universities, community psychology practitioners inherited a more difficult path. Practitioners had to work to be recognized on two fronts: by their academic community psychologist colleagues and in their work settings. At this point in the field's development, academics were making the case for a research basis for community psychology and practitioners did not always work from as explicit a research base; rather, they needed to grapple with local community needs and preferences. This was seen as weakening the case for the field within academia. At the same time, in their work settings community psychology practitioners found little value in identifying themselves as community psychologists in the communities and organizations they practiced in; the term *community psychologist* was unknown to those they worked with. For most of them, identifying themselves as a community psychologist did little to communicate their skills and abilities. Thus most of their colleagues in their work settings did not know them as community psychologists. Clearly it was their community psychology skills that got them hired and made them successful but that was not part of their identity at work. Instead, practitioners often took on the identity of their work, such as "community mental health," "public health," "community development," or "consultation/evaluation." Consequently, as the field of community psychology practice developed, it was mainly invisible.

Any field that wants to have an impact on individuals or community/systems levels needs a practice or applied aspect; this is especially true for fields such as community psychology, which define themselves as being dedicated to change. A look at other fields demonstrates the need for both academic pursuit and a developed practice: social work, public health, organizational psychology, anthropology, urban planning, and clinical psychology. Most of the work to advance the community psychology practice agenda occurs in the second half of our history; it is described later.

The Dominant Settings, Forms of Practice, and Exemplars in the Era

During these formative years of the field community psychology practitioners began to carve out roles for themselves in several unique practice settings (e.g., CMHCs and government) and around key community psychology principles (prevention, empowerment/self-help, and organizational change).

Community Mental Health Centers

As noted above, CMHCs were dominant settings for the practice of community psychology. At Yale University, the Consultation Center, which was the Consultation and Education unit of a local CMHC, was developed and run for many years by community psychologist David Snow. The Consultation Center provided not only models of service but also internships and postdoctoral trainings for graduate students in community psychology with a focus on practice.

Many other community psychology practitioners worked in CMHCs: Saul Cooper and Ruth Schelkun out of the Washtenaw CMHC in Michigan; John Kalafat and Bill Neigher of the Montclair CMHC in New Jersey; Anthony Broskowski of the Northside Community Mental Health Center in Tampa, Florida; Bill Berkowitz in Lowell, Massachusetts; and John Morgan at the Chesterfield CMHC.

Self-Help

Self-help was an area that began to capture the interest of community psychologists early on because of its focus on empowerment and giving psychology away. Self-help centers and networks were being created across the country as the legitimacy of self-help approaches began to emerge. Frank Reissman was a national leader who ultimately was honored for his work by SCRA. Ed Madera was the founder of the New Jersey Self-Help Group Clearing House. He started by keeping a list of groups and those wanting to start groups, then bringing them together with people who had experienced stressful life events and were looking for support groups. In 1980 they received funding from the New Jersey State Division of Mental Health to have one person keep this database of groups. The first self-help listing was published under a grant from Hoffman-LaRoche even prior to the first Self-Help Clearinghouse Directory (www.njgroups.org), and it was a list of local groups and best practice models from around the nation. Today there are more than 4,500 local New Jersey groups listed and about 1,100 national and online groups. Groups are started by people who need support after having gone through significant impactful life events. They pool general knowledge and experiences to provide mutual support.

Greg Meissen's work in creating the Self-Help Network in Wichita, Kansas, is covered in his previous Spotlight.

Government

Community psychologists found a natural home within government at many levels. As the field started out the most prominent government-based community psychologists worked for the National Institute of Mental Health, which managed research and community mental health grants critical to the field's start-up.

For example, community psychologist practitioner Gloria Levin was involved in the administration and review of research, training, and service demonstration programs and in policy development at NIMH. She had a long-standing interest in ethical implications of "outsiders" intervening in communities nurtured by her work as a community and labor organizer and her years in the Peace Corps.

Joyce Barham became the chief of the Prevention Branch at NIMH in 1985. The primary areas the Branch funded under her leadership were the prevention of conduct disorders and a major program directed to preventive interventions with depression and mental health. Barham developed the successful Depression Awareness and Treatment Program (D/ART), which changed the way treatment was given to people in the early stages of depression.

Steve Goldston was coordinator for Primary Prevention Programs at NIMH during this time. He traveled widely throughout the country promoting the government's support of prevention programs, encouraging psychologists at CMHCs to apply for federal grants directed to preventing mental health problems.

Organizational Development and Systems Change

For some community psychologists there was a natural affinity for the discipline of organizational development and change. This was a field with a literature and practice on consultation and systems change and thus an obvious partner to work with and within.

Don Klein was a founder of the field of community psychology, attending Swampscott and focusing his early work on prevention in mental health and community mental health. Don went on to consult to leaders in business, government, religious, health and human service organizations, and with citizens involved in local community development programs. He was a core faculty member of the Union Institute and University. In his later years Don focused on Appreciative Inquiry as the approach for his systems change work (Klein, 2001).

In the 1980s there was also a group of community psychologists at the Industrial Technology Institute in Ann Arbor, Michigan, who worked on social issues related to technological change, including doing consultations with industry. Louis Tornatzky headed the Center for Economic and Social Issues, staffed by community psychologists, economists, and other social scientists who collaborated with engineers and computer scientists from other divisions. Community psychologists such as Mitchell Fleischer and David Roitman continued to pursue this line of work throughout their careers, applying community psychology principles to facilitate organizational change.

Prevention

Prevention became a major focus for community psychology practitioners during this era. The "14 Ounces" book supported by APA highlighted 14 programs that were especially effective and reflected the emergence of prevention as a national priority. Many individuals developing those programs identified themselves as community psychologists, such as Bernard Bloom for his work on separation and divorce and Bill Davidson for his work on the prevention of juvenile delinquency. A number of the editors of the volume were also nationally recognized for their successful prevention work, including Emory Cowen for his work in schools and Rick Price for his work on the consequences of unemployment. Maurice Elias's prevention work on developing positive, constructive life paths for children, with a specific emphasis on social-emotional learning within the school setting, is a great example of the type of systematic, prevention efforts going on at this time.

Maurice Elias

Maurice Elias is a professor in the Psychology Department at Rutgers University. There he focuses on developing positive, constructive life paths for children, with a specific emphasis on social-emotional learning within the school setting. As an applied researcher, Maurice's work is enabled through strong partnerships with school administrators, teachers, and staff. He cites one partnership in particular, with the Plainfield, New Jersey, school system, as an exemplar of the collaborative processes necessary to successfully translate research into action within the school setting.

Before starting to work in Plainfield, Maurice had established an evidence-based school-based program aimed at enhancing students' decision-making skills (Elias & Bruene, 2005). Plainfield,

(Continued)

(Continued)

whose student body was predominantly African American, was intended to test a cultural adaptation of this program. However, what evolved instead was a systems-level intervention, championed by the superintendent of the Plainfield schools, geared toward incorporating social-emotional learning principles into the classroom, as well as building the capacity of staff.

Although the superintendent welcomed Maurice and his research team, entry into this setting was challenging as the district had a long history of strained relationships with outsiders. By spending time in the school buildings, talking and listening to teachers and administrators, and lending a helping hand where they could, Maurice and his team of graduate and undergraduate students from Rutgers were able to establish a culture of cooperation.

From an action-research perspective Maurice believed it was the role of his team to emphasize the theory and intent of social-emotional learning modules; the technical issues of how to teach the material were addressed by the teachers themselves. Using an empowerment model, leadership team structures were set up at the various buildings across the large district to facilitate the intervention and ensure responsibility for follow-through. Throughout an 8-year period, extensive quantitative and qualitative evaluation data were collected.

Looking back, Maurice recognizes that Plainfield was the first time he pushed past the "program" perspective and focused on helping make changes at the school and district level in a highly challenging context, to the culture and climate of the institution, a clear use of ecological principles and systems-level understanding. The experience validated what Maurice holds to be a cardinal principle of community psychology: that "no amount of skill on the part of the individual community psychologists is going to make something work without the full collaboration of those involved in the setting."

Maurice "Mo" Elias is a past president of SCRA, recipient of the 1993 SCRA Distinguished Contribution to Practice Award, and the 1998 SCRA Ethnic Minority Mentoring Award. Maurice's work has led to a national focus on social-emotional learning and school climate and has become even more critical as schools continue to face funding cuts, issues of violence, and poor performance.

THE LATER YEARS: 1990–PRESENT (2013): THE FURTHER DEVELOPMENT AND SHAPING OF COMMUNITY PSYCHOLOGY PRACTICE

Milestones of the Era

Looking at the years between 1990 and 2013 we see two decades highlighted by dramatic changes in the world that had a significant influence on community psychology practice:

- Globalization acknowledged a growing interdependence resulting in part from increasingly interconnected economic systems.

- The dramatic climate change crisis that threatens global survival gained increased attention and called for a global response.

- The Internet also facilitated globalization by creating a world intimately connected by newly found Internet access. It was now possible to actually carry on exchanges with colleagues around the world. As a result, global collaborations in community psychology increased.

- On September 11, 2001, midway through these two decades, the World Trade Center in New York and the Pentagon were attacked, the first foreign attack on mainland U.S. territory in modern history. This event shook the United States and shook the world. It triggered justification for the United States to begin a series of wars in Iraq and Afghanistan that consequently defined these years. With so much money tied up in wars and homeland security, resources for community building and community health became scarcer.

- There were numerous conflicts globally; much of the global conflict could be seen as wars fought over energy resources, directly related to the climate change crisis. Toward the end of these two decades the Arab Spring occurred with uprisings around the world for democracy.

A focus on liberation psychology, conflict resolution, community building, and violence prevention were some of the community psychology themes that emerged. A parallel focus on the plight of women across the globe raised the theme of liberation, which resonated in community psychology. All of these global events and more shaped the world that community psychology navigated.

On a domestic level in the United States, there was a significant demographic shift, with increasing numbers of communities of color across the country. The ever-changing U.S. population pushed issues of racial equality, citizenship and immigration policy, and representation back into the nation's attention. Policies and laws, such as the War on Drugs, which affected communities of color at a higher rate, were brought into the national conversation. This recalled the early civil rights roots of community psychology. Issues of discrimination, prejudice, white privilege, and systemic racism now emerged in discussions of health and educational disparities. Although many in the nation declared the issues of race as resolved (especially with the election of Barack Obama, a Black president), the data on racial and educational disparities illustrated the ongoing inequities in the nation and rallied many community psychologists in their work (Wolff, 2013).

Kien Lee's work on cultural competence in communities, highlighted in the following Spotlight, illustrates a community psychologist addressing these issues.

Kien S. Lee

Kien Lee found her home in community psychology via a roundabout pathway. Early in her career, she worked for a Washington, D.C–based evaluation and consultation firm; it was there where mentor, colleague, and friend David Chavis first introduced her to the field of community psychology. Now, almost 16 years later, Kien has gone back to school for formal training in community psychology and, together with David, oversees one of only a handful of businesses built on community psychology principles, Community Science.

Community Science (www.communityscience.com) is a research and development consulting organization, based out of Washington, D.C. What makes this business different is its use of community as the lens through which social problems and solutions are viewed. As Kien puts it, "Community Science is a proponent that research, evaluation, and other consultation services are something aimed at strengthening communities; the unique lens we bring to this work is that as we work with organizations, we are continually thinking both about the communities that these organizations are trying to impact as well as the communities which they are a part of."

The organization focuses on issues where senior staff has extensive knowledge and experience. For Kien, these issues include immigrant integration, cross-cultural competency, and health equity. The increasing attention to health equity and to the country's increasing racial and ethnic diversity has enabled her to find meaningful projects in these areas. This work ranges from working with nonprofits to increase their capacity to provide culturally competent services to helping facilitate immigrant integration processes, bringing both immigrants and longtime community residents together to find common ground to strengthen their communities.

As an organization, Community Science is careful to select projects that focus on community and systems change. Therefore, ecological perspectives drive her work. The ability to successfully manage multiple projects, including allocating time and resources, and keeping in mind the client's interests as well as the public's, are also important when working in the consulting field. Additionally, Kien advises students to find ways to get training and experience facilitating small- and large-group processes, something that community psychology students and graduates need but do not have sufficient opportunity to learn and practice in their graduate programs. She sees these skills as crucial in engaging communities as well as in translating research into practical actions.

While Kien and David have succeeded in creating a place for community psychologists to practice (about half of the company is made up community psychologists), Kien still worries about the visibility of the field. Although community psychology competencies, theories, and approaches are becoming more relevant to today's changing times, the visibility and value of the field has not increased. This gap creates the risk of "missing" future practitioners, which is something Kien relates to, as she was almost a near miss for the field.

In 2013, Kien received the SCRA Award for Distinguished Contributions to Practice in Community Psychology. Her work on immigration at the local level, specifically in facilitating processes through which communities and newer immigrant groups can come together, has become a national model for increasing integration and building culturally competent organizations.

A parallel civil rights battle was being fought over the LGBT (lesbian, gay, bisexual, and transgender) population. Community psychologists were engaged in all of these issues. The United States also saw changes in how we addressed health and human service issues. Across a broad range of health issues there was a renewed emphasis on prevention versus treatment that challenged the traditional treatment emphasis that had dominated the medical and mental health fields for so long. This emerged strongly in the public health arena and first addressed specific issues such as substance abuse and tobacco cessation. Comprehensive community approaches to substance abuse, alcohol, and drugs launched hundreds of comprehensive community substance abuse coalitions across the nation. This was also true in other public health arenas such as tobacco prevention. This focus on comprehensive community interventions opened the way for community psychologists to get involved in programming at the community/population level rather than just with individuals alone. Community psychologists became involved in various aspects of community programming including design, training, consulting, and evaluation.

The public health population-based approach was leading to the development of comprehensive community initiatives by foundations and government. The World Health Organization issued the Ottawa Charter, describing the prerequisites for health (elimination of poverty, sustainable environment, etc.), which opened the way for the emergence of the Healthy Communities movement, the basis of which paralleled community psychology principles and practices (Wolff, 2003).

The integration and overlap between community psychology and public health grew in this era with numerous collaborations both in academia and in the field. Community psychologists edited major public health journals (e.g., *Health Education and Behavior* edited by Mark Zimmerman). Community psychologists helped to create joint community psychology/public health programs (e.g., Vince Francisco at the University of North Carolina Greensboro). The public health arena became a significant location for the practice of community psychology. Not only did community psychology graduates work in that arena but community psychology ideas and writings were taught in public health and influenced the field. The community psychology program at Georgia State University took advantage of its co-location in Atlanta to work closely with the Centers for Disease Control and Prevention. Craig Blakely (2011, p. 20), working in a public health academic setting, talks of it as "dispersion of our skills into other disciplines." Both fields heartily embraced the idea of community-based participatory research as well.

The work in prevention that had been pioneered by community psychologists in the first 20 years of the field started to emerge in the new focus on prevention research centers and evidence-based prevention programs that had proven their effectiveness. This became the theme for numerous federal funding sources. Many community psychologists had developed prevention programs that qualified for these new criteria and began to have their work funded and widely disseminated across the country. Evidence-based programs picked up on the theme of our founders who had published the *14 Ounces of Prevention: A Casebook for Practitioners* (Price et al., 1988), which demonstrated that we could document outcomes from prevention programs.

The legacy of the mental health roots of community psychology was manifest in the ongoing involvement of many community psychologists with the mental health consumers movement and consumer-run organizations. This brought the grassroots empowerment theme of community psychology to the field of mental health.

Milestones in the World of Community Psychology

Events

The emergence of the SCRA Biennial Meetings, which were the first open (not by invitation only) meetings of community psychologists, created settings where academics and practitioners could exchange ideas and collaborate on equal ground. This provided settings for community psychology practitioners to gather, present, organize, exchange ideas, and become a more integral part of the field.

In 2005 at the Champaign Urbana Biennial a small group of practitioners and academics with the support of the SCRA's Executive Committee (EC) and President Cliff O'Donnell ran a series of visioning sessions that ultimately led to a revised vision for SCRA adopted by the EC and voted on by the membership. The original vision of SCRA had not been thoroughly re-examined for many years. The new vision (Wolff & Snell-Johns, 2005) emerged from this democratic participatory process and placed more emphasis on the "A" for Action in the name "SCRA." The new mission for SCRA was: "The Community Psychology of the future will be guided by four key principles: global in nature; use of multi-sectoral, interdisciplinary partnerships and approaches; a focus on creating policies informed by Community Psychology and social justice values; and research and action that promote social justice."

The process also led to a modification of the SCRA vision: "The Society for Community Research and Action (SCRA) will have a strong, global impact on enhancing well-being and promoting social justice for all people by fostering collaboration where there is division and empowerment where there is oppression."

Out of the visioning process a small group (that quickly grew) began having monthly calls in September 2005 on issues of community psychology practice. This was the first time in the history of community psychology that a group met consistently over a period of time to focus solely on practice. Those monthly calls evolved into the Practice Council and continue to this day, many years later, and generally have between 15 and 20 members on the call out of a pool of about 40 who attend (one-third of the members are graduate and undergraduate students).

This group asked fundamental questions and then acted to answer them, questions like: How do we define community psychology practice? What are the skills and competencies one would need to practice community psychology? Who considers themselves a community psychology practitioner and how did they get their skills? What is the status of community psychology education for practice in graduate programs?

The group started with basics—defining community psychology practice—and brought a draft definition to the first International Community Psychology Conference in Puerto Rico. At that meeting the participants helped refine the definition that then was published by David Julian (2006) in *The Community Psychologist*.

The more they pursued community psychology practice, the more they realized how little they knew about the state of practice and practice training in our field. Because of the disconnect between SCRA and practitioners, efforts were not made to track the settings where people were working, what they were doing, or their continuing professional needs. So a survey on practice was developed and analyzed (Gaitlin, Rushenberg, & Hazel, 2005).

The small practice-oriented group then decided it was time to pull SCRA together around "practice," so with the help of SCRA president Carolyn Swift, the Practice Group as they called themselves planned and conducted the first ever Summit on Community Psychology Practice at the Pasadena Biennial in 2007. The Summit was a huge success with over 100 people coming a day early to the Biennial. Those attending were energized; they focused their energy on three directions—publication, training, and practice. These three remain the foci to this day many years later. Over the next years this led to significant outcomes in each of the three areas:

1. Publications: These last two decades also finally saw the production of publications by community psychology practitioners that were clearly focused on the practice of community psychology. The most significant triumph was the creation of the *Global Journal of Community Psychology Practice* (www.gjcpp.org; Vince Francisco, editor), an international web-based journal appearing with about four issues a year beginning in 2010. Circulation has grown rapidly to between 1,200 and 1,600 readers per issue in over 100 countries around the world, which makes the journal in its first years competitive with other community psychology journals for readership.

The Community Psychologist (*TCP*), the internal organ of SCRA, also saw changes in the direction of acknowledging community psychology practice. The arrival of "The Community Practitioner" column within the *TCP* was a first step—originally edited by David Julian and later by Susan Wolfe. In recent years it has focused on examining how community psychology is practiced in various sectors (foundations, health care, nonprofits, etc.).

2. Training/education: The Practice Group then formed a collaboration with the SCRA Council on Education Programs on the competencies that are required for community psychology practice. The two groups first collaborated on a survey with a focus on competencies for practice and how community psychology students were being trained in the competencies. The results were presented at the 2009 Biennial in Montclair, New Jersey (Dziadkowiec & Jimenez, 2009). This collaboration ultimately led to a formal set of 18 competencies that were adopted by the SCRA Executive Committee and published in *The Community Psychologist* (Dalton & Wolfe, 2012). This was the first official listing of community psychology competencies; it has resulted in an active effort to systematically incorporate competencies into community psychology graduate training programs across the county.

3. Professional practice/careers in practice: The Practice Group developed a community practice webpage at the SCRA website, with job listings, vignettes, and resources. In *The Community Psychologist* they developed columns on various types of practice careers such as community psychologists in foundations, health care, and evaluation practices.

Finally, in 2008, the EC (under the leadership of Maurice Elias) adopted a proposal from the Practice Group that had them become the Community Psychology Practice Council with a voting seat on the Executive Committee, a position equal to that of the Council of Education Programs that represented the needs of the graduate programs. Throughout all these activities of the Practice Group, graduate students held critical roles—leading many of the initiatives.

In 2010 the Practice Council developed a Value Proposition for Community Psychologists. This effort was led by Al Ratcliffe and Bill Neigher. In their article titled "What Is a Community Psychologist? Why Should I Hire One?" (Ratcliffe & Neigher, 2010) they noted that a value proposition is a statement clarifying the distinctive value of a community psychologist for a prospective employer or for a whole sector of the economy. As Mo Elias (2009, p. 1) noted, "This statement should convince a potential consumer that one particular product or service will add more value or better solve a problem than other similar offerings." Here was a proactive stance to marketing community psychology practitioners to the employer market.

A final major set of events that crucially influenced the growth of community psychology practice in this era was the emergence of the International Community Psychology Conferences. These programs outside the United States have a greater emphasis on and regard for community psychology practice and systems change than U.S. programs, and thus provided excellent support for the community psychology practitioners. Taking advantage of the Internet, globally based practitioners were able to exchange information and collaborate. At the first International Community Psychology Conference, in Puerto Rico, the Practice Group held a series of workshops that allowed for the discussion and shaping of the definition of community psychology practice. This global influence continues in the work of the *Global Journal of Community Psychology Practice.*

Relationship Between Academic and Practice Community Psychologists

Over the last few decades the focus of the relationship between practitioners and academics has centered on the six key variables to developing a mature community psychology field of practice.

1. Defining a community psychology practice: For many decades there was no definition of community psychology practice. Thus, community psychology practice was anything that someone who declared themselves a community psychologist did in the field. This neglect created barriers for practitioners, because how can you develop an undefined field?

The Practice Group created a definition and solicited input from the field on the web and through the International Community Psychology Conference in Puerto Rico in 2004. This definition launched a discussion that has continued through the discussion of competencies.

2. Competencies: The competencies necessary to become a practicing community psychologist were also left undefined. This was the case even as graduate programs, both doctoral and master's, created programs that trained practitioners. They may have defined what their programs did but they did not define what the field expected of those going into practice. Some educators described their goal as teaching students to "think" like a community psychologist; this is clearly not enough to prepare students to practice community psychology in the real world. The SCRA Practice Group also tackled this issue, starting at the Pasadena Summit where a group worked to produce an original list of competencies, many drawn from parallel fields (Scott, 2007).

This was followed by valuable collaboration between the Council of Education Programs under the very able leadership of Jim Dalton, and the newly recognized

Photo 1.1   2013 Practice Council Summit held at the SCRA Biennial Conference in Miami, Florida.

Source: Carlos Luis.

Community Psychology Practice Council to develop an official definition of community psychology competencies for practice. These 18 competencies were then adopted by the SCRA Executive Committee (Dalton & Wolfe, 2012). Even with these significant steps on competencies many questions remain: What do we teach? When do we actually teach the competencies? What skills are needed? And when do community psychology practitioners get these skills—in graduate school or after they graduate? The excellent collaboration between practitioners and academics on the competencies illustrated the maturation of the relationships between these two groups.

3. Effectiveness: As an emerging field of practice, community psychology needed to demonstrate by anecdote and research that its community interventions resulted in observable, intended, positive community change; in other words to demonstrate its effectiveness. With no outlet for writing or presenting their work and discussing their outcomes it was hard for the field of community psychology practice to demonstrate its effectiveness and to grow as a field of practice. Thus effectiveness was unknown or unseen except in academic-based practice where it was more likely to be carefully evaluated, researched, and published. Part of the way the effectiveness of a practice

grows is through the sharing of stories and there was no place for that in community psychology publications and conferences. The onset of the SCRA Biennials began to change that status quo.

Even practice done by community psychology academics, unless researched and published, was not shared in the community psychology world. Many community psychology academics were very involved in practice but did not write or talk about it in the early community psychology years unless it was part of a research project. The Practice Group (later the Community Psychology Practice Council) created venues to publish—first "The Community Practitioner" column in *The Community Psychologist* and then the *Global Journal of Community Psychology Practice*. These created opportunities for sharing and learning.

4. Acknowledged and legitimate: The failure to acknowledge the contributions of community psychology practitioners was part of the professional organization's history: There was almost no presence of practitioners at the field's second national meeting, the historic Austin Conference in 1976. When the field created a category of SCRA Fellow, almost no practitioners qualified for many years (Wolff & Swift, 2008, p. 616). When SCRA created its award for Outstanding Contributions it was for research. Only after practitioners lobbied for mutual recognition was a new Practice Award created.

In the early years graduate students would often report to the few visible community psychology practitioners in SCRA that once they announced to their advisor that they were interested in a practice career path they felt they became second-class citizens in their academic departments. They often could not even find faculty willing to be their thesis advisor. The oft-repeated myth in the field was that those graduate students who could not get academic jobs went into practice—the myth represented the view that these were indeed second-class citizens.

The Practice Group, an informal gathering of practitioners, gained legitimacy by creating the first national gathering on community psychology practice. This Summit, attended by many academics, focused on the future directions for community psychology practice including publications, training, and support of practice in the field. Through their membership, activity level, and success the Practice Group carved a legitimate role for practice and finally achieved council status in SCRA on a par with the Council of Education Programs.

5. Visible: Community psychology practitioners were invisible to almost all audiences. Although valued by their employers, many were not known at their workplace as a community psychologist. Employers rarely advertised for professionals with community psychology titles for positions.

Within the field of SCRA there were few formal places for practitioners to gather and few where they could publish and share their work. In the early years of the SCRA Biennials graduate students would often approach the few practitioners who were there and be very curious as to who these "strange" community psychologists were since many had never met a community psychology practitioner in their years in graduate school.

So community psychology practitioners were invisible to employers, to the field, and to the public. They were seemingly a "stealth" profession, and academics hid the practice side of their work as well, rarely publishing it in SCRA venues.

6. Support: With all that is mentioned above it was hard for community psychology practitioners to find peer support in the field of community psychology. So the practitioners created it themselves—first with a practice interest group, then after the vision process they created the informal Practice Group that finally lobbied for and achieved status as the Community Psychology Practice Council. This group has gone beyond complaining and moved to create change to move the field of community psychology practice forward. It attracted large numbers of students. It is actively creating support settings where community psychology practitioners can share their work and learn from each other. It is important to note that academic community psychologists such as Greg Meissen, Vince Francisco, and Bill Berkowitz, with a deep investment in practice (their own and that of their students), have not only been very active members of the Practice Council but have been some of the group's most productive members.

The Dominant Settings, Forms of Practice, and Exemplars of the Era

Over the years from 1990 to 2013 the practice of community psychology began to spread to more and more fields and address a broader array of issues. The issues addressed were ones where the unique skills and competencies of a community psychologist turned out to be of special value to the work. By 1990 many community psychologists had been in the field long enough to find valuable work in a broad array of arenas. Over this time they were able to rise in their chosen field of practice to the point where their achievements could become visible and recognized. This occurred across a wide range of sectors including nonprofits, foundations, health-care settings, government, consulting firms, and more.

Major areas of focus of practice in this era covered a broad range of content areas including mental health, HIV, substance abuse, violence prevention, tobacco cessation, health issues such as asthma, social determinants of health, healthy communities, children and families, racism/health disparities, and others.

Challenges During These Years

The majority of career paths for community psychology graduates are outside academia (Elias, 2009). It is most likely accurate to say that most graduates of community psychology graduate programs take positions in practice rather than academia. This is due in part to the large number of graduates of master's programs, the limited number of academic positions, and the preference of many of those who complete their graduate training to go into applied work.

Unfortunately it is also true that it is very hard to track the graduates who go into practice rather than academic settings. Since there are almost no jobs for practitioners that are labeled as community psychology, these practitioners take on the identity or the issue of their work setting. Thus those who go into work on substance abuse prevention might affiliate with the Community Anti-Drug Coalitions of America or those who work in foundations will affiliate with a national organization of foundations (e.g., Council on Foundations). Those working on public health issues may become members of the American Public Health Association and those focusing their work on evaluation may affiliate with the American Evaluation Association. As adaptive chameleons, they change their colors to suit their new field. They keep their community psychology skills, values, and principles but slowly separate from SCRA, the field itself, and maybe even their identity as community psychologists. SCRA does not track graduates and surprisingly very few graduate programs actually keep a record of their graduates and where they are working.

The adoption of a set of community psychology competencies by SCRA does allow for practitioners to declare their proficiencies to potential employers and allows graduate students seeking their first job to emphasize their areas of skill. Thus, these competencies become one clear way to declare the skill set for community psychology practice (Dalton & Wolfe, 2012).

The most noteworthy aspect of practice from 1990 to the present is the vast array of settings where community psychologists now are having an impact, as illustrated below. This enhances the ability for community psychology thinking, principles, and practice to infiltrate many other fields.

Health Care

The health-care industry is a huge market in the United States and in most countries. Community psychologists have found a variety of valuable positions within that system. Bill Neigher (see accompanying Spotlight) is the vice president for system development at Atlantic Health Systems, the largest health-providing system in New Jersey and one of the largest in the United States. In that role he is charged with planning and supporting system development initiatives.

Others working in health care include Rebecca Lee, developing an ecological model for physical activity at the University of Houston, and David Lounsbury at Albert Einstein College of Medicine, engaged in multidisciplinary approaches to cancer prevention and control.

William Neigher

William (Bill) Neigher is currently the vice president for system development and chief strategy officer at Atlantic Health System (www.atlantichealth.org) in northwest New Jersey. Atlantic Health is a large multi-hospital system that offers services across the entire spectrum of care; there, Bill is responsible for overseeing growth as well as mission development. The organization's new vision statement, "empowering our communities to be the healthiest in the nation," is a direct reflection of Bill's own community psychology values.

As a practitioner, Bill is a great example of someone who advanced from doing community-based work, to managing others, to now creating the systems and environments that enable the value-driven initiatives he has devoted his career to advancing. Trained as a social psychologist, Bill was influenced early on by Emory Cowen and the value proposition he put forth for prevention. Bill got his start in health care in 1973 when he was   with the opportunity to work in a community mental health center in Passaic, New Jersey. There he collaborated with Charles Windle, of the National Institute of Mental Health, on evaluation research within the CMHC movement. Bill cites this early work as influential in bringing him to the field of community psychology; the ideas that he and Charles incorporated into their evaluation research, including transparency, public accountability, and community involvement in the research process, are still concepts that drive his work today.

From 1978 until 1998, the Community Systems Division of St. Clare Hospital CMHC (Denville, NJ) was an incubator for applied community psychology. Led by Bill, it was enabled by hospital executive Joseph Trunfio, a clinical psychologist who did his postdoctoral training in community psychology under SCRA's first president, Robert Reiff. Research and evaluation, consultation and education, and internal training were federal CMHC-funded elements that produced people and programs with national impact. Ed Madara founded the New Jersey and American Self Help Clearinghouses (www.selfhelpgroups.org), one of the first initiatives to enable the mutual aid and self-help movement (Madara won the SCRA Distinguished Contribution to Practice Award in 2001). John Kalafat and Maureen Underwood developed widely published training programs in crisis intervention and death and dying; Bill, along with NIMH's Charles Windle and others, provided a national sourcebook of CMHC program evaluation and published a symposium on the NIMH CMHC evaluation effort. For 7 years an annual postdoctoral fellowship led by John Kalafat trained community psychologists in applied settings, including a future president of SCRA (Ken Maton, in 1998).

Bill's current focus is preparing Atlantic Health for the changing model of health-care reimbursement under the Patient Protection and Affordable Care Act. As Bill puts it, "We currently have huge disparities in care: who gets care and what the outcome is . . . one of the tenets to healthcare reform is the value of prevention." Bill sees increasing access to health promotion services as a start to closing the gaps in care. Atlantic Health has been moving in this direction, even before the enabling legislation was passed; the system has begun to recognize that only a small fraction of "healing" and "health" happens within the walls of their facilities and has been reaching outward to engage and partner with the different parts of the community.

Looking forward, Bill anticipates new job settings opening to community psychology practitioners, especially those with an understanding of health promotion and prevention, in places such as with health insurance companies (Neigher & Kirk, 2013). However, in order for this to happen, we need a clearly articulated value proposition for the field.

Bill received the SCRA Award for Distinguished Contributions to Practice in Community Psychology in 2010. As a leader, Bill has made a sustainable impact on his organization, changing the vision statement from one that emphasized clinical care and treatment for the ill, to one that focuses on partnering with communities to promote health; this includes establishing the Atlantic Center for Population Health Sciences. The impact of this paradigm shift, in the era of the Affordable Care Act, is a model for how health systems across the country can interact with different sectors of the community.

Nonprofits

The domain of the nonprofit world is where many if not most community psychologists practice. Their activities can include evaluation and design of programs, organizational development, and management and leadership development for health and human service organizations, or initiation of community programming within the nonprofit realm. They can be staff, administration, board, volunteer, or consultant. An example of a community psychologist creating an actual nonprofit center for the practice and training of community psychology is the Center for Community Support and Research, developed by Greg Meissen (see his accompanying Spotlight) and affiliated with the Community Psychology Program at Wichita State. This Center, which evolved out of the Self-Help Network, combined practical community and organizational development practices with applied research and evaluation methods (Wituk, 2006). The Center has been involved in activities as broad as a visioning and planning process for the Wichita Mental Health Consumer Empowerment project and Compassion Kansas.

Government

Government at all levels has been a setting for practicing community psychologists. Rich Jenkins at the National Institute on Drug Abuse (Levin, 2007) works on HIV issues at the federal level. At the state level, Maria Chun (2012) writes of finding rewarding community psychology practice positions in state government, including roles as budget analyst, auditor/analyst, and regulatory reform director. Local government has also been a setting but at that level community psychologists have operated as elected officials: Thom Moore on the School Committee in Champaign/Urbana, Bill Berkowitz as a long-time Town Meeting member in Arlington, Massachusetts, and Debi Starnes an elected city councilor in Atlanta, Georgia, for over a decade. Debi (see her Spotlight) has written of her work (Starnes, 2004) on the Council with a major focus on homelessness but also on citizen participation and respect for human diversity and social justice.

Debi Starnes

Over the course of her career, Debi Starnes has served in both elected and policy advisory roles in the Atlanta, Georgia, city government. During her tenure in local government, she focused on issues related to community development, especially city-wide strategies to combat homelessness.

Trained in both clinical psychology and community/organizational psychology, Debi credits not her formal education, but rather the various leadership roles she has taken on in her local community, for propelling her into a career in city government. As Debi puts it, "I didn't get elected because I was a community psychologist, but being a community psychologist helped enormously in my perspective and how I approached different community issues or tasks, once elected." When running for office, it was just an aside that she had a PhD; voters evaluated her on the skills she brought to the table, including her reputation as a strategic thinker, a good collaborator, and a problem solver.

As a city council member (1994–2005), Debi strived to develop relationships between the homeless providers, business community, and residential neighborhoods in her district. In pursuit of this goal, she developed the Homeless Action Group, which brought together different sectors of the community to discuss issues related to homelessness on a monthly basis. The city, working with homeless providers and business leaders, developed a central intake and assessment facility called "The Gateway." This downtown facility has enabled homeless service providers to better match individuals with housing and services, and has allowed for improved communication between providers and the wider community (e.g., law enforcement, business). Throughout this effort, Debi relied on her ability to facilitate collaboration and bring diverse cohorts together to find common ground. Another competency essential to her work was translating scientific reports into usable information for the community.

Debi encourages other community psychologists to run for office, stressing that much improvement can be made on public issues and social problems from inside local governments. In terms of how to prepare for a career in local government? "There is no substitute," Debi says, "for rolling up your sleeves and getting involved at the grassroots level and letting your knowledge, skills, and abilities propel you forward."

Debi received the SCRA Award for Distinguished Contributions to Practice in Community Psychology in 2002. She currently stays busy managing her consulting firm of 25 years, EMSTAR Research, Inc. (www.emstarresearch.com/), which keeps several other community psychologists employed as well.

Foundations

Local, state, and national foundations are another arena where community psychologists have been employed and have been able to have significant influence. Some community psychologists run foundations: Judy Meyers, president and chief executive officer of the Children's Fund of Connecticut, and Sharon Rosen, executive director of the Sadie and Harry Davis Foundation focused on children's oral health in Maine.

Others have been project officers in larger foundations, like Ed Seidman and Vivien Tseng at the W. T. Grant Foundation, working on youth issues, and Adrienne Paine Andrews at the Kansas Health Foundation where she has responsibilities including leadership training, organizational capacity building, and food and fitness coalitions.

Judy Meyers (2011) describes it this way:

> Although a career in philanthropy is not one usually envisioned when in training to be a community psychologist, in point of fact there is no better match for the skills, knowledge, and values that encompass Community Psychology. Foundations come in many shapes and sizes, but at their core, they are about using resources to promote the public good and improve social or human conditions and the quality of life in communities. (p. 10)

Comprehensive Community Initiatives

The emergence of the healthy communities model from the World Health Organization and the funding by government and foundations of comprehensive community initiatives created community-wide settings for the practice of community psychology. Many community psychologists became involved in designing, training, studying, and evaluating community coalition efforts. Examples include Steve Fawcett and Jerry Schultz at the Work Group on Health and Development at the University of Kansas; Tom Wolff and Bill Berkowitz at Healthy Communities Massachusetts; and Vince Francisco with North Carolina's Healthy Carolinians.

Consulting and Evaluation Practices

Program evaluation is one of the strengths of community psychology graduate programs, so it is no surprise that many graduates of these programs become employed in the business of evaluating and designing programs. For some it can be an independent one-person practice doing program evaluations as well as program consultation (e.g., Ann Price at www.communityevaluationsolutions.com/). Others started by specializing in a single area, such as Emstar Research, a consulting firm run by Jim Emshoff and Debi Starnes (see Spotlight on Debi Starnes) that initially focused on substance abuse prevention. Their services include evaluation, data analysis, evaluation and research training, needs assessment, grant writing, and ongoing support. Although they began with a focus on substance abuse prevention, over the years they broadened widely from there.

Another prominent example is Community Science run by David Chavis and Kien Lee (see Spotlight on Kien Lee). Community Science's strategy is to provide an integrated approach to building the capacity of organizations and institutions to develop the health, economic equity, and social justice of communities. They combine evaluation, technical assistance, a support network, information technology, and educational services to build community capacity. Located outside of Washington, D.C., they do a lot of business with government agencies and foundations. Community Science is a unique community psychology–based organization that has many community psychologists on staff.

The Internet

In recent years the Internet has become a major setting for numerous forms of human interaction, information exchange, community building, and building community competencies. A bright example from community psychology is the Community Tool Box (CTB; http://ctb.ku.edu) developed by Steve Fawcett and colleagues (Jerry Schultz, Bill Berkowitz, Vince Francisco, Phil Rabinowitz, Christina Holt, Tom Wolff, and others). The CTB was designed to enhance the capacity of communities and community activists. Although begun as a domestic initiative it has rapidly become an international resource in English, Spanish, and Arabic with over seven million visitors a year, with half being from outside the United States.

Neighborhoods

Working in your own neighborhood as a community psychologist has been epitomized and written about by Bill Berkowitz (1984). Bill has been a long-term elected Town Meeting member in Arlington, Massachusetts, editor of a neighborhood newsletter, and co-creator of numerous community events in his community. He has written extensively on communities and neighbors sharing both how-to's and exemplars about how neighborhood leaders can create significant change (Berkowitz, 1987).

Global Climate Change, Sustainability, and Activism

Manuel Riemer and Stephanie Reich (2011) have been leaders in highlighting the role of community psychologists in issues of global climate change. Riemer (2010) has worked on national climate education efforts and local projects to develop local green project initiatives.

Gary Harper (see accompanying Spotlight) has taken his interest and commitment to HIV prevention work to opportunities in Kenya. There he has initiated grassroots community education programs that are run by the local Thigio youth themselves. "Thigio youth are actively engaged in a process that recognizes their individual and collective strengths and continually generates greater awareness of HIV/AIDS and more effective ways to combat the disease" (Bangi, Harper, & Callahan, 2006 p. 36).

Gary Harper

Drawing on his background in both public health and community psychology, Gary Harper has dedicated his career to advancing HIV prevention, specifically in adolescents and other marginalized groups, including gay/bisexual populations. Since 2004, these efforts have also included an international component, first in Kenya, and now in both Botswana and Zambia as well. What makes Gary's approach to this "international work" so fitting for the field of community psychology is how he frames it—it's about building capacity to prevent and cope with HIV at the local level.

Gary got his start working in Kenya through a university-sponsored trip. While there, he developed relationships with various groups, including a convent of nuns working to serve a rural community outside of Nairobi suffering with high rates of HIV; most of those initial relationships he still maintains today. Gary cites these relationships and others as crucial in enabling him to continue to successfully work in Kenya. In fact, many of his projects have been community initiated, with individuals approaching Gary, rather informally, based on their knowledge of his past work.

One lesson that Gary learned early in the process is that in order for groups to successfully collaborate across cultures, it's important to spend time together. Time working, but also time getting

(Continued)

(Continued)

to know one another and building the relationships that can sustain a partnership over time, over oceans, and over the numerous intercultural hiccups that are bound to occur.

Reflecting back on his work, Gary does not minimize the difficulty of this type of work, nor does he minimize the reward. "Doing international work has totally changed me as a human being. I am not the same person that I was when I first stepped off the plane in Kenya. It's changed the way that I look at the world, the way I look at myself, my friends, my family. . . . I will never be the same person I was the first time I stepped off the plane."

Gary Harper is currently a professor of Health Behavior and Health Education at the University of Michigan, School of Public Health. His research and community work both in the United States and in Kenya have given an empowered role within the prevention community to marginalized youth suffering from HIV.

FUTURE OF COMMUNITY PSYCHOLOGY PRACTICE

This history of community psychology practice covers four issues over the 40 years of the field. First we illustrated how the ecological stance of community psychology requires that the field and especially the practice be responsive to the environment, and thus we can see how community psychology practice has evolved over these 40 years in part by responding to the world events and issues occurring around the field—issues of war and peace, racism, sexism, homophobia, and a multitude of injustices.

The second focus of the chapter was on the evolution of the field of community psychology practice. With the practice of community psychology starting 40 years ago we track the pursuit by practitioners to create a new field of practice that was defined, skillful, effective, legitimate, visible, and supported. The outcomes of this pursuit include the creation and success of the *Global Journal of Community Psychology Practice,* an adopted set of community psychology practice competencies that has been approved by SCRA, and the creation of the Community Psychology Practice Council with a vote on the EC.

The third focus was a subset of the second and describes the tensions between academic and practice community psychologists and how those tensions evolved for the better over the last 40 years, to where we are today: with practice and academia coming together to improve training in the applied competencies.

The final focus of the chapter illustrated the growing breadth of impact of the field of community psychology practice over time. With time and the creation of more graduates, community psychology practitioners began to bring the principles and competencies of community psychology to a broader range of fields and settings, including public health, government, foundations, and global issues. The community-based impact of the field is illustrated through the practitioner Spotlights included in this chapter. While the breadth of subjects that practitioners tackle is wide, from health care to education, the approach is parallel and the skill set similar. Practitioners approach issues of shared social concern as collaborators, and work with community members and stakeholders to address environmental and systematic barriers to health and well-being.

As we reflect on the history of community psychology practice we go back to the origins and definitions of the field and ask: Has the field been able to address the core issues that were the impetus for its creation? Have we been able to fulfill Julian's definition: "to strengthen the capacity of communities to meet the needs of constituents and help them to realize their dreams in order to promote well-being, social justice, economic equity and self-determination through systems, organizational and/or individual change"?

As this chapter illustrates, community psychology practice has sterling examples of just such changes:

- The Community Tool Box that supports community development worldwide

- The self-help movement that is now a cornerstone of the nation's health and human service system

- Socio-emotional education, a prime example of prevention in school-age children

- A myriad of local community changes such as illustrated by Debi Starnes and her work on homelessness in Atlanta

- Major systems changes in the direction of community psychology principles, such as Bill Neigher's work with Atlantic Health System and their new Center for Population Health Sciences

- John Morgan's work on moving the state of Virginia to making a large commitment to prevention in children

Our hopes for the future are that this progress will continue and that:

- Community psychologists in their roles as practitioners will regularly publicly identify themselves as community psychologists, thus helping the practice of community psychology get long-deserved visibility.

- Employers will become aware of our "brand value" and consequently will seek to hire people called community psychologists and those with community psychology skills.

- Community psychology practitioners will be recognized for their skills by colleagues in allied fields.

- Based on the newly accepted community psychology competencies, graduate programs will become clearer about how they define community psychology practice, what competencies they teach, and how their students acquire those skills. More community psychologists will emerge with more community psychology competencies from graduate programs.

- And the adopted community psychology principles and competencies will be used more broadly to impact the major issues facing the globe including social justice, racial and economic inequity, and climate change.

RESOURCES

Recommended Reading

Hazel, K., Meissen, G., Snell-Johns, J., & Wolff, T. (2006). Without community practice, where art thou community psychology. *The Community Psychologist, 39*(2), 42–44.

Jason, L. (2012). *Principles of social change*. New York, NY: Oxford University Press.

Kelly, J., & Song, A. (Eds.). (2008). *Community psychology in practice: An oral history through the stories of five community psychologists*. New York, NY: Haworth Press.

Klein, D., & Goldston, S. (Eds.). (1977). *Prevention: An idea whose time has come*. Rockville, MD: National Institute of Mental Health.

Landsberg, G., Neigher, W. D., Hammer, R. J., Windle, C., & Woy, J. R. (Eds.). (1979). *Evaluation in practice. A sourcebook of program evaluation studies from mental health care systems in the United States* (DHEW Publication No. ADM 78–763). Washington, DC: U.S. Government Printing Office.

Meissen, G., Hazel, K., Berkowitz, B., & Wolff, T. (2008). The story of the first ever summit of community psychology practice. *The Community Psychologist, 41*(1), 40–41.

Neigher, W. D., Ciarlo, J., Hoven, C., Kirkhart, K., Landsberg, G., Light, E., . . . Woy, J. R. (1982). Evaluation in the community mental health center program: A bold new reproach? *Evaluation and Program Planning, 5*(4), 283–311.

Rappaport, J., & Seidman, E. (Eds.). (2000). *Handbook of community psychology*. New York, NY: Kluwer Academic.

Viola, J., & McMahon, S. D. (2009). *Consulting and evaluation with nonprofit and community-based organizations*. Boston, MA: Jones & Bartlett.

Wolff, T. (Ed.). (1994). Working in communities [Special issue]. *The Community Psychologist, 27*(3), 28–47.

Wolff, T. (2010). *The power of collaborative solutions: Six principles and effective tools for building healthy communities*. San Francisco, CA: Wiley.

REFERENCES

Albee, G. (1959). *Mental health manpower trends*. New York, NY: Basic Books.

Anderson, L., Cooper, S., Hassol, L., Klein, D., Rosenblum, G., & Bennett, C. (1966). *Community psychology: A report of the Boston Conference on the Education of Psychologists for Community Mental Health*. Boston, MA: Boston University.

Bangi, A., Harper, G., & Callahan, F. (2006). Community action in Kenya. *The Community Psychologist, 39*(1), 33–36.

Berkowitz, W. (1984). *Community dreams*. San Luis Obispo, CA: Impact.

Berkowitz, W. (1987). *Local heroes*. Lexington, MA: Lexington Books.

Blakely, C. H. (2011). Thoughts on community psychology 30 years later. *The Community Psychologist, 44*(1), 19–20.

Bronfenbrenner, U. (1979). *The ecology of human development: Experiments by nature and design*. Cambridge, MA: Harvard University Press.

Chun, M. (2012). A rewarding community psychology practice in state government. *Global Journal of Community Psychology Practice, 1*(1), 14–20.

Dalton, J., & Wolfe, S. (2012). Joint Column: Education connection and the community practitioner: Competencies for community psychology practice. *The Community Psychologist, 45*(4), 7–14.

Dziadkowiec, O., & Jimenez, T. (2009). Educating community psychologists for community practice: A survey of graduate training programs. *The Community Psychologist, 42*(4), 10–17.

Elias, M. (2009). Employability and community psychology: Why we need a value proposition. *The Community Psychologist, 42*(2) 1–3.

Elias, M. J., & Bruene, L. (2005). *Social decision making/social problem solving for middle school students: Skills and activities for academic, social, and emotional success.* Champaign, IL: Research Press.

Gaitlin, E., Rushenberg, J., & Hazel, K. (2005). What's up with graduate training? Results of the 2005 Graduate Program Survey. *The Community Psychologist, 42*(2), 10–17.

Hollingshead, B., & Redlich, F. (1958). *Social class and mental illness: A community study.* New York, NY: Wiley.

Iscoe, I., Bloom, B., & Spielberger, C. (Eds.). (1977). *Community psychology in transition: Proceedings of the National Conference on Training in Community Psychology.* Washington, DC: Hemisphere.

Joffe, J., Albee, G., & Kelly, L. (Eds.). (1984). *Readings in primary prevention of psychopathology: Basic concepts.* Hanover, NH: University Press of New England.

Julian, D. (2006). Defining community psychology practice: Meeting the needs and realizing the dreams of the community. *The Community Psychologist, 39*(4), 66–69.

Klein, D. (with Morrow, K.). (2001). *New vision, new reality—A guide to unleashing energy, joy, and creativity in your life.* Center City, MH: Hazelden.

Levin, G. (2007). Living community psychology: Featuring Richard Jenkins. *The Community Psychologist, 40*(3), 16–19.

Meyers, J. C. (2011). A community psychologist in the world of philanthropy. *The Community Psychologist, 44*(3), 10–11.

Neigher, W. D., & Kirk, C. M. (2013). Community psychology and the future of healthcare. *Global Journal for Community Psychology Practice, 4*(4).

Neigher, W. D., & Ratcliffe, A. W. (2011). Back to the future part III. *The Community Psychologist, 44*(1), 13–15.

Nelson, G., & Prilleltensky, I. (2010). *Community psychology in pursuit of liberation and well-being.* New York, NY: Palgrave Macmillan.

Price, R., Cowen, E., Lorion, R., & Ramos-McKay, J. (1988). *14 ounces of prevention: A casebook for practitioners.* Washington, DC: American Psychological Association.

Ratcliffe, A. W., & Neigher, W. D. (2010). What is a community psychologist? Why should I hire one? *The Community Psychologist, 43*(2), 5.

Riemer, M. (2010). Community psychology, the natural environment and global climate change. In G. Nelson & I. Prilleltensky (Eds.), *Community psychology: In pursuit of liberation, well-being* (2nd ed.). New York, NY: Palgrave Macmillan.

Riemer, M., & Reich, S. (Eds.). (2011). Community psychology and global climate change [Special section]. *American Journal of Community Psychology, 47*(3–4), 349–427.

Scott, R. (2007). Establishing core competencies for students in community psychology training. *The Community Psychologist, 40*(1), 38.

Slaikeu, K. (1977). Community-based community psychologists. In I. Iscoe, B. Bloom, & C. Spielberger (Eds.), *Community psychology in transition: Proceedings of the National Conference on Training in Community Psychology.* Washington, DC: Hemisphere.

Starnes, D. M (2004). Community psychologists—Get in the arena!! *American Journal of Community Psychology, 133*(1/2), 3–6.

Wituk, S. (2006). The self help center for community support and research at Wichita State University. *The Community Psychologist, 39*(3), 6–7.

Wolff, T. (1999). Practitioners' perspectives. In J. Rappaport & E. Seidman (Eds.), *Handbook of community psychology*. New York, NY: Springer.

Wolff, T. (2003). The healthy communities movement: A time for transformation. *National Civic Review, 92*(2), 95–113.

Wolff, T. (2013). A community psychologist's involvement in policy change at the community level: Three stories from a practitioner. *Global Journal of Community Psychology Practice, 4*(2). Retrieved from http://www.gjcpp.org

Wolff, T., & Snell-Johns, J. (Eds.). (2005). Creating a vision for the future of community psychology. *The Community Psychologist, 38*(4), 36–49.

Wolff, T., & Swift, C. (2008). Reflections on "real world" community psychology. *Journal of Community Psychology, 36*(5), 609–625.

Guiding Principles and Competencies for Community Psychology Practice

Maurice J. Elias, William D. Neigher,
and Sharon Johnson-Hakim

Is there a paying customer out there for those who practice community psychology? Not unique to other specialties within psychology, this fundamental question informs the process of defining the professional field of community psychology practice.

Our intention in this chapter is to take a long-distance look at the direction we believe the profession of community psychology practice should take for its sustained viability and relevance. We will first revisit earlier considerations about the marketability of psychology in general, as well as look at continuing discussions within the field about how to define a community psychology "practitioner." Next, we will summarize the important efforts taken to define a set of community psychology competencies and the distinctive way in which community psychologists apply the competencies in context. Finally, we close by presenting a collaboratively developed "value proposition" for community psychology practice and discussing our evolving view that even the notion of a value proposition is not sufficiently contextualized to serve as a model for our field. Included in this section of the chapter are several examples of applied value propositions, also known as "value-added" propositions, for community psychology practice in various work environments, including schools, clinical settings, academia, and health care. At the end of the chapter, we invite readers to create their own applied value propositions for the applied settings in which they work.

WHAT COMMUNITY PSYCHOLOGY PRACTITIONERS DO

Community psychology is a distinctive approach to understanding and solving community, organizational, and societal problems. While others also are concerned with community welfare, what makes community psychologists distinctive is that we apply well-established psychological principles and techniques, tested and proven in practice, to improve well-being and effectiveness at individual, organizational, and community levels. We do so with an explicit concern for social justice, inclusiveness and participation, the value of diversity, collaboration, and a focus on strengths.

Community psychologists work collaboratively with others to help strengthen systems, provide cost-effective services, increase access to resources, and optimize quality for individuals, private and governmental organizations, corporations, and community groups. Community psychologists build on existing strengths of people, organizations, and communities to create sustainable change. Practitioners of community psychology work as consultants, educators, grant writers, professors, human service managers, program directors, policy developers, service coordinators, evaluators, planners, trainers, team leaders, and researchers in all sectors including government and for-profit and non-profit organizations.

COMMUNITY PSYCHOLOGY: WHO WILL BUY?

In 1982, an article appeared in the journal *American Psychologist* (Fishman & Neigher, 1982, p. 533) with the provocative title, "American Psychology in the Eighties—Who Will Buy?" It questioned the relevance of American psychology for improving the public welfare (one of its fundamental missions) in a time of economic challenge for government spending during the Reagan administration. The article began with two quotations, reprised below:

> Not one rummy has been taken off the Baltimore streets by this research. Not one drunken husband has been dissuaded from beating his wife or one drunken mother from beating her child. These research projects are like exotic, expensively mounted butterfly collections, hidden away in vaults and only exhumed from time

Photo 2.1 Community psychologists work collaboratively with others to help strengthen systems, provide cost-effective services, increase access to resources, and optimize quality for individuals, private and governmental organizations, corporations, and community groups. They build on existing strengths of people, organizations, and communities to create sustainable change.

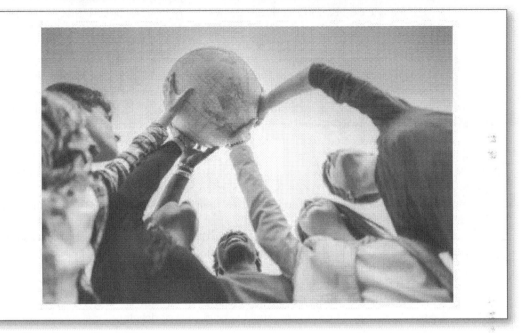

Source: iStockphoto.com/franckreporter.

to time to display to other collectors of the rare and unusual in mutual reaffirmation of their elite status. (p. 533)

The quote came from Representative Barbara Mikulski (D-MD) in 1979, today one of the longest-serving members of Congress. She was not the only legislator then or now to question the value of government spending on social science research. The second quote included in the article came from Morris Parloff (1980), a preeminent psychologist with a challenge to the field:

The basic question, then, is what must we as researchers do in order to respond more usefully to the pragmatic questions which now face the field. . . . We cannot remain in the aloof stance caricatured in the familiar picture of the basic scientist who prefers to seek after truth untrammeled by the noisy yammerings of the secular world. The fact is that in the practical world in which we must find support for our research we can only hope to settle for half-aloof. (p. 533)

THE PROFESSIONAL PRACTITIONER

The practice of community psychology as we describe it would seem to be very responsive to Parloff's challenge. Practice is applied, relevant, impactful, and responsive to community need, respectful of our principles, goals, and guiding concepts. We evaluate our programs for effectiveness and for improving future efforts, applying high standards of evaluation research in many cases. Parloff's comment, however, hints at a concern that also gripped community psychology as it approached its 20th birthday in 1985. The implication was that research was somehow separate from practice and needed to accommodate to the "secular world," mainly to get support. In a series of articles, Maurice Elias, James Dalton, Robert Franco, and George Howe (1984, 1986) attempted to examine what they referred to as the tension between community psychologists whose primary affiliation was in academic settings and those with primary affiliations elsewhere. From the authors' perspective, however, rather than viewing academia as separate from practice, they frame academia as a distinctive practice context. In fact, they argue, it is the only context in which community psychology is relatively well defined and the primary one for which there are clearly defined, reasonably well-paying jobs. Not only that, those community psychologists in academia have the easiest time "giving away" community psychology through working in nonpaying or lower-paying contexts when their work is subsidized. Community psychologists practicing in most other contexts must charge for their work or find someone who will pay them while they work on behalf of those with few resources. For a field that prides itself on not being tied to professionalization and professionals, and on the power of indigenous helpers, volunteers, community participation, and collaboration, we have had a hard time "marketing" what we do in contexts other than academia.

There is, of course, a history of how professions develop that can be instructive for community psychology practice at its relatively early stage of development. Two of the most common definitions of *profession* are:

> A calling requiring specialized knowledge and often long and intensive academic preparation; a principal calling, vocation, or employment; the whole body of persons engaged in a calling. ("Profession," 2013a)

> A paid occupation, especially one that involves prolonged training and a formal qualification. ("Profession," 2013b)

The idea that a profession is defined not only as individuals but also as collectives is, of course, very much in keeping with a community psychology perspective. This raises the question of how a profession evolves and strengthens. Greenwood's (1957) analysis of professions yielded five common characteristics: (1) systematic theory, (2) authority, (3) formal and informal community sanction, (4) ethical codes, and (5) a culture. Perks (1993) identified a set of milestones through which an occupation develops into a profession, including training schools, university schools, local and national associations, a code of professional ethics, and licensing laws. Bullock and Trombley (1999) also believe that formalization of qualifications, including education, time to learn from those already in the field, specific entry requirements, and regulation of who is and is not seen as a member of the field, marks the maturing of a profession. Yet by these definitions and milestones, community psychology practice does not bear all of the hallmarks of a mature, professional field.

Indeed, Elias and colleagues (1986) put forward some suggestions about what had to change both to resolve the academic-practitioner tension and to establish an integrative community psychology, characterized by the interplay and synergy of theory, research, and practice. Most of these were directed at formalization of practice and improving vehicles for communication and recognition among those who identify as community psychologists. Many of these have come to pass, and the current volume addresses many of the most important remaining areas. Other important developments within the Society for Community Research and Action (SCRA, Division 27 of the American Psychological Association) include:

- Establishing a Community Psychology Practice Council (CPPC), a magnet group where members can go to talk about issues pertaining to practice
- Establishing and regularizing the Practice Summit at biennial community psychology conferences
- Formalizing the role of the Practice Council as an official council of SCRA, with a voting representative on the Executive Committee of SCRA
- Creating an explicit connection between the Council of Education Programs (CEP) and Practice Council and links to the Executive Committee
- Evolving the publication *The Community Psychologist* as a vehicle for sharing the work of practice-related groups, CEP-CPPC collaborations, and developing ideas about community psychology competencies
- Adding two practice-related awards: the John Kalafat Award in Applied Community Psychology and the Award for Distinguished Contributions to Practice in Community Psychology
- Creating the *Global Journal of Community Psychology Practice,* a peer-reviewed e-journal for practitioners of community psychology and community improvement around the globe
- Collaborating and engaging with International Biennial Conferences on Community Psychology with a strong focus on practice
- Discussing concretely the skills and competencies necessary to practice as an applied community psychologist

For reasons that we believe are not difficult to discern, the aspect of community psychology practice that has been most clearly articulated is academia. Practice itself is applied, relevant, impactful, and responsive to contextual needs. And practice in the academic context is linked to a long history of traditional productivity standards:

- Producing new theory/knowledge from research and evaluation
- Teaching students at the undergraduate and graduate levels
- Publishing work in peer-reviewed journals and in "the new media"
- Enabling, directly or indirectly, positive change in individuals, families, communities, and society
- Serving on college or university committees and administration duties
- Obtaining grants and contracts

As we write this chapter (in 2013), cuts in federal and state statutory and discretional support to behavioral, social, and biomedical funding streams are concerning. A growing chorus of challenges to the value and future of college education has emerged recently; growing numbers of students are eschewing the liberal arts today, in favor of more secure and lucrative careers in business, computer sciences and technologies, and engineering (Bennett & Wilezol, 2013; Selingo, 2013). This means that the "revenue stream" from tuition that supports psychology department faculty positions may diminish accordingly. Within a threatened psychology field, community psychology, without a clear career path outside of academia, is on tenuous ground. Those practicing community psychology within academia find themselves departing from the traditional evaluative criteria at their peril, which of course creates constraints on the kind of "adventuresome research" that many have viewed as one of the hallmarks of the field (Tolan, Keys, Chertok, & Jason, 1990).

That said, the distinction between academically based and community-based practitioners is not always clear-cut. There are many academically based community psychologists who also practice as consultants, evaluators, researchers, and social action advocates outside the university setting. Income from these activities may go back to their colleges or universities, or be personally retained, depending on their contracts. Regardless of setting, for those who are in full-time community psychology practice, their livelihood depends on a stable or replenishing customer base. In academia, the consumers of practice are students and settings in which one carries out community psychology research or other forms of public scholarship; however, it is the judgment of professional peers, typically including some who are not community psychologists, that plays a significant role in professional advancement. In most other community psychology practice settings, such factors as reputation in the field, referral sources, demonstrable outcomes, fee schedule, and availability all come into play.

CREATING A BRAND IMAGE FOR COMMUNITY-BASED PRACTITIONERS

Referral sources are a marked difference between practice in academia and elsewhere. How do potential consumers find community psychologists? Does the field of community psychology have a "brand image" that helps the practitioner connect with potential customers? We will put that question in the larger context of psychology's public image, using the profession in general and then the subfield of clinical psychology as reference points.

The American Psychological Association (APA) engaged a group of consultants in 2008 to help create a public education campaign aimed at improving psychology's image as a science and profession:

> When it comes to the perception of psychology by the American public, there is good news and less-good news, to paraphrase the old comedy routine. The good news is that new research concludes that most Americans have a positive view of psychology and believe that studying human behavior can solve real-world societal issues. The less-good news is that they have a limited understanding of the depth and breadth of the discipline, and they don't view it as a hard science. (Mills, 2009, p. 28)

"Psychology in general is viewed as a career that treats 'the individual,' similar to psychiatry and social work, but not medicine," says Robert Green, a pollster with Penn, Schoen and Berland Associates, LLC. "This is in part because medicine is associated more with the use of scientific techniques that have real-world benefits. However, the public associates psychology with the study of human behavior a great deal." (Mills, 2009, p. 28)

The research comprised a baseline public opinion poll of 1,000 adults, followed by five focus groups scattered around the country.

We were heartened to learn that 82 percent of Americans rate psychology 'very favorably' or 'somewhat favorably,'" said Rhea K. Farberman, APA's executive director for public and member communications. "That's a great position from which to start a campaign. (Mills, 2009, p. 28)

But one place where Farberman saw a big challenge is in getting people to move beyond the somewhat stereotypical view of psychology that they have formed as a result of seeing psychologists, psychotherapists, or counselors on TV and in the movies. (We note that as of this writing, we are not aware of a TV movie, cable mini-series, or a motion picture featuring community psychology.) In fact, psychology itself is a diverse field; the American Psychological Association currently has 56 different recognized divisions/areas of study, community psychology being just one (APA, 2013).

If public perception of psychology as a field is positive, but somewhat diffuse, and clinical psychology is seen by other psychologists and the public as restricted to "mental health," what can we then infer about community psychology's recognition both within the field and among the general public? It seems clear that community psychology cannot easily capitalize on the brand image of psychology, and in fact, the latter may at times pose significant obstacles, particularly in international contexts where psychology can be associated with prevailing power structures (Cunningham, 2007; Perkins, 2009).

Ultimately, community psychologists as a community of professionals work in different settings. Some work in academia, others work in clinical settings, schools, health care, government, consulting, advocacy organizations, policy positions in government, and more. There is no hierarchy among these settings. Because each has its own distinctive skill set and application, it becomes challenging for the public to understand the commonalities in what community psychologists do. Price and Cherniss (1977) defined four domains of training necessary for a community psychologists—problem and resources analysis, innovation (intervention) design, conducting field trials, and innovation diffusion—and while we might disagree with the specifics, their conclusion is even more apt today: It is impossible for a single individual to be a fully trained, "complete" community psychologist. As we will discuss later, this is not unique to community psychology, but our field is only now coming to grips with this systematically. For that reason, we now turn to community psychology's systematic efforts to define competencies for practice.

One sobering stimulus for focusing on competencies is the result of job searches for "community psychology" on traditional websites like www.monster.com. They find little, if any employment opportunity under this heading. Perhaps what we do is better known by other job titles; perhaps we do not have a great handle on how our skills and competencies match up in a competitive market. To find out, a series of initiatives by SCRA and its membership looked to more carefully define the field of community psychology utilized a self-assessment to examine what we do as a profession, the skills and competencies we have to pursue our craft, the employment settings we work in, the values and guiding principles we share, and the vision we set for the field. The goal was to look at the factors that distinguish community psychologists from other practitioners, the skills and competencies that are foundational to our work, and the value we add to businesses and organizations.

Although the field of community psychology has existed for close to 50 years, it has not, until recently, explicitly outlined a set of competencies for community psychologists engaging in organizational or community-based practice. This is not to say that this conversation around competencies is brand-new; rather, discourse centered on carving the field's "niche" in the world of psychology and social service professionals has been ongoing since the founding of the field in 1965. In the early years of the field's development, this dialogue was intertwined with another debate: one around issues of accreditation for graduate programs and licensing for individuals (Newbrough, 1980). This second conversation was undoubtedly a vestige of our field's birthplace in clinical psychology and community mental health, and fueled by a desire to gain legitimacy and recognition within the broader field of psychology.

The current iteration of the competencies discussion is focused on outlining the work that community psychology practitioners do (skills/competencies) and defining how they do it (approach/values). The list of 18 competencies for community psychology practice presented in this chapter, and described in much greater detail in Chapters 3 through 13, is not intended for use in an accreditation or licensing process; rather, the goal of the list is to create an outline from which to talk about graduate and professional education, employment possibilities, and the evolving nature of community psychology practice (Society for Community Research and Action, 2012).

THE ROLE OF THE COMPETENCIES

Before presenting the set of competencies, it is important to understand their role, both what they are and what they are not. Questions worth considering include: How can they serve to advance the field as a whole? In what ways can they be used by individuals, both students and mid-career practitioners? What potential application do they have in undergraduate, graduate, and continuing education? Will they have an influence in how the field is perceived by outsiders? What potential issues arise from articulating a set of competencies, something that was not embraced by the field until relatively recently?

An established list of competencies has the potential to help define community psychologists' place in the broad realm of "helping" professions, all of which work in community, organizational, and governmental settings to advance issues of health, well-being, social justice, education, and inclusion in communities across the globe. While the field has done a sufficient job establishing itself within the domain of psychology, specifically by contrasting its approaches with those of clinical psychology, it has seen rather limited success in creating an identity of its own: one that is not reliant on comparisons with clinical psychology, one that is recognizable to the general public. Part of this invisibility is due to the "chameleon" effect described in Chapter 1; because practitioners work in a broad range of applied settings, they often adopt the identity of the specific setting in which they work, for example, public health professional, educational consultant, or evaluator, and drop the title "community psychologist" (Snowden, 1987). Although the skills might be highly relevant (and, one might argue, increasingly so in a fast-paced, interdependent world with growing inequities), the profession itself is not. Defining the applied work that community psychologists do in terms of the framework and skills they utilize is an important first step in creating a "brand promise" for the field (Neigher & Ratcliffe, 2010).

Outlining a set of competencies for community psychology practice is not the same as the field claiming exclusive ownership to these skills; there are members of other professional fields who have similar skill sets and approaches. Rather, this is part of setting the stage and garnering expectations, letting communities, employers, and potential partners from other fields know what they can expect from a community psychologist as a potential collaborator or employee. As we will discuss later, this is a crucial step in creating a value proposition for our field and is especially important since, while our skills may be applicable to various employment settings, the words "community psychologist" are rarely, if ever, used in a job ad. Further, there are few if any professional groups that effectively communicate "who they are" through a listing of competencies; who community psychologists are is defined by how we contextualize and integrate these competencies into the settings in which we work. However, without such a list, as noted earlier, a group of practitioners can hardly claim to be part of a profession.

EIGHTEEN COMPETENCIES FOR COMMUNITY PSYCHOLOGY PRACTICE

The list of 18 competencies (see Table 2.1) for practice was created in a collaborative and iterative manner. Members of the Community Psychology Practice Council, Council of Education Programs, and SCRA Executive Committee all contributed their unique perspectives. Additionally, the list was sent out for commentary and input from the general SCRA membership. Although this formal articulation of the competencies for community psychology practice is new, the skills emphasized in this list have been loosely agreed upon for some time (Kuperminc, 2011).

As you will experience in the following chapters, the objective of the book is not to simply describe these competencies, but to instruct readers on how to develop the knowledge, skills, and abilities needed to exercise these competencies in practice to further the vision, mission, and values of the field and demonstrate how these skills can be used to address social issues. Because of this, not every competency could be covered. However, we provide a broad overview of them here. The competencies are grouped into five categories: Foundational Principles, Community Program Development and Management, Community and Organizational Capacity Building, Community and Social Change, and Community Research.

Table 2.1   Eighteen Competencies for Community Psychology Practice

Foundational Principles	
1. Ecological Perspectives	The ability to articulate and apply multiple ecological perspectives and levels of analysis in community practice.
2. Empowerment	The ability to articulate and apply a collective empowerment perspective, to support communities that have been marginalized in their efforts to gain access to resources, and to participate in community decision making.
3. Sociocultural and Cross-Cultural Competence	The ability to value, integrate, and bridge multiple worldviews, cultures, and identities.
4. Community Inclusion and Partnership	The ability to promote genuine representation and respect for all community members, and act to legitimize divergent perspectives on community and social issues.
5. Ethical, Reflective Practice	A process of continual ethical improvement.
Community Program Development and Management	
6. Program Development, Implementation, and Management	The ability to partner with community stakeholders to plan, develop, implement, and sustain programs in community settings.
7. Prevention and Health Promotion	The ability to articulate and implement a prevention perspective and to implement prevention and health promotion community programs.
Community and Organizational Capacity Building	
8. Community Leadership and Mentoring	Leadership: The ability to enhance the capacity of individuals and groups to lead effectively, through a collaborative process of engaging, energizing, and mobilizing those individuals and groups regarding an issue of shared importance. Mentoring: The ability to assist community members to identify personal strengths and social and structural resources that they can develop further and use to enhance empowerment, community engagement, and leadership.
9. Small- and Large-Group Processes	The ability to intervene in small- and large-group processes in order to facilitate the capacity of community groups to work together productively.
10. Resource Development	The ability to identify and integrate use of human and material resources, including community assets and social capital.
11. Consultation and Organizational Development	The ability to facilitate growth of an organization's capacity to attain its goals.

Community and Social Change	
12. Collaboration and Coalition Development	The ability to help groups with common interests and goals to do together what they cannot do apart.
13. Community Development	The ability to help a community develop a vision and take actions toward becoming a healthy community.
14. Community Organizing and Community Advocacy	The ability to work collaboratively with community members to gain the power to improve conditions affecting their community.
15. Public Policy Analysis, Development, and Advocacy	The ability to build and sustain effective communication and working relationships with policy makers, elected officials, and community leaders.
16. Information Dissemination and Building Public Awareness	The ability to communicate information to various segments of the public, to strengthen competencies and awareness, or for advocacy. To give community psychology away.
Community Research	
17. Participatory Community Research	The ability to work with community partners to plan and conduct research that meets high standards of scientific evidence that are contextually appropriate, and to communicate the findings of that research in ways that promote community capacity to pursue community goals.
18. Program Evaluation	The ability to partner with community/setting leaders and members to promote program improvement and program accountability to stakeholders and funders.

The first category, Foundational Principles, includes five concepts—Ecological Perspectives, Empowerment, Sociocultural and Cross-Cultural Competence, Community Inclusion and Partnership, and Ethnical, Reflective Practice—that are core to defining the approach and perspective of community psychology. These Foundational Principles are reflective of the values of the broader field of community psychology and are essential to understanding the way in which community psychologists employ the other 13 competencies in community or organizational settings. Although these first five competencies are not distinct "action items," it is not sufficient to refer to them as "background" processes; rather, it is more appropriate to call them "foreground" processes. Community psychology practitioners need to pay constant attention to these principles, as they are not automatic. Practitioners must commit to "checking" themselves as work progresses to ensure that their actions are aligned with these principles; this process could include continuing education as well as peer consultation

The second category, Community Program Development and Management, refers to a practitioner's ability to assist communities and organizations in program development and implementation, from start to finish. This process includes partnering with stakeholders, helping to formulate program goals and measurable impacts, designing and researching best practices and adapting them to the setting, and training and supporting program staff, as well as assisting the stakeholders in thinking through the sustainability of the program. Also included in this set of competencies is an understanding of a prevention/health promotion framework and the ability to identify resources necessary to join this framework to program development processes, where applicable.

The third category of competencies is Community and Organizational Capacity Building and includes Community Leadership and Mentoring, Small- and Large-Group Processes, Resource Development, and Consultation and Organizational Development. Skills in this category concern the dynamic relationship between practitioners and the stakeholders they work with, and capture the myriad of roles a practitioner often plays. Because these skills involve interpersonal communication, teaching, and learning, they rely on the existence of a strong, trusting relationship between the community psychologist and the various groups of stakeholders.

The fourth category of competencies is Community and Social Change. One of the larger and more complicated groupings, it includes Collaboration and Coalition Development; Community Development; Community Organizing and Community Advocacy; Public Policy Analysis, Development, and Advocacy; and Information Dissemination and Building Public Awareness. These constitute a set of competencies directed toward "second-order change" processes, that is, processes focusing on ways to rearrange current relationships, roles, and power dynamics within a setting to establish a more just, inclusive, and health-promoting environment (Seidman, 1988). In order to succeed at creating sustainable, second-order change in communities or organizations, community psychologists must work with stakeholders to create systems that ensure that necessary resources and values are present and renewable.

The fifth and final category of competencies for practice is Community Research, which includes Participatory Community Research and Program Evaluation. This category of competencies reflects the goal of the field to apply tested psychological principles to promote the health and well-being of all people. Participatory Community Research meets that goal by marrying solid methodology with community voices; program evaluation allows us to effectively judge the merit of community-based or other initiatives and provide information in support of improvement, advocacy, or accountability (Windle & Neigher, 1978).

Yet as those who know the field of community psychology well will attest, there is an additional defining feature, captured well by Jim Kelly (1979) in the title of his seminal article: "'T'ain't What You Do, It's the Way You Do It." The competencies are employed in the context of a set of values that guide key decisions and choices, and temper how actions are carried out. The values of the field, explained by Kloos and colleagues (2011) and incorporated into the Value Propositions, are as follows:

1. Individual and family wellness: The physical and psychological health and well-being of individuals and the families that they belong to, as well as the recognition that these concepts can be interdependent.

2. Sense of community: This value refers to a perception of belongingness, interdependence, and mutual commitment that links individuals together.

3. Respect for human diversity: Acknowledging and valuing the differences that exist between members of groups, whether they are based on age, gender, socioeconomic status, ethnicity, sexual orientation, nationality, ability status, or other characteristics.

4. Social justice: Dedication to working toward equitable allocation of resources, opportunities, obligations, and power within a group or community.

5. Citizen participation: Allowing all members of a community/organization to have a meaningful say in decisions that will affect them.

6. Collaboration and community strengths: This value refers to the process through which community psychologists work with community members; although community psychologists bring expertise to the table, they strive to work collectively with community members so that they can build on existing strengths and knowledge. Included in this value is a "both/and" perspective (Rappaport, 1977), allowing for appreciation and integration of divergent viewpoints.

7. Empirical grounding: This is the process of ensuring that community-based actions are based on research findings whenever possible. Included in this value is the ability to translate research and apply it to various community settings, taking into account cultural, ethnic, and geographic differences, as well as improving the effectiveness of interventions.

These values become important aspects of the common identity of the field and, for those seeking to employ community psychologists, defining aspects of how they will work. As we will discuss later, these principles, used in combination, become the hallmark of the application of a sophisticated community psychology perspective and therefore create a distinction from others attempting to address the same issues or occupying the same roles, but without the community perspective. This distinctiveness becomes the defining aspect of a community psychology perspective and adds what we refer to later as "value-added" in the form of a value proposition for why one would want to select a community psychology–oriented colleague, versus someone else. (See Box 2.1 for an example of how a community psychology perspective affects a clinical-school case process.) If a prospective employer or consultee is not interested in respect for diversity, social justice, and collaboration and community strengths, just to name several of the values, then engaging a community psychology–oriented practitioner might not be the best idea. One can take an ecological perspective or seek to create community change (among other competencies) from an individualistic, power-focused, exploitative orientation or from a value position closer to that espoused by community psychologists. Understanding community psychology practice via competencies alone would not provide a full picture of its distinctive features.

IMPLICATIONS FOR USE AND TRAINING

Community psychologist practitioners are employed in diverse workplaces and adapt their skills and activities to the needs of these settings. The environment in which a person practices will often dictate which of the competencies he or she uses the most often; this flexibility is consistent with the guiding principles of the field, which encourage community psychologists to "meet people where they are," respond to the situation at hand, advance organizational vision, mission, and values, and collaborate with others to determine commonly agreed-upon work plans. An interesting way to think about the set of competencies for community psychology practice is as a "toolbox." Community psychologists have a certain number of skills they fill that box with and bring to any job for which they are hired. What they take out of that toolbox, however, and the order in which they use the tools, is dependent on the needs of the community at that time; we are not going to start hammering just because we brought a hammer with us. That said, many decades of hammering may leave one less prepared for more refined texturing work that might be required subsequently. Truth be told, some community psychologists are not good with hammers. Hence, as Price and Cherniss (1977) made clear, community psychology's core values become important in directing how its powerful tools will be used and are one of the driving forces behind the Value Proposition initiative.

As no individual community psychologist is expected to possess or flawlessly execute all of the current 18 competencies (and those that will emerge in the future), practitioners will vary in their level of expertise competency by competency, based on education, training, personal values, and experience. We adhere to the concept of viewing individual skill in terms of three levels: exposure, experience, and expertise (Kloos, 2010). All practitioners should have been exposed to the competencies, and their underlying values and principles, at some point in their career and ideally during their graduate-level professional training. However, the specific competencies they develop experience and expertise in are shaped by their training context, work settings, and the lifelong learning that they pursue. The only exceptions to this line of thinking are the competencies considered Foundational Principles.

For graduate and undergraduate education, a list of agreed-upon competencies brings with it both transparency and accountability. The competencies create a framework that graduate programs can use to define themselves and the training that they offer. For example, in which of the competencies can students hope to attain experience in their program? What are the expertise areas or strengths of the program? This transparency will help those who plan to enter the field formally to choose the best graduate program for them, based on the skills they see necessary for their future career path. Additionally, encouraging programs to define themselves using the competencies systematically creates a sense of accountability as well. Once programs have identified their training goals, and reflected on future work placements for their students, they can use the competencies as a roadmap for evaluating curriculum and community-based learning opportunities and filling in gaps wherever they might exist (Sarkisian & Taylor, 2011). Continuing professional education in combination with efforts at surveying employers' evolving needs will help the field grow in the right direction.

Articulating competencies in this manner and linking them to professional preparation for community psychology practice is an important benchmark in the evolution of the field. It is a statement that, while many individuals may be "doing" community psychology, there is a set of expectations that one can hold for someone who is recognized as a community psychologist. Right now, that recognition occurs primarily through membership in the Society for Community Research and Action and obtaining a degree from programs that are part of SCRA's Council of Education Programs. To a growing extent, there is similar recognition from international community psychology programs and national and regional associations sanctioning graduate training programs. This is a movement that we strongly encourage for the future growth of the community psychology field.

HOW DOES THIS ALL CONVERGE IN PRACTICE?

Consider this potential consulting engagement from a community action coalition in an inner city:

> Escalating episodes of violence against women, enduring in spite of numerous interventions by law enforcement and community groups, compel a more immediate solution. The coalition engages you as a community psychologist to look at the root causes, evaluate the ineffectiveness of current programs, and recommend an action plan. The coalition has a broad base of support from women's groups, community organizations, law enforcement, and faith-based communities. You accept, sign a contract, and begin the work.
>
> It quickly becomes clear that both the problem and the solutions are much more complex than was presented. Within some community sectors there is a permissive and even tolerant acceptance of physical violence, intimidation, and psychological abuse. In some cases they are faith-based; in others, cultural and economic. The consequences for women and family members who seek outside help can be profound and the fear to come forward is palpable. Attempts by law enforcement and prosecutors to allow anonymous reporting and mitigate retribution are politically confounded and highly controversial. The groups you meet with demand personal disclosure of your values and want transparency in your description of their conversations with you.

In every profession, case examples challenge the recipes and the linear outlines of how to proceed. While guided by core values, the community psychologist will find that in practice, values often conflict: "respect for diversity" and "social justice" may be in direct opposition with some in the community one is working with. As with other fields of psychology, for example, a clinical psychologist working with a client who is a "danger to others," or a pediatric psychologist working with a family around the terminal illness of a young child, or a gerontological psychologist advising a family about long-term care options for a parent with dementia, competing values from multiple perspectives must be considered. It is difficult to provide a priori, decontextualized recommendations about how to resolve these conflicts. Ultimately, this occurs through reflective practice, in terms of developing the habit of reviewing one's decisions and processes and also by seeking out peer and expert supervision as an ongoing part of one's professional functioning.

What community psychologists bring distinctly to such circumstances is an explicit focus on values, an awareness of how to differentiate one's own values from those of others operating in context, and a set of tools for proceeding, also guided by values such as collaboration, empowerment, respect for diversity, and an emphasis on strengths. By clarifying gateways in consulting agreements up front, by examining personal and community values when they are in conflict, by anticipating and disclosing situations where the practitioner will need to modify the scope of the engagement or step down, all parties are better informed as to the dynamics of commitment as the work evolves and expectations are clarified. This is a hallmark of value-added community psychology practice across a wide range of contexts.

For these reasons, in the Appendix at the end of this chapter, we present the introduction to the values proposition, followed by four context-specific versions of a value-added proposition for community psychology practice. If one were to hire a clinical psychologist (or clinician from other disciplines), a school psychologist (or a school counselor or school social worker), a health-care professional, or a faculty member in higher education (from a variety of disciplines), these value proposition statements articulate why hiring someone with a joint community psychology training background would bring distinct advantages to the employer. In arenas where there are already consumers, those prepared to "buy," a clear case can be made to engage a community psychology–oriented practitioner over their more traditional disciplinary-trained peers.

A LOOK AHEAD: TOWARD AN EXPANDED FUTURE FOR COMMUNITY PSYCHOLOGY PRACTICE

What is missing to further the advancement of community psychology as a profession without losing its essential character? We are not the only field facing these concerns and we have some lessons to learn from school psychology and even clinical psychology. Both of these fields have master's- and doctoral-level programs and both prepare practitioners. Both have skill sets that are as impossible as ours to provide to students within a graduate program time frame, especially at the master's level. These fields have lists of competencies required by their profession, and these lists are used to guide their training activities, but they do not say that these are competencies that are possessed by everyone as a graduation requirement. Rather, possessing the skill sets at a basic level prepares individuals for licensing or certification examinations that formalize individuals' entry into their fields, usually after an internship and sometimes post-degree supervision and training.

Community psychology has long resisted having a formalized entry credential for professional practice. However, for the field to evolve as a profession, greater formalization is necessary. One solution that occurs to us is that our field should strive to have master's and doctoral programs refer to competency clusters, sets of skills that they emphasize and that become the "trademark" of their graduates, while also ensuring that they impart to the students a commitment to operating by the community psychology Foundational Principles and values. Doing so will ensure that graduate programs are seen as credible and as sources of appropriate training. All programs will develop a "brand" and a procedure that will be transparent and accessible and for which the Council of Education Programs within SCRA can help through supportive feedback and evaluation for continuous improvement. Yes, this implies a more active role on the part of SCRA in assuring that programs have "truth in advertising." An example of this type of successful graduate program marketing can be seen in public health, where graduate programs list specialties such as epidemiology, behavioral health, or environmental exposure. All are "public health" degrees, but each one clearly states the path and skill set students will be best prepared to pursue.

Consequently, the SCRA Executive Committee has an important role to play in addressing the pull of centripetal forces on our students, and so we offer our thoughts to inform future deliberations. Upon graduation, our students want to be part of the SCRA field and family but know they must immerse themselves in the context of the communities/settings in which they want to have an impact. Community psychologist Roger Mitchell notes that it takes a long time to get the "reps" needed to understand settings and the configural relationships of relevant variables for change as well as veteran practitioners do (Personal communication, June 19, 2009). This comes from working with many organizations and a range of situations. Therefore, we strongly suggest a year of postgraduate supervision or mentoring, whether on-site or remotely, by an established community psychology practitioner as an additional credential to add value and ensure that graduates can solidify their identity as a community psychologist regardless of the setting that they work in. In this, we are explicitly including academia as a practice context. It is not rare that academic community psychologists are hired into departments where there are no other, or perhaps very few, community psychologists and those who are there may well have become over-assimilated as a survival strategy and not be ideal mentors to inspire their new colleague with the excitement and potential of focusing one's academic career strongly around community psychology.

And we also have to find ways to foster networking of experienced professionals in similar contexts. Just as SCRA has focused on being the networking vehicle for academic community psychologists, historically, SCRA resources and attention must be directed toward continuing the advances begun through the Community Psychology Practice Council and systematically and intentionally promote networking among those practicing community psychology in all contexts. We challenge community psychology to redefine professional competence in practice as something other than an individual variable. Competence in practice is a nested ecological and developmental process and it is our task as a field to be forward looking and create the support structures needed for our community psychology graduates and experienced professionals to practice synergistically. Early career mentoring and ongoing professional networking will help keep our practitioners connected to the SCRA core and allow our new professionals to be among and apart at the same time—a "both/and" solution in the spirit of Julian Rappaport.

REFERENCES

American Psychological Association. (2013). *Divisions of APA*. Retrieved from http://www.apa.org/about/division/index.aspx

Bennett, W. J., & Wilezol, D. (2013). *Is college worth it?* New York, NY: Thomas Nelson.

Bullock, A., & Trombley, S. (1999). *The Norton dictionary of modern thought*. New York, NY: W.W. Norton.

Cunningham, J. (2007). Centripetal and centrifugal trends influencing school psychology's international development. In S. Jimerson, T. Oakland, & P. Farrell (Eds.), *The handbook of international school psychology* (pp. 463–474). Thousand Oaks, CA: Sage.

Elias, M., Dalton, J., Franco, R., & Howe, G. W. (1984). Academic and nonacademic community psychologists: An analysis of divergence in settings, roles and values. *American Journal of Community Psychology, 12*(3), 281–302.

Elias, M., Dalton, J., Franco, R., & Howe, G. W. (1986). Divergence between community psychologists in academic and nonacademic settings: A closer look at the implications. *American Journal of Community Psychology, 14*(1), 113–118.

Fishman, D., & Neigher, W. (1982). American psychology in the eighties: Who will buy? *American Psychologist, 37*(5), 533–546.

Gladwell, M. (2000). *The tipping point: How little things can make a big difference*. Boston, MA: Little, Brown.

Greenwood, E. (1957). Attributes of a profession. *Social Work, 2*(3), 45–55.

Kelly, J. G. (1979). 'T'ain't what you do, it's the way you do it. *American Journal of Community Psychology, 7,* 339–261.

Kloos, B. (2010). Creating settings for training in collaborative community practice. *The Community Psychologist, 43*(2), 10.

Kloos, B., Hill, J., Thomas, E., Wandersman, A., Elias, M. J., & Dalton, J. (2011). *Community psychology: Linking individuals and communities* (3rd ed.). Belmont, CA: Wadsworth.

Kuperminc, G. (2011). Heeding the call to develop a model of professional training in community psychology. *The Community Psychologist, 44*(1), 17–19.

Mills, K. (2009). Getting beyond the couch: How does the general public view the science of psychology? *Monitor on Psychology, 40*(3), 28.

Neigher, W., & Ratcliffe, A. (2010). What is a community psychologist? Why should I hire one? *The Community Psychologist, 43*(2), 5.

Nelson, G., & Prilleltensky, I. (Eds.). (2005). *Community psychology: Towards liberation and well-being*. London, UK: Palgrave Macmillan.

Newbrough, J. R. (1980). Community psychology and the public interest. *American Journal of Community Psychology, 8*(1), 1–17.

Parloff, M. B. (1980). Psychotherapy and research: An anaclitic depression. *Psychiatry, 43,* 279-293.

Perkins, D. (2009). International community psychology: Development and challenges. *American Journal of Community Psychology, 44*(1), 76–79.

Perks, R. W. (1993). *Accounting and society*. London, UK: Chapman & Hall.

Price, R. H., & Cherniss, C. (1977). Training for a new profession: Research as social action. *Professional Psychology, 8,* 222–231.

Profession. (2013a). *Merriam-Webster.com*. Retrieved from http://www.merriam-webster.com/dictionary/profession

Profession. (2013b). *Oxforddictionaries.com*. Retrieved from http://oxforddictionaries.com/us/definition/american_english/profession?q = profession

Rappaport, J. (1977). *Community psychology: Values, research, and action*. New York, NY: Holt, Rinehart and Winston.

Sarkisian, G., & Taylor, S. (2011). Three steps for graduate training programs to strengthen their role in developing unified standards in community psychology education. *The Community Psychologist, 44*(1), 15–16.

Seidman, E. (1988). Back to the future, community psychology: Unfolding a theory of social intervention. *American Journal of Community Psychology, 16*(1), 3–24.

Selingo, J. J. (2013). *College (un)bound: The future of higher education and what it means for students.* New York, NY: New Harvest/Houghton Mifflin Harcourt.

Snowden, L. (1987). The peculiar successes of community psychology: Service delivery to minorities and the poor. *American Journal of Community Psychology, 15,* 575–586.

Society for Community Research and Action. (2012). *Competencies for community psychology practice.* Retrieved from http://www.scra27.org/practice/documents/practcompetenciestcpdraftaug2012.docx

Tolan, P., Keys, C., Chertok, F., & Jason, L. (Eds.). (1990). *Researching community psychology: Issues of theory and methods.* Washington, DC: American Psychological Association.

Windle, C., & Neigher, W. (1978). Ethical problems in program evaluation: Advice for trapped evaluators. *Evaluation and Program Planning, 1*(2), 97–107.

APPENDIX

THE GENERAL VALUE PROPOSITION AND CONTEXT-SPECIFIC VALUE-ADDED PROPOSITIONS FOR COMMUNITY PSYCHOLOGY PRACTICE

Introducing a Value Proposition for Community Psychology

A value proposition is a relatively brief statement that "makes the differentiated business case" for employers to hire us. What distinguishes us in that big stack of resumes? Is it the 18 competencies we say we have and practice, the context in community science we have for putting them together, or the values that underscore what we do? The value proposition (VP) is about establishing an identity for the field of community psychology among the many related fields of intellectual inquiry and practice that exist. We never grappled with Lonnie Snowden's (1987) wisdom when he spoke of the peculiar success of community psychology as a discipline in which centripetal forces actually remove people from the community psychology field because our emphasis on context takes people into other fields—unlike other fields that are built by centrifugal force, drawing people into a standard paradigm. Community psychologists often struggle with what seems to be a choice between being among community psychology colleagues but not immersed in their context of research, theory, and practice, or being apart from their community psychology colleagues out of respect for the community psychology principles of the importance of immersion in context.

A VP is a specialized statement that asks a field to state who we are as a discipline, how we go about our profession, where we work, the tools we use, and the values that drive our work. However, our audience is not our "choir"; the VP speaks to potential consumers or purchasers of our services who may not know anything about us. And it must also differentiate us from similar groups and speak directly to distinctive economic and market value. In our view, the VP is not only about value, it is about values. This was expressed by Jim Kelly (1979) when he identified our field with the song lyric, "'T'aint what we do, it's the way we do it." It may not seem rigorous or scientific to say this, but the uniqueness of our field is at least as strongly tied to our values as to our set of competencies. Our values are more than the Foundational Principles within our 18 competencies. Our values are the thread keeping community psychologists connected to a common core no matter where they are or what jobs they have. They are essential for connecting our education of future community psychologists to an intellectual core and practice base for future employment. Community psychology practice needs to expand its critical mass if our field is going to be able to have a significant impact on the issues we care about most, in a systematic way. But, as Snowden (1987) showed us, we cannot expand with a constantly eroding base. At the same time, we can draw some solace from the insights of Malcolm Gladwell (2000) and understand that we can reach the tipping point of influence for our field without a huge increase in numbers. That said, Gladwell's work also makes it clear that without a certain critical mass, which we surely have not yet attained, we will not increase our influence on the larger psychology field, let alone wider spheres of societal influence.

We begin below with an excursion through the general logic of a value proposition for community psychology. We then follow with our most recent and perhaps important insight: We will have our most powerful influence by adding value to other fields, disciplines, and perspectives. The value proposition is really a value-added proposition. What we need to be articulating is how the community psychology perspective and skill set create added value to other fields, positions, organizations, and approaches. We conclude with four illustrations of the overall value proposition explicitly tailored to illustrate the value-added proposition for community psychology for clinical and school psychology, health care, and higher education faculty.

What Is Community Psychology?

Community pychology is a distinctive approach to understanding and solving community, organizational, and societal problems. While others also are concerned with community welfare, what makes community psychologists distinctive is that we apply well-established psychological principles and techniques, tested and proven in practice, to improve well-being and effectiveness at individual, organizational, and community levels. We do so with an explicit concern for social justice, inclusiveness and participation, the value of diversity, collaboration, and a focus on strengths.

What Do Community Psychologists Believe? What Are Their Core Values?

We use *values* synonymously with *principles,* referring to ideologies, ethical standards, tenets, or beliefs. Importantly, just as we define our field as viewing individuals, behavior, and community in ecological context, we need to understand our values and their application in context as well. We embrace a pluralistic set of values, but with that inclusive perspective comes the potential for friction and conflict—within applications of the values themselves and in their contextual practice in settings where there are opposing or antagonistic values that may be as deeply held by others. Nevertheless, a field that stands for everything stands for nothing. To have a set of focal values does not invalidate the relevance of other values, nor does it prescribe how these values are used in the context of real-world, everyday practice. It does, however, provide some guidance for those practicing in the field as well as for those seeking to hire them and/or to collaborate with them.

Core values refers to the most fundamental set of beliefs shared by a group of individuals possessing a common identity. Drawing on the work of Nelson and Prilleltensky (2005), and on Kloos et al. (2011) in the third edition of their textbook on community psychology consider these seven values:

1. Individual and family wellness

2. Sense of community

3. Respect for human diversity

4. Social justice

5. Citizen participation

6. Collaboration and community strengths

7. Empirical grounding

There is consistency in looking at these core values through the lens of the Society for Community Research and Action, Division 27 of the American Psychological Association (www.scra27.org/about). In a broader context, SCRA intertwines them in its organizational principles and goals.

Four broad principles guide SCRA:

1. Community research and action requires explicit attention to and respect for diversity among peoples and settings.

2. Human competencies and problems are best understood by viewing people within their social, cultural, economic, geographic, and historical contexts.

3. Community research and action is an active collaboration among researchers, practitioners, and community members that uses multiple methodologies. Such research and action must be undertaken to serve those community members directly concerned and should be guided by their needs and preferences, as well as by their active participation.

4. Change strategies are needed at multiple levels in order to foster settings that promote competence and well-being.

Goals:

1. To promote the use of social and behavioral science to enhance the well-being of people and their communities and to prevent harmful outcomes.

2. To promote theory development and research that increases our understanding of human behavior in context.

3. To encourage the ongoing and mutual exchange of knowledge and skills among community psychologists, those in other academic disciplines, and community stakeholders so that community research and action benefits from the strengths of all perspectives.

4. To engage in action, research, and practice committed to promoting equitable distribution of resources, equal opportunity for all, non-exploitation, prevention of violence, active citizenry, liberation of oppressed peoples, greater inclusion for historically marginalized groups, and respecting all cultures.

5. To promote the development of careers in community research and action in both academic and applied settings.

6. To promote an international field of inquiry and action that respects cultural differences, honors human rights, seeks out and incorporates contributions from all corners of the world, and is not dominated by any one nation or group.

7. To influence the formation and institutionalization of economic and social policy consistent with community psychological principles and with the social justice values that are at the core of our discipline.

Clearly, the professional association of community psychologists and those training and practicing as community psychologists must operate under a shared belief system, and this appears to be taking place at present.

What Do Community Psychologists Do?

Community psychologists work collaboratively with others to help strengthen systems, provide cost-effective services, increase access to resources, and optimize quality for individuals, private and governmental organizations, corporations, and community groups. Community psychologists build on existing strengths of people, organizations, and communities to create sustainable change.

Community psychologists work as consultants, educators, grant writers, professors, human service managers, program directors, policy developers, service coordinators, evaluators, planners, trainers, team leaders, and researchers in all sectors including government, for profit, and nonprofit organizations.

In addition to a solid grounding in the science of psychology, most community psychologists can:

1. *Locate, evaluate, and apply information* from diverse information sources to new situations.

2. *Incorporate psychological, ecological, and systems-level understanding* into community development processes.

3. *Contribute to organizational decision making* as part of a collaborative effort.

4. *Evaluate programs/services* by developing evaluation designs; collecting, analyzing, reporting, and interpreting evaluation data.

5. *Plan and conduct community-based applied research*.

6. *Translate policy into community and organizational plans and programs* with observable outcomes.

7. *Provide leadership,* supervisory, and mentoring skills by organizing, directing, and managing services offered.

8. *Communicate effectively* in both technical and lay language with diverse stakeholder groups.

9. *Build and maintain collaborations* with a network of clients, communities, organizations, and other involved professions. Negotiate and mediate between different stakeholder groups around a particular issue.

10. *Demonstrate and teach* cultural competence and other key relationship skills to a wide range of constituencies.

11. *Develop social marketing* and other media-based *campaigns*.

Where Do Community Psychologists Work or Consult?

Community psychologists are found in a range of settings and find themselves in these settings via a diverse array of career paths. These settings include 2- and 4-year higher education; foundations; health and human service agencies; preschool and K–12 education systems; community development; architectural, planning, and environmental organizations; corporations; for-profit and nonprofit organizations; government systems—legislative and executive branches of local, state, and the federal government; research centers; independent consulting groups; evaluation firms; community-based organizations; advocacy groups; religious institutions; neighborhood groups; and public policy and community planning and development organizations.

How Do Community Psychologists Add Distinctive Value?

Community psychologists apply knowledge of community, social systems, and an ecological approach as our distinct value added. Community psychologists have the implementation skills to put theory, research, policy, and strategy into action in challenging and divergent settings. Community psychologists can be cost-effective additions to the workforce across a wide employment spectrum. Most importantly, community psychologists are adaptive, values-based professionals who tend to be mission-driven and thrive on working well with others.

Examples of Context-Specific Value-Added Propositions

By emphasizing ways in which community psychologists can contribute to various settings and work collaboratively with members of allied fields, the value proposition becomes the "value-added proposition." We offer the following four examples—clinical psychology, school psychology, health care, and universities—to illustrate how community psychology skills and perspectives can add distinctive value to work occurring in various sectors. Additionally, we invite other community psychology practitioners to create and circulate valued-added propositions for the setting in which they work; doing this will allow the field to create better brand identity, increase the marketability of graduates, and identify areas of emerging needs that can inform graduate training and continuing professional education.

Clinical Psychology

When clinical psychologists add the perspective and skills of community psychology, they will strengthen their ability to work in ecologically, culturally, and developmentally sensitive ways, promote strengths, and design and implement preventive and health promotion interventions. Most important, perhaps, is that clinical psychologists will think more about the interpersonal and structural supports needed to sustain changes that result from clinical intervention. This will be a growing concern, as clinical interventions are increasingly asked to justify their short- and long-term benefits and psychologists are challenged to differentiate their skill sets from those of other clinicians. The collaborative approach of community psychology helps to make clinical psychologists particularly valuable assets to teams and task forces, blending skill sets with those of other professions and working toward individual, familial, and community improvement.

There are five areas in which community psychology competencies are well allied with emerging opportunities in the clinical psychology field:

1. Foundational Principles: Use ecological perspectives to guide case-based conceptualization and intervention planning; create opportunities to empower patients in their various contexts; emphasize socio-cultural competence in providing clinical services; provide or seek to arrange clinical services and outside supports for those with income challenges

2. Community Program Development: Develop, implement, and manage evidence-based/best practice intervention programs and prevention/positive mental health promotion initiatives; provide collaborative outreach to those supporting mental health in the community; develop community supports for clients transitioning to community settings

3. Community and Organizational Capacity Building: Facilitate conversations around increasing interdisciplinary communication and collaboration; build capacity of clinical practitioners to emphasize prevention; engage other practitioners in professional support communities for supervision and professional growth; provide consultation and organizational development to settings such as schools, workplaces, medical settings, and community-based service organizations

4. Community and Social Change: Form essential collaborations including and beyond the confines of clinical offices for affecting population mental health; evaluate and advocate for health policy; spread public awareness to increase access and prevent illness and injury

5. Community Research and Evaluation: Evaluate case procedures and all programs for efficiency and effectiveness; create products useful to service recipients, allied mental health professionals, community residents, policymakers, and legislators

School Psychology

When school psychologists add the perspective and skills of community psychology, they will add to their ability to initiate and evaluate preventive and strength-promoting interventions; carry out consultation from an ecological, developmental, and systems perspective; and bring greater coherence to schools' efforts to promote social-emotional and character development and academic improvement in students. A community psychology perspective also contributes to a realistic understanding of what is required to create school infrastructures and professional development needed for sustainable change. The collaborative approach of community psychology helps to make school psychologists adaptive, values-based professionals who thrive on working well with others in teams and task forces, blending skill sets with those of other professions, and work collaboratively toward systems and community improvement.

There are five areas in which community psychology competencies are well allied with emerging opportunities in the school psychology field:

1. Foundational Principles: Use ecological perspectives to understand context of individual child and family circumstances; create opportunities to empower students and staff members; address disparities by emphasizing socio-cultural competence in providing educational and psychological services the value of reducing inequities

2. Community Program Development: Develop, implement, and manage evidence-based prevention/positive behavior promotion initiatives to promote overall school culture and climate as well as individual students' health and mental health; build networks of school psychology practitioners across localities and countries

3. Community and Organizational Capacity Building: Facilitate conversations around reform and organizational change; build capacity of school professionals to emphasize prevention; engage multiple stakeholders including students, all school staff members, administrators, school board members, parents, community organizations, community members, and media in supporting the school mission; provide teacher support/stress management/burnout prevention and coping strategies; develop school and community leadership competencies, including skills in small- and large-group processes; provide organizational-level consultation and development

4. Community and Social Change: Form essential collaborations including and beyond the confines of the school for affecting population health; evaluate and advocate for school mental health and education-related policy; spread public awareness of school identity, mission, vision, and motto to increase support and collaborative possibilities

5. Community Research and Evaluation: Assess school culture and climate and develop and evaluate improvement plans; evaluate all school programs for efficiency and effectiveness; create products useful to students, educators, community residents, policymakers, and legislators

Health Care

Community psychology is allied with the most fundamental realization in health care: most of sustainable healing and health occurs outside of medical settings. When health-care professionals add the perspective and skills of community psychology, they will add a focus on the emerging area of population health to traditional health-care foci of traditional medicine, preventive care, and population medicine. Population health management requires three basic competencies for success. First, health-care workers in this area must find ways to engage the community. Second, interventions (including policies, built environment, and programs) must emphasize both primary and secondary prevention in coordinated ways necessary for health-care systems to adjust to the wave of people with serious but preventable health concerns including diabetes and obesity. Population health management embraces the value of inclusion and finding ways to empower people to control their own health and wellness. A community psychology perspective strengthens one's ability to work in ecologically, culturally, and developmentally sensitive ways; promote strengths; and design, implement, and evaluate preventive and health-promoting interventions. The collaborative approach of community psychology helps to make health-care professionals particularly valuable assets to teams and task forces within and across organizational settings, blending skill sets with those of other professions, and having the skills to engage an array of stakeholders in communities, including governmental officials and advertisers and those providing consumer services (such as fast foods, construction design and implementation) with particular impact on population health and well-being.

There are five areas in which community psychology competencies are well allied with emerging opportunities in the health-care field:

1. Foundational Principles: Use ecological perspectives to guide the shift to population health; create opportunities to empower patients and community; address disparities by emphasizing socio-cultural competence in health-care and reducing inequities

2. Community Program Development: Develop, implement, and manage evidence-based prevention/health promotion initiatives to promote population health

3. Community and Organizational Capacity Building: Facilitate conversations around reform and organizational change; build capacity of medical practices to emphasize prevention; engage multiple stakeholders including patients, communities, organizations, staff, physicians, payers, and media by building on the competencies of community leadership, small- and large-group processes, and consultation and organizational development

4. Community and Social Change: Form essential collaborations including and beyond the confines of medical offices and hospitals for affecting population health; evaluate and advocate for health policy; spread public awareness to increase access and prevent illness and injury

5. Community Research and Evaluation: Conduct strengths-based, participatory research, needs and resources assessment, and program evaluation; evaluate all programs for efficiency and effectiveness; create products useful to community residents, service recipients, health-care professionals, policymakers, and legislators

Universities and Colleges

Community psychology is allied with the mission of most higher education settings: to prepare the next generation of leaders and citizens, locally and globally. Further, there is a commitment to social justice and educational equity. The doors of higher education must not only be open to diverse students and those whose families may not have college background, but there must be ways of ensuring that those who enter leave with degrees and a pathway to success. Higher education is changing and must adapt to those changes in both technological and human ways. Education extends beyond the college walls, and the responsibilities of effective universities of the future to their students will not cease upon their graduation. When higher education faculty add the perspective and skills of community psychology, they will add expertise and perspective in four essential areas: effective collaborative team/committee development and management, primary and secondary preventive approach to student mental health, action-research focus on university-based opportunities and problems, and service-learning paradigms. As colleges and universities enter a phase of challenge and competition, having faculty members whose expertise is aligned with larger institutional success as well as personal career success in a "both/and" way will be a considerable source of organizational strength.

There are five areas in which community psychology competencies are well allied with emerging opportunities in higher education:

1. Foundational Principles: Use ecological perspectives to guide comprehensive and multilevel planning; create opportunities to empower students and staff; reduce inequities by understanding socio-cultural competence and context and adding support resources and structures

2. Community Program Development: Develop, implement, and manage evidence-based prevention/health promotion initiatives to promote student and staff health, stress management, and nonviolent conflict resolution

3. Community and Organizational Capacity Building: Facilitate conversations around reform and organizational change; build capacity of university health and mental health and disabilities services, student and residence life, and commuter services for collaborative and coordinated efforts; engage multiple stakeholders for student success, including student support services, economic assistance, tutoring/mentoring/academic support, student advising, career services, and university communications by building on the competencies in community leadership, small- and large-group processes, and consultation and organizational development

4. Community and Social Change: Form essential collaborations including and beyond the confines of the university and foster experiential and service-learning paradigms; evaluate and advocate for higher education policy; find ways to share university expertise and knowledge widely and accessibly; spread public awareness about university programs and efforts and foster greater collaboration

5. Community Research and Evaluation: Conduct strengths-based participatory research, needs and resources assessment, and program evaluation; evaluate all programs for efficiency and effectiveness; create products useful to community residents, students, university staff, alumni, policymakers, and legislators

Box 2.1 A Clinical-School Referral Viewed From a Community Psychology Value-Added Perspective

Adam is a 12-year-old who has been referred to a psychologist for misbehavior in school. He has been inattentive in class and impatient with his peers to the point of having altercations during lunch and on the bus, resulting in frequent school detention. The school child study team is considering a special education referral but suggested an outside consultation to speed up the process. Adam has not had a prior history of difficulty. An older sibling is entering high school and a younger sibling is beginning a new school in third grade.

From a community-informed clinical perspective, conducting an ecological analysis of Adam's life situation would be a priority. How have his microsystems relationships changed? Is there a change in academic expectations? Are there new teacher relationships that might be troubling? What household responsibilities or other changes might result from the transitions being undertaken by his siblings? What are his parents' work situations and their time for interacting with him together or separately and how have they responded to the increased difficulties at school and whatever demands may have resulted from those? Are there changes in Adam's relationships with peers in and out of school as he begins to move into his teenage years? Is he under new peer pressures? Is he preparing for any religious ritual or rite of passage that may be causing added stress?

What other organizations does Adam participate other than school? Clubs? Religious? Youth groups? Talent classes? Sports? Have there been any meaningful changes in these areas of life? Have there been any changes in his parents' organizational situations? Are they under pressures that may translate into strained family interaction patterns? Are there any neighborhood matters that have changed? Might Adam be subject to bullying, harassment, or danger on his trip to and from school that he did not experience before?

All of these ecological considerations would be considered as factors interacting with Adam's own developmental trend and emerging identity issues. From a community psychology perspective, the individual level is not considered as a "main effect" but rather part of two-, three-, four-, or more-way interactions. And the best way to affect the individual level may be to work on aspects of the context, rather than aspects of the individual. A clinical or school psychologist or other related professional would certainly not ignore the individual level, but the addition of a community perspective widens the lens on interpreting the problem and places equal focus on finding solutions at multiple levels of analysis. Further, the community perspective recognizes that individual-level solutions have to be examined for their impact in the ecological surround, particularly at the microlevel, and potential obstacles anticipated and planned for.

CHAPTER 3

Understanding Ecological Systems

Stephen P. Stelzner and Richard M. Wielkiewicz

OPENING EXERCISE: WHERE DO WE PUT THE NEW SCHOOL?

Imagine your child attends "Taylor Open School," a local elementary school. You believe your child will remain at this school for several more years and your family has worked out a nice plan for getting your child to and from school. Then, with no warning, you receive an automated call from the school district office. A meeting will be held two nights hence to lay out a plan for the physical relocation of the elementary school. You are stunned and outraged along with most of the Taylor Open School parents. Parents are confused and worried. But most significantly, nobody understands how or why a decision has been made that will have a significant impact on their family. Not only has the decision come without warning, you must clear your schedule and set up child care for a meeting that occurs in two days. The stress and worry is enough to significantly disrupt your sleep.

So what had happened? A group of parents in another part of the district want to start a small charter school and they need a building. The district offered an older district-owned building that years ago served as a larger elementary school, but now stands empty. A match made in heaven? Not quite. The organizing parents feel the size, location, structure, and age of the building are unacceptable. The parents use their extensive social networking resources to put pressure on the district, particularly the district superintendent. At some point during the process, someone suggests that the site that houses Taylor Open School would be a perfect location for the new charter school. Taylor Open School could be moved to the older building since it has more children enrolled and would be a better "fit" for the former elementary school building. The superintendent agrees to draw up a plan to relocate Taylor to the old building and sets up the meeting to lay out the plan. Next, he authorizes the automated calls to the Taylor Open School parents, who are completely in the dark about the district's plans.

In the short term, this situation resulted in angry and distressed parents on both sides, confused and anxious children, a tense and emotional meeting, and an embattled and shaken district superintendent. How could this situation have been avoided? What could be done at this point to make both sets of parents happy or satisfied? Most importantly, what would/will help us understand the community so we can address concerns and student needs for both groups? A significant start would be to look at the situation from an ecological or systems perspective.

As is often the case in these situations, it was the squeaky wheel that got the grease. But unfortunately, the rest of the vehicle was ignored. In their book on behavioral economics, *Scarcity*, Sendhil Mullainathan and Eldar Shafir (2013) suggest organizations often engage in "firefighting"—that is, dealing with the most immediate problem because factors such as time or resources are scarce (or at least are perceived to be scarce). Mullainathan and Shafir argue that this leads to a reduced capacity to process information. The result is "the squeaky wheel gets the grease," but other parts of the organization (or community) are ignored, often with negative results. An ecological approach to community psychology shows us a different pathway, one that takes us away from the firefighting approach toward an understanding of the community as a social system.

OVERVIEW

Looking at communities and organizations through an ecological lens allows us to understand what happens in situations such as the one described above. But an ecological perspective—or systems perspective—also helps us think through how we can practice community psychology. The **ecological perspective** allows the community psychologist to gain an understanding of the multifaceted ways in which different elements of the community affect each other, and as result, that understanding allows us to know who, how, and when to engage with the community.

We begin with an introduction and conceptual definition of the ecological approach, describing its historical roots in biology and psychology. We then provide an overview of competencies needed to practice community psychology from an ecological perspective, focusing upon basic principles needed to think ecologically about communities. We then discuss skills and abilities needed to pursue an ecological approach, such as personality, mindfulness, systemic thinking, listening skills, and helping organizations and communities solve their own problems. Two applications of the ecological approach, school-based anti-bulling programs and a locally organized Healthy Start program, are discussed. The chapter ends with a discussion of future directions, a list of key terms and definitions, and other resources.

INTRODUCTION: CONCEPTUAL DEFINITION

The word *ecology* derives from the Greek word *oikos,* meaning "house," and thus literally would refer to the study of "houses." But in this case house refers to the habitats or environments in which organisms live. In psychology, and other social sciences, we are interested in "social ecology," or the study of environments in which human beings live and interact with one another. Historically, psychology began with the study of natural phenomena such as sensations (introspection) and consciousness (Freudian psychology), but these methods were banished from the mainstream of the field in favor of viewing psychology as a laboratory science. However, in the past several decades, the field has begun to incorporate ecological principles into mainstream branches such as community and environmental psychology.

A number of scholars have contributed basic ideas to the ecological perspective. Ludwig von Bertalanffy, a biologist, was one of the early founders of what has become known as general systems theory, a focus on the interrelationships between elements that together form a whole. He was an advocate for the study of interconnections among variables, especially for living species studied over time. He influenced many other scholars, including organizational psychologists Daniel Katz and Robert L. Kahn (1978), who employed Bertalanffy's framework in the preparation of their classic text, *The Social Psychology of Organizations.* James G. Kelly,

Photo 3.1 Monarch caterpillar.

Source: iStockphoto.com/brackish.nz.

whose ecological approach to community psychology will be addressed shortly, has acknowledged the influence of Bertalanffy—as well as Katz and Kahn—on his work.

Commoner's Four Laws of Ecology

Barry Commoner is also one of the pioneers in ecological thinking and his four laws of ecology have become a cornerstone of ecological thinking. His book *The Closing Circle* (1971) is one of the seminal works in this area. One of Commoner's lasting legacies is his four laws of ecology, as described in *The Closing Circle*. The four laws are:

1. Everything is connected to everything else.

2. Everything must go somewhere.

3. Nature knows best.

4. There is no such thing as a free lunch.

These four laws of ecology have been cited by several writers (e.g., Allen, Stelzner, & Wielkiewicz, 1998) to structure descriptions of the ecological approach to community psychology. Their meaning and application to community psychology are elaborated in a later section.

Bronfenbrenner's Developmental Approach

Urie Bronfenbrenner (1977, 1979) developed a framework for understanding human development from an ecological point of view. Bronfenbrenner felt it was critical to examine the development of individuals in the **context** of the environmental systems of which they are a part, starting with the individual, and gradually moving "out" to a nested framework of expanding contexts that influence development (microsystem, mesosystem, exosystem, macrosystem, later adding the chronosystem, as well as "biological" influences). Bronfenbrenner emphasized that not only is the individual influenced by the elements of each system, but that the systems themselves are connected and influence each other, and subsequently, individual development (keeping in mind that the individual is also part of the broader system). Since much of community psychology has focused on interventions in developmental settings (e.g., schools), Bronfenbrenner's theory provides a useful approach to understanding ecological influences.

Barker's Social Ecological Approach

Roger Barker (1965, 1968) was one of the early pioneers in the area of social ecology, laying out a comprehensive approach to quantifying social environments and studying the individual in context. One of the important contributions Barker made was coining the term *behavior setting* to describe the smaller social contexts in which behavior occurs over time, such as a waiting room, a playground, or his oft-cited example of a baseball game. In behavior settings, behaviors play out that are independent of the actual actors, but are prescribed elements of the setting. The settings can change over time, but it is the context of the setting that influences behavior in the setting. For example, the equipment, children, and parents all make up part of the behavior setting of a playground, but as the equipment is modernized, subtle changes in behavior occur.

Kelly's Ecological Approach to Community Psychology

James G. Kelly (Kelly, 1968, 1979; Kelly, Ryan, Altman, & Stelzner, 2000; Trickett, Kelly, & Vincent, 1985) laid out ecological principles for understanding community psychology, and his "ecological conception of preventive interventions" has been highly influential in the field and has inspired a great deal of thinking from an ecological and systems framework (e.g., Trickett & Rowe, 2012; Wielkiewicz & Stelzner, 2005). Kelly borrowed from principles in biology to lay out critical considerations for those working in community environments. An ecological approach, according to Kelly, "is useful to build a *community-based* community psychology. A psychology that is attentive to the promotion of competent individuals in responsive social systems" (Kelly et al., 2000, p. 133). Kelly and colleagues laid out four ecological principles for understanding, researching, and influencing human environments: interdependence, cycling of resources, adaptation, and succession.

The principle of **interdependence** states that any social system has multiple related parts and multiple relationships with other social systems. Thus, changes in one component of a social system affect and/or produce changes in other components of that system. This principle suggests that research and practice must examine the side effects (both positive and negative) of any type of intervention in the community. In addition, researchers/practitioners must understand that while they are attempting to affect the community, the community is also impacting the researcher/practitioner in serious and substantial ways.

Cycling of resources refers to how resources are used, distributed, conserved, and transformed in a social system. These resources may be personal, social, and/or physical. The transfer of energy (community resources) reveals the individual components that comprise the system and also their relationship to each other. In community practice, this means trying to build competencies in the individuals that make up a community, as well as creating competent communities. It also means that individuals, events, and settings in the community are potential resources that can facilitate attempts to have an impact on the community.

The principle of **adaptation** concerns the transactions between person and environment. The basic premise is that both person and environment influence each other, and each must adapt to input from the other. Thus, individuals vary their habits or characteristics to cope with changes that emerge from the environment, but the structures and processes of the environment also change as a result of individual behavior. Kelly and his colleagues suggest coping and adaptation are the dominant means for growth and change for both individuals and communities. It also means that community practice and research must be a flexible, improvisational process, as we adapt to changes in the system.

Social settings and social systems, and the individuals within them, change over time. Environments are not static; changes in the environment result in conditions that may be more favorable for one population over another, or may require some kind of adaptation. This is the essence of the principle of **succession**. As a result, those doing practice and research in communities must consider the impact of their work over time. Thus, it is important for the community practitioner to understand the community's history, but also to continue to monitor critical elements of the social system as it evolves. The dynamic nature of social systems means change is inevitable, and the community psychologist should try to anticipate future needs, resources, and structures.

Recent Applications of the Ecological Paradigm

A large number of community psychologists have applied either Kelly's ecological principles or social systems theory to their work in communities. Entire sections of the *American Journal of Community Psychology* have been devoted to theories, methods, and interventions aimed at "Systems Change" (June 2007) and "Social Ecological Approaches to Community Health Research and Action" (December 2009). Other recent examples include an application to sexual assault nurse examiners (Campbell, Patterson, & Fehler-Cabral, 2010), an ecological process model of systems change (Peirson, Boydell, Ferguson, & Ferris, 2011), and an ecological model of environmental stewardship behavior (Moskell & Allred, 2013).

Edison Trickett, an early collaborator of Kelly's, has been an important proponent of the ecological perspective and has written extensively about the application of ecological approaches to community research and intervention (e.g., Trickett, 1984, 2005, 2009a, 2009b; Trickett & Birman, 1989; Trickett, Kelly, & Todd, 1972; Trickett & Rowe, 2012; Trickett et al., 2011). In particular, Trickett has used the ecological paradigm to discuss interventions in school and public health settings (e.g., Trickett & Beehler, 2013). Trickett and colleagues (2011) have summarized the ecological/systems paradigm:

> [It] (1) focuses on the goal of increasing community capacity through interventions directed at specific community issues identified through community-engaged processes; (2) adopts an ecological and systemic perspective that assesses the influence of multiple levels of community ecology on the issue at hand and on community resources and capacities, research partners, community tensions and the relationship between the intervention team and the community; (3) focuses on the empowering role of community collaboration throughout the community intervention process; and (4) emphasizes the permeating role of culture and cultural history as both a resource for and an influence on the community-intervention process. (p. 1413)

Photo 3.2   Butterfly pupa: A time of change.

Source: iStockphoto.com/dossy.

DEVELOPING COMPETENCIES IN USING AN ECOLOGICAL APPROACH

The more we study the major problems of our time, the more we come to realize that they cannot be understood in isolation. They are systemic problems, which means that they are interconnected and interdependent.

Fritjof Capra

The first law of ecology is that everything is connected to everything else.

Barry Commoner

Knowledge Associated With an Ecological Approach

The purpose of this section is to introduce some basic principles of ecological thinking needed to address our adaptive challenges and overcome the cultural blinders created by our industrialized society (Benson, 2003). Other terms for this knowledge base are self-organization (Johnson, 2001), deep ecology (Capra, 1996), cybernetics (Bateson, 1972), chaos theory (Barton, 1994), complexity theory (Mathews, White, & Long, 1999), ecological theory (Commoner, 1971; Kelly et al., 2000), emergent processes (Johnson, 2001), and systems theory (Foster-Fishman, & Behrens, 2007; Foster-Fishman, Nowell, & Yang, 2007; Kelly, 2007; Tseng & Seidman, 2007). What these writers have in common is the view that understanding complex, interactive systems will lead us toward reasonable solutions and strategies for dealing with the adaptive challenges we face.

Systemic, Critical Thinking

Practically, approaching community psychology from an ecological perspective should include the ability to deal critically with complex events that have *multiple* causes and effects (e.g., Stanovich, 2013). For example, the idea that global warming is "caused" by carbon dioxide represents an oversimplification. Carbon dioxide emissions are the result of an energy-hungry and dynamic economic context. Global warming cannot be addressed by simply eliminating carbon dioxide emissions. Instead, we need to figure out how to supply the energy needed by our economic system while carbon dioxide emissions are lowered. This is likely to involve lowering the carbon dioxide emissions of the vehicles upon which American society is dependent and helping communities to develop less carbon-intensive transportation systems. Due to the complexity of the systemic causes of carbon dioxide emissions, multiple strategies must be developed to lower overall emissions of carbon dioxide to within acceptable limits. Thus, the critical thinking skills we apply to solving this complex adaptive challenge need to match the complexity of the original challenge.

Another critical thinking skill that will need to be developed is the ability to reflect upon your own "deepest prejudices, biases, and misconceptions" (Gong, 2005, p. 40) and learn to sympathize with opposing points of view in what Paul (cited in Gong, 2005) calls dialogical thinking. Another perspective on this problem is that community psychology graduate students and developing community practitioners need to make an accelerated transition from Bateson's (1972) Learning I in which problems are approached from a defined and limited set of alternatives to Learning II in which the set from which choices are made is, itself, changed such that the experience of the world encompasses a greater range of alternatives. In other words, we all need to adapt our style of thinking to the complexity of the issues we face. There are times when the complexity of the issues is so great that we can never really hope to understand them completely. Instead, we will need to be constantly revising our understanding according to the best available information. The implication is that we will often be required to let go of the knowledge that we have and replace it with new knowledge. We must expand the range of alternatives beyond conventional wisdom and experience because the adaptive challenges communities face are new and will require new strategies to meet them.

Principles of Ecology

At the level of human communities, we are connected to both the biological environment and each other. Imagine a community psychologist in the early stages of getting to know a community making an offhand comment such as, "The president seems to be rather dictatorial, from the way you describe her." While this may have been an innocent effort to paraphrase and reflect comments of an interviewee, the impact of the comment could be very profound. There is the distinct possibility of a "butterfly effect" (a butterfly flapping its wings in Brazil sets off weather events leading to a storm in the United States). The comment could be repeated and amplified through the social connections within the community until a figurative storm of controversy emerges (remember the open school example from the beginning of the chapter). An event like this early in the process of establishing a relationship between the community psychologist and the community could make it difficult to continue. On the other hand, it is possible that the community psychologist is purposefully trying to "shake things up." The connection of everyone in the community to everyone else can work to the advantage of the psychologist and to their disadvantage. It is important to be aware that the connections among community members are a key element of working with communities. A community is defined by the social connections among the members.

Biological, social, and community systems have *interdependent* components with bidirectional influences on each other. Humans influence biological systems through farming, carbon emissions, and other means, yet we are also dependent upon these same systems for meeting our physical needs for clean air, water, and food. Because the systems are interdependent, what we do to the systems comes back to influence our own health and survival. If pesticides are used to keep crops free of predatory insects, those same pesticides become part of the ecological system and may have an impact on our health and other components of the system. Similarly, people in a community influence and are influenced by others in the community. Teachers, for example, have an important influence upon students, but students also influence the ways that teachers go about teaching. In order to understand a school system, we need to look at the multiple components of the system and how they influence each other. We cannot understand the components of a system by studying them in isolation. We must look at the *context* and interdependencies as well.

One of the most challenging things that community psychologists need to do is to acquire an understanding of the relationships that exist within the community. Who talks to whom? What groups and individuals tend to avoid interactions with other groups and individuals? There is an endless degree of complexity involved in describing a community and almost no description is safe from criticism or revision because new information is likely to modify the picture of how the community components interact. How does one create consensus in the face of such complexity? (How can our superintendent create consensus among the various constituents—parents, children, teachers, etc.—in our opening vignette?) Understanding context is a key challenge for community psychologists.

Biologically speaking, there is no "waste" in nature and there is no "away" to which things can be thrown. In a natural system, waste products are used by other members of the system. Eventually, waste products (e.g., dead tree leaves) are broken down and become nutrients for other trees and plants in a sustainable process. When you put something in the garbage, wash it down the sink, flush it down the toilet, or dilute it in a river, it remains in the system. This leads to the accumulation of toxic substances in places where they do not belong, including our own blood because they are not broken down or used by other components of the system. In contrast, biological systems make multiple uses of resources. Waste material from one organism becomes nutrients for another in a sustainable cycle. Many environmental problems are created when waste material is not processed into a benign substance that can be used by other members of the system but is allowed to accumulate in the environment.

The people in a community are *resources* for the remainder of the community. They must go somewhere even when their current role in the community is no longer needed. Just as the goods and materials produced by society need to be recycled, so do the human resources in a community. Community interventions will sometimes lead to shifts in the roles assumed by individuals and subgroups within the community. A large part of the success of a community intervention may depend upon the ability of the community psychologist to keep individuals and groups whose roles have shifted integrated and interconnected with the group, in other words, *the human resources need to be recycled.* Even though roles change, the institutional memory and social connections of the individuals remain. If individuals are marginalized or isolated, that is, thrown away, some very unpleasant consequences could be the result. Such individuals could use their social connections to undermine or harm the community and the interventions developed by the community psychologist. On the other hand, when such individuals are recruited or trained for new roles in the community, the community benefits, as well as the individual who may develop new personal and professional skills. The core of any community is its human resources who must be recycled and retrained for new roles as the community moves forward.

Tensions can build within a community over a period of time. For example, an elected community leader could have a very hierarchical view of leadership processes, which leads the person to make a series of decisions that have the cumulative effect of building up resentment toward the leader. When community members are interviewed, they cannot point to any single decision that is "bad" or inappropriate, but they nevertheless develop a vague feeling that things are not quite "right." Because there is *no free lunch* there is eventually a cost of the leader's decisions, which could range from minor dissatisfaction to a major crisis when it is discovered that a decision has taken the community in an inappropriate direction that threatens its existence. As individuals who are trying to guide a community in a healthier direction, community psychologists take the same risks. Some interventions may be enthusiastically implemented by community members, while others, for reasons that are not known until later, are resented and ineffective. Each change in a system has a cost that can be unknown until its effects are observed. This is part of the excitement of being a community psychologist, but also keeps some of us awake at night with worry.

The concept of the **feedback loop** has many applications to understanding social systems. A simple feedback loop is illustrated by a thermostat that controls the heat in most houses. When the temperature falls below the set point, the heat comes on, which raises the temperature. Once the temperature is above the upper set point, the heat is turned off and remains off until the temperature drops below the lower set point. With this feedback loop in continuous operation, the temperature is maintained within comfortable limits. There are many feedback loops in the natural environment. Increasing carbon dioxide in the atmosphere creates a more favorable environment for plant growth, which in turn uses more carbon dioxide. However, this natural capacity for self-adjustment can be overwhelmed by human activity. According to Commoner (1971, p. 127), "Our task, then, is to discover how human activities generate *environmental impacts*—that is, external intrusions into the ecosystem that tend to degrade its capacity for self-adjustment."

One way to approach this concept from a community perspective is to ask to what extent the community welcomes new community members and simultaneously informs them about the community, while learning about the person (or people) and allowing them to influence the community. This creates a feedback loop: The person learns about the community and then exerts a small influence on it. The existence of such a feedback loop makes the community more adaptive and sustainable. On the other hand, if new members are not welcomed and integrated into the community, what is the likely long-term impact? In order to remain sustainable a community needs to welcome new members and allow their talents and abilities to influence it. If new members are not welcomed, they may have little motivation to remain actively involved. Then the community is likely to lose its coherence and fall apart as the remaining pool of members gradually shrinks through natural processes of attrition.

The concept of the feedback loop has multiple implications for community psychologists. The first contacts of a community psychologist with the community represent an intrusion of sorts and there is a lot to be learned from the way that the community responds. Does the community have an informal sequence of people to meet, giving the community a chance to get to know you and you to get to know the community? Do such meetings consist of interactive conversations? A lecture? A grilling? Do you feel welcomed into the community? Do you feel like an outsider? Answers to these questions can provide some key information about the nature of the community and how it responds to new challenges, both large and small, and it may point the way toward potential intervention strategies.

Another aspect of feedback loops is that they need to be created anytime community psychologists intervene with a community. In other words, measures that reflect the impact of the intervention need to be taken regularly to determine whether the intervention is a success (e.g., Wielkiewicz, 1995). When the feedback loop indicates the intervention is not succeeding, changes can be made to hopefully improve it, whereas when the feedback loop indicates success, the intervention can be continued. For an unsuccessful intervention, it may be necessary to create additional feedback loops, such as by holding meetings and getting qualitative feedback from community members to learn how the intervention might be improved. The creation of feedback loops greatly increases the probability of a sustainable community. (See Chapter 12 for more on the topic of evaluations.)

Every effect has multiple causes and every cause can ripple through the system with multiple influences. Since everything is connected to everything else, it follows that no single cause can account for any event. Thus, it is probably most accurate to state that variables influence, not cause, each other. Events within a community are complex, making it challenging to find effective interventions. For example, what are the causes of lack of jobs in a community? A long list of influencing factors could be developed: education, infrastructure, crime, motivation, leadership, lack of customers, fear, exporting of jobs to other countries, free trade treaties, lack of transportation, congressional actions, grants, vocational schools, public transportation routes, and others. It is an interesting exercise to create a list of influencing or causal factors for any community problem and then map the interrelationships of the various influencing factors. This map can be used to determine where effective interventions could be applied. The multiple influences involved in such problems do not make intervention impossible, just challenging and difficult.

Diversity is the substance out of which adaptation emerges (Capra, 1996; Klingsporn, 1973). Genetic, physical, intellectual, cultural, ethnic, biological, ideological, political, and educational diversity can all contribute to the adaptability of a system or species. When a system, species, or organization lacks diversity it is much less likely to adapt to changing conditions. Community systems benefit from diversity because a wide diversity in the individuals who make up the community provides more resources for developing adaptive strategies. Furthermore, individuals have talents that may not be known to the community, and the community needs to provide ways for those talents to be discovered and expressed. If the group has a wide variety of perspectives and beliefs about a challenge and its solutions, it is more likely that an adaptive solution will emerge. In contrast, a group having a limited range of knowledge and beliefs about the challenge will be less likely to produce an adaptive solution because the diversity of alternatives from which solutions can emerge is limited.

As an example, imagine that you are in charge of assembling a group to develop strategies for improving job and career opportunities in the community. If the group you assemble is composed only of individuals from the auto industry, the solutions likely to be proposed may be very limited. However, if the group includes people from the city government, education, planners, businesses located in or near the community, and others who are interested in the issue, the diversity of perspectives creates a wider range of possibilities from which solutions can emerge. Thus, individuals who are sincerely interested in solving problems engage a group with a wide range of opinions and perspectives in the process.

A monoculture is the opposite of a diverse system. A human monoculture consists of a highly restricted social group with a single-minded perspective. Since diversity of opinion and perspectives is not tolerated, groupthink and other signs of poor decision making are prevalent. Wielkiewicz and Stelzner (2005) argue that the complex problems faced by most organizations require diversity of perspectives and opinions in order to reach adaptive solutions and strategies. Thus, from a systems perspective, monocultures are to be avoided and diversity is to be valued.

Sometimes the components of a system fit together in such a way that a little thing can make a big difference. This is often referred to as the butterfly effect and comes from Commoner's first law of ecology that everything is connected to everything else and Kelly's parallel concept of interdependence. Being a community psychologist means searching for *tipping points* that might take the community in desirable directions. On the other hand, tipping points may work in the opposite direction. An intervention or change may have a drastic negative impact on a community that creates an immediate crisis. A natural or human-made disaster would be one example of such an event. While some writers describe tipping points that work against us, there are other ways that tipping points can work in our favor. One of the major issues in dealing with communities is to find small interventions with large impacts.

Donella Meadows (2001), writing in *Grist Magazine,* reminds readers that a wise approach to living is to slow down and maybe come to a complete stop when the route ahead is full of uncertainties and the pathway is dark. She suggests that this is the wisest approach to environmental issues. If actions contain a high risk of harm to the environment and the creatures that inhabit it, the best course of action is to slow down rather than go full speed ahead. She quotes Christine Todd Whitman, who was later appointed (and then resigned) as head of the Environmental Protection Agency: "We must acknowledge that uncertainty is inherent in managing natural resources, recognize it is usually easier to prevent environmental damage than to repair it later, and shift the burden of proof from those advocating protection toward those proposing an action that may be harmful." An ounce of prevention is worth a pound of cure. Thus, we should be much more cautious in putting new technologies and chemicals into our environment.

Working with communities is fraught with similar danger. Due to the complexity of community systems, it is impossible to accurately predict the impact of interventions before they are under way. Thus, it is important to examine interventions for unintended consequences. However, the complexity of human systems means that the process of examining the potential impact of the intervention strategy could occupy the team for a long time. All interventions involve an element of risk and community psychologists need to become comfortable with this idea or else they would be permanently engaged in the process of discussing potential impacts rather than actively involved in helping communities. There needs to be *a balance of precaution and risk taking* (Kelly, 1971). Once an intervention has been carefully vetted for its intended and unintended consequences and has the support of the community, it may be time to take a risk. If the team has adequate feedback loops in place, it should be possible to detect the impact of the intervention and make any needed corrections.

The Process of Leadership: Using an Ecological Approach

Trickett (2009a) has suggested that community capacity building can be defined in terms of "efforts to increase local resources for current and future problem solving or community betterment." One significant community capacity is leadership. Goodman et al. (1998, as cited by Trickett, 2011) have suggested leadership is one of the primary dimensions when discussing community capacities, while Dalton and Wolfe (2012) labeled "community leadership and mentoring" as one of the critical elements of community and organizational capacity-building. Moritsugu, Vera, Wong, and Duffy (2014) describe leadership as a significant element in organizational and community change. Kelly and colleagues (Kelly, Azelton, Lardon, Mock, & Tandin, 2004; Tandon, Azelton, Kelly, & Strickland, 1998) have researched and described the importance of community leadership in the African American community in Chicago.

Leadership is a key component in understanding how a community functions and how to intervene or change it. We will forgo a broad review of the vast leadership literature in favor of focusing on a model that is particularly relevant to the ecology of communities. The model is called **balanced leadership** (originally referred to as "ecological leadership") and is described by Wielkiewicz and Stelzner (2005). The core principle of the model is that organizations need to balance two different aspects of leadership processes: a more hierarchical/dustrial approach versus a more communal approach (the latter was labeled as "ecological" when first introduced, but because of the evolving nature of the model, and to avoid confusion with the use of the term *ecological* in this chapter, we will refer to it as a "communal" approach to leadership). Within this theory, **leadership** is defined as a process that emerges from the interactions and actions of people in an organization who contribute to leadership processes regardless of whether they are designated as "leaders." These interactions are then translated into formal decisions and actions, such as the implementation of new policies (e.g., an anti-bullying program in a school) or other organizational actions (Wielkiewicz & Stelzner, 2005).

The model begins with the assumption that communities are faced with a multitude of universal and local adaptive challenges. These challenges—such as an evolving global economy, growing recognition of our unsustainable use of natural resources, the interactions of diverse cultures, income gaps, and the increasing

Photo 3.3   Emergence in nature.

Source: iStockphoto.com/DougLemke.

tension between individual rights and the common good—have significant implications for leadership (Allen et al., 1998). A question for community psychologists is whether the leadership capacities of the community are being developed so it will be able to successfully cope with its adaptive challenges (e.g., bullying in schools, access to resources for the disadvantaged, empowering community members to have a voice in community issues). The main idea of balanced leadership is that leadership processes need to consist of an appropriate balance of hierarchical and communal processes. If key decisions are being made by one person or a small group of individuals with little or no input from others in the community (i.e., leadership processes are hierarchical), this could present a severe problem for the adaptability of the community because of the lack of diversity contributing to the emergence of potential responses to challenges. A key intervention for such communities may be to shift leadership processes toward a more communal model, while encouraging key individuals to give up some of their power. Community psychologists need to be spearheading efforts to improve the quality of leadership processes at all levels within and beyond communities.

Traditional hierarchical models of leadership are inadequate because they assume one individual can effectively direct an organization to long-term success (Allen et al., 1998; Wielkiewicz & Stelzner, 2005). When powerful individuals in positions of leadership make decisions that affect communities without adequate input from those affected by the decisions, or without input from those who have expertise to improve the quality of decisions, these decisions are likely to be maladaptive (Allen et al., 1998; Wielkiewicz & Stelzner, 2005). The results are events like the imposition of an undemocratic attempt to establish a charter school—as described in the opening vignette of this chapter—political contests that degenerate into vapid name-calling rather than informative debates on policy, and other signs of the absence of leadership for the common good. If the flow of information is restricted or ignored so only one or a few individuals are able to influence leadership processes, decisions are likely to be maladaptive because they are made with inadequate information.

Effective leadership facilitates the community's ability to adapt by valuing social responsibility, respecting all persons and the environment we depend upon, and respecting all community members (Astin & Astin, 2000; Wielkiewicz & Stelzner, 2005). Communality is the process by which effective leadership is manifested in contemporary organizations (Astin & Astin, 2000; Eagly, 2007). A communal approach to leadership empowers every individual as a potential leader through a shared vision, respectful dialogue, interdependence, and personal development (Astin & Astin, 2000; Heifetz, 1994). A communal approach increases the chances that the nature of the complex adaptive challenges that all communities face can be understood and effective adaptive strategies can be developed. Continued dependence upon positional leaders to provide "leadership" means that adaptive challenges will be met with an inadequate understanding of the nature of the problem, which leads to inadequate attempts to solve them.

The balanced leadership model (Allen et al., 1998; Wielkiewicz & Stelzner, 2005) proposes a tension between a communal approach and a hierarchical (industrial) approach. Positional leaders remain important, but their decision making should include a diversity of outlooks, and the value or effectiveness of the leader is determined by the followers' reactions and the response of the larger environment to the actions of the community. Positional leadership is necessary for planning strategy and managing crises, but is most effective when it does not stifle creativity in the community or organization (Uhl-Bien, Marion, & McKelvey, 2007). When a consensus cannot be reached, the leader needs to make a decision in an effective, timely manner. Relying on communal leadership alone can lead to the collapse of an organization because the amount of information that can be analyzed to address a problem or issue is infinite and constantly shifting and could engage the organization indefinitely. The best leaders balance the hierarchical and communal approaches and optimize this tension according to the circumstances (Wielkiewicz & Stelzner, 2005). Hence, Wielkiewicz and Stelzner (2005) have referred to such a model as a "balanced" or "sustainable" model of leadership—that is, the leader's role is to optimize or balance the tension between the traditional industrial approach, characterized by hierarchy and top-down decision making, and the communal approach, characterized by collaboration and consensus building. Neither approach can be pursued exclusively. Instead, an organization's leadership processes must strive to balance these processes according to the circumstances or context.

Although a balanced approach to leadership is optimal, it is relatively uncommon. Due to a number of societal and inherited characteristics and the ways that positional leaders are portrayed in the media, society has developed a distinct bias in favor of the hierarchical approach to leadership. This is not an effective approach to leadership, especially for the community psychologist. As a community member beginning his or her interaction with the organization from the outside, attempting to impose solutions or structure is almost certain to lead to failure. It is critical for community psychologists to see leadership from an ecological perspective and develop a communal approach to leadership. Furthermore, Wielkiewicz and Stelzner (2005) point out that the predominant model of leadership is hierarchical in which positional leaders are seen to be in charge of the organization and to make all the key decisions. Moving communities from a hierarchical approach to leadership toward a more communal approach may be a significant challenge for the community psychologist. Thus, it is extremely important for community psychologists to gain a thorough understanding of how decisions are made in the community or organization so they can understand the nature of leadership processes in the community. Here are some good questions to ask:

- How much community input was involved in the most recent decisions that impacted the community?
- Did broad-based community input have an observable impact on the decision?
- How was the decision implemented?
- Was the decision arrived at after discussion and debate?
- Does it represent a consensus point of view?
- Who made the decision? Was the decision made by an individual? A group?
- Is it possible to identify exactly when the decision was made or did it emerge as a consensus after considerable discussion?
- What processes were used to gain community input before the decision was made?
- How was the decision communicated to other community members?

- What was the reaction of community members to the decision?
- Are there individuals or groups who are grumbling or complaining about the decision?
- Are there individuals who believe others are undermining the implementation of the decision?
- To what extent does the entire community "buy into" the decision?

The balanced model of leadership posits that communality within organizations is imperative for long-term success (Wielkiewicz & Stelzner, 2005). Thus, the more communality observed in decision-making processes, the healthier the leadership processes. If signs of communality are nonexistent or difficult to identify, this is a problem that needs to be addressed. One solution is to bring representatives of various subgroups within the community together to discuss common needs and goals. However, strategies like this need to be approached cautiously because the established habits of the community are being challenged. The balanced model focuses on the context of leadership and de-emphasizes the importance of a single leader. It posits that leadership is an **emergent** process (more than the sum of its parts) formed by the interaction of the people in the organization. Every person has the potential to be a leader, and the synthesis of a variety of ideas and opinions creates the most useful solutions to new problems. For many reasons, shifting leadership processes in the communal direction can be challenging. For example, the community may have ostracized individuals who challenged existing leadership processes in the past. Establishing the community trust needed for communal leadership processes may be a long and difficult process. However, the greater the diversity of perspectives that contribute to leadership, the more likely that adaptive and sustainable community decisions will emerge. The challenge is to get those who may wield power to accept such diversity and to convince individuals who may have been marginalized in the past that the request for their input is genuine. Within the balanced model, leadership facilitates and is facilitated by the collaboration of many people with a wide range of diversity working together to make decisions (Allen et al., 1998; Wielkiewicz & Stelzner, 2005). The coalescing of diverse ideas, facilitated by communal leadership processes, allows communities to better adapt to their challenges.

The balanced model of leadership does not deny the importance of positional leaders. Wielkiewicz and Stelzner (2005) argue that, in contrast to traditional theories of leadership, the value of the positional leader should not be determined by the decisions of the leader alone. Rather, the effectiveness of the leader should be judged according to the way decisions emerge from the genuine sharing of ideas by the members within the organization, and whether the leader is able to marshal these processes to enhance the organization's ability to adapt. However, when the communal efforts of the members do not result in a timely consensus, an executive decision must sometimes be made because failure to execute adaptive strategies in a timely manner will interfere with the community's ability to adapt. Long-term over-reliance on communal leadership could lead to disintegration of the organization, because a complete consensus is nearly impossible to attain, excessively delaying decisions and execution of strategies. Thus, this model of leadership requires that organization members strive to maintain an appropriate balance between industrial/hierarchical and communal leadership processes.

One of the most important principles of this leadership theory concerns the importance of diversity and feedback loops. As Capra (1996) stated "[A] diverse community will be able to survive and reorganize itself. . . . In other words, the more complex its pattern of interconnections, the more resilient it will be" (p. 303). Drawing on this principle, Allen et al. (1998) posited that the key to effective organizational action is (a) to recognize that any decision is made in the context of many systems, such as the environment, the economy, local and world communities, and families, all interacting in highly complex, interdependent ways, and (b) to engage as many feedback loops from these systems as possible into organizational processes. Diversity in all of its forms (e.g., racial, ethnic, gender, sexual orientation, national origin, age, physical abilities, statistical) is a positive asset and a key element in adaptation (Ayman, 1993; Klingsporn, 1973). Leadership processes must encourage inclusiveness, which increases opportunities to learn through practice, and increases the quality of decisions by bringing more perspectives to the table (e.g., Finlay, 1991; Helgesen, 1995; James, 1996; Mai-Dalton, 1993; Paulus, 2000; Weisbord & Janoff, 1995).

The Environment and Leadership: An Example

Systemic and ecological thinking inevitably lead to thoughts about the dangers faced by individuals and communities from environmental crises (e.g., Brown, 2011). Effective community intervention needs to have elements of environmental sustainability built into it. Some interventions can directly address environmental issues, such as community solar projects, community gardens, political action against local polluters, and rehabilitating open spaces and parks for recreational use. At the same time some of the problems that communities face may be the direct result of environmental issues. For example, communities located near sources of air or groundwater pollution may have health issues that can only be addressed by eliminating the pollution. In such a case, the broader meaning of the word ecological extends to the physical environment that is essential to the survival and health of the human species. At the same time, such issues bring a load of systemic and leadership issues with them, including the role of corporations in daily life, state regulatory agencies, and politics, all centered on the need for community-based action. Any attempt to engage with a community must include some assessment of the local ecology identifying potential threats to physical health that come from the environment, such as air and water pollution, asbestos and lead paint, and proximity to manufacturing waste products.

SKILLS AND ABILITIES ASSOCIATED WITH AN ECOLOGICAL APPROACH

The following discussion is not meant to profile the successful community psychologist, but it is meant to inspire some self-examination and thought about the road ahead and some of the tools needed to successfully navigate it. The purpose of this section is to lay out some of those tools—skills and abilities—that could be useful to the community psychologist and would enhance an ecological approach.

Personality

We begin with personality because personality has such a strong influence on our pattern of interactions with others. The many contexts in which community psychology is practiced require a high degree of self-awareness because one is often gathering information through personal interactions or trying to influence others. Almost all psychologists are familiar with the five-factor model (FFM) of personality. The FFM originates from the lexical hypothesis, the notion that adjectives describing human personality characteristics contain a fairly complete catalog of human personality dimensions. Thus, by asking individuals to rate their own personalities on these common terms and then subjecting the data to factor analysis, the results should describe the basic dimensions of human personality. Currently, the findings of numerous researchers have converged on describing personality with five factors or dimensions (Donnellan, Oswald, Baird, & Lucas, 2006; Goldberg, 1992, 1993, 1999; McCrae, 2001; Paunonen & Ashton, 2001) although alternative models have also emerged (e.g., Ball, 1995; Block, 2001; Durrett & Trull, 2005).

The five factors are Openness to Experience, Conscientiousness, Extraversion, Agreeableness, and Neuroticism, which conveniently spell the acronym OCEAN for those who would like to remember them. Openness to Experience has also been called Intellect or Culture (Goldberg, 1993) and represents the degree to which an individual is intellectually curious, imaginative, and interested in abstract ideas. Conscientiousness reflects the extent to which an individual is dependable, organized, and task oriented. Extraversion is associated with being outgoing, sociable, and talkative. Agreeableness is associated with being cooperative, interested in others, and empathetic. Finally, Neuroticism is associated with being moody, and emotionally unstable.

Although no ideal profile exists and successful community psychologists would be expected to have the entire range of personality strengths and weaknesses, the nature of interventions with large groups and communities will likely place a certain set of demands upon the practitioner depending upon the context. For example, due to the necessity of at least occasionally interacting with large and medium-sized groups, a slightly or moderately extroverted personality would probably be an advantage for the community psychologist. Those who are highly introverted would, on the other hand, probably contribute greatly to the research process, as well as the reflective elements of any intervention. But those who are introverted may need to be aware of those occasions when being more outgoing is appropriate and develop those skills. Openness to experience and a positive attitude toward **lifelong learning,** or a belief that learning continues throughout a person's lifetime (e.g., Wielkiewicz, 2014), are necessities for life success, but are particularly important for a community psychologist because success requires that practitioners develop a deep understanding of the communities with which they interact. This may require becoming deeply involved in a variety of cultures and ethnic traditions. Openness to new experiences and a positive attitude toward learning as a lifelong endeavor would be essential for success.

The ability to get along with others (i.e., Agreeableness) is also essential for the community psychologist. A huge portion of the activity of a community psychologist consists of interactions with community members. If the practitioner is not able to at least maintain the appearance of being agreeable, it will be impossible to build the relationships upon which the community interventions will be based. The interventions are not imposed upon the community; they are developed in cooperation with the community members. Sometimes, however, advocacy or community work requires being comfortable with being less agreeable because there is a need to challenge the community to think differently about its problems. In other words, there is value to being able to function on both ends of the Agreeableness dimension. Sibley and Pirie (2013) added a sixth scale to the FFM, Honesty-Humility. A certain amount of humility when dealing with communities is probably a valuable personal asset. Community interventions are generally a cooperative activity and any attempt to impose upon the community is likely to be met with resistance that eventually results in a failure of the intervention. For the most part honesty is also the best policy. However, confidentiality will often need to overrule honesty. This is most likely to occur in the process of assessment of the community or organization. While compiling the results of surveys, interviews, and focus groups, a lot of valuable information is likely to be found that is best kept confidential. For example, two subgroups within the community may have hostile or negative feelings toward each other. Although the community psychologist may need to address this hostility, revealing its details to individuals is likely to do more harm than good. Thus, community practitioners need to find the appropriate balance between honesty and keeping information to themselves.

Mindfulness

Becoming aware of and to some extent controlling emotions is an essential skill for the community practitioner. Being mindful means to develop awareness of emotions, thoughts, feelings, and experiences and being in the moment and aware of what is happening around us. The central idea is that being aware of what is happening to us internally allows us to exercise control over emotions and keep a more level emotional keel. This is important in situations that can become emotional as individuals and subgroups within a community adjust and readjust to changes. At times it will be helpful for practitioners to distance themselves from the very community they are trying to help. For example, in establishing new lines of communication, the practitioners themselves may be the target of anger that has little or nothing to do with them. In such cases it may be particularly helpful to be objective and not get caught up in an emotional reaction that complicates matters rather than improving the situation. Again, appropriate distancing needs to be balanced with the ability to engage the community, which is an essential element of the ecological approach. It is also important to be aware of our own biases and the role of prior personal experiences on how we cognitively process contextual information. For those who would like to go deeper into this concept, Koerner (2012) and Tibbetts (2013) would be good starting points.

Systemic Thinking

The ability to think systemically about community issues at multiple levels of analysis (Dalton & Wolfe, 2012) might be the core skill in community psychology. It includes not only learning the terms and definitions included in the present chapter, but learning to see how they are relevant to understanding the communities with which one works. It also means the community psychologist must not only respond to the incidents in the community, but develop an understanding of the broader context of those incidents. This means striving to understand the **culture,** or customary traits, beliefs, behavior patterns, of the organization or community, how the organization has developed over time, and the relationships among its components.

Listening Skills

Community psychologists must also develop excellent listening skills. Just as clinical psychologists need to develop the skill to both hear the content of their client's spoken words and attend to the nonverbal aspects of communication, community psychologists must do the same. However, the task for community psychologists is much more complex. They must learn how to describe the general themes that emerge from a series of isolated conversations and develop a contextual understanding of these isolated conversations. There is no instructional package or procedure for accomplishing this goal. Each practitioner will need to develop skills and strategies with which he or she is comfortable. Taking notes of the conversations one has in different contexts of the organization or community may be a good beginning to the process. A list of questions that can serve as a starting point toward developing an understanding of community context follows:

1. What themes emerge from conversations with individuals?

2. What problems do individuals identify that need to be addressed?

3. Is it possible to identify groups or clusters of individuals who might be brought together for productive conversations about the community or organization?

4. What are the key tensions and conflict that exist within a community or organization?

5. Are key feedback loops being suppressed or ignored?

Empowering Organizations and Communities to Solve Their Own Problems

Although it may be tempting to simply tell community members what they need to do, solutions that come from the outside are not likely to be taken seriously. In fact such imposed solutions can seriously undermine relationships with the community. Instead, community psychologists need to learn how to help community organizations solve their own problems and promote their own welfare (Trickett et al., 2011). The strategies can range from reacquainting a community or organization with its mission statement, to a radical reconsideration of its purpose and strategies. In our experience there is considerable value in bringing members together and taking them through group processes designed to create consensus around goals, mission, problems to be solved, or other issues identified through an assessment. It may also be necessary to nurture feedback loops, especially those that are suppressed or ignored, so they can influence the community or organization (e.g., Morrison & Milliken, 2000).

The ability to see the difference between reactions to an event (e.g., a school's response to an incident of bullying or harassment) versus an ecologically valid, multilevel program of prevention is essential to **empowering** organizations and communities to solve their own problems. Again, if the intervention does not account for the overall context of the incident, how can it be viewed as ecologically valid? Community psychologists will need to be alert to this distinction at all stages of their interactions with the organization. It may be necessary to help organizations or communities convert an existing intervention from reactive to preventive, or it may be necessary to help create a new preventive program or intervention. This can be more challenging than it may appear. Reactive interventions have the advantage of immediately removing the problem situation, which can be very reinforcing because the organization does not recognize that the problem is occurring at a steady frequency or even increasing. Frequent and judicious use of the word *prevention* may assist the organization in moving in a different direction.

Facilitating Communication

Discovering communication techniques that are used by community members can help the psychologist learn about the organization. Knowledge of these same techniques can also be used to facilitate communication among community members. A significant component of many community interventions is to assist the organization members, subgroups, and the larger community to have better and more useful lines of communication. These strategies can involve making use of social media such as Facebook, taking advantage of formal and informal social networks, helping the organization to span artificial boundaries (Kelly et al., 2000), making good use of community celebrations (Kelly et al., 1988) by creating them if necessary, and engaging citizen advisory groups (Kelly et al., 1988).

Cross-Cultural Competence

Community psychologists need to be comfortable interacting with and understanding the unique cultures of communities. Fortunately, an entire chapter of this volume is devoted to this topic (see Chapter 4).

TRAINING, EDUCATION, AND EXPERIENCES TOWARD DEVELOPMENT OF ECOLOGICAL COMPETENCY

A community psychology curriculum needs to be very broad to allow future practitioners to develop a set of core skills while addressing their own needs and unique approach to community psychology. The list below is meant to be suggestive rather than prescriptive.

1. Experience or coursework in assessing community and organizational resources:

    a. Survey development and administration skills: One way to assess an organization or community is to develop a survey and ask as many individuals as possible to complete it. A survey can be valuable to gain a quantitative picture of the community (e.g., what percentage of individuals agree with a specific statement about the organization) and qualitative picture (e.g., include an open-ended question asking for suggestions for improving the organization or community). Surveys can also be used to create feedback loops that inform community psychologists about the efficacy of interventions.

b. Interview skills: Although surveys can provide a good picture of a community, interviews of selected members also can be extremely valuable. Community psychologists need to be skillful interviewers and these skills can be developed through practice and appropriate coursework. A key question that needs to be addressed is whether interviews will be highly structured with a predetermined set of questions or more open-ended and free-ranging.

c. Qualitative research skills: Community or organizational interventions often provide an opportunity for research that contributes to the empirical literature of community psychology. This requires an understanding of qualitative research methods because experimental interventions (i.e., randomly assigning the intervention to different groups) is usually not an option. However, establishing a control group, developing good measures of dependent variables, and other techniques can help demonstrate its usefulness in other contexts. Qualitative research skills are usually acquired via coursework.

d. Creating social settings (Kelly, 1987): In order for collaboration between community members and community psychologists to take place, there needs to be a context or social setting. One of the central ideas of the ecological approach to community psychology is that psychologists are not "experts" who impose solutions and strategies on communities; they are learners who must become engaged in the culture of the community or organization. This may require the assistance of "boundary spanners" who can help the community psychologist learn how to engage with the culture and provide basic services such as language translation (Kim, Kim, & Kelly, 2006). Furthermore, the community needs to discover or create social settings in which collaborative process can be developed via formal and informal interactions with community members. Because each community or organization has its own unique culture, it may take solid effort and the development of unique cultural competencies to discover or create these settings.

2. We have seen anecdotal evidence and theoretical support for the idea that one may have an easier time understanding ecological principles after recognizing a crisis in leadership at some level. Usually, this crisis involves a failure of leadership where the crisis or failure could have been avoided by paying attention to information that was ignored or suppressed by those in charge of making decisions. A crisis can be artificially created (e.g., by watching a movie of such a crisis) or one that has been directly experienced. Almost everyone has such experiences, and processing them with a mentor can facilitate insights into the nature of leadership and ecological approaches to community interventions.

3. Courses in group dynamics. Becoming familiar with group processes and especially how group processes can go astray (such as groupthink) is essential for community psychologists because so much can be learned by observing or engaging in group interactions.

4. Courses or workshops in group facilitation techniques. However, note that there are many models of how to facilitate group communication and the practitioner needs to find one with which he or she is comfortable.

5. Courses/workshops in community organizing and public policy. It is likely that many of the successful interventions undertaken by community psychologists will involve empowering communities to organize and influence public policy. Thus, coursework and workshops that improve such skills will be helpful.

6. Coursework or experience that assists in the development of cross-cultural competency. This is the topic of Chapter 4 of this volume.

7. Systemic and ecological thinking must also include knowledge of our environment and the many challenges we are facing to have a sustainable society. The history of the word *ecological* comes from writers who were addressing environmental issues.

8. Interdisciplinary courses in sociology, political science, biology, cultural studies, or other areas of interest and relevance.

Conclusion: Being a Lifelong Learner

Each time a community psychologist becomes part of a community, it is an opportunity to learn. No matter how much coursework and experience is accumulated, there is always more to learn. Each organization or community is unique and requires the practitioner to learn about it. Approaching the community with an open mind and allowing its members to become teachers is the best way to add to one's knowledge base. Furthermore, workshops, additional courses, and mentoring relationships also offer opportunities to become a more competent practitioner. Thus, we would like to summarize the training and experience needed to become a competent community psychologist with this reminder: Always be a lifelong learner.

APPLICATIONS

The ecological approach has become one of the primary models of community psychology and we expect it to remain so in the future. In order to say that an intervention is ecological, what conditions need to be met? Although there are numerous characteristics that relate to the quality and likelihood of success for a particular strategy, we believe that an ecologically based intervention would have at least the following five characteristics.

1. The intervention is multilevel and directed at all or most levels of the hierarchy of the community or organization. For example, a school district intervention

Photo 3.4   Interdependence: The loss of habitat and the threat to a species. A different kind of "butterfly effect"? Are there parallels in human habitats?

Source: iStockphoto.com/OGphoto.

would involve students, teachers, administration, parents, and possibly the larger community.

2. At each level the intervention is spread across subgroups. For example, if the intervention is taking place in a school, it would involve multiple classrooms and teachers.

3. There is more than one intervention or component of the program and interventions are tailored to particular subgroups. Clearly, a component of an intervention that takes place in classrooms and is directed at students would be different from the intervention as experienced by teachers.

4. Interventions are focused on prevention or systemic change as opposed to reacting to specific incidents.

5. The intervention creates feedback loops that can be used to evaluate effectiveness and lead to adjustments in the details of the intervention. In some cases, quasi-experimental designs are used to provide comparison and control so the impact can be evaluated in more detail. For example, within a school district, a random

selection of schools could experience all components of the intervention whereas other schools, serving as controls, would experience no intervention or only a portion of the entire intervention package.

In sum, an ecological intervention is multidimensional and multilayered and involves different components that are tailored to particular subgroups within the system.

An Ecological Perspective on Childhood Bullying

Physical, verbal, and cyber bullying are endemic problems in schools and communities around the world. In fact, if one searches the World Wide Web using the terms "bullying" and "suicide," millions of hits are obtained. The consequences of being bullied are very serious. Rigby (2003) reviewed the literature of school bullying with a focus on its consequences. The effects of bullying in school found in this review and others included the following:

- Low self-esteem

- A dislike for school and school avoidance

- Psychological distress including anxiety, depression, hopelessness, suicidal tendencies, anger, vengefulness, and self-pity

- Poorer physical health, psychosomatic symptoms associated with anxiety, headaches, lower resistance to infections, and other complaints

- Children bullied between 4 and 10 years of age "had highly increased odds" of showing symptoms of borderline personality disorder at age 11.8 years (Wolke, Schreier, Zanarini, & Winsper, 2012, p. 846). Borderline personality disorder is characterized by highly volatile relationships, difficulty in forming attachments, impulsivity, chronic feelings of emptiness, and emotional volatility.

Clearly, both anecdotal and empirical evidence indicate that bullying is a serious problem with serious consequences. Thus, it is imperative that effective anti-bullying interventions are developed.

Cross and colleagues (2011) reported results of an ecologically based anti-bullying study that involved randomized group assignment and several layers of intervention: whole school, classroom, parents, and individual students. The program is called the Friendly Schools program and was tested in elementary schools in Perth, Australia, and consisted of a 2-year intervention with an additional follow-up at one year. As a result of the program, self-reported victimization was reduced by 16% to 31%. Interestingly, the authors speculated that program implementation could have been higher except that teachers were overwhelmed by implementation of a new state-wide curriculum so they may have been too overloaded to effectively implement the program. It is not possible to escape the effects of systemic variables in any study. However, with moderate reductions in bullying and reporting of bullying this study provides general support for the idea that ecological approaches to prevention of bullying in schools can be effective.

A successful and frequently cited anti-bullying program has been described by Olweus (1993) and Kallestad and Olweus (2003). This is an excellent model for systemic anti-bullying interventions that was developed in Norway. Although various programs to prevent bullying had existed in Norway, anti-bullying efforts became more urgent after three widely publicized suicides were linked to bullying in the early 1980s. This led to the Olweus Core Program Against Bullying and Antisocial Behavior, or the Bullying Prevention Program. Core features of the program are listed below:

- All members of the community are involved and informed about the basic characteristics of bullying and how to respond to it.

- The goals are focused on both prevention and improvement of the general social climate of the school.

- A clear and consistent response to bullying is defined and established as policy throughout the system.

- School staff members are engaged in the program through conferences, discussion groups, and formation of a coordinating group.

- Adults who are part of the system are informed and enlisted to supervise and administer consequences.

- Adult supervision is provided during break times.

- An anti-bullying curriculum is presented to all children.

- Class rules against bullying are established.

- Parents become involved in anti-bullying efforts through their children's classrooms.

- Individual interventions are developed and administered for both victims and perpetrators of bullying.

- The intervention is conducted in the context of research so data are gathered and there is an opportunity for the program to be influenced and improved via feedback loops.

As can be seen from the list of components, the Olweus Bullying Prevention Program is easily categorized as an ecological intervention. The intervention was multilayered with components for the community, teachers, students, and staff. It took place across multiple groups within the system and had differing interventions for varying groups. Finally, the intervention was focused on the prevention of bullying rather than reactions to specific incidents. The impact of the initial application of this program was phenomenal with reductions in bullying of 50% or more. Thus, the program also included feedback to indicate its success (or failure).

A problem investigated by Kallestad and Olweus (2003) was to determine what variables were associated with implementation of the program's components by teachers in their classrooms. Listed in order of the magnitude of the path coefficients, these variables were positively associated with classroom implementation: perceived importance of the program, reading the materials describing the program, perceived level of bullying, having a history of victimization as a child, and a measure indicating how upset they were with bullying. A similar analysis showed that perceived level of bullying, perceived importance among staff, knowledge of students' break times, readiness to intervene, and being a regular (not a substitute) teacher predicted contact with individual students and their parents regarding bullying issues. At a higher systemic level, the authors examined predictors of classroom interventions at the level of the school, finding that openness in communication, teacher-to-teacher communication, and school attention to bullying problems predicted implementation of anti-bullying strategies at the school level. There are several important lessons to be learned from these results.

One lesson is that the authors reported a high degree of variation in the extent to which the entire anti-bullying program was practiced at the classroom and school levels. The authors also reported that the degree of reduction in bullying was substantially associated with the general index of classroom implementation but not any specific components of that measure. Thus, consistent with an ecological approach, it was the entire package that was effective, not any particular intervention. Furthermore, school climate was also a strong predictor of implementation, consistent with Pryce and Frederickson (2013) who found that declines in bullying were associated with improvements in school climate and a sense of school belongingness. Again, this is highly consistent with the **systemic** or ecological perspective. The context is just as important as the intervention itself. Finally, the prior history of victimization experienced by teachers was associated with greater likelihood to implement the anti-bullying program at the classroom level. The path coefficient was not huge (.19) but it was statistically significant and indicates the complexity of the general problem of obtaining reductions in bullying in a complex system.

Glover, Gough, Johnson, and Cartwright (2000) surveyed pupils attending 25 schools located in Staffordshire, England. A significant finding was related to bullies who are also victims. They found that bully victims, that is, bullies who were also bullied, were "four times more likely than other groups to lack a positive self-image and three times more likely to feel insecure in school" (p. 149). Furthermore, they were more likely to agree that those who are bullied actually deserve it. They were also more likely to express regret at perpetrating an act of bullying. Thus, victims who also become perpetrators of bullying may represent a downward spiraling behavior pattern that is not likely to respond to a reactive anti-bullying program. A whole-school, systemic approach that addresses the entire context of bullying would be needed to effectively address this systemic issue. This research showed that bullying has a strong negative impact on both bullies and victims. Furthermore they concluded

> anti-bullying policies are only effective where they have evolved from contributions to the debate made by all sections of the school community. It is evident that they need to be revisited on a regular basis and are ineffective unless backed up by continuous training not only for staff, but also for the pupils who might be involved in all forms of peer support. Above all, where staff are seen to be going through a process rather than working with conviction to implement an agreed policy, only the most extreme violations are dealt with and much antisocial behavior is driven underground. (pp. 155–156)

The evidence in this brief and noninclusive review is that ecological interventions have the potential to greatly reduce bullying that happens in schools but a lot of work remains. The program described by Olweus (e.g., Kallestad & Olweus, 2003; Olweus, 1993) has become the "gold standard" for ecological interventions to prevent bullying. The initial application of this program produced phenomenal results. It is also evident that a reactive anti-bullying program that ignores the ecological context of bullying is likely to be ineffective. Instead, an anti-bullying program needs to meet the criteria for an ecological intervention to meet with success, with school climate being one of the most important context variables identified so far.

These research findings are consistent with the behavior of a girl with whom one of the authors worked closely. Her parents were kind enough to provide a detailed history. Personal information has been altered. "Ellen" attended public schools in the Midwest and began experiencing social and physical bullying when she entered junior high school. The parents did not recognize that normal relationship conflicts had become severe bullying until she made a retaliatory threat that caused her to be suspended from school. Bullying and relationship problems continued unabated despite involvement of the legal system. She exhibited many of the problems associated with being a victim of bullying, such as absences from school, health problems, significant problems with anger while at home, and deterioration in school performance. She seemed to lack control and understanding of her own emotions.

The school district had what it called a "state of the art" anti-bullying program. A search of the district's website revealed a report on an anti-bullying video contest and efforts to reduce bullying in the schools that included presentations by the local police department, anonymous tip lines for reporting bullying, and administration of surveys in some schools designed to identity bullies and their victims. These efforts did not seem to be the components of a "state of the art" program. Ellen saw a sign advertising an anti-bullying week in the district and commented that is was nice to see that no bullying was allowed for a week, but it must be okay for the remaining weeks of the school year. Ellen's parents reported no evidence any district-wide interventions were occurring to prevent bullying.

The school district had armed community police officers stationed at junior and senior high schools. Interestingly, a pamphlet published by the U.S. Department of Justice, Office of Community Oriented Policing Services is available. The title is *Bullying in Schools* and it is Guide Number 12 in the Problem-Oriented Guides for Police Series (Sampson, 2012). The pamphlet describes a series of recommended effective interventions that can be carried out by the school-based officer and have most of the characteristics of an ecological intervention, but there was no evidence that policies toward bullying victims and bullying in general in Ellen's school district were influenced by these guidelines.

It appears that the presence of armed community police officers in the schools may have contributed to the administrative belief that the anti-bullying program was "state of the art." By engaging the legal system in responses to bullying the district may have believed that it had such a strong reaction to individual incidents that bullying behavior would be suppressed. Unfortunately, as argued by Glover et al. (2000), it appeared that the majority of bullying had been driven underground and that only the most severe, and sometimes retaliatory, incidents received a response. The perspective of each incident, encouraged by the presence of police officers, was so myopic that the system had no opportunity to see the ecological context of bullying. For example, data on the number of bullying incidents observed over time could have helped administrators to evaluate their program but there was no evidence that such data were being examined. In the face of these obstacles, the parents essentially withdrew their child from the system to participate in online education, and later attend an alternative school. At this point she slowly began to improve as she became more aware of her own emotions and how to control them. To say the least, there seems to be a discrepancy in the definition of "state of the art" that may need to be addressed by this system in the future.

An Ecological Perspective on Early Intervention Programs

One of the most important areas in which community psychology can make a difference is in the development of early intervention programs. The potential for significant impact is tremendous, because the developmental process at an early age allows for prevention in the truest sense of the word. Intervening in a child's life at that point in which adaptive capacities can be promoted, and maladaptive trends can be prevented, should be a primary focus of any healthy community (Moritsugu et al., 2014). While critical expertise will come from developmental psychology, pediatrics, public health, and other related fields, an ecological perspective provides the framework from which to understand the interacting systems in which a child's development is taking place. Bronfenbrenner (1979), of course, has provided a useful model of human development and the social systems that make up the ecological context of a child's development, while the ecological principles described in this chapter provide the framework for effective intervention.

One approach to early intervention—though the specific approach has varied from site to site and community to community—has been Healthy Start programs. The National Healthy Start Association reports over 100 Healthy Start "communities" funded by the U.S. Department of Health and Human Services (National Healthy Start Association, 2012). In a letter from David S. de la Cruz of the DHHS (Deputy Director, Division of Healthy Start and Perinatal Services, Maternal Child and Health Bureau), he states that Healthy Start began as "a demonstration program which utilized a community-driven, systems development approach to reduce infant mortality and improve the health and well-being of women, infants, children, and families" (National Healthy Start Association, 2012, p. 3). In 1991, 15 rural and urban communities were the beneficiaries of federal funding for Healthy Start initiatives. These communities were chosen because of their high infant mortality rates—1.5 to 2.5 times over the national average (National Healthy Start Association, 2012). Yet in many communities Healthy Start initiatives have become much more than an infant mortality and public health program. As de la Cruz states, "The mission of Healthy Start requires reaching beyond the well-being of newborns and addresses the well-being and empowerment of mothers, fathers, families, and entire communities" (National Healthy Start Association, 2012, p. 3).

The key method that has been common to Healthy Start programs has been the "home visitation services" approach, in which professionals in public health, nursing, and social work provide perinatal case management, risk management, depression screening, health education, and core outreach services. However, one of the most critical elements of

Healthy Start programs is the goal of remaining rooted in the community by creating community consortia of professionals, organizations, and community members who engage in efforts to improve overall perinatal care. For example, in 2011 one of the local consortia in the Big Island Perinatal Health Disparities Project was able to partner with the Hawai'i State Department of Labor and Industrial Relations and local businesses in promoting breast-feeding (National Healthy Start Association, 2012). Many Healthy Start programs have used these consortia to go beyond the basic home visitation approach. For example, Caughy, O'Campo, and Brodsky (1999) report that the Healthy Start program in Baltimore worked to develop jobs in the community and worked to improve housing options. Caughy et al. argue that wider environmental problems must be addressed if health interventions are to be effective. Later, a second version of the federally funded model required five core services "of outreach and client recruitment, case management, health education, screening for perinatal depression, and interconception continuity of care to all participants" (U.S. Department of Health and Human Services, 2010, p. 17), which took away some of the program flexibility. In addition to the core services, four core system efforts activities were required, including the consortia mentioned above, as well as the development of a local health systems action plan and a sustainability plan.

A Healthy Start initiative was developed within the array of programs that are part of the Anoka County Community Action Program (ACCAP). Anoka County is a northern metro county in the Twin Cities area (Minneapolis/St. Paul). It is the fourth most populous county in the state of Minnesota and borders on the two most populous counties in the state (Hennepin and Ramsey), which include Minneapolis and St. Paul, respectively.

In April 1996 a county commissioner in Anoka County became interested in Hawai'i's Healthy Start program. She had seen it replicated in another county in Minnesota and wanted to see if it could be established in Anoka County. Under the sponsorship of the county commissioner an initiative was begun in 1997 under the Anoka County Children and Family Council, with Anoka County acting as the fiscal "host" initially (the ACCAP Healthy Start has never received monies from the national DHHS). In January 2007, ACCAP became the fiscal host and supportive structure for the Anoka Healthy Start initiative.

The ACCAP Healthy Start initiative began with the standard home visitations similar to other Healthy Start programs around the country. The "Welcome Baby" visits were made available to every family living in Anoka County and were designed to provide support and information for expecting and new families on health and wellness, prenatal/child development, and parenting skills. The home visitors consisted of early childhood educators, public health nurses, volunteer family mentors, and family support specialists (R. Goodwin & P. Bohm, personal communication, November 8, 2007). Families also had access to infant massage therapy, doula birthing support, crisis funds, cribs, children's books, and other related resources (part of a "home visitor tool box"). Goals for the home visits included improved pregnancy and child health outcomes, teaching parents about early development and childhood learning environments, decreasing social problems (e.g., poverty, delinquency), and increasing families' use of community resources (Anoka County Healthy Start, 2006). Elements of the program were meant to be universal or preventive in nature (e.g., "developmental" mailings) and targeted for at-risk families (e.g., crisis support, long-term home visiting).

One goal of many of the Healthy Start programs nationwide is to help families take advantage of community resources and the service delivery system. This was also true of the Anoka program as they tried to develop system coordination of services. This led to a centralized database for enrollment, a website for community partners to access information, multidiscipline training for home visiting professionals, the development of brochures to assist families, a community needs assessment procedure, and the formation of committees devoted to communicating about and sharing resources (R. Goodwin & P. Bohm, personal communication, November 8, 2007).

Over time the latter committees began to develop into networks that allowed community partners to communicate in a variety of ways beyond the sharing of resources—referred to as "Champions" (R. Goodwin & P. Bohm, personal communication, November 8, 2007). This was facilitated by the Anoka County Children's Family Council and led to an attempt to identify and "plug" the gaps in service delivery available to families. Eventually these social network champions began an extensive systems coordination process that led to the inclusion of multiple community partners in the "champions" network (and, not coincidentally, an infrastructure diagram that closely resembles the ecological framework described by Bronfenbrenner). The network of partners fell into three categories: (1) the home visitors who worked directly with families, and included community partners such as Early Childhood Family Education (ECFE) and Head Start; (2) organizations that work closely with families, such as the school district and local schools, and social service departments (e.g., ACCAP, Family Support Services, Family Partners/Family Protection, Adult Mental Health); and ultimately (3) larger or less directly involved community institutions, such as local churches, physicians' offices and local hospitals, the corrections department, the local county library, the Minnesota Workforce Center, the Minnesota Family Investment Program (income maintenance), the local YMCA, local food shelves, three local police departments, the Salvation Army, Youth First (afterschool and asset-building program), Neighbors Helping Neighbors, and, significantly, local private businesses.

Has the Anoka County Healthy Start initiative been successful? Initiative "success" has been documented in a number of ways—parent surveys, community partner surveys, school transition successes, anecdotal evidence, and more. But one telling number is that from 2007 to 2009 the number of families served went from 797 to 2,931. Of course, this is not direct evidence of increased health outcomes or better child development outcomes (see Wolfe, 2014, for examples of Healthy Start outcomes elsewhere). But what is clear is that a large number of families have come into contact with a multitude of important community resources.

How did this happen? The ecological perspective provides a critical framework to understand the approach of Healthy Start. We can begin with Bronfenbrenner's ecological approach to human development. Many of the national Healthy Start programs began with the notion of reducing infant mortality, and all Healthy Start programs have been concerned with giving young children a "healthy start" in life (the scope of which has broadened to include physical health, mental health, school readiness, etc.). The Anoka initiative began with this same idea in mind, and therefore the home visits were an attempt to intervene early to make sure parents had the knowledge and resources to increase the probability that there would be healthy pregnancies and healthy infants. Thus, we begin with the young child, but it becomes immediately apparent that the child is part of a family, and so the parents become critical to any intervention, as do other members of the family. Of course, the child and his or her family are part of an extended family, a neighborhood, a larger community, a school district, and so on, each impacting the child's healthy development directly and indirectly in a multitude of ways. Thus, if we are to consider how we can influence the child's healthy development, we must consider the child's microsystem (family, home visit professionals, ECFE, Head Start, schools, physicians, churches, etc.), the mesosystem (the variety of ways in which these systems interact—e.g., the public health nurse and physicians or schools), the exosystem (social services, public health services, income maintenance services, etc.), and the macrosystem (the larger culture's attitudes and support structures for the healthy development of a child).

From a community psychology perspective this means putting into practice the elements we have discussed in this chapter. As Wolfe (2014) suggests, "it becomes obvious this is an area that is crying out for Community Psychologists' competencies, values, and perspectives" (p. 234). Initiatives like Healthy Start have moved toward systemic efforts to address the issue of children's health. While most of the early efforts focused on infant mortality, programs have evolved to focus on a broader range of health issues, targeting both physical and mental health outcomes, and developing intervention strategies that focus on multiple subgroups impacting the child's development. Using the Anoka Healthy Start as an example, the initiative expanded from the home visits with families to a multilevel, ecological approach to addressing the child and the family's needs. Not only did the family have access to information about a healthy pregnancy, but the Healthy Start initiative increasingly provided support and resources that facilitated physical, emotional, and cognitive development for these children. At the same time, parents had access to a network of resources dealing with income maintenance, parenting, adult mental health, and so on. Clearly, ACCAP satisfies all five criteria for an ecological intervention discussed at the beginning of this section.

The Anoka County Healthy Start tried to develop a systemic approach to children's health by creating the network of "champions" and other community resources. Further, this network expanded to include a wide array of community services and resources, and more importantly, there was a conscious effort to *think* about how these resources could be cycled or recycled through the system, as well as the critical interdependence that existed between the multiple community organizations and institutions in Anoka that could impact a child's healthy development. Families, schools, neighborhoods, health facilities, social service organizations, businesses, churches, food shelves, police departments, and many more were beginning to see the role they could play in this effort and become involved.

Unfortunately, the political tides shifted in Anoka County, and a new set of county commissioners had alternative priorities. In the spring of 2011, the loss of support from the county (fiscal and structural) resulted in the "end" of the Anoka County Healthy Start initiative. However, because of the feedback loops that had been generated within the community, various "constituencies"—professional and nonprofessional—have developed grassroots efforts to maintain many of the elements of Healthy Start (e.g., local school districts and public health nurses have continued doing variations on the home visits; many of the developmental resources were physically and structurally integrated into local Head Start programs). The lesson, of course, is that each component of a community system is interdependent and that interdependence can lead to unanticipated side effects, both positive and negative. Part of the lesson is that the community psychologist must facilitate a process in which all constituencies are considered as we try to understand and practice or intervene in the system, including government and other high-power institutions (e.g., see Barreiro & Stone, 2013; Kelly et al., 1988).

FUTURE DIRECTIONS

This chapter has focused on helping community practitioners develop an ecological perspective on the practice of their craft. However, we believe two critical groups have been neglected: undergraduates and the communities themselves. We begin with undergraduates because we have had extensive experience in struggling to encourage undergraduates to think ecologically about leadership and the world in general. Our initial anecdotal observations indicated that first-year students seemed to struggle to understand ecological concepts as we applied them to leadership processes, whereas seniors, particularly those with critical leadership experiences, had a much easier time grasping these ideas. A "critical experience" often consisted of club or group involvement in which an elected leader, such as a club or organization president, operated in a hierarchical manner, excluding the input of individuals with good ideas about the group. Having been excluded from leadership processes, such individuals seem to have an easier time understanding how and why an ecological approach to leadership might be superior to a hierarchical, top-down approach. These ideas have received both theoretical and empirical confirmation (Fischer, Wielkiewicz, Stelzner, Overland, & Meuwissen, in press; Komives, Owen, Longerbeam, Mainella, & Osteen, 2005; Wielkiewicz, Fischer, Stelzner, Overland, & Sinner, 2012).

With the understanding that learning to think ecologically about leadership seems to be a developmental process, well described by the Leadership Identity Development model (Komives et al., 2005), we wonder what implications this might have for the community psychologist. For example, is it helpful when community members learn to think ecologically? We would argue that communities are likely to function more sustainably when people in the community think in an ecological way because the community members themselves are likely to cooperate more with interventions when they can see that there is a context or general theme to them. Community members who understand this ecological context to interventions might also be able to contribute more to their success. We might also ask how many community members need to be thinking ecologically to have an impact—that is, is there a "tipping point"? Will a few key individuals be enough or is there a cumulative impact of having more and more community members thinking ecologically? If there is empirical confirmation that ecological thinking contributes to how well a community functions, we might then want to know what methods of encouraging ecological thinking are most effective.

Remembering that the default approach to leadership is the hierarchical model (Wielkiewicz & Stelzner, 2005), it seems reasonable to presume that many communities that could benefit from the services of community psychologists are likely to have serious issues with leadership processes. Yet it would be ineffective to directly challenge such processes because the community members are not likely to respond well. They may ignore the input of outsiders, or positional leaders could reject ideas that threaten their own authority. Thus, it seems that a more indirect approach is likely to be more successful. The question is exactly what approaches would work best. Perhaps having community members read a book, watch and discuss a movie, or look at the results of community surveys would be successful at shifting thinking in the ecological direction. Perhaps the measure developed by Wielkiewicz (2000) or a new measure of ecological thinking could contribute to improving community interventions. These are all empirical questions surrounding the core issue of how to shift the thinking of a community in an ecological direction, and whether such a shift toward ecological thinking helps community interventions succeed or takes the community in the direction of being more sustainable.

What does this mean for the community practitioner? For starters, of course, as we have outlined in this chapter, it is critical for community practitioners to develop the knowledge and skills necessary to use an ecological perspective themselves. But it also means that the practitioner needs to think developmentally about the community. How can community interventions lead to community structures, processes, settings, and events that have an ecological or systemic "flavor" to them? What would such community elements "look like" if we saw them or experienced

Photo 3.5   A monarch community.

Source: iStockphoto.com/PaulTessier.

them? In addition, how can the community practitioner provide developmental opportunities that facilitate both individual and communal thinking and action that is ecological?

SUMMARY

An ecological perspective—or systems perspective—helps us think through how we can practice community psychology. The ecological perspective allows the community psychologist to gain an understanding of the multifaceted ways in which different elements of the community affect each other, and as a result, that understanding allows us to know who, how, and when to engage with the community. We summarized some of the ideas of those who made valuable early contributions to the application of ecological thinking—for example, Barry Commoner and his four laws of ecology, Urie Bronfenbrenner and his ecological theory of development, and Roger Barker and his social ecological behavior settings—and these ideas remain valuable. In addition, the four ecological principles of *interdependence, cycling of resources, adaptation,* and *succession,* described by James G. Kelly, are particularly important in establishing an ecological perspective in community psychology. Many researchers and practitioners have been inspired by Kelly's work and have added to the ecological approach, notably Edison Trickett and his colleagues.

We described several other ecological principles that can be helpful to the community psychologist, such as systemic thinking, feedback loops, monocultures, context, multiple causation, diversity, and tipping points. Familiarity with these concepts and how they apply to understanding and intervening with communities is essential for the community psychologist. In addition, understanding a community's or organization's leadership processes can make a valuable contribution to comprehending it. A key question is the degree to which leadership is hierarchical and driven by a few positional leaders, or communal and driven by the input of many community members. There should be an adaptive balance in the application of these processes. Input of community members should be a high priority, but endless discussion is not practical, so executive decisions need to be made in a timely manner, which may require moving toward more hierarchical processes. The two processes should be in balance according to the context of the decisions being made.

As community psychologists enter the community, they need to be focused on developing collaborative relationships designed to empower community members. In order for collaboration between community members and community psychologists to take place, there needs to be a *context* or *social setting.* One of the central ideas of the ecological approach to community psychology is that psychologists are not "experts" who impose solutions and strategies on communities; they are learners who must become engaged in the culture of the community or organization (Kim et al., 2006). Furthermore, the community psychologist needs to discover or create social settings in which collaborative processes can be developed via formal and informal interactions with community members. Understanding context means to see not just an isolated social interaction, but the context or interdependencies that surround that interaction.

We identified a number of formal and informal skills, abilities, and training that can assist the community psychologist along his or her career path. Self-awareness is essential to interacting with others and we suggested that the five-factor model of personality provides a way to gain self-awareness. Mindfulness, becoming aware of and to some extent controlling emotions, is an essential skill for the community practitioner. Being mindful means to develop awareness of emotions, thoughts, feelings, and experiences that impact our work and daily lives, and being in the moment and aware of what is happening around us. It is another way of saying the community psychologist needs to be aware of the context of interactions with the community. Components of the community psychologist's training and experience include listening skills, cross-cultural competence, interviewing, research skills, and facilitation of groups. Finally, the community psychologist needs to be a lifelong learner. Learning should never stop. Community psychologists should be in constant pursuit of new competencies (e.g., social media skills, but also an awareness of the impact of social media on community life), while they continue to learn about the communities they serve.

The chapter concluded with two applications: school-based bullying and early intervention programs. Both of these applications illustrate that ecologically based interventions can be extremely successful at improving community health. We identified five common characteristics of ecologically based interventions:

1. The intervention is multilevel and directed at all or most levels of the hierarchy of the community or organization.

2. At each level the intervention is spread across subgroups.

3. There is more than one intervention or component of the program and interventions are tailored to particular subgroups.

4. Interventions are focused on prevention or systemic change as opposed to reacting to specific incidents.

5. The intervention creates feedback loops that can be used to evaluate effectiveness and lead to adjustments in the details of the intervention.

These characteristics were shared by both application examples. Our hope is that we have pointed toward a pathway of lifelong learning that will improve the health of communities around the world.

DISCUSSION QUESTIONS

1. Review the opening vignette describing the situation that occurred at Taylor Open School and imagine that you have been retained as a consultant to the district superintendent. Outline a process for addressing the immediate problem of where to place the new school and establishing a healthy school district community. What feedback loops can be created that enable the consultants to monitor the program?

2. Make a list of the factors that influenced you to be in this particular class at this time. Speculate on the possible influences that taking this class might have in the future.

3. Pick an organization, community, or group with which you or the discussion group is familiar and create a physical map of the interdependencies for it.

4. An examination of leadership process provides critical insight into how a community functions. Imagine an example of an organization or community with which the group is familiar and conduct an analysis of leadership processes for it. Determine the extent that leadership processes are hierarchical (top-down management, positional leaders make decisions, etc.) versus ecological or communal. Is there an appropriate balance between hierarchical processes and communal processes?

5. Take one of the online personality tests noted in the web resources section or find another and discuss the profile you obtain with respect to becoming a community psychologist.

6. Have you experienced or observed a crisis that was created by a failure of leadership? Describe that crisis and how leadership processes could have been improved by creating appropriate feedback loops to influence leadership processes.

7. The "Applications" section lists five characteristics of an ecological intervention. Expand upon this list by adding elements that you believe are also important to characterizing an ecologically based intervention.

8. The case study of Ellen, who was the victim of school-based bullying, illustrates a reactive rather than preventive approach to a serious problem. If you were invited to provide consultation to this school district, how would you influence this system, convinced that its program is "state of the art," to move in a healthier direction?

9. If you were a community practitioner working with the Anoka Healthy Start initiative, what could you do to engage governmental or other power brokers in an effort to support the work of Healthy Start?

10. What steps could you take to employ an ecological or systemic approach that might facilitate the grass roots effort to maintain the Healthy Start initiative?

KEY TERMS AND DEFINITIONS

Adaptation: The process of individuals varying their habits or characteristics to cope with changes that emerge from the environment. Kelly and his colleagues suggest coping and adaptation are the dominant means for growth and change for both individuals and communities.

Balanced leadership: When balanced leadership exists in an organization or community, both the hierarchical and communal nature of leadership processes are understood. Leadership processes then adjust leadership processes according to the context of the decision. Communal leadership processes are dominant as the organization struggles to understand the context and implications of decisions and policies. Hierarchical processes are predominant when consensus cannot be reached or a timely decision is essential.

Capacity building: Trickett et al. (2011) suggested that community capacity building increases the local resources that contribute to the ability to problem solve both now and in the future. Building leadership capacity has been identified by many writers as a key to capacity building.

Context: Understanding context consists mainly of moving back from the immediate situation and seeing the network of interdependencies and influences that surround it. Actively discovering informal social contexts within which informal interactions can take place is one of the early tasks of the community psychologist.

Culture: Culture consists of the customary traits, beliefs, behavior patterns, and normative behavior of an ethnic group, organization, or community.

Cycling of resources: In biological systems there is no waste; resources such as dead tree leaves are cycled and used by other organisms so there is no accumulation of waste products in the system. In human systems, the main resource is the people in the community, who also need to be recycled, that is, moved into alternate roles, when their current role in the community is no longer needed. A large part of the success of a community intervention may depend upon the ability of the community psychologist to keep individuals and groups whose roles have shifted integrated and interconnected with the group; that is, the human resources need to be recycled.

Diversity: To have individuals in a community who differ from each other along a variety of dimensions, such as gender, race, intelligence, experience, knowledge, skills, abilities, and other characteristics. The presence of diversity enhances adaptation.

Ecological perspective: The ecological perspective allows the community psychologist to gain an understanding of the multifaceted ways in which different elements of the community affect each other, and as result, that understanding allows us to know who, how, and when to engage with the community.

Emergent: Having a property that is more than the sum of the parts. Intelligence, for example, is an emergent property of the tissues and chemicals that make up the human brain.

Empowering or empowerment: A process whereby the community or organization is assisted in developing its own solutions to its problems and promoting its own welfare.

Feedback loop: When the output of a system feeds back to provide input for that same system. A thermostat uses a simple feedback loop to keep temperature within a specified range. Community psychologists can use feedback loops to monitor an intervention and make adjustments to improve it.

Interdependence: Describes the mutual dependence that exists among the members of a community or organization. One member may influence other members but that person is also influenced by other members. Communities and organizations are also interdependent with other communities and organizations. The interdependencies mean that an intervention does not have an isolated, fully predictable effect.

Leadership: An emergent process in organizations and communities through which decisions are made and policies implemented.

Lifelong learning: A belief or attitude that learning continues throughout a person's lifetime and does not end when schooling is over.

Systemic: Another term for ecological.

RESOURCES

Recommended Reading

Capra, F. (1996). *The web of life.* New York, NY: Anchor Books. This book provides an excellent and readable introduction to systems or ecological thinking.

For those interested in the environmental ecological crisis, especially the issue of global warming, these books are recommended: Brown, L. R. (2011). *World on the edge: How to prevent environmental and economic collapse.* New York, NY: W. W. Norton. Retrieved from http://www.earth-policy.org/images/uploads/book_files/wotebook.pdf; Wielkiewicz, R. M. (2015). *Sustainability and psychology.* St. Cloud, MN: Main Event Press.

Dalton, J., & Wolfe, S. (2012). Competencies for community psychology practice: Society for Community Research and Action Draft, August 15, 2012. *The Community Psychologist, 45(4),* 7–14. This article presents draft competencies for practicing community psychology. It notes that the document aims to enhance. An excellent resource for students, trainers, and practitioners.

Kelly, J. G. (2006). *On becoming ecological: An expedition into community psychology.* New York, NY: Oxford University Press. An excellent source for the pioneering work of Kelly as he articulates his conception of an ecological approach to community psychology. The book provides reprints of key articles and Kelly's perspectives of the context of each article.

Kelly, J. G., Ryan, A. M., Altman, B. E., & Stelzner, S. P. (2000). Understanding and changing social systems: An ecological view. In J. Rappaport & E. Seidman (Eds.), *Handbook of community psychology* (pp. 133–159). New York, NY: Plenum. This chapter is a nice introduction to the ecological perspective in community psychology.

Kelly, J. G., & Song, A. V. (Eds.). (2004). *Six community psychologists tell their stories: History, context, and narrative.* Binghamton, NY: Haworth. Valuable personal accounts relating to the journey of becoming a community psychologist, with some stories focusing on an ecological orientation.

Kelly, J. G., & Song, A. V. (Eds.). (2008). *Community psychology in practice: An oral history through the stories of five community psychologists.* Binghamton, NY: Haworth. Once again, valuable personal accounts relating to the journey of becoming a community psychologist, but with more of a practice orientation.

Kloos, B., Hill, J., Thomas, E., Wandersman, A., Elias, M. J., & Dalton, J. H. (2012). *Community psychology: Linking individuals and communities*. Belmont, CA: Wadsworth. Excellent text that introduces many of the concepts outlined in this chapter.

Moritsugu, J., Vera, E., Wong, F. Y., & Duffy, K. G. (2014). *Community psychology* (5th ed.). Boston, MA: Pearson. Excellent text that introduces many of the concepts outlined in this chapter.

Recommended Websites

There are several online resources for doing self-assessments of personality. One is located at http://personality-testing.info/ and another is at http://www.outofservice.com/bigfive/. Taking an online test may provide a baseline of personality characteristics to promote self-awareness and help you adjust to context in community situations.

The American Psychological Association has a number of online resources related to bullying that can be accessed here; http://www.apa.org/topics/bullying/index.aspx.

Division 27 of the American Psychological Association is the Society for Community Research and Action. It is an international society whose website, http://www.scra27.org, has a multitude of resources for students, practitioners, and trainers.

Suggested Activities for Further Competency Development

Film Discussion

Do the Right Thing: This 1989 film tells the story of the hottest day of the year in an African American community in Brooklyn, New York. The critically acclaimed film was directed by Spike Lee, who also plays a major role. It illustrates interdependencies and how an apparently small request can become a tipping point for profound and tragic actions.

Drumline: This movie tells the story of an elite marching band from the perspective of a talented first-year member of the band's drumline. The movie illustrates the multiple layers of a community and how an individual can struggle to find their place in a new community. There are also multiple leadership crises in the movie that can provide a starting point for discussions of leadership.

Exemplars of Community Psychology: A Video Introduction to the Field: Interviews with 21 professionals who have made significant contributions to the field of community psychology, including individuals considered instrumental in the "birth" of community psychology, such as Donald Klein and Jim Kelly, who does most of the interviewing, but is interviewed himself about the ecological approach.

Hoosiers: A new head coach with a checkered past is hired by an Indiana high school to lead an exceptionally talented group of players. This has an impact on multiple layers of the community. The movie illustrates a series of leadership crises and triumphs.

Madres Unitas: Parents Researching for Change: Documents the work of five Latina immigrant mothers as they start a school in Oakland, California, and learn to engage their neighbors, teachers, administrators, and other members of the community. The five women take part in participatory research and the film documents their personal development and empowerment.

Not in Our Town (series): Documents multiple community responses to hate crimes, including the original film that follows events in Billings, Montana, and the community's response to anti-Semitic graffiti and violence. Nice example of different levels and segments of the community coming together.

Promised Land: A salesman for a natural gas company arrives in a rural town to convince local land owners to sell drilling rights to their land. He encounters the varied interests that exist in the small town and ultimately the sale of rights comes to a community vote. Portrays community politics and the apparent conflicts between environmental issues and economic well-being. There is an odd plot twist at a critical point in the film, but the film allows for a discussion of a number of ecological principles, including interdependence.

Remember the Titans: Herman Boone, an African American, is hired to be head football coach at a previously segregated high school in the early 1970s. His task is to bring together a group of Caucasian and African American players and form a community of football players. Based on a true story, the movie shows the societal context of race relations in the 1970s while illustrating contrasting approaches to leadership.

Surviving the Good Times: A Bill Moyers report on two Milwaukee families that deal with layoffs and the resulting loss of income. Highlights multiple issues around family and community life that can be examined from multiple ecological levels.

Twelve Angry Men: Jury deliberations in a murder case highlight the prejudices and preconceived ideas a group can bring to any "community" discussion, as well as a lesson in group dynamics.

When the Levees Broke: Looks at New Orleans in the aftermath of Hurricane Katrina. Illustrates the role multiple constituencies (e.g., neighborhoods, government officials, military) played in both the events leading up to the disaster, as well as the recovery. The film also portrays the resilience of many of the citizens as they try to restore New Orleans' cultural heritage and rebuild the city with limited resources.

How Wolves Change Rivers: This film illustrates the "tropic cascade" that occurred when wolves were reintroduced to Yellowstone National Park. The film illustrates how one change can have a cascading effect on the entire environment. http://www .filmsforaction.org/watch/how-wolves-change-rivers/

Other Resources

a. Stelzner, S. P. (1996). The jigsaw exercise: A learning tool for the community psychology course. *The Community Psychologist, 29(4),* 26–29. Can be used as a strategy to read and reflect on the original articles that describe critical ideas about the ecological perspective.

b. Group exercise: Think of a social problem of concern to you. Draw a map of the specific social systems involved in the problem, then answer the following questions:

    i. What previous attempts have been used to solve the problem (to the best of your knowledge)?

    ii. Why does the problem seem to persist?

    iii. What are the ecological levels of analysis (ala Bronfenbrenner or those described in Kloos, Hill, Thomas, Wandersman, & Elias, 2011) that can be used to understand the problem?

    iv. Which levels would have the greatest impact on solving the problem?

  c. Bavelas, A. (1973). The five squares problem: An instructional aid in group cooperation. *Studies in Personnel Psychology, 5,* 29–38.) An interactive group exercise in collaboration. The exercise creates an artificial dependency among a small group of students. The problem cannot be solved until students recognize their interdependency and act cooperatively to solve the problem. The exercise can be used as a starting point for discussions of key ecological concepts.

A Checklist of Knowledge, Skills, Competencies, and Activities for Community Psychologists

Conceptual Definition

_____ Commoner's Four Laws of Ecology

   _____ Everything is connected to everything else.

   _____ Everything must go somewhere.

   _____ Nature knows best.

   _____ There is no such thing as a free lunch.

_____ Bronfenbrenner's Developmental Approach

_____ Barker's Social Ecological Approach

_____ Kelly's Ecological Approach to Community Psychology

   _____ Interdependence

   _____ Cycling of human resources

   _____ Adaptation

   _____ Succession, change over time

(Continued)

(Continued)

**Developing Competencies in Using an Ecological Approach:
Knowledge and Skills**

_____ Systemic, Critical Thinking

_____ multiple causation

_____ adapt thinking to the complexity of the issues

_____ willingness to let go of old ideas and conceptions

_____ Principles of Ecology

_____ beware of "butterfly effect"

_____ interdependency means that elements of a community are interconnected

_____ influences are bidirectional

_____ community practitioners strive to understand the *context* of interventions

_____ community members are community resources

_____ recycle the human resources as their roles change

_____ it is challenging to find the small events that accumulate a large impact

_____ identifying *feedback loops* helps immensely in understanding a community

_____ adaptation emerges out of diversity

_____ when diversity is low (monoculture) the community may be at risk

_____ balance precaution with risk taking

_____ Leadership Processes in Communities

_____ leadership processes provide a key context for understanding communities

_____ hierarchical/industrial processes are top-down and may inhibit adaptation

_____ communal processes involve everyone but can also inhibit adaptation

_____ ideally, leadership processes balance both approaches so decisions are well understood but implemented in a timely manner

_____ Key Characteristics of an Ecological Community Intervention

_____ the intervention is multilevel

_____ the intervention is spread across subgroups

_____ multiple interventions and tailored to particular community subgroups

_____ interventions focus on prevention or systemic change

_____ the intervention creates feedback loops

_____ used to evaluate effectiveness

_____ lead to adjustments in the details of the intervention

_____ Skills and Abilities Associated With an Ecological Approach

_____ personality: develop self-awareness of your own traits and habits

_____ adjust to the context of the situation

_____ mindfulness: being aware of one's internal emotions

_____ intense community engagement can elicit emotional responses

_____ practitioners need to develop awareness of the source of their emotions

_____ strive for a healthy balance of engagement and distancing

_____ excellent listening skills are essential for the community practitioner

_____ a primary goal is to empower communities to solve their own problems

_____ help communities or organizations to think systemically

_____ facilitate communication

_____ help the community to discover key feedback loops

A Checklist of Graduate Training and Lifelong Learning

_____ Course work in survey development, analysis, and interpretation

_____ Specific courses designed to develop interviewing skills

_____ Coursework in qualitative and quasi-experimental research techniques

_____ Learn to discover and create social settings

_____ Coursework in group dynamics and group processes

(Continued)

(Continued)

_____ Coursework in group facilitation techniques

_____ Develop a comfortable approach to group facilitation and consensus building

_____ Courses/workshops in community organizing and public policy

_____ Develop cultural competency

_____ The assistance of "boundary spanners" may be extremely helpful

_____ Become a lifelong learner

_____ Upgrade skills with new courses and workshops

_____ Let the community be the teacher

_____ Be open to new knowledge and new experiences; revise what you know

REFERENCES

Allen, K. E., Stelzner, S. P., & Wielkiewicz, R. M. (1998). The ecology of leadership: Adapting to the challenges of a changing world. *Journal of Leadership Studies, 5*(2), 62–82.

Anoka County Healthy Start. (2006). *Annual report 2006*. Anoka, MN: Author.

Astin, A. W., & Astin, H. S. (2000). *Leadership reconsidered: Engaging higher education in social change*. Battle Creek, MI: W. K. Kellogg Foundation.

Ayman, R. (1993). Leadership perception. The role of gender and culture. In M. Chemers & R. Ayman (Ed.), *Leadership theory and research: Perspectives and directions* (pp. 137–166). New York, NY: Academic Press.

Ball, S. A. (1995). The validity of an alternative five-factor measure of personality in cocaine abusers. *Psychological Assessment, 7*(2), 148–154.

Barker, R. G. (1965). Explorations in ecological psychology. *American Psychologist, 20,* 1–14.

Barker, R. G. (1968). *Ecological psychology.* Stanford, CA: Stanford University Press.

Barreiro, T. D., & Stone, M. M. (2013). *Social entrepreneurship: From issue to viable plan.* New York, NY: Business Expert Press.

Barton, S. (1994). Chaos, self-organization, and psychology. *American Psychologist, 49,* 5–14.

Bateson, G. (1972). *Steps to an ecology of mind.* New York, NY: Ballentine.

Benson, E. (2003). Thinking green. *Monitor on Psychology, 34*(4), 28–30.

Block, J. (2001). Millennial contrarianism: The five-factor approach to personality description 5 years later. *Journal of Research in Personality, 35,* 98–107.

Bronfenbrenner, U. (1977). Toward an experimental ecology of human development. *American Psychologist, 32,* 513–531.

Bronfenbrenner, U. (1979). Contexts of child rearing: Problems and prospects. *American Psychologist, 34,* 844–850.

Brown, L. R. (2011). *World on the edge: How to prevent environmental and economic collapse.* New York, NY: W. W. Norton. Retrieved from http://www.earth-policy.org/images/uploads/book_files/wotebook.pdf

Campbell, R., Patterson, D., & Fehler-Cabral, G. (2010). Using ecological theory to evaluate the effectiveness of an indigenous community intervention: A study of sexual assault nurse examiner (SANE) programs. *American Journal of Community Psychology, 46,* 263–276.

Capra, F. (1996). *The web of life.* New York, NY: Anchor Books.

Caughey, M. O., O'Campo, P., & Brodsky, A. (1999). Neighborhoods, families, and children: Implications for policy and practice. *Journal of Community Psychology, 27,* 615–633.

Commoner, B. (1971). *The closing circle.* New York, NY: Knopf.

Cross, D., Monks, H., Hall, M., Shaw, T., Pintabona, Y., Erceg, E., . . . Lester, L. (2011). Three-year results of the Friendly Schools whole-of-school intervention on children's bullying behavior. *British Educational Research Journal, 37*(1), 105–129.

Dalton, J., & Wolfe, S. (2012). Competencies for community psychology practice: Society for Community Research and Action. Draft, August 15, 2012. *The Community Psychologist, 45(4),* 7–14.

Donnellan, M. B., Oswald, F. L., Baird, B. M., & Lucas, R. E. (2006). The Mini-IPIP Scales: Tiny-yet-effective measures of the big five factors of personality. *Psychological Assessment, 18,* 192–203.

Durrett, C., & Trull, T. J. (2005). An evaluation of evaluative personality terms: A comparison of the big seven and five-factor model in predicting psychopathology. *Psychological Assessment, 17,* 359–368.

Eagly, A. H. (2007). Female leadership advantage and disadvantage: Resolving the contradictions. *Psychology of Women Quarterly, 31,* 1–12.

Finlay, J. S. (1991). Using the (Japanese) new management tools to solve organizational problems. *Organization Development Journal, 9*(1), 81–89.

Fischer, D. V., Wielkiewicz, R. M., Stelzner, S. P., Overland, M., & Meuwissen, A. S. (in press). Changes in leadership attitudes and beliefs associated with the college experience: A longitudinal study. *Journal of Leadership Education.*

Foster-Fishman, P. G., & Behrens, T. R. (Eds.). (2007). Systems change [Special issue]. *American Journal of Community Psychology, 46,* 191–418.

Foster-Fishman, P. G., Nowell, B., & Yang, H. (2007). Putting the system back into systems change: A framework for understanding and changing organizational and community systems. *American Journal of Community Psychology, 46,* 197–216.

Glover, D., Gough, G., Johnson, M., & Cartwright, N. (2000). Bullying in 25 secondary schools: Incidence, impact and intervention. *Educational Research, 42,* 141–156.

Goldberg, L. R. (1992). The development of markers for the big-five factor structure. *Psychological Assessment, 4,* 26–42.

Goldberg, L. R. (1993). The structure of phenotypic personality traits. *American Psychologist, 48,* 26–34.

Goldberg, L. R. (1999). A broad-bandwidth, public-domain, personality inventory measuring the lower-level facets of several five-factor models. In I. Mervielde, I. Deary, F. De Fruyt, & F. Ostendorf (Eds.), *Personality psychology in Europe* (Vol. 7, pp. 7–28). Tilburg, The Netherlands: Tilburg University Press.

Gong, R. (2005). The essence of critical thinking. *Journal of Developmental Education, 28,* 40.

Heifetz, R. (1994). *Leadership without easy answers.* Cambridge, MA: Belknap Press of Harvard University Press.

Helgesen, S. (1995). *The web of inclusion: A new architecture for building great organizations.* New York, NY: Doubleday/Currency.

James, J. (1996). *Thinking in the future tense: Leadership skills for a new age.* New York, NY: Simon & Schuster.

Johnson, S. (2001). *Emergence: The connected lives of ants, brains, cities, and software.* New York, NY: Touchstone.

Kallestad, J. H., & Olweus, D. (2003). Predicting teachers' and schools' implementation of the Olweus Bullying Prevention Program: A multilevel study. *Prevention & Treatment, 6*(1), Article 21.

Katz, D., & Kahn, R. L. (1978). *The social psychology of organizations* (2nd ed.). New York, NY: Wiley.

Kelly, J. G. (1968). Toward an ecological conception of preventive interventions. In J. W. Carter Jr. (Ed.), *Research contributions from psychology to community mental health* (pp. 74–99). New York, NY: Behavioral Publications.

Kelly, J. G. (1971). Qualities for the community psychologist. *American Psychologist, 26,* 897–903.

Kelly, J. G. (1979). T'ain't what you do, it's the way you do it. *American Journal of Community Psychology, 7,* 244–261.

Kelly, J. G. (1987). Seven criteria when conducting community-based prevention research: A research agenda and commentary. In *Preventing mental disorders: A research perspective* (DHHS Publication No. ADM 87-1493, pp. 57–72). Washington, DC: U.S. Government Printing Office.

Kelly J. G. (2007). The system concept and systemic change: Implications for community psychology. *American Journal of Community Psychology, 46,* 415–418.

Kelly, J. G., Azelton, E. E., Lardon, C., Mock, L. O., & Tandin, D. (2004). On community leadership: Stories about collaboration in action research. *American Journal of Community Psychology, 33,* 205–216.

Kelly, J. G., Dassoff, N., Levin, I., Schreckengost, J., Stelzner, S. P., & Altman, B. E. (1988). *A guide to conducting prevention research in the community: First steps.* New York, NY: Haworth.

Kelly, J. G., Ryan, A. M., Altman, B. E., & Stelzner, S. P. (2000). Understanding and changing social systems: An ecological view. In J. Rappaport & E. Seidman (Eds.), *Handbook of community psychology* (pp. 133–159). New York, NY: Plenum.

Kim, I. J., Kim, L. I. C., & Kelly, J. G. (2006). Developing cultural competence in working with Korean immigrant families. *Journal of Community Psychology, 34,* 149–165.

Klingsporn, M. J. (1973). The significance of variability. *Behavioral Science, 18,* 441–447.

Kloos, B., Hill, J., Thomas, E., Wandersman, A., & Elias, M. (2011). *Community psychology: Linking individuals and communities.* Belmont, CA: Wadsworth.

Koerner, K. (2012). *Doing dialectical behavior therapy: A practical guide.* New York, NY: Guilford Press.

Komives, S. R., Owen, J. E., Longerbeam, S. D., Mainella, F. C., & Osteen, L. (2005). Developing a leadership identity: A grounded theory. *Journal of College Student Development, 46,* 593–611.

Mai-Dalton, R. R. (1993). Managing cultural diversity on the individual, group, and organizational levels. In M. M. Chemers & R. Ayman (Eds.), *Leadership theory and research* (pp. 189–215). San Diego, CA: Academic Press.

Mathews, K. M., White, M. C., & Long, R. G. (1999). Why study the complexity sciences in the social sciences? *Human Relations, 52*(4), 439–462.

McCrae, R. R. (2001). 5 years of progress: A reply to Block. *Journal of Research in Personality, 35,* 108–113.

Meadows, D. (2001, January 9). Slow down, you move too fast: An ounce of prevention is worth a pound of cure. *Grist Magazine.* Retrieved from http://www.gristmagazine.com/citizen/citizen010901.asp

Moritsugu, J., Vera, E., Wong, F. Y., & Duffy, K. G. (2014). *Community psychology* (5th ed.). Boston, MA: Pearson.

Morrison, E. W., & Milliken, F. J. (2000). Organizational silence: A barrier to change and development in a pluralistic world. *Academy of Management Review, 25,* 706–725.

Moskell, C., & Allred, S. B. (2013). Integrating human and natural systems in community psychology: An ecological model. *American Journal of Community Psychology, 51,* 1–14.

Mullainathan, S., & Shafir, E. (2013). *Scarcity: Why having too little means so much*. New York, NY: Henry Holt.

National Healthy Start Association. (2012). *Saving our nation's babies: The impact of the Federal Healthy Start Initiative* (2nd ed.). Retrieved from http://www.nationalhealthystart.org/site/assets/docs/NHSA_SavingBabiesPub_2ndED.pdf

Olweus, D. (1993). *Bullying at school: What we know and what we can do*. Cambridge, MA: Blackwell.

Paulus, P. B. (2000). Groups, teams, and creativity: The creative potential of idea-generating groups. *Applied Psychology: An International Review, 49,* 237–262.

Paunonen, S. V., & Ashton, M. C. (2001). Big five predictors of academic achievement. *Journal of Research in Personality, 35,* 78–90.

Peirson, L. J., Boydell, K. M., Ferguson, H. B., & Ferris, L. E. (2011). An ecological process model of systems change. *American Journal of Community Psychology, 47,* 307–321.

Pryce, S., & Frederickson, N. (2013). Bullying behaviour, intentions and classroom ecology. *Learning Environments Research, 16,* 183–199.

Rigby, K. (2003). Consequences of bullying in schools. *Canadian Journal of Psychiatry, 48,* 583–590.

Sampson, R. (2012). *Bullying in schools*. Washington, DC: Community Oriented Policing Services, U.S. Department of Justice. Retrieved from http://cops.usdoj.gov/Publications/e07063414-guide.pdf

Sibley, C. G., & Pirie, D. J. (2013). Personality in New Zealand: Scale norms and demographic differences in the Mini-IPIP6. *New Zealand Journal of Psychology, 42,* 13–30.

Stanovich, K. E. (2013). *How to think straight about psychology* (10th ed.). Boston, MA: Allyn & Bacon.

Tandon, S. D., Azelton, S., Kelly, J. G., & Strickland, D. A. (1998). Constructing a tree for community leadership: Contexts and processes in collaborative inquiry. *American Journal of Community Psychology, 26,* 671–695.

Tibbetts, A. (2013). *A DBT skills workbook: You untangled: Practical tools to manage your emotions and improve your life*. Kansas City, MO: Lilac Center.

Trickett, E. J. (1984). Toward a distinctive community psychology: An ecological metaphor for the conduct of community research and the nature of training. *American Journal of Community Psychology, 12,* 261–279.

Trickett, E. J. (2005). The community context of disaster and traumatic stress: An ecological perspective from community psychology. In S. E. Hobfoll & M. W. deVries (Eds.), *Extreme stress and communities: Impact and intervention* (pp. 11–25). New York, NY: Kluwer Academic/Plenum.

Trickett, E. J. (2009a). Community psychology: Individuals and interventions in community context. *Annual Review of Psychology, 60,* 395–419.

Trickett, E. J. (2009b). Multilevel community-based culturally situated interventions and community impact: An ecological perspective. *American Journal of Community Psychology, 43,* 257–266.

Trickett, E. J., & Beehler, S. (2013). The ecology of multilevel interventions to reduce social inequities in health. *American Behavioral Scientist, 57,* 1227–1246.

Trickett, E. J., Beehler, S., Deutsch, C., Green, L. W., Hawe, P., McLeroy, K., . . . Trimble, J. E. (2011). Advancing the science of community-level interventions. *American Journal of Public Health, 101,* 1410–1419.

Trickett, E. J., & Birman, D. (1989). Taking ecology seriously: A community development approach to individually based preventive interventions in schools. In L. A. Bond & B. E. Compas (Eds.), *Primary prevention and promotion in the schools* (pp. 361–390). Thousand Oaks, CA: Sage.

Trickett, E. J., Kelly, J. G., & Todd, D. M. (1972).The social environment of the high school: Guidelines for individual change and organizational development. In S. Golann & C. Eisendorfer (Eds.), *Handbook of community mental health* (pp. 331–406). New York, NY: Appleton Century Crofts.

Trickett, E. J., Kelly, J. G., & Vincent, T. (1985). The spirit of ecological inquiry in community research. In E. Susskind & D. Klein (Eds.), *Community research: Methods, paradigms, and applications* (pp. 283–333). New York, NY: Praeger.

Trickett, E. J., & Rowe, H. L. (2012). Emerging ecological approaches to prevention, health promotion, and public health in the school context: Next steps from a community psychology perspective. *Journal of Educational and Psychological Consultation, 22,* 125–140.

Tseng, V., & Seidman, E. (2007). A systems framework for understanding social settings. *American Journal of Community Psychology, 46,* 217–228.

Uhl-Bien, M., Marion, R., & McKelvey, B. (2007). Complexity leadership theory: Shifting leadership from the industrial age to the knowledge era. *Leadership Quarterly, 18,* 298–318.

U.S. Department of Health and Human Services. (2010). Eliminating disparities in perinatal health (general population): New competition and competing continuations HRSA-10-153. *Catalog of Federal Domestic Assistance (CFDA) No. 93.926.* Retrieved from https://grants3.hrsa.gov/ 2010/Web2External/Interface/FundingCycle/ExternalView.aspx?&fCycleID = DE1F7436-67AF- 4DFA-952E-7BA53218F312&ViewMode = EU&GoBack = &PrintMode = &OnlineAvailabilityFlag = True&pageNumber = 1

Weisbord, M. R., & Janoff, S. (1995). *Future search: An action guide to finding common ground in organizations and communities.* San Francisco, CA: Berrett-Koehler.

Wielkiewicz, R. M. (1995). *Behavior management in the schools: Principles and procedures* (2nd ed.). Boston, MA: Allyn & Bacon.

Wielkiewicz, R. M. (2000). The Leadership Attitudes and Beliefs Scale: An instrument for evaluating college students' thinking about leadership and organizations. *Journal of College Student Development, 41,* 335–347.

Wielkiewicz, R. M. (2014). A lifelong learning scale for research and evaluation of teaching and curricular effectiveness. *Teaching of Psychology, 41,* 220–227.

Wielkiewicz, R. M. (2015). *Sustainability and psychology.* St. Cloud, MN: Main Event Press.

Wielkiewicz, R. M., Fischer, D., Stelzner, S. P., Overland, M., & Sinner, A. M. (2012). Leadership attitudes and beliefs of incoming first-year college students: A multi-institutional study of gender differences. *Journal of Leadership Education, 11*(2), 1–25.

Wielkiewicz, R. M., & Stelzner, S. P. (2005). An ecological perspective on leadership theory, research, and practice. *Review of General Psychology, 9,* 326–334.

Wolfe, S. (2014). The application of community psychology practice competencies to reduce health disparities. *American Journal of Community Psychology, 53,* 231–234.

Wolke, D., Schreier, A., Zanarini, M. C., & Winsper, C. (2012). Bullied by peers in childhood and borderline personality symptoms at 11 years of age: A prospective study. *Journal of Child Psychology and Psychiatry, 53,* 846–855.

Effecting Social Change in Diverse Contexts

The Role of Cross-Cultural Competency

Kien S. Lee

OPENING EXERCISE

This opening exercise illustrates the cultural forces, some of which may or may not be apparent to you, that can affect community interventions and their evaluation.

The evaluation findings for a national initiative intended to reduce the impact of exposure to violence on young children suggest that two grantees are not achieving the progress anticipated by the funder. One grantee serves primarily South Asian immigrants in Community A, while the other grantee serves a Native American tribe located in Community B. The evaluation team responsible for both grantees and sites found that the number of children who have been identified as exposed to violence, referred to services, and actually treated has been relatively low. They also found that the children and their families who have received treatment have not been able to stay engaged in the mental health services for more than two to four visits, on average. Further, the program managers in both communities appear to have focused more on community awareness activities and not on developing a system among law enforcement officers, child protective services, mental health providers, teachers, and anti-domestic violence advocates to identify and assist the children. The evaluation concludes that the programs in both communities are delayed in their implementation and require extensive technical assistance. What are the challenges faced by the two grantees? What are the evaluation team's assumptions about what is going on in the two communities? If you were the evaluator, what steps would you take to understand and address the concerns about the two grantees?

OVERVIEW

Community psychology focuses on the structures, functions, and processes of communities, and communities are comprised of people with common and distinct cultural beliefs and practices. According to Puddifoot (1996, p. 327), community psychology, as a field, is associated with those who see . . . a significance in "community" as a positive, meaningful entity in the ordering of our lives. It is generally assumed that if this sense of living in, belonging to, and having some commitment to, a particular community is threatened, the prospect of leading rewarding lives is to a greater or lesser extent diminished.

Gensheimer and Diebold (1997, p. 48) refer to community psychology as a field that focuses "explicitly on the broad range of human and social problems . . . , rather than traditional areas of psychological inquiry" and holds an ecological, problem-oriented research perspective that is stressed by examining the interplay of community, organizational, group, and individual factors, and uses an empirical approach to social intervention. Scholars of the field appear to agree that a sense of community is the over-arching value in community psychology (Chavis & Newbrough, 1986, p. 337; Lorion & Newbrough, 1996). Therefore, "community psychology can be a field for the study and development of communities" (Chavis & Newbrough, 1986).

Communities form the context in which people exist, and context contributes to individual and group behavior; this concept is unlike the older paradigms in psychology that linked behavior to genetics (Trickett, Watts, & Birman, 1994). Context also can cause the cultures of people to shift and as this occurs, the existence of the various groups living in that context changes relative to one another. The changes can cause the environment to become unstable and the people in it to experience stress, and in extreme cases, violence may erupt. Cross-cultural concepts; ecological frameworks; and sociopolitical, intergroup, and acculturation theories all attempt to understand how cultural and contextual changes affect human behaviors and their outcomes (Watts, 1994).

In short, the essence of community psychology is context and healthy, strong, and just communities. Community psychologists are trained to think in ecological terms to help people to identify problems and develop solutions that benefit their communities as a whole. They work as researchers, evaluators, advocates, service providers, community leaders, educators, policymakers, and so on. In these positions, they come across people from different cultures, histories, and experiences, and who work, live, learn, and age in all sorts of communities. It is inevitable that they have to develop the capacity to work across cultures and become cross-culturally competent.

This chapter focuses on questions, issues, and recommendations for developing the ability of community practitioners to work in culturally diverse settings. Given the growing diversity of communities across the United States and in other countries, it is essential that professionals who are working in communities as researchers, evaluators, organizers, policymakers, advocates, and program implementers understand the complex dynamics in these communities. As community practitioners, it is up to each of us to do our best to ensure that the individuals in these communities not only get along with each other but that they also live in healthy and just environments.

The aim of this chapter is to provide you with the knowledge and skills to ask questions and think critically about situations you are likely to encounter as you work in different communities and cultural settings. It is not to help you become knowledgeable about a particular culture (e.g., beliefs and traditions, clothing, food), which has been typical of existing training curricula for developing cultural competency. Two situations are presented to prompt your analysis of the cultural issues at play after an explanation about the concept of cross-cultural competency is provided. A list of print and web-based resources is also included for your reference.

DEFINING CROSS-CULTURAL COMPETENCY

Cross-cultural competency is the ability to interact, function, and work effectively among people who may not share your demographic attributes, language, beliefs, history, and experiences. It is impossible to become perfectly competent in your knowledge about another group of people, but it is possible to become sufficiently competent to cultivate mutual respect and promote behaviors and actions that ensure social justice and equity for the people with whom you are interacting and engaging. For this reason, it is preferable to use the term cross-cultural competency rather than cultural competency or cultural and

Photo 4.1 Cross-cultural competency is the ability to interact, function, and work effectively among people who may not share your demographic attributes, language, beliefs, history, and experiences.

Source: iStockphoto.com/fstop123.

linguistic competency, as "cross" emphasizes that the competency is embedded in exchanges and relations that are dynamic, and not static forms of knowledge with an "end" that marks competency. Additionally, because language is part of culture, it is unnecessary to separate "cultural" from "linguistic" competency.

There are three key components to cross-cultural competency development:

1. Understanding the definition of "culture"
2. Navigating the effects of social identities
3. Addressing privilege and power

Culture, social identity, and privilege and power are critical concepts because they have a powerful influence on people's interactions with one another. Your understanding of these concepts forms your perceptions of other people, and their understanding of these concept forms their perceptions of you. Your perceptions and theirs are then translated, in less than a second, into words and behaviors that sometimes make sense, and at other times, appear to be completely irrational to you and/or the people with whom you are interacting. Two key publications examine the role of culture, social identity, and privilege and power, discussing their importance in personal and group interactions:

- Stephan and Stephan (2001) provide a thorough review of the relations between groups of people in the United States and programs aimed at improving their relations. In doing so, they discuss theories and concepts like contact, prejudice, social identity, social dominance, and racism.

- Renzetti and Lee (1993) bring together a diverse group of scholars to discuss the effects of their race, ethnicity, gender, class, and other demographic attributes on their dual roles as researchers and change agents.

Culture

Culture is "a set of socially transmitted and learned behaviors, beliefs, institutions, and all other products and thoughts of a group of people that shape and guide the functioning of a particular individual, family, profession, organization, or community" (see, for example, "Culture," 2000; Cross, Katz, Miller, & Seashore, 1994; Hofstede, 1997). Culture comes in many forms and shapes that are constantly evolving. Some of the more apparent forms and shapes include: religion; language, clothing; celebrations of key events (e.g., birth, passage to adulthood), and food. There are forms of culture that require extensive inquiry and observation for someone who is not part of the group to understand, such as the meaning of leadership, family, and community; help-seeking behavior; beliefs about health; and gender roles.

Culture tends to be used interchangeably with demographic labels that distinguish groups from one another, such as race and ethnicity, sexual orientation, gender, nationality, or socioeconomic status. This is problematic because individual traits and the diversity within each of these groups are often ignored or misunderstood. Also, its use sometimes suggests that some groups are "cultureless" because they do not exhibit obvious differences in their skin color, language, clothing, or food. This can lead to stereotyping and misunderstandings among people of the same culture as well as between individuals in and outside the culture. The use of the label "Asian" in the United States is a common example of this problem. There is tremendous diversity among the groups of people that fit this label and their unique assets and needs are overlooked in their interactions with others, as well as in the development, implementation, and evaluation of programs and services intended to engage them. It is frequently assumed that a Chinese professional can easily work in a Vietnamese or Korean community when in fact, the Chinese, Vietnamese, and Korean cultures are vastly different.

At the same time, the misuse of the word *culture* to distinguish groups from one another can diminish the similarities they share, which are important for finding common ground to build community. Community psychologists and others can inadvertently overemphasize differences in language, traditions, and histories in order to be respectful, to the detriment of lifting up the deeper, less obvious similarities, such as values about family ties and children's well-being. Frequently, projects that attempt to bridge, for instance, Latino and White families start by engaging them in activities to share and celebrate their cultural traditions. This starting point immediately draws attention to their differences, rather than their similarities, such as their interest in a high quality education for their children. By focusing first on their aspirations for their children, the two groups of families will learn to perceive one another as allies and through the process of developing and collaborating on joint activities, they will have the opportunity to learn about each other's cultural values and traditions. In situations where the attention is focused primarily on cultural differences, the true source of group differences—disparities in privilege and power—may be masked and inadequately addressed.

Social Identities

Social identity is formed when a group of people attempt to see their group differentiated from other groups as a way to preserve and achieve group distinctiveness (Tajfel, 1981). This identity is shaped by culture, history, and context. People tend to have several social identities because they are likely to belong to two or more groups. A person's social identity can be based on a range of characteristics, from demographic attributes to beliefs and profession.

Social identity is complicated; it involves the person's self-identification with a particular social group relative to others' perceptions of the person's group membership. Stereotyping and unspoken and unrealistic expectations can arise from situations where people assume a person's social identity and conclude that he or she is "one of them" or "not one of them." For example, a gay man just got a job as senior program officer at a philanthropic institution; suddenly, the community-based organizations that work with lesbian, gay, bisexual, and transgender (LGBT) youth in the county are inviting him to meetings and lunches; they assumed, based on his demographic characteristics, that because he identifies as LGBT, he is more likely to listen and fund their work. He suddenly has a set of expectations placed on him solely because of his social identity. Community psychologists need to understand and be able to navigate the way social identities affect their interactions with individuals with whom they work in order to cultivate genuine relations.

Privilege and Power

The *American Heritage Dictionary* defines **privilege** as "the advantage granted to or enjoyed by a group of people beyond the advantage of all others" and **power** as "the ability or capacity to exercise authority, control, and influence" (see "Power," 2000: "Privilege," 2000). Privilege and power, based on a particular demographic and/or cultural attribute, complicate human interactions. If someone is perceived as part of the social group that has privilege and power, even if he or she does not self-identify with the group, his or her interactions with others may be affected.

History plays a big role in the creation of privilege and power and the marginalization, oppression, or even genocide of certain groups. The inequities that result from these events affect the labels and actions used to distinguish, divide, and/or discriminate against certain groups of people. These actions, in turn, often lead to institutional policies and practices that prevent certain groups of people from accessing resources and opportunities to better their lives and, therefore, maintain the status quo or perpetuate inequities (Trickett et al., 1994). Community psychologists need to understand and be skilled in dismantling and redistributing privilege and power as part of their responsibility to promote social justice and equity. This includes situations where community psychologists are researching or evaluating an issue or program; they have to be aware of how research has been used to harm certain disadvantaged communities (e.g., Native Americans) or cautious not to knowingly or unknowingly prevent the empowerment of some communities by mystifying science (Chavis, 1980).

DEVELOPING CROSS-CULTURAL COMPETENCY

Required Knowledge, Skills, Attitudes, and Practices

Remember and apply the definition of culture. An important step in developing cross-cultural competency is to remember and apply the definition of culture and to be cautious about its use. This helps to ensure that diversity within groups of peoples and similarities across groups and communities are not lost, and caution is exercised about the consequences of stereotyping.

Practice humility. In order to do this, you need to develop the following skills and to become aware of your behaviors by:

- Being mindful of the assumptions made about the cultures of another group of people
- Refraining from suggesting that the culture of one group of people determines the norm, and therefore the behaviors of another group of people are "deviant"
- Asking questions about the culture of another group of people in a respectful manner
- Listening and observing nonverbal communication and rules of conduct
- Identifying and working with people who are bicultural or multicultural—such as bridge builders, cultural brokers, or cultural translators—and can help you interpret verbal and nonverbal cues (Hofstede, 1997)

- Considering the development of cross-cultural competency a continuous process of self-reflection, awareness, and respectful partnering with people from different cultures (Dreachslin, Gilbert, & Malone, 2013; Tervalon & Murray-Garcia, 1998)

Pay attention to particular concepts and terms and do not assume that they mean the same thing for everyone. Literal translations of certain concepts and terms are not always appropriate and can cause misunderstandings, depending on the context in which the concepts and terms are used. Consequently, research and evaluation findings, program designs, and policies may inaccurately portray a group of people or improperly affect their lives. For example, in a study about the sense of home as a measure of immigrant integration, research showed that the concept of "home" in four different groups (Jamaican, Polish, Salvadoran, and Somali) was influenced by the circumstances under which their members migrated to Canada. Also, the term *home* may not exist in all languages (Murdie, 2004). In the Chinese language, it is synonymous with the word *family* while for Afghans, the literal translation is "house." There is potential for researchers who do not consider this in their studies to conclude that some immigrants do not consider their new country their home. Check the meaning of the word with bridge builders and professional translators and interpreters.

Pay attention to particular organizations and do not assume that they have the same function for everyone. Whether it is about community building, prevention services, or policy advocacy, certain institutions may play key roles as access points for a community. These include faith institutions, professional or trade associations, community centers, schools, sororities and fraternities, and civic groups. These organizations form the social support structure for members of a group or community; however, they may have different functions in different cultures. For instance, while the church in the Black/African American community plays an important role in organizing and advocating for their members, the role of the Buddhist temple in a Southeast Asian community or a mosque in a South Asian community tends to focus on providing spiritual and religious services to its members and to shy away from civic or political activities (Lee, 2004). This tendency, however, has gradually changed over time as Muslim faith leaders have had to address discriminatory acts against Muslims after 9/11.

Additionally, almost all groups or communities have a deeper layer of informal organizations that are not visible to the outsider. For instance, in immigrant communities, these informal organizations develop because immigrants may have an urgent need upon arrival in the United States that requires an immediate response (e.g., traditional burial services), or they relocate a network from their home country to their new place of residence (e.g., an alumni network of a university in the home country that has no need to seek nonprofit status). These informal organizations demonstrate the dynamic nature of culture.

Keep current on the dynamic context in which culture, social identities, and privilege and power are operating. These three core elements of cross-cultural competency do not occur in a vacuum; instead, they can change depending on domestic and global events such as political elections, war, economic recession, and social movements. It is critical for community psychologists, in order to be cross-culturally competent, to stay abreast of relevant issues and affairs that could affect the groups they work with or serve, and the context in which the groups live. They can do this by: reading relevant journal and newspaper articles, attending lectures and other presentations about the groups they work with or serve, joining discussion forums and communities of practice, and most importantly, participating in events that the groups sponsor or organize and conversing with the people there. Attending such events and interacting with the leaders and members of the group of interest is one of the best ways to learn about a local ethnic population (Dreaschslin et al., 2013).

Consider structural inequities and how they affect your work and its outcomes. Community psychologists need to be conscious of the inequities experienced by the groups or communities they work with or serve, how these inequities were created, and make sure that they do not inadvertently perpetuate them. **Structural inequities** are systems in which public policies, institutional practices, cultural representations, and other norms work in various, often reinforcing ways to perpetuate inequity among social groups. For instance, a study that compares the civic participation rates of two groups can be harmful if it is assumed that the playing field is equal for both groups, regardless of their cultural characteristics (e.g., race, ethnicity, religion, gender, age). Consequently, the study may wrongly conclude that one group is less civically engaged than another group because of its members' "apathetic" attitudes. Researchers who are cross-culturally competent will dig deeper and uncover that it is not the members' attitudes, but the way civic participation is defined and practiced in different cultures (but perhaps only one type of civic participation is considered "right" or the norm), as well as the unwelcoming practices of the civic institutions included in the study.

Another example is the design of strategies to address the high obesity rates in a particular community. Interventions targeting individuals' attitudes and behaviors (e.g., exercise programs, nutrition classes) are common and appropriate; however, such interventions alone are not enough. The cross-culturally competent health professional would study the problem from different angles, including the community infrastructure and policies that affect the high obesity rates. He or she may learn about the following interrelated situations, which contribute to the health problems experienced by the community members: the local farmers market does not accept food stamps because it operates in an environment with limited access to electricity and land-line telephones and, therefore, cannot process food stamp purchases, which are usually processed electronically; the school district has a policy that requires public schools to purchase food from vendors that charge the least, rather than from local farmers; the public resources allocated for restoring the park in the community have been reallocated to improving the park in a neighboring and wealthier community (whose members have the capacity to attend and voice their concerns at county meetings); a developer just bought land for an office building and tore down the only grocery shop that sold fresh vegetables and fruits.

Identify, recognize, and leverage the assets of a cultural group. Cross-culturally competent community psychologists pay equal attention to both the assets and needs of a cultural group, understand that assets can come in different forms (e.g., the cultural pride felt by its youth, a renowned leader who promoted the group's culture, the group's involvement in a historical event, the group's successful effort in preventing the construction of a highway through its town). Therefore it is essential to identify the assets available and ask how these assets can be leveraged to assist the group in achieving its goals.

Accept status differences and be honest about them. Some community psychologists and other professionals mistakenly believe that to be cross-culturally competent, they have to behave like people in the group. On the contrary, this behavior could be perceived as condescending or deceiving by the group members because the professionals may be ignoring differences in education level, authority, access to resources, and other key factors. It is better to accept than ignore the status differences, acknowledge them, and engage the group members in a discussion to ensure that the differences do not cause harm.

Suggestions for How to Develop Cross-Cultural Competency

The following are examples of practical ways, including key exercises, workshops, and other trainings, to develop your cross-cultural competency.

Engage in exercises that deepen your awareness about how your assumptions affect your work. Everyone has biases, unconscious or conscious, about different people within or outside their social groups. It is helpful for you to work toward understanding your biases and how they affect your perceptions, behavior, interactions, and use of language when working in communities (see, for example, Hopson, 2000). Project Implicit, a test about one's biases that are not always apparent (https://implicit.harvard.edu), is a helpful resource for testing yourself. Another helpful exercise is to always pause when you are constructing research questions, designing programs, developing theories, or conducting trainings, and ask yourself: What assumptions am I making? Is my choice of words implicitly assuming something about another group of people or community?

Here is an example of how biases can affect the interpretation and communication of a research study's findings. What biases and assumptions do you think are operating here and what impact can this potentially have?

> The total number of Asian Americans has reached a record high, according to Census data. By comparison, non-Hispanic Whites account for slightly more than one third of the U.S. population, while Hispanics and non-Hispanic Blacks account for a small percentage of the U.S. population. The percentages of Hispanics and non-Hispanic Blacks have decreased steadily over the past two years.

> A newspaper article concluded that "The influx of Asians reflects a slowdown in illegal immigration while American employers increase their demand for high-skilled workers."

> *Hint:* Asian immigrants come to the United States legally, while Hispanics do not. All Asians are lumped together into one category and assumed to be educated and skilled.

Attend trainings about human interactions and group processes to sharpen your ability to facilitate and navigate town hall meetings, community gatherings, reflective learning discussions, and any other processes that involve a diverse group of people. Trainings that include role plays, exercises, and experiential learning opportunities are helpful for honing this ability (Schön, 1983). The National Training Laboratory (NTL) is a useful resource (www.ntl.org); based on the principles of group relations espoused by Kurt Lewin, the NTL provides people with the theoretical knowledge and practical skills for facilitated group dialogues and processes. Its workshops are designed to help people experience firsthand, through simulations and other exercises, how their biases as well as other's perceptions about them, can unknowingly affect their interactions and behaviors.

Learn about theories and research regarding organizational behavior and organizational development. Organizations, regardless of their origin, type, or function, are an integral part of any group or community. Their relationships with one another, with the informal leaders of a cultural group, and with the larger systems operating in the community, can positively or negatively affect group dynamics and behaviors and community norms (Dreaschlin et al., 2013). The NTL and several universities (e.g., Temple University, American University) have training programs about organizational behavior and development and leadership and diversity management strategies.

Attend trainings about the structures and impacts of privilege and power. There has not been much training designed to help people understand the structures and impacts of privilege and power. The People's Institute (www.pisab.org) is an important resource in this area. It provides training on undoing institutional racism through dialogue, reflection, role playing, and knowledge exchange, teaching participants how to analyze the structures of privilege and power that undermine efforts to promote equity, especially racial equity.

The following is an example of how group facilitation skills and extensive understanding about privilege and power are critical.

A group of day laborers has been hanging out in front of a store in a suburban residential area waiting to be picked up for temporary work. Residents began to get agitated, citing incidents of inappropriate behavior (e.g., "cat calling," public urination) and describing the day laborers' presence as unsightly and detrimental to their neighborhood. They called for immediate action from the county government. The day laborers, on the other hand, told the community organizer who has been helping them that they needed work and had no place to go to be hired; in addition, they denied reports of public urination since the store owner had been kind enough to allow them to use the bathroom. The county government's community relations officer contacted you to convene a meeting between residents and day laborers to discuss and resolve the situation. How would you go about designing the meeting, taking into considering the diversity of the participants and the privilege and power dynamics at play?

Hint: Use simultaneous interpretation equipment and conduct half of the meeting in English (with an interpreter for the non-English speaking day laborers) and the other half of the meeting in the language of the day laborers (with an interpreter for the English-speaking residents). Arrange the seating such that neither the residents nor the day laborers are not sitting together with their own group; seat cultural brokers or bridge builders (e.g., advocates, service providers) in between the residents and day laborers.

THE IMPORTANCE OF CROSS-CULTURAL COMPETENCY IN COMMUNITY PRACTICE

Cross-cultural competency is essential in community practice because communities are comprised of people from many cultures and histories with varying levels of contact, trust, and social ties. Community psychologists must be able to negotiate and navigate the interactive effects of all these variables in order to continuously challenge the belief that people who do not fit the norms are lacking in capacity to live a successful life (Trickett et al., 1994), and to reduce the likelihood of certain individuals or groups being marginalized and oppressed. The following are vignettes that demonstrate how cross-cultural competency is critical for helping to ensure positive outcomes for a group of people or community.

Vignette 1: Parent Engagement in Schools

A school is struggling with parent engagement, especially with parents of their racial and ethnic minority students. A parent liaison is hired to communicate and work with these parents. The teachers complain that these parents are not interested in their children's schooling. Some of them even stopped bothering to send information home with the children, assuming that the parents will not read the information. Over time, the school's performance declines. The principal and some teachers blame the growing population of immigrant families in the surrounding area. The immigrant students perceive growing hostility toward them by some of their teachers, but they have nobody to talk to about their perceptions.

Your child attends the school and during a Parent Teacher Association meeting, you overhear two teachers complaining about "those" parents. Your concern about the school's declining performance also leads to a conversation with the school principal who shares her exasperation about the school climate, which she perceives as increasingly contentious and chaotic. More important, she is becoming very concerned about the students and their ability to learn and grow. You tell her that you would be willing to help her problem-solve and she eagerly accepts your offer. How would you go about assessing the problem, identifying solutions, and engaging the school personnel, parents, and students in the process? Why would you need cross-cultural competency to do this? Also consider the following questions to ensure a cross-culturally competent approach:

- What assumptions are in operation here about the role of school and parent engagement in different cultures? (*Hint:* What are the roles of schools, teachers, and parents in different cultures?)

- What might be affecting the parents' ability to participate in school events and become involved in their children's schooling? (*Hint:* Do some of the parents have more than one job, or have young children and cannot afford child care?)

- What are the differences in the social identities of the teachers, parent liaison, and parents, and the social groups to which they belong? (*Hint:* How do the teachers, parent liaison, and parents self-identify and what are the perceptions that each person might have about the other person's social identities?)

- Who has privilege and power and over whom? (*Hint:* What is the demographic makeup of the teachers and parents? What concerns might the parents have about how their children might be treated if they complain about a teacher?)

- What inequities developed and are perpetuated through the inconsistent sharing of information with certain parents? (*Hint:* What learning opportunities [e.g., field trips] might some of the children miss if they did not have their parents' consent to participate? How does this affect their grades?)

Vignette 2: Building Intergroup Relations in a Divided Community

A rural town where the majority of its White residents are descendents of German immigrants who resettled there many generations ago, is experiencing an influx of Latino immigrants. The community is segregated. Most of the White residents live in homes situated on the top of a small hill, while most of the Latino families live in rental homes located at the bottom of the hill. They don't attend each other's events and other than encountering one another in the schools where their children attend, cross-cultural interactions are minimal. A fight breaks out where a young Latino boy is badly hurt. The person who initiated the fight is another Latino youth. The incident is not properly handled by the police department. The story in the newspaper the next day suggests that these sorts of incidents are common and "gang problems," due to the arrival of immigrants, are affecting their once-quiet community. It goes on to denigrate the conditions of the area at the bottom of the hill, describing it as "unsafe" with "littered sidewalks."

The community center, which has been there for decades and is now led by a young Latina, reaches out to your organization for assistance. She had heard about your organization and its work from a colleague. She would like to put an end to the growing division but is not sure how. She invites you to visit the town and meet with her staff to get their perspectives of the situation. You accept the offer. As you drive through town, you notice a few things: a big mural behind the community center with illustrations of the German immigrants who first resettled in the town; a more diverse group of residents than you anticipated at the top of the small hill, including a number of South Asian and Black/African American families; signs for organizations, such as the Rotary Club, League of Women Voters; and several churches with announcements about community events. You also note that the area at the bottom of the hill has no sidewalks, street lights that do not appear to work, and young people hanging out at street corners after school chatting and laughing. Later, when you meet with the staff at the community center, you learn about the center's afterschool activities, parent leadership trainings, annual community picnics, and food drives. You also meet a staff person who discusses the lack of leadership capacity in the Latino community. You ask about the center's relations with the other organizations in the town (e.g., the ones that you saw signs for) and learn that they do not have any. How would you go about designing a strategy and process for bringing all the residents and leaders together to build relationships and trust? Why would you need cross-cultural competency to do this? Consider the following questions to ensure a cross-culturally competent approach:

- What assumptions and stereotypes are operating here about the residents who live at the top and at the bottom of the hill? (*Hint:* Is the divide here immigrant vs. non-immigrant, socioeconomic status, and/or ethnicity? Why does the staff person at the community center say that there is no leadership capacity in the Latino community?)

- What are the various social groups in the community? (*Hint:* Who participates in the organizations such as the Rotary Club and League of Women Voters? What types of organizations do the South Asian, African American, and Latino families participate in? Do they go to the churches in the community, or if not, where do they go for spiritual and faith services?)

- Who has privilege and power and over whom? (*Hint:* Why is it the families at the bottom of the hill don't have sidewalks or street lights? Who represents them on the city council?)

- What are the structures that are contributing to the status quo or perpetuating the unequal distribution of opportunities and resources? (*Hint:* What organizations, institutions, or avenues, similar to the Rotary Club and League of Women Voters, can the Latino and other low-income families turn to for voicing their concerns? Why is it that the community center does not have relationships with other organizations and leaders in the community? Why is it the newspaper can print a story that paints the image of "littered sidewalks" when there aren't even sidewalks?)

FUTURE DIRECTIONS

The vignettes above illustrate common occurrences in communities throughout the United States. The need for cross-cultural competency among community psychologists will become both more urgent and complex as communities become increasingly diverse in all aspects, from race and ethnicity to sexual orientation, and as community psychologists and other professionals' understanding of cross-cultural competency shifts from valuing diversity to promoting equity. The world has witnessed many events during the last several years—such as the election of the first African American president in the United States, economic recession, wars in Iraq and Afghanistan, and the Arab Spring—that will increase the need to discuss and act on problems that disproportionately affect certain groups of people and communities. The knowledge and skills to facilitate these discussions and actions must be considered part of cross-cultural competency.

SUMMARY

Key Points

- It is impossible to become perfectly competent in your knowledge about another group of people, but it is possible to become sufficiently competent to cultivate mutual respect and promote behaviors and actions that ensure social justice and equity for the people with whom you are interacting and engaging. The use of "cross" in cross-cultural competency emphasizes this point.

- The development of cross-cultural competency requires knowledge and skills in addressing three components: culture, social identities, and privilege and power.

- Culture comes in many forms and shapes that are constantly evolving; some of the forms and shapes are obvious to the outsider, while others require extensive inquiry and observation.

- Social identity is formed as a way to preserve and achieve group distinctiveness and is shaped by culture, history, and context. Individuals have many social identities.

- Stereotyping and unspoken and unrealistic expectations can arise from situations where people assume a person's social identity and concludes that the person is "one of them" or "not one of them."

- History plays a big role in the creation of privilege and power and the marginalization, oppression, or even genocide of certain groups. The inequities that result from these events affect the labels and actions used to distinguish, divide, and/or discriminate against certain groups of people.

- To practice cross-cultural competency means to

  o Remember and apply the definition of culture;
  o Practice humility;
  o Pay attention to particular concepts and terms and do not assume that they mean the same thing for everyone;
  o Pay attention to particular organizations and do not assume that they have the same function for everyone;
  o Keep current on the dynamic context in which culture, social identities, and privilege and power are operating;
  o Consider structural inequities and how they affect your work and the outcomes; and
  o Accept that there are status differences and be honest about them.

DISCUSSION QUESTIONS

1. In what situations has cross-cultural competency been practiced well? In what situations could the practice of cross-cultural competency have been improved? What were the outcomes? What could have been done differently to improve the application of this competency?

2. How might you apply the three components of cross-cultural competency (culture, social identity, and privilege and power) in your work?

3. How else could you hone your knowledge and skills in cross-cultural competency?

KEY TERMS AND DEFINITIONS

Cross-cultural competency: The ability to interact, function, and work effectively among people who may not share your demographic attributes, language, beliefs, history, and experiences.

Culture: A set of socially transmitted and learned behaviors, beliefs, institutions, and all other products and thoughts of a group of people that shape and guide the functioning of a particular individual, family, profession, organization, or community.

Power: The ability or capacity to exercise authority, control, and influence.

Privilege: The advantage granted to or enjoyed by a group of people beyond the advantage of all others.

Social identity: Something that is formed when a group of people attempt to see their group differentiated from other groups as a way to preserve and achieve group distinctiveness.

Structural inequity: A system in which public policies, institutional practices, cultural representations, and other norms work in various, often reinforcing ways to perpetuate inequity among social groups.

RESOURCES

Books and Articles

Allport, G. W. (1954). *The nature of prejudice*. Reading, MA: Addison-Wesley.

Black, J. S., & Mendenhall, M. (1990). Cross-cultural training effectiveness: A review and theoretical framework for future research. *Academy of Management Review, 15*, 113–136.

Bond, M. A. (1999). Gender, race, and class in organizational contexts. *American Journal of Community Psychology, 27*(3), 327–355.

Dreachslin, J. L., Gilbert, M. J., & Malone, B. (2013). *Diversity and cultural competence in health care*. San Francisco, CA: Jossey-Bass.

Gallagher, T. (2000). Building institutional capacity to address cultural differences. In R. Carter (Ed.), *Addressing cultural issues in organizations* (pp. 229–240). Thousand Oaks, CA: Sage.

Katz, J. H., & Ivey, A. (1977). White awareness: The frontier of racism awareness training. *Personnel and Guidance Journal, 55*, 485–489.

Kavanagh, K. H. & Kennedy, P. H. (1992). *Promoting cultural diversity: Strategies for health care professionals*. Newbury Park, CA: Sage.

Lederach, J. P. (1997). *Building peace: Sustainable reconciliation in divided societies*. Washington, DC: United Sates Institute of Peace.

Loden, M. (1996). *Implementing diversity*. New York, NY: McGraw-Hill.

Mindiola, T., Niemann, Y. F., & Rodriguez, N. (2002). *Black-brown relations and stereotypes*. Austin: University of Texas Press.

Potapchuk, M. (2001). *Steps toward an inclusive community*. Washington, DC: Joint Center for Political and Economic Studies.

Steinhorn, L., & Diggs-Brown, B. (2000). *By the color of our skin*. New York, NY: First Plume Printing.

Thornton, B., & Zambrana, R. (2009). *Emerging intersections*. New Brunswick, NJ: Rutgers University Press.

Manuals, Guides, and Case Studies

Annie E. Casey Foundation. (n.d.). *Race matters toolkit*. Baltimore, MD: Author.

Bond, M. A., & Harrell, S. P. (Eds.). (2006). Stories of diversity challenges in community research and action. *American Journal of Community Psychology, 37*(3/4), 157–365.

Bond, M. A., & Pyle, J. (1998). The ecology of diversity in organizational settings: Lessons from case study. *Human Relations, 51*(5), 589–623.

Chavis, D., Lee, K., & Buchanan, R. (2001). *Principles for intergroup relations projects*. Gaithersburg, MD: Community Science.

Lee, K. (2010). *The journey continues: Ensuring a cross-culturally competent evaluation*. Denver, CO: Colorado Trust.

Shapiro, I. (2002). *Training for racial equity and inclusion: A guide to selected programs*. Washington, DC: Aspen Institute.

St. Onge, P. (2009). *Embracing cultural competency: A roadmap for nonprofit capacity builders*. St. Paul, MN: Fieldstone Alliance.

Stewart, C. (1999). *Sexually stigmatized communities: An awareness training manual*. Thousand Oaks, CA: Sage.

Websites

Active Voice, a national organization that helps organizations tackle social issues through the use of story, film, and other multimedia tools: http://www.activevoice.net

The Applied Research Center, a national organization dedicated to racial justice. This website includes resources for training in racial justice and a link to the organization's publication, *Color Lines:* http://www.arc.org

The Aspen Institute, which provides information about seminars, publications, and initiatives about dismantling structural racism: http://www.aspeninstitute.org/policy-work/community-change/racial-equity

The Center for Social Inclusion, a national organization dedicated to identifying and supporting policy strategies to transform structural inequity and exclusion into structural fairness and inclusion: http://www.centerforsocialinclusion.org/

The American Evaluation Association's Task Force on Cultural Competence in Evaluation: http://www.eval.org/culturalcompetence.asp

U.S. Department of Health and Human Services, Health Resources and Services Administration, for health-care providers: http://www.hrsa.gov/culturalcompetence/

U.S. Department of Health and Human Services, Office of Minority Health's National Culturally and Linguistically Appropriate Services (CLAS) Standards in Health and Health Care. These CLAS standards are intended to advance health equity, improve quality, and help eliminate health-care disparities: http://minorityhealth.hhs.gov/templates/browse.aspx?lvl = 2&lvlID = 15:

National Center for Cultural Competence at Georgetown University, designed primarily for health and mental health professionals: http://www. nccc.georgetown.edu/

National LGBT Health Education Center, which offers educational programs and technical assistance to health care organizations in providing accessible, high-quality, and cost-effective care to lesbian, gay, bisexual, and transgender (LGBT) people: http://www.lgbthealtheducation.org

Worksheets

The websites and manuals listed above contain self-exploration or self-development assessment tools for building knowledge and skills around cross-cultural competency.

REFERENCES

Chavis, D. M. (1980). Returning research data to the community: Getting away from experimental colonialism. In R. R. Stough & A. Wandersman (Eds.), *Optimizing environments: Research, practice and policy.* Washington, DC: Environmental Design Research Association.

Chavis, D. M., & Newbrough, J. R. (1986). The meaning of "community" in community psychology. *Journal of Community Psychology, 14*(4), 335–340.

Cross, E. Y., Katz, J. H., Miller, F. A., & Seashore, E. W. (Eds.). (1994). *The promise of diversity.* Burr Ridge, IL: IRWIN Professional.

Culture. (2000). *American Heritage college dictionary* (3rd ed.). Boston, MA: Houghton Mifflin.

Dreachslin, J. L., Gilbert, M. J., & Malone, B. (2013). *Diversity and cultural competence in health care.* San Francisco, CA: Jossey-Bass.

Hofstede, C. (1997). *Culture and organizations.* New York, NY: McGraw-Hill.

Hopson, R. (Ed.). (2000). How and why language matters in evaluation. *New Directions for Evaluation, 86.*

Gensheimer, L., & Diebold, C. (1997). Free-standing doctoral programs in community psychology. In C. O'Donnell & J. Ferrari (Eds.), *Education in community psychology* (pp. 45–64). Binghamton, NY: Haworth.

Lee, K. (2004). *The meaning and practice of civic participation in four immigrant communities in the Washington metropolitan region* (Unpublished doctoral dissertation). The Union Institute and University, Cincinnati, OH.

Lorion, R. P., & Newbrough, J. R. (1996). Psychological sense of community: The pursuit of a field's spirit. *Journal of Community Psychology, 24*(4), 311–325,

Murdie, R. A. (2004, July). *House as home as a measure of immigrant integration: Evidence from the Housing Experiences of New Canadians in Greater Toronto Study.* Paper presented at the European Network for Housing Research Conference, Cambridge, United Kingdom.

Power. (2000). *American Heritage college dictionary* (3rd ed.). Boston, MA: Houghton Mifflin.

Privilege. (2000). *American Heritage college dictionary* (3rd ed.). Boston, MA: Houghton Mifflin.

Puddifoot, J. (1996). Some initial considerations in the measurement of community identity. *Journal of Community Psychology, 24*(4), 327–336.

Renzetti, C. M., & Lee, R. M. (1993). *Researching sensitive topics.* Newbury Park, CA: Sage.

Schön, D. (1983). *The reflective practitioner: How professionals think In action.* New York, NY: Basic Books.

Stephan, W., & Stephan, C. (2001). *Improving intergroup relations.* Thousand Oaks, CA: Sage.

Tajfel, H. (1981). *Human groups and social categories.* Cambridge, UK: Cambridge University Press.

Tervalon, M., & Murray-Garcia, J. (1998). Cultural humility versus cultural competence: A critical distinction in physician training outcomes in multicultural education. *Journal of Health Care for the Poor and Underserved, 9*(2), 117–125.

Trickett, E. J., Watts, R. J., & Birman, D. (Eds.). (1994). *Human diversity.* San Francisco, CA: Jossey-Bass.

Watts, R. J. (1994). Paradigms of diversity. In E. J. Trickett, R. J. Watts, & D. Birman (Eds.), *Human diversity* (pp. 49–80). San Francisco, CA: Jossey-Bass.

CHAPTER 5

Professional Judgment and Ethics

Michael Morris

Acknowledgment: The author thanks Karina V. Medved for the extensive background research she did in support of the preparation of this chapter.

OPENING EXERCISE: MY HOMEWORK IS DONE, BUT. . .

The community-based research organization you work for has recently completed an evaluation of an extended-day homework assistance program in a local public school system. In this pilot program, which focuses on three elementary schools, volunteer tutors work with children on their homework for up to two hours after the end of the school day. Your evaluation indicates that the program has a positive impact on the homework-completion rates of participants, but does not lead to higher grades. The superintendent of schools would like you to downplay the latter results in your written report and your in-person presentation to the city's board of education, which has provided funding for the program. She wants to expand the program to a dozen elementary schools in the coming year, a move that would require enhanced funding from the board and support from a local philanthropic organization to pay the high school students who serve as tutors. The superintendent is concerned that the no-impact-on-grades finding could dampen enthusiasm for the program among funders, leading to a premature termination of this worthwhile experiment. As she puts it, "I don't want to sink this program before we have a chance to improve it. And don't forget that an expanded program would provide valuable part-time work for high school students in an educational setting rather than in a fast-food joint. That's an important benefit in its own right."

As the superintendent is talking you're beginning to feel that the core objective of this intervention—to raise the academic achievement of elementary school students—is in danger of being lost, or at least compromised, amid a mix of secondary interests: a jobs program for teens, keeping elementary school children out of mischief for two additional hours every day, successfully courting funders, and so on. Although you don't wish to be insensitive to the superintendent's concerns, you have serious reservations about "burying" findings that you believe are of substantive importance.

What would you do in this situation? If you remain committed to giving these results the attention you believe they deserve, and the superintendent does not budge from her view, how would you respond? Is there anything you could have done that might have prevented this conflict from occurring?

OVERVIEW

This chapter explores the ethical dimensions of community psychology practice and considers strategies that can enhance the ethical quality of one's work in the community. The value and limitations of professional principles, guidelines, and standards dealing with ethics are discussed, and the distinctive challenges associated with community psychology's commitment to a social-justice agenda in multiple-stakeholder, culturally diverse environments are highlighted. The role of case analysis, journal keeping, and dialogue with colleagues in developing ethical competence is emphasized, along with the opportunities that the entry/contracting phase of community projects offers for preventing ethical conflicts.

Photo 5.1   Across an array of settings, community practitioners are required to address the question, "What is the (morally) right thing to do?"

Source: iStockphoto.com/RusN.

INTRODUCTION: CONCEPTUAL DEFINITION

Professional judgment and ethics in community psychology practice are topics that cut across all of the other core competencies addressed in this book. In community organizing, for example, the question of *whose* priorities and agenda are exerting the greatest influence on the change effort can raise significant ethical issues. Or consider the pursuit of social justice. Inherent in the concept of social justice is the claim that the cause of ethics is being served when one advocates for a more just society. And, of course, there is community-based research. How should a community psychologist react when grassroots stakeholders in a participatory action research (PAR) project lobby strongly for a methodology that runs a high risk of generating findings that would give the appearance of positive program impact in the absence of true change?

These are all situations that, at some level, require practitioners to address the question, "What is the (morally) right thing to do?" Thus, we are in the domain of ethics. Overall, **ethics** deal with "what is good and bad and with moral duty and obligation" ("Ethics," 2011, p. 429). Newman and Brown (1996) have noted that ethics can be viewed from three vantage points. The first encompasses core principles of moral behavior that should apply, at least in theory, to everyone. Thus, "Thou shalt not kill" is an admonition that finds expression in some form in all societies. The second pertains to principles and guidelines that members of a profession develop to inform their work. In medicine and research, for example, obtaining informed consent from patients and participants is generally regarded as a fundamental professional responsibility. Finally, ethics can refer to the study of individuals' beliefs and actions relevant to morality. For example, one can investigate empirically the extent to which informed consent is fully obtained from participants in a given intervention (e.g., Walker, Hoggart, & Hamilton, 2008). In this chapter the emphasis will be on competencies that are likely to contribute to effectiveness in the realm of ethical professional practice.

Before embarking on this journey we should note that ethical judgments in community psychology are a subset of professional judgments, in the sense that there are many occasions when a community psychologist might be called upon to exercise professional judgment with no particular ethical issue at stake. For example, a practitioner may be considering two different strategies for launching a community program in a situation where compelling arguments could be offered in support of both strategies. The practitioner's choice is likely to reflect his or her professional judgment about which strategy has the best chance of success in the current circumstances, but there is no strong sense here of an *ethical* imperative to select one strategy over the other. In this instance the practitioner is unlikely to perceive an ethical challenge. This chapter will focus on professional judgment in the realm of ethics, leaving to the authors of the other competency-based chapters the task of addressing professional judgment in those domains.

COMPETENCY DEVELOPMENT

Guidance for Ethical Practice

Community psychology has not developed an official set of ethical guidelines to inform practice, although the Society for Community Research and Action's (SCRA's) statement of goals refers to issues that have ethical implications.[1] For example, the field is "committed to promoting equitable distribution of resources, equal opportunity for all, non-exploitation, prevention of violence, active citizenry, liberation of oppressed peoples, greater inclusion for historically marginalized groups, and respecting all cultures" (SCRA, n.d.). The first five of these goals are seen as defining community psychology's commitment to social justice. Honoring human rights is also mentioned as an SCRA priority in both its goals and guiding concepts.

These general references do not provide specific ethical guidance, but they do suggest core **values,** which are strongly held ideals about what is moral, right, or good, that establish a foundation for ethical practice (see, for example, Nelson & Prilleltensky's (2010, chap. 3) delineation of personal, collective, and relational values). To the extent that other fields share these values, professional standards crafted in those arenas can assist community psychologists in addressing ethical concerns in their own domain. For example, both the American Evaluation Association (AEA; 2004) and the Joint Committee on Standards for Educational Evaluation (Yarbrough, Shulha, Hopson, & Caruthers, 2011) have developed guiding principles and standards, respectively, to support the ethical practice of program evaluation. **Principles** are broadly stated prescriptions of ethical conduct; **standards** are specific statements that provide guidance for ethical behavior. Given that community research is at the heart of SCRA's name and mission, it is not surprising that the AEA's Guiding Principles for Evaluators and the Joint Committee's Program Evaluation Standards offer a wealth of counsel relevant to community practice. For instance, the AEA principle of Responsibilities for General and Public Welfare includes the following assertion:

> Evaluators have obligations that encompass the public interest and good. . . .
> Because the public interest and good are rarely the same as the interests of any particular group (including those of the client or funder), evaluators will usually have to go beyond analysis of particular interests and consider the welfare of society as a whole. (AEA, 2004, E-5)

It is clear that this statement conceptualizes responsibility for the general and public welfare as an *ethical* responsibility. That is, evaluators who wish to be ethical must take into account the needs and perspectives of multiple stakeholders and, indeed, incorporate macro-level considerations ("society as a whole") as well. Of course, one can make a convincing case that program evaluators and community researchers are not the only groups that need to be sensitive to these issues. Anyone who endeavors to design and/or implement a community-based intervention has an ethical obligation to be mindful of the intervention's potential ramifications throughout and beyond the system where it is introduced. Thus, a principle such as Responsibilities for General and Public Welfare has implications for community psychologists in two of their most fundamental roles: researchers and change agents/facilitators.

This point is reinforced by analyses that target the ethical issues encountered by those in the latter role. For example, Rabinowitz, Berkowitz, and Brownlee (n.d.) identify a number of major ethical concerns that can arise in community interventions, including the following:

- Confidentiality, which can take multiple forms depending on the varieties of stakeholders involved, the sensitivity of the issues addressed (e.g., violence, substance use, sexual behavior), and the intervention context (e.g., information shared within programs, across programs, or even with external law enforcement officials in the case of mandated reporting)

- Consent, which can encompass both the informed consent of intervention participants and, in some instances, the wider community within which an intervention/ program takes place. Prevention programs, for example, are often implemented at multiple ecological levels, which can greatly complicate the task of obtaining informed consent. As Schwartz and Hage (2009) observe:

> Typically the target population is a group that is not actively seeking help. . . . The imposed nature of the intervention has the potential of exacerbating the typical power imbalance between a practitioner or researcher and participants, as the prevention practitioner is viewed as acting with expertise and authority to address a problem. . . . As the power differential increases, the ability of the participants to make autonomous decisions related to informed consent decreases. (p. 127)

In short, orchestrating informed consent in community practice can be a multi-layered, messy process, posing a significant challenge to practitioners who wish to be fully responsive to all community stakeholders.

• Competence, which refers to the adequacy of the education, training, and experience of the change agents/facilitators, as well as to the "due diligence" and proficiency that are displayed in the implementation of the intervention. As the content of this volume suggests, community psychologists need to be mindful of the wide range of competencies that the field encompasses, and be clear about which ones are called for in any given intervention they undertake.

• Conflict of interest, which involves situations where one's personal interests (financial, political, social, etc.) could influence one's objectivity or effectiveness in carrying out responsibilities related to the intervention. For example, being asked to provide a professional evaluation of the job performance of a close friend in a community program would represent a conflict of interest. Conflicts of interest are widespread in the world of community psychology practice, but the mere existence of such a conflict does not determine its ethicality. Rather, it is the *response* of the individual to the conflict that is crucial. In the present example, choosing to evaluate the friend would in most cases constitute unethical behavior, while declining the request would be deemed ethically appropriate.

• General ethical responsibilities, which to a great extent address the same domain as the AEA Guiding Principle of Responsibilities for General and Public Welfare. In both cases the emphasis is on the multiple stakeholders that must be attended to by practitioners. Viewing this issue from a program perspective, Rabinowitz et al. (n.d.) identify funders, staff members, program participants, and the community as a whole as key constituencies that must be taken into consideration.

Our discussion thus far suggests that community psychologists contend with many of the same ethical issues that confront those in other applied fields (e.g., program evaluation, public health). Confidentiality, informed consent, and conflict of interest, for example, are topics with a long history. To what degree do ethical concerns such as these take on a *distinctive* form in community psychology practice? The strongest case for distinctiveness can probably be made with respect to the interaction of five (of the seven) core values in community psychology identified by Kloos et al. (2012): social justice, empowerment/citizen participation, collaboration and community strengths, respect for human diversity, and empirical grounding. The field's commitment to social justice has historically been associated with advocating for disadvantaged, oppressed groups within society, and doing so in a way that enhances the ability of these groups to exercise power on behalf of their self-perceived interests and priorities. This process frequently involves community psychologists collaborating with the marginalized and disenfranchised, employing a knowledge of, and appreciation for, research that is relevant to the change effort. Ethical challenges that can arise in these situations include, but are by no means limited to, the following:

- Advocating for substantive change in ways that generate unrealistic expectations on the part of intervention participants. In participatory action research that emerges from a consciousness-raising strategy, for example, participants might be tempted to undertake projects that naively confront powerful and unyielding system stakeholders, resulting in failure-related demoralization and cynicism. In such circumstances, one might argue that the intervention actually had a *negative* impact on participants and thus represents a violation of the *do no harm* principle.

- Situations where community psychologists believe that important lessons from relevant research are being ignored or not taken seriously by participants in conceptualizing and/or implementing an intervention. How hard can we push without violating the collaborative spirit of the endeavor? Do we have a right to distance ourselves from a flawed intervention that might damage our professional reputation?

- Significant value conflicts emerge between the practitioner and community participants as the intervention unfolds. The community psychologist sees these differences as jeopardizing the intervention's ability to embody social justice. For instance, consider a conservative religious congregation that is lobbying vigorously to increase the supply of high-quality early childhood education in the community, but it has recently rebuffed attempts of same-sex parents to contribute to the effort. Should a community consultant who strongly supports gay rights continue to work with this congregation, assuming that the benefits of achieving the education goal would be available to all families, including gay ones? Would the ends justify the means in this case, or at least make the latter tolerable? If the consultant did remain involved, would it be ethically appropriate for him or her to try to change participants' views on gay rights while collaborating on the education intervention? Or would this constitute overstepping the agreed-upon boundaries for the consultation?

What we have in the third case is an instance where respect for diversity (the congregation's values) is at odds with a commitment to social justice (equality for same-sex couples). In the second case, the conflict is between empirical grounding, collaboration, and empowerment. And in the PAR example there is a tension between empowerment and the fundamental principle of *do no harm*. When faced with conflicts between values and/or principles, community psychologists must prioritize: What values/principles should be weighted more heavily when making a decision in this situation? Although many ethicists would argue that *do no harm* is the most fundamental ethical imperative (hence the phrase "*first,* do no harm"), the guidance provided by this principle, and most other principles and values, is so general that it can be of limited use when resolving conflicts among them in specific circumstances (e.g., see Mabry, 1999). And "specific circumstances" are where, by definition, ethical challenges take place in community psychology practice.

One implication of this discussion is that community psychologists need to be skilled at analyzing how the particular circumstances they find themselves in engage the values and principles relevant to community practice. For example, in the early childhood education case, would it make a difference if same-sex parents could, if excluded by the congregation, mobilize on their own to lobby for change, or does working with the congregation represent the only realistic option for their meaningful participation in this effort? What is the likelihood that, falling short of involving gay parents in the congregation's initiative, the community consultant might be able to begin fostering a climate of acceptance within the congregation that could lead to cooperative efforts with gay stakeholders at some point in the future? Finally, is the consultant's *personal* support for gay rights so strong, and central to his or her self-image, that working with a group that discriminates against same-sex couples would be extremely uncomfortable for him or her? The answers to these questions, and possibly others, would be important for the consultant to consider before making a decision on how to proceed ethically.

Ultimately, the distinctiveness of ethical challenges in community psychology practice is, to an appreciable degree, in the eyes of the beholder. As previously noted, many of these challenges are undoubtedly shared with other applied fields. However, insofar as community psychology often focuses on the welfare of society's most vulnerable groups, the consequences of not addressing ethical problems effectively take on special, disquieting significance. Questions such as whose interests are being served, and who has the power to make decisions relevant to an intervention (Roos, Visser, Pistorius, & Nefale, 2007), can be particularly daunting in a field whose practitioners have committed themselves to working with disenfranchised groups.

Ethics in the Community Psychology Literature

Analyses framed explicitly in ethical terms have not occupied a particularly prominent position in the writings of community psychologists, at least in the United States. In the widely used text by Kloos et al. (2012), for example, the terms *ethics* and *ethical* do not even appear in the index, although concepts with major implications for ethical practice, such as "core values," "social justice," and "cultural competence," do. Indeed, the observation by Levine, Perkins, and Perkins in 2005 that "ethical discussion is still rare" (p. 466) in community psychology remains largely true. Finding articles in community psychology journals with "ethics" in the title can be an intimidating task, given that so few exist (e.g., Helm, 2013; Hunter, Lounsbury, Rapkin, & Remien, 2011; O'Neill, 1989; Paradis, 2000; Serrano-García, 1994), and the last comprehensive treatment of ethics in the field appeared in 2000 (Snow, Grady, & Goyette-Ewing).

When one does encounter discussions of ethics in community psychology journals, they are usually part of an examination of the challenges faced when conducting community-based research. Hunter et al. (2011), for example, addressed the difficulties of establishing collaborative relationships with community partners in HIV prevention research in New York City. The dizzying array of stakeholders that participated in these interventions included AIDS service organizations, state and local public health agencies, hospitals/clinics, policymakers, and researchers from various institutions. These groups worked together to develop a Memorandum of Understanding (MOU) that addressed the myriad issues relevant to the research partnership, including privacy rights, confidentiality, risks and benefits to partners and clients, cultural sensitivity, ownership of data and intervention materials, and dissemination of program curricula and research findings. A hallmark of the collaboration was the participants' commitment to a long-term (2-year), transparent process in which their concerns, anxieties, interests, and priorities could be explored in depth. This significant investment of time undoubtedly led to ethical benefits in the MOU that was produced. (For an analysis of ethics in community-based participatory research from a public health perspective, see Buchanan, Miller, & Wallerstein, 2007.)

In another report, Lakes et al. (2012) examine the perspectives that different ethnic and cultural groups bring to informed consent, a core component of ethical research. The authors identify a number of themes, including perceived risks/benefits, participant burden, the meaning and ease of research participation, information needed to make a participation decision, and decision-making strategies. Not surprisingly, there were similarities and differences found on these dimensions between the White, Latina, and Asian American groups studied. This investigation highlights the limitations of believing that "a signed consent form documents shared understanding" (p. 227) and shows that community researchers must take into account the characteristics of the diverse groups they seek to recruit via informed consent.

Indeed, in recent years diversity and cultural competence have probably been the areas where community psychologists have, in their writing, most often tackled issues with direct relevance to ethics. Goodkind et al. (2011), for example, provide a detailed account of Project TRUST, a comprehensive intervention that attempted to address, from the vantage point of multiple stakeholders, health disparities experienced by American Indian/ Alaska Native (AI/AN) youth. At the heart of this endeavor was recognition of the estrangement of AI/AN youth from dominant-culture health-care approaches that marginalized their indigenous healing practices and cultural teachings. Although "ethics" per se is not employed as an explicit organizing concept in the analysis, it is clear that Project TRUST emerged from a belief that social justice, as well as ethical and effective community psychology practice, required greater responsiveness to, and embracing of, the culture of AI/ AN youth. At a more general level, the call for in-depth engagement of the cultures of groups that community psychologists develop interventions for and with constitute a dominant theme in the field (e.g., Aber, García, & Kral, 2011). In short, in order to be an ethical community psychologist one must also be a culturally competent one (see Chapter 4 for more about cross-cultural competence).

Ethical Competence

A review of the curricula of graduate programs in community psychology suggests that virtually all programs expose students to ethics in one or more courses. Consistent with this finding, Neigher and Ratcliffe (2011) report that at least 90% of their sample of 146 community psychologists indicated that training in "ethical professional practice" had been available to them. What is less clear is the extent to which ethics training goes beyond conventional topics in psychological research and practice or treats these topics in a distinctive fashion. As we have seen, traditional concerns such as informed consent, confidentiality/privacy, conflicts of interest, risks/benefits, professional competence, participation incentives, and reporting/dissemination of research results can all assume challenging forms in the multiple-stakeholder, culturally diverse environments in which community psychologists often work on behalf of social justice. Moreover, it is difficult to discern from most community psychology curricula how much attention is given to the ethics of social intervention, as opposed to the ethics of community research. Given the crucial role that such interventions play in the field, one hopes that students would have an opportunity to do more than simply explore the stigmatizing potential of primary and secondary prevention programs.

What Competencies Are Important?

Community psychologists should have an understanding of basic principles that underlie ethical behavior. The American Psychological Association's (APA's; 2010) Ethical Principles of Psychologists and Code of Conduct identify five such principles:

- Beneficence and Nonmaleficence: In essence, this involves acting in ways that benefit others ("doing good") rather than injure them ("doing no harm"). In practice, the goal is often one of maximizing benefits while minimizing harm. Consciousness-raising strategies, for example, can generate acute discomfort among participants, at least in the short term, as the personal consequences of social injustice are explored. In addition, some participants might even become estranged from friends and relatives *beyond* the short term, causing distress in both groups. What one hopes, of course, is that consciousness raising will generate a sense of efficacy and empowerment that, in the long term, will lead to positive social outcomes that significantly outweigh the strategy's costs.

- Fidelity and Responsibility: This principle emphasizes the need for psychologists to develop trusting relationships with others as a result of being seen as professionally responsible. For a community psychologist it requires, among other things, articulating to stakeholders the values that govern one's behavior and acting in accord with those values—for example, making clear how one will enact a collaborative role in working with stakeholders. In some cases this could entail explaining how one's values might *conflict* with stakeholders' values, setting the stage for a discussion of how this conflict should be handled.

- Integrity: Integrity focuses on "accuracy, honesty, and truthfulness in the science, teaching and practice of psychology" (APA, 2010, p. 3). Interacting with others in a transparent manner is key here. In the introductory exercise to this chapter, for instance, the evaluator might see his or her integrity being challenged by the superintendent's request to downplay certain results of the program evaluation (see, for example, Morris & Clark, 2013). And in the consciousness-raising example discussed under Beneficence and Nonmaleficence, integrity would require that participants be informed of the potential benefits *and* costs of consciousness raising.

- Justice: The concept of justice presented in the APA (2010) principles has an individualistic tone, calling for psychologists to "recognize that fairness and justice entitle all persons to access to and benefit from the contributions of psychology" (p. 3) and to "equal quality" in the work of psychologists. As a field, community psychology goes further, committing itself to *social* justice, a more macro-level concept that emphasizes the equitable allocation of resources, opportunities, obligations, and power throughout society (Prilleltensky, 2001), with special attention paid to marginalized groups and the advocacy that is often needed to achieve justice for them. To be sure, social-justice claims can be the subject of serious disagreement, resulting in situations where strategies based on those claims (e.g., affirmative action) are themselves criticized as unjust. This humbling realization complicates ethical practice, insofar as it reminds us that social justice is often a contested terrain and that one person's "moral right" can constitute another's "moral wrong."

- Respect for People's Rights and Dignity: This principle affirms the "dignity and worth of all people, and the rights of individuals to privacy, confidentiality, and self-determination" (APA, 2010, p. 4). It also asserts the need to be responsive to diversity, noting the various dimensions on which individuals can differ (age, gender, culture, race, disability, socioeconomic status, etc.). Once again, the emphasis appears to be primarily on the individual, in contrast to community psychology's framing such rights at the group and community levels.

Ethical competence, of course, requires more than just a *knowledge* of ethical principles, community psychology values, and the various subtopics (e.g., confidentiality, informed consent, cultural responsiveness) addressed in textbooks and relevant courses. One must become skilled at using this knowledge to guide decision making in the specific situations that community psychologists encounter in their work. The following questions can serve as a framework for addressing this task, focusing on circumstances where some type of ethical challenge or problem is involved.

How Do I Recognize an Ethical Challenge When I See One?

The answer to this question is not as simple as it might first appear; research indicates that individuals differ in their inclination to identify problems as ethical in nature (e.g., Desautels & Jacob, 2012; Reynolds, 2006). Indications that an issue may be an ethical one include:

- Most obviously, you believe (perhaps only intuitively) that something is "wrong" (unfair, unjust, inequitable, etc.) or threatens to become wrong if appropriate preventive action is not taken. For example, the voices of less powerful stakeholders are silent or are not being taken seriously by more powerful stakeholders.

- Stakeholders claim that an ethical issue has presented itself.

- Colleagues not directly involved in the situation, but who have knowledge of it, raise ethical concerns.

What Ethical Principles, Values, and Standards Are Most Relevant to This Situation?

The essential question here is *why* is this issue an ethical one? As we have seen, multiple principles, values, and standards can be relevant to any given case. In the introductory exercise, for example, the superintendent's request can be seen as engaging the principle of integrity (i.e., honesty in reporting findings), the community psychology value of empirical grounding (for the same reason), and perhaps even the principle of *do no harm* (e.g., current and future program participants might suffer if the homework assistance program is discontinued).

How Should These Principles, Values, and Standards Be Balanced Against One Another When Making a Decision?

It would be nice, or at least convenient, if there was a formula for combining a given set of ethical perspectives and then extracting a decision, but no such formula exists. Principles, values, and standards are inherently general and abstract; real life is not. The details of the case at hand must be examined, and a judgment reached concerning what, overall, would represent the most ethical course of action. In some instances one principle might emerge as foremost in importance, while in others a decision that honors multiple perspectives could be warranted. Thus, in the homework assistance case the community psychologist might believe that the modifications the superintendent is seeking in the evaluation report are so significant that they would undermine the report's fundamental credibility. In such a situation, altering the report in the manner requested might be regarded as simply unacceptable. On the other hand, the researcher might view the requested changes as undesirable but not so egregious that all other considerations should be discounted. In that case, the potential impact of the report on the program's continuation might be accorded greater importance, with the *do no harm* principle being invoked.

Reaching a decision based on a thorough analysis of the situation does not guarantee that others would necessarily arrive at the same conclusion (e.g., see Morris & Jacobs, 2000). Professionals can disagree on how to proceed, especially when the circumstances are complex. Individuals can vary in how they see a given principle or value applying to an ethical challenge, or even if they see it applying at all. This is to be expected when one is dealing with general principles. Individuals can also differ in how they *prioritize* certain values and principles in their own practice. Finally, the *personal* (as opposed to professional) values of individuals can vary, and in some cases these differences can play a major role in generating conflicting ethical decisions.

The fact that there is often no "one right answer" that all community psychologists would agree upon when dealing with an ethical challenge does not justify failing to explore the various dimensions of a given situation. Engaging in such exploration is what conscientious professionals do.

How Do My Personal Values Interact With the Ethical Challenge I Am Facing?

We do not bring just our education and professional training to the ethical dilemmas we encounter. We also bring our culture, our childhood, and a host of other formative experiences that have shaped our personal value system and sense of self. This value system has a legitimate role to play in decision making, especially when dealing with situations where professional and/or disciplinary values may conflict with one another. Thus, as was mentioned in the early childhood education case, what if the consultant's core self-image was intimately tied to his or her support for gay rights? That fact alone might be sufficient to generate a decision not to continue working with a congregation that declined to work with gay parents. Indeed, had the consultant been aware of the congregation's orientation toward gay rights during the entry/contracting stage of the intervention, it is likely that the consultant would not have agreed to take on the effort to begin with. This possibility underscores the importance of thoroughly investigating the ethical dimensions of a community intervention before committing oneself to it. Although community psychology training socializes us, and Institutional Review Boards frequently require us, to engage in this reconnoitering activity when conducting research, we are less likely to be prepared for it when undertaking other types of community interventions. The entry/contracting stage (see Block, 2011) is by far the best time to contemplate the ethical issues that an intervention might engage, because it provides the practitioner and other stakeholders with an opportunity to take actions that can prevent later problems.

Have I Solicited the Perspectives of Multiple Stakeholders, Including My Colleagues, on the Issue at Hand?

When facing difficult, stressful situations one can be tempted to think through the problem and come up with a solution without input from others, especially if one is afraid of being evaluated or judged. ("You were planning to do *WHAT*?") Not surprisingly, this can severely impair the quality of one's analysis and decision making. At a minimum, other stakeholders can provide perspectives on the ethical challenge that one may not have previously considered, helping to reframe the issue for you and those stakeholders. Such reframing can lead to strategies and solutions that otherwise would not have been contemplated.

In the homework assistance case, the evaluator could seek the superintendent's responses to the following questions:

- What do you mean, exactly, when you refer to "downplaying the findings"? Tell me more about why you think this would be a good thing to do.

- Are there ways of modifying the report to build support for the program that do *not* entail downplaying the findings on grades? What are they?

- In what ways could downplaying the findings on grades create problems for the program in the future?

- If our positions were reversed, how would you feel if I asked you to downplay the grade results? Would you think that you were being asked to do anything unethical? Why or why not?

- What concerns, if any, do you think the Board of Education or the foundation would have if they knew of your request?

Asking questions such as these not only can enhance the evaluator's understanding of the ethical issues involved, it might affect the superintendent's views as well. Of course, if the evaluator had engaged the superintendent during the entry/contracting stage in a discussion of how to deal with potentially unwelcome findings, there is a chance—perhaps a good one—that this entire episode might have been avoided.

How Do I Proceed if I Conclude That the Ethical Thing to Do Puts Me at Personal Risk?

The challenge of dealing with an ethical issue does not necessarily end when one identifies what one believes is the "right" course of action. The right course of action might have the potential to be personally costly. In the homework assistance case, the evaluator might fear that the superintendent would speak ill of the evaluator to others in the community if the report was not modified to the superintendent's liking. This could diminish the evaluator's chances of being hired for future projects.

Of course, when enmeshed in a stressful ethical dilemma, our perceptions can exaggerate the severity of the potential negative consequences of implementing a particular decision. Our imaginations can easily conjure up the worst possible scenario. It is nonetheless true that acting ethically can entail personal sacrifice. In these circumstances there is no escaping the fact that moral courage may be called for. As Kidder (2005) has observed, morally courageous behavior occurs when (1) an individual's motivation is rooted in ethical principles, (2) the individual is cognizant of the personal risk associated with supporting those principles, and (3) he or she is willing to accept that risk. Sometimes, the only reason for a community psychologist to do the right thing is that it is the right thing to do.

APPLICATION: STRATEGIES FOR DEVELOPING ETHICAL COMPETENCE

Enhancing one's ethical competence can be accomplished through reflection upon (1) fictional cases, (2) actual cases experienced by others, and (3) one's own experience. The scenario that began this chapter is a fictitious, point-of-decision case. It ends at the point where the evaluator must make a decision on how to proceed. The reader's task is to analyze the case utilizing relevant values, principles, and standards and offer a recommendation for what the evaluator should do. See Box 5.1 for another example of a fictional case.

Box 5.1 Herding Cats?

You have been asked by the executive director of an agency that provides community-based residential services to the seriously mentally ill to assist the agency in an organizational development project at one of its group homes. The executive director wants you to work with both the staff and residents there to strengthen programming. You and the executive director have been friends for

(Continued)

(Continued)

over a decade. An initial meeting with the group home manager reveals the following (according to the manager):

Most of the direct care staff believe that organizational development activities should focus on establishing more effective strategies for promoting responsible behavior among residents while they are in the home (e.g., performing household chores, attending group meetings). Turnover among direct care staff in this location is high when compared with the agency's other sites.

Some residents would like to have much more attention paid to developing social and recreational opportunities for them in the wider community. Others are more focused on vocational issues; they feel that little is done to help them obtain part-time work in the community that would provide them with more discretionary income. The manager maintains that this latter desire is largely unrealistic, due to the limitations imposed by the residents' mental illness.

Family members of residents believe that communication between them and the group home is far from optimal. The manager acknowledges that there may be some truth to this claim, but thinks that the impact of certain families on the lives of residents is so dysfunctional that less communication might in fact be better than more communication in those cases.

For his part, the manager sees a lack of qualified direct-care staff as the key to the group home's problems. "The agency's human resources department keeps sending me marginally qualified applicants. They may have been psychology majors in college but they have little practical experience. I end up hiring the best of a very mediocre lot." The manager also thinks the executive director has been aware of the challenges at the group home for over a year, but has chosen not to directly intervene. "She's either stretched too thin or just doesn't care. I'm not sure which."

As you leave the building a direct-care staff member approaches you, shakes your hand, and accompanies you onto the porch. "You're the consultant, aren't you? I took a community psychology course as an undergrad, and believe me, there is so much more we could be doing here to help these folks integrate into the community. But between you and me, that's never going to happen as long as the current manager is running things. He's clueless."

Questions to Consider

1. If you accepted this consultation, whose interests would you assign the highest priority to? The executive director? Group home manager? Direct-care staff? Residents? How would you decide?

2. What ethical principles and community psychology core values are most directly engaged by this case? Are any of them in conflict? If so, how would you address this conflict?

3. What would you say to the executive director the next time you meet with her?

Case-oriented reports in the community psychology literature can provide a wealth of material for ethical analysis, even when the reports do not foreground ethical concerns. One can explore the ethical dimensions of the case and critique, from an ethical perspective, the decisions made by the practitioners and others. Phillips, Berg, Rodriguez, and Morgan (2010), for example, describe an intervention in which the intervention team approached a middle school principal about "conducting a student-driven participatory action research project in collaboration with the teachers and students at her school" (p. 182). The principal was enthusiastic, and the PAR project was incorporated into an existing program that provided an accelerated academic curriculum for students who had lost a year of schooling. The core of the PAR curriculum consisted of four modules:

- *Building the Foundation* included "team building, ecological thinking and analysis, understanding identity and the cultural self, and an introduction to PAR" (p. 184).

- In *Issue Selection and Introduction to Research Modeling and Methods,* students identified a substantive issue that interested them and developed an approach to investigating it.

- *Research for Action* consisted of the students actually engaging in the research, including data collection and analysis.

- Finally, the objective of *Using the Data for Change* was to have students address the challenge of "how to translate their research findings into small scale action strategies . . . which they could implement and reflect [upon]" (p. 184).

Overall, the project aimed to "help facilitate youth development and empowerment, increase student efficacy, enhance school connectedness, and improve academic achievement" (Phillips et al., 2010, p. 184). In order to achieve this objective the intervention team tried to develop a strong collaborative and supportive relationship with the two classroom teachers participating in the project.

The project did not proceed smoothly for multiple reasons. For example, the teachers felt that certain aspects of the PAR approach (e.g., encouraging students to question basic assumptions and policies and explore controversial issues) "undermined their control" (Phillips et al., 2010, p. 186). Indeed, a number of topics that students felt strongly about were essentially deemed off-limits by the teachers, undermining a key component of the PAR philosophy embraced by the intervention team. At one point the project was suspended for 2 months because the teachers believed that more regular instructional time was needed to prepare students for upcoming state-wide standardized tests. In addition, in a few instances teachers performed research-oriented tasks for students rather than engaging in the more time-consuming activity of facilitating the development of the students' skills in those areas. Finally, as the intervention evolved it became clear to the team that "the teachers felt they did not have a choice whether they participated in either PAR or action research. They felt coerced by the principal into participation" (p. 192). Against this background, it is not surprising that the team reports that "our collaboration [with the teachers] never completely embodied unity of purpose" (p. 191).

The team's detailed account of this intervention, characterized by admirable candidness, provides readers with an opportunity to explore its ethical ramifications. Among the questions that might be addressed:

- Was the team so eager to launch the project and empower students that they failed to explore in sufficient depth, and with adequate competence, the teachers' feelings about the project? Were the rights of the teachers fully respected?

- What ethical responsibilities did the team take on when facilitating a climate that encouraged students to engage in conversations that could generate conflict, controversy, and confrontation with authority figures in a fairly rigid organizational hierarchy? If the team believed that students raised legitimate issues that were brushed aside by those in power, did they have an obligation to engage in some measure of advocacy on the students' behalf? Why or why not?

- If the team had known prior to the initiation of the PAR project that the teachers felt participation pressure, would that knowledge alone have been enough to justify not undertaking it? In this case it appears that the school district would have required the teachers to participate in an action research project of some sort, even in the absence of the PAR project. To the extent that this is true, does it alter the ethical status of the PAR project's coercive nature? Could the intervention team take ethical solace in the possibility that the PAR project promised to be a higher quality, more empowering experience for students than some other mandated project might prove to be? Or is that just a rationalization, given that a less ambitious alternative project might not have burdened the teachers with as much work as the PAR project did? Whose welfare should be accorded greater priority by the intervention team—the students or the teachers?

Questions such as these do not lend themselves to easy answers, but contemplating them can hone one's skills in analyzing the ethical dimensions of one's own community practice.

Keeping an "ethics journal" is another excellent method for developing skills in reflection and analysis. One can start such a journal at the beginning of any community project. Early entries should focus on the ethical issues that appear to be most prominent in the upcoming intervention, the values and principles that are involved, and how one plans to deal with those issues. Later entries report the outcomes of the strategies employed, how they might need to be modified, and any new ethical challenges that have emerged. Linking issues and actions to specific values and ethical principles can help one internalize the "frames of mind" a community psychologist should bring to the attempt to interact ethically with stakeholders. This should greatly enhance the entry/contracting stage of community interventions, when, as has been noted, the opportunity to *prevent* ethical problems, through open discussion with stakeholders, is greatest. See Box 5.2 for a case, adapted from an experience early in my community psychology career, where more effective management of the entry/contracting stage would have been ethically beneficial.

Box 5.2 It's the Students I'm Afraid Of. . .

A university colleague has asked you, a new arrival on campus, to partner with him on a needs assessment project that a local school district has hired him to conduct. The previous year a high school teacher was shot and killed by a non-student intruder during an attempted robbery in the high school. In the aftermath of this incident the district's school superintendent obtained a grant from a philanthropic foundation to support a study of teachers' views of safety issues within their schools and what steps might be taken to prevent future violence. You accept your colleague's invitation and embark upon a comprehensive study, using both interviews and surveys, of teachers' experiences and perceptions in six of the city's middle schools and high schools. The findings indicate that, for the most part, teachers regard the robbery/murder as a "freak" event with very little chance of reoccurring. What concerns teachers much more are the daily indignities they experience in interactions with many of their students: displays of disrespect and hostility, threatening (and profane) language and gestures, and the like, all taking place within a general school environment characterized by what might best be described as "chaotic incivility." Many teachers are scared, to be sure, but the source of their fear is not outsiders, but the youth they are supposed to be educating. You and your colleague prepare a report detailing these results and your recommendations and submit it to the superintendent.

Is there anything wrong with this picture? Some might assert that there is, and ask: Where are the voices of the students in this needs assessment? They were key stakeholders in these schools, yet their views of an issue with major implications for everyone in those buildings were not solicited. Here are a few questions worth pondering:

- Although the scope of the needs assessment had already been determined when you joined the project, should you have lobbied to broaden the focus of the study to include students as a condition of your participation? What would have been the benefits of broadening the focus?
- When it became clear that many teachers saw students as the source of the problem, did you and your colleague have a responsibility to explore with the superintendent the possibility of expanding the needs assessment?
- Does the inclusion of students in this investigation even represent an ethical issue to begin with? Can one argue that in this instance the foundation and the superintendent have the right to specify the parameters of the needs assessment as they see fit? Is this a situation where it might be wise, but it is not ethically required, to include student perspectives?

Finally, the value of consulting with experienced colleagues cannot be overestimated. The SCRA listserv, for example, is a rich resource for raising ethical questions and issues that others can respond to online and offline. When wrestling with ethical challenges, there is usually no need to "go it alone."

THE FUTURE OF ETHICS IN COMMUNITY PSYCHOLOGY PRACTICE

In their review, Snow et al. (2000) ask, "Why has a field that places a premium on social concerns and social impact neglected the development of ethical guidelines?" (p. 898). They observe that "while the complexity inherent to community psychology may complicate the actual development of ethical guidelines, these same unique characteristics create a compelling need to undertake that very task" (p. 898). That compelling need still exists. Community psychology has matured to the point where the absence of such guidelines threatens to limit the field's credibility as a source of informed, responsible social intervention. To be sure, the interdisciplinary orientation of community psychology will pose a challenge to those attempting to craft a set of ethical guidelines, but other interdisciplinary fields such as program evaluation have successfully addressed this task (e.g., AEA, 2004). The era of routinely complaining that the American Psychological Association's ethical principles and code of conduct are not a good fit for community psychologists must come to an end. Community psychology needs its own ethical principles.

The other major ethics-related item that should be on the agenda of community psychology is research. There is virtually no systematic research on the ethical challenges that community psychologists encounter in their practice. There are no large-scale, representative data sets describing the types of ethical problems that community psychologists confront, how they respond to those problems, and what the consequences of those responses are. Our ethical discussions tend to be theoretical and anecdote-driven. For a field that holds "empirical grounding" to be one of its core values (Kloos et al., 2012), this is distressing. When community psychology does finally undertake the task of establishing formal ethical guidelines, it would be wise, to put it mildly, if this effort were informed by a knowledge of what the field's members have experienced in this domain. There are more than a few doctoral dissertations waiting to be written here, dissertations that could help lay the foundation for enhanced ethical practice throughout the field.

More published case studies that focus on ethical issues in community interventions would also be welcome. Theoretical discussion of ethics is useful and engaging, but it is not a good substitute for exploring in detail the decision contexts that practitioners face as they negotiate ethical challenges. Such case studies would be especially helpful as a component of graduate training and professional development workshops in community psychology.

Finally, community psychology would be well served by increased dialogue on the relationship between ethics and the field's commitment to social justice. Inherent in the concept of social justice is the notion of a moral "ought" or "should"—the language of ethics—applied at the macro-level of analysis. As has been noted, however, competing visions of social justice abound, with each vision making its own claims of ethical superiority. Community psychology, for its part, has carved out a social-justice agenda that most observers would characterize as occupying the left/liberal side of the political spectrum. What are the implications of this reality for the ethics of community psychology practice within our ranks? To what extent do political conservatives feel comfortable and accepted in community psychology? Does respect for diversity, another community psychology value with ethical significance, call for the field to embrace diverse political orientations? Would the field be more ethical if it were more politically inclusive? Or is such a vision fundamentally unrealistic and perhaps undesirable? Ultimately, these are questions that go beyond the scope of this chapter, but they are worthy of a field that wishes to refine and articulate a distinctive ethical agenda for its practice.

SUMMARY

1. Ethics deals with "what is good and bad and with moral duty and obligation," and it is a domain that cuts across all of the other core competencies addressed in this volume.

2. Community psychology has not developed an official set of ethical guidelines, but it does encompass a set of goals and core values that establish a foundation for ethical practice, a foundation it shares, in part, with other applied fields such as program evaluation and public health.

3. Traditional topics in ethics such as informed consent, confidentiality, and conflict of interest can take on distinctive characteristics in the multiple-stakeholder, culturally diverse environments of community psychology practice where social-justice concerns are often highlighted.

4. Analyses framed explicitly in ethical terms have not occupied a prominent position in the writings of community psychologists, but when they do occur, the emphasis tends to be on ethical challenges encountered in community-based research.

5. Though they are largely framed in individualistic terms, the Ethical Principles articulated by the American Psychological Association represent a reasonable point of departure for conceptualizing the ethical competencies required of community psychologists.

6. Community psychologists should be skilled at recognizing ethical issues, identifying and balancing the principles/value/standards relevant to those issues, soliciting the perspectives of multiple stakeholders concerning them, incorporating personal (not just professional) values into their analysis, and understanding the role that personal risk-taking can play in making ethical decisions and acting upon them.

7. Strategies for developing ethical competence include reflecting upon fictional cases, analyzing actual cases experienced by others, examining one's community practice through an "ethics journal," and dialogue with colleagues.

8. The time has come for community psychology to develop its own set of ethical guidelines, one that is informed by sorely needed systematic research on ethical issues encountered in community practice. Increased attention to the relationship between ethics and the political implications of the field's commitment to social justice is also needed.

DISCUSSION QUESTIONS

1. In your view, is developing ethical competence more or less difficult than developing content-oriented expertise in areas such as policy advocacy, community organizing, and participatory research? Why?

2. Experienced professionals can disagree on how on a specific ethical challenge should be handled in community psychology practice. Overall, do you think this is a good thing or a bad thing for the field? Why?

3. If you were given the task of developing a set of guiding ethical principles for community psychology, what would be the first principle you would establish? Why would you make it the first?

4. Research on attribution theory tells us that many individuals tend to *externalize* problems; that is, they do not view their own behavior as causing the difficulties they experience. What are the implications of this finding for our understanding of the ethical challenges in community practice reported by community psychologists?

KEY TERMS AND DEFINITIONS

Ethics: Pertains to what is morally good and bad and to moral duty and obligation.

Principles: Fundamental, broadly stated prescriptions for ethical conduct.

Standards: Specific statements that provide guidance for ethical behavior, often framed in terms of ideal or model behavior.

Values: Strongly held ideals about what is moral, right, or good (Kloos et al., 2012, p. 25).

RESOURCES

Recommended Reading

American Psychological Association. (2010). *Ethical principles of psychologists and code of conduct.* Washington, DC: American Psychological Association.

Buchanan, D. R., Miller, F. G., & Wallerstein, N. (2007). Ethical issues in community-based participatory research: Balancing rigorous research with community participation in community intervention studies. *Progress in Community Health Partnerships: Research, Education, and Action, 1,* 153–160.

Fuqua, D. R., Newman, J. L., Simpson, D. B., & Choi, N. (2012). Who is the client in organizational consultation? *Consulting Psychology Journal: Practice and Research, 64,* 108–118.

Kidder, R. M. (2005). *Moral courage.* New York, NY: William Morrow.

Roos, V., Visser, M., Pistorius, A., & Nefale, M. (2007). Ethics and community psychology. In N. Duncan, B. Bowman, A. Naidoo, J. Pillay, & V. Roos (Eds.), *Community psychology: Analysis, context and action* (pp. 392–407). Cape Town, South Africa: UCT Press.

Schwartz, J. P., & Hage, S. M. (2009). Prevention: Ethics, responsibility, and commitment to public well-being. In M. E. Kenny, A. M. Horne, P. Orpinas, & L. E. Reese (Eds.), *Realizing social justice: The challenge of preventive interventions* (pp. 123–140). Washington, DC: American Psychological Association.

Snow, D. L., Grady, K., & Goyette-Ewing, M. (2000). A perspective on ethical issues in community psychology. In J. Rappaport & E. Seidman (Eds.), *Handbook of community psychology* (pp. 897–917). New York, NY: Kluwer Academic/Plenum.

Yarbrough, D. B., Shulha, L. M., Hopson, R. K., & Caruthers, F. A. (2011). *The program evaluation standards: A guide for evaluators and evaluation users* (3rd ed.). Los Angeles, CA: Sage.

Recommended Websites

American Evaluation Association: Guiding Principles for Evaluators: http://www.eval.org/publications/guidingprinciples.asp

American Evaluation Association: Guiding Principles Training Package: http://www.eval.org/GPTraining/GPTrainingOverview.asp

American Psychological Association: Ethical Principles of Psychologists and Code of Conduct: http://www.apa.org/ethics/code/index.aspx

Ethics in Community Psychology (G. Nelson & I. Prilleltensky): http://www.palgrave.com/psychology/nelson/students/ethics.html

Joint Committee on Standards for Educational Evaluation: Program Evaluation Standards Statements: http://www.jcsee.org/program-evaluation-standards/program-evaluation-standards-statements

Society for Community Research and Action Listserv: http://www.scra27.0rg/about/elistserves

The Community Tool Box: Ethical Issues in Community Interventions: http://ctb.ku.edu/en/tablecontents/sub_section_main_1165.aspx

COMPETENCY DEVELOPMET ACTIVITY

Interview a community psychologist about an intervention that he or she participated in where an ethical challenge emerged. Ask the interviewee to discuss the following issues:

- What was the nature of the challenge?
- What values or ethical principles did you see this challenge as threatening?
- How did you respond to the challenge? Why did you respond in the way that you did?
- How satisfied were you with the way things turned out? Why?
- In retrospect, do you think there is anything you could have done to prevent this challenge from occurring? If so, what?

Self-Exploration Worksheet

What personal values concerning right and wrong are most important to you? How do these values influence the way in which you approach your work?

Select a major ethical challenge that you have encountered in your personal or work life. When responding to that challenge, what were the major values or principles you were trying to uphold?

Have you experienced situations where your personal values and professional values have been in conflict? If so, how did you respond? What did you learn from this experience?

Have you ever been in a situation where, in order to do the morally right thing, you had to make a significant personal sacrifice? If so, what did you learn from the experience?

Have you ever *not* done the morally right thing because it would have been too personally risky? If so, what did that experience teach you?

Competency Assessment Worksheet

1. Read a detailed account of a community intervention in a community psychology journal or related publication.

2. Conduct an "ethics audit" of the intervention. How did the development and implementation of the intervention embody each of the following five ethical principles?

   - Beneficence/nonmaleficence
   - Fidelity and responsibility
   - Integrity
   - Justice/social justice
   - Respect for people's rights and dignity

3. Were there ways in which the intervention did not uphold one or more core values in community psychology, even though it lived up to the principles addressed in Question 2?

4. From an ethical perspective, are there aspects of the intervention that you would have handled differently? If so, what would you have done, and why?

NOTE

1. SCRA is the official "home" of Community Psychology (Division 27) in the American Psychological Association. It serves a variety of disciplines that focus on community research and action.

REFERENCES

Aber, M. S., García, J. I. R., & Kral, M. J. (Eds.). (2011). Culture and community psychology [Special issue]. *American Journal of Community Psychology, 47,* 46–214.

American Evaluation Association. (2004). *Guiding principles for evaluators* (Rev. ed.). Retrieved from http://www.eval.org/Publications/GuidingPrinciples.asp

American Psychological Association. (2010). *Ethical principles of psychologists and code of conduct.* Washington, DC: American Psychological Association.

Block, P. (2011). *Flawless consulting: A guide to getting your expertise used* (3rd ed.). San Francisco, CA: Jossey-Bass.

Buchanan, D. R., Miller, F. G., & Wallerstein, N. (2007). Ethical issues in community-based participatory research: Balancing rigorous research with community participation in community intervention studies. *Progress in Community Health Partnerships: Research, Education, and Action, 1,* 153–160.

Desautels, G., & Jacobs, S. (2012). The ethical sensitivity of evaluators: A qualitative study using a vignette design. *Evaluation, 18,* 437–450.

Ethics. (2011). *Merriam-Webster's collegiate dictionary* (11th ed., p. 429). Springfield, MA: Merriam-Webster.

Goodkind, J. R., Ross-Toledo, K., John, S., Hall, J. L., Ross, L., Freeland, L., . . . Becenti-Fundark, T. (2011). Rebuilding trust: A community, multiagency, state, and university partnership to improve behavioral health care for American Indian youth, their families, and communities. *Journal of Community Psychology, 39,* 452–477.

Helm, S. (2013). Ethics in community engaged scholarship—How to protect small rural communities? *The Community Psychologist, 46,* 33–35.

Hunter, J., Lounsbury, D. L., Rapkin, B., & Remien, R. (2011). A practical framework for navigating ethical challenges in collaborative community research. *Global Journal of Community Psychology Practice, 1*(3), 13–22.

Kidder, R. M. (2005). *Moral courage.* New York, NY: William Morrow.

Kloos, B., Hill, J., Thomas, E., Wandersman, A., Elias, M. J., & Dalton, J. H. (2012). *Community psychology: Linking individuals and communities* (3rd ed.). Belmont, CA: Wadsworth.

Lakes, K. L., Vaughan, E., Jones, M., Burke, W., Baker, D., & Swanson, J. M. (2012). Diverse perceptions of the informed consent process: Implications for the recruitment and participation of diverse communities in the National Children's Study. *American Journal of Community Psychology, 49,* 215–232.

Levine, M., Perkins, D. D., & Perkins, D. V. (2005). *Principles of community psychology: Perspectives and applications* (3rd ed.). New York, NY: Oxford University Press.

Mabry, L. (1999). Circumstantial ethics. *American Journal of Evaluation, 20,* 199–212.

Morris, M., & Clark, B. (2013). You want me to do what? Evaluators and the pressure to misrepresent findings. *American Journal of Evaluation, 34,* 57–70.

Morris, M., & Jacobs, L. (2000). You got a problem with that? Exploring evaluators' disagreements about ethics. *Evaluation Review, 24,* 384–406.

Neigher, W. D., & Ratcliffe, A. W. (2011). Back to the future: Part III. *The Community Psychologist, 44*(1), 13–15.

Nelson, G., & Prilleltensky, I. (2010). *Community psychology: In pursuit of liberation and well-being* (2nd ed.). New York, NY: Palgrave Macmillan.

Newman, D. L., & Brown, R. D. (1996). *Applied ethics for program evaluation.* Thousand Oaks, CA: Sage.

O'Neill, P. O. (1989). Responsible to whom? Responsible for what? Some ethical issues in community intervention. *American Journal of Community Psychology, 17,* 323–341.

Paradis, E. K. (2000). Feminist and community psychology ethics in research with homeless women. *American Journal of Community Psychology, 28,* 839–858.

Phillips, E. N., Berg, M. J., Rodriguez, C., & Morgan, D. (2010). A case study of participatory action research in a public New England middle school: Empowerment, constraints, and challenges. *American Journal of Community Psychology, 46,* 179–194.

Prilleltensky, I. (2001). Value-based praxis in community psychology: Moving toward social justice and social action. *American Journal of Community Psychology, 29,* 747–778.

Rabinowitz, P., Berkowitz, B., & Brownlee, T. (n.d.). Ethical issues in community interventions. Retrieved from http://ctb.ku.edu/en/tablecontents/sub_section_main_1165.aspx

Reynolds, S. J. (2006). Moral awareness and ethical predispositions: Investigating the role of individual differences in the recognition of moral issues. *Journal of Applied Psychology, 19,* 233–243.

Roos, V., Visser, M., Pistorius, A., & Nefale, M. (2007). Ethics and community psychology. In N. Duncan, B. Bowman, A. Naidoo, J. Pillay, & V. Roos (Eds.), *Community psychology: Analysis, context and action* (pp. 392–407). Cape Town, South Africa: UCT Press.

Schwartz, J. P., & Hage, S. M. (2009). Prevention: Ethics, responsibility, and commitment to public well-being. In M. E. Kenny, A. M. Horne, P. Orpinas, & L. E. Reese (Eds.), *Realizing social justice: The challenge of preventive interventions* (pp. 123–140). Washington, DC: American Psychological Association.

Serrano-García, I. (1994). The ethics of the powerful and the power of ethics. *American Journal of Community Psychology, 22,* 1–20.

Snow, D. L., Grady, K., & Goyette-Ewing, M. (2000). A perspective on ethical issues in community psychology. In J. Rappaport & E. Seidman (Eds.), *Handbook of community psychology* (pp. 897–917). New York, NY: Kluwer Academic/Plenum.

Society for Community Research and Action. (n.d.). *About SCRA.* Retrieved from http://www.scra27.org/about

Walker, R., Hoggart, L., & Hamilton, G. (2008). Random assignment and informed consent: A case study of multiple perspectives. *American Journal of Evaluation, 29,* 156–174.

Yarbrough, D. B., Shulha, L. M. Hopson, R. K., & Caruthers, F. A. (2011). *The program evaluation standards: A guide for evaluators and evaluation users* (3rd ed.). Thousand Oaks, CA: Sage.

CHAPTER 6

Participatory Approaches for Conducting Community Needs and Resources Assessments

Jomella Watson-Thompson, Vicki Collie-Akers, Nikki Keene Woods, Kaston D. Anderson-Carpenter, Marvia D. Jones, and Erica L. Taylor

Jomella Watson-Thompson, Department of Applied Behavioral Science, Work Group for Community Health and Development, University of Kansas; Vicki Collie-Akers, Work Group for Community Health and Development, University of Kansas; Nikki Keene Woods, Department of Public Health Sciences, Wichita State University; Kaston D. Anderson-Carpenter, Work Group for Community Health and Development, University of Kansas; Marvia D. Jones, Work Group for Community Health and Development, University of Kansas; Erica L. Taylor, Work Group for Community Health and Development, University of Kansas.

Correspondence concerning this chapter should be addressed to Jomella Watson-Thompson, Department of Applied Behavioral Science, Work Group for Community Health and Development, University of Kansas, Lawrence, KS 66045.

OPENING EXERCISE

Have you ever completed a community survey or participated in the census? Have you participated in a public forum, focus group, or listening session? If your response was "yes," then you have participated in some form of an assessment. Prior to reading this chapter, reflect on your experiences with participating in assessments. Consider the following questions: (1) When was the last time you participated in some component of a community assessment? (2) How were you involved in the assessment process? (3) Based on your involvement in the process, what worked well? (4) What aspects of the assessment process would you have changed? Why?

OVERVIEW FOR CONDUCTING NEEDS AND RESOURCES ASSESSMENT

It is important for community psychologists to be competent in the practice of conducting community needs and resources assessments. Needs and resources assessments are often an integral component of most community-based processes and support other competency areas including planning, capacity building, evaluation, and sustainability. The assessment process assists stakeholders in systematically examining the context, conditions, and magnitude of an issue, while identifying available resources for addressing the matter. In this chapter, the historical context of conducting needs and resources assessments in community psychology is presented. Then, an overview of the general tasks and activities that support a needs and resources assessment in the community is provided, as well as a case example. Both formal and informal training opportunities are discussed that may enhance the skills and experience of practitioners in supporting the competency. Lastly, considerations for the future direction of community needs and resources assessment in community psychology are presented.

History of Community Needs and Resources Assessments in Psychology

During the 1960s, there was dissension among psychologists regarding the most appropriate response for addressing gaps in mental health due to limited psychological resources, services, and social supports (Nelson & Prilleltensky, 2005). A confluence of factors advanced interest in community mental health services, including the return of veterans from World War II, social, economic and racial injustices, as well as legislative mandates. Community psychology in the United States, which evolved from the Swampscott Conference of 1965, offered an expanded approach for supporting mental health needs at the community level.

Evolution of Community Needs and Resources Assessment. Psychologists began to develop formal approaches to assess community mental health needs in response to the passage of the 1963 legislation mandating comprehensive community mental health centers and the corresponding Community Mental Health Amendments of 1975, which supported the deinstitutionalization of mental health services (Innes & Heflinger, 1989; Warheit,

Vega, & Buhl-Auth, 1983). One of the first integrated models for conducting community needs assessments was introduced in 1976; it included the following five methods: key informant interviews, community forums, social indicator analysis, community surveys, and rates-under-treatment approaches (Innes & Heflinger, 1989; Warheit, Bell, & Schwab, 1976). The mental health community needs assessment methods were later generalized and applied more broadly to analyze gaps in human services (Innes & Heflinger, 1989). Although approaches for conducting assessments have continuously evolved, the early models demonstrated the importance of using both qualitative and quantitative methods to examine needs and resources in the community.

Conceptual Definition

A **community needs and resources assessment** is a comprehensive analysis that examines the historical and existing context, conditions, assets, and capacity of the community to respond to a community issue. A **community need** is the discrepancy or gap between the existing situation (what is) and the optimum state (what it should or is desired to be; Innes & Heflinger, 1989). The assessment process aims to identify and validate whether a **community issue** is a concern that matters to individuals and groups in the community. A **community resource** refers to existing assets at the individual, organizational, or community levels that can be mobilized to address an issue. Examples of community resources or assets that enhance the quality of life in a community may include human resources such as neighborhood residents, youth, agency staff, and elected officials; facilities such as schools, churches, and businesses; or amenities like parks, community gardens, and bicycle paths. Community psychology takes a strength-based approach that not only identifies community deficits, but also recognizes existing and potential resources that may contribute to addressing an issue (Arthur & Blitz, 2000).

A community needs and resources assessment supports the facilitation of a process that may result in a variety of outcomes, including increased knowledge and awareness about an issue, collaboration and consensus for addressing the issue, as well as direct products such as a report. Through the assessment process information is systematically collected, reviewed, and analyzed to examine issues within the context of existing conditions and available resources in the community. A resulting assessment report, or related products, provides a summary of the information gathered to support data-informed decision making.

Community Psychology Values and Principles for Conducting Assessments

There are some core values and principles of community psychology that influences how community psychologists conduct needs and resources assessments. As a community psychologist, it is important to ensure that the assessment is developed, conducted, and utilized in a manner that promotes the values of community psychology and empowers the individuals and groups involved to better address the issue. Based on principles of community psychology, the assessment process should be participatory, prevention-oriented, support an ecological perspective, and be action-focused.

Participatory evaluation. **Participatory evaluation,** as a collaborative process of systematic inquiry, actively engages stakeholders in all phases of the assessment, and has with the shared goal of utilizing information to support action in addressing an issue (Israel, Schulz, Parker, & Becker, 1998; Minkler & Wallerstein, 2008). Based on principles of participatory evaluation, the assessment process is inclusive and engages those individuals and groups most affected by the issue, as well as those in a position to contribute to addressing the problem (Minkler & Wallerstein, 2008). The representation of diverse stakeholders in the assessment process reduces individual biases and assumptions, while ensuring different perspectives, knowledge, and expertise. Participatory approaches for assessing community needs and resources enhances community capacity to respond to issues by allowing community members and groups to shape both how the problem is defined and examined (Arthur & Blitz, 2000). Additional types of evaluation commonly used in community psychology include empowerment evaluation and utilization-focused evaluation, which also support a collaborative approach for building the capacity of stakeholders to assess and evaluate community efforts.

Prevention-oriented. Based on a **prevention-oriented approach**, the potential antecedents (i.e., precursors) that serve as risk or protective factors associated with behaviors of interest in the community are examined as part of the assessment. Arthur and Blitz (2000) suggest, "the nature of prevention requires a slightly different approach to needs assessment . . . there is a fundamental difference between prevention and treatment that leads to different methods for needs assessment and service planning" (p. 243). Prevention-oriented assessment requires not only examining the present rate or incidences of problem behaviors, but also the future probability of needs and resources related to a community issue. For instance, examining adolescent substance abuse in the community cannot merely focus on existing rates of use, but must also consider the future probability of drug use by youth in the community to be preventative (Arthur & Blitz, 2000). Therefore, a prevention-oriented assessment permits understanding of community needs and resources across multiple levels of prevention including at the primary (i.e., protection from experiencing a problem), secondary (i.e., detection of elevated risk for problem), and tertiary (i.e., treatment and rehabilitation to minimize effects and reduce problem) levels.

Ecological perspective. Based on a holistic approach, behaviors and conditions are examined across multiple ecological levels as part of the assessment. An **ecological perspective** recognizes "the interaction between individuals and the multiple social systems in which they are embedded" (Nelson & Prilleltensky, 2005, p. 71). Risk and protective factors related to a community issue are examined across multiple socio-ecological domains including at the individual (e.g., history, experience), relational (e.g., family, peers), community (e.g., neighborhood, associations), and societal (e.g., culture, norms) levels.

Action-focused assessment. The community needs and resources assessment should provide information to identify and validate community issues to be addressed. The goal of the assessment is to support a collaborative process that enables informed decision making for planning and taking action on issues that matter to the community. The engagement of community stakeholders, including those most affected by the problem, is important for ensuring the assessment will lead to mobilization and action in the community.

TASKS AND SKILLS FOR CONDUCTING NEEDS AND RESOURCES ASSESSMENTS

In this chapter, eight key tasks, activities, and skills that guide the process of conducting needs and resources assessments are presented and are displayed in Figure 6.1.

Task 1: Identify the Purpose of the Assessment

Prior to engaging in assessment-related activities, the purpose of the assessment should be identified. A shared understanding among stakeholders of the intended function and uses of the assessment from the onset permits examination of the community issue in a way that guides decisions regarding stakeholder participation, assessment methods, and information collection, analysis, and presentation approaches. To identify the purpose of the assessment, determine why the assessment is being conducted, what will be better understood about the community issue and by whom, and how stakeholders will know if the assessment process and outcomes are achieved. Consider, "what should be known after conducting the assessment that is presently unknown?" To assist in examining the purpose, it is important to identify the conditions occasioning the assessment, as well as the level, scope, and time period of the assessment.

Examine the Context and Conditions Influencing the Assessment Process

The intended function of the assessment should be determined, which may include validating whether a new or present issue is a community problem, examining the need for new or existing community services and programs, and/or studying and gaining consensus on changing needs and resources in the community. The individuals or groups supporting the assessment should also examine the impetus of the assessment to minimize potential barriers and biases that could influence the process. Illustrative examples of factors that may occasion an assessment include the occurrence of either a positive (e.g., new leadership) or negative event (e.g., death in community) allocation of resources related to an issue, media attention to an issue, and/or interest and support for an issue by individuals or groups. Engaging community stakeholders from the onset in identifying the purpose and potential uses of the assessment enhances coordination and community support. **Stakeholders**, those individuals or groups who care about and have an interest in the issue, should include people who are most affected or have experienced the issue, as well as agency representatives and officials.

Identify the Level and Scope of the Assessment

A **community** is defined as individuals or groups who share a common place, interest, and/or experience (Fawcett et al., 2000). How the community is defined, and by whom, has

Figure 6.1 Tasks and Activities for Conducting a Community Needs and Resources Assessment

Tasks	Related Activities	Necessary Skills
Task 1: Identify the Purpose of the Assessment	• Examine assessment context and conditions • Identify the level and scope of the assessment • Identify the assessment time period	Listening to community members; facilitating dialogue; identifying and communicating with stakeholders; consensus building; collection and review of archival records
Task 2: Determine Assessment Components	• Identify questions to be answered by the assessment • Identify appropriate components of the assessment	Developing assessment questions; information gathering; categorizing and organizing information; consensus building
Task 3: Identify Appropriate Methods	• Ensure a participatory approach • Identify factors influencing appropriateness of methods • Select appropriate assessment methods	Active listening; group facilitation; public speaking, quick summation of ideas and conclusions; note-taking; consensus building; data collection and review
Task 4: Enhance Community Capacity to Assess	• Examine assessment capacity of partners • Enhance community capacity	Information collection; develop and maintain relationships; interpersonal communication; facilitate or identify training and technical support; assess individual and group skills
Task 5: Develop and Implement Assessment Plan	• Determine the objectives of the assessment • Identify strategies and develop action steps • Implement and regularly review plan	Developing measurable objectives; developing action plan; establish process to review and use plan; implementing or supporting assessment methods
Task 6: Analyze Assessment Results	• Identify appropriate analytic tools • Use appropriate analytic methods • Ensure accurate data citation and crediting	Data collection; data recording; data analysis and interpretation; identifying data limitations; citing and crediting sources
Task 7: Communicate the Results of the Assessment	• Engage stakeholders in determining report format • Disseminate report using multiple channels • Publicly present assessment for dialogue	Developing graphs; developing tables, visual displays of information; writing professional and community reports; presenting to community audiences; organizing and facilitating public dialogues; information dissemination
Task 8: Use Assessment to Guide Planning and Action	• Frame the issue and goals based on the assessment • Use the assessment for planning and evaluation • Regularly review and update the assessment	Information synthesis and analysis; active listening; group facilitation; consensus building; collecting and updating information

implications for how the issue will assessed. It is most common to consider the geographic scope (e.g., neighborhood, county) or boundaries of the community. Also, determine if the assessment is intended to better understand the needs and resources based on the experiences (e.g., race/ethnicity, education ability/disability) and interests (e.g., substance abuse, safety) of individuals and groups in the community.

Identify the Assessment Time Period

There are two aspects of the time period that are helpful to clarify prior to beginning the assessment process. The projected duration of the assessment process should be determined to inform the selection of appropriate and feasible assessment methodologies. There should also be some rationale in determining the retrospective period for which information will be collected. The time range being examined influences the analysis and assessment results. For instance, a community issue over the past 5 years may provide markedly different results than reviewing trends over a 10-year period.

Task 2: Determine the Appropriate Components of the Assessment

The type of information examined and presented in the assessment is determined by what needs to be further understood about the issue both in the community and by stakeholders. For each assessment component, appropriate questions are identified to guide data collection.

Identify Questions to Be Answered by the Assessment

The components of the assessment (e.g., community description, problem analysis) are determined based on the types of questions to be examined, which are identified by the individuals and groups conducting the assessment. To begin determining questions to be answered through the assessment, consider the basic prompts for information gathering: who, what, when, where, why, and how. Table 6.1 provides a brief summary of some initial questions that may be considered when probing for the types of information the assessment may address. Identifying the questions to be examined assists in determining appropriate components to be included in the assessment. For instance, if you are interested in knowing who and what types of people live in the community, then a community description should be developed as part of the assessment. Whereas a problem analysis should be included in the assessment if you want to know who is engaged in certain types of behaviors and the prevalence of problem behaviors in the community related to an issue.

Identify Appropriate Components of the Assessment

Core components often included in an assessment are a community description or profile, problem analysis, and a resource assessment. The appropriateness of various assessment components is guided by the type of questions to be answered based on the purpose of the assessment.

Table 6.1   Common Types of Questions Addressed by Community Assessment Components

Standard Prompts for Information Gathering	Community Description	Resource/Asset Analysis	Problem Analysis
Who?	❑ Who is in the community? ❑ Who are key people and leaders in the community? ❑ Who cares about the issue in the community?	❑ Who (individuals or groups) in the community have and/or can contribute to addressing the issue? ❑ Whom do people go to in the community for assistance?	❑ Who is presently engaged in the behavior(s) of interest? ❑ Who may be at risk for engaging in the problem behavior(s) now or in the future?
What?	❑ What are the characteristics of the people and groups in the community? ❑ What issues matter to people in the community?	❑ What resources/assets are present in the community? ❑ What skills or capabilities are present in individuals and/or groups in the community?	❑ What are the level, scope, and magnitude of the problem behavior(s)? ❑ What are the effects and results of the problem(s) in the community?
When?	❑ When was the community and/or group(s) established?	❑ When are resources available/unavailable?	❑ When do the behavior(s) of interest occur, and for how long?
Where?	❑ Where is the community located?	❑ Where are the resources/assets in the community?	❑ Where do the behavior(s) of interest occur?
Why?	❑ Why do people care about the issue in the community? ❑ Why is the issue a concern?	❑ Why are some individuals or amenities (e.g., open field for kids to play) identified to be assets?	❑ Why do people engage in the behavior(s) of interest?
How?	❑ How has the community changed or stayed the same? ❑ How has the nature of the issue changed?	❑ How are resources/assets in the community used? ❑ How much is allocated to the community or issue?	❑ How many people are involved in the behavior(s) of interest? ❑ How many people are affected by the issue?

Developing a community description. Most assessments include some information describing the people in the community. The **community description** provides an analysis of the environmental context and people in the community. Generally, the community description includes information pertaining to the demography, economy, geography, history, politics, governance, and leadership. The changes experienced in the environment or by people in the community over time are examined to provide a historical context. As part of the community description, the community being examined is clearly defined in terms of geographic and social boundaries. Ensure that the community description reflects the perspectives of individuals in the community based on how they view and describe the community.

Conducting a resource assessment. A resource assessment provides a systematic examination of capacity (i.e., collective skills, capabilities, and resources) in the community that can be used to address an issue. Community resources include both recognized and underutilized assets in the community that can be evoked in response to a problem. Engage the community in identifying the formal and informal resources that may exist in a community. Types of community resources are individuals, groups, physical structures, social networks, and institutions that can be used in responding to an issue. A resource assessment includes, but is not limited to an assessment of available services in the community.

Conducting a problem analysis. A **problem analysis** is the collection of information about a community issue to define and validate the level, severity, magnitude, and social concern in the community. The problem analysis dissects the community issue by examining the gap between the present and ideal state for behaviors and conditions that matter to people in the community (Innes & Heflinger, 1989; Work Group, 2010). Inherently, a needs assessment is conducted as an element of the problem analysis. The first step in conducting a problem analysis is to gather information that indicates the level and social importance of the issue. As summarized in Table 6.2, information is collected to examine the frequency, duration, scope, severity, impact, perceptions, and social concern related to the issue (Work Group, 2010). Information gathered to suggest the frequency of a behavior or condition should indicate how frequently the behaviors of interest occur. For instance, based on the example of underage drinking, it would be appropriate to examine how often youth are drinking.

There are two dimensions related to the duration or length of occurrence of the problem to be examined. Information is gathered about how long the behaviors of interest have occurred in the community to provide an historical context of the issue, and to determine if the issue is a new or is a persistent problem. The length of time that individuals engage in the behaviors is also identified to better understand if the behaviors are cyclical or occur during certain periods of time (e.g., adolescence) or over the life course.

In examining the scope and prevalence of the issue, determine how many individuals are involved (or not involved) in the behaviors of interest. Since there are multiple levels of prevention (i.e., primary, secondary, tertiary), examine the number of individuals presently engaged in the problem behaviors, as well as the range of individuals who may be at risk or universally affected by the issue (Arthur & Blitz, 2000).

Table 6.2   Categories of Types of Data to Examine in Conducting a Problem Analysis

Categories of Types of Data to Examine	Basic Questions to Answer Based on Collected Information	Some Appropriate Types of Assessment Methods to Consider
Frequency	• How frequently does the behavior(s) of interest occur? • How often do individuals engage in the behavior(s) of interest? • How has the occurrence of the behavior(s) changed over time?	• Survey, direct observation, review of secondary data
Duration	• How long does the behavior(s) of interest last? • How long has the behavior(s) been present (or not present) in the community?	• Review of seconday data, direct observation, interviews
Prevalence or Scope	• How many people are affected by the issue? • How many people are involved in the behavior(s) of interest? • How many people are at risk for engagement in the problem behavior in the future?	• Survey, direct observation, review of secondary data, mapping
Severity or Magnitude	• What are the effects or results of the issue to people and in the community? • What is the magnitude of (how large are) the effects? How substantial and significant are the effects?	• Survey, direct observation, review of secondary data, focus groups
Impact	• What are the positive and negative results related to the issue and efforts to address the problem in the community? • How does the behavior(s) or environmental condition(s) of interest relate to or influence other community issues? • Are there modifiable factors (i.e., risk and protective factors, personal and environmental factors) that can be addressed related to the issue that may be co-occurring with other community problems?	• Interviews, focus groups, listening sessions, photo voice
Social Concern	• Is the issue perceived to be a problem by individuals and groups in the community? • Are individuals and groups in the community aware of the issue? • How has the issue been validated or justified to be of community concern?	• Interviews, focus groups, listening sessions, review of secondary data (e.g., media outlets), Photovoice

Examine the severity and impact of the issue on individuals and groups in the community to better understand not only who is affected (i.e., scope), but how severely individuals and groups are impacted by the problem. In examining the severity, consider how the problem disturbs or disrupts the quality of life for those in the community. For some issues, particularly those related to mortality, there may be low prevalence of the problem, but the severity of the issue, such as for homicides, may be unacceptable in the community.

An analysis of the impact of the problem requires examining the consequences for addressing the issue in the community. Consider both the intended and unintended consequences, which may positively or negatively influence the issue and efforts to address the problem. In addition, it is critical to understand the interaction of the issue with other community problems. Determine risk and protective factors associated with the issue to identify if there are modifiable factors to address that may also contribute to improvements in other areas of concern.

A key element of a problem analysis is to examine the social significance or importance of the issue to determine if it is perceived by the community to be a problem. Often, the assessment process in itself increases awareness and provides validation for the issue as a community concern. It is critical to assess how individuals and groups both perceive and define the issue. The community issue should be defined in a manner that names and frames the problem in terms of environmental conditions and behaviors to be changed in the community. The way an issue is defined influences whether it is deemed to be a problem, the types of individuals and groups who care about the issue, as well as what may be appropriate intervention responses.

Task 3: Identify Appropriate Methods for Conducting Assessments

Ensure a Participatory Approach for Assessing Community Needs and Resources

Often, identifying methods to be used in an assessment can be a daunting task due to the sheer number of available methods and varied considerations related to the community context (e.g., size of community, subpopulations to be sampled). A participatory orientation can increase accessibility and social validity by engaging stakeholders who have knowledge of culturally appropriate approaches and access to different populations. A preliminary step before selecting methods to implement for a community needs and resources assessment is to determine the stakeholders, including organizational and community representatives, who are priority participants in the assessment. A community might choose to emphasize particular subpopulations (e.g., those whose voices are underrepresented, racial and ethnic minorities) or take a generalist approach to describing the needs and resources of the community as a whole. Regardless, being clear about who is afforded the opportunity to participate in the assessment is an important step in making decisions about what methods are used and with whom.

Identify Factors Influencing the Appropriateness of Methods

Historical, cultural, and political factors may influence the appropriateness of a method. Communities with a history of exploitation or unethical treatment may be less willing to complete some assessment methods that seem to be more research-oriented. Engaging stakeholders in the assessment process can help determine those methods that may be more comfortable, less risky, or generally more acceptable to certain populations. Communities, particularly those experiencing poor outcomes, can be over-assessed through top-down or external assessments that do not ultimately result in community interventions or improvement. Engaging community members from the populations most affected by the issue in the selection of methods may help eliminate unnecessary barriers.

The feasibility of conducting assessment approaches in terms of both human and financial resources is another important consideration. The budget available to support the assessment may inform the appropriateness of various types of methods. For instance, conducting and analyzing individual interviews and surveys may be time and resource intensive, whereas focus groups and listening sessions engage more people, which may make them more cost-efficient. Many secondary data sources are available at no cost or for small fees.

Select Appropriate Assessment Methods

The combined use of quantitative and qualitative methods, referred to as **mixed methods**, enhances the completeness of the data and permits a deeper understanding of the issue (Jick, 1983). Table 6.3 provides a brief overview of basic components of common types of qualitative and quantitative methods.

Qualitative methods generally employ narrative descriptions or thematic analyses to characterize the perceptions, attitudes, or beliefs of an individual or group. Qualitative methods assist in examining the context and conditions related to an issue, and aid in answering questions pertaining to the impact and social concern or validity for a community issue. Traditional forms of qualitative methods include interviews, focus groups, and listening sessions, while nontraditional approaches include observational methods. Interviews are a data collection method that provide insight into a person's experiences and perceptions about an issue by prompting the respondent to answer a series of open-ended questions.

Similar to interviews, focus groups ascertain perceptions, beliefs, and attitudes regarding issues, but convene a small group of people to discuss a specific topic and are moderated by a facilitator who helps guide the conversation. One type of focus group format is the root cause ("but why") analysis, which collects information about the conditions and factors underlying why a community problem exits by asking a series of "but why" questions to identify the root causes of an issue (Work Group, 2010). Then, after a listing of contributing factors or root causes has been developed, the facilitator can support a similar pattern of questioning to explore "if so, then what" can be done about each factor or cause. Listening sessions, also called public forums, gather information about perceptions of community needs and resources from a large number of people. Listening sessions are often useful before implementing other methods because the generative discussion resulting from broad questions asked in a public forum can be more deeply explored through other methods.

Method Components	Types of Qualitative Methods						Types of Quantitative Methods			
				Observational and Visual Analyses			Surveys			Secondary Data Sources/Archival Records
	Interview	Focus Group	Listening Session	Direct Observation	Geospatial Mapping	Photovoice	Cross-sectional (census survey)	Concerns Survey	Stakeholder Survey	
Requires facilitator/administrator	X	X	X			X	X	X	X	
Requires some type of recording or note-taking	X	X	X	X						
May be administered as group	X	X	X			X				
Collects information from/about individual	X			X			X	X	X	
Uses open-ended question format	X	X	X						X	
Uses close-ended questions and response options							X	X	X	
Records observed behaviors and environmental conditions				X		X				X
Data in form of number and statistics				X			X	X	X	X
Data in form of words, pictures, or objects	X	X	X	X	X	X				X

Photovoice, direct observation, and geospatial mapping are examples of qualitative methods that employ visual-based or observational approaches. Researchers or practitioners implementing a photovoice project engage community members in photographing the conditions that surround a topic of interest. After the completion of photo-taking, the facilitator guides participants through a process of selecting and making sense of photos that best depict the phenomena of interest. Direct observation can be another useful method for assessing community needs and resources. Observational approaches range from informal data collection methods such as windshield tours, which provide brief observations of community challenges and strengths identified while riding through a community, to more formal (and quantitative) applications in which the occurrence of behaviors (e.g., number of people smoking) or products of behavior (e.g., cigarette butts on the ground) are recorded. A way to represent the assets or needs of a community identified using any of the qualitative methods is to depict them on a map to visually show the geographic locations and distribution within the community.

Quantitative methods provide numerical and statistical data that assist in examining the frequency, prevalence, duration, and magnitude of specific behaviors (e.g., the proportion of adults in a community who are current smokers), which are often referred to as population-level outcomes. A couple of common types of quantitative methods include surveys and secondary data analyses. Surveys are a structured data collection approach that ask specific questions about behaviors (e.g., have you used alcohol in the past 30 days), experiences (e.g., have you been at a party where alcohol was provided to minors by an adult), and/or perspectives (e.g., do you think it is wrong for other youth your age to drink alcohol) related to an issue. There are several types of surveys that might be used including cross-sectional (census) surveys, stakeholder surveys, and concerns surveys. Through a cross-sectional survey information is collected at one point in time from a broad range of individuals from the population or community of interest. A stakeholder survey is used to obtain feedback from individuals in the organization or community, which may include community residents, service providers, field experts, and/or community partners. The aim of a concerns survey is to quantify community members' perceptions by having respondents rate 25 to 40 community issues for both importance and satisfaction with how well they are addressed in the community. Items rated as high importance and high satisfaction with implementation are identified as strengths, and items rated with high importance and low satisfaction are considered relative problems or needs for the community (Work Group, 2010).

Secondary data sources. Secondary data analysis refers to data collected by one entity and analyzed by another party to answer different questions. A number of federal, state, and local entities collect data regarding community health and development issues that may aid in understanding the needs and assets of a community. Examples include the Behavioral Risk Factor Surveillance System, Point-in-Time Counts of Homelessness, or Uniform Crime Reports. A common challenge with using public or archival records is that data may be analyzed at a level different from the unit of analysis for the assessment. Organizations collecting and managing these data sources often have procedures in place for other organizations to request de-identified data that can be analyzed locally. When developing the assessment plan, determine available, feasible, and appropriate data sources.

Task 4: Enhance Community Capacity to Assess

Community capacity is the collective skills, capabilities, and resources of a group to promote positive change and improvement in the community over time and across place. The community assessment process can enhance community capacity to both identify and address community issues.

Examine Assessment Capacity of Partners

Examine the capacity of the groups that have come together in common purpose to ensure sufficient support for the assessment process. Based on the goals of the assessment, the partnering organizations should also do a completeness check to identify additional stakeholders to include in the process, including those individuals and groups most affected by the issue. The participation of diverse stakeholders in the process will reduce the common challenge of redundancy in information collection across the community due to separate and uncoordinated efforts.

The complementary skills, experiences, and expertise of individuals and groups partnering to support the assessment process should be identified. For instance, if one of the identified assessment methods is geospatial mapping of resources, but the collaborative partners supporting the assessment do not have experience in this area, then it may be appropriate to identify others in the community with the desired skill who can assist or provide support. The individuals and groups supporting the assessment should also discuss and delineate clearly defined roles, responsibilities, and expectations. For instance, if a partner has skills in survey administration, it should be clearly understood by all parties the expectations for compensation, time commitment, and resources needed.

Enhance Community Capacity

The capacity of the partnering organizations and individuals, including those most affected by the problem, should be enhanced through the assessment process. A common method to increase the capacity of community members and groups is through training or technical assistance. According to Jackson et al. (2003), "enhancing 'capacity' involves training in 'needs assessment,' by which community deficits might be systematically identified" (p. 340). Through the assessment process, partnering individuals and groups gain skills and knowledge in the development and implementation of assessment methods. The completed assessment provides information that enhances the ability of the community to address the issue.

Task 5: Develop and Implement a Plan for Conducting the Assessment

Determine and State the Objectives of the Assessment

Develop a detailed plan to guide the assessment process and to ensure a shared understanding between stakeholders regarding the purpose and goals of the assessment. As a part of the plan, develop clear objectives that specify the timeframe in which the major goals of the assessment will be accomplished. It is helpful to develop written objective statements that are specific, measurable, attainable or achievable, realistic, timed, and challenging (SMART + C). An example of an objective statement to support the assessment is as follows: By March (within two months), information from five identified assessment methodologies will be collected and analyzed.

Identify Assessment Strategies and Develop Action Steps

In the plan, the strategies or data-gathering methods (e.g., focus group, archival records) selected to support each component (e.g., problem analysis, community description) of the assessment are identified. Then, for each strategy or assessment method, action steps are developed indicating the individuals or groups responsible for implementing specific assessment activities within a certain timeframe. Identify who will be responsible for conducting the assessment methods. In the plan, clearly specify the resources and collaborators needed to support each activity. In developing the action plans, community stakeholders should realistically consider the levels of support that are necessary and available to ensure the feasibility of the proposed assessment methods and components.

Implement and Review the Assessment Action Plan

The development and implementation of the action plan facilitates a consensus building process to support conducting the assessment. It is important to involve key stakeholders in the development, implementation, and regular review of progress in supporting the assessment action plan. As part of implementing the action plan, the assessment methods are conducted and the components of the assessment (e.g., problem analysis, community description) are developed, summarized, and presented. Stakeholders should ensure collective accountability in implementing, reviewing, and making adjustments to the plan. Figure 6.2 provides an illustrative example of an action plan to support implementation of one assessment method.

Task 6: Analyze the Results of the Assessment

Although it is important to identify appropriate analytical approaches to categorize and present the data, the primary function of the analyses is to occasion examination and use of the data to enhance community knowledge and understanding of the issue, as well as inform the decisions of individuals and groups to further address the issue. To guide and focus the analyses, the key questions sought to be answered by the assessment should continuously be reviewed to minimize the likelihood of analytic drift (i.e., the analyses do not answer the questions identified to be examined through the assessment). If necessary, the assessors should modify or update the questions to be answered as part of the assessment process to ensure the types of data collected align with the analysis plan for each component of the assessment. Some key activities that can assist in preparing the group to analyze assessment data include identifying analytic tools, using appropriate analytic methods, and ensuring accurate citation of referenced data.

Identify Appropriate Analytic Tools

Identify appropriate data analytic tools to assist with organizing, analyzing, and presenting the data. Statistical packages commonly used for analyzing quantitative data may include relatively simple tools such as Microsoft Excel and GraphPad Prism with more user friendly and attractive graphing options, to more robust data analytic programs such as SPSS, SAS, Statistica, MATLAB, and Mathematica. There are also computer assisted qualitative data analysis software (CAQDAS) packages such as ATLAS.ti, MAXqda, NVivo, N6 (NUD*IST), and Qualrus, which can be used to organize qualitative data from a variety of

Figure 6.2 Illustrative Example Action Plan for One Assessment Method

Assessment Method: Photovoice

Purpose of Methodology: The use of Photovoice will assist in gaining a youth perspective of the community conditions that contribute to or detract from health.

Objective: By April 1, 2012, 30 youths from the community will participate in Photovoice to collect and analyze images depicting community conditions about health.

Proposed Implementation Plan

Action Step	Who Will Implement	Date of Completion	Tools/ Resources Needed	Who Needs to Know
1. Develop clear description of procedures	Vicki/Work Group	12/1/2011	Photovoice protocols/methods	Health Department
2. Develop promotional material	Vicki/Work Group	12/1/2011	Computer, paper, printer	Health Department
3. Identify ways of recruiting youth from middle or high school	Jamie/ YWCA	12/1/2011	List of youth program participants, promotional material	Health Department, YWCA, local schools, parents
4. Identify "champions" who might promote involvement with youth and in the community	Keith/Health Department	12/1/2011	List of partners and stakeholders	Health Department, local schools
5. Purchase materials	Keith/Health Department	1/7/2012	Cameras/photo paper	Health Department fiscal personnel
6. Develop training materials	Vicki/Work Group	1/7/2012	Existing training materials	Not applicable
7. "Train" youth in conducting Phototvoice	Vicki/Work Group	1/5/2012	Meeting (facility, refreshments, projector, and computer)	YWCA, parents, youth photographers

Action Step	Who Will Implement	Date of Completion	Tools/ Resources Needed	Who Needs to Know
8. Conduct data collection by taking photos in community	Youth participants	1/16- 2/16/2012	Camera, youth photographers	YWCA, parents, youth photographers
9. Develop/print photos and display	Keith/Health Department	2/17/2012	Printer, paper	Not applicable
10. Hold group process meetings to analyze photos	Jamie/ YWCA	2/22/2012	Meeting room	YWCA, parents, youth photographers
11. Prepare photos with assigned captions	Youth participants	2/27/2012	Photos, papers, poster board	YWCA, parents, youth photographers
12. Prepare final presentation display of photos	Youth participants	3/15/2012	Photos, papers, poster board	YWCA, parents, youth photographers
13. Post overall presentation online and obtain community feedback on Photovoice display using an online discussion board	Vicki/Work Group	3/20/2012	Website, online discussion board	Health Department, youth, parents, community residents

sources including text, audio, and visual presentations. Although it is often appropriate that individuals or groups partnering to support the assessment have some familiarity with the use of appropriate software packages, the data analytic packages merely assist with organizing, computing, and presenting the data. The analyses require the ability to make sense and meaning of the data, as well as to recognize limitations in the data collection procedures, results and analyses.

Use Appropriate Analytic Methods

When analyzing data, carefully review and examine the data to identify both strengths and limitations of the information collected. For example, a strength could be that a large sample from an often excluded segment of the population (e.g., individuals who dropped out of high school) participated in data collection. Whereas, a limitation could be that the quantity of participants across race/ethnicity was too small to draw any conclusions for a subset of the participants. Consider and acknowledge the limitations regarding the inferences that can be made with the data collected. Inappropriately addressing these limitations can cause incorrect conclusions or attributions in the interpretation of the data. In order to generalize data to a broader population, evidence must be provided to ensure that data were collected from a representative sample. Also, it is important to be cautious about extrapolating data from small sample sizes. When communicating information about the analyses, clearly describe how data were collected and with whom to minimize overstating or misinterpreting the conclusions. For example, if characterizing findings from two focus groups, do not say, "Washington County residents feel that a critical need is to address transportation," but rather a more accurate characterization would be, "Focus group participants, who were elderly residents of Washington County, identified a critical need for addressing transportation."

Ensure Accurate Data Citation and Crediting

Establish the credibility and validity of the methods used by ensuring appropriate data citation and crediting of source information (Nelson & Prillelnetsky, 2005). Clearly indicate all sources of data included in the reported findings and acknowledge secondary data sources. The data collection methods used should be clearly noted in the assessment, as well as in communications with others to support further exploration of the data by individuals and groups, as well as permit ongoing updates or extensions to the assessment. For example, the use of geospatial mapping of outcomes may result in knowing that a particular neighborhood experiences disproportionate rates of violence, but may not provide much explanatory information, thus requiring additional data collection to better understand the implications of the findings.

Task 7: Communicate the Results of the Assessment

Engage Stakeholders in Determining the Report Format

After assessment data are collected, analyzed, and reviewed, the remaining task is to communicate the results of the assessment back to key stakeholders. Present the content in the assessment components (e.g., community description, problem analysis) in a format that is simple, concise, and visually appealing. Remember, the audience for the assessment report is community residents, including those affected by the problem, as well as organizational stakeholders. Write the summary findings using language and a format that is appropriate for a community audience. Visually display data including graphs, tables, and figures in a format that does not require a lot of interpretation or background reading. Also, consider the use of quick summary tools such as poster formats or infographics, which briefly summarizes information using visuals and concise statements. Infographics provide a series of integrated graphics and visual displays of information to succinctly communicate a story that efficiently presents complex information. For instance, the Robert Wood Johnson Foundation used an infographic saying "Better Education = Healthier Lives" to provide a visual story that depicts the relationship between education and the health of individuals and communities. The infographic provided visual images that depicted how college graduates live longer lives and have reduced risk for chronic illness.

Disseminate the Report Using Multiple Channels

Dissemination of the assessment data is an important step for increasing awareness about a community issue. It can also prompt community stakeholders to mobilize and advocate for new or expanded efforts. A core function of the data dissemination process is to support conditions that ensure the outcomes of the assessment matter to people in the community. The data from the assessment are a resource that may be used to build the capacity of stakeholder groups and the community. It is important to identify the key stakeholders to engage in dissemination, including those individuals and groups that participated in the assessment process.

Although reports are a commonly used mechanism for communicating the results of the assessment, they may not be the format preferred by stakeholders. Additional formats to consider include community report cards, fact sheets, and media releases. Use multiple formats and channels for communicating the results of the assessment to various community audiences.

Publicly Present the Assessment for Community Dialogue

Ultimately, the goal of disseminating the assessment findings is to occasion dialogue about the problem in the community. Community psychologists do not merely provide the data to community stakeholders, but also work with partners to support mechanisms (e.g., public forums, media releases) that ensure information is appropriately presented to and interpreted by broader audiences. The presentation and delivery of information contributes to how the issue is named and framed in the community as a problem, which later informs the selection of appropriate strategies to address the issue. For instance, when providing data related to community issues such as racial disparities in infant mortality, the initial response by the community may be blaming the victims (pregnant women), rather than also examining the context in which the problem occurs (e.g., disparities in access to care). The facilitation of presented information and resulting dialogue is critical and informs the approaches that will be taken to support future action related to the issue.

Task 8: Use the Needs and Resources Assessment Results for Improvement

The findings presented in the needs and resources assessment set the stage for community action and collaborative problem solving. Once the community issue has been defined within the context of needs and available resources, the assessment findings are used to support meaningful change and improvements in community outcomes. The needs assessment is a mechanism that can move stakeholders from problem and resource identification to planning and mobilizing resources to support community action.

An example of a practitioner reflection of assessment follows:

> Though the process of conducting a community assessment to understand needs and resources for after-school programs for youth, I learned the importance of providing services deemed important by the people you want to serve versus providing a service that you think the people need. . . . I also valued the process of selecting appropriate tools to use in gathering information that reflected the audience or could be done in a specific timeframe to allow us to get the best response from the community. Most importantly, the value of developing the report, provided a resource for the community that could be used for multiple purposes including: to serve as benchmarks, to avoid duplication of services, and to better understand groups of people in the same community, who often may have different experiences, outlook and often desiring different outcomes. (Dola Gabriel, Community Mobilizer)

Frame the Community Issues or Goals Using the Assessment

The assessment results inform or validate the naming and framing of the community issues or potential goals (Work Group, 2010). **Problem framing** refers to the process of creating a description of a problem or goal in a manner that occasions future action. An appropriate framing of a problem or goal can attract participation from diverse community members and stakeholders interested in addressing the problem. In framing the problem, avoid assigning blame. Consider the following two framings: Schools are not doing enough to ensure that students complete high school. Or there are too few community supports to ensure that students complete high school, with the result that students are dropping out of school. The first framing infers that schools alone are responsible for ensuring that students complete high school. Conversely, the second statement supports the open involvement of a broader set of partners in collaborating to address the issue. The framing of the issue begins to inform what can be done to address the problem. Based on an ecological perspective, framing the issue more broadly makes it more likely that strategies will be identified that address the issue, at not only the individual level (e.g., knowledge and skills of students), but also to promote change within the environment (e.g., family support, school policy) and broader context (e.g., disproportionate allocation of resources across schools).

Use the Assessment to Guide Planning and Evaluation Activities

Following the community assessment, community stakeholders and collaborative partners should begin to immediately examine appropriate intervention responses and develop a course of action. To ensure that the assessment can be appropriately used in decision making, it is necessary to broadly disseminate the report to multiple and diverse community audiences and stakeholders. The community needs and resources assessment is a tool that can be used to support planning, implementation, and evaluation activities. During planning, the data from the assessment may serve as baseline indicators from which objectives are developed. Data presented in the assessment may also support evaluation by providing indicators of intervention effectiveness.

Regularly Review and Update the Assessment

The assessment should be regularly reviewed and updated by partners and key stakeholders to celebrate accomplishments, and to make necessary adjustments to increase the likelihood of effectiveness. It is critical that stakeholders are continuously informed of the progress toward improvements in outcomes, as well as any challenges experienced in responding to the community issue. Determine a mechanism for regularly communicating and providing feedback to community audiences and stakeholders about the assessment, which will make it more likely that partners integrate the use of the assessment in practice, and will support actions resulting from the assessment.

Over time, the needs and resources present within a community may change. There are a variety of environmental factors that influence the needs and resources of a community, such as demographic shifts and changes in funding. Review and regularly update the assessment components, at an interval agreed upon by collaborative stakeholders, to support continued use and accuracy of the information. Stakeholders should agree upon feasible methods for updating the assessment. An ongoing and coordinated plan between collaborative partners to contribute to updating the assessment can feasibly ensure current information is available for decision making.

APPLICATION SCENARIO: LAWRENCE-DOUGLAS COUNTY COMMUNITY HEALTH ASSESSMENT

Douglas County is a mid-sized Midwestern county in Kansas with a population of approximately 110,000 residents. The Lawrence-Douglas County Health Department (LDCHD) facilitated a collaborative process for conducting a community health assessment as part of the requirements for Public Health Accreditation. The accreditation process required an assessment of health status, including the community conditions that contribute to or detract from health, and the assets available in the community to address health.

The LDCHD established a multi-sector steering committee to guide the overall approach to assessment and supported implementation of different assessment methodologies. In addition to meeting criteria for Public Health Accreditation, the administration of the LDCHD endeavored to examine health disparities present in the county using a mixed methods approach for collecting data, particularly from underrepresented populations (i.e., racial and ethnic minorities, low-income populations, and residents of the small communities outside the main population center in the county).

To provide technical assistance in conducting the assessment, the LDCHD established a relationship with a local academic partner, the University of Kansas Work Group for Community Health Department. The academic partners assisted the LDCHD by preparing plans and tools (e.g., structured interview scripts, survey drafts) for implementation of several different assessment methodologies. The steering committee identified several appropriate methods including: concerns surveys, key informant interviews, focus groups, photovoice, geospatial depictions of health care utilization data, a Local Public Health

System Assessment, and a compilation of community and health status indicators from secondary data sources. The integration of both quantitative and qualitative methods permitted LDCHD to examine different aspects of health disparities in the county. The steering committee was extensively engaged in developing and providing feedback on the assessment plans.

Quantitative methods were used to examine the frequency, scope, prevalence, and magnitude of the community health issues. The concerns survey provided a quantitative description of perceived strengths and problems encountered in Douglas County. Secondary data sources regarding demographics, health status, health behaviors, and clinical indicators were compiled to provide a quantitative set of data reflecting the health of county residents. Sources of data included the U.S. Census Bureau, the Kansas Department of Health and Environment, the Kansas Bureau of Labor Statistics, and the Centers for Disease Control and Prevention.

A combination of qualitative methods was used to provide opportunities for diverse engagement to permit a deeper understanding of the data. Through the focus groups, qualitative information was collected. Focus groups were conducted at various sites including the public housing authority, Native American college, and African American churches to help the LDCHD meet its goals of ensuring that people generally underrepresented in assessment data participated in data collection. To engage youth, another underrepresented voice, photovoice was used as a nontraditional assessment method. The LDCHD partnered with a local youth-serving organization that had a specific focus on the arts to train and involve youth in photovoice methodology, analysis, and reporting of results to depict problems in the community.

Based on a partnership established between the LDCHD and the local hospital, information was compiled about how health care utilization varies geographically within the county. This method, also referred to as hotspotting (Gwande, 2011), mapped de-identified data regarding health care utilization at the census tract level to reveal small pockets of the community in which health care utilization was concentrated.

In total, more than 1,500 community residents were engaged in some form of assessment data collection. The steering committee was satisfied that the assessment revealed disparities and that underrepresented groups participated in the assessment. Using both quantitative and qualitative data, 13 issues related to health or social determinants of health were identified. Four open community forums were held to review the assessment findings, and participants attending the forums prioritized the issues. Based on community prioritization, the following five community issues were identified: access to healthy foods, engagement in physical activity, poverty and the lack of jobs, access to mental health services, and access to health-care services.

TRAINING, EDUCATION, AND EXPERIENCES TO FACILITATE THE DEVELOPMENT OF THE COMPETENCY

There are a variety of formats including training, technical assistance, and applied experiential learning opportunities that can provide specialized knowledge and skills required for

Photo 6.1   Community members come together to engage in a community needs assessment.

Source: Jomella Watson-Thompson.

conducting community needs and resources assessments. Training can be supported through informal mechanisms, such as technical assistance offered by local government or formal offerings by academic partners through certifications or academic courses (Israel et al., 2010). The appropriateness of various types of training and support depends on several factors including availability of funds, depth of knowledge needed, available time, and immediacy of the need.

Technical assistance, the provision of supports to offer advice, consultation, training or resources by an individual or group with expertise, may enhance the capacity of the community to support an assessment, as well as offer a less expensive option for supporting specific assessment needs. Technical assistance (TA), as a form of support, is beneficial to practitioners and others working in the field, including community residents. Consider obtaining TA by hired consultants or academic partners who work with individuals or groups to increase skills to support conducting an assessment. A strength of TA is it provides just-in-time supports to meet very specific capacity needs by focusing on the development of a subset of skills. At times, it is appropriate for the TA provider to directly perform the needed function such as with data analysis. The time allotted for the assessment process is an important consideration when identifying appropriate opportunities for types of training and/or TA.

Training opportunities are often available in the form of certification options for practitioners and residents as an incentive for completing training. Certifications may be related to professional standards for practitioners or community-level certifications for residents who may not have formal academic degrees. There are a number of academic courses available to both traditional and nontraditional students. The courses sometimes provide opportunities for formal certification in service learning or are part of a series of courses for a more advanced certificate (Buckner, Ndjakani, Banks, & Blumenthal, 2010). Academic courses are also available that include an emphasis on experiential learning, such as community cooperative courses or practicum experiences. These experiential courses provided the learner the opportunity to work directly with a community-based organization to enhance specific capacities. As an example, the University of Kansas offers a graduate certificate program in community health and development for non-degree seeking graduate-level students, which allows professionals not enrolled in graduate school to obtain training in competencies, including community assessment. The certificate program includes a series of three courses, including one lecture course in community health and development competencies, followed by two semesters of a practicum in which the students receive technical assistance from the instructors in applying the competencies to address a community issue. Other formal instances of community needs assessment training include workshops at professional conferences or memberships in professional associations. For instance, the Community Anti-Drug Coalitions of America offers several types of training and technical assistant platforms for individual community leaders, stakeholders, or groups affiliated with a community anti-drug coalition.

FUTURE DIRECTIONS FOR COMMUNITY NEEDS AND RESOURCES ASSESSMENTS

Conducting community needs and resources assessments remains critical for addressing community health and development issues. Understanding the characteristics of community-determined issues, including the level, scope, and magnitude, is fundamental to appropriately define the problem in ways that permit the mobilization of assets and resources. Although the general purpose for conducting needs and resources assessments has remained relatively consistent over time, there is an expanded array of approaches and methods available to employ. The visual display of data continues to advance options for both assessment methods and analytical techniques. Community practitioners need to continuously advocate for and support appropriate assessment methods that ensure community sensitivity and cultural appropriateness. By engaging community stakeholders in the assessment process, community practitioners can continue to advance the use of innovative, feasible, and sensitive approaches that do not compromise community access and participation in assessments.

As technology continues to advance, the methods and tools used to conduct assessments will continue to become more robust. The integration of technology for both collecting and visually displaying information advances the assessment process. For instance, the use of word clouds, which graphically display the frequency and prominence of key words used by participants of qualitative methods, has become an innovative approach to quickly summarize and present information from thematic analyses. There are now a variety of free online word tools that can assist in developing word cloud displays.

Although the integration of technology to strengthen and modernize assessment methods is important, the deployment of technological advances must be balanced with ensuring equitable participation in the assessment process. Technology-based approaches are appropriate to use when they enhance the process and do not limit equitable participation. For instance, the administration of a web-based survey or focus group in a low-income community may be inappropriate. Community practitioners should ensure that the technology used to support assessments allows the participation by the least resourced members of the community.

It is important that community practitioners continue to uphold values and principles, like those of community psychology, when conducting community needs and resources assessments to support processes that are participatory, prevention-oriented, ecological-based, and action oriented. Although participatory approaches to assessment may require more time to equitably involve multiple and diverse community representatives, they are necessary in addressing problems related to community health disparities. Partnerships between community stakeholders and academic partners, as well as other technical assistance providers, are important to continuously enhance the assessment capacity of communities.

SUMMARY

- Conducting community needs and resources assessments is a fundamental competency integral to supporting other competencies, including planning and evaluation.

- The assessment process occasions systematic information gathering, review, and analysis to examine issues within the context of community conditions, needs, and resources.

- Based on the values of community psychology, it is important to ensure that the assessment process is participatory, is prevention oriented, supports an ecological perspective, and is action focused.

- Standard components of an assessment generally include a community description, problem analysis, and resources assessment.

- The eight tasks that support conducting a community needs and resources assessment are: Task 1: Identify the purpose of the assessment; Task 2: Determine assessment components; Task 3: Identify appropriate methods; Task 4: Enhance community capacity to assess; Task 5: Develop and implement the assessment plan; Task 6: Analyze assessment results; Task 7: Communicate the results of the assessment; and Task 8: Use the assessment to guide planning and action.

- The combined use of quantitative and qualitative methods, referred to as mixed methods, enhances the completeness of the data and permits a deeper understanding of the issue.

- The deployment of technological advances in supporting the assessment must be balanced with ensuring equitable participation in the assessment process, including by the least resourced individual(s) or group(s) in the community.

- Both formal and informal supports are available to develop the skills of individuals and groups to conduct assessments, including through training, technical assistance, and experiential learning opportunities.

DISCUSSION QUESTIONS

1. What are the three most important things you learned about conducting a resources and needs assessment, and why?

2. In what ways can practitioners uphold the values and principles of community psychology when conducting community needs and resources assessments?

3. How would you determine the most appropriate methods to use in conducting an assessment? And how would you engage underrepresented populations in the assessment process through the use of the selected methods?

4. What can be done to support the use of the community assessment by key audiences and stakeholders to ensure its use in decision making?

5. What specific resources are available to you to further develop your ability to conduct a community resources and needs assessment? Be sure to consider both local and global (Internet) resources.

Table 6.4 Rapid Survey of Task Competence in Conducting a Community Assessment

Tasks and Related Activity Components for Conducting a Community Needs and Resources Assessment
Task 1: Define the assessment purpose. To support implementation of this task, you should be able to conduct the following activities: (a) Examine the context and conditions regarding why an assessment should be conducted; (b) Identify the level and scope of the assessment; and (c) Identify the time frame for conducting the assessment. *Rate your ability to implement this task and related activities.* ☐ **Poor**　　☐ **Fair**　　☐ **Good**　　☐ **Very Good**　　☐ **Excellent**

Task 2: Enhance organizational and community capacity to conduct a needs and resources assessment.

To support implementation of this task, you should be able to conduct the following activities:

(a) Examine the capacity of partners to conduct an assessment; (b) Enhance the capacity of partner organizations to conduct the assessment; and (c) Use the assessment process to build the capacity of the community to address the issue.

Rate your ability to implement this task and related activities.

☐ **Poor**   ☐ **Fair**   ☐ **Good**   ☐ **Very Good**   ☐ **Excellent**

Task 3: Determine the components of the needs and resources assessment.

To support implementation of this task, you should be able to conduct the following activities:

(a) Determine if a community description is appropriate to include in the assessment; (b) Determine if a problem analysis will be included in the assessment; and (c) Determine if a resources assessment will be included.

Rate your ability to implement this task and related activities.

☐ **Poor**   ☐ **Fair**   ☐ **Good**   ☐ **Very Good**   ☐ **Excellent**

Task 4: Identify appropriate assessment methods.

To support implementation of this task, you should be able to conduct the following activities:

(a) Promote use of participatory methods; (b) Identify appropriate use of mixed methods (i.e., quantitative and qualitative data collection); and (c) Determine appropriate methods to be used to support each component of the assessment.

Rate your ability to implement this task and related activities.

☐ **Poor**   ☐ **Fair**   ☐ **Good**   ☐ **Very Good**   ☐ **Excellent**

Task 5: Develop and implement the assessment plan.

To support implementation of this task, you should be able to conduct the following activities:

(a) Determine the objectives for conducting the assessment; (b) Identify strategies and develop action steps for implementing the assessment; and (c) Implement and regularly review the plan for conducting the assessment.

Rate your ability to implement this task and related activities.

☐ **Poor**   ☐ **Fair**   ☐ **Good**   ☐ **Very Good**   ☐ **Excellent**

Task 6: Analyze the assessment results.

To support implementation of this task, you should be able to conduct the following activities:

(a) Identify and review the key questions to be answered by the assessment; (b) Use appropriate analytical methods to examine assessment results; and (c) Provide accurate citations and crediting for assessments data.

Rate your ability to implement this task and related activities.

☐ **Poor**   ☐ **Fair**   ☐ **Good**   ☐ **Very Good**   ☐ **Excellent**

(Continued)

Table 6.4 (Continued)

Task 7: Communicate and disseminate assessment findings.

To support implementation of this task, you should be able to conduct the following activities:

(a) Engage stakeholders in determining appropriate format for the report or related materials summarizing assessment results; (b) Disseminate the report through multiple channels and stakeholders; and (c) Publicly present the assessment to occasion community dialogue.

Rate your ability to implement this task and related activities.

☐ Poor   ☐ Fair   ☐ Good   ☐ Very Good   ☐ Excellent

Task 8: Use the assessment results for improvement.

To support implementation of this task, you should be able to conduct the following activities:

(a) Frame the problem based on the assessment findings; (b) Use the assessment to guide planning and evaluation; and (c) Regularly review and update the assessment with community partners and stakeholders.

Rate your ability to implement this task and related activities.

☐ Poor   ☐ Fair   ☐ Good   ☐ Very Good   ☐ Excellent

KEY TERMS AND DEFINITIONS

Community: Individuals and groups who share a common place, interest, or experience.

Community capacity: Collective skills, capabilities, and resources of a group to promote positive change and improvement in the community over time and across people.

Community description: Analysis of the environmental context and people in the community.

Community issues: Community needs that have been identified to be of concern and matter to individuals and groups in the community.

Community need: Discrepancy or gap between the existing situation (what is) and the optimum state (what it should or is desired to be be).

Community needs and resources assessment: A comprehensive analysis that examines both the historical and existing context, conditions, assets, and capacity of the community to respond to a community-level problem.

Community resource: Existing asset present at the individual, organizational, or community level that can be mobilized to address a community issue.

Ecological perspective: Recognizes the interaction between individuals and the multiple social systems in which they are embedded.

Mixed methods: The combined use of quantitative and qualitative methods.

Participatory evaluation: Collaborative process of systematic inquiry that engages stakeholders in all phases of the assessment, with the goal of using information to address the issue.

Prevention-oriented approach: Examines the potential antecedents (i.e., precursors) that serve as risk or protective factors associated with behaviors of interest in the community.

Problem analysis: Collection of information about a community issue to define and validate the level, severity, magnitude, and social concern for the issue as a problem in the community.

Problem framing: The process of creating a description of a problem or goal in a manner that occasions future action.

Qualitative methods: Information-gathering approaches that provide narrative descriptions or thematic analyses characterizing the perceptions, attitudes, or beliefs of an individual or group.

Quantitative methods: Data collection approaches that provide numerical and statistical data describing the frequency and scope of particular behaviors.

Stakeholders: Those individuals or groups who care about and have an interest in an issue.

Technical assistance: The provision of supports to offer advice, consultation, training, or resources by an individual or group with expertise.

RESOURCES AND EXAMPLES

Resources and Toolkits for Developing Community Assessments

Centers for Disease Control and Prevention. *Community health assessment and group evaluation (CHANGE): Building a foundation of knowledge to prioritize community needs*: http://www.cdc.gov/healthycommunitiesprogram/tools/change.htm

Community Anti-Drug Coalitions of America. *Assessment primer: Analyzing the community, identifying problems and setting goals*: http://www.cadca.org/resources/detail/assessment-primer

Community Tool Box. *Developing a plan for assessing local needs and resources*: http://ctb.ku.edu/en/tablecontents/sub_section_main_1019.aspx

University of Wisconsin Population Health Institute. County Health Rankings: http://www.county-healthranings.org/

Examples of Community Needs and Resources Assessments

Lawrence-Douglas County Health Department. *Douglas County community health assessment report*: http://ldchealth.org/download/Information/About%20The%20Community/Community%20Health%20Improvement%20Plan/2012%20Community%20Health%20Assessment.pdf

Minnesota Department of Health. *Community assessment*: Accessed from http://www.health.state.mn.us/divs/hpcd/chp/hpkit/text/phase1.htm

Rotary International. *Community assessment tools*: http://www.rotary.org/ridocuments/en_pdf/605c_en.pdf

Resources for Training Opportunities

Community Anti-Drug Coalitions of America. *National Coalition Academy training for coalitions*: http://www.cadca.org/trainingevents/training-coalitions

REFERENCES

Arthur, M., & Blitz, C. (2000). Bridging the gap between the science and practice in drug abuse prevention through needs assessment and strategic community planning. *Journal of Community Psychology, 28*(3), 241–255.

Buckner, A., Ndjakani, Y., Banks, B., & Blumenthal, D. (2010). Using service-learning to teach community health: The Morehouse School of Medicine Community Health Course. *Academic Medicine, 85*(10), 1645.

Fawcett, S. B., Francisco, V. T., Hyra, D., Paine-Andrews, A., Schultz, J. A., Roussos, S., . . . Evensen, P. (2000). *Building healthy communities*. In A. R. Tarlov & R. F. St. Peter (Eds.), *The society and population health reader: A state and community perspective* (pp. 314–334). Itasca, IL: F. E. Peacock.

Gwande, A. (2011). The hot spotters. *The New Yorker*. Retrieved from http://www.newyorker.com/magazine/2011/01/24/the-hot-spootters

Innes, R. B., & Heflinger, C. A. (1989). An expanded model of community assessment: A case study. *Journal of Community Psychology, 17,* 225–235.

Israel, B., Coombe, C., Cheezum, R., Schulz, A., McGranaghan, R., Lichtenstein, R., . . . Burris, A. (2010). Community-based participatory research: A capacity-building approach for policy advocacy aimed at eliminating health disparities. *American Journal of Public Health, 100*(11), 2094.

Israel, B. A., Schulz, A. J., Parker, E. A., & Becker, A. B. (1998). Review of community based research: Assessing partnership approaches to improve public health. *Annual Review of Public Health, 19,* 173–202.

Jackson, S. F., Cleverly, S., Poland, B., Burman, D., Edwards, R., & Robertson, A. (2003). Working with Toronto neighbourhoods towards developing indicators of community capacity. *Health Promotion International, 18,* 339–350.

Jick, T. (1983). Mixing qualitative and quantitative methods: Triangulation in action. In J. Van Maanen (Ed.), *Qualitative methodology* (pp. 135–148). Beverly Hills, CA: Sage.

Minkler, M., & Wallerstein, N. (Eds.). (2008). *Communication based participatory research for health: From process to outcomes*. San Francisco, CA: Wiley.

Nelson, G., & Prilleltensky, I. (2005). Community psychology: Journeys in the global context. In G. Nelson & I. Prilleltensky (Eds.), *Community psychology in pursuit of liberation and well-being*. New York, NY: Palgrave Macmillan.

Warheit, G. J., Bell, R. A., & Schwab, J. J. (1976). *Needs assessment approaches: Concepts and methods*. Washington, DC: National Institute of Mental Health.

Warheit, G. J., Vega, W., & Buhl-Auth, J. (1983). Mental health needs assessment approaches: A case for applied epidemiology. *Prevention in Human Services, 2,* 9–34.

Work Group for Community Health and Development. (2010). *Promoting community health and development: The community tool box curriculum*. Lawrence: University of Kansas.

Organizational and Community Capacity Building

*Scotney Evans, Catherine Raymond,
and Douglas D. Perkins*

OPENING EXERCISE

East Nashville teenagers and their families are angry. The local neighborhood public high school serving mostly low-income youth is not adequately preparing students for post-secondary education. Results of a recent student survey indicate that while 90% of students at the school aspire to post-secondary education, only about one third had met with a guidance counselor to make a plan for how to get there. Those that did meet with guidance counselors had, on average, only met with counselors between two and four times for about an hour total. Additionally, many students reported that they do not know how they would pay for college even if accepted. School administrators feel they are constrained by the limited funds and lack of support coming from the school district. Students and their parents just want a dedication to college readiness equal to that of schools in more affluent neighborhoods. One local organization—Community IMPACT (CI) Nashville— is determined to do something about this problem.

CI is a small, grassroots, neighborhood-based nonprofit organization that has a mission to engage marginalized young people in creating community change on the issues that affect their lives. Due to limited resources, CI has only a small staff of young community organizers and limited organizational capacity to affect change on this complex issue. While youth and families in the community want to play a role, CI has been unable to create and implement a strategy to meaningfully engage local youth in this issue in a sustainable way. Additionally, the East Nashville community has a high number of families living in poverty and many are disconnected from the discussions and decisions that affect their lives. Although they care about this issue, very few feel that they have the knowledge, skills, and support they need to take coordinated action.

Now imagine that you've been asked to help CI, the local high school, and the residents build capacity to be able to affect change on this issue. Where would you start? How would you go about building organizational and community capacity for change? What knowledge, skills, and attributes would *you* need to be able to work alongside them to build their capacity to get what they need on this issue? We'll explore answers to these questions in this chapter.

OVERVIEW

Organizational and community capacity are closely linked due to the fact that much action to improve communities occurs in, and through, organizations. Strong, effective organizations can play a significant role in building and supporting community capacity. For example, organizations are instrumental in building local capacity for community engagement in planning and governance, for the production of services such as housing or job training and placement, and for the capacity to inform, organize, and mobilize residents toward shared goals (Chaskin, 2001). Nonprofit, community-based organizations, with their community-oriented missions, can be particularly important to the development and maintenance of community capacity. Additionally, given the complexity of social and environmental problems and the unrelenting pressure to reduce the cost of creating and implementing solutions, interorganizational collaboration and working through networks offer ways to develop and share knowledge and weave together capacities that can achieve greater impact (Plastrik & Taylor, 2006; Scearce, Kasper, & Grant, 2009).

In this chapter we first introduce the concepts of *organizational capacity* and *organizational capacity building* and explore these in some detail. Then we explore the related concepts of *community capacity* and *community capacity building*. From there we highlight the specific practitioner knowledge, skills, and abilities associated with the competency and identify the training, education, and other experiences that facilitate the development of these competencies. We end with a look at a real-world application of this competency and a discussion of future trends in organizational and community capacity building. While the ideas presented in this chapter can be applied to many different types of organizations in communities, we focus specifically on the organizational capacity of nonprofit organizations to provide effective services, build community capacity, and promote social change. Nonprofits are those community-based organizations that operate exclusively for charitable, community-building, advocacy, or educational purposes and are neither traditional for-profit businesses nor governmental agencies. Examples include many community organizations with which you frequently interact, such as social service agencies, religious organizations (e.g., churches, temples), or museums.

CONCEPTUAL DEFINITIONS

Organizational Capacity

What do we mean by *organizational capacity*? Although there is not one commonly agreed-upon definition, recognized leaders in the field generally focus on an organization's ability to "do things"—to achieve, perform, or be effective in executing actions that support an organization's goals, mission, and sustainability. For instance, Dougherty and Mayer (2003, p. 2) define **organizational capacity** as the "the combined influence of an organization's abilities to govern and manage itself, to develop assets and resources, to forge the right community linkages, and to deliver valued services—all combining to meaningfully address its mission." For Letts, Ryan, and Grossman (1999), organizational capacity is reflected in an organization's "ability to develop, sustain, and improve the delivery of a mission" (p. 4). Or Light (2004), who describes capacity as "everything an organization uses to achieve its mission, from desks and chairs to programs and people" (p. 14).

Conceptually, we think of organizational capacity as consisting of distinct domains that each represents an aspect of an organization such as governance, organizational culture, or technical abilities. While there is certainly overlap and interdependence among the various domains, segmenting organizational capacity can be helpful when assessing an organization's capacity and designing and implementing interventions to build capacity.

Researchers and practitioners have developed a number of frameworks to conceptualize organizational capacities that differ primarily in how the different aspects of an organization are emphasized and grouped into domains. With its focus on adaptation and leadership, the authors of this chapter have found Connolly and York's (2003) framework to be very relevant to organizational and community capacity building and simple to use in practice. Connolly and York describe four core domains of organizational capacity: adaptive capacity, leadership capacity, management capacity, and technical capacity. **Adaptive capacity** refers to "the ability of a nonprofit organization to monitor, assess, and respond to internal and external changes" (p. 20) through activities such as strategic planning, developing beneficial collaborations, scanning the environment, and assessing organizational performance. **Leadership capacity** is "the ability of all organizational leaders to inspire, prioritize, make decisions, provide direction and innovate, all in an effort to achieve the organizational mission" (p. 20) through activities such as promoting the organization within various stakeholder (i.e., constituent) communities, and setting and communicating organizational priorities. **Management capacity** refers to "the ability of a nonprofit organization to ensure the effective and efficient use of organizational resources" (p. 20) through, for example, effective personnel and volunteer policies. And finally, **technical capacity** is "the ability of a nonprofit organization to implement all of the key organizational and programmatic functions" (p. 20) such as delivery of programs and services, effectively managing organizational finances, conducting evaluation activities, and raising funds.

Organizational capacity is not static: It changes over time. To a significant extent, organizational capacity is developmental in the sense that it is, in part, a function of organizational age and size. As organizations mature and grow, their capacities and capabilities change, much as an individual's capacities and capabilities change over time. Organizations can also lose capabilities and capacities through, for example, staff turnover, lack of organizational learning systems, a reduction in resources, or the failure to update technology systems.

Organizational capacity also varies from organization to organization. There is not a universal standard—a single "right way"—by which all organizations should operate. Different organizations provide different types of services and face different circumstances and operating environments. For example, the Building Movement Project (www.buildingmovement.org)

has a specific framework for thinking about the organizational capacities, strategies, and structures needed to facilitate the process of building momentum toward social change. Thus, an organization's capacity *needs* at any particular moment will depend on a wide variety of factors (Sussman, 2008), in part because each organization's environment and circumstances are constantly changing—client and community needs and assets change, organizations grow and evolve, and economic and political conditions change. In order to survive, organizations must constantly adapt and build new capacities. This adaptive process of developing new capacities is called *organizational capacity building.*

Organizational Capacity Building

Now that we have discussed organizational capacity and how, over time and with changing circumstances, organizations must develop new capacities, we can shift our focus to organizational capacity building. Backer (2001) writes that capacity building involves "strengthening nonprofits so they can better achieve their mission" (p. 38). Blumenthal (2003) defines capacity building as any "actions that improve nonprofit effectiveness" (p. 5). Typically, building organizational capacity is an ongoing, often complex developmental process: There is no final destination. At its most basic level, **organizational capacity building** is the process of *identifying* what organizational capacities to target for strengthening and *applying* targeted strategies most likely to build those capacities.

Identifying Organizational Targets for Capacity Building

The development of a plan for capacity building and the delivery of capacity building should always be preceded by a formal assessment of a nonprofit's needs and strengths. Assessing needs can help highlight organizational capacity targets for change. Identifying strengths can point to potential capacity-building strategies. The **organizational needs** assessment should be conducted collaboratively with nonprofit staff and be utilized to develop an individualized capacity building plan (Backer, Bleeg, & Groves, 2004, 2010; Blumenthal, 2003; Innovation Network, 2001; Joffres et al., 2004). There are a number of organizational capacity assessment tools freely available for use, which can help identify organizational strengths and areas in need of attention (Marguerite Casey Foundation, 2005; Venture Philanthropy Partners, 2001). The Marguerite Casey Foundation (2005) recommends a two-step process of assessing organizational capacity that includes a first step having key personnel individually use the tool to rate the organization on different capacity dimensions. Upon completing the assessment on an individual basis, participants then gather to discuss their ratings and reach consensus on one set of ratings that best represents the organization. They believe that completing the assessment using a team approach both improves validity and reduces individual biases. This process also serves as a catalyst for key organizational stakeholders to engage in a rich dialogue about the organization.

Many capacity-building efforts focus on incremental change targeting technical or operational organizational components such as improving accounting systems or implementing program evaluation activities. It is often easier to obtain funding for this type of capacity-building effort and it can be completed in a relatively short timeframe—although some question whether these incremental capacity-building projects have significant impact on overall organizational effectiveness. Many experts support capacity building that focuses on more fundamental or transformative change in culture, mission, strategies, and structures, with particular attention paid to adaptive and leadership capacities (such as governance and strategy) in the belief that building these capacities is more likely to have long-term positive impact on an organization's effectiveness (Blumenthal, 2003; Connolly & York, 2003; Letts et al., 1999; Venture Philanthropy Partners, 2001).

One simple model for understanding different targets within an organization for capacity building and each target's potential effect on organizational effectiveness and impact is the "pyramid of organizational capacity building" that comes from St. Luke's Health Initiatives (2011). They suggest that it is helpful to conceptualize capacity building on three distinct levels. First is the *base level*. This level contains the basic strategic direction, management capacities, financial support, program execution, infrastructure, and relationships that all organizations need to function effectively in community settings and make progress toward their missions. Basic capacities and infrastructure at the base level are necessary for survival, but insufficient for creating social impact. Second is the *intermediate level*. This is where the adaptive capacities come into play. All organizations need to remain flexible and open to discovery, innovation, and learning. They need to adopt the best emerging practices that lead to high impact and foster a culture of innovation and adaptability to changing circumstances. Lastly, they stress the importance of building capacity at the *top level*. We know that community-based organizations are attempting to address complex, changing, and entrenched social problems. This requires that organizations participate in a network of stakeholders who are focused on higher-order systems change. Thus, organizations need to build collaborative capacity to engage effectively with other social change partners to build collective efforts that can really made a difference.

Strategies for Organizational Capacity Building

While the three levels described above help us identify *what* areas to target for change in organizations, *how* to go about building capacity is another question worth exploring. Whether focusing on incremental change or deeper transformative change, when people think of organizational capacity building, the activities that generally come to mind are training workshops and technical assistance. However, in practice, there is a wide range of actions that can be taken to build organizational capacity. In addition to the assessment of organizational needs, strengths, and readiness for change described above, capacity-building practices and processes can be grouped into two major categories: (1) technical assistance and organization development consultation (e.g., training, coaching, peer networking, provision of resource materials, convening) and (2) direct financial support (Backer et al., 2004). We'll discuss the former briefly below.

After assessing the organization to determine capacity-building needs, we can apply the activities or strategies most likely to affect the change needed. Given the diversity of capacity-building needs, a "one size fits all" approach is believed to be less effective. Thus, individualization, that is, customization of capacity-building activities to align with organizational needs and circumstances, is important (Backer et al., 2010; De Vita, Fleming, & Twombly, 2001; Innovation Network, 2001; Light, 2004; Sobeck, 2008). When developing capacity-building efforts, capacity builders should take into account identified nonprofit capacity-building needs and strengths; nonprofit staff members' learning styles; and non-profit history, culture, life stage, and environment. This individualization should also include flexibility to alter an initial capacity-building plan as needed (Backer et al., 2010; Blumenthal, 2003).

Technical assistance and organization development consultation in the form of training, coaching, and peer networking are common capacity-building strategies. Often an assessment will reveal that an organization's capacity needs are interrelated, which means a combination of approaches may be warranted. For example, a consultant may be brought in to help an executive with board development and strategic planning while managers attend training on developing logic models and theories of change for programs. While narrowly defined strategies can work, the most impactful capacity-building activities include a comprehensive range of approaches (Backer, 2001).

Strategies that include opportunities for peer-to-peer learning have been cited as an important capacity-building success factor (Backer et al., 2010; Connolly & Lukas, 2002; Innovation Network, 2001; Joffres et al., 2004). Peer-to-peer learning opportunities such as roundtables, communities of practice, or learning circles are seen to reduce isolation as well as promote collaboration and problem solving. St. Luke's Health Initiatives (2011) has found success with its "Learning Through Networks" approach to building organizational and community capacity. In its TAP (technical assistance partnerships) approach, nonprofits work together in small teams or "learning circles" to identify and implement solutions for common organizational and community development issues. Once they settle on needed capacities, teams are matched with consultants who help them work collaboratively through the challenges and opportunities. This collaborative capacity-building approach had its challenges, but they found that over time (1) participants acquire specific knowledge and skills to increase organizational and community capacity; (2) participants broaden their community connections; (3) participants are able to translate learning into plans and activities at their agencies and in their communities; and (4) organizational capacity and performance are improved.

Keys to Success in Organizational Capacity-Building Efforts

Several factors are thought to be important in the successful design and implementation of capacity-building efforts. Those most consistently cited include (in no particular order) individualization of capacity building, capacity-builder qualifications, relationship quality, dosage of capacity building, peer-to-peer learning, evaluation, and organizational needs **assessment,** which in the context of organizational capacity building generally involves engaging staff, and often other stakeholders, in critically examining an organization's management and governance structures and processes. It is usually guided by an assessment tool and forms the basis for development of a capacity-building plan. Some of these are covered elsewhere in this chapter but we'll briefly discuss a few additional factors below.

Relationship quality. First, the quality of the relationship between the capacity builder and organizational staff is thought to be an important factor in capacity building. *Capacity builders* is the term commonly used in reference to those organizations and individuals that deliver capacity building to nonprofits. They may include staff from the organization providing the funding for capacity building (e.g., foundation staff) but in most cases funders contract with intermediary organizations or consultants to provide capacity building to grantees/contractors (Blumenthal, 2003; Connolly & York, 2002). Organizations may also utilize their own staff to serve as internal capacity builders. The strongest relationships involve ongoing collaborations characterized by trust and mutual respect between a qualified capacity builder and an organization in need.

Dosage and duration. Second, the design of any capacity-building strategy must plan for a sufficient amount and duration of capacity building so that new practices can be learned, practiced, and implemented (Chinman et al., 2008; Leake et al., 2007; Mitchell, Florin, & Stevenson, 2002). For example, while a one-off training session can be useful to increase staff knowledge, it is unlikely to build capacity unless training sessions are coupled with additional skill building and supports that increase the likelihood that the knowledge gained will result in tangible organizational change. The amount of time over which capacity-building practices are provided (duration) is also important. Capacity-building strategies delivered over time allow for the development of a high-quality relationship between the capacity builder and recipient and for new practices to be institutionalized (Backer et al., 2010; Blumenthal, 2003; Innovation Network, 2001; Venture Philanthropy Partners, 2001).

Evaluation. And finally, conducting both process and outcome evaluations is also believed to be an important factor (Backer et al., 2010; Blumenthal, 2003; De Vita et al., 2001). A process evaluation generates valuable information about the implementation of the capacity-building effort and how it may be improved. An outcomes evaluation assesses the extent to which the capacity-building effort resulted in the desired outcomes and can identify any unanticipated outcomes. Evaluations increase understanding of the dynamics of capacity building and document whether or not the desired changes have occurred. Process evaluations, in particular, can provide important ongoing data to improve capacity-building practices by learning from the successes, failures, and unanticipated outcomes in a program of capacity building. Process evaluations gather perceptions of those involved in the capacity-building effort to learn how things are going.

Community Capacity

Much of the interest in community and organizational capacity building has been in response to a professionalized model of community programming and research that over time has not produced the community well-being and development gains desired. In the 1990s evaluators realized community partners needed more training, resources, leadership, and "social capital," in the form of community participation and networks of information and influence, to effectively implement comprehensive substance abuse prevention and other health promotion programs and coalitions. Most definitions of community capacity focus on commitment, skills, resources, and problem-solving abilities of particular programs or institutions or community participation in a process of relationship building, community planning, decision making, and action (Goodman et al., 1998).

Fawcett et al. (1995) defined community capacity as "the community's ability to pursue its chosen purposes and course of action both now and in the future" (p. 682) and suggested it is influenced by a variety of personal, group, and environmental factors, such as relationships with, and support and other resources from, all relevant sectors and agencies within the community, including educational, health, religious, and business organizations. Community capacity grew as a prominent phrase and focus in the academic literature starting in 2001 with publications by Robert Chaskin and others. Chaskin (2001) offers a definitional framework for community capacity based on the literature and case studies from a comprehensive community initiative. He defines **community capacity** as

> the interaction of human capital, organizational resources, and social capital existing within a given community that can be leveraged to solve collective problems and improve or maintain the well-being of a given community. It may operate through informal social processes and/or organized effort. (p. 295)

Chavis, Speer, Resnick, and Zippay (1993) suggest that a community has the capacity to take action on social concerns if (1) the institutional and social relations are in place to reach all community members; (2) the institutions are accountable to their constituents (members, consumers, citizens); (3) the institutions, collectively and individually, have the ability to mobilize resources to respond to changing conditions; and (4) there is an enabling system (Chavis, Florin, & Felix, 1992) in place to develop and maintain community development and problem-solving initiatives.

While these definitions provide rich theoretical grounding for our understanding of community capacity, we appreciate the simplicity and clarity of the framework developed by the Aspen Institute (1996) that focuses on the combined influence of a community's commitment, resources, and skills that can be deployed to build on community strengths and address community problems and opportunities. *Commitment* is the collective will to act, based on a shared awareness of problems, opportunities, and possible solutions. *Resources* are the financial, natural, and human assets and methods to deploy them intelligently and fairly. *Skills* are all the assets, talents, and expertise of individuals, organizations, and networks that can be marshaled to address problems and seize opportunities. Taking strategic action to build commitment, resources, and skills is called **community capacity building.**

Community Capacity Building

Community capacity-building efforts can encompass a wide range of activities, from formal leadership development efforts to community-wide planning to a wide variety of less formal activities that build trust and social capital among citizens. The purpose of community capacity building is to create opportunities for people in a community to work together, develop a vision and strategies for the future, make collaborative decisions, and take action while building the individual skills and capabilities of a range of participants and organizations within the community (Aspen Institute, 1996). Community capacity-building efforts to improve marginalized communities face two related but different tasks: building common purposes, useful relationships, and capacities within the community; and connecting the community to external resources and influence (Saegert, 2005). Building capacity in a community is about developing common purpose, relationships, resources, and skills. The challenge for those on the outside wanting to help is to partner appropriately to create the conditions for a community to grow in capacity (Aspen Institute, 1996).

The Aspen Institute suggests there are eight outcomes to consider as goals for community capacity building: (1) expanded diverse and inclusive citizen participation; (2) expanded leadership base; (3) strengthened individual skills; (4) widely shared understanding and vision; (5) strategic community agenda; (6) consistent, tangible progress toward goals; (7) more effective community organizations and institutions; and (8) better resource utilization by the community. Community capacity-building efforts can focus on one or more of these outcomes as part of any capacity-building initiative. Community capacity is realized through a combination of three levels of social agency: individuals, organizations, and networks (Chaskin, 2001). These levels are also interconnected points of entry for strategic capacity-building interventions.

Strategies for Community Capacity Building

Community-building efforts tend to focus on some combination of four major strategies: leadership development, organizational development, community organizing, and fostering inter-organizational collaboration (Chaskin, Brown, Venkatesh, & Vidal, 2001). While targeting one of these areas for change might bring some level of benefits, building community capacity is most effective when a comprehensive approach is taken. Because of the difficult nature of community change, community capacity building requires simultaneous attention to strengthening individuals, formal organizations, and the relational networks tying them to each other and to the broader systems of which they are a part (Chaskin, 2001).

Leadership development. Neighborhoods and communities need local leaders who are willing and able to assume some responsibility for community betterment by being out front to ignite and facilitate action (Chaskin et al., 2001). Building the capacity of local leaders involves enhancing the skills, knowledge, commitment, and access to information and resources of individual residents in the community and providing opportunities to increase their active participation in community-improving activities (Chaskin, 2001). The best leadership development initiative is not a stand-alone activity but rather embedded in the development of organizations and networks. Embedding leadership development in these activities provides practical opportunities for individuals to try out and hone various skills (Chaskin et al., 2001).

Chaskin and his colleagues make the distinction between formal training and on-the-job engagement strategies. *Training* refers to structured activities to convey information and to build confidence and skills for civic participation that includes instrumental skills (public speaking, writing, organizing, producing materials, and research), as well as process skills (negotiation, compromise, running meetings, problem solving, power analysis, and navigating community systems). *Engagement* provides opportunities for people to learn on the job while working on efforts to benefit the community. Leadership development in this case is a process of learning while doing, and reflection plays a key role. In the end, Chaskin and his colleagues recommend combining the two approaches to get the best of both worlds.

Additionally, there is great benefit to preparing groups of individuals in a community for leadership roles versus focusing on individual leaders. Leaders can then engage in the public sphere not as disconnected individuals but as embedded members of a connected community (Warren, 2001). Finally, Chaskin et al. (2001) remind us that whatever approach is utilized, developing individual leaders does not automatically translate into stronger community capacity. New leaders must be willing to use their skills to benefit others and the community at large and be committed to engaging others to play an active role in community betterment, gaining strength from solidarity.

Community organizing. The second strategy for community capacity building—organizational capacity building—was covered at length in the first part of this chapter, so we will not review it here. The third strategy for building community capacity is community organizing. Community organizing is "the process of bringing people together to solve community problems and address goals" (Chaskin et al., 2001, p. 93). Community organizing seeks to alter the relations of power between the groups that have traditionally controlled decisions and the residents of marginalized communities. Community organizing involves putting relationship building, social capital development, and partnerships at the core of community building (Gittell & Vidal, 1998) and capitalizes on individual, organizational, and community strengths. Drawing again on the excellent book on this topic by Chaskin and his colleagues (2001), we know that employing a community organizing strategy for community capacity building forces us to confront several choices for how we go about it. We'll highlight two of these: (1) whether to use a conflict or consensus approach and (2) whether to focus on single or multiple issues.

Conflict versus consensus strategies. Conflict approaches utilize oppositional tactics to bring about desired ends. Examples include marches, sit-ins, and mass protests or "actions." The rationale for using a conflict strategy is the understanding that powerful people and institutions will not work to reduce injustice unless direct pressure is applied (Chaskin et al., 2001). This method seeks to build social power capable of leveraging resources and negotiating improvements for a community (Speer, Hughey, Gensheimer, & Adams-Leavitt, 1995). Consensus-based strategies on the other hand do not presume that conflict is required to stimulate change. Rather, change is sought by promoting mutual respect and positive interaction among residents, organizations, and other stakeholders by focusing on opportunities for mutual benefit in order to get things done (Chaskin et al., 2001). Cooperation is the operating principle instead of confrontation. The current trend in community capacity building is to rely more on consensus strategies, as they are more useful in building the capacity of individuals, networks, and communities to seek common ground and develop solutions that benefit communities.

Single versus multiple issues. Community organizing efforts can focus on a single issue (e.g., vacant lots) through targeted strategies or take on a wider range of concerns over time. Single-issue strategies bring people together and promote unified action around a specific concern. Unfortunately, some single-issue campaigns can be highly targeted and short-lived. When the issue is resolved, the capacity generated may dissipate (Chaskin et al., 2001). However, single-issue efforts can also become a starting point for building capacity for sustained efforts on multiple issues. Multiple-issue strategies attempt to build a membership base and local capacity to address issues of concern noted by residents over time. If done well, these actions provide the opportunity for enhancing collective problem-solving capacities while strengthening community bonds and commitment. The best organizing efforts are not just about winning one victory, they are about building power and winning in ways that enhance a community's capacities for winning again in the future. This means that how communities organize around particular issues is just as important as what they win.

Strengthening Organizational Collaboration and Networks Community capacity building is an approach that emphasizes relationships, coalitions, and consensus building (Gittell & Vidal, 1998; McNeely, 1999). At the organizational or institutional level of community, building and strengthening inter-organizational partnerships and networks is a critical strategy for community capacity building. Networks, coalitions, alliances, and other forms of inter-organizational collaboration are seen as effective strategies for building power to affect the broader systems and policy change needed to benefit marginalized communities. They have been shown to build capacity of the community through strengthening organizations and institutions (Butterfoss, Goodman, & Wandersman, 1993; Chavis et al., 1993). Bringing together organizations with similar missions, goals, and concerns makes better use of limited resources and increases the chances that a shared agenda can be achieved. Building this type of collaborative capacity in communities requires a focus on the relationships between organizations and the creation of a shared purpose, shared objectives, and collective power. Inter-organizational capacity building is about the creation and maintenance of spaces that provide the opportunity for a variety of community organizational actors to coordinate resources and action (Foster-Fishman, Salem, Allen, & Fahrbach, 2001).

The "backbone" organization. Gray (1989) stresses the importance of a legitimate and skilled convener with process capacity that is given authority to have the role of convener. The recent literature on collective impact refers to this convening role as the "backbone" organization (Kania & Kramer, 2010). The backbone organization utilizes a dedicated staff that can plan, manage, and support the initiative through ongoing facilitation, technology and communications support, data collection, reporting, and handling logistical and administrative details needed for the initiative to function smoothly (Kania & Kramer, 2010). The need for a skilled convener with existing relationships within a community and strong process capacity is a persistent theme in the collaboration, network, and collective impact literatures. A convening agency must have sufficient organizational capacity, experience, commitment, leadership, and vision to form and build an effective coalition (Butterfoss & Kegler, 2009). McGuire (2002) characterizes lead organization activities as: identify and bring in the people, organizations, and resources needed (activation); generate agreement on network structure, operating rules, principles, and values (framing); induce and maintain commitment to the network (mobilizing); and facilitate relationships among participants and create an environment conducive to productive interaction (synthesizing).

Inter-Organizational Structure. Weaving a cohesive inter-organizational coalition or network with a shared purpose where there is none requires building relationships, skills, resources, and enabling structures to assemble and coordinate the specific elements necessary for collective learning and action. The establishment of an overarching organizational structure and processes to guide coalition functioning in communication, decision making, and conflict resolution is an important factor in the success of collaborative entities (Kegler, Rigler, & Honeycutt, 2010). Maintaining inter-organizational relations and mobilizing members relies on the availability of resources to provide staff, maintain good communication, and support collective activities (Chaskin et al., 2001). Coalitions can promote communication through newsletters, television and community radio programs, conferences, and electronic discussion boards and social media. Community coalitions can also benefit from the help of an outside facilitator who can support the process and help connect the group to other allies and necessary resources.

Tools for Community Capacity Building

There are specific technologies that can be used to further the strategies mentioned above. For example, Internet-based resources, such as the *Community Tool Box* (http://ctb .ku.edu/), provide an effective means for transmitting skills, information, and other resources widely and inexpensively (Francisco et al., 2001). Community capacity-building efforts that can be enhanced through such web supports include community needs/ assets assessment, resource development, project planning, community recruitment organizing and mobilization, intervention strategies, implementation and marketing, advocacy, and evaluation. *Community-based participatory research,* when done well, can also help build community capacity to engage with research as both consumers and participants. For example, Cashman et al. (2008) illustrate how the roles and skills of community and academic partners are complementary and that meaningfully involving community members in data analysis and interpretation, while it may lengthen project time, can strengthen community capacity in various ways as well as provide unique and valuable insights into the research results, which can lead to better outcomes for all. *Asset-based community development* (Kretzmann & McKnight, 1993) is another specific approach that starts with the capacities of the residents, organizations, local culture, and physical features of an area and engages in a process of connecting, organizing, and orchestrating instrumental links among them to build local definition, investment, creativity, hope, and control.

Keys to Success in Community Capacity-Building Efforts

Comprehensive community capacity-building efforts are complex, multifaceted, and, depending on the context, may be limited in what they can accomplish. Three ingredients increase the likelihood that community capacity-building initiatives will be successful: community engagement, a relationship-driven approach, and linking strategies.

Community engagement. A core principle of community capacity building is that residents should be engaged in the work of improving their own communities (Kubisch, Auspos,

Photo 7.1 Community meetings create opportunities for members to come together to discuss their interests and concerns and can be an effective way to engage in community organizing.

Source: Photo courtesy Victory Heights Blog.

Dewar, & Taylor, 2013). Significant community improvement takes place only when local community people are committed to investing themselves and their resources in the effort. Engaging community residents and other stakeholders in identifying and prioritizing needed changes and devising and implementing strategies to build capacity has long been a cornerstone of community-building work. Broad-scale mobilization of residents in community-building efforts is critical for building overall community capacity and key to the long-term success of these types of initiatives (Chaskin, 2001; Foster-Fishman et al., 2006). While outside assistance can be invaluable, community capacity is never built from the top down, or from the outside in. Meaningful community participation extends beyond physical involvement to include generation of ideas, contributions to decision making, and sharing of responsibility for action.

Relationship-driven approach. A critical task for any community capacity-building effort is to constantly build and rebuild the relationships between and among local residents, local associations, and local institutions. Relationships provide the medium for collaborative work, facilitate access to needed resources, and promote commitment and satisfaction. The key is bridging differences and finding common ground, shared interests, and a sense of mutual self-benefit. Capacity builders can provide the supports that facilitate networking among residents and organizations in a community. They can use their resources to support community-building and community-organizing activities directly as well as by creating opportunities and spaces for residents to get to know each other and come together in collective action. It is in these face-to-face interactions that residents build trust and cooperation around a community-based agenda. In order for relationships to be developed and take root, there is a need for safe places for people to congregate to get to know each other, to discuss, to exchange, to argue, to debate. The existence of a "safe space" or a "system of safety" within communities is often cited as fundamental to promoting or inhibiting the growth or engagement of community capacity (Chaskin et al., 2001).

Linking strategies. As has been described in this chapter, community capacity building involves some combination of four strategies: leadership development, organizational development, community organizing, and inter-organizational collaboration. Working in an integrated fashion across these four major strategies increases the likelihood that efforts to build community capacity will endure and succeed (Chaskin et al., 2001). For example, productive inter-organizational collaborations require organizations with sufficient capacity. And the success of any community-organizing effort requires capable leaders. In turn, organizational and community development activities provide opportunities for leadership development. Recognizing how these four strategies complement and depend on each other and integrating these strategies for maximum benefit are critical factors in community capacity-building efforts.

COMPETENCY AND COMPETENCY DEVELOPMENT: ORGANIZATIONAL AND COMMUNITY CAPACITY BUILDING

Whether external or internal to organizations or communities, effective capacity builders demonstrate certain competencies. One of the most consistent shortcomings identified in the organizational capacity-building field is the lack of competent providers, especially in terms of their specialized knowledge of the nonprofit community (Backer, 2001). In this section, we'll highlight some of the requisite knowledge, skills, and abilities needed for organizational and community capacity building.

KNOWLEDGE FOR ORGANIZATIONAL AND COMMUNITY CAPACITY BUILDING

The most frequently cited knowledge base and experience thought to support successful capacity building include expertise in change management, expertise in the subject area of the capacity-building effort, and relevant local knowledge (Backer et al., 2010;

Blumenthal, 2003; Kibbe et al., 2004). Competencies for organizational and community capacity building have been more broadly identified for community psychology practice through a collaborative process organized recently within the Society for Community Research and Action (SCRA) and published in draft form in the Fall 2012 issue of *The Community Psychologist* (Dalton & Wolfe, 2012). Those competencies include an understanding of foundational principles in the field (e.g., ecological perspectives, empowerment, cross-cultural competence, inclusion and partnership, ethical-reflective practice) as well as knowledge of specific aspects of community program development, community and organizational capacity building, community and social change, and applied (especially participatory) community research. "Practitioner" competencies relate to more technical knowledge and skills in the areas of communication, research, and community and organizational processes and interventions. "Specialist" competencies are knowledge and skills specific to practitioners' particular role and setting. Specialist knowledge may include an understanding of the larger institutional context beyond the practitioners' organizational setting, relevant regulatory and policy frameworks and players, and theoretical and research literature relevant to one's area of practice.

Skills and Abilities for Organizational and Community Capacity Building

In the category of skills and abilities particular to community and organizational capacity building, the following practice competencies were identified by SCRA: community leadership and mentoring, small- and large-group processes, resource development, and consultation and organizational development. *Leadership* in this context is defined as "the ability to enhance the capacity of individuals and groups to lead effectively, through a collaborative process of engaging, energizing and mobilizing those individuals and groups regarding an issue of shared importance" (Dalton & Wolfe, 2012, p. 11). Competent capacity builders are able to establish trusting relationships and work with community partners and differing stakeholders to assess issues and priorities. They are able to work across diverse groups to find productive ways to address organizational and community concerns and they support the planning and implementation of specific actions to address an issue. *Mentoring* is defined as "the ability to assist community members to identify personal strengths and social and structural resources that they can develop further and use to enhance empowerment, community engagement, and leadership" (Dalton & Wolfe, 2012, p. 11). Competent capacity builders advise and support organizational and community leaders and help them develop and utilize forms of collaborative leadership in their efforts. As part of the organizational and community capacity-building process, mentoring also includes the ability to model the practice of critical reflection in one's own work.

The ability to intervene effectively in *small- and large-group processes* was also seen as important skill "in order to facilitate the capacity of community groups to work together productively" (Dalton & Wolfe, 2012, p. 11). Related skills are effective interpersonal communication, facilitation of meetings, group decision making, action planning, consensus building, and conflict analysis and resolution. One recent graduate of a community psychology program who is now running her own community consulting practice reported to us that her training in facilitation methods and the "technology of participation" through the Institute of Cultural

Affairs (http://ica-international.org/top/top-intro.htm) was invaluable, providing the tools she needed to help groups and organizations process experiences, plan together, make decisions, and build capacities. Often in our work with community groups we are using facilitation and workshop methods that can be modeled and taught to others to use in their own community efforts. One of the authors (Evans) often uses a process called "exploding the issue" with groups of staff in organizations to explore root causes of some of the problems their constituents face. Once organizations see and experience this group process it becomes part of their toolbox to use with each other and with community constituents.

Resource development is defined as the "ability to identify and integrate use of human and material resources, including community assets and social capital" (Dalton & Wolfe, 2012, p. 11), and includes fundraising knowledge and skills. *Consultation and organizational development* is defined as "the ability to facilitate growth of an organization's capacity to attain its goals" (Dalton & Wolfe, 2012, p. 12) and includes the ability to assess organizational capacity, issues, needs, and assets; create and sustain effective partnerships; and facilitate learning, problem-solving, and collaborative strategic planning of goals and actions. In organizations, capacity builders help determine an organization's capacity-building needs through an assessment process. This process is often guided by a capacity-building assessment tool and may also involve quantitative and/or qualitative data collection such as surveys, interviews, document reviews, and observations from internal and external stakeholders. The goal is increased understanding of the organization's current and desired status, including its readiness to engage in capacity-building activities. Thus, capacity builders must have the ability to create and use tools for data collection and understand how to collect, manage, analyze, and report findings in formats that can be utilized by community and organizational partners. Capacity builders then work with organizations to develop an appropriate plan for building capacity that is based upon the results of the assessment process. The plan details the specific actions that the organization will undertake to address its capacity-building needs, the anticipated results, the timeline, and the resources needed. Capacity builders have the knowledge, skills, and tools to move organizations from assessment of developing capacity-building needs to the implementation of strategies to address those needs.

The importance of relationships. The quality of the relationship between the capacity builder and community partner is also thought to be an important factor in successful capacity building (Blumenthal, 2003; Innovation Network, 2001; Kegeles, Rebchook, & Tebbetts, 2005). One thing that we've learned in our years of working with and studying organizational and community processes is that relationships are fundamental. First and foremost, any effort to build capacity in community contexts is grounded in an enduring relationship of trust and mutual respect. Community psychologists have long espoused the importance of taking the time to establish long-term, caring, committed relationships with community partners in order to work in solidarity for social change (Kelly, 1979; Nelson & Prilleltensky, 2005; Rappaport, 1990; Trickett, 1984). As community researchers and practitioners, we often find ourselves connected with community partners long before and after a specific project. When we develop committed relationships with community partners that allow us to be seen as equals and as friends and companions in the process, we enable open and honest dialogue.

Evans (2014) suggests that those of us working in communities should be skilled at playing the role of "critical friend" to help community partners better work toward social justice objectives. In the context of an enduring relationship of trust and mutual respect, gentle critique of current practices can be a tool that can bring shared assumptions and beliefs into the foreground for examination. It's about working alongside individuals, organizations, and communities to reveal how the beliefs and attitudes that inform their action may help to preserve a social order that is antithetical to their collective experiences and goals (Carr & Kemmis, 1986). We can be outspoken critics of the status quo as well as trusted friends with high expectations for organizational and community change.

Critical competencies. In a similar vein, Kagan, Burton, Duckett, Lawthom, and Siddiquee (2011) add the following "critical" competencies, which are important for building capacity in many organizational and community contexts. *Critical analysis and reframing* is the ability to conduct social analysis of authority and power in communities and to examine the larger social and political forces at play. It is also the ability to reframe problems too often described in individual or family-level terms through the lens of deficiencies in systemic conditions. *Critical reflection* is the ability to critique and learn from our practice, and make sense of successes and failures alongside those with whom we make alliances. For critical theorists, critical reflection has no meaning unless it is accompanied by awareness of power relationships and sociopolitical realities (Reynolds, 1998). Another recent master's-level graduate in community psychology suggested to us that he considered reflective practice to be a key competency in his own consulting practice and something that was encouraged and cultivated through his academic program. Being able to critically self-reflect on experiences can help identify new insights as well as gaps for future learning. He's been continuing this practice through his consulting blog (www.strongrootsconsulting.ca/blog), which then has an additional capacity-building impact by sharing resources with a nonprofit audience, both locally and beyond. Lastly, *critical reflexivity* is the capacity to make positions of power and privilege (including one's own) transparent in change processes as well as the awareness of the assumptions, positions, and values we bring to the process. It's about questioning, examining, and becoming aware of personal assumptions and values as well as taken-for-granted dominant professional constructions influencing practice (Brechin, 2000).

Training, Education, and Experiences That Would Help Strengthen This Competency

Those wanting to build competencies in the area of organizational and community capacity building develop knowledge and skills through a combination of formal education, professional development training opportunities, and practical field experiences.

Formal Education

Seeking master's-level training in community psychology and related fields is an excellent way to build a solid knowledge base, theoretical grounding, and practical skills for organizational and community capacity building. Not to mention that obtaining a graduate degree brings with it credentials that, to some degree, help when building relationships with community partners. Programs in community psychology, community sociology, urban and regional planning, urban affairs, urban geography, applied anthropology, community (macro) social work, public health, and public administration all provide some emphasis on building knowledge and applied skills for this kind of work. Many of these programs can be completed in one year and some are now being offered online or through a hybrid model (some online, some face-to-face).

When exploring graduate programs that can offer solid training in capacity building, look for programs that have a strong experiential component built into their course plan. For example, many programs require students to complete a community-based practicum experience where they work alongside community partners to help them accomplish a goal while learning from the experience. This field experience is designed to integrate students' didactic learning with practical experience and translate community and organizational skill-building and leadership tools to a real-world environment. Additionally, look for key course offerings on the following topics:

- Organizational development or organizational change
- Community psychology or community development
- Community organizing
- Action research
- Applied research
- Program development and evaluation
- Leadership
- Group dynamics or group process
- Nonprofit management
- Community consultation
- Diversity or multiculturalism

Professional Development

In addition to formal coursework, there are also ways to build competencies through participation in specialized training events. As was mentioned earlier, training in group facilitation, action planning, and innovative participatory and self-organizing group processes such as Open Space Technology (Owen 2007, 2008), World Café (Brown, Isaacs, & World Cafe Community, 2005) and Dynamic Facilitation (Rough, 2002) are process skills that can be applied to a host of organizational and community contexts and situations. Capacity-building and philanthropic organizations in communities often offer training on a variety of topics and skills at an affordable price. For example, many of the United Way branches and local, state, and national nonprofit alliances either maintain or partner with a training center that provides public workshops, customized workshops tailored to specific needs, technical assistance, consulting, and other resources to build competencies in people and organizations. Additionally, national organizations like the Interaction Institute for Social Change (www.interactioninstitute.org), the Foundation Strategy Group (www.fsg.org), 4Good (https://4good.org), and Vibrant Communities Canada (http://vibrantcanada.ca) offer in-depth training, webinars, podcasts, and online resources on important skill and topics. A sampling of learning opportunities recently offered by these organizations includes:

- Facilitative Leadership for Social Change
- Whole Measures: Transforming Communities by Measuring What Matters Most
- Community-Building Curriculum
- Strategic Drivers for Comprehensive Community Change
- Essential Facilitation
- Civic Leadership Lab
- Strategic Planning Part 1: Cultivation and Organizational Development
- Connecting Strategy, Evaluation, and Learning in Your Organization
- Diversity in the Collaborative Organization
- Strategic Drivers for Comprehensive Community Change
- Social Media for Social Good

These and other similar organizations maintain extensive resource libraries on their websites and can provide a wealth of useful information and strategies. A recent graduate of a community psychology graduate program who received training in "Facilitative Leadership for Social Change" from the Interaction Institute reported that she learned tangible skills that she can use to facilitate different groups of people and some specific techniques on how to set up and execute meetings. She felt that the training really complemented her master's degree.

Attending local, regional, and national conferences on issues and topics related to organizational and community capacity building is also a great way to learn new skills and strategies and can help build and expand your professional network. For example, The Alliance for Nonprofit Management's 2014 national conference is centered on the theme "Capacity Building for Collective Impact." Other national associations such as The Society for Research and Action (www.scra27.org), the American Evaluation Association (www.eval.org), Community-Campus Partnerships for Health (http://ccph.info), the Organizational Development Network (www.odnetwork.org), Independent Sector (www.independentsector.org), and the Urban Affairs Association (http://urbanaffairsassociation.org) to name but a few, offer annual or bi-annual conferences with presentations and workshops by researchers, practitioners, and entrepreneurs from around the world.

Field Experience

While formal education and professional development are invaluable, direct experience in organizations and communities is perhaps the best training in the complexities and messiness that is organizational and community capacity building. Direct experience with organizational and community development, consultation, local policy development, administration, advocacy, and community organizing helps one become aware of the assets, needs, and challenges of capacity building and planned change in organizational and community contexts. Moreover, experience with applied research and evaluation—designing research, collecting, analyzing, and communicating data—helps the capacity builder learn the intricacies of utilizing research for organizational and community change. On-the-job training in the research philosophies and methodologies of needs assessment, program evaluation, policy analysis, community surveys, interviewing, focus groups, accessing and analyzing social indicator data (census, education, crime, health), and basic qualitative and quantitative analysis could come through participating as a member of a research or evaluation team. Direct experiences of this nature can happen through internships, volunteering, or paid work experiences. Organizations and community groups would typically welcome volunteers or interns willing to contribute to the cause while learning valuable knowledge and skills.

APPLICATION

The Importance of the Competency to Community Practice

Community psychologists and other community practitioners engaged in organizational and community settings are consistently faced with the question: How do we help create change? Whether it's change related to reduction of negative community indicators such as levels of youth violence or positive change such as increasing civic engagement, this process ultimately requires people, programs, organizations, and communities with sufficient capacity to create and sustain change. Organizations without sufficient capacity in key domains will struggle and will be unable help their constituents or fulfill their missions. Communities with weak organizations and disengaged residents will be unable to determine their future or effectively address the critical needs and aspirations of the people who live there. Community practitioners with the core knowledge, skills, tools, and attributes described above can help organizations and communities build sufficient capacity to create the kind of change they need to promote well-being.

Although we've highlighted some ideas and key principles to help guide our thinking about this type of community practice, there is no single template for how to engage in capacity building in real-world settings. Often our capacity building efforts are less systematic and more opportunistic in that we are infusing capacity building in all of our engagements with community partners. Below we provide a brief example of this competency in practice in which Catherine describes the way that organizational capacity building often happens as part of consultation engagements not specifically focused on capacity building.

A Real-World Application of the Competency: Organizational Capacity Building

I (Catherine) am a consultant to nonprofit organizations and have a strong professional interest in strengthening our local nonprofit sector and the local community. As such, I am always on the lookout for how I can opportunistically infuse organizational capacity building into my consulting assignments (most often these are for program evaluation or strategic planning). In this way, the nonprofit benefits from increased staff and organizational capacity as a secondary outcome of the contract—at no additional out-of-pocket cost. As they walk hand-in-hand with me through the evaluation or strategic planning, we also talk about how they can internally manage the process in the future—with no, or reduced, external assistance.

In some cases when there is a small budget for the work, staff participation is imperative to stretch the budget, and with some simple modifications to the contract design I can create learning experiences within the staff involvement. For example, in an evaluation, staff might participate in the design of the plan and measures, collecting and managing some of the data, and reflecting on the results and utilization of the data. In effect, staff build capacity as they work with me to implement the contracted evaluation or strategic planning process. This type of capacity building is not about systematically assessing an organization and then developing and implementing a capacity-building plan. Rather, it is about looking for any opportunity that presents itself to build staff and organizational capacity. Evaluation theorists have long recognized the potential for participatory forms of organizational development and evaluation and capacity building to foster collective learning and development (Cousins & Earl, 1992; Patton, 1998; Preskill, 1994; Preskill & Torres, 1999).

With some nonprofits, it has been relatively easy to do this, whereas others have not been interested. Some clients really just want me to come in, do my thing, and leave. In other organizations, there might be interest but usually due to staff being "stretched too thin" the organization may be unable to participate. In my experience, leaders at small to medium nonprofits have been more interested in this participatory capacity-building approach but small organizations sometimes have the most difficulty participating due to lack of staff availability.

In reflecting on my work, I have identified a number of factors—both on my end, as the consultant, and on the client's end—that appear to impact the likelihood of success. These factors, discussed below, represent in-the-field applications of the content presented earlier in this chapter.

As the consultant, I must first determine to what extent, if any, my client is interested in adding a capacity-building component to my consulting contract. In cases where the client has a small budget, I introduce the idea as a way to get more "bang for the buck" since staff involvement reduces my work and thus my fee. For many, this argument is very persuasive. I must also assess to what extent the client has the internal capacity, or "readiness," to engage in capacity-building activities. Is the organizational leadership supportive? Does there appear to be an organizational culture of learning so that staff are accustomed to participating in learning processes? Are the staff who would be involved willing and do they have the time to participate? What relevant skills and experience do they have?

If the client is interested and appears to have the capacity to participate, I design the project to be very collaborative and participatory from the first through the final stages. The project scope is modified to encompass the stated purpose of the contract (e.g., evaluate a program, create a strategic plan) and the secondary purpose of building capacity. This type of design involves some changes in my roles such, as ceding some level of control over the process; effectively and efficiently engaging staff in meaningful activities; providing monitoring, oversight, and feedback to ensure quality; and being particularly sensitive to staff's ability and level of participations (e.g., time, skills, interest). Of most significance, in this approach, my role expands to include a training and coaching role. I have both academic training and professional experience in adult education and professional development so this is a role in which I am comfortable. Not all consultants would be.

Both evaluation and strategic planning involve data collection, management, analysis, and utilization so these skills and processes tend to be the focus of the capacity-building work I do with organizations. Data collection and management activities may be shared activities while data analysis is most often done by me. Interpreting and utilizing the results is generally a shared activity.

A core staff group is created that works closely with me to design the project, including data collection tools. My experience indicates to me that engaging staff in the process right from the onset has many benefits. It increases staff learning outcomes and staff willingness to participate and also results in a better project design and analysis because the design and analysis reflect the knowledge of those who are actually engaged in the work.

In any consulting contract, communication is always important, but when capacity building is added to the work scope, communication becomes a key success factor. In addition to periodic meetings for planning, training, and interpretation, I create detailed written instructions and often provide training to prepare staff for their roles.

In closing these field-based reflections, a few concluding remarks are in order. Building capacity is a necessary, ongoing organizational process. However, there is less and less external funding available for "capacity-building projects" and some argue that these discrete projects often do not result in meaningful, enduring increases in capacity. Thus, an opportunistic approach to capacity building is a sustainable strategy—looking for opportunities to create capacity-building experiences within the ongoing, or periodic, activities of the organization. However, "it takes two to tango." No matter how skilled a capacity builder one is, the organization must be willing and able to engage in capacity-building activities. And finally, not all external consultants make good capacity builders. It requires a consultant who is willing and able to work collaboratively and can serve as a coach.

FUTURE DIRECTIONS

An emerging view of capacity building places it within a broad theoretical framework that links organizational and community capacity building to a vital civil sector and a strong democratic society. Researchers and practitioners are moving to conceptualize capacity building in collective and holistic terms, recognizing the relationships among and between individual, group, organizational, and community development. In the nonprofit sector, there is a growing understanding that building communities and networks among practitioners strengthens the potential impact of the sector. Many funding agencies are recognizing that philanthropy needs to focus on developing learning systems across organizations and networks in communities in order to fully leverage their investments in social change. Thus, there is an increasing focus on building collaborative capacity (Himmelman, 2001)—the capacity of organizations and institutions to work together across sectors with communities to achieve results.

Capacity-building practitioners should also note the increasing importance of digital technologies and digital literacy. More and more, organizational and community change efforts are being informed and aided by technology, digital tools, and social media. Those of us working to build capacity of organizations, networks, and communities should be skilled at using new digital tools such as email, blogs, wikis, YouTube, Twitter, and Facebook that encourage conversations between people, and across people and organizations, to enlarge their efforts quickly, easily, and inexpensively (Kanter & Fine, 2010). In community capacity-building efforts in particular, these technologies reduce the reliance on traditional organizations and contribute to the ease and speed with which individuals and groups can be mobilized for action (Shirky, 2008). The speed and strength of communication these tools facilitate enables organizations to both harness the power of their networks and involve their community more fully.

SUMMARY

Organizational and community capacity building are key strategies for promoting community empowerment and well-being. Capable and effective organizations can play a leading role in building and supporting community capacity. Communities can better address community problems, build on community strengths, and seize opportunities when the necessary commitment, resources, and skills can be deployed. Contributing to the development of capacity in organizations and communities takes skilled and knowledgeable leadership acting in the context of relationships built on trust and mutual respect. In this chapter we provided definitions of organizational and community capacity and capacity building and attempted to highlight the individual practitioner competencies needed to fully engage with organizational and community partners in the capacity-building endeavor. We hope readers will make use of the material in this chapter as well as the resources provided at the end to further their exploration and develop their own talents as agents of change in organizations and communities.

Key Points

- Organizational and community capacity are linked because much action to improve communities occurs in the context of organizations.

- Organizational capacity is everything an organization uses to achieve its mission.

- An organization's capacity needs at any particular moment will depend on a wide variety of factors.

- Organizational capacity building is the process of identifying what organizational capacities to target for strengthening and applying targeted strategies most likely to build those capacities.

- Community capacity is the combined influence of a community's commitment, resources, and skills that can be deployed to build on community strengths and address community problems and opportunities.

- Community capacity building is taking strategic action to build commitment, resources, and skills in community settings.

- Those wanting to increase their ability to lead capacity-building efforts can develop knowledge and skills through a combination of formal education, professional development training opportunities, and practical field experiences.

DISCUSSION QUESTIONS

1. The authors note that a "one size fits all" approach to organizational capacity building is believed to be less effective. However, given the limited funding for organizational capacity building, a "one size fits all" approach would most likely be more efficient and less expensive. Why would it be less effective?

2. How might organizational capacity needs differ between a young organization and a mature organization? Between a small organization and a large organization? Between an organization providing mental health services and an organization working with constituents to advocate for policy change? Think about the needed capacities in each of these cases using Connolly and York's (2003) four capacity domains.

3. What are the challenges of working to build capacity in a community as an outsider? Which of the competencies outlined in this chapter would be of particular importance in this situation? Why?

4. How could one use social media when attempting to build community capacity through community organizing? What are the benefits and drawbacks of this strategy?

KEY TERMS AND DEFINITIONS

Adaptive capacity: "The ability of a nonprofit organization to monitor, assess, and respond to internal and external changes" through activities such as strategic planning, developing beneficial collaborations, scanning the environment, and assessing organizational performance (Connolly & York, 2003, p. 20).

Community capacity: The interaction of human capital, organizational resources, and social capital existing within a given community that can be leveraged to solve collective problems and improve or maintain the well-being of a given community.

Community capacity building: Taking strategic action to build commitment, resources, and skills in community settings.

Leadership capacity: "The ability of all organizational leaders to inspire, prioritize, make decisions, provide direction and innovate, all in an effort to achieve the organizational mission" (Connolly & York, 2003, p. 20).

Management capacity: "The ability of a nonprofit organization to ensure the effective and efficient use of organizational resources" through, for example, effective personnel and volunteer policies (Connolly & York, 2003, p. 20).

Organizational capacity: The combined influence of an organization's abilities to govern and manage itself, to develop assets and resources, to forge the right community linkages, and to deliver valued services—all combining to meaningfully address its mission.

Organizational capacity building: The process of identifying what organizational capacities to target for strengthening and applying targeted strategies most likely to build those capacities.

Organizational needs assessment: In the context of organizational capacity building, this generally involves engaging staff, and often other stakeholders, in critically examining an organization's management and governance structures and processes. It is usually guided by an assessment tool and forms the basis for development of a capacity-building plan.

Technical capacity: "The ability of a nonprofit organization to implement all of the key organizational and programmatic functions" such as delivery of programs and services, effectively managing organizational finances, conducting evaluation activities, and raising funds (Connolly & York, 2003, p. 20).

RESOURCES

Effective Capacity Building in Nonprofit Organizations: http://www.vppartners.org/learning/reports/capacity/assessment.pdf

The Aspen Institute—Community Building Publications: http://www.aspeninstitute.org/policy-work/community-change/publications

The Aspen Institute. (2006). *Measuring community capacity building: A workbook in progress for rural communities*: http://www.aspeninstitute.org/sites/default/files/content/docs/csg/Measuring_Community_Capactiy_Building.pdf

The Foundation Center Capacity Building for Nonprofit Organizations: A Resource List: http://foundationcenter.org/getstarted/topical/capacity.html

The Alliance for Nonprofit Management: http://www.allianceonline.org

Recommended Reading

Blumenthal, B. (2003). *Investigating capacity building: A guide to high-impact approaches.* New York, NY: Foundation Center.

Chaskin, R. J., Brown, P., Venkatesh, S., & Vidal, A. (2001). *Building community capacity.* New York, NY: A. de Gruyter.

Connolly, P., & Lukas, C. A. (2002). *Strengthening nonprofit performance: A funder's guide to capacity building.* St. Paul, MN: Amherst H. Wilder Foundation.

Kretzmann, J. P., & McKnight, J. L. (1993). *Building communities from the inside out: A path toward finding and mobilizing a community's assets.* Chicago, IL: ACTA.

Recommended Websites

Community Toolbox, Chapter 3. Assessing Community Needs and Resources: http://ctb.ku.edu/en/tablecontents/chapter_1003.aspx

Community Toolbox, Chapter 8: Improving Organizational Management and Development: http://ctb.ku.edu/en/improve-organizational-management-and-development

Free Management Library section on capacity building: http://managementhelp.org/organizationalperformance/nonprofits/capacity-building.htm

Capacity Building Resource List at The Foundation Center: http://foundationcenter.org/getstarted/topical/capacity.html

Other Recommended Materials

Building Movement Project—Tools: http://buildingmovement.org/our_tools/entry/service_and_social_change

Suggested Activities for Further Competency Development

- Attend one of the conferences listed in the section above on Professional Development. Set goals ahead of time for what knowledge and skills you want to learn from the conference and preview the program before attending to map out your learning agenda.

- Practice assessing organizational capacity and use one of the assessment tools suggested below to conduct an organizational assessment of a nonprofit organization with which you are familiar. Based on your assessment of the organization, develop several capacity-building recommendations.

- Improve your group process skills by attending a training on facilitation skills. Alternatively (or additionally) shadow an experienced facilitator in the community from whom you can learn new techniques and strategies.

Worksheets

The One Hour Organizational Assessment: https://www.ideaencore.com/item/one-hour-organizational-assessment/?utm_source = Consumer&utm_medium = newsletter&utm_campaign = 2013-03-12

Marguerite Casey Foundation Organizational Capacity Assessment Tool: http://caseygrants.org/resources/org-capacity-assessment/

McKinsey Capacity Assessment Grid: http://www.vppartners.org/sites/default/files/reports/assessment.pdf

Social Venture Partners Organizational Capacity Assessment Tool: http://www.socialventurepartners.org/seattle/news-events/reports-and-tools/

Community Engagement Strategies Assessment Worksheet: http://www.buildingmovement.org/pdf/Community_Engagement_Assessment_Worksheet.pdf

For Self-Exploration or Self-Development

- Put yourself in the role of someone who is working in an organization or community and is seeking outside help with a capacity-building effort. What type of person would you want to engage? What characteristics would be important? Now reflect on your own attributes: How do they match with what you imagined in the role-play above? What characteristics make you capable to be a leader in capacity building? What things do you need to work on?

- Take in one of the many online trainings related to various aspects of organizational or community capacity building. Check out some of the offerings through the organizations listed in the Resources.

For Assessment of Knowledge, Skill, and Abilities Relating to the Competency

- Self-assess your ability to provide capacity-building assistance to an organization or local community. In making this assessment, consider both the capacity builder qualifications discussed in the chapter and the case example. In what areas do your strengths lie? In what areas would you need to further develop your capacities and capabilities?

- Come up with several examples of organizational activities or functions for each domain within the Connolly and York organizational capacity framework.

- In what ways might the levels of nonprofit organizational capacity within a community be important to community capacity-building efforts?

REFERENCES

Aspen Institute. (1996). *Measuring community capacity building: A workbook in progress for rural communities.* Retrieved from http://www.aspeninstitute.org/publications/measuring-community-capacity-building

Backer, T. E. (2001). Strengthening nonprofits: Foundation initiatives for nonprofit organizations. In J. De Vita & C. Fleming (Eds.), *Building capacity in nonprofit organizations* (pp. 33–84). Washington, DC: Urban Institute. Retrieved from http://www.urban.org/uploadedpdf/building_capacity.pdf

Backer, T. E., Bleeg, J. E., & Groves, K. (2004). *The expanding universe: New directions in nonprofit capacity building.* Washington, DC: Alliance for Nonprofit Management. Retrieved from http://www.handsonnetwork.org/files/resources/RS_New_Directions_in_Nonprofit_Capacity_Building_2004_Alliance.pdf

Backer, T. E., Bleeg, J. E., & Groves, K. (2010). *Evaluating foundation-supported capacity building: Lessons learned.* Encino, CA: Human Interaction Institute. Retrieved from http://www.humaninteract.org/images/finalrep129c.pdf

Blumenthal, B. (2003). *Investing in capacity building: A guide to high-impact approaches.* New York, NY: Foundation Center.

Brechin, A. (2000). Introducing critical practice. In A. Brechin, H. Brown, & M. Eby (Eds.), *Critical practice in health and social care* (pp. 25–47). London, UK: Open University Press. Retrieved from http://openlearn.open.ac.uk/file.php/3924/!via/oucontent/course/302/k315_1_001.pdf

Brown, J., Isaacs, D, & World Café Community. (2005). *The World Café: Shaping our futures through conversations that matter.* San Francisco, CA: Berrett-Koehler.

Butterfoss, F. D., Goodman, R. M., & Wandersman, A. (1993). Community coalitions for prevention and health promotion. *Health Education Research, 8*(3), 315–330.

Butterfoss, F. D., & Kegler, M. C. (2009). Community coalition action theory. In R. J. DiClemente, R. A. Crosby, & M. C. Kegler (Eds.), *Emerging theories in health promotion practice and research: Strategies for improving public health* (pp. 238–276). New York, NY: Wiley.

Carr, W., & Kemmis, S. (1986). *Becoming critical: Education knowledge and action research.* Philadelphia, PA: Falmer Press.

Cashman, S. B., Adeky, S., Allen, A. J., 3rd, Corburn, J., Israel, B. A., Montano, J., . . . Eng, E. (2008). The power and the promise: Working with communities to analyze data, interpret findings, and get to outcomes. *American Journal of Public Health, 98*(8), 1407–1417.

Chaskin, R. J. (2001). Building community capacity—A definitional framework and case studies from a comprehensive community initiative. *Urban Affairs Review, 36*(3), 291–323.

Chaskin, R. J., Brown, P., Venkatesh, S., & Vidal, A. (2001). *Building community capacity.* New York, NY: A. de Gruyter.

Chavis, D. M., Florin, P., & Felix, M. R. (1992). Nurturing grass roots initiatives for community development: The role of enabling systems. In *Community organization and social administration: Advances, trends, and emerging principles.* Binghamton, NY: Haworth.

Chavis, D. M., Speer, P. W., Resnick, I., & Zippay, A. (1993). Building community capacity to address alcohol and drug abuse: Getting to the heart of the problem. In R. C. Davis (Ed.), *Drugs and the community: Involving community residents in combatting the sale of illegal drugs* (pp. 251–284). Springfield, IL: Charles C Thomas.

Chinman, M., Hunter, S. B., Ebener, P., Paddock, S. M., Stillman, L., Imm, P., & Wandersman, A. (2008). The getting to outcomes demonstration and evaluation: An illustration of the prevention support system. *American Journal of Community Psychology, 41*(3–4), 206–224.

Connolly, P., & Lukas, C. (2002). *Strengthening nonprofit performance: A funder's guide to capacity building.* St. Paul, MN: Amherst H. Wilder Foundation.

Connolly, P., & York, P. (2002). Evaluating capacity-building efforts for nonprofit organizations. *OD Practitioner, 34*(4), 33–39.

Connolly, P., & York, P. (2003). *Building the capacity of capacity builders: A study of management support and field-building organizations in the nonprofit sector.* Retrieved from http://www.tccgrp.com/pdfs/buildingthecapacityofcapacitybuilders.pdf

Cousins, J. B., & Earl, L. M. (1992). The case for participatory evaluation. *Educational Evaluation and Policy Analysis, 14*(4), 397–418.

Dalton, J., & Wolfe, S. M. (2012). Joint Column: Education connection and the community practitioner. *The Community Psychologist, 45*(4), 7–14.

De Vita, C. J., Fleming, C., & Twombly, E. C. (2001). Building nonprofit capacity: A framework for addressing the problem. In C. J. De Vita & C. Fleming (Eds.), *Building capacity in nonprofit organizations.* Washington, DC: Urban Institute Press. Retrieved from http://www.urban.org/uploadedpdf/building_capacity.pdf

Doherty, S., & Mayer, S. E. (2003). *Results of an inquiry into capacity building programs for nonprofit programs.* Minneapolis, MN: Effective Communities. Retrieved from http://wwweffectivecommunities.com/E CP_CapacityBuildingInquiry.pdf

Evans, S. D. (2014). The community psychologist as critical friend: Promoting critical community praxis. *Journal of Community and Applied Social Psychology.* doi 10.1002/casp.2213.

Fawcett, S., Paine-Andrews, A., Francisco, V. T., Schultz, J. A., Richter, K. P., Lewis, R. K., . . . Lopez, C. M. (1995). Using empowerment theory in collaborative partnerships for community health and development. *American Journal of Community Psychology, 23*(5), 677–697.

Foster-Fishman, P. G., Fitzgerald, K., Brandell, C., Nowell, B., Chavis, D., & Egeren, L. A. V. (2006). Mobilizing residents for action: The role of small wins and strategic supports. *American Journal of Community Psychology, 38*(3–4), 143–152.

Foster-Fishman, P., Salem, D., Allen, N., & Fahrbach, K. (2001). Facilitating interorganizational collaboration: The contributions of interorganizational alliances. *American Journal of Community Psychology, 29,* 875–905.

Francisco, V. T., Fawcett, S. B., Schultz, J. A., Berkowitz, B., Wolff, T. J., & Nagy, G. (2001). Using Internet-based resources to build community capacity: The community tool box. *American Journal of Community Psychology, 29*(2), 293–300. Retrieved from http://ctb.ukans.edu/

Gittell, R., & Vidal, A. (1998). *Community organizing: Building social capital as a development strategy.* Thousand Oaks, CA: Sage.

Goodman, R. M., Speers, M. A., McLeroy, K., Fawcett, S., Kegler, M., Parker, E., . . . Wallerstein, N. (1998). Identifying and defining the dimensions of community capacity to provide a basis for measurement. *Health Education and Behavior, 2*(3), 258–278.

Gray, B. (1989). *Collaborating: Finding common ground for multiparty problems.* San Francisco, CA: Jossey-Bass.

Himmelman, A. T. (2001). On coalitions and the transformation of power relations: Collaborative betterment and collaborative empowerment. *American Journal of Community Psychology, 29*(2), 277–284.

Innovation Network. (2001). *Echoes from the field: Proven capacity building principles for nonprofits.* Retrieved from http://www.innonet.org/client_docs/File/Echoes_Full.pdfs

Joffres, C., Heath, S., Farquharson, J., Barkhouse, K., Latter, C., & MacLean, D. R. (2004). Facilitators and challenges to organizational capacity building in heart health promotion. *Qualitative Health Research, 14*(1), 39–60.

Kagan, C., Burton, M., Duckett, P., Lawthom, R., & Siddiquee, A. (2011). *Critical community psychology.* Chichester, UK: Wiley-Blackwell.

Kania, K., & Kramer, M. (2010, December). Collective impact. *Stanford Social Innovation Review..* Retrieved from http://www.ssireview.org/articles/entry/collective_impact/

Kanter, B., & Fine, A. H. (2010). *The networked nonprofit: Connecting with social media to drive change.* San Francisco, CA: Jossey-Bass.

Kegeles, S. M., Rebchook, G. M., & Tebbetts, S. (2005). Challenges and facilitators to building program evaluation capacity among community-based organizations. *AIDS Education and Prevention, 17*(4), 284–299.

Kegler, M. C., Rigler, J., & Honeycutt, S. (2010). How does community context influence coalitions in the formation stage? A multiple case study based on the Community Coalition Action Theory. *BMC Public Health, 10*(1), 1–11.

Kelly, J. G. (1979). T'ain't what you do, it's the way you do it. *American Journal of Community Psychology, 7*(3), 244–258.

Kibbe, D. B., Enright, K. P., Lee, J. E., Culwell, A. C., Sonsini, L. S., Speirn, S. K., & Tuan, M. T. (Eds.). (2004). *Funding effectiveness: Lessons in building nonprofit capacity.* San Francisco, CA: Jossey-Bass.

Kretzmann, J. P., & McKnight, J. L. (1993). *Building communities from the inside out: A path toward finding and mobilizing a community's assets.* Chicago, IL: ACTA.

Kubisch, A. C., Auspos, P., Dewar, T., & Taylor, S. (2013). *Resident centered community-building—What makes it different? A report from the connecting communities learning exchange.* San Diego, CA: Jacobs Center for Neighborhood Innovation. Retrieved from http://www.aspeninstitute.org/policy-work/community-change/publications#sthash.lAbKxpML.dpuf

Leake, R., Green, S., Marquez, C., Vanderburg, J., Guillaume, S., & Gardner, V. A. (2007). Evaluating the capacity of faith-based programs in Colorado. *Research on Social Work Practice, 17*(2), 216–228.

Letts, C. W., Ryan, W. P., & Grossman, A. (1999). *High performance nonprofit organizations: Managing upstream for greater impact.* New York, NY: Wiley.

Light, P. C. (2004). *Sustaining nonprofit performance: The case for capacity building and the evidence to support it.* Washington, DC: Brookings Institution Press.

Marguerite Casey Foundation. (2005). *Organizational capacity assessment tool.* Retrieved from http://www.caseygrants.org/pages/resources/resources_downloadassessment.asp

McGuire, M. (2002). Managing networks: Propositions on what managers do and why they do it. *Public Administration Review, 62*(5), 599–609.

McNeely, J. (1999). Community building. *Journal of Community Psychology, 27*(6), 741–750.

Mitchell, R. E., Florin, P., & Stevenson, J. F. (2002). Supporting community-based prevention and health promotion initiatives: Developing effective technical assistance systems. *Health Education and Behavior, 29*(5), 620–369.

Nelson, G. B., & Prilleltensky, I. (2005). *Community psychology: In pursuit of liberation and well-being.* New York, NY: Palgrave Macmillan.

Owen, H. (2007). Open space technology. In P. Holman, T. Devane, & S. Cady (Eds.), *The change handbook: The definitive resource on today's best methods for engaging whole systems* (2nd ed., pp. 135–148). San Francisco, CA: Berrett-Koehler.

Owen, H. (2008). *Open space technology: A user's guide* (3rd ed.). San Francisco, CA: Berrett-Koehler.

Patton, M. Q. (1998). Discovering process use. *Evaluation, 4*(2), 225–233.

Plastrik, P., & Taylor, M. (2006). *NET GAINS: A handbook for network builders seeking social change.* Retrieved from http://networkimpact.org/downloads/NetGainsHandbookVersion1.pdf

Preskill, H. (1994). Evaluation's role in enhancing organizational learning: A model for practice. *Evaluation and Program Planning, 17*(3), 291–297.

Preskill, H., & Torres, R. T. (1999). Building capacity for organizational learning through evaluative inquiry. *Evaluation, 5*(1), 42–60.

Rappaport, J. (1990). Research methods and the empowerment social agenda. In P. Tolan, C. Keys, F. Chertok, & L. Jason (Eds.), *Researching community psychology: Issues of theory and methods* (pp. 51–63). Washington, DC: American Psychological Association.

Reynolds, M. (1998). Reflection and critical reflection in management learning. *Management Learning, 29*(2), 183–200.

Rough, J. (2002). *Society's breakthrough! Releasing essential wisdom and virtue in all the people.* Bloomington, IN: 1st Books Library.

Saegert, S. (2005). *Community building and civic capacity.* Retrieved from http://www.aspeninstitute.org/sites/default/files/content/docs/rcc/CommunityBuildingCivicCapacity.pdf

Scearce, D., Kasper, G., & Grant, H. M. (2009). *Working Wikily 2.0: Social change with a network mindset.* Retrieved from http://www.workingwikily.net/Working_Wikily_2.0.pdf

Shirky, C. (2008). *Here comes everybody: The power of organizing without organizations.* New York, NY: Penguin.

Sobeck, J. L. (2008). How cost-effective is capacity building in grassroots organizations? *Administration in Social Work, 32*(2), 49–68.

Speer, P. W., Hughey, J., Gensheimer, L. K., & Adams-Leavitt, W. (1995). Organizing for power: A comparative case study. *Journal of Community Psychology, 23*(1), 57–73.

St. Luke's Health Initiatives. (2011). *TAP: Learning through networks.* Retrieved from http://slhi.org/wp-content/uploads/2011/06/TAP-learning-through-networks-2011.pdf

Sussman, C. (2008). *Building adaptive capacity: The quest for improved organizational performance.* Boston, MA: Management Consulting Services. Retrieved from http://www.barrfoundation.org/files/Building_Adaptive_Capacity.pdf

Trickett, E. J. (1984). Toward a distinctive community psychology: An ecological metaphor for the conduct of community research and the nature of training. *American Journal of Community Psychology, 12*(3), 261–279.

Venture Philanthropy Partners. (2001). *Effective capacity building in nonprofit organizations.* Retrieved from http://www.vppartners.org/learning/reports/capacity/capacity.htmls

Warren, M. R. (2001). *Dry bones rattling: Community building to revitalize American democracy.* Princeton, NJ: Princeton University Press.

CHAPTER 8

Community Organizing

Paul W. Speer and Brian D. Christens

OPENING EXERCISE

You are a middle-aged homeowner. You have owned a home (in three different cities) over the course of your adult lifetime—a 26-year period. In all that time you never filed a homeowners claim, but in the last 4 years you have filed three claims. The first was from your neighbor's tree blowing over in a big storm and destroying your detached garage. The second was from a major flood that affected much of the city you live in, and specifically ruined the heating and air-conditioning, and part of the foundation, in your basement. The third was for a massive hailstorm that punched holes through your roof, broke car a windshield, and created major damage for you and your neighbors. In each case, a claims adjuster inspected the damage and approved claims. Each claim was for a weather-related event that also impacted many others in your community. You are then notified that your insurance company has dropped your coverage for excessive claims. You contact an insurance broker, who informs you that you will not be able to obtain coverage from any other primary insurance carrier because of your excessive claims. The best you can do is to obtain coverage that triples your insurance rate, with a deductible five times greater than your previous deductible. Your broker, when asked, shares that this is happening to many others in your community. You reflect that insurance is supposed to be a collective contribution to a pool of funds that distributes risk across a whole community. You come to realize that the pooled risk notion of insurance is simply an illusion; although it serves as a psychological security blanket for individuals, at a systems level, insurance is a source of profit—not a mechanism for distributing risk. Realizing many others in your community are in the same position, what steps would you take to organize your community?

OVERVIEW

Community organizing is one of the central practice approaches utilized by community psychologists. Organizing is an intervention frequently employed by community psychologists when tackling the diverse social problems that our field addresses: alcohol and substance abuse, teen pregnancy, domestic violence, violent crime, affordable housing, and many others. Though there are many different approaches and varieties of community organizing, a common thread in these approaches is the engagement of individuals and communities affected by social problems in the definition, analysis, and solution to those problems (Stoecker, 2009). This emphasis on engagement of the individuals and communities affected by problems, as opposed to experts or political leaders, is resonant with community psychology's emphasis on citizen participation, empowerment, sense of community, and social justice (Maton, 2000). The alignment of these central tenets of community psychology makes community organizing a natural tool or, in Newbrough's words, a "found object," that "allows for psychology and community to be pursued at the same time" (Newbrough, 1992, p. 20). This chapter begins by describing what community organizing is. Competencies required in community organizing are then described, followed by an example of how community organizing was applied in community context. Next, future challenges to the field and practice of community organizing are identified. Finally, key terms, and sources of more information and training opportunities are provided.

CONCEPTUAL DEFINITION

Community organizing is a process through which people impacted by common concerns work together to build the social power necessary to achieve a series of partial solutions to those concerns. These common concerns, or shared self-interests, are perceived in community organizing as requiring change in community contexts or structural conditions, rather than in the modification of individual behaviors exclusively (Maton, 2000). Community psychologists assist members of a community to take sustained collective action to gain the power and resources required for improving conditions affecting their community.

Key Features of the Conceptual Definition

This conceptual definition has several key components that anchor it to community psychology practice. One critical component of community organizing is the collaboration among people affected by a particular social problem. This collaboration is more than a tentative or episodic coming together; rather it is focused on building a sustainable and cohesive collective. Developing cohesiveness within a collective aligns closely with the concept of "sense of community."

A second critical component to organizing is that people affected by a problem are the ones to address that problem. This is perhaps best contrasted with advocacy where individuals and groups act on behalf of others. Advocacy is certainly an important, valued, and necessary approach to solving some problems, particularly with vulnerable populations who may not be capable of acting for themselves (e.g., vulnerable children, the elderly, those with intellectual disabilities). In contrast to advocacy, organizing emphasizes the central role of those directly affected by social problems. Organizing holds that those directly affected by particular problems are most suited to understand and find appropriate solutions for those problems. In community organizing there is a so-called **iron rule** that holds that we should never do for others what they can do for themselves (Cortes, 1993). So organizing is very clear that the issues addressed must be those that directly affect members of the organizing group; organizing does not take on issues, however worthy, that primarily impact others. This view in organizing is consistent with the community psychology value of emphasizing community strengths and in developing empowerment.

A third critical component to organizing is the development of power. Social power, which represents the ability to influence the behavior and perceptions of others (in contrast to electoral power, economic power, or military power), is understood in community organizing as the most fundamental and necessary instrument for making social change (Warren, 1998). From the perspective of organizing, social change does not occur through empirical or rational processes, and social change does not occur through moral or value-based reasoning (Speer, 2008). It is important to understand that organizing embraces and values both empiricism and moral judgments, but those are not sufficient to produce social change. For community organizing, the most important factor in producing change is social power and the goal of organizing is to build power among those most oppressed, forgotten, and exploited in society. This component of organizing resonates strongly with community psychology's emphasis on empowerment and social justice. Although this perspective may be understood to challenge community psychology's emphasis on research, the prominence placed on values in community psychology is consistent with this understanding.

A final key component to organizing is an emphasis on systems change. Community organizing understands that many social problems require change on the part of individuals affected by those problems. However, like community psychology, community organizing understands that many social problems are actually symptoms of maladaptive settings and institutional arrangements. Exploring institutional arrangements and social systems represents an ecological view (see Chapter 3 in this volume) consistent with community psychology. The perspective held by organizing is perhaps best expressed by the sociologist C. Wright Mills (1959, p. 187), who asserted:

> Whether or not they are aware of them, men in a mass society are gripped by personal troubles which they are not able to turn into social issues. They do not understand the interplay of these personal troubles of their milieu with problems of social structure.

Mills was advocating for the development of a **sociological imagination**—a capacity to understand the connection between personal struggles and the social conditions and systems that contribute to those individual struggles. This component to organizing aligns with the ecological analysis practiced by community psychologists (Christens, Hanlin, & Speer, 2007; Maton, 2000), as well as an understanding of primary prevention and first- and second-order change.

COMPETENCY AND COMPETENCY DEVELOPMENT

Community organizing competencies can be conceptualized at several levels of analysis. Organizing starts with people (Checkoway, 1997) and community psychologists working in organizing settings must have competencies in listening, building relationships, challenging others, and understanding the perspectives of others. At an organizational level of analysis, organizers need to develop competencies that are appropriate for voluntary, participatory settings. Competencies for these settings include building shared leadership, developing accountability, and cultivating setting-level qualities that encourage participation. At the community level, organizers must possess an ability to build relationships with other organizations, challenge authority, understand power, and understand ecological or systemic analyses of community issues.

This description of competencies at various levels of analysis touches on some of the more critical competencies required for building a successful community organization. Although there are many varieties and approaches to community organizing, and many historical actors who have influenced community organizing (e.g., Dorothy Day, A. Philip Randolph, Bayard Rustin, Fannie Lou Hamer), perhaps none has been as influential as Saul Alinsky. Alinsky was important for many things, but perhaps most critical was his understanding that community organizing was a dynamic, context-dependent process. Alinsky (1971) emphasized that the practice of organizing was based on a set of principles rather than conducted in a sequential or fixed linear process. Alinsky was very sensitive to context—an approach that dovetails with the ecological approach in community psychology.

Individual-Level Competencies

At the individual level, participation in community organizing provides a range of experiences that challenge common perceptions of social power and provides a collective context through which emotional reaction(s) to that power can be processed or reflected upon. Freire (1970) described this action-reflection process as "dynamic praxis." At the psychological level, empowerment is a phenomenon that entails the development of leadership competencies as well as a belief in the capacity to affect change in the political and community realm.

Skills for Community Organizing

For community psychologists working as organizers, there are several skills that are important for developing emotional and cognitive empowering processes within individuals.

Listening. First, organizers must be capable of listening—this listening requires sensitivity to the challenges, beliefs, and values held by individuals. Listening, however, also requires candid dialogue. Candid dialogue is a challenge inherently, but to have such dialogue across race and gender and class makes this a particularly important skill. This kind of listening is consistent with the community psychology emphasis on cross-cultural competencies. However, listening in community organizing is more daunting than just respectful engagement and thoughtful attention to others. Organizers must also be skilled in challenging others and, at times, agitating others as part of the listening process.

Building relationships. How can an organizer be culturally sensitive and inclusive while at the same time challenging? This raises another organizing competence: building relationships. Organizers have to be capable of building relationships that entail honesty, trust, sharing, empathy, challenge, and acceptance. Building relationships is what organizers do. Listening is a key piece of building relationships, but being a good listener will not organize a community.

Challenging. The ability to challenge someone—someone you are listening to, and over the longer term someone you are building a relationship with—is a critical competency in organizing. An organizer typically challenges an analysis, assumption, perception, or belief. The purpose of challenging is to advance an understanding of the causes of the issues confronted by an individual, and to deepen the reflection individuals have on their own values and their place in the community in relation to these issues. The capacity for an organizer to challenge or agitate comes in proportion to the strength of relationship an organizer has with an individual. The organizer is always seeking to deepen this relationship, and that means the organizer typically "pushes" or advances this relationship through a willingness to test this relationship with a challenge. A challenge or agitation is not a harsh interaction, but it is often direct—frequently a direct question posed in a thoughtful way. Sometimes people shy away from a direct question—a question that might ask how they feel about an event that happened or a circumstance in the community. At other times, a challenge might ask what people did in a particular circumstance, or why they didn't do something in a particular circumstance.

Clarifying self-interest. The issue of challenges and agitations blends into the organizing concept of self-interest. Organizers in the relationship-building process are listening for the self-interest of the individuals they are meeting with. Self-interest is not selfishness or myopic advantage over others; in organizing, self-interest is understood as those things that are important to an individual. Organizers discern self-interest by listening to the stories, experiences, and priorities that individuals share in conversation. Within this sharing, people communicate what they value—caring for an elderly parent or a child's struggles in school or a neighbor's victimization from crime. Listening for self-interest allows an organizer to understand what people in the community are capable of doing together. By listening to stories, self-interest can be discerned. As relationships are developed, self-interests can be connected to values. Organizers care about values because people act on values.

Finally, these skills and competencies must be blended together as organizers interact with community members. Through careful listening, organizers discern the self-interest of individuals and begin to build the relationships necessary for developing sustainable organizations. Community organizers must also have the capacity to challenge and agitate so that community members address serious yet often suppressed issues. Challenge is possible in proportion to the depth of relationship developed, which connects back to the ability to listen for the self-interest of others. Self-interests reflect deeply held values; these may be about family or children, economic security, neighborhood stability, or other aspects of life that provide meaning.

Organizational-Level Competencies

At the organizational level, empowerment theory is relevant to community organizing because it involves the development of collective or organizational power that can change policies or practices of communities (Peterson & Zimmerman, 2004). Empowerment is a process that can be cultivated by specific settings, or what is termed "empowering organizations" (Peterson & Speer, 2000; Zimmerman, 2000). For example, a feature of an empowerment setting would be "opportunity role structure" (Maton & Salem, 1995, p. 643), which refers to the roles available within organizational settings that encourage individual participation (Speer & Hughey, 1995). These structures are qualities or characteristics of organizations that shape the amount, accessibility, and arrangement of formal positions or roles within an organization and that provide chances or opportunities for members to cooperate and build relationships, and strengthen their leadership skills and competencies.

When thinking about the organizational-level competencies required in community organizing, organizational empowerment theory articulates intra-, inter-, and extra-organizational components of organizational empowerment (Peterson & Zimmerman, 2004). **Intraorganizational empowerment** refers to characteristics about the structure and function of organizations (e.g., opportunity role structure). Some characteristics of organizations lead to greater participation and development of individuals within organizations. Organizations possessing characteristics that support and develop member skills and competencies are called "empowering organizations" (Zimmerman, 2000, p. 51). Here, organizers must possess the necessary skills and competencies to develop settings within organizations that have the characteristics of empowering settings. As an example, some organizing efforts avoid electing formal officers of the organization, and instead focus on formal roles required within the organizing process. These roles, then, are intentionally rotated among individual members each meeting as a method of building collective capacity, developing skills across a broad cross-section of the membership, and inviting new members into the organization (Speer & Hughey, 1995).

Interorganizational empowerment refers to linkages organizations have with other organizations in a community. Organizers possess competencies to understand power relations between actors and institutions in communities. **Power mapping** is a specific technique for diagramming the relationships between entities that play important roles in relation to issues of community concern. Understanding power relations at the organizational level allows organizers to strategically target their action and their research. For example, an organizing group in Minnesota advanced a major transportation initiative, and ensured that transportation was available to low-income communities of color, by studying powerful actors shaping transportation policy. Organizers built close relationships with health professionals, national research groups, as well as other community groups, and successfully pressured for the changes they sought (Speer, Tesdahl, & Ayers, 2014). Finally, **extraorganizational empowerment** refers to methods and actions organizations employ to shape or alter the broader environments in which they are embedded. For organizers, this entails alteration of the power relations within the community systems that perpetuate problems and disparities among groups. For example, an organizing group in Kansas City was, over several years, able to alter the city's system for developing and implementing housing policy (Speer & Christens, 2012).

Community-Level Competencies

One of the first community psychologists to elaborate on an understanding at the community level of analysis was Ira Iscoe (1974) and his articulation of the competent community. Iscoe was concerned with the ways in which community psychologists could work in productive and helpful ways with disenfranchised communities. He was quite attentive to issues of social class and the need for community psychologists to respect the particular values and priorities held by different communities. He was also well aware of the way that economic and material distress led to psychological harm and feelings of hopelessness and powerlessness among individuals within a community. Additionally, Iscoe understood that successful efforts to empower lower income and impoverished communities would lead to tension and conflict with the power structure. So, the key competencies for Iscoe were sensitivity to the priorities and values of impoverished communities, an understanding of developmental stages that communities move through as they build power, and an understanding of the resistance to empowering a community by the power structure. In the end, the criteria for a competent community, according to Iscoe, is a shift to a greater balance of power between what Alinsky would term "the haves" and the "have nots."

Another community psychologist who has emphasized community-level interventions is Kenneth Heller (1989, 1992). The central competencies for working at the community level for Heller include the building of collective power, preparation for resistance from the power structure, and forming coalitions. Community psychologists are required to build collective power if they want to affect the quality of life for individuals in that community. Importantly, to build stable and sustainable collective power requires cultivating a sense of community. For community organizing there is a reciprocal relationship between building

Photo 8.1 Community Organizing Meeting or "Action."

Source: iStockphoto.com/EdStock.

social power and developing a sense of community. Like Iscoe, Heller understands that the exercise of collective power will inevitably entail conflict. A critical competency for community psychologists practicing community organizing is to understand this inevitability, and to develop skills at addressing—not avoiding—conflict.

Finally, skills at building coalitions are critical at the community level of analysis. Coalition development is an extremely challenging process. Kadushin, Lindholm, Ryan, Brodsky, and Saxe (2005) provide a very important analysis of the socio-structural barriers to coalition development that community psychologists must be aware of in developing strong coalitions. One critical competency for building coalitions is the ability to understand organizational self-interest. Just as individuals have self-interest, so too do organizations. For example, many organizations are interested in expanding the services they provide, increasing budgets, and getting recognition for the work they do. Those building coalitions, however, rarely address these interests and instead focus on a particular goal, assuming organizations will join together because they want the same outcomes (e.g., more affordable housing, crime reduction). Another critical competency is coalition management. Coalitions are different from organizations, and coalition development requires an awareness and sensitivity to the variation in organizational forms and processes among organization members of the coalition. Relatedly, coalition management needs to reflect the particular organizational members composing that coalition. Competent coalition management is more than simply a standardized "Robert's Rules of Order" approach to structure. Organizational members will vary in numerous ways—along race, class, geographic scale, organizational scale (budget, staff size)—and competent coalition management must tailor a coalition's functioning to those members rather than a one-size-fits-all approach.

Training, Education, and Experiential Opportunities to Facilitate Organizing Competencies

Organizing competencies can best be obtained through training and experience in community organizing. Although university-based classes may offer insights into the history, theories, and models of community organizing—and may develop some of the skills of a competent community organizer—we believe that there is no substitute for engagement in actual community organizing processes to hone the competencies that are required for successful community organizing.

Many networks exist that educate and train community members in community organizing (see Summary section for potential resources). In some cases, students and community psychologists may be able to attend these trainings. Most importantly, we'd encourage students and other community psychologists to seek out experiential learning through involvement in community organizing, and to treat opportunities for engagement with organizing as learning opportunities, as well as venues for action-oriented research and practice. Participating in community organizing efforts will provide direct experience in many of the competencies described (discerning individual and organizational self-interests, building relationships, challenging others, and strengthening organizations).

As an example, one common organizing setting that could develop many competencies would be research efforts. It is common for organizing groups to invite an official or expert to meet about questions the organizing group has developed. Prior to this meeting, community members develop questions for public officials or experts about a matter of concern. Different community members prepare to ask different questions, and getting an answer to the question posed (rather than obfuscation) develops the skill of challenging. Careful listening to responses provides an opportunity to discern the self-interest of the organization represented in the research meeting. Finally, the way the organizing group presents itself to the official or expert provides an opportunity for the organizing group to build its organization and the relationship between the organization and the invited official or expert. Engagement in this way provides an opportunity for experiential learning—not only from the direct experience through participation, but from the engagement with the organizing group as it processes and interprets the experience itself.

APPLICATION

There are many historical antecedents to community organizing practice in the discipline of community psychology. Roger Barker was a scholar who heavily influenced the development of community psychology. Barker's ecological psychology (1968) elevated the influence and role of community contexts and settings in the shaping of individual behavior. This perspective, like that embraced by community psychology, sought to balance an overemphasis on individualism with a focus on how environments shape and constrain individual behaviors. Similarly, the preventive orientation of community psychology aligns with the focus in community organizing on systems analysis that seeks to address causes of social problems, rather than treatments. One common critique of organizing efforts by those in positions of power is that organizing groups should help directly in the problems surfaced (work at soup kitchens to help the hungry; picket drug houses instead of altering police and court practices; build housing with Habitat for Humanity rather than altering affordable housing policies). The perspective of community organizing aligns strongly with community psychology's primary prevention orientation, addressing conditions that contribute to maladjustment before they become problems rather than treating people after problems have emerged, and the understanding that second-order change, altering systems and structures that contribute to problems rather than adapting individuals to unhealthy conditions, is required to have a chance at impacting the social issues of concern (Christens & Freedman, 2014).

Just as Barker's view contributed to the systems analysis practiced in community psychology, community mental health movements and the war on poverty emphasized the inherent skills and capacities of all people as well as the importance of citizen participation. The practice competencies associated with these various strands of community psychology history blend in the practice of community organizing.

Real-World Applications of Competencies

As an example of how organizing puts into practice the competencies of organizing, the following is a story about an organizing effort during the crack cocaine epidemic. At this time, many in working-class and low-income communities were confronting drug houses, addicted drug users, prostitution, crime, drugs in schools, and many other intolerable circumstances. On the one hand, many communities called the police with minimal or no response. On the other hand, these same communities often experienced an elevated police presence with frequent stops and searches. As an example, a woman in one community who had repeatedly called for police action on her street around blatant drug dealing and drug use, got no response to her calls but found herself frequently detained by police roadblocks where she was stopped, questioned, detained, and eventually let go. During one of these stops she was given a citation for a taillight that was not functioning.

The community organizing group described here sought to address the crack epidemic because this was overwhelmingly the issue of greatest concern to members. To launch work on this issue, the group held about 80 research meetings with police, prosecutors, public defenders, judges, prisons, schools, hospitals, treatment centers, and the like. One of the things they discovered in this research was that judges were not issuing warrants for drug arrests without at least two undercover drug purchases. Judges had made this more stringent requirement for two purchases because they had discovered in the past that the police sometimes misrepresented facts to justify the issuance of judicial warrants. In the case of the drug houses on the street of the woman described earlier, the police acknowledged that they knew these were drug houses but were unable to obtain warrants. Instead, police set up roadblocks in an attempt to find drugs, but, even according to police, these strategies were ineffective. This led to a perverse situation in which active citizens were bearing the brunt of an increasingly intrusive police presence that was ineffective in addressing the crime problem and resulting in harassment of innocent citizens while drug dealing continued unabated.

This was a period of time when the ideology of the "drug war" was in ascendance. Throughout the research process, members of the organizing effort began to piece together an analysis of the distinct responses of different institutions and how these institutions came to behave as they were confronted with the crack cocaine epidemic. When viewed individually, some institutional actions made sense. When viewed systemically, the behavior was counterproductive and had no coordination or larger vision or understanding about this epidemic. In response, the organizing effort developed a push toward a comprehensive and coordinated effort across local institutions—an effort that included enforcement, education, prevention, and treatment. Furthermore, the organization pushed back against the "war on drugs" narrative and developed an analysis they termed "a public health epidemic."

The goal of the organizing effort was to develop a more coordinated and comprehensive approach to the crack epidemic across local institutions. Efforts to develop this coordination were met with support by some actors in the establishment, but derision by most officials. For example, at one meeting of city council members, a council member shouted at the group after a presentation about the group's findings. This city councilwoman yelled that the group should be picketing drug houses in their own neighborhood rather than trying to tell the council what to do.

After several requests that the mayor work to develop more coordination across many city departments were rebuffed, the group decided to mobilize their organization to have a public meeting to present their analysis and push the mayor to take some initiative in planning and coordinating a comprehensive citywide strategy in response to the crack epidemic. As preparations for this event were taking place, the organizing group continued meeting with officials. The media began to report on stories based on the analysis developed by the organizing group. Reporters following this analysis began to independently verify the perspective of the organizing group.

As an example of a leadership development challenge, one particular leader was profiled in a newspaper article about the experiences she and her family confronted in a working-class neighborhood with regard to the crack epidemic. It was a powerful story that integrated the ways in which the contradictory policies and practices of local institutions contributed to the degraded quality of life experienced by this leader and her family. It turns out that this particular leader was employed as a secretary at a large, prestigious law firm. This woman was relatively unrecognized within this large firm but when this story made the newspapers, the law firm made her story a centerpiece of the firm's newsletter. As a result, this leader became identified within her firm and received several forms of recognition at work, including a special acknowledgment at an important luncheon of the partners. Attorneys and others spoke to her more frequently on elevators, in hallways, and generally her workplace quality of life was elevated.

This leader then, however, became motivated in her organizing efforts to get more attention through the media. Unbeknownst to other members of the organizing effort or the community organizing staff, she began pushing others in her organizing group to allow her to speak to the media and make other media contacts. As noted in the section on organizational competencies, to develop an empowering organizing context, leadership roles must be rotated among members and new participants should be encouraged to build their skills by taking on diverse leadership roles. Having a single individual do a single high-profile job undermines this organizational development competency.

As the organizing effort was building toward a large public meeting with the mayor, it became apparent that this individual leader was demanding to handle media relations in the organizing process. This leader was questioned about her actions, but she was adamant on doing the media work. Surprisingly, this leader refused to give up her insistence on covering media relations. After several conversations with this woman and those closest to her, the organizer began to hear stories about the workplace profile and the work recognition this woman received from the organizing effort. The organizer and several other leaders challenged her directly about this insistence on media interactions, raising the deeper goal of the organization to build power and the importance of rotating roles in developing new leadership in the process of building such power. This leader became angry and stopped participating with the group.

This example—detailing both the issue work of a community organization and the organizational development challenge with respect to an individual leader—provides an illustration of how some competencies are put into practice. The organizational development challenge posed by this individual leader is a rare event, but illustrative of an organizational development lesson. As noted in the section on competencies, knowing the self-interests of people is critical in engagement and leadership development. However, self-interest can change. For the leader working at the law firm, we might understand her self-interest shifting from ameliorating the blight of drug crime in her neighborhood to the esteem derived in her workplace. Importantly, value for the organizing process, development of the organization, and efficacy in altering city policies was elevated over the transformed interests of an individual leader. The process of challenging this leader about the goals of building power and developing new leaders was a difficult and painful process for the organizer and other leaders. People cared for this particular individual and wanted a workable resolution to her drive for media attention. On the other hand, when leaders become fixed in organizational roles, the development of emerging leaders stagnates, the openness of the organization to the broader community becomes constrained, and established leaders evolve into "gatekeepers" who control and limit both perspectives and participation. The act of challenging individuals about their behaviors—of keeping everyone in an organization honest and accountable to collective goals—is an essential organizational competency.

At the community level, the work on the crack epidemic demonstrates the value of prevention and a systemic approach to understanding social problems. Often, particular community issues are understood as caused by a single actor or entity. Though this may be the case, cultivating a broader systemic analysis is a key community-level competency. This example also demonstrates the natural fit between community organizing and community psychology. The values of primary prevention, citizen participation, empowerment, systems change, and promotion of well-being within community psychology are demonstrated in this case.

FUTURE DIRECTIONS

The field of community organizing, as with all organizations and institutions in society, is confronting major challenges. Economic restructuring, globalization, and the entrenchment of neoliberal policies represent the biggest sources of challenge to organizing. In response to this challenge, organizing must confront the capacity to operate at larger scales (Christens & Collura, 2012; Orr, 2007). Efforts within the field of community organizing have already undertaken many efforts to mobilize and build power at regional levels (Kleidman, 2004; Osterman, 2002; Pastor, 2001; Warren, 2001; Wood, 2007). Additionally, statewide and national-level organizing efforts are emerging (Gecan, 2002; Swarts, 2007; Wood, 2007).

Efforts to build power at larger scales will require new kinds of competencies to be effective and sustainable. One type of competency will be the development of strategic partnerships with key actors. Although community organizing as a field has extensive experience and knowledge in developing partnerships at local levels, the types of partnerships required to work at larger scales will require new types of organizational partners. For example, partners might be supportive in relation to the administrative needs, technical capacities, research skills, issue expertise, as well as grassroots partnerships with others in different locales.

In looking to the future, there is space for community psychologists to support the development of competencies needed for the discipline of organizing as it advances in the future. The use of technology and social media will become important, particularly the manifestation of these tools in the context of low-income populations who may have access issues and particular social media preferences. With regard to capacities that support organizing's ability to increase the scale of its efforts, research and support in the area of collaboration across extended networks will be valuable. It is important to note that many community organizing networks (PICO, Gamaliel, NPA, IAF, OFA, NOI) already possess capacities in this regard. Nevertheless, as efforts at larger scales become more central to the success of organizing, a deeper understanding and broader scope of practices and competencies will be required. One such understanding will be how extended networks of organizing groups across broad geographic scales can collaborate on issues anchored in diverse ecological contexts. Similarly, operations at multiple political scales must integrate the diverse ecological forces driving the interests of actors at macro, meso, and micro scales. Additionally, competency in operating at such scales necessitates competency in other domains as well, such as cultural understanding, management, policy analysis, and group process.

SUMMARY

Key Points

- Community organizing is a dynamic process, driven by a set of principles around which people, organizations, and communities behave and function.

- Organizing addresses individual and collective processes simultaneously.

- Organizing understands social power as the critical component to achieving the necessary change in addressing social problems.

- Organizing requires the development of strong organizations, and this requires intentional development of organizational processes that encourage participation and development of skills among individual participants.

DISCUSSION QUESTIONS

1. What kinds of community psychology competencies are associated with the organizing process of challenge and agitation?

2. How might the self-interest of an individual or an organization change over time?

3. Can you describe an example of changing self-interest that you have experienced?

KEY TERMS AND DEFINITIONS

Community organizing: Process by which individuals and communities affected by problems collaborate to analyze this problem and exercise social power to address this problem.

Extraorganizational empowerment: Organizational actions that make changes in the policies or systems that affect communities.

Interorganizational empowerment: Relationships, collaborations, and alliances across organizations.

Intraorganizational empowerment: Characteristics that represent the internal functioning and viability of empowering organizations.

The iron rule: A principle in organizing that prioritizes power and responsibility to those directly impacted by social issues, as long as these individuals are capable of addressing those issues.

Power mapping: A practice in community organizing of identifying the relative power and position of various community actors and decision makers.

Sociological imagination: Understandings of how social-structural forces are manifested in the lives of individuals.

RESOURCES

Recommended Reading

Alinsky, S. D. (1971). *Rules for radicals: A pragmatic primer for realistic radicals.* New York, NY: Vintage Books.

Wood, R. L., Fulton, B., & Partridge, K. (2013). *Building bridges, building power: Developments in institution-based community organizing.* Retrieved from http://www.soc.duke.edu/~brf6/ibcoreport.pdf

Organizing Networks and Training Websites

Center for Third World Organizing: http://ctwo.org
Direct Action & Research Training Center: http://www.thedartcenter.org
Gamaliel Foundation: http://www.gamaliel.org
IAF: http://www.industrialareasfoundation.org
National Organizers Alliance: http://noacentral.org
National People's Action: http://npa-us.org
New Organizing Institute: http://neworganizing.com
PICO Network: http://www.piconetwork.org

Other Recommended Materials

COMM-ORG: The online conference on community organizing: http://comm-org.wisc.edu
Community Toolbox: http://ctb.ku.edu/en

Suggested Activities for Further Competency Development

- Practice the skill of discerning the self-interest of others.

- Examine the organizational processes of the groups in which you belong. How do these processes support or discourage participation and skill development among members?

For Self-Exploration or Self-Development

- Think about your own self-interests—how do you know what they are? Think about how you spend your time and the activities you are involved in—are these consistent with what you identify as your self-interest?

- Practice your listening skills with friends by having serious conversations— challenge people in these conversations about why they act or feel the way they do. How do you feel in asking those challenging questions?

For Assessment of Knowledge, Skill, and Abilities Relating to the Competency

- Reflect on the organizations of which you are a part—in what ways do you contribute to those organizations? Do you bring in more members? Are you a leader in some capacity? Are you able to bring people together? Are you able to get the organization to reflect or reconsider their actions?

REFERENCES

Alinsky, S. D. (1971). *Rules for radicals: A pragmatic primer for realistic radicals.* New York, NY: Vintage Books.

Barker, R. (1968). *Ecological psychology: Concepts and methods for studying the environment of human behavior.* Stanford, CA: Stanford University Press.

Checkoway, B. (1997). Core concepts for community change. *Journal of Community Practice, 4*(1), 11–29.

Christens, B. D., & Collura, J. J. (2012). Local community organizers and activists encountering globalization: An exploratory study of their perceptions and adaptations. *Journal of Social Issues, 68*(3), 592–611.

Christens, B. D., & Freedman, D. A. (2014). Community organization and systems intervention. In T. P. Gullotta & M. Bloom (Eds.), *Encyclopedia of primary prevention and health promotion* (2nd ed.). New York, NY: Springer.

Christens, B. D., Hanlin, C. E., & Speer, P. W. (2007). Getting the social organism thinking: Strategy for systems change. *American Journal of Community Psychology, 39*(3–4), 229–238.

Cortes, E. (1993). Reweaving the fabric: The iron rule and the IAF strategy for power and politics. In H. G. Cisneros (Ed.), *Interwoven destinies* (pp. 294–319). New York, NY: W. W. Norton.

Freire, P. (1970). *Pedagogy of the oppressed.* New York, NY: Continuum.

Gecan, M. (2002). *Going public.* Boston, MA: Beacon Press.

Heller, K. (1989). The return to community. *American Journal of Community Psychology, 17*(1), 1–15.

Heller, K. (1992). Ingredients for effective community change: Some field observations. *American Journal of Community Psychology, 20*(2), 143–163.

Iscoe, I. (1974). Community psychology and the competent community. *American Psychologist, 8,* 607–613.

Kadushin, C., Lindholm, M., Ryan, D., Brodsky, A., & Saxe, L. (2005). Why is it so difficult to form effective community coalitions? *City & Community, 4*(3), 255–275.

Kleidman, R. (2004). Community organizing and regionalism. *City & Community, 3*(4), 403–421.

Maton, K. I. (2000). Making a difference: The social ecology of social transformation. *American Journal of Community Psychology, 28*(1), 25–57.

Maton, K. I., & Salem, D. A. (1995). Organizational characteristics of empowering community settings: A multiple case study approach. *American Journal of Community Psychology, 23*(5), 631–656.

Mills, C. W. (1959). *The sociological imagination.* New York, NY: Oxford University Press.

Newbrough, J. R. (1992). Community psychology in the postmodern world. *Journal of Community Psychology, 20*(1), 10–25.

Orr, M. (Ed.). (2007). *Transforming the city: Community organizing and the challenge of political change.* Lawrence: University Press of Kansas.

Osterman, P. (2002). *Gathering power: The future of progressive power in America.* Boston, MA: Beacon Press.

Pastor, M. (2001). Common ground at ground zero? The new economy and the new organizing in Los Angeles. *Antipode, 33*(2), 260–289.

Peterson, N. A., & Speer, P. W. (2000). Linking organizational characteristics to psychological empowerment: Contextual issues in empowerment theory. *Administration in Social Work, 24*(4), 39–58.

Peterson, N. A., & Zimmerman, M. A. (2004). Beyond the individual: Toward a nomological network of organizational empowerment. *American Journal of Community Psychology, 34*(1/2), 129–145.

Speer, P. W. (2008). Social power and forms of change: Implications for psychopolitical validity. *Journal of Community Psychology, 36*(2), 199–213.

Speer, P. W., & Christens, B. D. (2012). Local community organizing and change: Altering policy in the housing and community development system in Kansas City. *Journal of Community & Applied Social Psychology, 22*(5), 414–427.

Speer, P. W., & Hughey, J. (1995). Community organizing: An ecological route to empowerment and power. *American Journal of Community Psychology, 23*(5), 729–748.

Speer, P. W., Tesdahl, E. A., & Ayers, J. A. (2014). Community organizing practices in a globalizing era: Building power for health equity at the community level. *Journal of Health Psychology, 19*(1), 159–169.

Stoecker, R. (2009). Community organizing and social change. *Contexts, 8*(1), 20–25.

Swarts, H. J. (2007). Political opportunity, venue shopping, and strategic innovation. ACORN's national organizing. In M. Orr (Ed.), *Transforming the city: Community organizing and the challenge of political change* (pp. 134–161). Lawrence: University Press of Kansas.

Warren, M. R. (1998). Community building and political power: A community organizing approach to democratic renewal. *American Behavioral Scientist, 42*(1), 78–92.

Warren, M. R. (2001). *Dry bones rattling: Community building to revitalize American democracy.* Princeton, NJ: Princeton University Press.

Wood, R. L. (2007). Higher power: Strategic capacity for state and national organizing. In M. Orr (Ed.), *Transforming the city: Community organizing and the challenge of political change* (pp. 162–192). Lawrence: University Press of Kansas.

Zimmerman, M. A. (2000). Empowerment theory: Psychological, organizational and community levels of analysis. In J. Rappaport & E. Seidman (Eds.), *Handbook of community psychology* (pp. 43–63). New York, NY: Kluwer Academic/Plenum.

CHAPTER 9

Building and Strengthening Collaborative Community Partnerships

Judah J. Viola, Bradley D. Olson,
Suzette Fromm Reed,
Tiffeny R. Jimenez, and Christina M. Smith

OPENING EXERCISE

The focus of this chapter is on building and strengthening community partnerships from the perspective of community psychologists embedded in or collaborating with cultural institutions, government, and nonprofits. Let's begin with an exercise to explore one form building partnerships can take. Take the perspective of an early career community practitioner. Imagine you have a few years of experience working as a consultant independently or as part of a small firm. Your focus is on program evaluation and community-based research across a variety of content areas such as health, education, and housing. A previous program evaluation client (the education director of a local museum) knows of your community connections. You are aware the museum has historically not been as accessible as it could be to large portions of the city's population. The goals of the museum include expanding its reach beyond its traditional audience and serving as a resource that is both accessible and relevant to as much of the city's diverse groups as possible. The museum has some strong ties with high performing schools and science clubs, but little connection to community-based agencies that work with the audience they are trying to reach. The client asks for assistance in finding and developing partnerships with community organizations across the city.

In effect you are being asked to take on the role of "community liaison." Jot down some ideas of how you would address the following questions and then, as you read the chapter, see how your approach might evolve. *What knowledge, skills, and abilities will you need to be an effective liaison and capacity builder to assist in this partnership-building endeavor? How do you begin to build the necessary partnerships to make this goal a reality? Finally, how do you develop a sustainability plan for ensuring that the client has what is needed to maintain these partnerships after your consultation work has ended?*

OVERVIEW

The chapter begins with conceptual definitions of partnerships and collaboration as well as aspects of the community psychology practice competencies most related to developing consulting and evaluation partnerships (i.e., collaborative consultation and group process skills). As you will read here and in other chapters, each competency requires an extensive set of knowledge, skills, and abilities that directly connect to building and sustaining effective working relationships. Next, the chapter moves into our four-stage model of partnership building that stems from our practice work in consultation and evaluation. Examples from our own community psychology practice work are provided to illustrate some of the questions, concerns, challenges, and rewards involved when trying to apply these skills to building community partnerships. We close the chapter with a brief summary of the main points, followed by a set of recommended resources for further exploration and consideration.

CONCEPTUAL DEFINITIONS

Partnerships are dynamic and reciprocal relationships of two or more people or organizations with a shared set of goals that are developed to find mutual and practical solutions. Partnerships can also be seen as a network of constructive working relationships with clients, communities, organizations, and professional colleagues across diverse sectors and academic frames of reference. For the purposes of this chapter *partnerships* and *relationships* are used interchangeably. **Collaboration** refers to the nature of the mutually beneficial relationships and processes in which community partners engage. The knowledge associated with collaboration involves exchanging information, sharing resources, and enhancing the capacity of others to achieve a common purpose by sharing risks, resources, responsibilities, and rewards (Himmelman, 2001; see also Wolff, 2009).

Partnerships, at their core, are dynamic because they are defined by reciprocal relationships with a shared set of goals (Mumford, Zaccaro, Harding, Jacobs, & Fleishman, 2000). While there is not one right way to build relationships, we believe there are competencies made up of knowledge, skills, and abilities that can be developed to make you more effective in building strong, sustainable partnerships. In addition to competencies, as community psychology practitioners we value shared power and a collaborative approach to decision making (Kloos et al., 2010; Nelson & Prilleltensky, 2010).

New partnerships may bring diverse perspectives, political connections, technology, energy, audience members, money, experience, content expertise, and a sense of ownership to a collaborative endeavor. Partnerships may help an agency establish greater legitimacy throughout the community and make sure that the agency is effective and accessible for an array of populations (National Council on the Aging, 2003, p. 8). In effect, partnerships are tools as well as transformative learning opportunities to achieve mutual and/or individual goals (Compassion Capital Fund [CCF] National Resource Center, 2010). When discussing partnerships it is important to consider the different forms of mobilizing power to address community issues, pool resources, enhance coordination for planning and implementation, and minimize the duplication of efforts (Sofaer, 1999).

In our approach, a community practitioner first builds a relationship with an organization and then works with that organization to build further relationships. Consistent with our museum example in the opening exercise, working with the education department of a major cultural institution (e.g., a museum of natural history, an art museum, an aquarium) to act as a community liaison and reach out to the broader community, one would likely develop partnerships with individuals, community organizations, primary and secondary schools, school systems/districts, universities, other museums and cultural institutions, coalitions, and funders.

Each partner and partnering organization has a unique history, set of norms, interests, and context, all of which are helpful to know. The size, budget, and other resources (e.g., time, volunteers) and policies of organizations may differ in relevant ways, and those variables may influence how connected a consultant or evaluator becomes with the organization. The strength of your relationships, and who you have relationships with, matters. For instance, having partnerships with different gatekeepers and decision makers who have greater or less power to get things done—or to obtain approval using a collaborative leadership approach—impacts the influence of the partnership.

Nonprofits and local government agencies can enhance their individual and collective capacity to have an impact through building partnerships. Studies of partnership dynamics suggest that participants manage the complexity of partnerships by adopting a long-term, flexible approach that is responsive to the need for change (CCF National Resource Center, 2010).

The vast majority of nonprofits are small, local organizations that will rarely be able to take advantage of economies of scale. Thus, a small nonprofit may achieve greater impact by coordinating some aspects of its work with related providers. Beyond simply reducing redundancies, these partnerships can generate synergies that magnify the impact of each individual member (Wei-Skillern & Marciano, 2008).

In sum, navigating partnerships at individual, organizational, and community levels is a complex exercise, with a great number of contextual differences in each relationship at each level. Take a moment to reconsider the questions at the opening to this section in light of the material presented in this section: What do you want to know about the resources of the museum as well as of potential partner agencies (diversity, political connections, technology, energy, audience members, money, experience, content expertise, and a sense of ownership)? What community change might occur from a partnership between the museum and any community organization?

PRACTICE COMPETENCIES

It is valuable to embed community psychology competencies in the context of a community practitioner's mind-set, knowledge, and skills. Community psychologists have a unique vantage point, which includes a focus on systems (an ecological level of analysis), and an appreciation for diversity. In addition to core research and evaluation skills, our training emphasizes capacity building, group facilitation skills, data collection skills, and knowledge of the collaborative process. While knowledge and skills can improve, they are sometimes context specific, and each consultation/evaluation project is different. One project may strengthen our partnership abilities in community-organizing skills, which, for instance, may not translate well to building collaborative relationships with elected officials. Nevertheless, two common and generalizable competencies within the partnership literature are (1) collaborative consultation and (2) group facilitation.

Collaborative Consultation

With our own consulting work, we try to acknowledge openly, particularly at the beginning of the process, that the partners who are engaging our services are the content experts. We do gain some level of expertise in the program efforts we evaluate, but there are certain forms of knowledge held only by those entrenched in the work for a long period of time. Understanding an organizational culture, its goals and plans, and ways of functioning, takes a great deal of time. We feel we bring value to the relationship by viewing the organization from a fresh perspective and by articulating that view to our partners—often presented as a visual model, logic model, or report. Our strengths as consulting community psychologists make us just one more partner in a larger process. We would not say that we "empower" our partners, but when the partnership works in a collaborative way, we all feel empowered by the partnership.

Collaborative consultation, a form of consultation that uses a shared decision-making process and feedback loops throughout the work with the goal of helping all partners more toward a mutually desired goal and empowerment, may take more time and communication than a more hierarchical relationship. With collaboration there is a shared decision-making process and feedback loops throughout the phases of the work. Also, buried within the collaboration competency is the ability to demonstrate leadership/management skills, to resolve conflict, to engage in problem solving, and to help all the partners move toward a mutually desired action.

Collaboration is not just a "feel good" term. When done right, it is a process very different from the more hierarchical approaches represented in government and private enterprise. As Wolff (2009) explains, collaborations allow us to move away from the traditional, ineffective models of solving problems to a more hopeful and sustaining process. With effective collaboration, Wolff explains, existing fragmentation can move toward more holistic solutions, and usual limits to information sharing can be transformed into more effective and accessible forms of communication. In addition, duplication of efforts can shift to coordination, competition to cooperation. A crisis orientation can be countered through prevention, lack of stakeholder involvement turns into a citizen-driven process, and lack of cultural competence can transform to culturally relevant and respectful approaches. Moreover, excessive professionalization can shift to the greater use of both formal and informal helping networks, and the too often loss of spiritual purpose can be reworked to align with a collaborative effort's goals and its process (Wolff, 2009, p. 23).

Gray (1991) identified several benefits that were more commonly available through a collaborative approach: (1) a more comprehensive ability to analyze social issues, leading to higher quality solutions; (2) the greater ability to reframe social problems differently from more adversarial approaches; (3) a process that better ensures various stakeholder interests are shared; (4) solutions provided by those who are closest to the issues, which enhances community members' willingness to collaborate further; (5) an increased potential for improving relations among stakeholders; and (6) the potential for developing mechanisms for future partnership-based action.

Collaboration can occur with or without a facilitator, liaison, or mediator. However, a community psychologist-practitioner can be effective in helping to bring people together, to help structure the dialogue within the context of a specific meeting or set of meetings, and to gain insight from community members to work together more effectively (see Gray, chap. 7). What it takes to support a collaborative process varies substantially with context.

Mattessich, Murray-Close, Monsey, and Wilder Research Center (2001) identified five key factors for success of community collaborations: (1) mutual trust and respect among the partners, (2) an appropriate mix of stakeholder representation, (3) membership cohesion, (4) collaborators who value cooperation and see advantages to participation, and (5) members who are able and willing to compromise. Whether it is ensuring representation or encouraging compromise, a community psychologist who is attempting to enhance these conditions requires a complex set of valuable skills. *How might the collaborative approach play out in the museum example at the beginning of this chapter? Revisit your answers to the questions raised earlier. Jot down any new ideas.*

Group Facilitation

One of the challenges of playing a consultative role in a collaborative effort can simply involve knowing who to bring together and how to arrange a new group of people. Even more challenging, however, is the conflict, anxiety, inertia, or role confusion that is sometimes unavoidable within a partnership. Having knowledge of group dynamics and processes, in addition to tailoring your approaches to those people and situations, can help you assess almost any group-related situation. Some key group facilitation process skills include:

- **Diverse decision-making:** Ensuring that a wide range of people are engaged in decision making and can have helpful dialogue in a safe environment

- **Interpersonal communication:** Utilizing effective interpersonal communication skills (e.g., active listening, paraphrasing, reframing, challenging, moving on)

- **Conflict analysis:** Assessing the issues, players' concerns, and positions of stakeholders to better understand conflicts and assist in resolutions

- **Animating consensus building:** Facilitating and energizing consensus-building processes

- **Facilitation:** Using a diversity of techniques (e.g., circles, mediation, interviewing, use of narrative) to enable groups to achieve their goals for dialogue, planning, and decision making

- **Crisis intervention:** Applying problem-solving and clinical skills when appropriate to address major problems that arise and become barriers to progress

It is also useful to be well versed in foundational theories to help provide a lens from which to understand how groups work. For example, **group dynamics,** the behaviors and psychological processes that occur within or between social groups, is a foundational area (e.g., see Lewin, 1947) underlying much of today's organizational development literature. Additional related theories such as group cohesion and social identity theory (Dion, 2000; Hogg, 1992; Tajfel, 1979) incorporate the ideas of group bonds, identities, and in-group/out-group relations. **Normative social influence** focuses on the influence of expectations on group and individual attitudes and behaviors (Crutchfield, 1955; Latane, 1981) and of course **sense of community**, the notion that an important factor in any group relationship is the extent to which individuals feel they are fully connected to an interdependent community (Chavis & Pretty, 1999; McMillan & Chavis, 1986; Sarason, 1974, 1986).

COMPETENCY DEVELOPMENT

In addition to gaining a strong research and theoretical training in community psychology, we recommend taking the time to seek out training in group process and collaboration in order to gain the important knowledge, skills, and abilities. Sometimes these are part of one's graduate program, but if not it is also possible to take such courses in other programs or departments within the university. In particular, departments within your university may offer specific courses in group processes, or more general courses such as social psychology, organizational development, and organizational leadership may cover group process and group relations in their curriculum.

Sources of Training Beyond Academia

Furthermore, professional organizations in your academic field or allied disciplines often offer workshops, webinars, or training institutes that cover group facilitation skills, leading difficult dialogues, mediation, and negotiations that often involve role-play or apprentice-style learning opportunities (see American Evaluation Association, Evaluator's Institute, American Public Health Association, American Psychological Association, American Society for Training and Development).

Trainings are also offered by individual practitioners or organizational development companies. Community organizing groups such as the PICO National Network or the Industrial Areas Foundations or their affiliates offer many valuable leadership trainings. Specifically, we suggest you become trained in using methods that foster cooperation, collaboration, and dialogue. Areas that may help here include those focusing on empowerment evaluation, operative groups, appreciative inquiry, restorative justice, peace circles, community organizing leadership, World Café facilitation, and diversity training. At the end of the chapter we include recommended resources on partnerships, collaboration, and group facilitation and trainings that cover many of these topics.

Reading theory, attending workshops, and gaining firsthand community experiences, advocacy, and community-based research will lead to better knowledge of and skill sets on a variety of topics: conflict resolution/intergroup relations, community organizing, and human diversity. There are community-based trainings offered through teach-ins, community organizing leadership trainings, and peace circles (see Peacemaker Institute International, http://peacemakerinstitute.org/).

APPLICATION

In considering how to bring together all of the knowledge, skills, and abilities associated with the competencies for building and maintaining partnerships regardless of where they are gained, we find it helpful to explore existing models for guiding our actions and then adapt those models to our own contexts and experiences. Thinking temporally, there are stages of developing partnerships. For instance, Tuckman's five-stage model of small-group development includes *forming, storming, norming, performing,* and *adjourning* (see Tuckman & Jensen, 1977) and has been very useful in thinking about group processes. Additionally, classic social and contemporary organizational development and management consultants present models of how groups form, interact, face challenges, and succeed. These models include the group needs model (Bellman & Ryan, 2009), complexity theory (Anderson, 1999), action research (Lewin, 1947), appreciative inquiry (Coghlan, Preskill, & Catsambas, 2003; Cooperider, Whitney, & Stavros, 2008), organizational change theories (Rafferty, Jimmieson, & Armenakis, 2013), systems theory (Checkland, 1981; Holland, 1992; Reynolds, 2008), and field theory (Lewin, 1947). All of these models/theories, from diverse fields, offer opportunities to better understand partnerships. The process model outlined below is intended to be pragmatic by keeping the basic stages consistent with our experiences of partnership-building, evaluation, and consultation in the community.

Four-Phase Model of Collaborative Consulting and Evaluation Partnerships

The pragmatic four-phase process model we suggest be used for developing partnerships and working collaboratively includes (1) seeking; (2) connecting and negotiating; (3) implementation and maintenance; and (4) ending and capacity building (see Figure 9.1).

While the phases imply linearity, the process tends to be iterative—earlier phases, more often than not, end up being revisited to clarify (or adjust to) changing circumstances or needs.

First, we will explore the values and assumptions embedded in the client-consultant process from the perspective of a community psychologist—values such as relationship building and empowerment span all phases of the model. We then move into the specifics of each stage/phase using the example in the opening exercise.

Values and Assumptions Embedded in the Client-Consultant Process

Partnerships are a type of relationship, as are networks, or community coalitions, and there are many models of partnerships that can be successful. Applying a community psychology frame of reference means making use of core values that guide the client-consultant process, including developing and maintaining trust, as well as encouraging an empowering process. Providing equity of information and lateral decision-making power

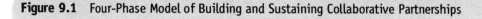

Figure 9.1   Four-Phase Model of Building and Sustaining Collaborative Partnerships

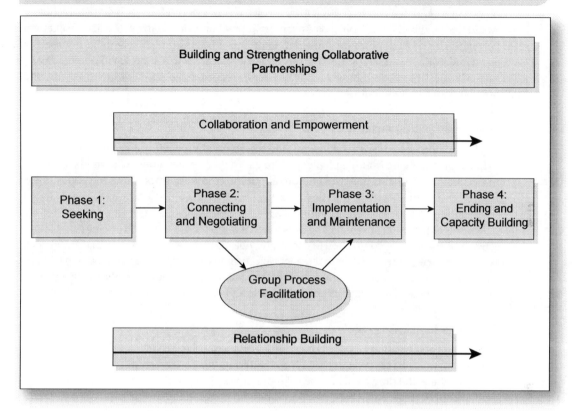

through collaboration creates a more empowering process. The goal is to consistently help partners make contributions and feel a sense of ownership of group successes. As community psychologists we believe that authentic ongoing communication among all partners and a true collaborative process will transform a sense of oneness and independence into a sense of community, interdependence, and empowerment among partners. This process will, ideally, positively influence other stakeholders impacted by the partnership. Furthermore, regular contact, whether face-to-face or virtual, is important to maintain energy, transparency, and investment. *Consider your role as community liaison from the opening exercise. Will your role shift from a "community liaison" for the museum to a consultant to the partnership as a new entity, or will you become one partner among many?*

Phase 1: Seeking

Often the seeking phase begins with exploring the landscape of potential partners. If there is a competency involved, it includes using one's interpersonal skills, existing professional networks, and research acumen. You need to quickly assess a partner's organizational strengths. What programs, resources, or connections will complement your partnership-related goals? Such a determination may involve a series of brief initial inquiries, including web-based and individual conversations to help build and then narrow the list of potential partners. The seeking phase may overlap with later phases and is likely to be returned to again and again. Phase I typically finds temporary resolution in a short list of potential partners who possess assets that will add value for the partnership and a desire to explore the possibility of a more enduring relationship.

Challenges and Opportunities

The seeking phase has its challenges. One is simply in convincing busy potential partners to find a time to meet. Another challenge is to gain a greater awareness of potential partners in the area, which helps in learning more about the resources throughout the community. Even if partners do not emerge at first, you will have gained contacts at agencies with shared goals, adding to your awareness, your network, as well as visibility within the community.

Consider the opening exercise: The museum has strong ties to high-performing schools and science clubs, but little connection to community-based agencies that work with the audience you are targeting. You reach out to ten agencies, meet with several. You find that only two are interested in collaboration. It might feel like time was wasted, but now the other eight agencies may have become part of your informal network, and you have opened doors for the future.

Questions to Ask/Answer

- What organizations exist in the content or geographic area?
- What are the probable benefits from fostering this relationship?
- What are the drawbacks of the relationship (e.g., economic as well as other resource costs, such as time commitments, or credibility and trust)?
- Is the geographic location of potential partners an important factor?
- Once you have identified an organization to approach, consider:

  o Who are the gatekeepers at these organizations?
  o What is the best level of entry within the organization (frontline staff, management, executives, board members)?
  o When doing your background research, explore the range of activities, reputation, structure, culture, values, and approach of partner organizations, including the history of partnerships and the nature of those past collaborations.

Examples From Our Practice

As consultants to museums, schools, and social service institutions we are often asked to help identify potential partners and locations for programming. Geographic proximity is often a factor. We were once asked to explore all neighborhood parks on the south and west sides of Chicago for bodies of water youth could engage with for exploring aquatic ecosystems. Our list of suitable locations was then cross-referenced with local community-based organizations, parks department field houses, and schools that might partner with the museum. Schools, parks, and other organizations within walking distance were researched, as was the number of youth served by these institutions and whether the potential partners were interested in building their capacity through train-the-trainer environmental programs led by the museum.

Practice Recommendations Based on Lessons Learned

Within the seeking phase, utilize existing networks. Make use of your own and/or your client organization's reputation. Do not hesitate to make "cold calls" or emails and move beyond your area of comfort and expertise. While the calls may be "cold" in the sense that you will not personally know the contact, it is helpful to do your homework beforehand. The more information you have up front, the less likely you will approach organizations that are not a good fit with your group or your partnering organization.

As you are learning about your potential partners, look to match goals and find synergies. Partners should bring assets neither you nor your client has internally. Before agreeing to partner, ask the potential partners to reaffirm their own vision and goals. This will allow each party to establish its own priorities and expectations (Wild Rose Foundation, 2001). However, priority clarification cannot happen in isolation. Each group needs to be flexible to move beyond their initial expectations.

Recognizing the interdependence within our work is an important part of understanding partnership building. Thus, letting others know what you are looking for in the partnership is important. Community psychology practice, even for consultants who work "independently," includes regular contact with a variety of colleagues, current and past partners, subcontractors, clients, and friends. In the seeking phase, people in your existing network are likely to have good recommendations. Use a snowball technique that will assist you in building new connections and following up on each expanding set of recommendations.

Phase 2: Connecting and Negotiating

The second phase, *connecting and negotiating,* is crucial to setting up effective partnerships. Initial meetings help partners get to know each other and learn about mutual values, culture, strengths, and challenges. Trust between partners and a clarified commitment to a shared vision should be established. Determining the roles and responsibilities of each partner and setting up a basic framework for communication and follow up are needed. Depending on the nature of the project, the relationship may or may not be formalized during this connecting and negotiating phase. The connecting and negotiating may end with a contract or merely a verbal agreement to move forward, though returning to the original agreement is common in later phases.

Challenges and Opportunities

Initial challenges tend to take extremes. Mistrust can lead to resistance, whereas unrealistic positive expectations can lead to overambitious goal setting. Competing priorities and demands on participants' time and resources are often major challenges.

Photo 9.1 Connecting and negotiating are crucial to setting up effective partnerships.

Source: iStockphoto.com/ClarkandCompany.

Some Phase 2 opportunities include an increased sense of power that comes with joining forces to accomplish a goal, increased resources (e.g., staff, time, money), and increased access to people with shared goals. Strategies, cultures, and other ways of doing the work more effectively (i.e., regularities) often emerge at this time.

Questions to Ask/Answer

- What are the benefits to target groups (primary stakeholders) in establishing this partnership?

- What have been the experiences with partnerships in the past? What went well? What did not go well?

- How will you make decisions as a partnership? Will the other partner(s) agree to collaborate? How will you communicate? How will you build accountability into the process?

- Considering power differentials: When and where should meetings occur? Who should you bring to the meetings and who should you request attend? Does the potential partner organization operate only during business hours?

- Where might organizational adjustments on either side need to be made?

- At what level are you initiating the relationship?

- Are there signs of charisma, excitement, or reliability in the leadership?

- Is there hope for future capacity building expressed by the partner?

- Is there value in using a Memorandum of Agreement (MOU) or some other written contract to clarify roles and responsibilities as well as a system to ensure accountability?

Examples From Our Practice

In the case of our museum example, we chose to partner with three different types of organizations to expand the diversity of museum volunteers. The museum partnered with (1) a school system service learning office that helped connect with service learners and program participants; (2) a county forest preserve department to expand offerings and trainings available to the audience they each served; (3) a community development corporation to provide options for and access to job training programs through an internship process.

While there were overlapping goals, the organizations were very different from each other and the museum chose to work separately with each group rather than bring all parties together in a single group.

Given the highly structured school office, the initial negotiations with the school partner centered on coming to clear agreements about eligibility rules and requirements for participants. With the forest preserve, the connecting and negotiating phase was used to learn about the strengths of each organization and carefully consider opportunities for synergy. With the community development organization partnership, there was need to take additional time to establish rapport, build trust, and learn about the differing organizational cultures before a realistic agreement and plan could be reached. As community psychology practitioners, in our role as community liaisons we encouraged museum staff to attend events sponsored by the community development corporation and really take the time to understand the strengths and culture of the organization.

Practice Recommendations Based on Lessons Learned

- Do your research: Learn what is important to each partner organization. Use their goals and objectives and continuing dialogue to find possible connections that strengthen relationships, build trust, and identify synergies. Learn the context of the organization's past partnerships. This is a way to build deeper buy-in to the partnership, plan for success, and avoid making mistakes that can be avoided.

- While trying to build a new relationship there is a natural tendency to want to put your best foot forward and look your best. However, it is very important, particularly at this early stage, not to over-promise. Start with open brainstorming. Look realistically at what each side can commit to the project. Keep in mind that it is easy to overestimate what an organization will contribute to the effort, so consider potential barriers or competing priorities. Nonprofit executive staff may run into challenges with their board, or government agencies may get slowed down as approvals are needed or legal agreements must be reviewed. These concerns rarely arise in the excitement of early collaborative planning.

- Set ground rules for conducting meetings. These can vary from respecting diverse perspectives and cultures to respecting time by agreeing to begin and end meetings on time and stay on task, sharing responsibilities for setting agendas, maintaining minutes, and hosting and/or staffing meetings.

- Develop a shared decision-making process in which partners have equal power (i.e., be collaborative).

- Consider exploring innovative models of communication (e.g., Women's Leadership Circles, difficult conversations, crucial conversations).

- Recognize and make explicit the limitations of the partnership, and reflect and re-strategize on these limits when necessary. Acknowledge the existence of separate organizational aims and objectives as well as disconnects between policy and practice. Blending organizational policies and regularities requires knowing your own program capacity and understanding the capacity of each partner. Time will be needed to understand differing cultural norms, resources, and capacities.

- If all parties are not committed to the process after a few meetings, or do not see the potential for synergy resulting from the partnership, it is fine to agree to go your separate ways until a better opportunity presents itself. You are aiming for a high commitment level from all partners. If this is not found, then it is best to consider other partners.

- Further identification of resources, such as geographic asset mapping or community or neighborhood profiles, can be helpful for identifying mutual resources and planning where to target efforts.

- If the partnership takes the form of a new entity outside the partner organizations, this can add a level of complexity to the decision making, roles and responsibilities, and accountability issues. In these cases, it might make sense to develop an MOU. At the very least, clear procedures are helpful for all parties to understand how decisions will be made and actions taken and to help create a sense of shared responsibility. Depending on the formality and size of the partnership, more explicit contracts can provide the partnership structure and yet still allow for flexibility.

- Make commitments specific and explicit, with timelines. If those in the room do not have the authority to make such commitments, develop a clear timeline for obtaining those commitments and/or a plan for getting the necessary decision makers briefed to support the decisions needed.

Phase 3: Project Involvement, Implementation, and Maintenance

The third phase of the model involves doing the work of the partnership. Now that the plans are laid out, this is when implementation occurs. During this phase you may need to return to the negotiations to clarify or reestablish roles, responsibilities, and commitments. Norms that were developed in Phase 2 are often cemented in Phase 3. This is typically the period where it is possible to assess the effectiveness of a partnership. Implementation and maintenance is typically the lengthiest phase.

Challenges and Opportunities

Phase 3 can begin with a feeling of relief that partners can actually get to work on their mutual projects. Fear and anxiety can arise around whether partners will fulfill their commitments. Communication is critical during all phases; all partners need to be clear about challenges, small wins, and any changes that occur when executing plans. Communication breakdowns during the implementation and maintenance phase can be a major barrier to successful outcomes. Opportunities abound during this phase of the partnership. Partners will continue to learn about themselves, their partners, and how to work together. As new information surfaces, partners may need to revisit previously developed plans in order to attend to the new information. Over time, partners will start to see the fruit of their labor in action.

Questions to Ask/Answer

Keep asking questions about ways to improve the relationship. For example:

- How is the partnership mutually beneficial?
- How are our abilities strengthened through the partnership?
- How are our partners strengthened through this relationship?

Organizational partners are not the only stakeholders and thus it is important to consider how the work of the partnership is involving or impacting other stakeholders.

Examples From Our Practice

The consultant often takes responsibility for facilitating group dynamics in a way that will lead to continued results. Revisiting the strengths, benefits, and small wins as the "sparks" of the partnership can go a long way in helping to maintain the collaborative spirit needed to reach long-term goals. For example, beginning regular meeting sessions by reflecting on achievements or showing a timeline of the progress achieved to date has been helpful for us in the past. Additionally, focusing on using terms such as *we* and *ours* is a simple though subtle way of further promoting a positive sense of community. In the case of our work with the museum and schools partnership we were aware from previous work with the schools that high turnover and high-stress times of year (i.e., testing periods and budgeting periods) would be barriers to meeting goals. Thus we encouraged both the museum staff and the school staff to map out their timelines to allow for periods of hibernation. Yet we emphasized the need to stay in regular contact for brief check-ins even when no partnership work was planned for completion at that particular time. The continued dialogue allowed for news of barriers or problems to be shared and addressed quickly.

Practice Recommendations Based on Lessons Learned

• Formally or informally develop and maintain partnership norms. This should include following the ground rules that were originally set, reminding partners of shared values and revisiting if necessary. Some guides suggest documenting the norms with "I will" or "we will" statements to increase ownership. Others recommend positively reiterating the agreed-upon norms regularly to reinforce their centrality to the success of the partnership.

• Check in often to keep all parties on track—just reach out.

• Maintain multiple points of contact. Having several layers of contacts at the organization helps most in cases where there is turnover or when staff responsibilities are reassigned.

• Use multiple channels for communication (e.g., phone, email, in-person).

• Work to maintain a presence at the partner organization. This might mean stopping by to say hello or attending partner events. Having a presence helps build and maintain trust with primary contacts as well as other staff and stakeholders.

• Promote an atmosphere of learning. This allows partners to reflect on and learn from successes and failures with the opportunity to make necessary mid-course corrections.

• Map out your process over time; visual depictions of your plans can give you a more integrated sense of your path.

• Use a timeline and stick to it; use concrete and time-sensitive goals and reminders. When tasks take longer than planned, communicate changes and update timelines.

• Document plans to ensure institutional memory (and institutional-partnership memory).

• If formality is required, use MOUs to clarify roles and responsibilities.

Phase 4: Ending and Capacity Building

There tends to be much more enthusiasm around starting new initiatives, relationships, and collaborative projects than winding down projects or ending partnerships. Determining when to end a partnership is context specific. At times, changes in strategic directions or a sudden shortage of resources can lead to a partnership's end. In an ideal world, partnerships would always evaluate the effectiveness of the partnership as well as the project. When a formal evaluation is not feasible, periodic check-ins can help reassess the benefits of maintaining the partnership over the long term.

Community psychologist practitioners should always be focused on the long view of any community relationship. We realize our time is limited, that it is important to do our best with the time we have. By being attuned to the importance of capacity building, we can better ensure the sustainability of successful interventions. Ideally, capacity building occurs during all phases of the project, but it is in Phase 4 when these systems are given explicit attention and implemented.

Challenges and Opportunities

The main challenges in this phase are determining when and how to end the project (if not the relationship itself). Organizational learning often occurs when the high activity of a partnership goes on hiatus or when little more than occasional capacity-building check-ins occur.

Questions to Ask/Answer

- When is it time for the relationship to move into a temporarily inactive state?
- What norms were developed around decision making and leadership?
- How did the partners ensure that all work from all partners was completed?
- Did the partnership meet its intended goals?
- What were the unintended consequences of the partnership (positive or negative)?
- What benefits are expected by keeping open future possibilities of re invigorating the partnership (e.g., co-writing new grants)?
- How can we sustain the benefits gained from the partnership once we are on our own?
- What have we learned about partnerships and collaboration in general?

Examples From Our Practice

Oftentimes initiatives succeed because of a few very passionate and committed individuals across the organizations. While this is a good thing, keeping the long view requires that we see beyond the people and personalities involved to create the higher-level connections that will sustain the momentum of the work achieved thus far. From our experiences, timelines of project phases help clarify when discussions of ending the project should occur. In one project, we developed, with other partners, an advisory board for a community-based disability-leadership training program. All of the main disability organizations in the state supported this effort. The entire disability community shared an interest in building the next generations of leaders and devoted to the project a portion of their resources (e.g., time on the advisory board, small amounts of matched funds). The advisory board ended up being a good place to seek advice from partners, discuss developing disability leadership over the long term. It also became a time to develop the higher-level connections across organizations to sustain the momentum of the work.

Capacity building was intentional at the outset. Each of the early phases of the project specified how partners would work together to develop materials based on the strengths they brought to the collaboration. By the end of the project, each partner believed that positive impacts at individual, organizational, and interorganizational levels were due to the focus on capacity building from the beginning to the end of the project. The shared sense of value for the partnership helped further support and sustain innovative leadership development opportunities for the disabilities community across the state.

Practice Recommendations Based on Lessons Learned

- Keep an eye out for long-term benefits of relationship building.

- Reflection and evaluation lead to more effective future partnerships. Simple reflections can happen individually or in concert with partners, but bringing a critical eye to the process and determining lessons learned is a useful exercise for future collaborations. More comprehensive and thorough evaluations will require additional resources and involvement of voices and perceptions of multiple stakeholders.

- Multiple projects can occur with the same partnership over time. Therefore, aim to enhance the transferability of knowledge from the current project to future contexts.

- Utilize long-term data collection/tracking systems in order to provide information to contact stakeholders in the future, contribute to collection of successes and narratives of impact, and help evaluate the effectiveness of partnerships.

- Using open honest communication with partners is helpful at every stage of the partnership. Seek honest and straightforward feedback from all the partners. Such debriefing discussions allow for closure of the partnership and open each partner to inform future work.

FUTURE TRENDS FOR COLLABORATIVE COMMUNITY PARTNERSHIPS

The need for community organizations, educational and cultural institutions, and government agencies to build and sustain effective partnerships is an area of growing interest (Stewart, 2013). In times of shrinking resources and expanding social and economic inequalities those interested in social justice must focus more on collaboration as opposed to competition. Funders such as foundations and governments aim to expand their reach and measure their **collective impact,** which is the result of organizations from different sectors agreeing to solve a specific social problem using a common agenda, aligning their efforts, and using common measures of success. While evaluating programs are essential, measuring collective impact across whole coalitions is a growing topic of interest. There is increasing recognition that organizations will not have their desired impact on their own and there is a need for people with a variety of collaborative skills to bring organizations together effectively (Brown et al., 2012). In fact, recent federal Requests For Proposals (RFPs) have included requirements for measuring collective impact; for example, the Office of Special Education Programs of the U.S. Department of Education funded the Center for Effective Collaboration and Practice; the Center for Mental Health Services funds grants under the Comprehensive Service System for Children's Mental Health Program to build local, county, and statewide systems of care; and the U.S. Department of Justice funds Safe Futures and Safe Start Programs, which build local collaborations to intervene with young children and with youth to keep them in school and to prevent juvenile delinquency. For example a recent RFP from the Health Resources and Services Administration reads: "To maximize opportunities for community action to address social determinants of health and achieve collective impact, HS grantees will support coordination, integration, and mutually reinforcing activities among health, social services, and other providers and key leaders in the community" (U.S. Department of Health and Human Services, 2014).

Collective efforts typically begin with a goal and then the building of a network of non-profits, government agencies, schools, businesses, philanthropists, faith communities, and key community leaders who create common strategies and coordinate collective activities to achieve goals over time. Hanleybrown, Kania, and Kramer (2012) cite five required conditions for collective impact: (1) common agendas, (2) shared measurement systems, (3) mutually reinforcing activities, (4) continuous communication, and (5) "backbone" organization support. Collective impact efforts address social, educational, economic, and health issues in a way consistent with other community partnerships. Clearly, community psychology practitioners have a role to play in supporting the development and measuring the impact of such efforts.

SUMMARY

The role of the community practitioner may take many forms (e.g., liaison or connector, consultant, evaluator, research partner). The ability to build and sustain partnerships is essential across each of these roles. This chapter presented definitions, benefits, and best practices from the literature on important factors for building and strengthening partnerships and collaboration. We introduced and connected the work of partnership building with core competencies of community psychology practice, and presented a four-phase model of partnership building through the lens of community psychology practitioners. We discussed challenges and opportunities that arise in each phase of partnership building, questions to ask oneself, examples from our practice, and recommendations for working through each phase successfully. Finally we discussed suggestions for training that can help develop skills to strengthen partnership building, and we close, beyond this section, with some suggested additional resources to further explore the topic and competencies on your own.

DISCUSSION QUESTIONS

1. What are the similarities and differences between a partnership and collaboration?

2. What are key factors for successful community collaborations? Do any of these particularly resonate with you and your community experiences? How so?

3. What are some key group facilitation process skills?

4. Describe the four-phase model of collaborative consulting and evaluation. Are there particular aspects of the model that you find to be more or less useful to your work in the community?

KEY TERMS AND DEFINITIONS

Collaboration: The nature of the mutually beneficial relationships and processes in which community partners engage. Collaboration involves exchanging information, sharing resources, and enhancing the capacity of others to achieve a common purpose by sharing risks, resources, responsibilities, and rewards.

Collaborative consultation: A form of consultation that uses a shared decision-making process and feedback loops throughout the phases of the work with the goal of helping all the partners move toward a mutually desired action and empowerment.

Collective impact: The result of having organizations from different sectors agree to solve a specific social problem using a common agenda, aligning their efforts, and using common measures of success.

Conflict analysis: Assessing the issues and players' concerns and the positions of stakeholders to better understand conflicts and assist in resolutions.

Crisis intervention: Applying problem-solving and clinical skills when appropriate to address major problems that arise and become barriers to progress.

Diverse decision making: Ensuring that a wide range of people are engaged in decision making and can have helpful dialogue in a safe environment.

Facilitation: Using a diversity of techniques (e.g., circles, mediation, interviewing, use of narrative) to enable groups to achieve their goals for dialogue, planning, and decision making.

Group dynamics: Behaviors and psychological processes that occur within a social group or between social groups.

Normative social influence: The influence of expectations on group and individual attitudes and behaviors.

Partnerships: Dynamic and reciprocal relationships of two or more people or organizations with a shared set of goals that are developed to find mutual and practical solutions.

Sense of community: The extent to which individuals feel they are fully connected to an interdependent community.

RESOURCES

Trainings

Obtain training in methods that foster cooperation and collaboration, such as empowerment evaluation (Fetterman, Kaftarian, & Wandersman, 2014), Appreciative Inquiry, restorative justice, peace circles, World Café, salons, chataquas, or other empowering dialogue approaches that allow for power sharing as issues are defined and framed and decisions are made.

Different organizations offer trainings and workshops on the topic of partnering across nonprofits as well as nonprofits partnering with government (see www.independentsector .org/ for schedules and details). Training workshops range from week-long in-person courses costing over $1,000 to free 1-hour webinars and everything in between. Below are some specific examples.

Group facilitation workshops:

1. The Center for Appreciative Inquiry: http://www.centerforappreciativeinquiry.net/ offering/appreciative-inquiry-facilitator-training-aift/

   - Uses Appreciative Inquiry for individuals to build organizations and influence positive changes. Typically 4 days long and includes learning processes, research, principles, practice/strength building, planning, and practice/ practicum.
   - Certification included, experiential, relationship focused. Trainers and mentors assist in learning and demonstrating techniques.

2. 450 FAST Professional Facilitation Workshop Training: http://www.mgrush.com/ content/view/11/26/

   - Held monthly; 5-day seminars. Uses the Facilitated Application Specification Technique (FAST) approach, which is a facilitated interactive model, and information gathering for consensus, communication, and group dynamics.
   - Day 1 includes facilitations skills learning and orientation; Day 2, facilitation skills and practice; Days 3 and 4 involve methodology (e.g., designing meetings, facilitation, proper questioning; Day 5 includes student skills and practices, critiques on student's skills, and improvement techniques.

3. Insight Prison Project: http://www.insightprisonproject.org/restorative-justice-facilitator-training-for-incarcerated-populations.html

   - Insight Prison Project has a restorative justice, victim/offender education group model for facilitators aimed at incarcerated populations.
   - Multi-phased 1–3, ranges between 3- and 5-day sessions.
   - Phase 1 overviews the model, guest speakers on victimization, and graduates prisoners from the program. Phase 2 focuses on small-group facilitation, organizations culture impacts, how to implement model in new sites, and assessing developmental stages. Phase 3 involves training, case consultations, evaluation by trainers.

4. University-based Group Facilitation certificate seminars (e.g., DePaul University): http://www.learning.depaul.edu/standard/content_areas/continuity_application/ coursegroup.asp?group_number = 205&group_version = 1

   - Based on the international facilitators and competencies; two required seminars, two elective seminars, and an annual symposium must be completed to receive a certificate.

- Topics covered include relationship building, group process, environment, effective outcomes, and teams. Also, facilitating change in the organization and supporting practices of facilitation.

5. Interaction Institute for Social Change: http://www.interactioninstitute.org/

   - Three-day general facilitation workshop on the essential strategies and skills for helping groups solve problems, resolve conflict, and build agreement.
   - They also offer facilitation training specific to racial justice work.

Online Tools

1. The Community Toolbox's Chapter 1 Section 7, "Working Together for Healthier Communities: A Framework for Collaboration Among Community Partnerships, Support Organizations, and Funders" (available at http://ctb.ku.edu/en/tablecontents/sub_section_main_1381.aspx) is essential reading for someone doing community research, consultation, or organizing with a focus on community health. Two great aspects of the toolbox are the simple and straightforward language used to describe very complex processes and the interactive nature of the toolbox. If you have questions about the content within a given section you can always use the "ask an advisor" feature.

2. National Council on the Aging: The Partnerships Analysis Tool for Partners in Health Promotion: http://www.ncoa.org/improve-health/center-for-healthy-aging/content-library/PartnershipAnalysisTool.pdf. Also see the lists they provide in appendixes C and D: http://www.ncoa.org/improve-health/center-for-healthy-aging/content-library/HA_CommunityPartnerships.pdf.

3. The Annie E. Casey Foundation has some good tools that provide benchmarks for and preparation ideas to build partnerships from the perspective of a child welfare agency; see their appendix B "An Overview for Self-Assessment on Building Community Partnerships" and appendix C "Possible Benchmarks in Phases of the Development of Community Partnerships" at http://www.aecf.org/upload/pdffiles/familytofamily/finalcptool_append71606.pdf.

4. The Center for the Advancement of Collaborative Strategies in Health provides a set of tools that are available for download to be used by members of a partnership to assess how well a collaborative process is working and to identify specific areas for partners to focus on to make the process work better. The directions and tool files can be found at http://www.PartnershipTool.net.

5. Torres, G., & Margolin, F. (2003). *The collaboration primer: Proven strategies, considerations, and tools to get you started.* Health Research & Educational Trust. This manual provides assessment tools, checklists, and models of collaboration to help plan successful partnerships: http://www.hret.org/upload/resources/collaboration-primer.pdf.

6. Virginia Health Care Foundation 2002 Annual Report titled, *A Decade of Making a Difference, One Life at a Time,* features the GAIT Program, the precursor to the

JABA Health Services, as "A Model That Made It." The report can be found at the Foundation's website: http://www.vhcf.org.

7. Wild Rose Foundation, Alberta, Canada, offers a workbook titled *Working in Partnership: Recipes for Success, Designed to Provide Assistance in Developing and Sustaining Partnerships With Community Agencies and Businesses.* Available at http://www.cd.gov.ab.ca/building_communities/volunteer_community/resources/partnership_kit/index.asp.

Other Recommended Websites

For a grounding on ten core theories within organizational development, see brief explanations and connection to other resources for organizational development practitioners: http://organisationdevelopment.org/?page_id = 31

For guidance on the facilitation of peace circles, see Peacemaker Institute International's website. Specifically, they discuss the "five simple guidelines": http://memosrwanda.wordpress.com/bearing-witness-retreats/peace-circles/peace-circle-guidelines-for-facilitators/

Recommended Reading

Bellman, G. M., & Ryan, K. (2009). *Extraordinary groups: How ordinary teams achieve amazing results.* San Francisco, CA: Jossey-Bass.

Bennis, W., & Biederman, P. W. (1997). *Organizing genius: The secrets of creative collaboration.* New York, NY: Perseus Books.

Block, P. (2008). *Community: The structure of belonging.* San Francisco, CA: Berrett-Koehler.

Gray, B. (1991). *Collaborating: Finding common ground for multiparty problems.* San Francisco CA: Jossey-Bass.

Wolff, T. (2009). *The power of collaborative solutions: Six principles and effective tools for building healthy communities.* San Francisco, CA: Jossey-Bass.

REFERENCES

Anderson, P. (1999). Complexity theory and organization science. *Organization Science, 10*(3), 216–232.

Bellman, G., M., & Ryan, K. D. (2009). The group needs model: A new tool for creating extraordinary groups. *OD practitioner, 41*(4), 45–50.

Brown, P., Green Brody, J., Morello-Frosch, R., Tovar, J., Zota, A. R., & Rudel, R. A. (2012). Measuring the success of community science: The Northern California Household Exposure Study. *Environmental Health Perspectives, 120*(3), 326–331.

Chavis, D. M., & Pretty, G. (1999). Sense of community: Advances in measurement and application. *Journal of Community Psychology, 27*(6), 635–642.

Checkland, P. (1981). *Systems thinking: Systems practice.* Chichester, UK: Wiley.

Coghlan, A. T., Preskill, H., & Catsambas, T. T. (2003). An overview of appreciative inquiry in evaluation. *New Directions in Evaluation, 100,* 5–22.

Compassion Capital Fund National Resource Center. (2010). *Strengthening nonprofits: A capacity builder's resource library.* Washington, DC: U.S. Department of Health and Human Services. Retrieved from http://strengtheningnonprofits.org/resources/guidebooks/Leading_a_Nonprofit_Organization.pdf

Cooperider, D. L., Whitney, D., & Stavros, J. M. (2008). *Appreciative inquiry handbook: For leader of change.* San Francisco, CA: Berrett-Koehler.

Crutchfield, R. (1955). Conformity and character. *American Psychologist, 10,* 191–198.

Dalton, J., & Wolfe, S. (Eds.). (2012). Competencies for community psychology practice: Society for Community Research and Action. *The Community Psychologist, 45*(4), 7–14.

Dion, K. L. (2000). Group cohesion: From "field of forces" to multidimensional construct. *Group Dynamics: Theory, Research, and Practice, 4*(1), 7–26.

Donors Forum & Wallace Foundation. (2010). *Fair and accountable: Partnership principles for a sustainable human services system.* Retrieved from http://www.wallacefoundation.org/knowledge-center/after-school/financial-management-for-nonprofits/Documents/Partnership-Principles-for-a-Sustainable-Human-Services-System.pdf

Fetterman, D. M., Kaftarian, S. J. & Wandersman, A.H. (2014). *Empowerment evaluation: Knowledge and tools for self-assessment, evaluation capacity building, and accountability.* Thousand Oaks, CA: Sage Publications.

Gray, B. (1991). *Collaborating: Finding common ground for multiparty problems.* San Francisco, CA: Jossey-Bass.

Hanleybrown, F., Kania, J., & Kramer, M. (2012). Channeling change: Making collective impact work. *Stanford Social Innovation Review.* Retrieved from http://www.ssireview.org/blog/entry/channeling_change_making_collective_impact_work

Himmelman, A. T. (2001). On coalitions and the transformation of power relations: Collaborative betterment and collaborative empowerment. *American Journal of Community Psychology, 29*(2), 277–285.

Hogg, M. A. (1992). *The social psychology of group cohesiveness: From attraction to social identity.* New York, NY: New York University Press.

Holland, J. H. (1992). Complex adaptive systems. *Daedalus: A New Era in Computation, 121*(1).

Kania, J., & Kramer, M. (2011). Collective impact. *Stanford Social Innovation Review, 60.* Retrieved from http://www.ssireview.org/articles/entry/collective_impact

Kloos, B., Hill, J., Thomas, E., Wandersman, A., Elias, M. J., & Dalton, J. (2010). *Community psychology: Linking communities and individuals* (3rd ed.). Belmont, CA: Wadsworth.

Latane, B. (1981). The psychology of social impact. *American Psychologist, 36,* 343–365.

Lewin, K. (1947). Frontiers in group dynamics I: Concept, method and reality in social science: Social equalibria. *Human Relations, 1,* 5–40.

Mattessich, P. W., Murray-Close, M., Monsey, B. R., & Wilder Research Center. (2001). *Collaboration: What makes it work?* (2nd ed.). Saint Paul, MN: Amherst H. Wilder Foundation.

McMillan, D. W., & Chavis, D. M. (1986). Sense of community: A definition and theory. *Journal of Community Psychology, 14*(1), 6–23.

Mumford, M. D., Zaccaro, S. J., Harding, F. D., Jacobs, T. O., & Fleishman, E. A. (2000). Leadership skills for a changing world: Solving complex social problems. *Leadership Quarterly, 11*(1), 23.

National Council on the Aging. (2003). *Partnering to promote healthy aging: Creative best practice community partnerships.* Retrieved from http://www.ncoa.org/improve-health/center-for-healthy-aging/content-library/HA_CommunityPartnerships.pdf

National Resource Center. (2010). Partnerships: Frameworks for working together. *Strengthening Non-Profits: A Capacity Builder's Resource: Part 10.* Retrieved from http://strengtheningnonprofits.org/resources/guidebooks/Partnerships.pdf

Nelson, G., & Prilleltensky, I. (2010). *Community psychology: In pursuit of liberation and wellbeing* (2nd ed.). New York, NY: Palgrave Macmillan.

Rabinowitz, P. (2013). Coalition building I: Starting a coalition. In T. Wolff (Ed.), *The community tool box*. Retrieved from http://ctb.ku.edu/en/tablecontents/sub_section_main_1057.aspx

Rafferty, A. E., Jimmieson, N. L., & Armenakis, A. A. (2013). Change readiness: A multilevel review. *Journal of Management, 39*(1), 110–135.

Reynolds, M. (2008). Response to paper "Systems Thinking" by D. Cabrera et al.: Systems thinking from a critical systems perspective. *Journal of Evaluation and Program Planning, 31,* 323–325.

Sarason, S. B. (1974). *The psychological sense of community: Prospects for a community psychology.* San Francisco, CA: Jossey-Bass.

Sarason, S. B. (1986). Commentary: The emergence of a conceptual center. *Journal of Community Psychology, 14,* 405–407.

Sofaer, S. (1999). *Working together, moving ahead: A manual to support effective community health coalitions.* New York, NY: Baruch College School of Public Affairs. Retrieved from http://www.policy archive.org/handle/10207/bitstreams/21720.pdf

Stewart, S. D. (2013). United Way, Healthy Communities, and collective impact. *National Civic Review, 102*(4), 75–78.

Tajfel, H. (1979). Individuals and groups in social psychology. *British Journal of Social and Clinical Psychology, 18,* 183–190.

Tuckman, B., & Jensen, M. A. (1977). Stages of small group development revisited. *Group and Organizational Studies, 2,* 419–427.

U.S. Department of Health and Human Services. (2014). *Healthy Start initiative: Eliminating disparities in perinatal health. Funding opportunity announcement* (Announcement Numbers HRSA-14-121, HRSA-14-120, HRSA-14-122). Retrieved from https://grants3.hrsa.gov/2010/web2External/ Interface/FundingCycle/ExternalView.aspx?fCycleID = b11968f7-eae-4993-be01-7973c4f5c7ba

Wei-Skillern, J., & Marciano S. (2008). The networked nonprofit. *Stanford Social Innovation Review.* Retrieved from http://www.ssireview.org/images/articles/2008SP_feature_wei-skillern_marciano.pdf

Wild Rose Foundation. (2001). *Working in partnership: Recipes for success.* A project for Alberta [Canada] Community Development. Retrieved from http://www.orgwise.ca/sites/osi.ocasi.org .stage/files/resources/Working%20in%20Partnership%20-%20Recipes%20for%20Success.pdf

Wolff, T. (2009). *The power of collaborative solutions: Six principles and effective tools for building healthy communities.* San Francisco, CA: Jossey-Bass.

CHAPTER 10

Advocacy and Social Justice

Leonard A. Jason, Christopher R. Beasley, and Bronwyn A. Hunter

OPENING EXERCISE

You are at home reading a book when you hear a knock on your door. You open it to find several neighbors who appear upset. "The house down the street is going to be a sober house!" one of them angrily explains, "We don't want a bunch of people who used drugs living on our street. Property values will go down and the neighborhood will be over-ridden with drugs and crime. Come help talk to city officials in order to support an ordinance that will not allow this recovery home to be located in our middle-class neighborhood or any others in town." You have a brother who for years had a substance abuse problem and has just begun turning his life around with the help of self-help groups. You have also read about some of the benefits of recovery homes for people with substance use disorders and other types of community-based housing for people with severe mental illness and developmental disabilities. You believe it is important to support the integration of vulnerable people back into community settings and disagree with your neighbors that a sober house will increase drugs and crime in your neighborhood. You also believe that men and women in recovery deserve an opportunity to live in safe, residential homes in your community.

- Is this an issue you are interested in advocating for?
- Do you think you have the personal disposition to be a successful advocate on the issue?
- What knowledge, skills, and abilities do you think would be required to successfully advocate on this issue?
- How would you plan efforts to advocate for the establishment of recovery homes in your town?

OVERVIEW

Advocacy is important to community practice because it furthers the social justice goals of practitioners and their community partners (Maton, Humphreys, Jason, & Shinn, in press). First and foremost, advocates may promote community psychology values when efforts are directed toward changing systems that perpetuate social problems. Advocacy may also help practitioners and community members secure resources and reduce barriers for the populations they serve. These types of efforts may influence the social environment as they create dialogue between community practitioners, community organizations, and policymakers, which has the potential to frame how the issue is discussed. Nonprofit organizations and citizen action coalitions are often closest to the problem and can serve as a bridge between government officials and the people they serve. Furthermore, advocacy can be an important service to the community when practitioners act as a resource to policymakers by providing knowledge, guidance, and mobilization. Finally, advocacy may be an opportunity to develop knowledge, skills, and abilities for community psychologists as well as their partners in the community.

In this chapter we present a foundation for advocacy and social justice in community psychology practice. We first define advocacy and social justice and follow with descriptions of the skills and abilities necessary to this work. We then discuss training, education, and experiential opportunities that may lead to the incorporation of advocacy and social justice with community practice. Drawing from the first author's experiences, we end with two distinct case examples where advocacy strategies were used to promote social justice among underserved and marginalized populations.

DEFINING ADVOCACY AND SOCIAL JUSTICE

In a recent book by the first author, titled *Principles of Social Change* (Jason, 2013), five orienting principles were described that form the basis for much of the work reviewed in this chapter and will be amplified throughout in the sections below. Those five principles of social change are:

1. Develop a clear vision of second-order change (changing systems that create problems).
2. Focus interventions on those who perpetuate powerlessness, poverty, and other forms of oppression.
3. Work with citizens and organizations to create coalitions. Coalitions can successfully confront power abuses.
4. Remain persistent, patient, and willing to do what is necessary over the long haul. Maintain long-term commitment to change.
5. Continuously evaluate and refine strategies and tactics to find the most effective means of bringing about change.

Conceptual and Historical Definition

Social justice, generally defined, means equal treatment of and opportunities for all individuals, groups, and communities. Scholars consider the broad term, social justice, to encompass both distributive and procedural justice. Along these lines, **distributive justice** refers to fair access to tangible and material goods including housing, medical care, education, and employment (Vasquez, 2012) while **procedural justice** represents the fairness involved in power and decision-making processes that determine who benefits from those resources. Embedded within these definitions is an implicit motivation to take action to change social structures, policies, and practices that are unfair and limit access to goods and services (Goodman et al., 2004; Vasquez, 2012).

Social justice has been identified as a core value of community psychology (Kloos, Hill, Thomas, Elias, & Dalton, 2012; Prilleltensky & Gonick, 1996). Community psychologists frequently work to promote justice through prevention and intervention to support the health and well-being of historically disadvantaged groups (Fondacaro & Weinberg, 2002). Despite discourse toward the integration of research and practice to promote social change (Fondacaro & Weinberg, 2002; Prilleltensky, 2001), social justice is often a controversial topic in psychology. This is because social justice is a value that requires psychologists to take a social and political stand on debated social issues, which may cross psychologists' boundary lines in certain settings (Bradley, Werth, Hastings & Pierce, 2012). For example, Bradley and colleagues (2012) found that psychologists in rural communities believed that advocacy for contentious issues could adversely impact their personal and professional lives. These psychologists reported that their advocacy activities had the potential to limit the community's willingness to use mental health services in geographic areas where services were scarce. In similar fashion, social justice has been criticized as a moral value that exists in contrast to traditional scientific objectivity (Fondacaro & Weinberg, 2002). Nonetheless, in recent years, the American Psychological Association (APA) has called for continued focus on promoting social justice across sub-disciplines of psychology (e.g., Mays, 2000; Vasquez, 2012). Furthermore, the American Counseling Association has created a set of guidelines for counseling psychologists who engage in advocacy activities related to social justice (Lewis, Arnold, House, & Toporek, 2003).

Social justice cannot be understood without a conceptual understanding of social and political systems and how these systems have historically created unequal power differences that impact resources and opportunities for individuals, groups, and communities (Jason, 2013). As such, an early step toward social justice practice is an awareness of **oppression,** or unequal treatment and access to resources because of individual or group identities. It is also critical to understand how oppression affects human development and well-being in addition to the limitations it imposes upon an oppressed group. Oppression exists due to differences assigned to both individual and group identities. Prilleltensky and Gonick (1996, pp. 129–130) defined oppression as a

> state of asymmetric power relations characterized by domination, subordination, and resistance, where dominating persons or groups exercise their power by restricting access to material resources and by implanting in the subordinated persons or groups fear or self-deprecating views about themselves.

Therefore, oppression greatly impacts the well-being of individuals who belong to groups that have limited access to resources and power. Further, the dominant group often imposes restrictions to limit access to power and opportunities that could shift the power away from members of the dominant group (Nelson, Prilleltensky, & McGillivary, 2001).

Forms of oppression include racism, sexism, classism, heterosexism, and ageism, among others, where individuals who belong to the marginalized group experience limited resources and unequal power and decision making because of their group memberships or social and cultural identities (Crethar, Torres Rivera, & Nash, 2008). For example, African Americans have an extensive history of unequal treatment and oppression evidenced by slavery, segregation, and laws restricting the right to vote. This oppression is referred to as racism, because the unequal treatment and power distributions are based solely on race. Sexism identifies the unequal status between males and females; classism denotes unequal power among individuals who live in poverty and those who do not; heterosexism exemplifies the unequal power status between heterosexual individuals and those who identify as lesbian, gay, bisexual, or transgender (LGBT); and ageism represents discrimination and unequal access to resources based on age. Individuals who identify with the group that has less power are limited in their social and political power and thus have limited opportunities when compared to their dominant counterparts. It should also be noted that group membership is not mutually exclusive. That is, individuals can be members of more than one group and thus experience multiple forms of oppression.

Social justice is therefore a response to oppression that requires active work with individuals, groups, and communities to shift the distribution of power and increase access to tangible and material resources (Prilleltensky, 2001; Vasquez, 2012). With a broad understanding of the historical, social, and political underpinnings of social justice, advocacy takes center stage. Advocacy consists of an understanding of the socio-political environment; the individual, group, and community, as well as a passion to create and move toward social change. Advocacy encompasses community psychology values such as empowerment, citizen participation, health and wellness, and respect for diversity (Maton, Strompolis, & Wisniewski, 2013; Nelson et al., 2001; Prilleltensky, 2001). The goal of **advocacy** is to work with individuals, groups, and communities to change existing social structures, policies, and practice to promote social justice (Toporek, Lewis, & Crethar, 2009). Community psychology advocacy attempts to move beyond **first-order change**, which is defined as an effort to eliminate deficits and problems for individuals while neglecting to address the causes that contribute to those problems (Watzlawick, Weakland, & Fisch, 1974). **Second-order change,** which focuses on changing systems that create problems rather than addressing the problematic symptoms, moves beyond a reactive response and involves efforts to alter shared goals, roles, and power relationships (Seidman, 1988).

Glidewell (1984) discussed the history of advocacy and noted that advocacy emerged from the legal arena where clients were represented by attorneys who possessed expertise to change an aspect of the clients' life. Through this process, clients did not necessarily develop the skills and abilities that they needed to advocate for themselves (Glidewell, 1984). Community psychology facilitated an expansion of the advocate role by promoting equitable access to resources for disadvantaged groups and individuals (Rappaport, 1981). In this sense, advocacy consisted of spending time building long-term relationships with clients while supporting the clients' own strengths and building their capacity to create social change (Glidewell, 1984). Goals for this type of advocacy work include serving the interests of oppressed groups, sharing power with clients, and fostering collective action.

Following Glidewell's (1984) guidelines, advocacy can be differentiated between individualistic client-centered treatment strategies and large-scale political movements. Individualistic approaches to social justice include working with clients, one-on-one, to increase their access to tangible resources and empower them to make choices (Burnes & Singh, 2010; Lewis et al., 2003). In this context, advocacy could include helping clients not only to obtain funds to pursue educational and vocational opportunities but also to bring about social justice for themselves and others.

Individuals operate within social systems, and community psychologists are most often interested in the context of the individual and how this context shapes well-being and life experience. Often, larger political, social, and systems change is achieved through collaboration with groups to make changes in policies, procedures, or existing social structures (Toporek et al., 2009). Therefore, a collectivist approach to social justice could include partnering with community groups and collaborating with group members. Characteristics that promote social justice include shared power and decision making, advocacy, empowerment, and respect for diversity (Nelson et al., 2001).

Bradley and colleagues (2012) provided useful tips for assessing willingness to engage in advocacy work. Building your capacity to act as an advocate requires an in-depth awareness of your values and traits and how they influence you and your ability to collaborate with groups to promote social change. As such, it is also important to clearly identify your desire to assume an advocacy role with an awareness of how the role may impact your personal and professional roles (Bradley et al., 2012). Advocacy work is a time commitment; thus, be realistic about your willingness to devote time to the issue at hand. Jason (2013) has argued that advocacy often begins with a strong, passionate personal interest in a topic, as this type of passion can help sustain the advocacy through the often needed long time commitments to a cause.

Lewis and colleagues (2003) identified seven core competencies that promote and impact on social change in a large, public, policy-driven arena. These include: (1) identifying issues that require political intervention and action; (2) finding appropriate methods to address these issues; (3) seeking out and collaborating with others who have similar advocacy goals; (4) supporting alliances and organizations that promote change; (5) collaborating with allies to provide evidence and prepare data reports to support the need for change; (6) collaborating with allies to lobby legislators and other policymakers; and (7) maintaining an open line of communication with individuals, groups, and organizations to ensure what you are advocating is consistent with goals for social action. These guidelines highlight several competencies and strategies that can be useful for engaging in advocacy in the policy arena.

In summary, prior to engaging in political advocacy to achieve social change it is imperative to develop an understanding of the social, historical, cultural, and political context of oppression. It is also essential to identify ways in which oppression impacts members of disadvantaged groups and how you would like to intervene as an advocate. Advocacy consists of integrating core community psychology values, such as empowerment, social justice, citizen participation, and respect for diversity to promote social change. Advocacy can occur in an individual relationship and/or collectively with a group or community and requires broad skills and abilities. When dealing with unequal distributions of power, it is often critical to work collaboratively with community groups and organizations that have the resources to bring about structural second-order change. Having a long-term time perspective is often needed to bring about these types of changes, and using feedback and evaluation can aid in fine-tuning efforts over time. These skills and abilities include effective relationship building, communication, and persuasion. It is also essential to be aware of, listen to, and follow your instincts as you attempt to navigate complex social systems to advocate for change (Jason, 2013). As shown in Table 10.1, there are 12 key components of successful advocacy (Cohen, Lee, & McIlwraith, 2012). These competencies will be discussed in the following sections.

Table 10.1   Twelve Key Components of Successful Advocacy (Cohen et al., 2012)

- Find out what the Society for Community Research and Action (SCRA) and other associations are doing about the issue
- Coordinate with local, regional, and national associations for additional resources and support
- Identify yourself as a professional in interactions with others
- Learn something about those whom you are asking such as where they stand on issues
- Understand policies and procedures of the setting the other person is in
- Give background information about yourself before meetings with stakeholders
- Consider what is important to the other person to develop understanding and a sense of reciprocity
- Be clear and succinct in written and verbal communications
- Accompany a request with an offer
- Find ways to agree to some requests even when doing so may seem challenging
- Follow up with requests and follow through with promises
- Mentor others about advocacy

COMPETENCY AND COMPETENCY DEVELOPMENT

Competencies

Core competencies. The field of community research and action has developed a set of core competencies for practice in this area. These include (1) collaboration and coalition development; (2) community development; (3) community organizing and community advocacy; (4) public policy analysis, development, and advocacy; and (5) community education, information dissemination, and building community awareness (Dalton & Wolfe, 2012). Change agents collaborate with communities to learn about issues important to the communities and to assist them in organizing coalitions. Advocates also help develop cohesive communities to take on powerful political forces that may stand in the way of change. With cohesive communities and coalitions needed for action, community practitioners analyze existing policy around the issue and help others develop a plan to implement alternatives. Finally, advocates educate communities about existing policies to build awareness about action strategies to build capacity for change initiatives. In the following section, we will expand on these competencies and introduce additional proficiencies community practitioners may want to consider.

Disposition. Advocacy requires a desire for social justice, and the personal disposition, knowledge, skills, and abilities necessary to carry out a policy agenda (Trusty, 2005). Paulo Freire (1970) indicated that change begins by helping people identify issues for which they have strong feelings and actively searching for solutions to those issues. First and foremost, advocates must be committed to eliminating social inequities and barriers to well-being. This requires both a capacity and an appreciation for suffering (Kiselica & Robinson, 2001), awareness that something is fundamentally wrong, and dedication to initiate the journey to action. However, a commitment to social justice continues to be vital long after the beginnings of change are set into motion. Commitment sustains these efforts by providing much needed energy when challenges seem too daunting to overcome.

Advocacy efforts are sustained by self-confident idealism, which is manifested in a strong belief that the world not only *can* but also *will* be a better place in the future (Trusty, 2005). Advocates should have a vision of the future that is just and empowering. Oppression creates a pessimistic view of the future and weakens individual and collective confidence that change is possible to achieve. Therefore, it is the advocate's role to break free of the confines of this oppression, and convey this idealism and self-confidence to others.

Advocates must draw from a keen intuition and a strong ethical foundation to navigate challenges and dilemmas. The public policy landscape is littered with misleading information, paradoxes, and obstacles that inhibit change. It is sometimes impossible to understand all the complexities and nuances of a given issue, so advocates often rely on their intuition to guide them through uncertainties and help them make urgent decisions (Jason, 2013). There are sometimes opportunities for action that must be seized upon with urgency. During these times, it is important that advocates trust their instincts to help themselves and community organizations through the maze of conflicting information and efforts to derail social change by those upholding the status quo.

Similarly, urgent action and complexity may create conditions that demand advocates to be flexible and receptive. The setting and environment will provide clues to practical pathways for change, and advocates should be responsive to these signs and learn from the environments in which they are embedded. At times, the complexities of working with and in systems may require compromise to satisfy collaborators and other stakeholders. It may be necessary to give way on an issue in order to obtain a stakeholder's support on another issue. During these times, it is important to keep a broad strategy in mind so as not to get bogged down in individual battles that may have little impact on long-term goals.

Advocates often have a sense of autonomy that is balanced with a value for collaborative action. Early in an advocacy effort, it may feel like a lonely journey if few others express the same passion for change that you possess. During this time, it may be especially important to have a sense of autonomy and determination to continue. Having a deep-seated interest in the cause is often critical to sustaining the long-term commitment that may be needed for social change. There may be other times in the change process when collaborators no longer seem as motivated or supportive of the cause. In these situations, advocates must follow their intuition and have faith that change can occur in order to forge ahead. However, this autonomy must be balanced with a value for collaborative action.

Finally, advocates must be patient and perseverant during sometimes lengthy policymaking efforts. For example, in the third section of this chapter, the first author discusses his experiences in developing a collaborative team of scholars and patients who obtained funding to document the prevalence of chronic fatigue syndrome (CFS). In this example, he delineates the patience and perseverance required to gain the community-based data to ultimately challenge inappropriate myths about and portrayals of patients with CFS. Change often requires persistent pressure on those unwilling to change the status quo. Therefore, advocates should develop the endurance to achieve small wins to sustain their confidence and maintain commitment from others. This is particularly important in today's increasingly stressful environment, where advocates and collaborators often have fewer resources to accomplish their goals. An exemplar in the change arena is Nelson Mandela, whose social change efforts took place over decades while he was incarcerated, and required strong networks of community activists to challenge oppressive apartheid in South Africa.

Knowledge. Advocacy can occur at various levels of government, administration, and social systems that could include legislative bodies, government agencies, organizations, and communities (DeLeon, Loftis, Ball, & Sullivan, 2006). Roles for community psychologists and practitioners in this process may include assessing issues and their political landscapes, teaching others about advocacy, organizing community groups, and modeling the character and actions needed to be successful (Cohen et al., 2012). For example, community advocates can assess the size of the problem, determine effective interventions, and open the door to opportunities for other practitioners and organizations (Cohen et al., 2012). Success in this role would require a comprehensive knowledge of resources, government processes, conflict resolution, advocacy models, and systems change principles (Trusty, 2005).

Importantly, community practitioners must have knowledge of the power system they are attempting to reform. The power system includes principal power holders and administrative bodies as well as public policy rules and procedures (Mooney & Van Dyke-Brown, 2003; Moore, 2011; Trusty, 2005). Knowledge of these systems encompasses their history, operational structure, and reason for existence (Mooney & Van Dyke-Brown, 2003). Knowledge may also include the rulemaking process of related entities, how and where rules are recorded, committees overseeing the rules, and public commenting processes for potential new rules (Mooney & Van Dyke-Brown, 2003). It is also important to understand legislative processes such as the pathways from the introduction of legislative bills to implementation of new laws (Mooney & Van Dyke-Brown, 2003). For example, committees often make policy recommendations, but the amount of power committees wield varies. Therefore, lower-level committees may sometimes be used by those in power to appease dissatisfied groups by making inconsequential decisions. Thus, understanding the legislative process and power of related committees can inform advocates about the appropriate course of action and significance of decisions.

Advocates should understand these processes and the structural and functional aspects of political systems, in addition to the key stakeholders who manage them, in order to identify power allocations and analyze strategies and tactics for redistribution. Redistribution is particularly important when enacting large-scale **second-order change**—a focus on changing systems that create problems rather than solely attributing problematic symptoms to an individual. Those who can negotiate power are sometimes expected stakeholders such as politicians but, at other times, these power brokers may have unexpected and unassuming roles. Unassuming stakeholders may have acquired respect and commitment through lengthy tenure in institutions. Thus, understanding the norms and values of communities and systems allows advocates to better understand formal and informal sources of power and the dynamics associated with power distributions.

In addition to understanding the political process, advocates should understand how to campaign for change. The status quo is often upheld by powerful entities that benefit from existing policy. Taking on these figures is no slight task, but passionate commitment combined with sustained systematic action can and will lead to policy change. Advocacy models and methods can act as a guide for such sustained action. For example, after developing a strong disposition for advocacy and discovering an issue they feel strongly about and have resources to tackle, advocates can build the knowledge and relationships necessary to develop an action plan (Trusty, 2005). This plan is then enacted through collaboration to change policy and is followed by a celebration, or by regrouping when plans do not produce desired change. However, the process does not end with success or obstacles. Advocates should also evaluate successes and challenges in the change process to strengthen future endeavors. Furthermore, it is important to remain vigilant to ensure change is sustained over time and not undermined by shifting social trends. Lastly, this learning can be institutionalized in organizations and communities as well as passed along through mentoring so others can carry action forward.

It is also useful to know tactics and strategies specific to lobbying (Mooney & Van Dyke-Brown, 2003). Advocacy requires knowledge of how to have one's views recognized by key stakeholders (Cohen et al., 2012). For example, advocates lobbying for a policy may be able to get access to politicians through personal connections or supportive advocates who are constituents. They may also be able to get access by campaigning for politicians during elections or helping evaluate and implement policies. Such service might include providing background information for potential legislation, analysis of bills, and providing fact sheets for representatives to use when learning about policies and communicating with others. If these efforts are not sufficient, advocates may be able to get access by bringing public attention to an issue and/or mobilizing broad community support. Public awareness efforts may range from letters to editors to television debates and community forums. Advocates can more effectively create awareness if they know how to use media, the Internet, and other technology (Kiselica & Robinson, 2001) as well as how to engage with popular and social media in terms of current political priorities, using bipartisan terms (DeLeon et al., 2006). Researchers who strive to influence policy may benefit from knowledge of how to synthesize and communicate complex policy issues to a lay audience (DeLeon et al., 2006). Although policy decisions are often not based on research (DeLeon et al., 2006), findings are valuable when they are consistent with politicians' prior conclusions and can support change efforts when paired with other power holders who have similar views (Jason, 1991).

Specific techniques for lobbying include letters, emails, calls, and visits to politicians, as well as testimony at legislative hearings and ongoing relationships with representatives. Additional techniques for local lobbying include attendance at city council meetings and petitions to get issues onto the ballot. It is important to know the process and strategy for each of these communication tactics as well as how interpersonal factors can strengthen or weaken change efforts. The Ten Commandments of Lobbying (see Table 10.2) suggest these and other tips for successful lobbying.

Community advocates must also understand principles of systems change (Kiselica & Robinson, 2001; Moore, 2011; Trusty, 2005). **Systems change** is a fundamental shift in how systems functions (www.ccitoolsforfeds.org/systems_change.asp). For advocacy, this includes a change in the distribution of power structures and decision making. It can

Table 10.2 Ten Commandments of Lobbying (Mooney & Van Dyke-Brown, 2003, p. 41)

1. Never lie or mislead about facts, importance, position strengths, or anything else

2. Look for friends in unusual places

3. Never cut off anybody from permanent contact

4. Don't grab credit

5. Make your word your bond

6. Don't lobby opponents publicly committed to their position

7. Always notice and thank everyone who has helped you

8. Don't gossip

9. Do your homework

10. Be there

include changing parts of a system or the sequence of actions within a system. For example, advocates could promote shared decision making between politicians and constituents to give community members greater input on policy. Systems change may also include a shift in interactions between parts of the system. In this context, advocates could campaign for greater community member access to representatives. Further, systems change could alter society by shifting underlying policy choices. As such, advocates could campaign for new health-care delivery options (Shinn, 2007). Lastly, systems change could include different feedback channels. For example, advocates could change processes through which citizens give feedback to legislative bodies. By further understanding these principles, advocates can work for second-order change that remedies the fundamental structures that either lead to problems or create barriers to citizen participation in solutions.

Successful advocates tend to be resourceful and seek allies for a policy agenda (Trusty, 2005). To do so, community practitioners often need to know potential allies on the issue (e.g., supportive regional, state, and national organizations) and how to form collaborations with these allies. This process also requires knowledge of community organizing principles discussed in Chapter 8 of this book, such as how to build community networks of people and organizations and develop consensus among varied groups. This collaborative work can be informed by knowledge about individual, group, and organizational processes and interventions (Kiselica & Robinson, 2001). For example, knowledge of consultation processes can be important when providing services for stakeholders in key areas of an issue (DeLeon et al., 2006).

Community advocates should also understand how to share their knowledge with stakeholders closest to the issue. In addition, advocates should be aware of barriers to self-advocacy and ways to address these barriers. For example, past research on advocacy among women living with HIV/AIDS demonstrated that barriers to participation in the decision-making process included feelings of submissiveness, a lack of acceptance by decision makers because of these women's marginalized status, and input not being taken into consideration or being implemented (Bell, 2005). These women felt they were excluded from the decision-making community dominated by men who addressed only male issues. Their advocacy efforts were also hindered because of the burden of their life circumstances compounded by a lack of knowledge and skills specific to advocacy. However, these barriers could be reduced by expanding outreach and creating self-help groups to decrease isolation and hopelessness as well as efforts to increase self-esteem, self-efficacy, networking skills, and knowledge of advocacy methods (Bell, 2005).

Skills. While advocacy knowledge may be acquired fairly quickly, skills take more time to develop. The first skills involved in a change effort are problem assessment (Trusty, 2005), information gathering, and analysis (Moore, 2011). Advocates should develop competency in assessing social trends and observing patterns that may be problematic or unjust. Although an issue may, at first glance, appear to be a considerable problem, information gathering will validate this observation and provide substantive evidence that will help convince others of the problem. During this process, advocates should use analytical skills to evaluate evidence and determine patterns from observations.

Some information may not be readily available, so it may be advantageous for advocates to develop assessment and research skills to produce the type of information necessary to support the change effort. Applicable research may range from documenting of prevalence and related factors (as will be illustrated in the case example discussed below on CFS) to assess intervention effectiveness. Research may also be used to understand the underlying meaning of problems and the appropriateness of current tools used to assess them.

Problems do not exist independent of their socio-cultural context, so advocates should have the ability to identify cultural factors related to both the problem and potential strategies for redress. For example, Gandhi, one of history's most successful change agents, familiarized himself with cultural, class, political, and religious institutions in order to develop a detailed analysis of the social infrastructure (Toit, 1996). Using this assessment, he was able to tailor his interventions to the needs of the people. He welcomed the views of different religious and political factions and worked toward meeting the needs of each group.

Once a problem has been identified and the supporting assessment has taken place, executive skills come to the forefront. Executive skills include problem solving, organization (Trusty, 2005), and management (Moore, 2011). Advocates often shift from information gathering to planning and implementation. During the planning phase, advocates need experience and skill in devising various strategies to solve problems. This skill includes creating scenarios of obstacles and barriers and tailoring solutions to each scenario. Given the complex nature of problems and various scenarios of action, advocates could draw from strong organizational skills used to organize ideas, materials, and people. During an ongoing change initiative, advocates may also utilize management skills to implement and alter strategies as well as to coordinate efforts of groups and organizations.

Throughout the change effort, advocates should demonstrate excellent communication skills (Moore, 2011; Trusty, 2005) for listening to and interacting with both collaborators and key stakeholders who are in positions of power. These include both verbal and nonverbal communication skills (Kiselica & Robinson, 2001). During communications with those in power, advocates should concisely express an authoritative position (Cohen et al., 2012) and make it clear that they will not be defeated. Advocates should also time their communication appropriately to take advantage of social and political trends as well as stages of relationship development with collaborators and power holders.

As mentioned previously in this chapter, advocacy campaigns are often fraught with setbacks. Family and other interpersonal relationships could become strained when time is devoted to change efforts, particularly if urgent action is needed to seize opportunities. Similarly, advocates' psychological well-being may become strained. Therefore, it is also essential for advocates to engage in self-care to maintain their psychological and social well-being (Trusty, 2005).

Advocates also need to be able to come up with solutions that are both imaginative and out-of-the-box thinking. Often, when dealing with power structures that want to maintain the status quo, efforts to confront power brokers in imaginative and unexpected ways can prove effective, as evidenced by Saul Alinksy (1969) in many of his social organizing campaigns for social justice.

Abilities. Advocates need knowledge and skills as well as an ability to perform in the moment. This ability is a combination of both innate characteristics and the refinement of skills over time. Abilities related to advocacy center on strategy, communication, and collaboration. At its core, social change is a strategic process that begins with a critical examination of conventional thinking to identify problems and power abuses. Successful advocates select targets for change that are appropriate for the available resources and timing in the maturation of social movements. As mentioned before, large-scale second-order change is exceedingly complex, and advocacy could take a number of directions. Successful advocates have an ability to know where to start in working with coalitions in the face of complexity and seemingly insurmountable challenges. Similarly, advocates and community organizations often set realistic goals (DeLeon et al., 2006) and take small manageable steps such as learning about issues in the immediate environment. Advocacy often requires working on intermediate challenges while keeping a long-term structural goal in mind. Advocates must be able to persevere through challenges to sustain their vision of second-order change. During these sustained efforts, advocates will likely have numerous opportunities but should focus on those most critical to the change effort.

Advocates also need to be able to understand and communicate with a wide array of stakeholders. However, aspiring advocates sometimes overlook the importance of being able to communicate with those who oppose their change efforts. At times, mutually agreeable solutions can be achieved through dialogue and compromise. This dialogue requires an understanding not only of the issue at hand but also of the people and organizations involved. Below the surface, these entities are swayed by underlying values, biases, and assumptions. Advocates must be able to recognize and respect these to negotiate (DeLeon et al., 2006). Doing so helps advocates not only form strategy but also speak the language of the opposition when presenting problems and solutions.

Those in power may sometimes be open to dialogue and compromise, but they are often less amenable to compromise on important policy implications unless challenged by coalitions that hold leverage. Such efforts benefit immensely from sustained collaborative action that provides additional resources and opportunities to empower communities. Therefore, community advocates often have an ability to organize and work collaboratively to make structural change. They are able to successfully mobilize community support to restructure power. Whereas elected officials sometimes impose first-order interventions through top-down strategies, community advocates have the potential to lead grassroots efforts to enact second-order social change. A classic example of such change was Reverend Martin Luther King Jr.'s use of bottom-up coalition building to fight for civil rights in the 1950s and 1960s.

To create conditions for grassroots action, advocates could foster trust and openness to build cohesive communities focused on social change (Lorion & Iscoe, 1996). Collaborations often begin with people from diverse backgrounds, so advocates may learn to understand multiple perspectives and guide stakeholders through a process of compromise and consensus to build long-term relationships (DeLeon et al., 2006). This requires an understanding of others as well as an ability to demonstrate empathy, warmth, concreteness, and understanding (Ponzo, 1974). It also requires an ability to reflect on people's strengths and weaknesses in order to devise ways of enabling them to do either less or

Photo 10.1   A grassroots effort to advocate for social peace.

Source: © Ragesoss/Wikimedia Commons/CC-BY-SA-3.0.

more (Lorion & Iscoe, 1996). These communities may develop through a series of socio-political stages ranging from acritical to adaptive/pre-critical, and finally liberation (Watts & Abdul-Adil, 1994). During the process, change agents must be able to help people, organizations, and coalitions move through these stages.

The process of advocacy and social change can sometimes appear chaotic and unfocused, and those in the status quo might lack an appreciation of this process. Community psychologists can be clear with their values so that they do not usurp the power of those advocating for community change. One of the case studies presented below involved the Oxford House network of recovery homes. The first author was approached by an official from the Substance Abuse Mental Health Services Administration who wanted to considerably expand the Oxford House program, using data from our studies. However, he concluded that the Oxford House organization was disorganized, lacked sufficient infrastructure, and had poor leadership. Such problems, he thought, would inhibit expansion to thousands of homes across the United States. He proposed that the first author take over the process of training and monitoring recruiters for the expansion. But if a researcher took over this vital function of the Oxford House organization, it would betray the fundamental relationship that the first author had with the democratically run Oxford House organization. Help from the federal government should never involve eliminating the authority or leadership of a successful grassroots organization, as this official wanted to do.

Training and Experiences to Develop Advocacy Competency

Training. The aforementioned knowledge, skills, and abilities can be developed through both training and experience. Training can take place through traditional workshops and classes as well as extracurricular opportunities. Although stand-alone advocacy workshops are hosted by universities and community organizations, they also take place during local, regional, national, and international conferences for action-related organizations. These workshops provide an opportunity to learn about the process and strategy of advocacy as well as an opportunity to practice basic skills. For example, the Biennial Conference of the Society for Community Research and Action (SCRA) frequently hosts such workshops. Materials from these sessions can be found on the policy page of SCRA's website (http://www.scra27.org/what-we-do/policy). Workshops such as these also take place online through webinars and other online formats.

Another way to learn about the process and strategy of advocacy as well as systems of change is through formal coursework. For example, advocacy courses often provide opportunities to learn about government systems and the process of policy development. Advocates can also develop skills and techniques in these courses. As an example, Jason et al. (2002) taught a graduate class where individual students selected a social change advocate, investigated what they had accomplished, and then presented to the class lessons that were learned from these community activists. However, advocacy courses alone may not provide the knowledge and skills needed for collaboration and community development. These can be learned through consultation courses that emphasize collaborative relationships and capacity building or community organizing courses that focus on coalition building. However, none of these courses provide the knowledge and skills needed to pass advocacy along to community members. The capacity for such training can be strengthened through courses in empowerment and instruction. Although coursework has traditionally been inaccessible to many because of time, geographic, and financial barriers, recent trends in online learning may provide opportunities for advocates to participate in online courses at their own pace for minimal or no cost. Courses using models such as the Massive Open Online Course framework are likely to provide new resources for advocates. Other opportunities could be provided by podcasts offered for free through iTunes and other application programs.

Advocacy knowledge and skills can be further developed through independent learning. We have included several advocacy-related websites at the end of this chapter so advocates can find additional information on relevant knowledge and skills. We have also included suggested books for aspiring advocates to learn from. However, websites and books provide only a cursory knowledge of the advocacy process, as they portray this process in a linear and concrete manner. The nuances and complexities of advocacy and strategies for navigating them are best learned from advocates who are experienced. People such as these can be found online through social networks as well as in person at conferences. By building these networks, aspiring advocates can not only learn the process of advocacy but also build the resources necessary for action and obtain support for sustained and sometimes stressful efforts.

Experience. Training through workshops, coursework, and extracurricular learning and mentoring will provide advocates with a basic foundation from which to act; however, experience is necessary to refine skills. Advocacy competencies can be developed through graduate training as well as practitioner experiences. During graduate training, students can become involved in administrative responsibilities and graduate student associations to gain practice in defending needs, activities, and requests (Cohen et al., 2012) as well as develop proficiency in communicating with diverse groups of stakeholders and forming strategy and coalitions. Students can also gain advocacy experience through coursework by drafting policy briefs and other reports for evaluation and fieldwork courses.

Practitioners can gain advocacy experience by joining others' advocacy efforts or enacting change on a smaller scale. The process can begin with local issues and progress to state and federal issues as practitioners gain advocacy experience. What better time than now to begin to change the world? Aspiring change efforts can start immediately by writing, calling, and lobbying local, state, and federal representatives to promote social change. They can assess issues and develop policy briefs as well. These policy briefs may carry even more weight when supported by international organizations such as SCRA, which now has a rapid response process for expediting advocacy efforts. The first author helped to write one such policy brief on Recovery Residences. Any SCRA member can submit a rapid response brief to the policy committee, who will decide within days whether to elevate the brief to the executive committee level, which will similarly decide whether SCRA will support the brief (see www.scra27.org/policy/documents/rapid-response-position-statements/rapidresponsecalltomembershiptocontactlegislaturesandpublicforumsreg). Briefs can be used to inform legislative action or court cases, so aspiring change agents could also draft court briefs to advocate for justice-related action.

Community practitioners can also gain immediate advocacy experience in the field by consulting for action-oriented organizations. After developing the knowledge and skills necessary for social change efforts, practitioners can begin to organize communities into action and train community members to both practice advocacy and spread these skills to other members.

ADVOCACY IN ACTION: REAL-WORLD USES OF ADVOCACY

We now present two case examples that show how advocacy has been used by community researchers. The first involves a controversial illness known as chronic fatigue syndrome (CFS). The second case study deals with alcohol and substance abuse, which affects approximately 22 million (9%) Americans.

Case Study 1: Chronic Fatigue Syndrome

Many health-care professionals continue to doubt the scientific validity of this diagnosis. The social construction of this disorder as a "yuppie flu" illness contributed to the negative attitudes that health-care providers have toward those with this syndrome (Richman & Jason, 2001). This has had serious negative impacts on patients with this illness. For example, Green, Romei, and Natelson (1999) found that 95% of individuals seeking medical treatment for CFS reported feelings of estrangement, and 70% believed that others uniformly attributed their CFS symptoms to psychological causes. Twemlow, Bradshaw, Coyne, and Lerma (1997) found that 66% of individuals with CFS believed that they were made worse by their doctors' care. In addition, studies by the CDC in the 1990s suggested that only about 20,000 people had this illness. If medical personnel believed that CFS was a relatively rare disorder primarily caused by psychiatric symptoms, then physicians might minimize or misinterpret the physical complaints of patients with CFS. This could underlie the mistrust and lack of communication that has been reported between patients and medical personnel.

The studies on CFS prevalence estimates carried out by scientists at the CDC used case ascertainment methods where physicians identified patients who presented with unexplained fatigue-related symptoms. Those patients were then referred for a medical examination to determine whether they met criteria for CFS (Reyes et al., 1997). Many low-income individuals did not have access to medical settings and thus may not have been included in the prevalence studies. Moreover, because many physicians doubted the existence of CFS, they might not have even made referrals to CFS prevalence research studies.

From these studies, it was clear that such social trends were unjust and marginalized a subsection of the population. A group of investigators in Chicago, including an epidemiologist, a biostatistician, a physician, a psychiatrist, a survey researcher, and a community psychologist (the first author) and his students decided to tackle this problem by writing and submitting a National Institutes of Health (NIH) grant to challenge the low CFS prevalence rates by conducting the first community-based study based on a random community sample. The NIH reviews were very critical, and they said that since the CDC prevalence studies had found so few people with CFS in a random sample of 30,000 individuals, the investigators would not find any patients with this illness. Thus, the research team had to be skilled in devising new strategies to validate the information gathered from their problem assessment. Notably, more evidence was needed to convince others of the problems that this illness was actually causing in society. In an effort to refute this criticism, in 1993, with financial support from the largest CFS patient self-help organization, the first author and a collaborative team conducted a small prevalence study that consisted of interviewing a random community-based sample of approximately 1,000 adults (Jason et al., 1995). Those individuals who self-reported having CFS or many of the symptoms of CFS were examined by a physician and interviewed by a psychiatrist in order to determine whether they met case criteria for CFS. The research team's diagnosis rate was considerably higher than the rate originally reported by the CDC.

With these pilot data, the research team approached the program officials at NIH with intent to resubmit a larger CFS prevalence grant. Yet, the investigators were informed that NIH was not very interested in a CFS epidemiology study. Despite this setback, the research team was not deterred and continued to resubmit grants until they were successful in securing NIH funding. In the grant-funded study conducted from 1995 to 1998, a large community random sample was screened for CFS symptomatology, and then those with CFS symptoms were medically and psychiatrically examined. With such a large study, the investigators had to be skilled in organizing and implementing their planned strategies. Using their research and analytical skills, approximately 42% of the sample was determined to have CFS, with rates being higher among Latino and African American respondents compared to White respondents (Jason et al., 1999). The results of this epidemiological study suggested that this illness may affect approximately 800,000 people in the United States. Women, Latinos, middle-aged individuals, and persons of middle to lower socioeconomic status were found to be at higher risk for CFS. The findings directly contradicted the perception that middle to upper-class Caucasian women were most at risk for this illness. Moreover, about 90% of people who were identified as having CFS in this sample had not been previously diagnosed by a physician prior to participation in the study. The largest self-help organization widely publicized these other findings indicating that ethnic minorities had higher CFS rates than European Americans, and that CFS rates were not greater among those with higher incomes. This study was used by advocates to counter the notion that CFS was a rare "yuppie flu."

It is easy to become overwhelmed when confronting complex problems or power holders, but by focusing on one small piece at a time, tangible change and success can be achieved. In addition, because of the wide attention that was given the community-based CFS prevalence research, the first author was appointed the chairperson of the Research Subcommittee of the Chronic Fatigue Syndrome Advisory Committee, which makes recommendations regarding CFS to the U.S. Secretary of Health and Human Resources. In this capacity, he was able to adeptly communicate the research findings to those in power and work on other policy-related issues such as the stigmatizing name given this illness.

In this case study, a collaboration of professionals and the major CFS self-help organization developed a clear vision of possible second-order objectives, as the group worked to decrease stigma associated with this illness. With that vision intact, the team realized that the forces that had trivialized this illness were strong. Power structures such as the CDC had to be confronted in order to change inappropriate attributions of CFS. The advocacy approach used coalitions working together to take advantage of collecting and disseminating new findings. Obstacles to change were overcome by collaborations that provided critical pilot funding for the research efforts. The team also maintained a long-term commitment to change, as the entire effort took almost a decade of work. Finally, the investigators used feedback in the form of constant communication about research findings among important players and community partners and patient organizations. These principles, and especially the focus on power abuse, were all vital to this success.

Case Study 2: Addiction Recovery Supports

For many people with substance use disorders, treatment begins in a detoxification program to remove substances from the body. Typically, a time-limited therapeutic program will follow. However, these programs are becoming briefer as funding has decreased. For many addicted persons, detoxification does not lead to sustained recovery. Instead, these individuals repeatedly cycle through service delivery systems (Vaillant, 2003). The missing element for many patients is a supportive, cohesive setting following treatment for substance abuse. The Oxford House network represents one model for a recovery home organization as it provides affordable and safe housing for individuals recovering from substance use disorders (Jason, Olson, & Foli, 2008). This self-help organization has grown over the last two decades from 18 Oxford Houses to over 1,600. Residences are rented, single family homes with a gender-segregated capacity for 6 to 12 individuals. Over 10,000 people live in these recovery homes, making them the largest single self-help residential recovery program in the United States. Houses are self-supporting and democratically run with no staff presence. This was an example of how out of the box thinking may be able to solve some types of societal problems.

In 2001, the first author was watching CBS's *60 Minutes* and saw a man by the name of Paul Molloy talking about his unique creation. Intrigued, he contacted Paul, and out of that initial conversation grew a long-term collaborative partnership between a university-based research team and a grassroots, community-based organization. Before embarking on the project, Oxford House representatives and the research team spent a year getting to know each other by attending each other's team meetings. This type of information gathering was necessary in order to skillfully plan plausible steps for change efforts. Oxford House members helped the research team fashion and adapt interview questions. After collecting pilot data, several years were spent submitting and resubmitting proposals in hopes of receiving a federal grant to more intensely study the effectiveness of Oxford Houses. Similar to the difficulties with obtaining federal grant funding for the CFS prevalence research, this team had to persevere and not lose sight of their goals in these advocacy efforts despite multiple setbacks and rejections. Again, when problems arose, the research team had to find strategies to overcome obstacles.

The research team finally received federal funding for a study, for which 150 people were who were finishing addiction treatment at alcohol and other drug use treatment facilities in Illinois were recruited. After careful organization and management for the study, half were randomly assigned to live in an Oxford House, while the other half received standard, traditional aftercare services. Participants were interviewed every 6 months for 2 years; it was found that those assigned to a communal living Oxford House had less substance use, were less likely to commit a crime, and found better jobs than those in traditional aftercare (Jason, Olson, Ferrari, & LoSasso, 2006). Together, the productivity and incarceration benefits yielded an estimated $613,000 in savings. These findings suggested that there are significant public policy benefits for these types of lower cost, non-medical, community-based care options for individuals with alcohol and other drug problems. Through the use of assessment and analytic skills, these data validated the advantages of Oxford Houses to addiction recovery efforts. As a result of this research, the Oxford House recovery model was placed in SAMSHA's National Registry of Evidence-Based Programs and Practices (www.nrepp.samhsa.gov/ViewIntervention.aspx?id = 223)

In this work with the Oxford House organization, there were many opportunities to collaboratively influence both judicial decisions as well as state-level policies to support the expansion of the Oxford House organization. Given the continuing stigma toward those with addictions, some communities oppose sharing their neighborhood with group homes like Oxford House, and they use maximum occupancy laws in efforts to close these homes. Cities and towns pass laws that make it illegal for more than five or six unrelated people to live in a house—and deliberately target Oxford House, which usually needs seven to ten house members to make rent affordable. After the release of the NIH funded outcome study, the first author was called by a lawyer who asked if his team could help resolve a dispute involving a town trying to close down the local Oxford House by claiming that there could be no more than five unrelated individuals living in one home. The DePaul research team examined a national Oxford House data set, and assessed how the number of residents in an Oxford House affected residents' individual outcomes for recovery (Jason, Groh, et al., 2008). They found that larger house sizes of eight to ten residents corresponded with less criminal and aggressive behavior. These results were used in five court cases, which successfully argued against closing Oxford Houses that had more than five or six nonrelated residents. Again, the research team was able to effectively communicate their research findings to sway political and social trends. After providing material for several lawyers working on the zoning case in North Carolina, the first author received a letter from Paul Molloy, reading in part:

> The dispute has been ongoing for six years! The town will pay attorney's fees, which are about $105,000 and a fine to the Department of Justice. The key to their decision appears to be your research showing that larger houses had better outcomes than the smaller ones. Thanks. Once again reason and logic prevailed and more folks are able to benefit.

The DePaul research team also visited the Illinois Department of Alcohol and Substance Abuse to present some of the study's findings. The director subsequently restarted a $100,000 loan program to provide Oxford Houses $4,000 loans to open up recovery houses, and the State of Illinois hired an Oxford House alumnus to begin starting new houses. The advocacy engaged in by community coalitions such as Oxford House and

DePaul University can change power structures that perpetuate institutional ways of treating people. Bottom-up social change movements can create inexpensive, community-based, structured programs that allow people to be reintegrated into society.

Clearly, allowing vulnerable people suffering from addiction to be discharged from substance use treatment settings or jail into dangerous, nonsupportive, and often desperate living situations is not acceptable. There is a need to work for second-order change, and provide new settings for these most vulnerable citizens. Yet, it is only by working with community coalitions, such as Oxford House, that we can begin to change power structures that perpetuate first-order institutional ways of treating people. Bottom-up social change movements, such as Oxford Houses, have the capacity to create alternative programs that help people in recovery integrate back into safe and supportive communities with low-cost housing options. The DePaul research team committed over 20 years to this partnership with the Oxford House organization, and they have successfully documented that providing housing and job support is critical to helping people with substance use disorders regain the skills and foundation needed to lead productive lives.

Non-Research Advocacy. Central to our discussion of advocacy and social justice is the importance of research evidence to support the need for social change. Despite this focus, it is possible to advocate for change without the ability to create research to support a vision (Humphreys & Piot, 2012). We believe that research can be a fundamental part of the process, and community psychologists function best as scientist-practitioners with an empirical underpinning for advocacy efforts. We believe that the Oxford House researcher-organization collaboration is a good example of the benefits that both groups can gain. Clearly, community practitioners can be effective in advocacy even if they don't have research skills, as they can partner with those who have these skills. Each member of a coalition can bring different resources and experiences to the advocacy effort in order to influence social change.

FUTURE TRENDS FOR ADVOCACY

Advocacy has evolved from the legal arena through civic protest to a more systematic process of enacting change from within a policy-making framework and is continuing to adapt to social changes and communication technologies. As with much of our society, advocacy has become more specialized and professionalized over time. Advocates now often serve in managerial roles focused on single issues while collaborating with other people and organizations to achieve broader goals. These collaboration trends include an increasing global network of change agents and not-for-profit organizations. There has also been increasing emphasis on monitoring advocacy cost-efficiency and effectiveness over time. These trends of specialization, professionalization, collaboration, and evaluation are likely to continue into the future.

Advocacy has similarly adapted to advances in communication tools. While long-distance communication strategies were once limited to postal and telephone interactions, developments in Internet technology have created cost-efficient opportunities for mass communication. Websites and email listservs served as tools to keep collaborators informed and motivated. In recent years, social networks were developed to help people stay connected and were quickly adopted by advocates to keep communities of change agents connected, informed, and motivated. More recently, social networks have begun to become more specialized with particular interests being targeted by the network and increasing interconnection between social media websites. These social networks have proven themselves to be valuable resources for recruiting new members for advocacy initiatives.

In the future, social media are likely to continue as a tool for change efforts. The recent Arab Spring that saw the toppling of many dictators was very much influenced by the social media that helped mobilize youth to bring about change. However, advocacy collaborators will likely form specialized social networks that integrate with other social networks for recruitment of advocates and dissemination of information. Lastly, Internet communications are entering into a post-email era where communication channels are specific to the task at hand. For example, social media are often used for personal communication while email is increasingly relegated to commercial and business purposes. As part of this trend, organizations are adopting collaborative project management tools for organization and task-specific communications. While these have thus far been centered on business projects, advocacy-specific project tools are likely to develop in the future. As with recent business management tools, advocacy project tools are likely to be hosted online and to integrate both project and stakeholder relations tools.

Finally, the nature and targets of change have evolved over time. In response to global financial pressures in recent years, advocacy has increasingly emphasized cost-efficient remedies for social problems. For example, our society is still reliant on an 1800s model of expensive institutional remedies to deal with crime and our educational system. These systems will change over time. The targets of change have evolved from a focus on national problems to an emphasis on global issues. In the future, change efforts will continue to highlight global problems with emphases on overpopulation, water and food access, international mobility, economic and technological disparities, health care, and global warming.

SUMMARY

In summary, community practitioners advocate for policies to address unjust distributions of power, decision making, and resources. Second-order change efforts facilitate the liberation of oppressed groups. Advocacy is a process that begins with a self-assessment of core values and motivations that are likely to sustain long-term change initiatives and then learning more about the issue and its context. Working with coalitions provides the ability to confront powerful vested interests that support the status quo. The change process proceeds by working collaboratively with community groups and organizations in planning before cycling back to action-based evaluations of successes and challenges. It is important for community advocates and their community partners to understand the dispositions, knowledge, skills, and abilities not only for their own advocacy efforts but also to pass along the craft to future generations of change agents.

Table 10.3   Disposition, Knowledge, Skills, and Abilities for Advocacy

Disposition	Knowledge
Value for social justice and well-being Self-confidence Autonomy balanced with collaboration Urgency balanced with patience Perseverance Commitment Appreciation for human suffering Strategic sensibility and judgment	Resources Government processes Conflict resolution Advocacy models Systems change principles Models and methods of advocacy Individual and group interventions Media, Internet, and other communication technologies Political priorities and social trends Self-understanding
Skills	Abilities
Collaboration Problem assessment Organization Self-care and coping Communication Information gathering and analysis Management	Identifying problems Relating to others Working with diverse groups Working in complex environments Adopting languages of others Listening and building consensus Detecting biases Being flexible and adaptable

DISCUSSION QUESTIONS

1. What is social justice, and why is it important to community practitioners?

2. What is advocacy, and in what situations might it be useful for promoting social justice?

3. What knowledge, skills, and abilities are needed to engage in second-order change?

4. How does working collaboratively with community organizations help to deal with power abuses?

5. What helps advocates and community groups sustain efforts over long time periods?

6. How might you refine and fine-tune your advocacy efforts over time using research methods?

KEY TERMS AND DEFINITIONS

Advocacy: Working with or for a client (individual, group, community) to change existing social structures, policies, and practice to promote social justice.

Distributive justice: Equal access to tangible and material goods.

First-order change: Efforts to eliminate deficits and problems for individuals while neglecting to address the causes that contribute to those problems.

Oppression: Unequal treatment and access to resources because of individual or group identities.

Procedural justice: The fairness involved in power and decision-making processes that determine who benefits from these resources.

Social justice: Equal treatment of and opportunities for all individuals, groups, and communities.

Second-order change: A focus on changing systems that create problems rather than addressing the problematic symptoms.

Systems change: A fundamental change in how systems are structured and operate.

RESOURCES

Recommended Reading

1. Agendas, Alternatives, and Public Policies

2. Lobbying Illinois: How You Can Make a Difference in Public Policy

3. Teaching for Diversity and Social Justice

Recommended Websites

Society for Community Research and Action public policy website: http://www.scra27.org/what-we-do/policy/

Community toolbox guide to advocacy: http://ctb.ku.edu/en/tablecontents/chapter_1030.aspx

American Public Health Association advocacy tips: http://www.apha.org/advocacy/tips/

Stop Violence Against Women advocacy resources: http://www.stopvaw.org/the_advocacy_process

American Alliance of Museums advocacy educational materials: http://www.aam-us.org/advocacy/resources/online-training

Online tools for advocacy campaigns: http://www.socialbrite.org/2012/02/23/the-best-tools-for-advocacy-campaigns/

Federal legislators' search engine: http://www.congress.org/congressorg/directory/congdir.tt

Library of Congress archive of federal regulations: http://thomas.loc.gov/home/thomas.php

Project and stakeholder management tools:

- http://civicrm.org
- http://freedcamp.com
- https://do.com
- http://asana.com
- http://www.apollohq.com

Suggested Activities for Further Competency Development

- Indicate five issues you would be interested in advocating for

  o Complete the Advocacy Self-Assessment Tool for each issue

- For the issue you score highest on, develop a plan to advocate directly and indirectly around that issue using the principles for social change.

  o What persons, organizations, or institutions would be involved?
  o What resources are available?
  o What is a reasonable working time frame for enacting change?
  o What are anticipated barriers and how will you address them?
  o What advocacy knowledge, skills, and abilities do you need to further develop and implement your plan?
  o Where can you access resources for additional advocacy training?
  o Worksheets
  o For assessment of knowledge, skill, and abilities relating to advocacy on the issue and needs for further development

Advocacy Self-Assessment Tool

For each section below, rate your agreement to each question for your chosen issues with a score ranging from 1 to 5, with 1 = *I do not agree* and 5 = *I strongly agree*. Then, total your responses. For the issue you score highest on, develop a plan to advocate directly and indirectly around that issue using the principles for social change (refer to number 2 in Suggested Activities for Further Competency Development).

COMMITMENT

1. Are you strongly committed to working on this issue?

2. Are you willing to put in a great effort to achieve this goal?

3. Would you be willing to spend many years working on this issue?

4. Do you have a sense of obligation to continue working on this issue above all others?

CENTRALITY

1. Is what you have listed more important than any other issue you could work on?

2. Is this matter of great personal meaning to you?

3. Do you have passion and a burning desire to see this issue addressed?

4. Is this an issue that you devote a lot of time to thinking about?

RESOURCES

1. Are you a member of or do you work with any activist groups or community organizations that are dealing with the topic you have selected?

2. Are you aware of any friends, family members, or colleagues who are either working on this issue or interested in doing so?

3. Do you have access to resources that might be applied to working with this topic? Resources can be defined rather broadly as time, energy, funds, or materials.

4. Do you feel that you have the capabilities and confidence to engage in work with the issue that you have mentioned?

REFERENCES

Alinsky, S. (1969). *Reveille for radicals*. New York, NY: Vintage.

Bell, E. (2005). Advocacy training by the international community of women living with HIV/AIDS. *Gender & Development, 13*(3), 70–79.

Bradley, J. M., Werth, J. L., Jr., Hastings, S. L., & Pierce, T. W. (2012). A qualitative study of rural mental health practitioners regarding the potential professional consequences of social justice advocacy. *Professional Psychology: Research and Practice, 43*(4), 356–363.

Burnes, T. R., & Singh, A. A. (2010). Integrating social justice training into the practicum experience for psychology trainees: Starting earlier. *Training and Education in Professional Psychology, 4*(3), 153–162.

Cohen, K. R., Lee, C. M., & McIlwraith, R. (2012). The psychology of advocacy and the advocacy of psychology. *Counseling Psychology, 53*(3), 151–158.

Crethar, H. C., Torres Rivera, E., & Nash, S. (2008). In search of common threads: Linking multicultural, feminist, and social justice counseling paradigms. *Journal of Counseling & Development, 86*, 269–278.

Dalton, J., & Wolfe, S. (2012, August 15). Joint Column: Education connection and the community practitioner. Competencies for community psychology practice. Society for Community Research and Action. Draft. *The Community Psychologist, 45*, 7–4. Retrieved from http://www.scra27.org/practice/documents/practcompetenciestcpdraftaug2012docx

DeLeon, P. H., Loftis, C. W., Ball, V., & Sullivan, M. J. (2006). Navigating politics, policy, and procedure: A firsthand perspective of advocacy on behalf of the profession. *Professional Psychology: Research and Practice, 37*(2), 146–153.

Fondacaro, M. R., & Weinberg, D. (2002). Concepts of social justice in community psychology: Toward a social ecological epistemology. *American Journal of Community Psychology, 30*(4), 473–492.

Freire, P. (1970). *Pedagogy of the oppressed.* New York, NY: Continuum.

Glidewell, J. C. (1984). Training for the role of advocate. *American Journal of Community Psychology, 12*(2), 193–198.

Goodman, L. A., Liang, B., Helms, J. E., Latta, R. E., Sparks, E., & Weintraub, S. R. (2004). Training counseling psychologists as social change agents: Feminist and multicultural principles in action. *The Counseling Psychologist, 32,* 793–837.

Green, J., Romei, J., & Natelson, B. J. (1999). Stigma and chronic fatigue syndrome. *Journal of Chronic Fatigue Syndrome, 5,* 63–75.

Humphreys, K., & Piot, P. (2012, February 27). Scientific evidence alone is not sufficient basis for health policy. *British Medical Journal, 344,* e1316.

Jason, L. A. (1991). Participating in social change: A fundamental value for our discipline. *American Journal of Community Psychology, 19,* 1–16.

Jason, L. A. (2013). *Principles of social change.* New York, NY: Oxford University Press.

Jason, L. A., Groh, D. R., Durocher, M., Alvarez, J., Aase, D. M., & Ferrari, J. R. (2008). Counteracting "not in my backyard": The positive effects of greater occupancy within mutual-help recovery homes. *Journal of Community Psychology, 36,* 947–958.

Jason, L. A., Najar, N., Porter, N., & Reh, C. (2009). Evaluating the Centers for Disease Control's empirical chronic fatigue syndrome case definition. *Journal of Disability Policy Studies, 20,* 93–100.

Jason, L. A., Olson, B., Ferrari, J. R., & LoSasso, A. T. (2006). An evaluation of communal housing settings for substance abuse recovery. *American Journal of Public Health, 91,* 1727–1729.

Jason, L. A., Olson, B. D., & Foli, K. (2008). *Rescued lives: The Oxford House approach to substance abuse.* New York, NY: Routledge.

Jason, L. A., Pratt, T., Ware, C., Chimata, R., Bangi, A., & Johnson, D. (2002). Social activists: Lessons for community psychology. *International Journal of Group Tensions, 31,* 103–122.

Jason, L. A., Richman, J. A., Rademaker, A. W., Jordan, K. M., Plioplys, A. V., Taylor, R., . . . Plioplys, S. (1999). A community-based study of chronic fatigue syndrome. *Archives of Internal Medicine, 159,* 2129–2137.

Jason, L. A., Taylor, R. R., Wagner, L., Holden, J., Ferrari, J. R., Plioplys, A. V., . . . Papernik, M. (1995). Estimating rates of chronic fatigue syndrome from a community based sample: A pilot study. *American Journal of Community Psychology, 23,* 557–568.

Kiselica, M. S., & Robinson, M. (2001). Bringing advocacy counseling to life: The history, values, and human dramas of social justice work in counseling. *Journal of Counseling and Development, 79,* 387–397.

Kloos, B., Hill, J., Thomas, E., Elias, M. J., & Dalton, J. H. (2012). *Community psychology: Linking individuals and communities.* Belmont, CA: Wadsworth.

Lewis, J., Arnold, M. S., House, R., & Toporek, R. L. (2003). *Advocacy competencies: American Counseling Association Task Force on Advocacy Competencies.* Retrieved from http://www.counseling.org/Resources/

Lorion, R. P., & Iscoe, I. (1996). Reshaping our views of the field. In R. P. Lorion, I. Iscoe, P. DeLeon, & G. R. VandenBos (Eds.), *Psychology and public policy: Balancing public service and professional need.* Washington, DC: American Psychological Association.

Maton, K. I., Humphreys, K., Jason, L. A., & Shinn, B. (in press). Advocacy and social policy. In C. Keys, M. Bond, & I. Serrano-Garcia (Eds.), *Handbook of community psychology.* Washington, DC: American Psychological Association.

Maton, K. I., Strompolis, M., & Wisniewski, L. (2013). Building advocacy and policy capacity: A survey of SCRA members. *The Community Psychologist, 46,* 13–16. Retrieved from http://scra27.org/policy/documents/marketplace/surveyofscramembershipcapacitybuildingreport

Mays, V. M. (2000). A social justice agenda. *American Psychologist, 55*(3), 326–327.

Mooney, C. Z., & Van Dyke-Brown, B. (2003). *Lobbying Illinois: How you can make a difference in public policy.* Springfield: University of Illinois at Springfield.

Moore, S. (2011). Can public-policy advocacy be taught? or learned? *The Philanthropist, 23*(4), 471–480.

Nelson, G., Prilleltensky, I., & MacGillivary, H. (2001). Building value-based partnerships: Toward solidarity with oppressed groups. *American Journal of Community Psychology, 29*(5), 649–677.

Ponzo, Z. (1974). A counselor and change: Reminiscences and resolutions. *Personnel and Guidance Journal, 53,* 27–32.

Prilleltensky, I. (2001). Value-based praxis in community psychology: Moving toward social justice and social action. *American Journal of Community Psychology, 29*(5), 748–778.

Prilleltensky, I., & Gonick, L. (1996). Polities change, oppression remains: On the psychology and politics of oppression. *Political Psychology, 17,* 127–147.

Rappaport, J. (1981). In praise of paradox: A social policy of empowerment over prevention. *American Journal of Community Psychology, 9,* 1–25.

Reyes, M., Gary, H. E., Jr., Dobbins, J. G., Randall, B., Steele, L., Fukuda, K., . . . Reeves, W. C. (1997, February 21). Descriptive epidemiology of chronic fatigue syndrome: CDC surveillance in four cities. *Morbidity and Mortality Weekly Report Surveillance Summaries, 46*(No. SS2), 113.

Richman, J. A., & Jason, L. A. (2001). Gender biases underlying the social construction of illness states: The case of chronic fatigue syndrome. *Current Sociology 49,* 15–29.

Seidman, E. (1988). Back to the future, community psychology: Unfolding a theory of social intervention. *American Journal of Community Psychology, 16,* 3–24.

Shinn, M. (2007). Waltzing with a monster: Bringing research to bear on public policy. *Journal of Social Issues, 63,* 215–231.

Toit, B. M. D. (1996). The Mahatma Gandhi and South Africa. *Journal of Modern African Studies, 34*(4), 643–660.

Toporek, R. L., Lewis, J. A., & Crethar, H. C. (2009). Promoting systemic change through ACA advocacy competencies. *Journal of Counseling and Development, 87,* 260–270.

Trusty, J. (2005). Advocacy competencies for professional school counselors. *Professional School Counseling, 8*(3), 259–265.

Twemlow, S. W., Bradshaw, S. L., Jr., Coyne, L., & Lerma, B. H. (1997). Patterns of utilization of medical care and perceptions of the relationship between doctor and patient with chronic illness including chronic fatigue syndrome. *Psychological Reports, 80,* 643–659.

Vaillant, G. E. (2003). A 60-year follow-up of alcoholic men. *Addiction, 98,* 1043–1051.

Vasquez, M. J. T. (2012). Psychology and social justice: Why we do what we do. *American Psychologist, 67*(5), 337–346.

Watts, R. J., & Abdul-Adil, J. (1994). Psychological aspects of oppression and socio-political development: Building young warriors. In R. Newby & T. Manley (Eds.), *The poverty of inclusion, innovation, and interventions: The dilemma of the African American underclass.* New Brunswick, NJ: Rutgers University Press.

Watzlawick, P., Weakland, J. H., & Fisch, R. (1974). *Change: Principles of problem formation and problem resolution.* New York, NY: W. W. Norton.

CHAPTER 11

Planning, Implementing, and Developing Evidence-Based Interventions in the Context of Federally Funded Programs

Richard A. Jenkins

The author wishes to thank Augie Diana, Belinda Sims, and Lori Ducharme for their helpful input regarding considerations for the funding and implementation of substance use prevention programs. Harold Perl, Wilson Compton, Gaya Dowling, Jack Stein, and the editors provided helpful editorial comments for this chapter.

Disclaimer: The views expressed are those of the author and do not necessarily represent those of the National Institute on Drug Abuse, the National Institutes of Health, the U.S. Department of Health and Human Services, or the U.S. government.

OPENING EXERCISE

You are a community psychology practitioner consulting with a regional health agency that serves several counties in a rural part of your state, where most resources are based in county seat towns, one of which has a state university. The agency began as a regional public health authority, but recently was reorganized as part of a state effort to consolidate health and public health services. The agency now includes mental health and substance abuse services that formerly were part of other agencies that had had different geographic structures. Only a few staff from these former agencies are based in your catchment area and their backgrounds are in treatment or community support programs. The newly reorganized agency receives drug and alcohol prevention funds, but no one has expertise in these areas. The "prevention" staff in the regional health agency is concentrated in areas like childhood vaccination, HIV prevention, and contraception distribution.

The state health department not only wants the regional agency to provide drug and alcohol prevention services, but now also wants these to be evidence-based interventions (EBIs). Its expectations are more prescriptive about the programs it wants funded than those of its federal funder. The state previously had encouraged EBIs, but had never made them a funding requirement. The one ongoing drug use prevention program in the area uses educational outreach by the police. It is based on a national program that has little evidence of effectiveness and had been adapted to the local area without evaluation. This program is low in cost and popular with most of the school boards, which only need to

Photo 11.1 The U.S. Capitol, Washington, D.C.

Source: Susan M. Wolfe.

provide classroom time. You have been told that some of the police chiefs like the outreach aspect of the program, although the police officers who conduct the program feel it is outside their normal duties. The regional health agency is concerned about the cost and resources required for implementing new services, but recognizes that what it has inherited from the other agencies is not adequate and will not be eligible for future funding.

Given these circumstances, where do you start in order to identify programs that would be supported? How do you deal with the resource demands of implementing new programs, especially in a place where the population is relatively dispersed? What steps can you take to ensure that once these programs are started, they will be sustained? How do you go about building support in the community for something new and unknown if the current intervention is relatively popular?

OVERVIEW

This chapter will focus on competencies needed for the **implementation,** which refers to the use of strategies to adopt and integrate evidence-based interventions (EBIs) and change practice patterns within specific settings. This includes program planning and implications for the development of new interventions, as well as changes to patterns of service delivery practice. Federally funded services in the United States provide the context here, which includes most services for prevention, treatment, and care services directed at health, behavior, or social problems. Many of the lessons here apply outside of federal programs (particularly in the foundation sector) and similar issues can occur in international settings, particularly where bureaucratic structures resemble those in the United States. Researchers, policymakers, and much of the service provider community endorse EBIs as the most efficient and effective way to deliver services; however, the actual process of placing EBIs in the field is not simple. Despite incentives and **technical assistance** from funders to adopt EBIs, implementation continues to lag in many areas (e.g., Institute of Medicine [IOM], 2000, 2009). Technical assistance includes providing information, instruction, feedback, and/or training to assist providers in developing strategic plans or implementing interventions. Hence, competencies in a variety of areas are needed, as well as adequate resources.

This chapter reviews principles rather than focusing on specific EBIs or the particular details of their implementation. Concepts and frameworks for implementation tend to reflect features of the systems where they were developed and the roles of their developers (see "Evolution of Implementation Frameworks," below). Consequently, numerous roles and tasks have been identified that vary by conceptualization and framework (Damschroder et al., 2009; Powell et al., 2012; Rabin & Brownson, 2012). This chapter will focus on the most common roles and tasks that present themselves to practitioners, the associated competencies, and the most recognizable contexts for them: planning, implementation (the actual putting in place of interventions), and development of new EBIs (see Table 11.1). Development sometimes is placed at the beginning of the implementation process; however, development of new EBIs tends to draw lessons from existing EBIs and their implementation in the field, so it will be treated last.

Table 11.1 summarizes the most common implementation roles and tasks, organized by setting. Some practitioners may work within federal or state agencies (e.g., administering, planning, or funding EBIs; evaluating EBI implementation and delivery; or developing new EBIs). Others may work at **enabling agencies** that are responsible for policies that govern the provision of resources for services and how they are accessed. Examples include mental health boards or health departments (e.g., providing training and technical assistance, serving as a board or committee member). Providers also may be employed by **provider organizations** that deliver services to the public. In addition, practitioners may work in independent practice or as academic researchers performing consultative functions to one or more of these settings.

Graphics cannot capture sufficiently the complexity of all the potential roles and tasks, or all of the institutional relationships and their various feedback mechanisms that exist in the implementation process. The approach here is narrative rather than schematic, and relational/contextual rather than purely technical; indeed, the limitations of the purely technical perspective that guides most frameworks will be made clear. The chapter presents the simplest cases of each step (planning, implementation, or development of EBIs) with a description of common variations on these cases, the common tasks for practitioners, and their necessary competencies.

The chapter begins with an overview of the funding, resources, and systems for EBIs in federally funded services. These provide the foundation for understanding any implementation process and provide the structures and contexts used for planning, implementation, and development of EBIs. This is followed by discussions of planning for implementation of EBIs (usually done on a state or community level), implementation of specific programs, and development of new EBIs. The chapter is primarily written for training community psychology practitioners and for experienced practitioners seeking to refine their capacities for engaging in EBIs

Table 11.1 Roles and Tasks for Community Practitioners

Stage	Roles and Tasks and Most Common Associated Contexts
Planning of EBIs	• Review EBIs and related literature (F, EA, AC, I) • Identify and aggregate data for strategic planning (F, EA, AC, I) • Analyze and interpret data for strategic planning (F, EA, AC, I) • Collect new data (surveys, rapid assessment) for strategic planning (F, EA, AC, I) • Analyze and interpret program data for strategic planning (F, EA, AC, I) • Collect new program data for strategic planning (F, EA, AC, I) • Organizational development work related to advisory groups (organizing new groups, helping existing groups reorganize) (F, EA, AC, I) • Assist advisory groups with using data (F, EA, AC, I) • Assist advisory groups with selection of EBIs (F, EA, AC, I) • Evaluate planning processes (F, EA, AC, I) • Contribute to strategic plan development as an advisory group member (AC, I) • Contribute to strategic plan development as a staff member (F, EA)
Implementation of EBIs	• Review available EBI packages (F, EA, PO, AC) • Administer funding of EBIs (F, EA) • Develop funding announcements for EBIs (F, EA) • Develop guidelines for implementation practices (F, EA) • Consult with external training and technical assistance programs (AC) • Provide training and technical assistance to managers and/or frontline staff (F, EA, PO, AC, I) • Develop monitoring systems for process and outcome evaluation (F, EA, PO, AC, I) • Analyze monitoring data and evaluate implementation quality (F, EA, PO, AC, I) • Participate in quality improvement (F, EA, AC, PO, I) • Oversee development of supports such as implementation packages, training, and technical assistance (F, EA) • Develop implementation packages (AC) • Grant writing (PO, AC, I)
Development of EBIs	• Review EBIs and related literature (F, EA, AC, PO, I) • Develop funding announcements for new or adapted EBIs (F, EA, AC, PO, I) • Identify gaps in populations, modalities, issues addressed (F, EA, AC, PO, I) • Design new or adapted interventions (AC, I) • Grant writing (AC, I) • Organize community advisory groups (AC, I)

Note: Contexts: F = Funder; EA = Enabling agency; PO = Provider organization; AC = Academic; I = Independent Practitioner

(*practitioner* will be used instead of the longer term incorporating community psychology); however, much of the content is applicable to related and overlapping fields and this will be discussed at the close of the chapter (see "Planning, Implementation, and Development of EBIs: Summary and Consideration of Community Psychologists and Other Disciplines").

DEFINING IMPLEMENTATION

The implementation field has responded to the needs of funders, practitioners, and researchers with a variety of definitions and frameworks (e.g., Damschroder et al., 2009; Powell et al., 2012; Rabin & Brownson, 2012). The chapter uses a colloquial definition of implementation: *putting interventions in place.* This incorporates *adaptation* of interventions to novel settings and populations, *dissemination* across various kinds of service delivery settings and systems, and the tools that enable quality improvement and sustainability over time, such as *monitoring* and technical assistance. **Adaptation** refers to modifying an EBI so that it is responsive to particular needs of a target audience or settings. This is particularly important where the population or setting is different from the one where the EBI was originally developed or previously implemented. **Dissemination** involves the active efforts to spread EBIs so that they reach their target audience. Adaptation and dissemination sometimes are treated as concepts separate from implementation, although they are intrinsic to implementation practice. Implementation is treated here as a transactional, social change process embedded in a variety of systems, but one that is viewed from the perspective of a practitioner. **Monitoring** is the process by which implementation of EBIs and their outcomes are measured so that these data can inform further refinement of the implementation of those EBIs and determine their effects.

THE STRUCTURE OF FUNDING, RESOURCES, AND SYSTEMS FOR EBIs

The Structure, the Players, and Their Roles

Planning, implementation, and development of EBIs requires an understanding of how health and social service delivery systems are organized and funded along with the requirements that may be attached to funding. At its simplest, funding usually involves a federal agency providing grants to a state for the delivery of a specific category of services. States administer the grants and provide services or they contract with local provider organizations to carry out the services, while providing technical assistance and oversight. Examples of federal funders include the Centers for Disease Control (CDC); the Substance Abuse and Mental Health Services Administration (SAMHSA); and the Health Resources and Services Administration (HRSA). Provider organizations can include small single-site community organizations, national networks of locally based voluntary organizations (e.g., Young Men's Christian Association), large health-care organizations with numerous branches and affiliates (e.g., Kaiser Permanente, academic medical systems such as Cleveland Clinic Foundation), and city, county, or regional public bodies.

These are **categorical** funding streams which support services for specific conditions (e.g., HIV as opposed to other sexually transmitted diseases) and/or particular service delivery systems (e.g., HIV prevention vs. HIV treatment and care). Multiple funding streams may originate from different parts of a single federal agency. For example, injury prevention and HIV prevention are funded by CDC, but originate in different parts of the agency. State and local governments often supplement federal funding and may be the primary source of funds for some services, such as those not funded by federal programs (e.g., syringe and needle exchange services for HIV prevention among people who inject drugs). Some federal programs also directly fund individual provider organizations such as clinics, school districts, and community organizations or consortia of these organizations such as regional Head Start agencies.

Regardless of the recipient, federal grants typically have multiyear cycles and include conditions on the nature and scope of services to be provided. These grants often are administered as **cooperative agreements** in which the federal funder plays significant oversight and technical assistance roles with states or directly with provider organizations. Cooperative agreements are grant mechanism that include substantial participation from a funder, which often includes direct, active involvement in oversight and technical assistance for program practice that goes beyond periodic progress monitoring. Grant requirements typically include language regarding the use of EBIs to deliver services, and criteria or compendia that define these EBIs. Use of EBIs may be a specific requirement of funding, or EBIs may be expected to represent a certain proportion of services delivered in the community. The guidance and expectations of federally funded programs evolve over time, often in response to research on the implementation and planning processes. Federal agencies sometimes supplement their normal categorical grants with other, usually competitive, funding to help states introduce or increase the use of EBIs. Some federal agencies fund independent technical assistance centers to provide training to the staff of provider organizations (see "Recommended Websites" for examples). Technical assistance centers usually provide training for specific EBIs as well as for skills generally needed to identify, adapt, and implement EBIs.

State and federal bureaucracies usually have parallel categorical structures (e.g., CDC's HIV prevention program interacts with state health department HIV/AIDS programs), although state governments have been consolidating related agencies (e.g., HIV and sexually transmitted infection [STI] bureaus). Federal agencies also have begun to consolidate some program and planning functions, which creates some synergy with changes at the state level. For example, CDC recently began funding states to consolidate functions such as disease **surveillance** and data systems that support related areas of chronic disease prevention (e.g., tobacco control, diet and nutrition; CDC, 2011). CDC and HRSA have issued common guidelines for developing epidemiological profiles to reduce duplication between HIV prevention (CDC) and HIV care (HRSA) planning processes (CDC & HRSA, 2004).

As mentioned previously, state and local governments often supplement federal funding. The roles of state and local governments are governed by state laws, which vary by state. There may be city, county, or regional bodies empowered to act as enabling agencies such as regional health districts or county mental health boards. These establish local priorities and make local funding decisions, often providing most of the oversight and technical assistance for EBIs. State funding agencies sometimes also serve as the primary enabling agencies. States, cities, counties, or enabling agencies may raise funds through legislative action or tax levies voted by the public.

State agencies and/or local enabling agencies often have stakeholder-based advisory groups, which may be a funding requirement for service planning. **Stakeholders** are persons, groups, organizations, members, or systems that affect or can be affected by an organization's actions. These groups may include a narrow range of participants, such as representatives of provider organizations in the case of substance abuse coalitions. In the cases of HIV community planning groups for prevention or treatment and care (CDC & HRSA, 2004), membership is broader and includes providers, advocates, academic researchers, and consumers. The roles and organization of these advisory groups vary widely and tend to reflect how services are administered within states, as well as federal funding requirements and historical trends such as patterns of community activism (Chung & Lounsbury, 2006).

Competencies for Understanding Funding, Resources, and Systems

Practitioners interested in planning, implementing, or developing programs need to know

- the scope of funding (i.e., size and scope of different funding streams; duration of funding);
- funding requirements including definitions of "evidence"; compendia of recommended EBIs, as well as

  o guidelines for the selection of EBIs;
  o programs funded by local rather than federal funds and how they are integrated into planning;
  o funding mechanisms (grants, contracts, cooperative agreements);
  o funding formulae (e.g., per client, per service, per encounter, forms of capitation);

- training and technical assistance activities that are supported by funders and/or enabling agencies, including

  o costs for training and technical assistance borne by funders and enabling agencies versus those borne by provider organizations;

- funders' financial support for planning and evaluation activities.

Information about systems, resources, and funding is foundational for almost all of the roles practitioners are likely to have in the implementation process. All of this information is publicly available from funders at the state and federal level in their funding announcements. These, as well as supporting materials related to the specifics of funding and technical assistance, should be online along with examples of EBIs that are supported and/or required. The specificity and detail of available information will vary widely. Practitioners should follow up with their contacts in the various systems involved in funding (funders, enabling agencies) as well as stakeholders to fully understand the resources available for EBIs as well as the funding guidelines and requirements. Beyond collecting factual information, this process of becoming acquainted with funder expectations, resources, and systems is useful for establishing relationships, understanding roles and expectations, and beginning to comprehend how implementation systems are organized.

THE PLANNING PROCESS FOR EBIs

The planning process provides a variety of roles for practitioners and often provides their introduction to systems for implementing services. Planning affects the selection of EBIs and their ultimate implementation, although planning roles may be several steps removed from the field implementation of specific interventions. Planning usually is framed as a technical process but is affected very much by social processes like group dynamics and benefits from an understanding of human judgment and decision making (Jenkins et al., 2005). These social and psychological processes usually are unappreciated or only naively addressed in funder guidance. Consequently, this section includes a segue into these areas and the overall length of this section reflects the outsized role that planning processes can play in practitioners' work.

Components of the Planning Process

The planning process usually has multiple steps that incorporate funding guidelines and requirements. State agencies may need to approve decisions made by local enabling agencies that use federal funds that are administered by the state. Enabling agencies may have their own internal review processes for funding programs, although major financial decisions may require approval by a board of directors. Depending on funding requirements, advisory groups associated with enabling agencies or state funding agencies may play purely advisory roles or may vote to approve or concur with plans made by a state or an enabling agency.

Planning for EBIs usually begins with a synthesis of data that document need, current responses in the community, and what should be addressed by programs. This is often described as a **gap analysis** because it indicates the "gaps" (unmet or underserved needs) that should be addressed by new services or modification of existing services. These data and the gap analysis are then integrated into a plan for addressing these unmet or underserved needs, based on available EBIs, the appropriateness of EBIs for populations or settings of interest, and indications of EBIs' **effectiveness** (evidence of significant preventive or therapeutic effects when delivered under real-world conditions). This is often called a **strategic plan**; in the past this often was described as a **logic model**. The term "logic model" remains helpful because the strategic plan is meant to provide a logical, step-by-step explanation of how the gap analysis has made use of existing data, informed the selection of specific EBIs, and will measure the effect of these EBIs. Strategic plans vary in duration depending on the funding stream, but usually anticipate work that will take place over a period of several years.

Strategic plans usually serve as the basis for grant applications to funders, as well as the bases for annual progress reports that are submitted after funding occurs. Funders may prescribe particular data elements or the use of a particular data-based algorithm to guide the plan, but the general structure tends to be common across funders and funding streams. The strategic planning model has been built into some programs, like Communities That Care (Hawkins & Catalano, 1992), that integrate planning and implementation at the community level. There also have been attempts to mechanize this process through computerized **decision support systems,** which help decision makers select among alternative ways to address a problem; however, this approach has limitations such as grading the quality of supporting research for EBIs (Sorensen, 2011).

One assumption of the strategic plan/logic model approach is that the plan should reflect a **theory of change** that accounts for how the EBIs will ameliorate problems of interest and is related to supporting data. A theory of change should incorporate **core elements,** (i.e., essential ingredients), as well as what is known generally about factors that lead to better outcomes, such as mitigation of risk factors and enhancement of protective factors. For example, EBIs that use methods known to change sexual risk behavior should lead to fewer cases of HIV (IOM, 2000). Similarly, early childhood interventions that address protective factors like parenting or classroom behavior should affect later drug use and abuse (IOM, 1994, 2009).

Advisory Group Approaches to Program Planning

Planning processes may involve working primarily with representatives of a funder, enabling agency, or provider organization or perhaps interacting with a board of directors for one of these, but often planning makes use of advisory groups. Practitioners may work directly with these advisory bodies or they may find that the deliberations of these groups shape work that needs to be done. The advisory group approach in planning has a long history in federally funded programs, going back to anti-poverty programs in the 1960s (Gans, 1973; Moynihan, 1969), and is commonly used outside of federal funding streams such as neighborhood economic development (Milligan, Coulton, York, & Register, 1999) and land use planning (Steinmann, Smith, Jurdem, & Hammond, 1977).

Because advisory groups often are a required part of the planning process, funders usually provide guidance and resources for their organization and function (e.g., CDC's HIV prevention community planning and some related technical assistance materials are included under "Recommended Websites"). These groups should be contrasted with groups that form on a grassroots, bottom-up basis or evolve out of existing coalitions (e.g., substance abuse coalitions that evolve out of "drug-free communities" groups). This distinction is important because the roles, commitment, and engagement of a directed advisory group in a planning process may be very different from what is seen in a grassroots mobilization process. There often is ambiguity about the roles of advisory groups and how these are reconciled with the data-driven process that usually is expected in a strategic planning process. Advisory group members often feel that a data-driven process favors predetermined outcomes, especially where data are limited or presented in ways that seem divorced from what they see as the primary planning objectives.

Data for EBI Planning and Decision Making

Practitioner roles in planning often involve various approaches to existing data (identifying data sources; aggregating, analyzing, and/or interpreting data), or collection of new data. Practitioners also may be asked to help analyze data for developing plans (at the funder, enabling agency level, or provider organization level) or grant writing (at the provider organization level, helping them apply for funds to provide EBIs). Data elements for the planning process may be specified, to some extent, by funders and there may be algorithms provided by federal funders to guide data use. Briefly, data sources may include census or other demographic data; disease surveillance, vital statistics, or other mandated reporting; population-based surveys; program data; resource compilations; and data related to evaluation and **cost-effectiveness.** The latter refers to the estimation of how the costs (labor, materials, overhead costs) associated with an intervention relate to its measurable outcomes. Commonly used data sources are summarized in Table 11.2 and these are in addition to research data on particular EBIs.

A significant, common barrier to effective planning is the availability of appropriate local data (Mrazek, Biglan, & Hawkins, 2003; Rugg et al., 2000). There are numerous limitations to data at the local level, and the most common include:

- Data on small but epidemiologically important populations often are lacking (e.g., young African American gay men, who constitute the largest fraction of new HIV/AIDS cases; CDC, 2012).

Table 11.2   Common Data Elements for EBI Planning Processes

- Demographic data such as census data to characterize populations and geography
- Local disease surveillance (cases reported for diseases like HIV, sexually transmitted infections, or tuberculosis that may be relevant)
- Other conditions reported to government agencies (requirements will vary by state)
  - o Conditions reported on a mandatory basis (e.g., many forms of abuse, crime)
  - o Conditions reported on a voluntary basis (e.g., suicide, drug overdose)
- Vital statistics (i.e., births, deaths, causes of death)
- Program data (usually from publicly funded service delivery systems; e.g., hospital admissions, emergency department visits, unique users of mental health centers, juvenile or adult cases, persons under court or social welfare supervision)
- Population-based surveys that identify problem areas, as well as risk or protective factors (see "Resources" for examples)
- Enumeration and mapping of community resources
- Data on program evaluation and cost-effectiveness of existing programs (usually collected for specific interventions or estimated on a regional basis based on program data for specific classes of interventions)

- Local data such as vital statistics, disease surveillance, and other reporting of conditions may be constrained by confidentiality concerns that limit demographic or geographic breakdowns where there are small numbers of cases.

- Program data usually are limited to publicly funded facilities, which is a limitation where the public sector is relatively small or only somewhat relevant.

- Census data can be broken down into small geographic areas that may be useful but outdated.

- Population-based surveys sometimes provide breakdowns for states and some larger cities or counties, but sampling and confidentiality concerns may limit what is available.

- Surveys often are performed on a repeated cross-sectional basis rather than longitudinally, and those with a longitudinal component often have insufficient sample sizes for state or local breakdowns.

- Sentinel data (e.g., drug overdoses in emergency departments) may be useful in tracking trends but may reflect only certain classes of problems or populations and may be lagging rather than emergent indicators of trends.

- Data often are limited or nonexistent for conditions such as psychiatric disorders or homelessness, which may contribute to risk for a wide variety of problems.

- Program evaluation and cost-effectiveness data for existing programs often are absent or are of limited usefulness (e.g., constructed from regional or state-wide service data that may not fully capture costs or effectiveness of individual programs). There may be efforts to extrapolate program effects from indicators such as program data, surveillance, or case reporting, but the nature of these data usually make it difficult to estimate the effects of any one program.

Limitations associated with individual data sources may be compounded by issues in the integration of data. Different data sources may or may not overlap in terms of whom they sample (in the case of population-based data) or who enters into their reach (in the case of surveillance or program data). Data sharing between agencies that do not regularly collaborate may be problematic. For example, substance use agencies and public health agencies often do not routinely share data although this may be of importance for areas such as HIV or viral hepatitis prevention. Data sharing can be complicated by incompatibilities in data management systems, reporting requirements, as well as differences in data elements that limit geographic or demographic breakdowns.

Local **data warehouses** have been created to overcome data integration problems, usually on a metropolitan area basis, and most notably through the Urban Institute's National Neighborhood Indicators Partnership (www.neighborhoodindicators.org/). These usually include vital statistics, census data, and locally generated indicators such as reported crimes or school attendance data. These data often are geocoded to enable layering of different data on each other, and some warehouses permit simple online data cuts and analyses such as crosstabs. Federal agencies have supported demonstration projects to develop public health data warehouses such as CDC's Project OASIS (Gaffga, Samuel, Stenger, Stover, & Newman, 2009), which incorporated STI, tuberculosis, and other data in geocoded formats; these projects often have been continued with local support from state or local health departments.

Addressing Gaps and Limitations in Data

Some local data gaps may be filled if funders or enabling agencies have the resources to perform one-time or periodic surveys (Mrazek et al., 2003, provide a framework) or conduct small-scale, multimethod rapid assessments (Beebe, 2001). Conducting these supplemental studies is among the most frequent roles for practitioners in the planning process. These studies may include documenting local needs, suggesting ways to improve existing programs, and/or providing data to adapt EBIs to populations, venues, or other locally important circumstances. These studies also may lead to opportunities to improve data collection systems; improvements in the quality of program data can help in monitoring the implementation of EBIs as well as informing the planning process.

Data for EBI Planning: Implications of Data Limitations

Ideally, data uses should drive data collection for planning as well as evaluation. Unfortunately, planning often relies on data collected for other purposes, such as administration or disease surveillance, and opportunities for supplemental data collection often are limited. Even under better circumstances, data use is suboptimal (e.g., Weiss, 1980, 1998). Decision makers involved in the planning process often have had limited exposure to research such as undergraduate courses in research methods or a single research course in a practitioner training program, and some will not have had any exposure, particularly community members who may participate in advisory groups. Researchers who provide data, such as state epidemiologists or academic researchers, often do not routinely participate in planning activities beyond supplying data tables or technical reports and may have a limited understanding of how those data are to be used. The mismatch between data suppliers, users, and the planning process, combined with the limitations of data themselves, create many situations where the **utilitarian** approaches prescribed in federal programs become complicated in practice. Utilitarianism assumes that one can maximize potential benefits and minimize potential harms based upon consideration of available data.

Decision Making Under Uncertainty: An Important Segue

The gaps in available data and the usual planning contexts create situations that Tversky and Kahneman (1974) described as "decision making under uncertainty." Decision makers are expected to integrate a variety of data, and these data may be limited in their ability to inform major planning tasks, which accounts for the "uncertainty" in their use. The idea that having data is necessary, but not sufficient to promote evidence-based planning and policy is well known (e.g., Hammond, 1996), but fundamental issues such as helping non-researchers frame more researchable questions and helping researchers understand how data must be used for planning rarely have been addressed (see "Recommended Reading" for a case study that attempted to address these problems).

Decision making under uncertainty often leads to reliance on personal biases or shortcuts that limit deliberations about the available data or distort their meaning (Kahneman, 2011; Tversky & Kahneman, 1974). Common biases include the tendency to dismiss data that do not confirm experience or prior beliefs. Common shortcuts in decision making include considering anecdotal information to be more representative than is true, or adopting the first acceptable decisional alternative rather than evaluating all possible options. Basic processes in human memory also may lead to bias; hence, data are more easily recalled if they are vivid, recently or repeatedly presented, or can be incorporated into an existing understanding of a problem.

Individual-level issues in decision making can be compounded by the additional challenges posed by decision making in advisory groups. Decisions may be swayed by individuals who are the most vocal or otherwise influential within a group (Plous, 1993). There may be competing agendas or worldviews, such as the differing perspectives of researchers and non-researchers (Weiss, 1980), although disagreement within a group can be constructive and may prevent social dynamics such as "groupthink" (Janis & Mann, 1977) that lead to opinions being ignored or dismissed. Nonetheless, creating and maintaining an atmosphere where varied opinions can be offered and considered is difficult in practice (Cherniss & Deegan, 2000; Kreuter, Lezin, & Young, 2000; Roussos & Fawcett, 2000). Apart from the planning decisions they must make, advisory groups need to develop their own internal organization, procedures, and policies, which is time consuming but essential for groups to fulfill their mandated mission (Cherniss & Deegan, 2000; Dearing, Larson, Randall, & Pope, 1998). Guidance for these processes often is inadequate and their importance often is underappreciated by funders or enabling agencies until problems are evident.

Identifying and Selecting EBIs for Implementation

The selection of EBIs may be an explicit outcome of the strategic plan process or it may be something that provider organizations do in response to a strategic plan that identifies classes of interventions or other requirements. EBI selection increasingly is driven by funder definitions of research evidence and compendia of EBIs that have been assembled through synthesis of available research, based on these definitions. Some compendia are driven by evidence of efficacy while others are driven by effectiveness outcomes. Most compendia are updated on a regular basis. Examples of these compendia include SAMHSA's NREPP and CDC's compendium of HIV prevention interventions (see "Recommended Websites"). Some, but not necessarily all, of the interventions in these compendia are likely to be supported through implementation packages. These typically provide materials for conducting the intervention, training onsite staff, and providing public information as well as information on core elements, applicable populations, and supporting research. These packages usually have been developed by the originators of the EBIs or with their collaboration and are available from the originators or from third-party vendors.

If funder-based compendia have not been developed or where their rigor has been questioned, there may be other compendia that have been compiled by professional organizations (e.g., Flay et al., 2005), foundation funders, or expert panels. There also are authoritative reviews that have been compiled by organizations like the Cochrane Collaboration (see "Recommended Websites"), which is devoted to compiling these kinds of compendia. The criteria used by Cochrane, in particular, increasingly drive the ways in which these compendia are compiled by others. Finally, there may be key academic literature reviews that guide a particular class of interventions.

Once authoritative compilations have been identified that are consistent with funding requirements, selection of EBIs can proceed. Selection should be consistent with planning data and EBIs should demonstrate applicability in terms of populations, resources, delivery methods, and provider settings. Provider organizations should engage frontline providers and their supervisors as the planning process goes forward so that they understand the factors driving this process and ensure that these staff can inform selection and actual implementation. Unfortunately, consultation with frontline staff often is handled poorly and tends to occur in a top-down manner. Because not all EBIs are packaged and not all EBI packages are supported by funders with training or technical assistance, the availability of these supports also is important in making final selections of EBIs. The absence of readily available technical assistance often leads to the engagement of practitioners to fill this gap, which will be discussed below under "Implementation of EBIs."

Practitioner Roles, Tasks, and Relevant Competencies

Planning is part of the routine work for practitioners who are employed by funders and enabling agencies or work in management capacities at provider organizations. Planning often is the point of entry into implementation work for academics or independent practitioners working as consultants, and graduate students often become involved with planning-related tasks such as data analysis or conducting needs assessments. The tasks that are asked of practitioners are wide in variety and often broad in scope. They may range from simple literature reviews or data analysis tasks to more complex efforts to integrate data or reorganize advisory groups. Secondary analysis of public or program data and small supplementary studies to fill data gaps are common, as is assistance in integrating planning data and report writing. Table 11.1 provides a summary and illustrates the range of tasks that can be taken on within a broad spectrum of roles.

Roles and relationships are simplest when a discrete project such as a review of literature on EBIs has been requested by a funder, enabling agency, or provider organization. This kind of task has clear technical requirements such as knowledge about a discrete range of EBIs, makes clear who is seeking the assistance, and sets an endpoint for the relationship. There are, of course, other obligations, including considering the best interests of the affected population, the integrity of the available research, and the ability of the individual practitioner to conduct the work. Roles become more complex when they involve relatively open-ended relationships such as providing technical assistance on an ongoing basis to an enabling agency for strategic plans and progress reports or work that involves multiple participants in the planning process such as advisory groups and enabling agencies or funders. Open-ended relationships may need periodic renegotiation, while those with multiple participants need clarity in terms of who is providing funding, who receives services, and how those people or groups interact. In complex situations, the practitioner needs to sort out obligations and relationships and be clear about these with all parties involved.

Planning tasks easily become complex and often require expertise in areas such as decision making where few practice benchmarks exist. The large descriptive literature on decision making under uncertainty has led to few individual-level interventions and most of those have not demonstrated efficacy. People working in the field have become more optimistic about the ability of people to overcome these challenges than in the past (Kahneman, 2011), but limited expertise is available and much of the academic work in this area relies on laboratory tasks and other approaches with limited generalizability. Hence, exposure to relevant but broad foundational areas in social and behavioral research such as attitude change and behavior change principles is valuable for filling these gaps. Knowledge of decision-making research is useful for recognizing the presence of uncertainty and its outcomes such as heuristics and biases and developing ways to challenge them (e.g., providing multiple perspectives, repetition of novel or critical points, breaking material down into smaller sequential steps to improve comprehension). Research related to the advisory group process has not focused on decision making and data use, per se, but does provide useful if somewhat general guidance regarding factors that make groups function better (e.g., Foster-Fishman, Berkowitz, Lounsbury, Jacobson, & Allen, 2001; Kreuter et al., 2000; Roussos & Fawcett, 2000).

Common requests to practitioners often involve collection of new data or providing technical assistance (e.g., analytic or interpretive assistance) to make the best use of what is available. This frequently occurs in the context of trying to integrate data into "strategic plans" or grant applications that need to be responsive to these plans. These tasks require technical knowledge about specific data (e.g., measurement, sampling, generalizability) as well as an understanding of how data are used to meet funders' planning requirements. Hence, knowledge of the broad planning process (noted earlier under "The Structure of Funding, Resources, and Systems for EBIs," including the competencies under subhead "Competencies for Understanding Funding, Resources, and Systems") is imperative. As noted there, it is important that practitioners attend to data users and their knowledge and experience in working with data, particularly in a planning context. The perspectives of researchers who supply data to the planning process also need attention because they often have limited insight as to how data may be used for planning purposes and may be concerned about the potential for misinterpretation of data by other parties during the planning process.

Exposure to the planning process and opportunities to observe and interact with key participants are essential for any tasks involving the planning process and these should occur before getting deeply involved with data tasks. The ability to observe and recognize patterns of behavior benefit from exposure to ethnographic methods as well as areas related to group process such as organizational development and group dynamics. At the individual level, it is important to recognize limitations in the human capacity for recalling and combining large amounts of data, as well as affective and attitudinal barriers to data use, and environmental influences such as time pressure and features of the planning environment (see Kahneman, 2011, for an overview).

The planning process itself has been the subject of research; however, the way in which this research has evolved often serves as a barrier to its use. Most of this research is descriptive and there are few systematic research studies, most of which use nonexperimental designs. Research most often has occurred early in a new planning process, when requirements are novel and advisory groups are first organized, which limits its value for considering how planning processes evolve over time. Studies also tend to be specific to a particular funding stream and its particular requirements, which means that previous research from other funding streams is ignored and funders and enabling agencies "reinvent the wheel" when a new planning program is initiated. Therefore practitioners should attend to the broad range of literature rather than just those studies related to the categorical funding stream where their assistance is requested.

There have been some efforts to organize and synthesize research on the planning process. In particular, several literature reviews have focused on issues that are valuable in helping groups function (Cherniss & Deegan, 2000; Foster-Fishman et al., 2001; Kreuter et al., 2000; Roussos & Fawcett, 2000); however, it may be difficult to find case material to make these concepts more concrete. Much of the case material exists in a gray literature of technical reports that may be available from funders or their consultants, but not widely distributed. This material has begun migrating to the web, although its lifetime often is limited. Despite the emphasis on the formation of planning processes and advisory groups there are some examples of how advisory groups have evolved and reinvented themselves (e.g., Dearing et al., 1998) and the "Recommended Reading" contains two related case studies that were published as a special issue of the journal *AIDS & Behavior.*

The transactional nature of planning tasks such as working with advisory groups and boards of directors provide good opportunities for integrating research and related training (e.g., literature reviews, needs assessments) with training in administrative and program-focused consultation (Caplan, 1970; O'Neill & Trickett, 1982). There also may be opportunities to be engaged in community mobilization. Practitioner roles in the planning process (see Table 11.1) can become complex because of the various entities that may be part of the planning process and the variety of often interrelated tasks that they may perform.

Overall, participation in planning for EBIs requires an understanding of funder requirements generally, as well as the elements that fulfill those requirements such as data elements, compendia of EBIs, and advisory groups. The integration of data for gap analysis, EBI selection, and strategic plan development requires both technical skill and an understanding of how decision making under circumstances of uncertainty can bias the planning process. Organizational development skills may be needed, as well as consultation skills and the ability to build working alliances with a variety of actors in complex organizational settings. Planning provides a good example of how a seemingly technical set of tasks, often arranged in a stepwise manner, requires a broad range of foundational skills in a variety of areas and an ability to use them in the context of complex transactional relationships.

IMPLEMENTATION OF EBIs

Many practitioners who begin with an interest in program implementation find themselves more involved with preliminary steps, like planning. This preliminary work can be valuable to actually putting programs in place inasmuch as effective planning should include selection of programs that are feasible to implement in particular settings and locales. Planning also should facilitate organizational support for EBIs by provider organizations, anticipate resource needs such as training and technical assistance, and provide the bases for monitoring systems, quality improvement, and EBI sustainability. Stakeholder concerns, particularly those from frontline service providers, expressed during planning may be good predictors of concerns that will surface during program implementation. This section will focus primarily on the simplest case of implementing a single EBI in a single setting, although considerations for larger scale implementation will be discussed. Implementation practice is heavily influenced by available funding resources and service delivery systems (see "The Structure of Funding, Resources, and Systems for EBIs").

The Evolution of Implementation Practice

The current state of implementation practice involves a sometimes bewildering array of concepts and frameworks. Each approach usually has its own terminology despite often substantial overlap with concepts and frameworks found in other approaches. The specific implementation approaches and terminology that are used in any one funding stream reflect past or present funding requirements as well as the customs of provider organizations and dominant service provider professions. Practitioners need to understand and respect this context and its perceived importance for continued funding of programs while drawing on a breadth of approaches that may help in creatively solving implementation problems.

Implementation practice evolved from the realization that research publications often had limited effects on the services that were put in place (IOM, 1994, 2000, 2009). The field began by focusing on frontline providers and their supervisors, and started with the manualization of EBIs and the relatively haphazard distribution of manuals (usually provided only on request). The limitations of this approach quickly became evident and formalized manual-based training programs combined with more systematic distribution of EBI manuals became common. Later, simple manuals were replaced with comprehensive packages that included manuals, materials for staff training and public education, as well as access to various forms of technical assistance.

Training and technical assistance methods have progressed from single-session training programs built around manuals to training programs that are integrated with ongoing technical assistance to provide coaching, feedback, and reinforcement. Training used to be largely the province of intervention developers, but now technical assistance often is available from funders, enabling agencies, and/or senior provider staff. Technical assistance modalities have evolved from single-session in-person approaches to those that include telephone and information technology–based methods. Unfortunately, this can mean that technical assistance is provided by a variety of sometimes contradictory sources, with often poor communication and coordination. There also has been greater recognition that EBIs may need to be adapted to settings, populations, and other local conditions, although preservation of core elements remains important, which creates its own problems (see "Core Elements").

The Evolution of Implementation Frameworks

The relatively low level of implementation of EBIs, in practice, and the variable quality of implementation led to research regarding "what works" and, from this, frameworks to guide and monitor implementation. This research often has driven the changes in implementation delivery that were described in the previous section. Another major impetus has been authoritative reviews such as those conducted by the Institute of Medicine (e.g., IOM, 1994, 2000, 2009). These reviews have tended to reach similar conclusions and this may account for some of the similarities across frameworks. Specific funding streams or particular types of settings also have influenced some frameworks. Glasgow's RE-AIM model (Belza, Toobert, & Glasgow, 2007) evolved out of efforts to measure dimensions of implementation in health-care settings, while adaptation and implementation were built into Hawkins and Catalano's (1992) "Communities That Care" system for local implementation of substance abuse prevention programs. The field has grown to the point that there are not only reviews of the literature (Damschroder et al., 2009; Powell et al., 2012) but also at least one "review of reviews" (Rabin & Brownson, 2012), which has attempted to identify common terminology and features of implementation models.

Funders may emphasize one implementation framework over another, particularly those that have their roots in a particular funder's programs; however, it is useful to be familiar with a variety of frameworks. The strengths and weaknesses of individual frameworks are likely to draw from their respective roots and some models may be stronger in some areas such as measurement or attention to research-practice collaboration than others. Some funders may use an approach that originally drew from multiple frameworks and knowledge of the original sources will provide more depth than simply following funder requirements.

Most implementation frameworks focus on identifying barriers and facilitators to implementation. These may focus on frontline service providers (training, responsiveness to specific interventions), organizational issues (leadership and support for EBIs, resources, experience with similar programs), cultural considerations (organizational culture, cultural backgrounds of providers and members of the target population), and/or individual-level preferences of target populations. Early work focused primarily on frontline service providers, while more recent models have included organizational and cultural factors, as well as structural/systemic considerations such as funding, policy, and technical assistance systems. Over time, frameworks have tended to grow more complex as more factors have been identified and more interactions among various actors in funding and service delivery systems have been recognized. An exception is Wandersman and colleagues' "Getting to Outcomes" (Wandersman, Imm, Chinman, & Kaftarian, 2000), which evolved out of work with technical assistance programs at SAMHSA and has attempted to simplify the approach to addressing questions regarding need, selection, adaptation, integration, monitoring, and quality improvement for a single EBI.

Actually Putting EBIs in Place

After interventions have been selected, provider organizations need to begin the process of determining how to integrate the EBIs into their settings. This may involve adaptation to their particular modalities for delivering service (office-based; outreach; family, group, or individual delivery), their clientele (socio-cultural or clinical considerations), or resource issues such as staffing, space, and programmable times of the day.

Core Elements

Research generally supports **fidelity** to core elements, the degree to which core elements of an intervention are preserved when an EBI is implemented in a novel setting, as critical to the preservation of program effectiveness (Dusenbury, Brannigan, Falco, & Hansen, 2003). Therefore, core elements have to be considered in any adaptation, although there are a number of factors that make this complicated. The degree to which core elements are adequately specified varies substantially by intervention. Some interventions are highly structured with clear conceptual bases while others may be designed in ways that allow wide latitude in terms of actual content. Less structured interventions can be problematic to adapt unless the underlying behavior change principles for the EBI are clear. The relative importance of different core elements usually has not been rigorously investigated and individual EBI developers often have identified core elements in unsystematic ways. This is particularly true of interventions that were developed before the various IOM reports and other reviews highlighted the importance of core elements. In these cases, core elements often have been identified post hoc, on a "rational" or experiential basis; it has not been unusual for intervention developers to change their minds about the core elements based on subsequent research or experience in the field.

Identification of core elements may require a certain amount of "detective work" and judgment on the part of provider organizations and practitioners who may be working with them. Taxonomies such as the National Institute on Drug Abuse (NIDA; 2003) approach may be helpful. NIDA's taxonomy breaks core elements into structure (audience, setting), content (information, skills), and delivery (setting, special features like booster sessions). Consideration of conceptual frameworks and behavior change theories also is important, because these usually are intrinsic to the intervention and may drive delivery approaches. EBIs targeting individuals, families, and small groups typically utilize social learning principles (e.g., Bandura, 2001) such as skill building, as well as attitude change approaches (e.g., theory of reasoned action/theory of planned behavior; Ajzen, 1991; Fishbein & Ajzen, 1975), and these may be complementary. Network-based interventions may include social influence approaches such as diffusion of attitudes, norms, and behaviors (Kelly et al., 1991; Rogers, 2003). One aid to decoding core elements is the increasingly common practice of incorporating mediation/moderation analyses (e.g., Fairchild & Mackinnon, 2009) into intervention trials that often test elements of conceptual frameworks. Some EBIs have been adapted to different settings or populations, although descriptions of how adaptations have been made often are limited in research papers and practitioners should contact investigators for more detail. Some interventions have been evaluated in different delivery formats (e.g., nurse vs. paraprofessional delivery of home visitation health programs; Olds et al., 2002), although this often occurs, in practice, without systematic evaluation.

When systematic evaluation of core elements is not available for a specific EBI, relevant research may be available for interventions that are similar in terms of conceptual basis, methods of delivery, activity types, or outcomes. Interventions in a wide variety of topical areas may target similar health behaviors such as management of emotion or utilize common approaches like skill development drawn from widely used theoretical roots such as social learning theory. EBIs also may have commonalities because of similarities in setting and delivery methods (e.g., paraprofessional delivery in the community vs. professionals in office settings). Consequently, knowledge of EBIs should extend beyond the narrow range of interventions supported by any one funder or funding stream, although practitioners should be knowledgeable about the most applicable EBIs, including any materials and technical assistance that are available for them.

Reinventing EBIs: Two Case Studies

The converse of understanding core elements is understanding how reinvention of EBIs occurs. Venigas, Kao, and Rosales (2009) have described the process of how HIV prevention interventions were reinvented under relatively optimal conditions. This occurred in a relatively well-resourced context where multiple EBIs were available, and supportive guidance was available along with packaged EBIs and technical assistance programs. The presence of resources to pilot-adapted interventions was critical in this example for maintaining core elements, but many implementation barriers remained. There was some resistance to adopting some of the EBIs based on providers' previous experiences and some early discontinuation occurred based on negative experiences. Reinvention often was guided by cultural and linguistic considerations, as well as integration with other services offered by provider organizations. In some cases, state and local funders added their own requirements, which included activities that were not original parts of the EBIs. Pilot testing of adapted interventions often indicated that the time needed to conduct interventions originally constructed as single-session interventions now required multiple sessions, which required the addition of strategies for retention. Some EBIs were implemented in ways that included changes that intervention developers had identified as inappropriate, but it was difficult to know how these might have affected outcomes, based on the intervention guidance and available monitoring and outcome systems.

Shea, Callis, Cassidy-Stewart, Cranston, and Tomoyasu (2006) examined implementation of some of the same EBIs as Venigas et al. (2009) from the perspective of state health departments in Maryland and Massachusetts. They also found instances of implementation that were not consistent with core elements of EBIs, which they linked to gaps in available training and support materials. Some EBIs were prohibitively expensive to implement with fidelity or were deemed by provider organizations to be inappropriate for populations of interest. Many of the EBIs were more expensive than the programs that they replaced, such as traditional outreach or education, and the EBIs required more engagement of target populations. The availability of new EBIs was hampered by resource constraints for providing technical assistance. Despite these barriers, the presence of detailed protocols and materials associated with the EBIs, as well as outcome monitoring systems that facilitated program improvement and accountability were seen as supporting adoption of the EBIs. Significantly, both states also had program leadership that was strongly committed to research-based prevention programs.

Practical Limitations of Implementation

These case studies illustrate some of the real-world implementation barriers that practitioners are likely to encounter when working with provider organizations, whether as consultants or employees. Even where there is institutional support and resources exist to facilitate evidence-based practice, gaps can occur. Interventions may be dismissed as inappropriate without efforts to address ways to adapt them to local circumstances. Cost, integration with local services, and the addition of new requirements over time may create systemic barriers to implementation with fidelity. Past experience with similar interventions and early failures are other barriers, while structural supports such as monitoring systems and provision of training and technical support may have limits. Adaptation is an issue and models for adaptation such as Wingood and DiClemente's (2008) ADAPT-ITT approach often are a better fit for research settings, although they may have heuristic value in practice settings.

Practitioner Roles, Tasks, and Relevant Competencies

Practitioners have many opportunities to participate in actually putting EBIs into practice and integrating them within various settings. These most often occur in the context of consultation with provider organizations or technical assistance components of funders or enabling agencies, but a wide variety of roles and contexts are possible (see Table 11.1). Practitioners also may work in program administration for funders or enabling agencies and develop policies, guidelines, and monitoring systems or conduct research related to implementation. Practitioners in academia also may be involved in evaluation of implementation processes and development of implementation packages for existing EBIs. Implementation practice can involve putting a single EBI in place in one program setting or the dissemination and implementation of one or more EBIs across a large region in different types of settings.

Implementation practice tasks and roles vary to some extent, depending on whether someone is employed by a funder or enabling agency, as opposed to being part of a provider organization or an independent practitioner (see Table 11.1). Nonetheless, practitioners in all these roles may be called upon to provide training and technical assistance for EBIs and may be involved in development of monitoring systems or the analysis of monitoring data. Regardless of role, there will be a need to understand the specifics of the EBI being implemented and any supporting materials (e.g., implementation packages, manuals, training and client information materials provided outside of packages) as well as related research. Familiarity should include an understanding of core elements, how these have been derived, and how they relate to relevant processes such as training, technical assistance, and monitoring, as well as to any previous efforts to implement these EBIs.

There may be a particular framework that guides implementation in the setting where practitioners work; however, they should have familiarity with other frameworks, a process that has been helped by the recent proliferation of reviews of the literature (e.g., Damschroder et al., 2009; Powell et al., 2012; Rabin & Brownson, 2012). Familiarity with other EBIs also is desirable, especially where there are significant similarities to the EBI of interest. This is particularly helpful where there is limited knowledge about the EBI of interest on the part of enabling agencies and/or provider organizations in terms of core elements as well as adaptation to different settings and populations. The presence of EBI compendia can be helpful for identifying these kinds of cognate interventions and is helpful if it becomes apparent that the EBI of choice is not working out and a suitable alternative needs to be identified. The broader knowledge and skill areas in implementation benefit from a general understanding of behavior change principles, with particular attention to those used in the EBI of interest. This is particularly important where information about core elements from intervention developers is limited. Knowledge about the systems within which implementation is embedded also is important, including funding requirements or local policies that may lead to reinvention of interventions in significant ways.

Skill sets in funding and enabling agencies typically draw heavily on their existing policies and the nature of their relationships with each other or with provider organizations. On the other hand, development of implementation packages and technical assistance benefit from the broad areas of knowledge and skill noted above, as well as familiarity with how services are provided in practice. The same is true of efforts to develop monitoring and outcome evaluation systems, although these may draw on data collection instruments already used by a funder or enabling agency for other evaluation purposes.

Where practitioners are working directly with provider organizations, they will find that they need to understand implementation at multiple levels of an organization even if they are engaged primarily to work at one level. For example, working with program managers to develop an organization's policies around implementation monitoring will require understanding the experience of providers who will carry out the EBI, as well as the perspective of the consumers who will receive services based on the EBI. Efforts to help frontline providers adapt an EBI are likely to be more productive with an understanding of how the organization is supporting the adoption and adaptation of the EBI, how much the frontline providers have been engaged in the adoption process, and whether there is policy support from leadership for using EBIs. Previous experience as a service provider can be desirable, particularly with prior exposure to different settings, although some former providers may become too bound by past experience as opposed to adequately understanding the experiences of others.

Despite recent research that suggests that organizational factors like leadership, supervisor support, and interactions within provider organizations are important for successful implementation of EBIs (Asgary-Egan & Lee, 2012; Damschroder et al., 2009; Torrey, Bond, McHugo, & Swain, 2012), practitioners' entry into implementation is often at the level of working with individual service providers. The bulk of technical assistance resources remain geared toward these individuals, and problems often are conceptualized in terms of individual providers (e.g., self-efficacy, experience with similar interventions, previous experience with the population). Frequently, problems conceptualized as at the individual provider level are more complex and involve providers as a collective group and/or relations between different levels of an organization, which are aspects of implementation that have had relatively little investigation. EBIs may have been chosen with little input from frontline providers and efforts to adapt EBIs may not have taken into account their knowledge of the population or past experience with similar interventions. Efforts to monitor fidelity or outcomes may be novel and viewed as employee performance measurement rather than as feedback and quality improvement tools. In some cases, monitoring tools actually may be part of an employee's evaluation and the limitations of this needs to be addressed with supervisory staff, especially where an EBI represents a departure from past activities.

There may be other issues whereby practitioners may find themselves dealing with implementation issues on an organizational basis, working with people across different levels of an organization to find solutions. There may be disagreements about the training needs of staff and the degree to which interventions need to be adapted to particular circumstances. A commitment to EBIs on the part of leadership in an organization may be difficult to disseminate to others in the organization. There also may be preexisting problems in an organization that reflect factors like hierarchy and bureaucracy in a large organization or the limitations of charismatic leadership in a small one. Practitioners need preparation in how to quickly assess organizational issues and how to intervene in ways that will foster organizational development and program implementation objectives rather than further discord. A focus on organizational issues may require renegotiation of a consultation relationship that initially had been based on limited objectives such as providing technical assistance for a single EBI to frontline service providers. The reception of a change like this may be complicated if the practitioner originally was engaged as a consultant by a funder or enabling agency on which a provider organization is dependent for much of its funding.

Implementation of EBIs in multiple settings compounds many of the issues that arise within a single setting. Multiple settings often translate into differing organizational climates, variations in resources, and greater diversity among client populations and providers. Adaptation and fidelity to core elements become more complicated with multiple sites, and the importance of well-designed monitoring systems becomes more important. Tailored technical assistance is particularly important in multisetting implementation and usually produces better fidelity than single-session training or distribution of manuals (Kelly et al., 2000). Unfortunately, resources may be limited for this purpose, particularly where there are few opportunities to become acquainted with staff personally and understand the organizational features of their workplaces as well as the particular needs of their populations. When resources vary across provider organizations and individual service delivery sites, practitioners may need to fill gaps in low-resource settings that a larger organization would have covered by itself, such as gaps in training, technical assistance, or case consultation. Technology-based technical assistance is increasingly common and has become more feasible through widely available technology such as Skype; however, technical problems remain common and the use of lower-tech approaches like telephone conferencing may be necessary.

In general, implementation requires a thorough understanding of funder requirements, relevant compendia of EBIs, and available supports such as packages, training, and technical assistance. Practitioners may be asked to extend the reach of supports to provider organizations with limited resources or to help larger organizations better stretch these resources across sites. Maintaining fidelity to core elements of EBIs may require judgment and investigation in order to establish what elements are truly core and how modifications to interventions can be made without losing fidelity. This may include investigation of EBIs that are different but share structural or conceptual similarities to those that have been chosen for implementation. It often is necessary to develop monitoring systems and these need to relate to core elements as well. Implementation also requires an understanding of the settings where EBIs will be put in place in terms of the organization, its mission, and its service delivery model as well as the needs of individuals at different levels of the organization. Skills in organizational development and consultation are essential for these functions, as well as technical knowledge and skills related to specific EBIs and broad knowledge of the principles underlying the EBIs of interest.

DEVELOPING NEW EBIs

General Considerations for Developing New EBIs

Community practitioners in training often are involved in the development of new EBIs through pilot work or specialized and/or supportive roles within clinical trials built around testing efficacy, effectiveness, or specific adaptations of EBIs. This work typically is funded by research agencies like the National Institutes of Health (NIH); agencies that principally fund services like CDC or HRSA also may fund research on new or adapted EBIs. Occasionally, funders may have specific requests for applications (RFAs) for intervention development; however, this more often is covered by standing funding announcements, especially from primary research funders like NIH. Development may be seen as an "upfront" step (preceding implementation), but in most fields, new interventions continue to be developed even after many EBIs have entered the field. Previously developed EBIs often are used as points of departure and many new EBIs begin as attempts to fill gaps left by existing interventions or to adapt EBIs for delivery with new technologies. Adaptation of existing EBIs to new populations or settings is increasingly common and provides an important gateway to implementation by providing principles for how to implement them in new contexts. All of these approaches require a broad understanding of existing research on EBIs and downstream considerations for implementation.

Current funder guidelines for EBIs should not preclude development of new interventions that go outside the scope of existing delivery methods or theories, although many researchers are cautious about going beyond what is currently funded for implementation. Technology has stimulated new approaches to intervention and there are many trials in the field using information technology approaches (SMS texting, web-based social networking, interactive video, and virtual reality) to a variety of health and social conditions (e.g., tobacco cessation, nutrition, reduction of HIV/STI sexual risk behavior). Still, it is unclear how these can be integrated into existing settings and funding streams, which makes it important to document resource needs for establishment and maintenance of new programs like these and to identify ways to conduct cost-effectiveness estimation. The Affordable Care Act (www.hhs.gov/healthcare/rights/law/index.html) is likely to stimulate new approaches to intervention both because it will provide new sources of service revenue and because it may reshape services and their relationship to the health-care system, particularly where services previously have not been linked to health care (e.g., substance abuse prevention).

Practitioner Roles, Tasks, and Relevant Competencies

The development of new EBIs should draw from foundational skills in behavior change theory, research design, methodology, and measurement. General considerations for the creation of settings, particularly any contextual factors that may confer protection or risk for a particular problem, also are necessary. Interventions intended to be implemented through a distinct funding stream should take into consideration funder guidelines for interventions that currently are supported, with particular attention to criteria for "evidence" (see "Recommended Websites" for examples). Practitioners should review the standards of evidence and the EBIs (from compendia or other sources) that meet these guidelines, with particular attention to gaps such as those based on population, setting, or modality in available EBIs. These guidelines will influence research designs and outcome variables. Experience with existing EBIs also may be helpful in terms of understanding limitations of existing EBIs, especially if that experience has occurred in the context of field implementation.

Consultation with persons responsible for program oversight at the local, state, or federal level may be helpful in gauging how funding requirements have been evolving over time and the implications this evolution may have for new EBIs. For example, requirements for HIV prevention grants from CDC have increasingly focused on programs that meet more and more specific evidence criteria, and state health departments often initiated these policies ahead of CDC. Peer reviews of research grant applications for new EBIs by federal research funders like NIH and major foundations often include reviewers who are experienced with EBI implementation. Reviewers like these are likely to consider funder guidelines as well as practical aspects of implementation (e.g., core elements, feasibility of manualization, common provider organization resources) when evaluating new research proposals. Hence, consultation with researchers who serve as peer reviewers and program staff at research funders is likely to be valuable.

Developers of new EBIs need to consider how to establish core elements of the intervention and use appropriate methods to demonstrate their centrality, such as mediation/moderation analyses (Fairchild & Mackinnon, 2009) or research designs that enable component analysis of such disaggregation studies, as well as comparisons of delivery or setting. New clinical trial designs that investigate ways to optimize interventions or test different combinations or sequelae of interventions (Collins, Murphy, & Strecher, 2007) also hold promise for helping inform how to implement interventions in resource constrained environments or populations with complex problems. The issues that provider organizations face in adapting EBIs should be considered, so that core elements are well specified and evidence based where possible. Clear conceptual models that link directly to process and outcome evaluation measures usually are expected by research funders and peer reviewers as part of the effort to test core elements. This is especially true where novel elements such as cultural adaptations or changes in mode of delivery, such as a change from face-to-face to online, are introduced. Engagement of target audiences at an early stage, stakeholder participation throughout the research process, and efforts to test interventions with populations and settings approximating an EBI's ultimate uses increasingly are expected both in developing new EBIs and in conducting adaptation research.

Research funders and many academic researchers have adhered to the stepwise pattern of research from identification of risk/protective factors through pilot and efficacy research to effectiveness trials (IOM, 1994). There now is more attention to early identification of implementation issues (Glasgow, Lichtenstein, & Marcus, 2003) and some areas such as HIV prevention have emphasized efficacy data as the primary basis for adoption rather than waiting for large-scale effectiveness trials. Other factors that are related to adoption such as cost-effectiveness are increasingly expected even in efficacy studies. All of this requires simultaneous attention to traditional concerns with theory testing and comparative intervention designs, as well as more attention to the ultimate uses and users of an intervention and concern with the types of research evidence expected by funders and enabling agencies.

SUMMARY AND CONCLUDING COMMENTS

Planning, Implementation, and Development of EBIs: Summary and Consideration of Community Psychologists and Other Disciplines

Hopefully, this chapter has provided an introduction to the roles, tasks, and competencies that are needed to bring EBIs into practice or develop new ones. It should be evident that there are a great many technical and regulatory considerations that need to be met, and that these exist among often overlapping systems that include funders, enabling agencies, and provider organizations. Many frameworks and concepts have evolved to capture the implementation process, but often they fail to capture the background of technical or funding requirements, the culture of different systems. They also tend to neglect the experiences of providers and consumers, as well as the ways in which the evolution of provider roles and professions have shaped service delivery. Practitioners need to be aware of these background and contextual factors while also attending to the immediate needs of the people and organizations who engage them. Funders, enabling agencies, practitioner organization staff, and advisory group members often are keenly aware of the technical, regulatory, or professional/cultural factors that shape their world, but may benefit from the bigger picture that a practitioner can bring. At the same time, practitioners need to be aware that the work occurs in a social, transactional context where the imperative of evidence-based practice is only one consideration and often is overridden by more immediate concerns even when it has been embraced.

This chapter has been written primarily for the professional development of community psychologist practitioners; however, the roles here frequently are filled by persons in other disciplines. These often are in applied subfields of disciplines that have considerable overlap with community psychology, such as applied anthropology, applied sociology, public health behavioral and social science, health education, applied communication, education evaluation, community nursing, and social welfare.

Community psychology emphasizes levels of analysis above and more complex than individuals and their immediate environment, but community psychologists may find opportunities to draw on skills that are foundational to psychology or more characteristic of other psychology subdisciplines such as behavior change theories, research in judgment and decision making, measurement, and basic concepts in research design. Practitioners in other disciplines also may find themselves drawing on foundational areas of their field, as well as applied areas that enable them to work in complex environments. For example, applied sociologists may draw on survey methodology and conceptualization of roles and statuses, while applied anthropologists may draw on areas like inductive inquiry, a focus on social organization, and the use of varied qualitative methods and analytic tools. Persons trained in public health may find both public health practice and foundational work in epidemiology to be useful, while the orientation to systems and the community in social welfare may be of particular value. Practitioners trained as clinicians (e.g., clinical/community psychologists, social workers, nurses, health educators) also may draw on their clinical experiences in terms of understanding provider perspectives, financing and reimbursement practices, the organization of service delivery settings, and the day-to-day details of performing interventions. Disciplines that give particular attention to program administration, such as social welfare, also may find that those skills add unique contributions.

Planning, implementation, and development of EBIs are likely to draw on a great many things that practitioners have learned, in coursework and in their professional or other life experiences, rather than reflecting simple sets of technical skills normally taught in any one discipline. Conversely, work in these areas requires that one be multidisciplinary in outlook, open to new areas of skill and inquiry, and not constrained by one's disciplinary identity and original training. A final consideration is that early direct experience in the planning, implementation, and development of EBIs is essential, along with opportunities to take that experience to build a bigger picture of the contexts where this work occurs.

Back to the Beginning

The opening exercise of this chapter offered the unhappy task of helping a regional health agency fulfill a mandate to implement EBIs for the prevention of drug and alcohol use in a resource-constrained environment. The first question to consider was whether EBIs were available, perhaps the easiest question to answer. There was a large literature on this (e.g., NIDA, 2003) and the state had provided guidance; there were a number of EBIs that could be selected, although only a few of them had technical assistance support from the state or federal government. Information about these programs also was available from SAMHSA's NREPP compendium as well as the NIDA review.

Building community support and acquiring resources to begin implementation are more challenging than identifying new programs. The current program was cheap, easy to implement, and popular with some stakeholders, but not with everyone who actually carried out the intervention. In searching for different approaches to community mobilization around EBIs for drug and alcohol prevention, the consultant learned about PROSPER, an integrated approach to evidence-based planning, selection, and implementation of drug and alcohol prevention programs (Spoth, Greenberg, Bierman, & Redmond, 2004;

Spoth et al., 2013; see also "Recommended Websites"). PROSPER had been tested in towns about the size of smaller communities in the region and makes use of cooperative extension staff from land grant state universities, who provided technical assistance to communities on a variety of issues (originating in agriculture but more recently entering arenas related to child development). PROSPER provided tools for conducting needs assessments, which also could be used to measure population-level outcomes, and the PROSPER trial had supported interventions that were on the state's list. In addition, PROSPER emphasized implementation with fidelity and focused on partnerships with schools, which also were seen as assets.

The PROSPER trial was done in other states and although PROSPER had collaborations with some state governments, there was not an active collaboration in the practitioner's state. Even so, when the practitioner contacted people at the state substance abuse agency, they were interested in trying this approach and had experience with a program that included some similar elements, Communities That Care (Hawkins & Catalano, 1992). The state also was interested in possibly developing a formal PROSPER collaboration.

The practitioner used the PROSPER model to organize local teams that included school boards and law enforcement agencies to work toward implementation of EBIs for substance use prevention in the community. Although some of these stakeholders were happy with their existing program, they recognized that it no longer would be funded in the future and that committing to something new would be in their interest, as well as that of their communities.

The local university had some relevant faculty who were engaged by the practitioner who also identified a local extension service agent with interest in child development. The university was not a land grant institution (which is the base for cooperative extension services), but there was no objection from the extension service to the local agent collaborating with this university. The practitioner began meeting with technical assistance staff from the state and local stakeholders to organize a program, find resources for data collection, and conduct a needs assessment. Because this was a new direction for the health agency and immediate funding was limited, they decide to concentrate on two counties in the catchment area rather than all of them. These counties differed somewhat in terms of demographics and resources and were viewed as good starting places. All parties are concerned about funding despite the cost information they have been able to obtain from other PROSPER sites. The schools in the pilot areas identified willing teachers to deliver interventions that might be selected from the PROSPER menu. The university partners volunteered to help with analysis of the needs assessment; staff training will come out of normal training funds, while technical assistance will be partially a function of a normal state grant.

The use of a structured package including assessment materials and a menu of interventions supported by funders increased the likelihood that the new intervention would get off to a good start and be implemented with fidelity. The use of the cooperative extension service and the engagement of stakeholders increased the likelihood that the EBI could be sustained once implemented. A next step for the practitioner might be to help with collection and analysis of the assessment data and help the stakeholders choose among the supported EBIs and make local adaptations that preserve fidelity to core elements. Later tasks for the practitioner may include working with technical assistance providers to ensure fidelity or assisting with quality assurance processes or outcome evaluation.

DISCUSSION QUESTIONS

1. Are evidence-based interventions readily available to communities?

2. Why are there so many models of implementation and why are they so complicated?

3. Why don't data-driven planning processes lead to more evidence-based services?

4. What is the best way to make sure evidence-based services are implemented and kept in place?

5. What skills are essential for effective implementation of evidence-based interventions?

KEY TERMS AND DEFINITIONS

Adaptation: Modifying an EBI so that it is responsive to particular needs of a target audience or settings, particularly where the population or setting is different from the one where the EBI was originally developed or previously implemented.

Categorical (as in categorical funding): Funding for a particular class of services, usually determined by the condition that the funding is meant to improve (e.g., child welfare) or ameliorate (e.g., HIV prevention). The "category" also may be a particular class of service delivery settings (e.g., community health centers) that deliver a specified range of services.

Cooperative agreement: Grant mechanism that includes substantial participation from a funder, which often includes direct, active involvement in oversight and technical assistance for program practice that goes beyond periodic progress monitoring.

Core elements: The "active ingredients" of an EBI, which may include the underlying mechanisms of behavior change, and features such as structure, content, and delivery and which should be preserved during adaptation and implementation to a new setting or population.

Cost-effectiveness: The estimation of how the costs (labor, materials, overhead costs) associated with an intervention relate to its measurable outcomes, and whether savings outweigh new costs attributable to the intervention. A novel intervention usually will be compared with the service that is typically available or with the case where no service is offered and its absence is associated with costs, (i.e., costs of incarceration or other forms of institutionalization; medical costs associated with acquiring a disease; costs associated with metrics such as disability-adjusted life years [DALYs] or lost quality-adjusted life years [QALYs]).

Data warehouse: A central repository of data that is created by integrating data from one or more disparate sources such as health department vital statistics or disease surveillance, census data, and program data from sources such as courts, social service agencies, or hospitals. Data warehouses typically store current as well as historical data and make them available for analysis. They may combine data based on geocodes such as zipcodes or census tracts.

Decision support system: Broadly, a resource to help decision makers such as administrators or advisory groups select among alternative ways to address a problem. Such systems help decision makers use their available data to select interventions using algorithms based on population, setting, or desired outcomes.

Dissemination (of EBIs): Active efforts to spread EBIs so that they reach their target audience. This may involve distributing manuals or "packages" that include manuals and supporting training materials, as well as training professionals who may potentially deliver EBIs in their settings.

Effectiveness: Evidence that an intervention has significant preventive or therapeutic effects when delivered under real-world conditions, as in delivery by providers in clinics, schools, or community organizations.

Enabling agency: An agency that is responsible for policies that govern the provision of resources for services and how people access services. Examples include mental health or substance abuse boards, regional authorities, or school boards. These agencies usually are organized in a manner established by state law and respond to state authorities and their funding requirements, although they may be empowered to raise funds locally through taxes. An enabling agency provides proximal oversight and technical assistance for implementing EBIs. Local enabling agencies have been emphasized here although state government often fulfills this function as well as being the primary funder to local provider organizations.

Fidelity: The degree to which **core elements** of an intervention are preserved when an EBI is implemented in a novel setting, particularly when the EBI has been adapted to a setting or population that differs from where it has been used in the past.

Gap analysis: A common planning process whereby unmet or underserved needs are identified through consideration of relevant data (e.g., epidemiological data and program data from existing services). This serves as the basis for planning and selecting EBIs to address the unmet or underserved needs.

Implementation: The use of strategies to adopt and integrate evidence-based health interventions and change practice patterns within specific settings. Use of the term here subsumes adaptation and dissemination under implementation, while some commentators would treat one or both of these as processes separate from implementation.

Monitoring: The process by which implementation of EBIs and their outcomes is measured so that these data can inform refinement of the implementation of those

EBIs and establish how and why the EBIs have an effect. A **monitoring system** is a standardized set of monitoring measures.

Provider organization: An organization that delivers services to the public. This can range in size from a small community organization that operates from a single site to a large local organization such as a school system, as well as organizations that deliver a variety of services such as hospitals or community mental health centers, or health-care networks.

Stakeholder: In general, a person, group, organization, member, or system that affects or can be affected by an organization's actions. Someone who provides services affected by implementation of EBIs or someone who administers an agency proving those services may be considered a stakeholder. Stakeholders also can include those who advocate for populations to be served by EBIs, as well as consumers. Elected officials whose jurisdiction includes agencies or entities that provide services also would be considered stakeholders.

Strategic plan: An integrated plan that is meant to guide implementation of EBIs in a particular categorical funding mechanism. This usually incorporates a variety of data as inputs to define gaps in local services (epidemiological data, program data) and serve as the basis for selecting EBIs to address these gaps. The plan usually includes steps for monitoring the implementation of EBIs and measuring their outcomes.

Surveillance (in public health): The process of continually observing the occurrence of a particular condition. This may be done through voluntary or mandatory reports of occurrences of that condition (e.g., HIV cases). Surveillance also may be conducted through periodic, population-based surveys of health conditions as well as the occurrence of risk or protective factors.

Technical assistance: Providing information, instruction, feedback, and/or training to assist providers in developing strategic plans or implementing interventions. Technical assistance is sometimes contrasted with training in that it may be more of a recurring, transactional relationship, with much briefer encounters than those that occur in training; however, training activities such as instructional workshops often are subsumed under technical assistance.

Theory of change: A component of the logic model or strategic plan that specifies the processes by which a condition can be ameliorated or changes can be affected in risk or protective factors related to that condition. The selection of EBIs should reflect the use of interventions that are consistent with the theory of change and address the factors and conditions specified in it.

Utilitarian (as in utilitarian reasoning): In a planning context, the notion that one can maximize potential benefits and minimize harms based on consideration of available data. This presumes that adequate and appropriate data are at hand and that data can be used to identify specific outcomes in a consistent manner, conditions that often cannot be met.

RESOURCES

Recommended Reading

Institute of Medicine reports that have influenced research on implementation of EBIs:

Institute of Medicine. (1994). *Reducing risks for mental disorders: Frontiers for preventive intervention research.* Washington, DC: Author.

Institute of Medicine. (2000). *No time to lose: Getting more from HIV prevention.* Washington, DC: Author.

Institute of Medicine. (2009). *Preventing mental, emotion, and behavioral disorders among young people: Progress and possibilities.* Washington, DC: Author.

A useful introduction to conducting multimethod rapid community assessments:

Beebe, J. (2001). *Rapid assessment process: An introduction.* Walnut Creek, CA: Alta Mira.

Useful overviews of decision-making research:

Kahneman, D. (2011). *Thinking, fast and slow.* New York, NY: Farrar, Straus and Giroux.

Plous, S. (1993). *The psychology of judgment and decision making.* New York, NY: McGraw-Hill.

Reviews of the literature on the use of advisory group approaches to intervention planning:

Roussos, S. T., & Fawcett, S. B. (2000). A review of collaborative partnerships as a strategy for improving community health. *Annual Review of Public Health, 21,* 369–402.

Kreuter, M. W., Lezin, N., & Young, L. (2000). Evaluating community-based collaborative mechanisms: Implications for practitioners. *Health Promotion Practice, 1,* 49–63.

Articles from a case study of working with community planning groups and provider organizations to increase use of data for planning purposes; These articles (except for Mejia et al.) appeared in a special issue of the journal *AIDS & Behavior:*

Amaro, H., Conron, K. J., Mitchell, E. M. H., Morrill, A. C., Blake, S. M., & Cranston, K. (2005). HIV prevention community planning: Challenges and opportunities for data-informed decision-making. *AIDS & Behavior, 9*(Suppl. 2), S9–S27.

Batchelor, K., Freeman, A. C., Robbins, A., Dudley, T., & Phillips, N. (2005). A formative assessment of the use of behavioral data in HIV prevention in Texas. *AIDS & Behavior, 9*(Suppl. 2), S29–S40.

Batchelor, K., Robbins, A., Freeman, A. C., Dudley, T., & Phillips, N. (2005). After the innovation: Outcomes from the Texas Behavioral Data Project. *AIDS & Behavior, 9*(Suppl. 2), S71–S86.

Batchelor, K., Freeman, A. C., Robbins, A., Dudley, T., & Phillips, N. (2005). A formative assessment of the use of behavioral data in HIV prevention in Texas. *AIDS & Behavior, 9*(Suppl. 2), S29–S40.

Jenkins, R. A., Cranston, K., Robbins, A., Amaro, H., Morrill, A. C., Batchelor, K., . . . Carey, J. W. (2005). Improving the use of data for HIV prevention decision making: Lessons learned. *AIDS & Behavior, 9*(Suppl. 2), S87–S99.

Jenkins, R. A., Robbins, A., Cranston, K., Batchelor, K., Freeman, A. C., Amaro, H., . . . Carey, J. W. (2005). Bridging data and decision making: Development of techniques for improving the HIV prevention community planning process. *AIDS & Behavior, 9*(Suppl. 2), S41–S43.

Mejia, R., Jenkins, R. A., Carey, J. W., Amaro, H., Morrill, A. C., Krech, L., . . . Cranston, K. (2009). Longitudinal observation of an HIV Prevention Community Planning Group (CPG). *Health Promotion Practice, 10,* 136–143.

Morrill, A. C., Amaro, H., Dai, J., Dunn, S., Blake, S. M., & Cranston, K. (2005). HIV prevention community planning: Enhancing data-informed decision making. *AIDS & Behavior, 9*(Suppl. 2), S55–S70.

Reviews of the literature on implementation including terminology and models:

Damschroder, L. J., Aron, D. C., Keith, R. E., Kirsh, S. R., Alexander, J. A., & Lowery, J. C. (2009). Fostering implementation of health services research findings into practice: A consolidated framework for advancing implementation science. *Implementation Science, 4,* 4–50.

Powell, B. J., McMillen, J. C., Proctor, E. K., Carpenter, C. R., Griffey, R. T., Bunger, A. C., . . . York, J. L. (2012). A compilation of strategies for implementing clinical innovations in health and mental health. *Medical Care Research and Review, 69,* 123–157.

Rabin, B. A., & Brownson, R. C. (2012). Developing the terminology for dissemination and implementation research. In R. C. Brownson, G. A. Colditz, & E. K. Proctor (Eds.), *Dissemination and implementation research in health* (pp. 23–51). New York, NY: Oxford University Press.

Widely cited articles related to standards for implementation:

Dusenbury, L., Brannigan, R., Falco, M., & Hansen, W. (2003). A review of research on the fidelity of implementation: Implications for drug abuse prevention in school settings. *Health Education Research: Theory & Practice, 18,* 237–256.

Flay, B. R., Biglan, A., Boruch, R. F., Castro, F. G., Gottfredson, D., Kellam, S., . . . Ji, P. (2005). Standards of evidence: Criteria for efficacy, effectiveness, and dissemination. *Prevention Science, 6,* 151–175.

A frequently cited model for cultural adaptation of EBIs:

Wingood, G. M., & DiClemente, R. J. (2008). The ADAPT-ITT model: A novel method of adapting evidence-based HIV interventions. *Journal of Acquired Immune Deficiency Syndromes, 47*(Suppl. 1), S40–46.

Recommended Websites

Population-based surveys and disease surveillance examples of commonly available epidemiological data related to health:

Youth Risk Behavior Surveillance System (Youth, Cross-sectional, Annual): http://www.cdc.gov/HealthyYouth/yrbs/index.htm

National Longitudinal Study of Adolescent Health (Youth Cross-sectional, Longitudinal, Annual): http://www.cpc.unc.edu/projects/addhealth

Monitoring the Future (Youth, Cross-sectional & Longitudinal, Annual): http://www.monitoringthefuture.org/

Behavioral Risk Factor Surveillance System (Adults, Cross-sectional, Annual): http://www.cdc.gov/brfss/

National Survey on Drug Abuse and Health: https://nsduhweb.rti.org/

National Survey of Family Growth: http://www.cdc.gov/nchs/nsfg.htm

CDC HIV/AIDS Case Reports (updated annually): http://www.cdc.gov/hiv/topics/surveillance/

CDC Surveillance of Injury and Causes of Death: http://www.cdc.gov/nchs/fastats/injury.htm

Examples of sample measures for population-based research and outcome studies:

CDC's Compendium of Measures Related to Violence: http://www.cdc.gov/ncipc/pub-res/measure.htm

Cochrane Collaboration Effective Practice and Organization of Care Group's Data Collection Checklist: http://epoc.cochrane.org/sites/epoc.cochrane.org/files/uploads/datacollectionchecklist.pdf

Communities That Care Youth Survey: http://www.sdrg.org/ctcresource/CTC_Youth_Survey_2006.pdf

Phen-X Toolkit: Health and substance use measures designed for population-based health research: https://www.phenxtoolkit.org/

U.S. Census Bureau American FactFinder search engine for local data (includes access to annual economic reports and the American Community Survey which supplements the regular decennial census): http://factfinder2.census.gov/faces/nav/jsf/pages/index.xhtml

Data Warehouses (Composite databases of population-based data, typically organized by geographic area, although not always geocoded)

National Neighborhood Indicators Partnership: http://www.neighborhoodindicators.org/

Examples of Data Reporting for Program Planning:

Community Monitoring Systems: Tracking and Improving the Wellbeing of America's Children and Adolescents: (Author: Society for Prevention Research) http://www.preventionresearch.org/CMSbook.pdf

Guidance for planning, including technical assistance materials:

Guidance for CDC HIV Prevention Community Planning: http://www.cdc.gov/hiv/topics/cba/resources/guidelines/hiv-cp/pdf/hiv-cp.pdf

Additional tools related to this guidance:

Integrated Guidelines for Developing Epidemiological Profiles: HIV Prevention and Ryan White Community Planning (CDC & HRSA): http://www.cdc.gov/hiv/topics/surveillance/resources/guidelines/epi-guideline/index.htm

Orientation guide: http://www.cdc.gov/hiv/topics/cba/resources/guidelines/Orientation_Final.pdf

Facilitating planning group meetings: http://www.cdc.gov/hiv/topics/cba/resources/guidelines/facilitating%20meetings%20version_2005.pdf

Compendia of EBIs

Agency for Health Care Quality National Guideline Clearinghouse (primarily concerned with biomedical screening and treatment): http://www.guideline.gov/resources/ahrq-evidence-reports.aspx

CDC Compendium of Evidence Based HIV Behavioral Interventions (Prevention & Treatment Adherence): http://www.cdc.gov/hiv/topics/research/prs/compendium-evidence-based-interventions.htm

The Campbell Collaboration. This is a social/behavioral science counterpart to the better known Cochrane Collaboration, which solicits reviews and provides resources for compiling and synthesizing information on effective interventions in education, social welfare, and more: http://www.campbellcollaboration.org/

The Cochrane Collaborative performs authoritative reviews of interventions, most but not all of which are biomedical. Cochrane's general approach to conducting reviews has been adopted by government agencies and professional organizations: http://www.cochrane.org/

National Institute on Drug Abuse. (2003). *Preventing drug abuse among children and adolescents: A research based guide for parents, educators and community leaders* (2nd ed.). Bethesda, MD: Author. Availble at http://www.drugabuse.gov/publications/preventing-drug-use-among-children-adolescents (abridged version of above document)

SAMHSA's NREPP: http://www.nrepp.samhsa.gov/Index.aspx

U.S. Preventive Services Task Force Recommendations (primarily screening prevention and early intervention for biomedical conditions, although future guidelines are likely to specifically include behavioral health): http://www.uspreventiveservicestaskforce.org/recommendations.htm

University of Kansas Community Toolbox Links to databases of best practices: http://ctb.ku.edu/en/promisingapproach/Databases_Best_Practices.aspx

Examples of TA programs:

American Psychological Association's Behavioral and Social Science Volunteer program to support HIV prevention (funded by CDC): http://www.apa.org/pi/aids/programs/bssv/index.aspx).

CDC's National Network of Prevention Training Centers for HIV/STI: http://nnptc.org/

SAMHSA's Collaborative for the Application of Prevention Technologies: http://captus.samhsa.gov/about-us

University of Kansas Community Toolbox (resources for planning, implementation, and development of EBIs; oriented to general tools rather than those specific to particular conditions or diseases): http://ctb.ku.edu/en/default.aspx

Video and PowerPoint Presentations from Introductory Course on Implementation (NIH Office on Behavioral and Social Science 2012 Training Institute on Dissemination and Implementation in Health: http://conferences.thehillgroup.com/OBSSRinstitutes/TIDIRH2012/agenda.html

Examples of Integrated Systems for Implementation:

Communities That Care (University of Washington Social Development Research Group; program for implementation of EBIs to prevent substance use and psychiatric disorder includes measures, manuals, program description, and other resources): http://www.sdrg.org/ctcresource/index.htm

National Public Health Partnership Performance Standards Program (a framework for quality improvement, not specifically related to implementation of EBIs; provides sample documents for planning and evaluation): http://www.cdc.gov/nphpsp/index.html

PROSPER (PROmoting School-community-university Partnerships to Enhance Resilience; a partnership that began with Iowa State University and Penn State University, based on earlier work on implementation of school-based substance abuse prevention interventions, with fidelity, using university-community collaborations that engage cooperative extension services as well as other state resources): http://www.prosper.ppsi.iastate.edu/default.asp?home http://www.prevention.psu.edu/projects/PROSPER.html

SUGGESTED ACTIVITIES

- Attend a public meeting of an advisory group for your state or metropolitan area, such as a substance abuse coalition (prevention), a Ryan White Council (HIV treatment and related services), or an HIV prevention community planning group. These can be identified with a simple web search.

- Attend a public meeting of an enabling agency such as a county mental health board, regional health authority, substance abuse agency, or city/county health department. These can be identified through simple web searches.

- Do a web search for a strategic plan or related documents that cover your state or local area and review the content. For example, the key words "strategic plan," "substance abuse," and your state will yield the state plan; the keywords "HIV prevention" and your state will provide the state's HIV prevention plan; larger cities like New York City and Los Angeles also will have plans.

- Volunteer to be a member of a local advisory group for an enabling agency. The possible opportunities for this will become evident after attending a public meeting.

REFERENCES

Ajzen, I. (1991). The theory of planned behavior. *Organizational Behavior and Human Decision Processes, 50,* 179–211.

Asgary-Eden, V., & Lee, C. M. (2012). Implementing an evidence-based parenting program in community agencies: What helps and what gets in the way? *Administration and Policy in Mental Health, 39,* 478–488.

Bandura, A. (2001). Social cognitive theory: An agentic perspective. *Annual Review of Psychology, 52,* 1–26.

Beebe, J. (2001). *Rapid assessment process: An introduction.* Walnut Creek, CA: Alta Mira Press.

Belza, B., Toobert, D. J., & Glasgow, R. E. (2007). *RE-AIM for program planning: overview and applica-tions.* Washington DC: National Council on Aging Center for Healthy Aging.

Caplan, G. (1970). *The theory and practice of mental health consultation.* New York, NY: Basic Books.

Centers for Disease Control and Prevention. (2011). *Prevention and Public Health Fund Coordinated Chronic Disease Prevention and Health Promotion Program Department of Health and Human Services Centers for Disease Control and Prevention. CDC-RFA-DP09-9010301PPHF11.* Retrieved from http://www.grants.gov/web/grants/view-opportunity.html?oppId = 98533

Centers for Disease Control and Prevention. (2012). Estimated HIV incidence in the United States, 2007–2010. *HIV Surveillance Supplemental Report, 2012, 17*(4).

Centers for Disease Control and Prevention & Health Resouces and Services Administration. (2004). *Integrated guidelines for developing epidemiologic profiles: HIV prevention and Ryan White CARE Act community planning.* Atlanta, GA: Authors.

Cherniss, C., & Deegan, G. (2000). The creation of alternative settings. In J. Rappaport & E. Seidman (Eds.), *Handbook of community psychology* (pp. 359–377). New York, NY: Kluwer Academic/ Plenum.

Chung, K., & Lounsbury, D. W. (2006). The role of power, process and relationships in participatory research for statewide HIV/AIDS programming. *Social Science and Medicine, 63,* 2129–2140.

Collins, L. M., Murphy, S. A., & Strecher, V. (2007). The Multiphasic Optimization Strategy Trial (MOST) and the Sequential Multiple Assignment Randomization Trial (SMART): New methods for more potent health interventions. *American Journal of Preventive Medicine, 32,* S112–118.

Damschroder, L. J., Aron, D. C., Keith, R. E., Kirsh, S. R., Alexander, J. A., & Lowery, J. C. (2009). Fostering implementation of health services research findings into practice: A consolidated framework for advancing implementation science. *Implementation Science, 4,* 4–50.

Dearing, J. W., Larson, R. S., Randall, L. M., & Pope, R. S. (1998). Local reinvention of the CDC HIV prevention community planning initiative. *Journal of Community Health, 23,* 113–126.

Dusenbury, L., Brannigan, R., Falco, M., & Hansen, W. (2003). A review of research on the fidelity of implementation: Implications for drug abuse prevention in school settings. *Health Education Research: Theory & Practice, 18,* 237–256.

Fairchild, A. J., & Mackinnon, D. P. (2009). A general model for testing mediation and moderation effects. *Prevention Science, 10,* 87–99.

Fishbein, M., & Ajzen, I. (1975). *Belief, attitude, intention, and behavior: An introduction to theory and research.* Reading, MA: Addison-Wesley.

Flay, B. R., Biglan, A., Boruch, R. F., Castro, F. G., Gottfredson, D., Kellam, S., . . . Ji, P. (2005). Standards of evidence: Criteria for efficacy, effectiveness, and dissemination. *Prevention Science, 6,* 151–175.

Foster-Fishman, P. G., Berkowitz, S. L., Lounsbury, D. W., Jacobson, S., & Allen, N. A. (2001). Building collaborative capacity in community coalitions: A review and integrative framework. *American Journal of Community Psychology, 29,* 241–261.

Gaffga, N. H., Samuel, M. C., Stenger, M. R., Stover, J. A., & Newman, L. M. (2009). The Oasis Project: Novel approaches to using STD surveillance data. *Public Health Reports, 124*(Suppl. 12), 1–4.

Gans, H. J. (1973). *More equality.* New York, NY: Parthenon.

Glasgow, R. E., Lichtenstein, E., & Marcus, A. C. (2003). Why don't we see more translation of health promotion research to practice? Rethinking the efficacy-to-effectiveness transition, *American Journal of Public Health, 93,* 1281–1287.

Hammond, K. R. (1996). *Human judgment and social policy.* New York, NY: Oxford University Press.

Hawkins, J. D., & Catalano, R. F. (1992). *Communities That Care: Action for drug abuse prevention.* San Francisco, CA: Jossey-Bass.

Institute of Medicine. (1994). *Reducing risks for mental disorders: Frontiers for preventive intervention research.* Washington, DC: Author.

Institute of Medicine. (2000). *No time to lose: Getting more from HIV prevention.* Washington, DC: Author.

Institute of Medicine. (2009). *Preventing mental, emotion, and behavioral disorders among young people: Progress and possibilities.* Washington, DC: Author.

Janis, I. J., & Mann, L. (1977). *Decision making: A psychological analysis of conflict, choice, and commitment.* New York, NY: Free Press.

Jenkins, R. A., Cranston, K., Robbins, A., Amaro, H., Morrill, A. C., Batchelor, K., . . . Carey, J. W. (2005). Improving the use of data for HIV prevention decision making: Lessons learned. *AIDS & Behavior, 9*(Suppl. 2), S87–S99.

Kahneman, D. (2011). *Thinking, fast and slow.* New York, NY: Farrar, Straus and Giroux.

Kelly, J. A., Somlai, A. M., DiFrancisco, W. J., Otto-Salaj, L. L., McAuliffe, T. L., Hackl, K. L., . . . Rompa, D. (2000). Bridging the gap between the science and service of HIV prevention: Transferring effective research-based HIV prevention interventions to community AIDS service providers. *American Journal of Public Health, 90,* 1082–1088.

Kelly, J. A., St. Lawrence, J. S., Diaz, Y. E., Hauth, A. C., Brasfield, T. L., Kalichman, S. C., . . . Andrew, M. E. (1991). HIV risk behavior reduction following intervention with key opinion leaders of population: an experimental analysis. *American Journal of Public Health. 81,* 168–171.

Kreuter, M. W., Lezin, N., & Young, L. (2000). Evaluating community-based collaborative mechanisms: Implications for practitioners. *Health Promotion Practice, 1,* 49–63.

Milligan, S., Coulton, C., York, P., & Register, R. (1999). Implementing a theory of change evaluation in the Cleveland Community-Building Initiative: A case study. In K. Fulbright-Anderson, A. C. Kubisch, & J. P. Connell (Eds.), *New approaches to evaluating community initiatives: Vol. 2. Theory, measurement, and analysis* (pp. 45–85). Washington, DC: Aspen Institute.

Morrill, A. C., Amaro, H., Dai, J., Dunn, S., Blake, S. M., & Cranston, K. (2005). HIV prevention community planning: Enhancing data-informed decision making. *AIDS and Behavior, 9*(Suppl. 2), S55–S70.

Moynihan, D. P. (1969). *Maximum feasible misunderstanding.* New York, NY: Free Press.

Mrazek, P., Biglan, A., & Hawkins, J. D. (2003). *Community-monitoring systems: Tracking and improving the well-being of America's children and adolescents.* Fairfax, VA: Society for Prevention Research. Retrieved from http://www.preventionresearch.org/CMSbook.pdf

National Institute on Drug Abuse. (2003). *Preventing drug abuse among children and adolescents: A research based guide for parents, educators and community leaders* (2nd ed.). Bethesda, MD: Author.

Olds, D. L., Robinson, J., O'Brien, R., Luckey, D. W., Pettit, L. M., Henderson, C. R., . . . Talmi, A. (2002). Home visiting by paraprofessionals and by nurses: A randomized, controlled trial. *Pediatrics, 110,* 486–496.

O'Neill, P. I., & Trickett, E. J. (1982). *Community consultation.* San Francisco, CA: Jossey-Bass.

Plous, S. (1993). *The psychology of judgment and decision making.* New York, NY: McGraw-Hill.

Powell, B. J., McMillen, J. C., Proctor, E. K., Carpenter, C. R., Griffey, R. T., Bunger, A. C. . . . York, J. L. (2012). A compilation of strategies for implementing clinical innovations in health and mental health. *Medical Care Research and Review, 69,* 123–157.

Rabin, B. A., & Brownson, R. C. (2012). Developing the terminology for dissemination and implementation research. In R. C. Brownson, G. A. Colditz, & E. K. Proctor (Eds.), *Dissemination and implementation research in health* (pp. 23–51). New York, NY: Oxford University Press.

Rogers, E. M. (2003). *Diffusion of innovations* (5th ed.). New York, NY: Free Press.

Roussos, S. T., & Fawcett, S. B. (2000). A review of collaborative partnerships as a strategy for improving community health. *Annual Review of Public Health, 21,* 369–402.

Rugg, D. L., Heitgerd, J. L., Cotton, D. A., Broyles, S., Freeman, A., Lopez-Gomez, A. M., . . . Page-Shafer, K. (2000). CDC HIV prevention indicators: Monitoring and evaluating HIV prevention in the USA. *AIDS, 14,* 2003–2013.

Shea, M. A., Callis, B. P., Cassidy-Stewart, H., Cranston, K., & Tomoyasu, N. (2006). Diffusion of effective HIV prevention interventions—Lessons from Maryland and Massachusetts. *AIDS Education and Prevention, 18*(Suppl.), 96–107.

Sorensen J. L. (2011). From Cat's Cradle to Beat the Reaper: Getting evidence-based treatments into practice in spite of ourselves. *Addictive Behavior, 36,* 597–600.

Spoth, R., Greenberg, M., Bierman, K., & Redmond, C. (2004). PROSPER community-university partnership model for public education systems: Capacity-building for evidence-based, competence-building prevention. *Prevention Science, 5,* 31–39.

Spoth, R., Redmond, C., Shin, C., Greenberg, M., Feinberg, M., & Schainker, L. (2013). PROSPER community-university partnership delivery system effects on substance misuse through 6 1/2 years past baseline from a cluster randomized controlled intervention trial. *Preventive Medicine, 56,* 190–196.

Steinmann, D. O., Smith, T. H., Jurdem, L. G., & Hammond, K. R. (1977). Application of social judgment theory in policy formulation: An example. *Journal of Applied Behavioral Science, 13,* 69–88.

Torrey, W. C., Bond, G. R., McHugo, G. J., & Swain, K. (2012). Evidence-based practice implementation in community mental health settings: The relative importance of key domains of implementation activity. *Administration and Policy in Mental Health, 39,* 353–364.

Tversky, A., & Kahneman, D. (1974). Judgment under uncertainty: Heuristics and biases. *Science, 185,* 1124–1131.

Venigas, R. C., Kao, U. H., & Rosales, R. (2009). Adapting HIV prevention evidence-based interventions in practice settings: An interview study. *Implementation Science, 4,* 76.

Wandersman, A., Imm, P., Chinman, M., & Kaftarian, S. (2000). Getting to outcomes: A results-based approach to accountability. *Evaluation and Program Planning, 23,* 389-395.

Weiss, C. H. (1980). *Social science research and decision-making.* New York, NY: Columbia University Press.

Weiss, C. H. (1998). Have we learned anything new about the use of evaluation? *American Journal of Evaluation, 19,* 21–33.

Wingood, G. M., & DiClemente, R. J. (2008). The ADAPT-ITT model: A novel method of adapting evidence-based HIV interventions. *Journal of Acquired Immune Deficiency Syndromes, 47*(Suppl. 1), S40–S46.

Empowerment Evaluation and Community Psychology

*An Alignment of Values and Principles
Designed to Improve the Human Condition*

David M. Fetterman

OPENING EXERCISE

A state department of health–funded tobacco prevention initiative focused on preventing minorities from using tobacco. The initiative included strategies ranging from smoke cessation programs to a host of tobacco prevention activities, such as establishing smoke free parks, educating youth, and influencing legislation. The grantees consisted of 20 different community-based organizations, including churches, hospitals, and nonprofit social service organizations. Previous to this effort, these organizations competed with each other for funding. They also had no incentive to collaborate or communicate with each other.

Initially, program performance was uneven across the state. A few organizations were productive; however, most of the agencies were not able to accomplish their objectives. In addition, there was no systematic record of their progress or accomplishments. This made them vulnerable when compared with other legislatively funded efforts.

The agency responsible for coordinating these individual organizations invited proposals to evaluate the initiative. An evaluator was selected to conduct the evaluations because the agency learned that he uses an empowerment evaluation approach. What is an empowerment evaluation? How does it align with the needs of community initiatives? How do you conduct one? What are the competencies required of an empowerment evaluator? What were the challenges for the evaluation? How important were facilitation skills in this evaluation? How could the department of health get a picture of the entire initiative, to monitor its progress? What kinds of outcomes were realistic given this decentralized configuration of talent and resources?

OVERVIEW

Empowerment evaluation is practiced throughout the United States and the world, ranging from Baltimore to San Diego and Australia to Japan. It has been applied to a wide variety of settings, including Stanford University's School of Medicine (Fetterman, Dietz, & Gesundheit, 2010), Arkansas's tobacco prevention programs (Fetterman, Delaney, Triana-Tremain, & Evans-Lee, 2014), Native American reservations (Fetterman, 2013), Hewlett-Packard's $15 million Digital Village Initiative (Fetterman, 2013, 2014), NASA/Jet Propulsion Laboratory's prototype Mars Rover (Fetterman & Bowman, 2002), and townships and squatter settlements in South Africa.

The chapter begins with the definition of empowerment evaluation and a list of empowerment evaluation's ten guiding principles. A few empowerment evaluation principles have been selected to highlight the underlying similarities between empowerment evaluation and community psychology, including: inclusion, capacity building, evaluation, and empowerment. The convergence of these empowerment evaluation principles and community psychology values is synergistic. A brief discussion about the similarities between the empowerment evaluator and the community psychologist provide additional insight into some of the competencies required of these complementary roles. The chapter provides additional depth into empowerment evaluation competencies by summarizing knowledge, skills, and abilities required to conduct an empowerment evaluation. The chapter concludes with case examples, demonstrating the utility of the approach and significance of selected competencies.

EMPOWERMENT EVALUATION: DEFINITION

Evaluation is typically defined as making a judgment about the amount, number, value, or worth of something. **Empowerment evaluation** is defined as the use of evaluation concepts, techniques, and findings to foster improvement and self-determination (Fetterman, 2001, p. 3). Building on this definition, with an emphasis on outcomes, empowerment evaluation is further defined as:

> An evaluation approach that aims to increase the probability of achieving program success by (1) providing program stakeholders with tools for assessing the planning, implementation, and self-evaluation of their program, and (2) mainstreaming evaluation as part of the planning and management of the program/organization. (Wandersman et al., 2005, p. 28)

EMPOWERMENT EVALUATION: GUIDING PRINCIPLES

A movement, as it has been called, this large in scope and depth requires some guidelines to: (1) provide additional conceptual and methodological clarity and (2) guide practitioners in the field. Empowerment evaluation is guided by ten principles (Fetterman & Wandersman, 2005), specifically:

1. Improvement: Help people improve program performance and achieve desired results in the lives of those affected by the community programs

2. Community ownership: Community stakeholders control and own the evaluation, with the assistance of an empowerment evaluator

3. Inclusion: Stakeholders and staff from a variety of levels are included in program planning and decision making

4. Democratic participation: Community members participate in the initiative and assessment in an open and democratic fashion, which is based on a faith in the capacity of human beings to exercise intelligent judgment and action if proper conditions are furnished

5. Social justice: Community members, program staff, and the evaluator make a commitment to addressing social inequities, sharing a commitment to a fair, equitable allocation of resources, opportunities, obligations, and bargaining power

6. Community knowledge: Community members' expertise is valued and used to inform planning, program decision making, and program evaluation

7. Evidence-based strategies: Evidence-based strategies, or conventional research and scholarship, are used to inform program practice (and assessment)

8. Capacity building: Community members and staff members learn and apply new program and evaluation skills (in order to enhance their communities)

9. Organizational learning: Using data to inform organizational decision making and improve organizational practice while developing a reflective organizational culture

10. Accountability: Sharing responsibility for results and outcomes

These principles represent a deep respect for people and their right to self-determination. Empowerment evaluators respect community knowledge. It is the foundation on which much conceptual understanding is constructed. Empowerment evaluators also, in contrast with some community-based evaluators, value evidence-based strategies. Empowerment evaluators believe there is no sense in throwing the baby out with the bath water, just because some research has done more damage than good. In addition, there is also no sense in reinventing the wheel. Empowerment evaluators are pragmatic. If useful knowledge, skills, or abilities exist, they should be mined and used—whether community or research-based.

Empowerment evaluations are not neutral experiments. Although, they are characterized by honesty, clarity, and transparency, they have a bias toward improving the human condition and helping people help themselves. Empowerment evaluators believe that people should be in charge of their own evaluations. It is one of the most authentic and effective ways people develop their own capacity. People learn by doing. Empowerment evaluators do not abdicate their responsibility. They help guide community-based evaluation, serving as "critical friends." They help keep things on track and rigorous.

On an organizational level, empowerment evaluation contributes to organizational learning (organizational self-reflection, systematic inquiry, and action; Fetterman, 2005, pp. 49–50). Community and staff members find it is an engaging and often enlightening process. Community and staff members, in conjunction with the empowerment evaluator, contribute to organizational learning to produce outcomes. The questions at the end of the day remain the same for community members, staff members, donors, policymakers, and evaluators: Did you do it? Did you do what you said you were going to do? Did you have the intended impact on the community? These are some of the core principles guiding empowerment evaluators.

The relationship between empowerment evaluation principles and community psychology become more evident after placing empowerment evaluation within the context of other stakeholder involvement approaches to evaluation.

STAKEHOLDER INVOLVEMENT APPROACHES TO EVALUATION AND COMMUNITY PSYCHOLOGY: COMPATIBILITY WITH EMPOWERMENT EVALUATION

Collaborative, participatory, and empowerment evaluation approaches are stakeholder involvement approaches to evaluation. They are all compatible with community psychology. However, the evaluator plays a significantly different role in each of these approaches, which has implications for use by community psychologists. For example, the evaluator is in charge of the evaluation in collaborative evaluation. Participatory evaluators share control of the evaluation. In empowerment evaluation, the community and staff members are in control of the evaluation and the empowerment evaluator is a critical friend, much like community psychologists who facilitate the process without being in charge of it. (The role of the critical friend is discussed in greater detail later in the chapter.) In addition, empowerment evaluation is designed to build capacity and is the only approach that is explicitly designed to foster self-determination. The role of the empowerment evaluator (placing control in the community's or participants' hands) and the value position of the approach (to foster self-determination) make empowerment evaluation the most aligned approach for community psychologists.

EMPOWERMENT EVALUATION AND COMMUNITY PSYCHOLOGY: VALUES IN ALIGNMENT

Empowerment evaluation has roots in community psychology and action anthropology, which accounts in part for many of the similarities between them (Fetterman, 1996, p. 7). Empowerment evaluation is designed to help people help themselves. It values the emic or insider's perspective of reality. It respects community knowledge. Empowerment evaluation places the tools of evaluation in the hands of community members in order to help them monitor and evaluate their own performance. This evaluative eye is used to help people pursue their dreams, accomplish their objectives, and produce real-world outcomes or results.

Community psychologists, similar to empowerment evaluators, have a deep respect for the autonomy, independence, and growth of the individual (and community). Similar to empowerment evaluators, community psychologists value inclusion, participation, collaboration, capacity building, evaluation, and empowerment. Moreover, there is a common understanding that no one can empower another. People must empower themselves. In this regard, however, both empowerment evaluators and community psychologists strive to create an environment that is conducive to people empowering themselves (see the *Handbook of Community Psychology,* Rappaport & Seidman, 2000).

Empowerment evaluators' principles are in alignment with community psychology values and principles as represented by the proposed competencies for community psychologists (Dalton & Wolfe, 2012). A few empowerment evaluation principles have been selected to highlight the underlying similarities between empowerment evaluation and community psychology, including: inclusion, capacity building, evaluation, and empowerment. Together they are designed to help improve the human condition.

Inclusion

Inclusion and participation are guiding principles in empowerment evaluation and community psychology. Strength and power are derived from the collective participation of a large and diverse pool of talents spread across the community (Wandersman & Florin, 2000). There is always strength in numbers. In addition, inclusion and participation cultivate a sense of ownership and responsibility for the outcome of a community initiative. Inclusion and participation are also the basis of or foundation for capacity building.

Capacity Building

Capacity building is a hand up, not a hand out. Empowerment evaluation and community psychology are committed to helping people help themselves. Once community members acquire new skills and competencies, often learning by doing, they are in a better position to chart their own way in the future. They become independent rather than dependent human beings.

Evaluation

When we honestly reflect on how we arrived at the place we are now in work and family life, we are compelled to attribute no small part of it to evaluation. Wherever we were when we started the journey (our baseline), we had to have a dream we aspired to (a goal). We also had to determine what was reasonable progress toward that goal (benchmarks). We conscientiously compared our accomplishments (actual performance) with those benchmarks to determine if we were on track and likely to make our dreams come true. Mistakes required midcourse corrections, sometimes changes in the goals themselves. This is monitoring and evaluation. The same data driven decision making, self-monitoring, and evaluation are advocated for community use by both empowerment evaluator and community psychologist alike.

Empowerment

The empowerment evaluator and community psychologist partner with community leaders, mentors, and most importantly help community members learn how to do things by encouraging them to do things for themselves. Empowerment evaluators help build capacity by advocating for the use of self-evaluation to monitor and evaluate performance. This kind of experiential, life-long learning approach often pushes people to engage in activities outside their comfort zone. This is where real learning takes place, as well as empowerment and sustainability.

EMPOWERMENT EVALUATOR: ROLE

Empowerment evaluators and community psychologists do not empower anyone. However, they do create a climate that is conducive to people empowering themselves. The role they play to help facilitate this process is strikingly similar. In empowerment evaluation, **critical friends**, as discussed earlier (Fetterman, 2009) are friends of the program or type of program. However, they are highly critical of program performance because they want the program to perform and produce the desired results. Empowerment evaluators are involved, committed, and interested in program outcomes and help to establish a reliable feedback system to guide community decision making.

Zimmerman (2000) describes the role of the community psychologist in empowering activities. He highlights, in the process, the similarity between the community psychologist and the empowerment evaluator roles:

> An empowerment approach to intervention design, implementation, and evaluation redefines the professional's role relationship with the target population. The professional's role becomes one of collaborator and facilitator rather than expert and counselor. As collaborators, professionals learn about the participants through their culture, their world view, and their life struggles. The professional works *with* participants instead of advocating *for* them. The professional's skills, interest, or plans are not imposed on the community; rather, professionals become a resource for a community. This role relationship suggests that what professionals do will depend on the particular place and people with whom they are working, rather than on the technologies that are predetermined to be applied in all situations. While interpersonal assessment and evaluation skills will be necessary, how, where, and with whom they are applied can not be automatically assumed as in the role of a psychotherapist with clients in a clinic. (pp. 44–45)

Photo 12.1 Dr. Fetterman serving as a critical friend in an empowerment evaluation with a community member as part of a comprehensive community-wide initiative.

Source: David M. Fetterman.

The empowerment evaluator and community psychologist both set the tone for inclusion, capacity building, evaluation, and empowerment by modeling and informally articulating the philosophy behind the approach. Specifically, they help to establish a positive learning climate in which the views of all stakeholders are respected, input from all parties is solicited, and the conversation is guided so as to encourage comments that are constructive and improvement oriented. Both use a communication style that is inviting, unassuming, nonjudgmental, and supportive, so that stakeholders will feel comfortable in speaking openly about issues and concerns. Empowerment evaluators and community psychologists are able to remind members of the group about what they have in common, including long-range goals, dreams, and aspirations (see Cox, Keener, Woodard, & Wandersman, 2009, for guidance on hiring an empowerment evaluator).

EMPOWERMENT EVALUATION: KNOWLEDGE, SKILLS, AND ABILITIES

The basic competencies of the empowerment evaluator are categorized below in terms of knowledge, skills and abilities.

Knowledge

- Fundamentals of evaluation
- Empowerment evaluation theories, principles, concepts, and steps

A basic knowledge about evaluation is required to conduct an empowerment evaluation. This includes learning how to co-create a theory of change and action (James, 2011) and develop a logic model or at least a programmatic chain of reasoning. In other words, the evaluator should learn how to determine or help a community determine for themselves, if they begin at X (baseline) and do Y (an intervention), it is logical and likely to produce Z (an outcome). It is also important to learn how to conduct interviews, develop surveys, analyze data, and report on findings.

In addition to this general background in evaluation, a specific knowledge about stakeholder involvement approaches to evaluation is required, such as collaborative, participatory, and empowerment evaluation. Learning about the theory, principles, concepts, and steps associated with empowerment evaluations will maximize the synergistic combination of empowerment evaluation and community psychology.

This type of knowledge can be acquired by reading empowerment evaluation textbooks, chapters, articles, and websites. In addition, knowledge and skills can be acquired experientially by attending a formal educational program, participating in workshops, and participating in an evaluation (under the supervision of an experienced evaluator). For example:

Empowerment Evaluation Books

Empowerment Evaluation: Knowledge and Tools for Self-assessment, Evaluation Capacity Building, and Accountability (Fetterman, Kaftarian, & Wandersman, 2014)

Empowerment Evaluation in the Digital Villages: Hewlett-Packard's $15 Million Race Toward Social Justice (Fetterman, 2013)

Evaluation for Improvement: A Seven-Step Empowerment Evaluation Approach for Violence (Cox, Keener, Woodard, & Wandersman, 2009)

Empowerment Evaluation Principles in Practice (Fetterman & Wandersman, 2005).

Foundations of Empowerment Evaluation (Fetterman, 2001)

Empowerment Evaluation: Knowledge and Tools for Self-Assessment and Accountability (Fetterman, Kaftarian, & Wandersman, 1996)

Empowerment Evaluation Articles

Fetterman, D. M. (2009). Empowerment evaluation at the Stanford University School of Medicine: Using a critical friend to improve the clerkship experience. Rio de Janeiro: *ENSAIO: Avaliação e Políticas Públicas em Educação, 17*(63), 197–204.

Fetterman, D. M., Dietz, J., & Gesundheit, N. (2010). Empowerment evaluation: A collaborative approach to evaluating and transforming a medical school curriculum. *Academic Medicine, 85*(5), 813–820.

Fetterman, D. M., Rodriguez-Campos, L., Wandersman, A., & O'Sullivan, R. (2014). Collaborative, participatory and empowerment evaluation: Building a strong conceptual foundation for stakeholder involvement approaches to evaluation [Letter to the editor]. *American Journal of Evaluation, 35*(1), 144–148.

Fetterman, D. M., & Wandersman, A. (2007, June). Empowerment evaluation: Yesterday, today, and tomorrow. *American Journal of Evaluation, 28*(2), 179–198.

Web-Based Sources

Empowerment Evaluation Blog: http://eevaluation.blogspot.com
Collaborative, Participatory, and Empowerment Evaluation webpage: http://www.davidfetterman.com/
    empowermentevaluation.htm
Facebook: Collaborative, Participatory, and Empowerment Evaluation page
Wikipedia: Empowerment Evaluation

Skills

- Interpersonal and communication skills
  - o Being respectful of individuals' feelings and sensitivities when speaking with them; being sensitive to cultural differences and nuances
- Group facilitation
  - o Ensuring everyone has the opportunity to speak and contribute
  - o Moderating conflict and encouraging constructive dialogue
- Advising groups concerning data collection, analysis, and reporting
  - o Keeping the group in charge but guiding it in terms of the systematic and rigorous nature of data collection, analysis, and reporting, as well as the ethics associated with each stage of the work
- Creating safe, self-critical, and constructive environments
  - o Modeling constructive criticism; being honest but diplomatic in exchanges and dialogue
- Cultivating organizational learning
  - o Helping members of the group generate useful data and use the data to inform organizational decision making

Skills and knowledge go hand-in-hand. Skills required of an empowerment evaluator include: interpersonal, communication, group facilitation, and research and evaluation skills. Empowerment evaluators also serve as "coaches" and "critical friends." Critical friends need to be able to create psychologically safe environments in order to foster open dialogue and self-critique. Critical friends also need to know how to help people use data to inform decision making and cultivate organizational learning. Many of these skills can be acquired by participating in formal educational programs, workshops, and empowerment evaluations. In addition, a mentor or peer can provide invaluable guidance and feedback concerning skill acquisition, development, and refinement. For example:

Graduate Courses

Graduate courses in evaluation focusing on collaborative, participatory, and empowerment evaluation can be found at: Claremont Graduate University, Stanford University, San Jose State University, Charleston University, University of Arkansas, University of South Carolina, University of South Florida, and University of North Carolina.

Workshops

Empowerment evaluation workshops are available annually at the American Evaluation Association (AEA). They are also available online in webinar format on the AEA website. Recordings of UNICEF's empowerment evaluation webinars are also available online. They are at: http://www.mymande.org/content/empowerment-evaluation-0

Presentations

The American Evaluation Association, UNICEF, and Claremont University maintain e-libraries containing empowerment evaluation slides, blog posts, recorded exchanges, and products of other e-learning activities.

An empowerment evaluation Ignite lecture is available online. It is a rapid presentation of the approach, consisting of 20 slides in 5 minutes. It is at: http://www.youtube.com/watch?v = fjUvV4HHH38

The American Evaluation Association's empowerment evaluation slides are available at: http://comm.eval.org/communities/resources/viewdocument/?DocumentKey = 2fab05ef-6ecc-4e62-b858-118e01096486

UNICEF's empowerment evaluation slides are online at: http://www.mymande.org/sites/default/files/UNICEF[1]fetterman.pdf

Claremont Graduate University's empowerment evaluation debate, with critical friends Michael Scriven and Michael Patton, is available online at: http://ccdl.libraries.claremont.edu/cdm/singleitem/collection/lap/id/69

Abilities

- Sociocultural competence
- Motivation (groups)
- Cultivate ownership and commitment
- Help people implement plans
- Continuous learning

In addition to formal training, informal experiential training is useful, particularly concerning the cultivation of empowerment evaluation abilities. Empowerment evaluators need to demonstrate sociocultural competence throughout an engagement. It is a form of respect for the community. It is best learned through immersion, working in multicultural communities with the guidance of a mentor, critical friend, or knowledgeable peer or colleague (see Chapter 4 in this volume for more information). Empowerment evaluators also need to be able to motivate groups, particularly when enthusiasm wanes at various stages in the process. Empowerment evaluators need to be educators and assistants, helping people develop, implement, and assess their programs or activities. Empowerment evaluators also need to be committed to lifelong, continuous learning. Everyone learns from each other in empowerment evaluations, they are not linear or one-way paths to enlightenment. A few experiences that merit consideration concerning the development of empowerment evaluation abilities include:

Experiential

Interview empowerment evaluators about their abilities and experience

Participate in an ongoing empowerment evaluation

Executive Coaching

Hire an experienced empowerment evaluation coach or critical friend to: train, critique, and coach throughout an empowerment evaluation

Facilitation

Facilitation training or experience is critical. The focus should be on learning how to help a group establish its own goals, instead of creating goals for them. Empowerment evaluators should practice facilitation skills at non-threatening community events. They should also participate in projects that rely on facilitation skills—learning from experienced facilitators.

Related Training Activities

Participate in cross-cultural experiences (within or outside the United States). Working with culturally diverse groups helps empowerment evaluators develop, refine, and improve their abilities, enhancing the quality of their work in multicultural settings.

Participate in ethnographic or qualitatively oriented fieldwork. It prepares evaluators for the complexity and uncertainty of working in community settings. It also helps evaluators learn how to apply critical abilities: adopting a nonjudgmental orientation, listening to the emic or insider's perspective or reality, contextualizing data, and taking time to become immersed in the life of the people you are working with.

These competencies, and the rationale for recommended training opportunities to develop and enhance these competencies, are more meaningful when placed in the context of concrete case examples.

EMPOWERMENT EVALUATION: CASE EXAMPLES

Empowerment evaluation has been successfully applied in a wide variety of settings. A few case examples of the utility of the approach include: a $15 million Hewlett-Packard initiative, Stanford University's School of Medicine, and Arkansas's school system. However, the Arkansas tobacco prevention empowerment evaluation is also used to highlight specific empowerment evaluation competencies.

Utility of Empowerment Evaluation Approach

Empowerment evaluation has been used in a $15 million Hewlett-Packard Digital Village Initiative, designed to bridge the digital divide in communities of color. One of the digital villages, called the Tribal Digital Village (composed of 18 tribes), built one of the largest unlicensed wireless systems in the country, according to the head of the FCC. They also operated a digital printing press. These successful ventures help the tribes communicate outside of the reservation and build a stable local economy (Fetterman, 2013, 2005, pp. 98–107).

Empowerment evaluation was used to help evaluate and transform a Stanford University School of Medicine's curriculum. Internal metrics demonstrated how empowerment evaluation's impact was statistically significant. External metrics also supported the utility of the approach. Applying this approach fostered greater institutional self-reflection, led to an evidence-based model of decision making, and expanded opportunities for students, faculty, and support staff to work collaboratively to improve and refine a medical school curriculum (Fetterman, Deitz, & Gesundheit, 2010).

This approach has also been used to help schools emerge from academic distress, improving standardized test scores in math and literacy in Arkansas (Fetterman, 2005, pp. 107–121). Previous to an empowerment evaluation, scores had steadily declined resulting in state take-overs of entire school districts in Arkansas. Another state-wide initiative in Arkansas focused on tobacco consumption. Empowerment evaluation helped community-based organizations reduce tobacco consumption throughout Arkansas, saving millions of dollars in excess medical costs. This case example highlights both the utility of the approach and specific competencies.

Tobacco Prevention Intervention: Highlighting Empowerment Evaluation Competencies

The Arkansas tobacco prevention initiative was introduced at the beginning of this chapter. A number of questions were raised about how best to approach the evaluation in the introductory exercise. This case example responds to many of those questions.

As stated earlier, the Arkansas tobacco prevention initiative consisted of 20 grantees from across the state. They included various community-based organizations, including faith-based institutions, hospitals, schools, and cessation centers. They began as a confederation of independent, competing agencies. They had no experience working together on common objectives, sharing data, or conducting evaluation.

Empowerment evaluation was selected to help unify the group and provide the members with the tools needed to accomplish their goals. A critical friend was selected to facilitate the group discussion as they worked to establish a common mission: helping minority communities reduce their consumption of tobacco. Then the coach or critical friend guided their discussion about the status of their work. Some grantees rated their work quite favorably, others were less generous with their self-assessments. The coach asked for evidence to support their ratings. This made some people defensive; however, the majority of grantees found it a refreshing approach compared with past experiences characterized by unsubstantiated positions, personal opinions, and political maneuvering. After engaging in a dialogue about their individual agency efforts, they evaluated their work as a group. This was the first time they even thought of themselves as group. Initially, they did not rate themselves very highly as a unified body, but the process rapidly created solidarity across grantees and a sense of ownership for what they were doing as a group.

The critical friend helped to make a transition in the discussion from self-assessment to plans for the future. The group came up with goals to improve their efforts, specific strategies, and proposed credible evidence. For example, if communication was a problem when they were discussing the quality of their work, then the goal was to improve communication as part of their plans for the future. Strategies to improve communication were linked to the evidence provided during their self-assessments. For example, if the reason communication was rated low was because they did not have an agenda for group meetings, then an agenda was suggested as a strategy. Similarly, if they thought email and videoconference communications were insufficient, they recommended increased and more effective use of these communication tools, as well as an electronic bulletin board to reach the community. Suggested evidence included: the use of agendas, increased use of emails and videoconference sessions, as well as the installation of an electronic bulletin board. The critical friend confirmed the value of some forms of evidence and questioned other forms of evidence, suggesting substitutions in those cases.

This set the stage for even more substantive discussions about their daily work. They had the tools to assess their work: creating smoke-free parks, building coalitions with similar groups, promoting the Quitline (a phone line to call if a person wanted to quit smoking), and influencing legislation concerning smoke prevention policies. They used these tools to create a collaborative and cooperative atmosphere, replacing in large part the heavily independent and competitive spirit that dominated the group interaction in the past. For example, they initially rated themselves poorly when it came to creating smoke-free parks. However, as part of a newly formed group, they realized that their fate depended on everyone in the group, even their weakest link (since we aggregated the data across grantees for the legislature). Instead of competing with each other, members of the group shared their most effective strategies with each other. One grantee said she recruited students to pick cigarette butts off the ground in selected parks, bring them to city council meetings, and then have them use the bags of butts symbolically to strengthen their request for a policy change—banning all smoking in city parks. Others listened to her story, shared it in their communities, and replicated this strategy successfully across the state.

Once the group finished establishing their goals, it was important to help them monitor their progress. The group, with the assistance of their empowerment evaluator, established their baseline (0 smoke-free parks in the county), goal (12 smoke-free parks each year), and benchmarks (3 smoke-free parks each quarter). The group entered their actual performance data into this evaluation dashboard (number of smoke-free parks they were able to establish each quarter) and compared it with their benchmarks and goals. The critical friend facilitated a discussion about the group's progress and midcourse correction options.

The outcomes of the effort were remarkable. Approximately 95% of the group was able to meet their annual goals in Centers for Disease Control recommended intervention areas, including creating smoke-free environments such as smoke-free parks. In addition, grantees learned to trust the process and agreed to pool their data in a number of areas. For example, the number of minority youth they helped to stop consuming tobacco, once combined across grantees, translated into over $90 million saved in excess medical costs across the state. The group also agreed to work together to improve minority evaluation skills, as applied to tobacco prevention. They proposed the creation of the Arkansas Evaluation Center. It passed the state House and Senate and was signed into law by the governor. These are just a handful of outcomes resulting from this evaluative collaboration.

Competencies

The tobacco prevention empowerment evaluation highlighted a number of competencies. They are organized according to knowledge, skills, and abilities categories.

Knowledge. The coaches or empowerment evaluators needed a basic knowledge of evaluation to help the group monitor their performance with baselines, goals, benchmarks, and actual performance. However, they also needed a specific knowledge about empowerment evaluation to help people use these tools to monitor and assess their own performance. (See the Appendix for a description of the three steps of empowerment evaluation used in this case example: mission, taking stock, and planning for the future.)

Skills. The empowerment evaluators also demonstrated a variety of skills in this tobacco prevention initiative. They demonstrated their interpersonal and communication skills working with diverse community participants, sponsors, and staff members. They had to communicate honestly, but constructively, when grantees proposed less than optimal forms of evidence. Facilitation skills were also critical at helping the group come to a consensus about their mission, their assessment of their performance, and their plans for the future.

The empowerment evaluator displayed methodological expertise, advising the group concerning data collection, analysis, and reporting. During the planning for the future step, the group had to collect relevant data, analyze them, and report on them in order for the group to determine if their strategies were working. The self-critique stages of the process required the construction and maintenance of a safe environment to facilitate an open dialogue. The empowerment evaluator encouraged the group to compare their actual performance data with their goals and benchmarks to contribute to organization learning. The information allowed the individual member groups to learn from each other and enabled the entire group to monitor their progress over time.

Abilities. The tobacco prevention example also highlighted a number of abilities required of empowerment evaluators. The cultural sensitivity competence was critical while working with economically disenfranchised communities of color. Insincerity or insensitivity would have undermined the entire initiative. The empowerment evaluator's ability to motivate was critical when encouraging staff and community members to launch this initiative and when enthusiasm waned due to normal organizational disappointments, missed benchmarks, and psychological setbacks. In addition, the ability to motivate was critical when encouraging program staff and community members to monitor their own performance.

The critical friend helped the grantees take ownership of the initiative by encouraging them to take charge of their own programs and conduct their own evaluations (instead of fostering dependency by doing it for them). The continuous learning competency was probably one of the most important competencies demonstrated in this empowerment evaluation. The evaluator and the grantees were continually learning how best to monitor and assess their performance. The political and economic landscape was constantly changing, requiring continual adaptation to the environment. In addition, every year clients, program staff members, and funders changed, requiring new strategies, allegiances, and practices. There were also new tobacco prevention and cessation strategies introduced each year, requiring continual learning to keep up with the strengths and weaknesses of specific interventions.

There are many more case examples demonstrating the practicality, utility, and effectiveness of this approach in real-world settings (Fetterman, 2001, 2009; Fetterman, Kaftarian, & Wandersman, 1996; Fetterman & Wandersman, 2005). They also provide additional insight into the competencies required of empowerment evaluators.

SUMMARY

There is an important synergy that is created by aligning the strengths of the community psychologist with the knowledge, skills, and abilities of an empowerment evaluator. They are separate strands of the same social fabric. They are both committed to inclusion, capacity building, evaluation, empowerment, and improving the human condition. Together they can help communities mend wounds that have ripped through their communities and weave ornate tapestries of hope, resilience, self-reliance, and self-determination, producing healthier families and more prosperous communities.

DISCUSSION QUESTIONS

1. What is empowerment evaluation? Why is it particularly useful as an evaluation approach for community psychologists?

2. How might you use this approach in your own personal and professional life?

3. What is the role of a critical friend in the empowerment evaluation approach?

4. How would you cultivate self-determination in a group or community?

5. How do you see your role in facilitating community ownership? Who should be in control?

6. How to you internalize and institutionalize evaluation?

7. How do you ensure quality and rigor in this work?

KEY TERMS AND DEFINITIONS

Critical friends: Evaluation coaches and facilitators who help stakeholders conduct their own evaluation of their programs to improve performance. They are friends of the program who are highly critical of program performance because they want the program to perform and produce the desired results.

Empowerment evaluation: Using evaluation concepts, techniques, and findings to foster improvement and self-determination. Empowerment evaluators view program staff members, program participants, and community members as in control of the evaluation. However, empowerment evaluators do not abdicate their responsibility and leave the community to conduct the evaluation solely by itself. They serve as critical friends or coaches to help keep the process on track, rigorous, responsive, and relevant.

Participatory evaluation: Participatory evaluators jointly share control of the evaluation. Participatory evaluations range from program staff members and participants participating in the evaluator's agenda to participation in an evaluation that is jointly designed and implemented by the evaluator and program staff members.

RESOURCES

Recommended Reading

Cox, P. J., Keener, D., Woodard, T., & Wandersman, A. (2009). *Evaluation for improvement: A seven step empowerment evaluation approach for violence prevention organizations.* Atlanta, GA: Centers for Disease Control and Prevention.

Fetterman, D. M. (2013). *Empowerment evaluation in the digital villages: Hewlett-Packard's $15 million race toward social justice.* Stanford, CA: Stanford University Press.

Fetterman, D. M. (2014). Hewlett-Packard's $15 million digital village: A place-based empowerment evaluation initiative. In D. M. Fetterman, S. Kaftarian, & A. Wandersman (Eds.), *Empowerment evaluation: Knowledge and tools for self-assessment, evaluation capacity building, and accountability.* Thousand Oaks, CA: Sage.

Fetterman, D. M., Delaney, L., Triana-Tremain, B., & Evans-Lee, M. (2014). Empowerment evaluation and evaluation capacity building in a 10 year tobacco prevention initiative. In D. M. Fetterman, S. Kaftarian, & A. Wandersman (Eds.), *Empowerment evaluation: Knowledge and tools for self-assessment, evaluation capacity building, and accountability.* Thousand Oaks, CA: Sage.

Fetterman, D. M., Dietz, J., & Gesundheit, N. (2010.) Empowerment evaluation: A collaborative approach to evaluating and transforming a medical school curriculum. *Academic Medicine, 85*(5), 813–820.

Fetterman, D. M., Kaftarian, S., & Wandersman, A. (2014). *Empowerment evaluation: Knowledge and tools for self-assessment, evaluation capacity building, and accountability.* Thousand Oaks, CA: Sage.

Fetterman, D. M., & Wandersman, A. (2005). *Empowerment evaluation principles and practice.* New York, NY: Guilford.

Recommended Websites

Wikipedia (empowerment evaluation)
Collaborative, Participatory, and Empowerment Evaluation website: http://www.davidfetterman.com
(search for empowerment evaluation)
Empowerment Evaluation Blog: http://eevaluation.blogspot.com

Other Recommended Materials

Radio Interviews: http://www.davidfetterman.com (search for radio interviews)

NOTE

1. See Scriven (1998) and Sechrest (1997).

REFERENCES

Cox, P. J., Keener, D., Woodard, T., & Wandersman, A. (2009). *Evaluation for improvement: A seven step empowerment evaluation approach for violence prevention organizations.* Atlanta, GA: Centers for Disease Control and Prevention.

Dalton, J., & Wolfe, S. (2012). Joint Column: Education connection and the community practitioner. *The Community Psychologist, 45*(4), 7–14.

Fetterman, D. M. (1996). Empowerment evaluation: An introduction to theory and practice. In D. Fetterman, S. Kaftarian, & A. Wandersman (Eds.), *Empowerment evaluation: Knowledge and tools for self-assessment and accountability.* Thousand Oaks, CA: Sage.

Fetterman, D. M. (2001). *Foundations of empowerment evaluation.* Thousand Oaks, CA: Sage.

Fetterman, D. M. (2009). Empowerment evaluation at the Stanford University School of Medicine: Using a critical friend to improve the clerkship experience. *Avaliação e Políticas Públicas em Educação, 17*(63), 197–204.

Fetterman, D. M. (2013). *Empowerment evaluation in the digital villages: Hewlett-Packard's $15 million race toward social justice.* Stanford, CA: Stanford University Press.

Fetterman, D. M. (2014). Hewlett-Packard's $15 million digital village: A place-based empowerment evaluation initiative. In D. M. Fetterman, S. Kaftarian, & A. Wandersman (Eds.), *Empowerment evaluation: Knowledge and tools for self-assessment, evaluation capacity building, and accountability.* Thousand Oaks, CA: Sage.

Fetterman, D. M., & Bowman, C. (2002). Experiential education and empowerment evaluation: Mars Rover educational program case example. *Journal of Experimental Education, 25*(2), 286–295.

Fetterman, D. M., Delaney, L., Triana-Tremain, B., & Evans-Lee, M. (2014). Empowerment evaluation and evaluation capacity building in a 10 year tobacco prevention initiative. In D. M. Fetterman, S. Kaftarian, & A, Wandersman (Eds.), *Empowerment evaluation: Knowledge and tools for self-assessment, evaluation capacity building, and accountability.* Thousand Oaks, CA: Sage.

Fetterman, D. M., Dietz, J., & Gesundheit, N. (2010). Empowerment evaluation: A collaborative approach to evaluating and transforming a medical school curriculum. *Academic Medicine, 85*(5), 813–820.

Fetterman, D. M., Kaftarian, S., & Wandersman, A. (1996). *Empowerment evaluation: Knowledge and tools for self-assessment and accountability.* Thousand Oaks, CA: Sage.

Fetterman, D. M., Rodriguez-Campos, L., Wandersman, A., & O'Sullivan, R. (2014). Collaborative, participatory and empowerment evaluation: Building a strong conceptual foundation for stakeholder involvement approaches to evaluation [Letter to the editor]. *American Journal of Evaluation, 35*(1), 144–148.

Fetterman, D. M., & Wandersman, A. (2005). *Empowerment evaluation principles and practice.* New York, NY: Guilford.

James, C. (2011). *Theory of change review: A report commissioned by Comic Relief.* London, UK: Comic Relief.

Rappaport, J., & Seidman, E. (Eds.). (2000). *Handbook of community psychology.* New York, NY: Kluwer Academic/Plenum.

Scriven, M. (1998). Empowerment evaluation examined. *Evaluation Practice, 18*(2), 165–175.

Sechrest, L. (1997). Book review of empowerment evaluation: Knowledge and tools for self-assessment and accountability. *Environment and Behavior, 29*(3), 422–426.

Wandersman, A., & Florin, P. (2000). Citizen participation and community organizations. In J. Rappaport & E. Seidman (Eds.), *Handbook of community psychology.* New York, NY: Kluwer Academic/Plenum.

Wandersman, A., Snell-Johns, J., Lentz, B. E., Fetterman, D. M., Keener, D. C., Livet, M., . . . Flaspohler, P. (2005). The principles of empowerment evaluation. In D. M. Fetterman & A. Wandersman (Eds.), *Empowerment evaluation principles in practice.* New York, NY: Guilford.

Zimmerman, M. (2000). Empowerment theory. In J. Rappaport & E. Seidman (Eds.), *Handbook of community psychology.* New York, NY: Kluwer Academic/Plenum.

APPENDIX

Empowerment Evaluation Exercise

Mission. Convene a group with something in common. Ask them to describe their purpose or mission. Have one of them write key phrases on poster paper in front of everyone. Take an hour to conduct this exercise and place the poster sheets on a wall within sight.

Take Stock. Next ask the group to make a list of the most important activities associated with making that mission a reality. After they list 20 or more activities, give them each 5 dots. Ask them to vote for the most important activities on the list that they think they need to evaluate as a group. They can put all five dots on one activity or spread them out evenly. Once they have placed their dots on the poster paper list of activities, count the dots. The top 10 activities (the ones with the most dots) should be written on a separate sheet of poster paper (resembling an Excel spreadsheet). Create enough individual rows and columns for everyone to rate how well the group is doing concerning each activity.

Then ask each member of the group to rate the activities on a 1 (low) to 10 (high) scale. Make sure they put their initials at the top of each of their columns, so you can call on them to engage in a dialogue. Once all the ratings are placed on the poster sheet, calculate the average across activities and down each column by person. Then look for an activity with a very high or very low overall average rating. Select an activity with a lot of variation in ratings. Ask a person why they rated the activity low. For example, if they gave "communication" a 3 ask them why they gave it a 3 and have a colleague record the response. Also ask them why they did not give it a 1 or 2, suggesting that there must be something positive going on there as well (building on strengths). Then ask another member of the group why they gave "communication" a high rating. The evidence they provide can be used in the next step of the empowerment evaluation process. You do not have to exhaust the group; stop once they begin to slow down.

Planning for the Future. Finally, ask the group to select three of the activities they want to work on and improve. If "communication" is one of them, ask them to specify the goal for the activity (e.g., improve communication). Then ask them what strategies they would use to improve communication. The strategies can be drawn from the evidence they provided in the taking stock step of the exercise. For example, if they said the reason they gave communication a low rating was because they never had an agenda, then a strategy might be to start creating agendas. In addition, ask the group what would be credible evidence that the strategies are being implemented and working (e.g., an agenda is created and a survey of the group suggests that agendas are an improvement in group communication).

In a real empowerment evaluation, individuals would then be assigned responsibility for reporting progress on their activity at their next normal staff meeting. This internalizes evaluation as part of the planning and operations of the group or organization.

CHAPTER 13

Dissemination and Sustainability

Changing the World and Making It Stick

Susan M. Wolfe, Louis G. Tornatzky, and Benjamin C. Graham

OPENING EXERCISE: INNOVATION U

It is the third year of a massive economic recession and national legislators from both sides of the aisle are looking for solutions and working with presidential and agency staffers. One spending program is particularly attractive for reduction by legislators who resent the arrogance of the recipients. That is the over $40 billion spent by the federal government on university research projects and programs. Members of Congress are skeptical about positive economic impacts, a position that is shared by many big city mayors who need fiscal relief for welfare programs and support of police departments. At the meetings a small group of university administrators, joined surprisingly by some CEOs of famous and profitable technology companies, argue that *some* universities are very effective in fostering technology innovation that is directly traceable to professors' research and being clever about converting patented technology to real startup companies, wealth creation, and jobs for constituents. During the heated discussions, several people point to the relationship between Stanford University and Google as an example, but others argue that Stanford is a special case and one can't readily replicate its culture and history. While others mention more case examples, the meetings are not conclusive and participants retire to cocktail lounges in downtown Washington to nurse their disappointment before their plane leaves Reagan National. One theme that keeps bubbling up in their conversation is "if we could only replicate what Stanford does, then we could fix the economy." Eventually this discussion reaches the level of governors. They not only want to figure out what to do to leverage their universities' points of excellence but to also stem the tide of their best and brightest young people leaving many of their states and heading to California or points north and east (Tornatzky, Gray, Tarant, & Howe, 1998). What steps would need to be taken to package what Stanford and other successful universities are doing? How could this be disseminated to other universities? What would it take to sustain these efforts in the settings in which they are adopted?

OVERVIEW

Chapter 11 in this book provided a description of how federally funded programs are developed, implemented, and disseminated. However, many community psychology practitioners are developing new programs, policies, and initiatives outside of the federal funding realm. There are also examples such as the opening exercise whereby others are funding individuals and institutions that are doing things that work. The focus of this chapter will be dissemination (how we take "what works" and systematically spread it around) and sustainability (once spread around, how we keep it in place). The main focus of the discussion will be at the program level, although the concepts are also applicable to policies and larger initiatives. We will begin by defining the key relevant concepts, then describe what dissemination and sustainability competence looks like (including examples), provide information about how to develop competence, and then discuss the future of dissemination and sustainability.

In this chapter, many of our examples will go beyond typical programs community psychology practitioners work with (e.g., poverty, mental health) and extend into areas such as technological innovation and business. The purpose will be to encourage community psychology practitioners to extend their competencies into areas where there has been little engagement by our field. For example, there are community psychologists who have ventured into areas such as the workplace (Bond, 2007), technological innovation (Tornatzky & Fleischer, 1990), and the role of universities in fostering community impact in jobs and business expansion (Tornatzky & Rideout, 2014). These are areas that are ripe for the application of community psychology practice competencies as well as how community psychology could learn and practice in new problem domains. We will take the liberty of addressing other issues including how community psychology might define itself differently, work in partnership with other entities and disciplines, and, hopefully, have a larger impact on improving life chances and happiness in society.

CONCEPTUAL DEFINITIONS

Extrapolating from the spread of innovation within agriculture, in 1962 Everett Rogers published the seminal text on dissemination, *Diffusion of Innovations*. Dissemination models in community psychology were developed based on Rogers's earlier work, Havelock's (1971) work in the educational field, and later work described by Fairweather and Tornatzky (1977) and Fairweather and Davidson (1986). More recent work is based in the growing field of dissemination and implementation science—the study of how ideas are promulgated across a broad diversity of contexts, inherently requiring an ecological lens (Ruzek & Rosen, 2009).

Dissemination refers to the intentional, systematic distribution of interventions to a targeted group of stakeholders for the purpose of changing or influencing practice or policy (Chambers, Ringeisen, & Hickman, 2005, p. 313; Lomas, 1993). Not simply the study of how to best broadcast a good idea, dissemination science is a complex process in which strategies found to work are diffused within complex systems, including addressing features both universal and unique to the specific neighborhoods, community organizations, clinics, or other "on the ground" contexts. In this way, dissemination science underscores an effort's ability to promote adoption of evidence-based programs across settings and services while maintaining fidelity of key program components.

Community psychology is no stranger to thinking in complex ways about context (Trickett, 1996). That said, the dissemination literature utilizes a host of specific but often confused terms and it is worthwhile to differentiate between similar terms used in the field. One such term is **diffusion**, which is distinct from dissemination in that it refers to a more general, not always intentional spreading of innovation (Schoenwald, McHugh, & Barlow, 2012). Dissemination is perhaps most frequently paired, and commonly confused, with implementation. **Implementation** refers to "the use of strategies to adopt and integrate evidence-based health interventions and change practice patterns within specific settings" (Chambers, 2009). The concepts of dissemination and implementation meet at the intersection of the specific context/setting; dissemination science studies how we get the word out and primes unique contexts for adopting innovations, while implementation science examines the specific contextual variables and processes that influence how the intervention is adopted and integrated.

The competency as defined by the Society for Community Research and Action (SCRA) Task Group on Defining Practice Competencies (Dalton & Wolfe, 2012) expands on this definition to include dissemination of community education, information, and building public awareness. The communication of information aspect of dissemination includes sharing knowledge with community members and engaging diverse groups in dialogue about information, diffusion of innovation (including using training and technical assistance), and social marketing.

While there is no universally agreed-upon definition, **sustainability** in program implementation refers to "the continuation of activities or benefits for target recipients after an initial period of funding ends or following the initial implementation of a new program or procedure" (Scheirer, 2013, p. e1). A related term is **sustainability capacity**, which refers to the structures and processes that allow a program to harness resources to effectively implement and maintain a program (Schell et al., 2013). As a competency, sustainability refers to the ability to "ensure sustainability of programs (e.g., through best practices management, community buy-in, securing funding and regulatory compliance)" (Dalton & Wolfe, 2012, p. 11).

In the world where most of us practice and conduct interventions or research, the unit of activity is more often than not the program. In this chapter we will primarily examine dissemination and sustainability through this lens, while incorporating other dimensions, including the incorporation of research findings, impact of policy, and other activities operating on various ecological levels of analysis/intervention.

A **program** can be defined as a set of resources and activities directed toward a set of common goals (Newcomer, Hatry, & Wholey, 1994). Exploring the complex challenge of sustainability through the lens of the program helps focus on what community psychologists can do to maximize a program's impact. Later in the chapter we will explore several concrete examples of how the components described here apply in real-world examples.

DISSEMINATION AND SUSTAINABILITY: KNOWLEDGE, SKILLS, AND ABILITIES

Dissemination

The knowledge, skills, and abilities (KSAs) needed for dissemination in practice are largely dependent upon the framework employed, the approach taken, and what is being disseminated. Early models developed and employed by community psychologists, which are still often the models employed today, extended Rogers's (1962) innovation diffusion model and Havelock's (1971) dissemination review. This systematic approach was primarily utilized to disseminate programs as described by Fairweather and Tornatzky (1977) and involved a four-stage model: approach, persuade, activate, and diffuse. A more recent model is Wandersman and colleagues' (2008) Interactive Systems Framework (ISF), which combines aspects of the aforementioned research in practice models and community-centered models. Another recent model proposed by Sandler (2007) integrates dissemination with theories of power and justice, and is consistent with community psychology values and goals as described in the Preface to this book.

The Approach, Persuade, Activate, and Diffuse Model

Prior to disseminating an **innovation**, or a situationally new knowledge-derived tool, artifact, or device by which people extend and interact with their environments, its readiness should be assessed. Before initiating the approach phase, the following criteria should be determined for whether the innovation has evidence of effectiveness: the innovation has the ability to go to scale (e.g., program materials, services and support); clear cost information is available; and monitoring and evaluation tools are prepared. Equally important is whether the innovation has a clearly defined model to ensure **implementation fidelity.** If these criteria are met, the innovation is ready for dissemination. The KSAs for this phase are those required for program development, implementation, and evaluation.

The knowledge required for program development is an expert-level comprehensive understanding of the literature in order to create the theory of change that will underlie the program. In other words, fully grasping the mechanisms that explain why doing one thing should result in another. Foundations, research centers, and others offer a wealth of resources to help organizations create theories of change, such as the Aspen Institute's *The Community Builder's Approach to Theory of Change: A Practical Guide to Theory Development* (Anderson, 2005).

Skills at this stage in the process include program planning, project management, logic model or similar framework development, budgeting, possibly preparing funding applications, and research and program evaluation skills. The abilities include developing and leading a team to develop and implement the program (often an interdisciplinary endeavor), and the ability to implement and evaluate while maintaining objectivity if the community psychology (CP) practitioner was also a member of the development and implementation team. It requires the ability to be able to always keep in mind the recipients of what is being done and the need to be sure that what you do is in their best interest and to make all decisions regarding whether to disseminate or sustain the program from that perspective.

Approach phase. The approach phase is where the potential target population moves from being unaware of the innovation to awareness. It may engage a personal approach whereby an advocate for the innovation approaches the target population in person and creates awareness through direct information sharing in meetings with groups or individuals. The indirect approach is where other media are employed such as mass media (television, newspapers), group approaches (workshops, professional meetings), or publication in the professional literature.

Historically, much of the work that has been performed by researchers has been published in the professional literature and presented at professional conferences where the likelihood of reaching the target audience of practitioners and community members is small; therefore, there is an abundance of knowledge and practices that has been produced by researchers that has gone no farther than university libraries (Kreuter & Bernhardt, 2009). The KSAs required are primarily communication, diffusion of innovation, and social marketing (Dalton & Wolfe, 2012). Communication may entail utilizing an educational approach to provide information to community members. It may also require engaging diverse groups in dialogue through consultation, public speaking or community forums, writing editorials or utilizing social media, or utilizing the media via press releases and public service announcements.

Communicating information that has been produced and published in academia requires the CP practitioner to have translation skills and be able to "speak both languages"—academic and practice. Professionals at community-based organizations and community members will likely want to know that what you are communicating has an evidence and theoretical foundation, but they will not be so interested in the details. The information that will matter will be what the program can do for them, how much it will cost, whether it will fill their need, and whether it will be culturally relevant to their community. Effectively communicating such information requires the CP practitioner to first examine the extent to which this program will truly fit the community and meet its needs, including the practitioners' self-examination of his or her motives for communicating this specific program to this specific community.

If a CP practitioner utilizes the diffusion of innovation approach it will require systematic identification of stakeholders and their interests and a strategy for tailoring messages to them. It may also require providing capacity-building training and technical assistance. Throughout this process the CP practitioner will need the KSAs to evaluate the dissemination process and outcomes. The evaluation should include the use of information and reevaluation of stakeholder needs and interests in order to revise the program as needed (Dalton & Wolfe, 2012).

Kreuter and Bernhardt (2009) described a marketing and distribution system approach that draws upon a business model. The KSAs described as necessary for creating awareness of research-based products are customer research and segmentation, packaging, and promotion. Fairweather and Davidson (1986) recommend testing different approaches experimentally to determine which works best with the targeted population. KSAs would include knowing how to research the relevant characteristics of various populations; understanding how to prepare and package information, programs, or policies in a way that will appeal to various audiences; and knowledge of a variety of promotion techniques. It would also require knowledge of how to empirically test dissemination strategies and determine their effectiveness.

Persuasion phase. This phase is when the target population moves from the state of awareness to making a decision whether to adopt the innovation (Fairweather & Davidson, 1986). The adoption decision is the "point in the process where the user moves from not having the innovation to having it" (Wolfe, Fleischer, Morrell, & Eveland, 1990, p. 179). The ability to research the target population and tailor messages appropriately is also necessary during this phase. It is critical to match the target population to style of persuasion, the content, and the legitimacy of the advocate.

Understanding potential roles and interpersonal dynamics in each situation is critical. First, it is important to know who the **gatekeepers** are (individuals or groups who control the amount and content of information that may be utilized in the decision process). Being able to cultivate effective relationships with gatekeepers and to persuade them to move the process forward is a necessary step. To move any innovation forward the gatekeepers must not only allow the information in, but also positively support the change. The availability of an **innovation champion** or an advocate who works at gaining support for the change is important, especially if an **innovation assassin** or someone attempting to maintain the status quo is working to undermine the process.

Three core behaviors during the adoption process are (1) defining a problem or determining that something needs to be changed; (2) searching for solutions and finding ways to solve the problem; then (3) choosing among the potential alternative solutions (Wolfe et al., 1990). Included in this process are the strategic-financial component, an interpersonal component, and a political component. The proposed innovation needs to fit with the strategic mission of the targeted group. One of the chapter authors has witnessed far too many instances whereby an organization pursued funding for a program simply because it was available, even when it did not fit with the organization's mission or other services. Too often after the organizations receive the grant monies and implement the programs, they realize they have gained nothing. The result is that they do not apply for continuation grants and the communities lose the services.

To address the interpersonal component, the primary skill is that of building relationships that foster trust and understanding. Building such relationships requires the CP practitioner to be genuine when interacting with and to strive to develop an understanding of the target population at a deeper level. It also requires that should the increased understanding indicate that the innovation is not appropriate for the target population, the CP practitioner be willing to make significant adaptations, identify more appropriate innovations, be honest in communicating limitations of the innovation for that specific population, and be willing to walk away. In regard to the political component, through the relationship-building process the CP practitioner needs also to learn about competing agendas, who will benefit most from adopting the innovation, and who will benefit more from adopting alternatives or maintaining status quo.

Activation phase. In this important phase the innovation moves from adoption to implementation. With the implementation KSAs as described in Chapter 11 of this book, the CP practitioner facilitating the implementation needs to be able to assess fidelity, support adaptations, and evaluate the outcomes. Even with evidence-based innovations, each time they are applied to new settings or new populations, they must be evaluated utilizing the most stringent designs feasible for the setting and resources available.

Diffusion phase. In this last phase the target population spreads the innovation by either expanding it within their own organization or persuading other groups or organizations to adopt it. During this phase the CP practitioner role will be that of a technical advisor who encourages and monitors dissemination to ensure that fidelity to the core of the model is maintained and evaluation is continued with each new implementation. The CP practitioner might also assist the target population with developing the dissemination strategy and the approach and persuasion phases with these additional potential adopters. The KSAs are those associated with consultation and organizational capacity building as described in Chapter 7 of this book.

One of the problems in effectively diffusing and fostering the robust program implementation of innovations is that the necessary behaviors are not always consistent with fostering the academic career of the university-based CP practitioner. Harken back to the opening exercise for a real example. Coauthor Tornatzky has been involved for over a dozen years in defining replicable "best practices" on the part of universities that will encourage technological innovation and economic impact in the "real world." The results of these efforts are actively disseminated through free mailings, Internet postings (www .innovation-u.com), consultations, and briefings to individuals who are in positions to implement the best practices and policies. These include reaching out to university leaders, state and local government officials, and the policy community (see Tornatzky & Rideout, 2014; Tornatzky, Waugaman, & Gray, 2002). The language and style of this information emphasizes readability and not academic turgidity. Publishing this type of information (not peer reviewed) and presenting it to such audiences is not considered valuable toward tenure and promotion in the university environment. For CP practitioners who are not in academic settings, other constraints, such as competing priorities and supervisor direction may prohibit engagement in such a long-term enterprise.

The Interactive Systems Framework

This framework was developed for dissemination of programs, policies, process, and principles, collectively referred to as "innovations" (Wandersman et al., 2008). Its value is that it recognizes and addresses the complexity of disseminating innovations at various levels and it provides a structure for understanding the systems, functions, and relationships that are operational during dissemination and implementation. This framework consists of three systems or sets of activities. First, the **prevention synthesis and translation system** extracts information about innovations and prepares them to be implemented. The associated KSAs are knowledge of existing research in the area of interest, skills in synthesizing the research, and the ability to translate it so that it is understandable and applicable by practitioners. These skills are the same as those needed during the *approach phase* in the previous model described in this chapter. Critical to this process is the ability to identify and clearly define core elements of innovations or those features of the innovation that are linked with its effectiveness and an expert understanding of the underlying theory of change. Ideally, the CP practitioner needs collaboration skills to work with the intended audience and produce information that is both understandable and applicable by end users.

The second system is the **prevention support system,** which supports the work of those who will implement innovations in practice (Wandersman et al., 2008). This system involves going beyond providing information to provide both innovation-specific and general capacity-building support to end users. For innovation-specific support the CP practitioner needs skills in training, providing technical assistance, and coaching/consultation. General capacity building includes enhancing the organizational infrastructure, skills, and motivation of the organization based on the assumption that a well-functioning organization will better support the innovation. General capacity building requires skills in assessing organizational needs and capacity, understanding the organizational culture and the extent to which it is able to support innovation, the knowledge and the ability to utilize organizational change methods, and resource development skills.

The third system, **the prevention delivery system** is where innovations are implemented in the field (Wandersman et al., 2008). This may occur in an organization, community, state, or at the national level. At the individual level, this system requires education, experience with the innovation (or a similar innovation), and motivation to implement. At the organization level leadership, program goals, commitment, skills for planning, implementation and evaluation, climate, structure, and innovation-specific factors are all critical.

The KSAs required by the CP practitioner at this stage include those associated with implementation as described in Chapter 11 of this book. The CP practitioner also needs the ability to understand organizational context and how it may fit, or not fit, with a specific innovation or a core feature of an innovation. At the community level, the CP practitioner needs to have KSAs to assess community needs and resources, leadership, participation, sense of community, and be willing and able to intervene directly in community problems. Many of the KSAs needed for community organizing, building community collaborations, and cross-cultural competence that were described in earlier chapters will be required for implementing innovations at the community level. One important issue that is relevant to field implementation is long-term survival and support. If an innovative system works now and is effective, it can potentially provide that value-adding outcome for years to come. The CP practitioner needs the ability to go beyond giving lip service to long-term survival and sustainability, and commit to providing long-term support.

Dissemination and Theories of Power and Justice

In keeping with CP values and goals, dissemination practice must draw on a **critical psychology** perspective to resolve tensions between community-based and evidence-based practices (Sandler, 2007). Disseminating and implementing programs and policies within structures of inequality can legitimize these structures. For the most part, addressing structural inequity has been ignored in dissemination literature and the literature relevant to evidence-based practice. Taking this one step further, the dissemination of evidence-based practices is primarily a top-down endeavor whereby "experts" determine community needs and solutions.

CP practitioners who approach dissemination from a critical psychology perspective need to develop a deep understanding of and ability to recognize and gain insight into structural injustices and to develop practices that will address them. Sandler (2007) describes elements of community-based practices that incorporate this perspective. First, the composition of the dissemination and implementation team must be inclusive of the community. Too often dissemination of an innovation is a process whereby the innovation moves from one professional to another and is subsequently implemented on behalf of those experiencing the problem, with little or no input from the individuals or communities that are affected. Sandler refers to this as the paternalism and disempowering professionalization of services. It more often serves the needs of the professionals to create jobs and maintain their power relations. The role CP practitioners may play is to promote full participant and community inclusion in this process. This must go beyond getting their input via focus groups or interviews to advocating for their full participation on boards and committees with full decision-making authority. The KSAs may include community leadership, advocacy, and mentoring skills, as well as knowledge of group dynamics and the ability to intervene or lead the group in a manner that will ensure full community member inclusion.

Sandler's (2007) second insight addresses fragmentation of services from the market-model social service and education sector. To reduce fragmentation, the adoption and implementation team must include representation from all relevant organizations in the community. For example, when programs to address children's social needs are implemented in schools, the implementation team should include professionals from mental health, health care, social service, substance abuse, and other agencies that will work with the families and children involved. The goal is to create a more holistic approach that is collaborative rather than competitive between agencies and is inclusive of community members and to develop the leadership capacity of the marginalized families. Professional partners must extend beyond their individual missions and adopt the mission of the program or initiative in a way that merges their diverse expertise. For the CP practitioner, the KSAs required are those needed for building collaborative partnerships, as described in Chapter 9 of this book.

A third insight especially relevant to dissemination is the differential local resources and agencies across communities (Sandler, 2007). When outsiders such as universities and national program staff are disseminating innovations to communities there is an inherent power differential. They often determine which organizations and individuals to include, legitimizing some and excluding others based on a team composition framework that was pre-decided outside of the specific community. According to Sandler (2007), these teams often reproduce hierarchical, racialized power dynamics whereby service providers are White and service recipients are people of color. The top-down approaches to adaptation seldom incorporate the expertise of local service providers and program recipients.

Limitations associated with the traditional top-down dissemination models are that they maintain the divide between experts and recipients and do not recognize the expertise within the community; they assume that all members of a racial or ethnic group are the same and require the same adaptations; and they ignore the unique dynamics and challenges of each specific community. To overcome these limitations requires true cultural representation on the implementation team. The KSAs required for the CP practitioner include those associated with cross-cultural competence as described in Chapter 4 of this book. The CP practitioner must be able to comfortably discuss sensitive topics such as race and ethnicity and be able to promote inclusiveness among groups that have historically not fully embraced the concept. True inclusion of the community will require facilitating a culture shift whereby professionals are trained and socialized to effectively partner with individuals in a way that promotes mutual power relations between themselves and the population being served. It also requires the CP practitioner to mentor and develop the traditionally marginalized local community members so they can fully embrace their new roles and power relations. But most importantly, bridging the gap between professionals

Photo 13.1 Sustainability: Ensured continuation.

Source: Susan M. Wolfe.

who are used to being in the driver's seat and community members who have historically accepted their disempowered roles will require training and resocialization of the helping professionals in their new roles as community collaborators, as well as careful monitoring to ensure that they do not undermine the empowerment process.

Sustainability

CP practitioners should be planning for sustainability throughout the program development, implementation, and dissemination processes. If a program, policy, or other change is found to be effective, the ultimate goal should be to keep it in place, either as value-added or as the new way of doing business. In practice, sustainability should often be an important goal of the dissemination process. Critical to the goal of sustainability is *which* program or policy elements are key predictors of outcomes that are of interest to sustain, and how sustainability capacity can be garnered to support these elements. This becomes more and more difficult as program elements (participants, treatments or events, context) become more complex and difficult to manage.

There is great value that can be gained from the cumulative knowledge garnered from spending years or decades unraveling a problem, understanding the ingredients, experimenting with different potential solutions or different versions of a single solution to determine relative efficacy, and then spending years getting the results used widely. That path tends to be similar whether one is trying to cure a deadly disease, develop the penultimate solution to low-energy personal transportation, or comprehensively address community violence in urban communities. The next couple of pages describe how this process might unfold.

Sustainability in Ideal and Not-So-Ideal Settings

There is no substitute for what Fairweather called experimental social innovation (Fairweather & Tornatzky, 1977) or others have simply referred to in terms of field experimentation or quasi-experimentation. These approaches assume a lengthy process of getting from problem awareness to validated program solutions that may include all of the following, and not necessarily in this order:

- In-the-wild observation of a problem and its processes and ad hoc events that seem to address those processes or attenuate negative outcomes

- More structured and focused case analyses of the problem, its processes and potential solutions, or contributing factors in a single site (e.g., a specific community or city). This might include needs and resource assessments, case studies, or other quantitative, qualitative, and mixed methods approaches to gather a deeper understanding of the problem at hand, its associated dynamics, and potential solutions.

- Developing measurement instruments and measuring the problem and related phenomena across a number of settings using methodologically sound procedures (e.g., mixed modeling) to sort out via relational statistics what might be related to potential solutions

- Designing a structured intervention and then testing it at a single site in one form

- A series of related experiments or quasi-experiments to further test the intervention and its components, test each component to determine its relative impact, and developing a clear model with clearly defined components after determining "what works

- Developing related materials and guidelines for core components to facilitate maintaining fidelity, and identifying what may be suitable to adapt to each setting and defining the boundaries of potential adaptations. For example, producing an implementation handbook that very clearly describes what each core component is and what must be done consistently to maintain fidelity, while also presenting descriptions of acceptable adaptations.

- Replication of the intervention over many sites and settings, and many years of effort while consistently evaluating the impact

- Creation, implementation, replication, and dissemination of a guidebook for solving the problem under consideration with descriptions of the potential solutions

If the above outline approximates the path for program development, why don't we see it very often? Actually, we do see it relatively often, and with a lot of money and person-years behind it, in problem domains that are deemed more critical than are those typically addressed in community psychology. If we look at the development of programs of medical treatment, pharmaceuticals, or surgical devices as an example, they take years to go through true experimental trials. If such innovations are successful they can be hugely beneficial to society—and remunerative to the developers. Unfortunately this is not so much the case in the typical program set that community psychology is wont to address.

The years-long process described above is a sizeable challenge for CP practitioners in both academic and practice settings. CP practitioners in academic careers are required to publish three or four peer-reviewed journal articles per year. Publishing a book every 4 years that approximates the long incubation, implementation, and validation process of a community psychology innovation adds very little to their tenure folders or promotion portfolios. Additionally, conducting research and social innovation through long community partnerships is rarely conducive to the timelines of theses or dissertations (Stamatakis, Norton, Stirman, Melvin, & Brownson, 2013). Outside of academia, CP practitioners rarely find work in settings that support the lengthy and costly process required to develop such social innovations.

Challenges to Sustainability

Increasingly, the validity of a program innovation (particularly in the context of an era of declining public investment) is better measured by *how long* the program is viable at an acceptable level of impact. This lies in the domain of program *sustainability*. Answering that question takes a lot of investment and patience, and it is rarely answered. If it were, the sunk costs in program development and verification might have a better public return on what is often public investment from federal or state agencies. However, as noted above, verification of longitudinal program impact is too often not consistent with an academic or practice career, and oddly enough it is sometimes not within the patience, interest, and budget priorities of federal agencies or other program development funders.

Additionally, CP practitioners are often working with grant-funded programs and initiatives with a limited shelf-life. If these programs are being implemented within the context of a larger organization or a nonprofit community-based organization, there is little likelihood that the program will be sustained when the grant funding ends. Grant-funded programs are often add-ons or enhancements to existing services. In some instances, organizations may see the value-added from the program and retain at least some elements of it if they have the resources. Too often, such programs are implemented by organizations that are operating on a shoestring and are unable to maintain even a component of the program.

In her review of the literature on sustainability, Scheirer (2005) found that securing funding or other resources was frequently cited as the greatest challenge to sustainability. Obtaining long-term funding to support and sustain systematic development, implementation, and dissemination of programs can present obstacles. Funders want to see positive outcomes after the first year of funding, leaving no room for trial and error or continuous development. They rarely fund the lengthy process involved in the development and validation of new programs.

One of the authors of this chapter recently worked with two programs that received funding for 18 months to form a community coalition and provide services that produced measurable outcomes. By the time the programs reached the point where they had fully implemented the programs and worked out the bugs, the funding ended. In this specific instance, the state issued a new request for proposals several months after the programs ended, and it required an entirely different approach that was so far removed from what had been done that neither organization reapplied for funding. One organization maintained the program and the other has funding from the parent organization to continue temporarily pending the outcome of a grant proposal that was submitted. Circumstances such as this present additional challenges for the sustainability of a systematic plan of action to target and reduce a specific problem. CP practitioners working toward sustainability need knowledge of funding streams and their workings, skills to navigate such systems, and the ability to formulate and implement a plan of action to ensure permanence of "what works."

Scheirer (2005) found that sustainability was primarily influenced by organizational context and the people within and outside the organization that influenced such context. The fit between the program and the organization's mission and procedures and the extent to which the program was modifiable to fit were important. As with the initial adoption of the program, leadership and the presence of a champion were also important. The ability to demonstrate benefits of the program to internal and external stakeholders, including external organizational support in terms of securing resources and mobilizing support for continuation, were also important.

Solutions for Sustainability

Based on her findings, Scheirer (2005) offers recommendations to increase the likelihood of program continuation to developers at the local level. First, she recommends they choose programs that relate to the organization's mission and culture to increase the likelihood of support from upper management and so that the program fits with the skills and workloads of available staff members. The implication for the CP practitioner is that skills in organizational assessment to gaining a full understanding of mission and culture, organizational resources, and the daily workings of the organization are necessary. Additionally, an in-depth understanding of the program and its adaptability to fit the target organization are critical. Sustainability will be compromised if this fit is not maximized at the adoption and implementation phases.

If the CP practitioner enters the situation after the fact and is asked to promote sustainability of an already adopted and implemented program, skills might require those needed to adapt an existing program to the extent that the likelihood of sustainability is increased. Scheirer's second recommendation is that modifications to fit the organizational context must maintain the core components that contribute to effectiveness of the original design.

The third recommendation (Scheirer, 2005) is to identify and support a program champion that can take a leadership role in sustainability planning. This may be the same champion that supported the initial adoption and implementation, or it may require identifying or developing a new champion. The CP practitioner may take on this role, which would require leadership skills, among many others. The alternative would be to facilitate the development of leadership, communication, and program advocacy skills among a key stakeholder. The CP practitioner would need the ability to identify an individual who both has the capacity to develop such skills and is in a position to assume this role. Understanding the organizational politics is important so as not to set up members of the organization to either fail or possibly compromise their employment position. It would also require the CP practitioner to understand the dynamics between the organization and external stakeholders in the event that external stakeholders may be able to more effectively champion the sustainability of the program.

Scheirer's (2005) fourth recommendation extends the potential role that external stakeholders may play in promoting sustainability. She recommends that the benefits of the program for various groups of stakeholders (internal and external) be publicized throughout the design and implementation phases. Gathering feedback from program participants via surveys and focus groups and including them on advisory boards requires skills in cross-cultural competence and program evaluation methods as well as the ability to build inclusive community partnerships. Forming an active coalition or participating in an existing coalition provides a supportive group that can rally resources and political support. This requires skills in coalition development and developing community partnerships as described in Chapter 9 of this book. The program design should include linkages to other community-based organizations and mechanisms that serve their interests.

The final recommendation is to consider institutionalizing the program into the core operations of the organization rather than keeping it as a stand-alone program. The program should be shifted from soft money to hard money and built into the parent organization's budget cycle. This can be done gradually over the life of the funding cycle or at one time, perhaps replacing the old way of doing business. Budget development and planning skills combined with overall strategic planning skills are needed to accomplish this. The CP practitioner can play a role by facilitating the strategic planning process to incorporate the program into the larger plan and ensure that the organization ties its strategic planning process to its budget planning process. Understanding accounting and financial systems and strategic planning is helpful.

Institutionalization can be facilitated by building program activities into existing personnel's job descriptions. The fewer new personnel needed to maintain the program the greater the likelihood the program will survive. Similarly, incorporating existing supplies and technology into the program and sharing them across activities reduces costs. Cross-training staff within the organization to the extent possible so that the program skills become part of the required professional standards will facilitate sustainability in the face of turnover. Finally, including the program in organizational governance documents, such as policies and procedures, will further institutionalize it (Yin, 1981). KSAs include knowledge of business and management practices and the development of business management skills.

Education, Training, and Experiences That Facilitate Development

Education

Most master's and doctoral level CP programs provide some of the KSAs relevant to dissemination and sustainability. They provide training in community research and program evaluation in addition to the ecological theories that provide the foundation for such work. Taking classes in other departments, including Social and Organizational Psychology, the School of Management, Public Health, and Communications, may also be useful. Courses in group process, organizational psychology, organizational assessment, marketing, communication, and management all provide useful knowledge.

Another area of education that provides skills for dissemination and sustainability is found in the business school and focuses on entrepreneurship. As noted earlier in this chapter, there are few settings CP practitioners work in that would support the lengthy process of developing, disseminating, and sustaining social innovations. Recent trends suggest that entrepreneurship may be an especially lucrative path for female practitioners. Despite the national trends that indicate that female students are a growing majority in colleges, tend to get better grades on average, and are the most capable team leaders and managers when in school and in the workplace, they are underrepresented in the entrepreneurial economy (e.g., new startup companies, angel and venture investment, technology-intensive ventures). This is not attributable to capability, but to choices made. Organizations such as the Kaufman Foundation (www.kauffman.org/) provide tools and training specific to social entrepreneurship that can supplement what is learned in a business, engineering, or life science curriculum. One of the more interesting trends (and positive outcomes) in entrepreneurship education is the dramatic expansion of co-curricular and extra-curricular learning opportunities. That is, don't just read and discuss entrepreneurship, but "learn by doing" via no-credit competitions, participating in business incubators, and interning with real live entrepreneurs. Another important trend is moving the locus of entrepreneurship education out of the business schools and into colleges of engineering and other disciplines. The interesting question is whether it is easier to teach a business student requisite engineering knowledge or vice versa.

Additional Training

While few in number, some resources for specialized training in dissemination and implementation science exist, such as those offered by the Prevention Research Center, a joint collaboration between St. Louis University and Washington University (http://prcstl .wustl.edu/training/Pages/MTDIRC.aspx). Additionally, several national conferences in dissemination and implementation science are offered each year (see "Resources" section). Otherwise, much of the training that is useful for dissemination and sustainability can be obtained through professional development opportunities such as workshops and continuing education classes. Writing is an example of one of the core skills that can be refined through workshops and extra training. Writing workshops can be useful to learn about how to write for different audiences and to more clearly convey your message to the public. One of this chapter's authors had always been told that she was a good writer, but when she worked for the government was mandated (along with the entire office) to attend a writing workshop. Now she recommends that every professional attend such a workshop because writing is a skill that can be continually refined throughout a career.

Writing development should include workshops for grant writing. Being able to get money is foundational for dissemination and sustainability. Not only is it helpful to be able to write grants for dissemination and sustainability, but being a good grant writer can often help the CP practitioner to gain entry into a community or organization. Grant writing skills should include learning how to write large federal grant applications, complete state funding applications, and write foundation grants. Each of these has a very different set of associated skills.

Dissemination involves sharing information. Taking workshops to refine presentation skills and prepare appealing materials (e.g., graphics, brochure layout) can empower the CP practitioner to create presentations and written materials that appeal to a wide variety of audiences. Becoming skilled with various presentation and publication software makes more tools available and there are often training programs and workshops available to learn to use all of their features effectively.

Coalition development is another area where there are workshops available through professional associations and other organizations. More information about how to develop this competency can be found in Chapter 9. Policy and advocacy are other skills that CP students report are not always available in their graduate programs, but they are offered through workshops and other professional development opportunities. More about developing this competency can be found in Chapter 10.

Finally, although as CP practitioners we like to think of ourselves as being cross-culturally competent, attending workshops and other trainings in this area on a continuing basis is always useful. Chapter 4 of this book provides good information about this competency and also how it might be developed. Attending local workshops serves more than one purpose. First, even if you are already cross-culturally competent, such workshops serve as reminders and refreshers. Second, it is helpful to attend such workshops that are being provided to the local professional community to understand the messages they are receiving about this topic and determine the extent to which it will adequately prepare them for the next step—true collaboration with the community. Also, the nature of the conversations and comments made provides additional insight into the local community's perspective on race, ethnicity, and culture.

Experience

For many of the KSAs required for dissemination and sustainability there is no substitute for experience. Experience can be obtained through internships, paid employment, and taking advantage of volunteer opportunities. If there is a skill you want to cultivate, find someone in your community who is considered an exemplar and find a way to work with that person in whatever capacity is possible and feasible. Volunteering or interning as an advocate under the tutelage of someone who is really good at it and is willing to mentor can provide the KSAs needed to advocate for programs and policies across settings.

To gain experience with managing programs and projects, implementing new initiatives, and managing staff and volunteers, you most often will be required to enter a setting in a lower level position and work your way up to such opportunities. You will likely be more effective at convincing others to adopt programs or policies into settings if you have walked their walk. Being experienced at managing projects and programs imparts the insights needed to provide technical assistance for implementing the program you are disseminating. Having worked in an organization and experienced the various constraints provides valuable contextual information for promoting sustainability as well.

Engaging in organizations and participating on coalitions and other collaborative efforts provides opportunities to observe and navigate a variety of interpersonal and politically charged situations. Gaining this experience as a student or through internships provides safe opportunities to remain quiet and observe because nobody will expect you to generate solutions or manage the politics yet. To learn from these experiences, work to identify those who are skilled at managing politically charged situations and disagreements, building alliances, and keeping even the most challenging personalities on task and positive. Once you have identified them, observe the nuances of their communication styles and strategies employed.

APPLICATION

Two case examples are presented in this section of the chapter. The first, the work of Bill Fairweather, provides insight into the lengthy dissemination process required to create adoption of a social innovation and its subsequent sustainability. The second is a description of a series of events one of the authors encountered during the writing of this chapter. It provides an example of the challenges to sustainability of federally funded programs within the context of community-based organizations.

Dissemination of the Fairweather Community Lodge

An exemplary example of dissemination and sustainability is the historically and methodologically important work of Bill Fairweather and colleagues. This endeavor resulted in an experimentally validated program that enabled chronic mental hospital patients to attain some degree of secure relative freedom in the so-called real world. Fairweather (1980) and colleagues spent over 25 years encompassing hospital-based true experimentation focused on group problem solving among hospitalized mental patients, which was followed by another 10 years of experimentation that extended those processes into a community-based living and working situation known as the Community Lodge. This in turn enabled those ex-patients involved to persist and thrive economically, socially, and personally in the community for years. For those who are not familiar with the body of work you should think of the program as a very effective entrepreneurial kibbutz for people with mental disorders.

It was a process that involved *years* of field-based trial and error, data collection and analysis, and resulted in *one* model program. The point being made here is that many problems are big enough and some program solutions profound enough to justify this level of time and money. Aspiring new practitioners can benefit by considering dissemination and sustainability issues in evaluating, designing, and learning from the projects they engage in that are similar to Fairweather and colleagues' work.

In their book *Innovation and Social Process: A National Experiment in Implementing Social Technology,* Tornatzky, Fergus, Aveliar, Fairweather, and Fleischer (1980) describe results of studies over several years that included a national experiment to compare various technical assistance strategies to facilitate adoption and implementation of Fairweather's Community Lodge and studies of service providers to determine their capacity to engage in innovation. To fully understand the most effective dissemination methods required a series of studies that ultimately found that much of what is done to disseminate innovations does not work. KSAs primarily utilized over this time were those associated with conducting community-based research as well as those associated with the Approach-Persuade-Activation-Disssemination phases described earlier. Their findings included:

1. Assistance, encouragement, or support is necessary to ensure the establishment of a peer-to-peer innovation network. Networks tend to be geographically bound and confined in other ways. For example, Veterans Administration hospitals confined their peer network to the federal system.

2. Disseminating innovations via informative newsletters and print media was found to be ineffective. Yet to this day much of what is learned from research and practice is still disseminated passively in journals, reports, newsletters, and conferences.

3. Even when a number of organizations adopt an innovation, if it does not reach a reasonable level of institutionalization and is not legitimized and supported, it will likely not last.

4. Providing workshops and site visits may not be sufficient to ensure full implementation and sustainability. A more concentrated, on-the-ground approach may be necessary with adequate resources devoted to supporting innovations.

Sustainability and the Healthy Start Programs

In Chapter 3 of this book, Stelzner and Wielkiewicz described the federally funded Healthy Start initiative as an example of the application of an ecological model to reducing infant mortality disparities in communities. This program began in 1991 with 15 projects and in 2010 there were 104 projects. This program has evolved over the years, and coauthor Wolfe, who has worked with Healthy Start programs intermittently since 1994, has had the opportunity to observe this evolution. The first phase of Healthy Start was implemented before there was much demand for accountability. Local evaluation was required, but the role of the evaluator was to simply describe what the project had done and how many people were served. Money was provided to communities and they decided what to do with it. The requirement was that they form a "consortium" of interested parties to collaborate to reduce infant mortality.

The project this particular author worked with at that time used the money to fund teen pregnancy prevention projects, a program providing prenatal education and support to adolescent mothers, a low-birth-weight center, transportation services for pregnant women and new mothers, parent aides, visiting nurses, and male health risk reduction services (e.g., teach them to use condoms). Each year the program issued a request for proposals and funded the best proposals received from a variety of community-based organizations. While this sounds like a haphazard approach, keep in mind that it is reflective of the level of sophistication of service funding at the time.

Around 1998, U.S. Department of Health and Human Services (DHHS) Health Resources and Services Administration (HRSA) gathered a group of the local evaluators together to discuss the development of common outcome criteria and introduce a new tool called "a logic model." The evaluators sat in a room for a couple of days working to determine (other than a reduction in the infant mortality rates) what could be measured that would indicate the projects had been successful. The underlying problem was that each community was doing something different, so it was like trying to compare apples and oranges. Without a single "model" with an underlying theory of change, this was essentially an impossible task.

Within the next couple of years Healthy Start 2.0 was rolled out. This version of the initiative provided grantees with clear guidelines and expectations that included core service and core systems requirements, but still allowed flexibility for local adaptation. Grantees were required to report progress on a set of performance measures that had been developed for all maternal-child health programs funded by HRSA. Projects were funded at the same levels throughout this period with no increases in their allocations. Project managers utilized KSAs associated with implementation. As local evaluator, co-author Wolfe took on a variety of roles, depending upon what each site requested and needed. They included evaluation activities (e.g., focus groups, surveys, appreciative inquiry), collaborating to develop the local health systems' action plan, facilitating strategic planning and staff development workshops, coalition development technical assistance, and helping to write grant proposals to expand or enhance services, and each role required a different set of KSAs depending upon the tasks at hand. Some skills included facilitation, evaluation design, coalition development, grant writing, program development, and collaboration.

While there were changes to the program requirements for Healthy Start 2.0 that requested projects do more (with the same amount of funding) and performance measures, this model was operational until late 2013 when HRSA released the request for proposals (RFP) for competitive applications for Healthy Start 3.0. This time they changed the game.

First, in prior years existing Healthy Start projects received priority points on their applications and most projects retained their funding across each 5-year cycle. For this round of applications existing projects were informed that they would no longer receive priority points. Although there had always been a performance measure that had programs rate themselves on the degree to which they worked to promote program sustainability beyond the life of the HRSA funding, most programs remained in denial that they would ever actually have to consider this. Second, the model was changed and additional requirements for increasing collective impact and implementing evidence-based components were added. For the new model, skills in community organizing and inclusion of community members in coalitions were needed. The funding level for the basic program remained the same, and the maximum was actually less than some programs had been receiving. Third, programs were given the option to apply at three different levels. The first was the most basic level program similar to what they were already doing. This was the funding level with a maximum that was less than what a large proportion of projects were receiving. The second level required additional activities, including more required data collection and analysis components and serving even more program participants. Ten projects would receive this level of funding. The third level required the project to assume a regional and national leadership role in addition to requirements for the first two levels. Each level increased the number of participants programs were required to serve and required fatherhood programs to be implemented, although the fathers served were not to be included in the increased numbers of required participants.

Shortly after the proposals were submitted, while programs were waiting to learn of their fates, HRSA sent each a set of guidelines for a sustainability plan they referred to as a Transition Plan. Projects were required to answer a series of questions if they (a) applied for a level that represented a reduction in funding; (b) received no funding but planned to continue some or all of the services; (c) received no funding and planned to discontinue services; and (d) received funding but for a different project area. Questions included how they planned to phase the program out, whether they would transition services to another organization, funding sources for the closeout transition, and plans to complete a final Local Impact report.

At the time this RFP was issued, coauthor Wolfe was serving as the local evaluator for four Healthy Start programs—three of which decided to reapply for funding, and one of which decided to discontinue services. The parent organization for the discontinued project was Catholic and it would not be able to fully implement the reproductive life planning and Affordable Care Act requirements, so the organization made a logical decision to not apply for the funding. Given these limitations, it would not have been competitive. Fortunately, in this case a local school of public health with an area focused on maternal-child health decided to adopt the program and submitted the grant application. Staff from the existing program dedicated countless hours to working collaboratively with the university staff to write the proposal and share their experience. In this instance, sustainability for at least another 5 years will be assured, pending the outcome of the grant proposal. Why? Because the host organization (1) found another organization willing to pursue the grant and (2) collaborated to share its knowledge and experience with the program, and gave its endorsement to transfer the program.

After the proposals were submitted, the parent organization of another of the projects the author works with decided that it was no longer interested in hosting the program. It contacted the funding agency and withdrew the application, then called the program staff to tell them to prepare to shut it down. The rationale was that this specific program did not fit with their mission and other services, and the funding (which had not changed in over 10 years) was not enough to do what was required anyway. In this case, it was too late to hand the program off to another organization, so this city will lose the services altogether and nothing will be sustained.

The Healthy Start example is representative of the way services and programs are often provided to communities to combat social ills. Requests for proposals are issued, community-based organizations apply for funding, and if the funding is approved, they have services for 3 to 5 years at a time. At the end of that time, the RFP may or may not be renewed, the community may or may not apply, and the proposal may or may not be approved. Notably, although the federal funding agency included a performance measure related to sustainability, there was really no requirement or guidance issued for a solid sustainability plan, no technical assistance was provided, and no actual planning was done with the projects. Projects set their own goals for this measure, most set them relatively low, and HRSA did not push for anything more. Projects had been funded for so many years that, although in the backs of their minds they knew that losing the funding was always a possibility, staff still did not take steps to prepare for it (despite the urging of their local evaluator). The new RFP was going to fund fewer projects, which means that some programs that have existed for over a decade will close with little or no components sustained, and their communities will lose valued services. Because the Healthy Start initiative has never invested in an intensive evaluation, it has not been accepted as an evidence-based program, which further compromises the communities' ability to attract funding to retain the program or its components.

The Healthy Start example offers food for thought regarding what could be done to ensure sustainability. If you were a CP practitioner in a role that was peripheral to this project, what would and could you have done? In this instance, the CP practitioner assisted the projects with writing their proposals by reviewing and commenting on drafts, writing the needs assessment, and writing the evaluation plan; provided guidance for developing the community impact section; helped with selection of areas to be served; and advised on which level the programs were most suited to apply for. As an external partner, she had little say in what the organization would do if the funding application was not successful.

What is the lesson in here regarding the application of the competencies? There are two ways a CP practitioner can go. The first is to adopt the Fairweather model, dedicate yourself to the problem, and spend a large chunk of your career systematically developing an innovative, replicable, and sustainable solution, such as the Community Lodge. It is notable that many graduates from the Michigan State University doctoral program who studied with Fairweather took this path. For example, Denis Gray got involved early on in the Industry-University Collaborative Research Centers program at the National Science Foundation (NSF), and has spent over 35 years improving assessment practices, identifying paths for program enhancement, and disseminating what is being learned. In other words he is engaging in long-term advocacy efforts that include studying the problem and gathering data, developing policy alternatives to address it, then advocating for policy change, as Jason, Beasley, and Hunter described in Chapter 10.

The second direction that may be taken is to go beyond "program" development to addressing root causes of the problems. For example, there is increasing evidence that the stress of racism plays a role in continuing the health disparities between Whites and Blacks. Programs are not going to fix this. The solution will entail long-term, systematic identification and eradication of institutionalized racism that is prevalent in our schools, criminal justice system, workplaces, and even our medical care. One potential shortcoming of this path is that the links between presumed causal relationships and programs that might provide tangible improvements in life chances are often very weak. It may lead to a career of feckless ranting without getting into the guts of the problem environment.

THE FUTURE OF DISSEMINATION AND SUSTAINABILITY IN COMMUNITY PSYCHOLOGY PRACTICE

Dissemination and sustainability have received relatively little attention within CP practice or, for that matter, within the social innovation fields overall. The bourgeoning field of dissemination and implementation science originates within the university, and government realms can run the risk of promulgating the top-down approach. This leaves a great deal of room to develop better strategies and competencies in this area. Before discussing why this is so and what we can do about it, the term *program replicates* needs further discussion. Earlier in this chapter we described the need to understand and hopefully quantitatively verify the key program activities and activities that produce outcomes. There is an interesting research literature that points out that partial or *faux* replicates do not yield the same positive outcomes with clients or participants. The work of Blakeley, Emshoff, and Roitman (1984) is very illustrative in the area of social and educational programs, indicating that the extent of deviation from the original model program is associated with an attenuation of positive outcomes.

Scheirer (2013) has focused on health-related interventions and commented extensively on the linkages between the complexity and scope of interventions and their likelihood to be soundly replicated and continued. In effect, one may spend lots of time trying to foster replicates, but if not focused on the specific practices and procedures that are associated with positive program outcomes, the results may be weak or disastrous. So, one may achieve "sustainability" in terms of ostensible replicates dotting the landscape but many will be faux replicates and weak in terms of results.

Sometimes there are programs or organizational functions that are embedded within a much larger organizational context, and where there are clear differences in desirable outcomes, but where the potential impacts of causal variables are difficult to sort out. In other words, something good is happening in settings A, B, C, and D, but it is not clear why outcomes are better than those in settings E, F, G, and H. It is not clear where the boundaries of the "program" lie and what the key causal elements are. In terms of classic research design, we might want to set up a matched and random assignment experimental design to see what impacts what. However, while that might be great for rabbits and rats, it is not usually viable for problems in which the experimental unit is much larger.

Answering this question and others like it gets tricky. For one, the relevant activities and variables are not easily confined in one organizational locus. While all research universities have something called a technology transfer office (TTO) where a lot of dissemination happens, some of the most relevant behavior occurs elsewhere, such as back in the faculty inventor's department. There are often wide differences of opinion across department heads and deans, within the same institution, about the desirability of spending time on dissemination and sustainability. This sometimes gets expressed formally or informally in tenure track evaluation criteria. In addition, changes in senior university leadership—president, provost, vice president for research—are often accompanied by changed views about whether or not a faculty member should pursue an innovation.

Some of the relevant behavior for disseminating innovations occurs outside the organizational context of the university per se, in the density of relationships between TTO staff and external stakeholders, which introduces interesting causal relationships. Or even if we have a TTO that is richly staffed in terms of head count, TTOs differ in the extent of relevant knowledge in those heads or whether they will engage in transferring social technologies that will likely bring little or new return for the investment. For example, if the TTO head has started two companies over the past 10 years or, in the case of transferring social technologies, worked in nonprofit community-based settings, she or he may better advise and encourage others. And it also seems to be the case (a working hypothesis at least) that universities that are good at this often have presidents who serve as champions and create a rewarding organizational culture. Finally, in a big university of thousands of faculty and students and large budgets, it is really mostly impossible to stop the existing program in order to do experiments.

There are a lot of program and problem settings where this is the case, particularly when addressing the usual practice domains of community psychology, as well as the more expanded problem set which we will advocate at the end of this chapter. The community is a messy venue. Lots of things are happening and it is hard to sort stuff out while they are.

Typically the developer and disseminator of an innovation might want to track a number of program examples in parallel and/or over time, keeping track of some hopefully quantitative outcomes, but also—most importantly—developing longitudinal histories of what is happening in terms of events or program activities that might be influencing outcomes. In effect, she or he could and should do some parallel case studies to see what can be teased out in terms of Yes-No or ordinal metrics and that might be related to differences in outcomes across sites and settings.

This is considered testing the *counterfactual case*. That is, trying to identify which qualitative phenomena, which might be converted into a quantitative metric, are instrumental in outcomes of interest to us, and there is much support for mixed-method designs in implementation and dissemination research (Palinkas et al., 2011). It means laboring over very rich descriptive cases of a sample of organizations, holding constant what would obviously be causal in our outcomes of interests (such as the amount of research in this example), and then sorting out evidence of practices, policies, cultural values, and the like being related to the outcomes of interest.

The converting of qualitative information to something that can be counted has much utility for verifying some outcomes of interest. But the value of qualitative analysis and descriptions goes beyond the situation just described. One really can't express the nuances of a complex community or organizational program in summary statistics. The more qualitative examples we have of programs having impact, but in perhaps slightly different ways and nuances, the richer portfolio we have of what a community program is all about.

Take an example that has preoccupied one of the authors for over 20 years, and that is approximated by the Innovation U example in this chapter that, truth be told, is not really "fake." That is, the relative ability of universities to encourage faculty invention, protect those inventions, and "transfer" those inventions to established or new companies so that wealth and/or jobs might result and there are more paths in a society via which to prosper. While this work has been primarily conducted in regard to hard technologies, social sciences could also benefit from such approaches and lessons learned regarding the transfer and sustainability of social technologies.

The literature on sustainable programs is probably more focused forward (what are features of sustainable programs) then demonstrating long-term sustainability achieved. Recently Denis

Gray and colleagues (Gray, Sundstrom, Tornatzky, & McGowen, 2011; Gray, Tornatzky, McGowen, & Sundstrom, 2012) have been conducting a series of case studies of the latter phenomenon to see if there are predictors or after-the-fact explanations of program sustainability.

In the early 1980s the National Science Foundation launched and supported a division that was focused on "industrial" programs, and several of the constituted programs still survive. It was and is called the Industry-University Cooperative Research Centers (IUCRC) program (see www.nsf.gov/eng/iip/iucrc/ for more information about this initiative). Most important for our discussion here, after a 1- to 2-year trial run in the 1980s most of the program features and procedures were pretty much locked in place. In addition, from the onset of the program there has been an annual process-outcome evaluation research data-gathering program that was overseen by the NSF program. This was supplemented by occasional policy/practice research projects that addressed a question of interest to the company members, the NSF, and the participating universities. A program practice and policy book was commissioned in the 1990s and has been the cookbook of the program ever since. Each of the Centers has a designated center evaluator who is on a separate contract with the NSF and data were gathered on technical and attitudinal outcomes from both university and industry participants. That data set now encompasses outcomes and processes for over 30 years and has been mined for ideas to tune the program in terms of procedures and approaches.

In the last 5 years an opportunity emerged for looking at long-term sustainability of this kind of program innovation. It was discovered that among the Centers that were launched in the 1980s a number were still in operation, still executing for the most part the original IUCRC program, many with much larger budgets coming exclusively from member companies and looking forward to continuing on after many of the original founding faculty had retired or died. The implications are astounding. Thus, after a modest initial public investment many of the Centers persist as industry cooperatives with significant positive outcomes for companies.

Recently, a 2-year study was commissioned by the NSF to explore why/how a number of early Centers had survived and often prospered. This effort is summarized in detail in the cited works above but some findings seem to stand out. This entire group of "long-term sustainers" had developed very excellent approaches to leadership continuity and transfer—there was no hiatus. All had been responsive to national or international shifts in the locus of relevant industry partners and program tactics were tuned accordingly. For example, as big steel moved from a predominately North American industry to an international industry, the Center shifted accordingly. All the long-term sustainers had supplemented their program approaches beyond the all-members-deciding-on-projects model to one that had different kinds of cooperative models that companies could choose from.

The point is that here is a great example of a program innovation that was explicitly modeled and structured from the onset based on research findings, where the key operating and structural variables were maintained over time and ongoing outcome and process variables were closely monitored. It has lasted and thrived for over 30 years. There are potential lessons here for community psychology.

While CP practice is often to some extent interdisciplinary, our collaborations are usually with disciplines that are similar to our own, such as public health and social work. Some of the examples and lessons shared in this chapter come from business and industry. In the future, CP practitioners might benefit from hanging out with those in disciplines that are outside of the social science realm, such as physicists, engineers, urban planners, graphic designers, and English majors.

Take for example the field of marketing. Over years we have all watched corporations convince the masses that cereals comprised primarily of sugar are healthy for children and all little girls require paraphernalia that will transform them into Disney princesses. We snarl about corporate greed and how it capitalizes on brainwashing small children. What we do not admit is that they have found very effective ways to influence thinking and they are essentially the masters of the science of persuasion en masse. In the future, it may be beneficial for aspiring CP practitioner training to venture into the marketing field, such as taking marketing classes or interning in corporate marketing departments so as to better incorporate its substantial knowledge into one's community work.

As demonstrated in the Healthy Start example, the future of social innovation will not lie in government-funded 5-year programs. It will lie in creating more "programmatic" solutions that assess what is being done, what works and does not work, and then finding ways to replace what is not working with innovative, systematically developed alternatives. Rather than developing programs that are asides from business-as-usual and serve 200 people a year, we need to address the root causes of social ills. It will also require working toward larger scale change such as that described by Jason, Beasley, and Hunter in Chapter 10. It will require a paradigm shift from the individual approaches of changing people to a systems approach to changing the context and systems.

Finally, while CP has, as a rule, paid little attention to dissemination methods and done little to promote sustainability, this is an area that is deserving of more attention and development. When we find something that works well and can have a major impact on our world, we need to consider it our moral obligation to disseminate and sustain it. What if Jonas Salk discovered and developed the polio vaccine, published it in some obscure journal, and went on to study something else? What if Charles Drew never shared his method of separating red blood cells from plasma, other than to present it at some obscure regional conference? While what we are doing does not "save lives" in the way that medical practices do, social innovations potentially save and/or transform lives in equally valuable ways. Future CP practitioners who are developing and implementing programs or advocating for local policy changes might consider extending their work to include a commitment to disseminating and sustaining "what works." They might also consider seeking a work setting that will allow them to conduct research that will advance our knowledge of effective dissemination and sustainability practices.

SUMMARY

Key Points

- Prior to disseminating a program or policy it is important to identify and clearly define the core components.
- Successful dissemination requires a systematic, long-term, hands-on approach that is attentive to the match between the features of the innovation being disseminated and

the features of the community or organization adopting and implementing it.

- Sustainability should be considered from the moment an innovation is conceptualized and should be built into the design, implementation, and dissemination processes.
- Innovations that change existing structures and that are set in policy are more sustainable than programs that are add-ons to institutionalized practices.
- We still know little about effective dissemination and sustainability strategies; there is room for a lot more work in this area.
- Dissemination and sustainability practice would benefit from a more interdisciplinary approach that includes going outside of the social sciences for training and collaboration.

DISCUSSION QUESTIONS

1. You are interested in reducing poverty in your community. What steps would you take to develop an innovative solution, disseminate, and sustain it?

2. In looking at the current system for funding social innovation (e.g., government and foundation grants), what could be done differently that would promote dissemination of social innovations that work and their sustainability?

KEY TERMS AND DEFINITIONS

Activation phase: The phase in which an innovation moves from adoption to implementation.

Approach phase: The phase in which the potential target population moves from being unaware of an innovation to awareness.

Critical psychology: A variety of approaches that challenge mainstream psychology's assumptions and practices that help sustain unjust political, economic, and other societal structures.

Diffusion: The distribution of practices or natural phenomena across broad systems via methods that may or may not be intentional.

Diffusion phase: The phase in which the target population spreads an innovation by expanding it within their own organization or persuading other groups or organizations to adopt it.

Dissemination: The intentional, systematic distribution of interventions to a targeted group of stakeholders for the purpose of changing or influencing practice or policy.

Gatekeepers: Individuals or groups who control the amount and content of information that may be utilized in the decision process.

Implementation: "The use of strategies to adopt and integrate evidence-based health interventions and change practice patterns within specific settings" (Chambers, 2009).

Implementation fidelity: The degree to which an intervention or program is delivered as intended.

Innovation: The situationally new development and introduction of knowledge-derived tools, artifacts, and devices by which people extend and interact with their environment.

Innovation assassin: A person or persons who attempt to influence decision makers to reject an innovation.

Innovation champion: An advocate who works at gaining support for change.

Persuasion phase: When a target population moves from a state of awareness about an innovation to making a decision about whether to adopt the innovation.

Prevention delivery system: A system whereby innovations are implemented in the field.

Program: A set of resources and activities directed toward a set of common goals.

Sustainability: "The continuation of activities or benefits for target recipients after an initial period of funding ends or following the initial implementation of a new program or procedure" (Scheirer, 2013, p. e1).

Sustainability capacity: The structures and processes that allow a program to harness resources to effectively implement and maintain a program.

RESOURCES

Classic Books

Fairweather, G. W., & Davidson, W. S. (1986). *An introduction to community experimentation: Theory, methods and practice*. New York, NY: McGraw-Hill. [See chap. 11 for a model for an experimental approach to dissemination.]

Fairweather, G. W., Sanders, D. H., & Tornatzky, L. G. (1974). *Creating change in mental health organizations*. Elmsford, NY: Pergamon. [This book describes the first national experiment that systematically evaluated social change processes. It provides a case example of the authors' research on disseminating the lodge society to 255 mental health hospitals throughout the United States.]

Tornatzky, L. G., Fergus, E. O., Avellar, J. W., Fairweather, G. W., & Fleischer, M. (1980). *Innovation and social process: A national experiment in implementing social technology*. New York, NY: Pergamon.

Websites

Anderson, A. A. (2005). *The community builder's approach to theory f change: A Practical guide to theory development*. Washington, DC: Aspen Institute. http://www.aspeninstitute.org/sites/default/files/content/docs/rcc/rcccommbuildersapproach.pdf

Global Implementation Conference: http://globalimplementation.org/gic/

Prevention Research Center: http://prcstl.wustl.edu/training/Pages/MTDIRC.aspx

Seattle Implementation Research Collaborative (SIRC): http://www.seattleimplementation.org/

REFERENCES

Anderson, A. A. (2005). *The community builder's approach to theory of change: A practical guide to theory development*. Washington, DC: Aspen Institute.

Blakely, C. H., Emshoff, J. G., & Roitman, D. B. (1984). Implementing innovative programs in public sector organizations. *Applied Social Psychology, 5*, 87–108.

Bond, M. A. (2007). *Workplace chemistry: Promoting diversity through organizational change*. Lebanon, NH: University Press of New England.

Caroll, C., Patterson, M., Wood, S., Booth, A., Rick, J., & Balain, S. (2007). A conceptual framework for implementation fidelity. *Implementation Science, 2*(40). Retrieved from http://www.implementation science.com/content/2/1/40

Chambers, D. A. (2009, January). *Dissemination and implementation research in health: An overview of PARs 06-520, 06-521, 07-086*. Paper presented at the 2nd Annual NIH Conference on the Science of Dissemination and Implementation: Building Research Capacity to Bridge the Gap from Science to Service, Bethesda, MD. Accessed at: http://obssr.od.nih.gov/news_and_events/conferences_and_ workshops/DI2009/02_Speaker%20Presentations/Plenary/Opening_Day2_Chambers.pdf

Chambers, D. A., Ringeisen, H., & Hickman, E. E. (2005). Federal, state, and foundation initiatives around evidence-based practices for child and adolescent mental health. *Child & Adolescent Psychiatric Clinics of North American, 14*(2), 307–327.

Dalton, J., & Wolfe, S. (Eds.). (2012). Joint Column: Education connection and the community practitioner. *The Community Psychologist, 45*(4), 7–13.

Fairweather, G. W. (Ed.). (1980). *The Fairweather Lodge: A twenty-five year retrospective*. San Francisco, CA: Jossey-Bass.

Fairweather, G. W., & Davidson, W. S. (1986). *An introduction to community experimentation: Theory, methods and practice*. New York, NY: McGraw-Hill.

Fairweather, G. W., & Tornatzky, L. G. (1977). *Experimental methods for social policy research*. New York, NY: Pergamon.

Fox, D., Prilleltensky, I., & Austin, S. (2009). *Critical psychology: An introduction*. Thousand Oaks, CA: Sage.

Gray, D. O., Sundstrom, E., Tornatzky, L. G., & McGowen, D. (2011). When triple helix unravels: A multi-case analysis of failures in industry-university cooperative research centers. *Industry and Higher Education, 25*(5), 333–345.

Gray, D. O., Tornatzky, L., McGowen, L., & Sundstrom, E. (2012). *Research center sustainability and survival: Case studies of fidelity, reinvention and leadership of industry/university cooperative research centers*. Arlington, VA: National Science Foundation.

Havelock, R. G. (1971). *Planning for innovation through dissemination and utilization of knowledge*. Ann Arbor: Center for Research on Utilization of Scientific Knowledge, Institute for Social Research, University of Michigan.

Kreuter, M. W., & Bernhardt, J. M. (2009). Reframing the dissemination challenge: A marketing and distribution perspective. *American Journal of Public Health, 99*(12), 2123–2127.

Lomas, J. (1993). Diffusion, dissemination, and implementation: Who should do what? *Annals of the New York Academy of Sciences, 703*(1), 226–237.

Newcomer, K. E., Hatry, H. P., & Wholey, H. P. (1994). Meeting the need for practical evaluation approaches: An introduction. In J. S. Wholey, H. P. Hatry, & Newcomer, K. E. (Eds.), *Handbook of practical program evaluation* (pp. 1–10). San Francisco, CA: Jossey-Bass.

Palinkas, L. A., Aarons, G. A., Horwitz, S., Chamberlain, P., Hurlburt, M., & Landsverk, J. (2011). Mixed method designs in implementation research. *Administrative Policy Mental Health, 38*(1), 44–53.

Rogers, E. M. (1962). *Diffusion of innovations*. New York, NY: Free Press.

Ruzek, J. I., & Rosen, R. C. (2009). Disseminating evidence-based treatments for PTSD in organizational settings: A high priority focus area. *Behaviour Research and Therapy, 47*(11), 980–989.

Sandler, J. (2007). Community-based practices: Integrating dissemination theory with critical theories of power and justice. *American Journal of Community Psychology, 40,* 272–289.

Scheirer, M. A. (2005). Is sustainability possible? A review and commentary on empirical studies of program sustainability. *American Journal of Evaluation, 26*(3), 320–347.

Scheirer, M. A. (2013). Linking sustainability research to intervention types. *American Journal of Public Health.* doi:10.2105/AJPH.2012.300976

Schell, S., Luke, D., Schooley, M., Elliott, M., Herbers, S., Mueller, N., & Bunger, A. (2013). Public health program capacity for sustainability: A new framework. *Implementation Science, 8*(1), 15.

Schoenwald, S. K., McHugh, R. K., & Barlow, D. H. (2012). The science of dissemination and implementation. In R. K McHugh & D. H. Barlow (Eds.), *Dissemination and implementation of evidence-based psychological interventions* (pp.16–42). New York, NY: Oxford University Press.

Stamatakis, K., Norton, W., Stirman, S., Melvin, C., & Brownson, R. (2013). Developing the next generation of dissemination and implementation researchers: Insights from initial trainees. *Implementation Science, 8*(1), 29.

Tornatzky, L. G., Fergus, E. O., Avellar, J. W., Fairweather, G. W., & Fleischer, M. (1980). *Innovation and social process: A national experiment in implementing social technology.* New York, NY: Pergamon.

Tornatzky, L. G., & Fleischer, M. (Eds.). (1990). *The processes of technological innovation.* Lexington, MA: Lexington Books.

Tornatzky, L. G., Gray, D. O., Tarant, S. A., & Howe, J. E. (1998). *Where have all the students gone? Interstate migration of recent science and engineering graduates.* Research Triangle Park, NC: Southern Technology Council.

Tornatzky, L. G., & Rideout, E. (2014). *Innovation U 2.0: Reinventing university roles in a knowledge economy.* Research Triangle Park, NC: Southern Growth Policies Board.

Tornatzky, L. G., Waugaman, P. G., & Gray, D. O. (2002). *Innovation U: New university roles in a knowledge economy.* Research Triangle Park, NC: Southern Growth Policies Board.

Trickett, E. J. (1996). A future for community psychology: The contexts of diversity and the diversity of contexts. *American Journal of Community Psychology, 24*(2), 209–234.

Wandersman, A., Duffy, J., Flaspohler, P., Noonan, R., Lubell, K., Stillman, L., Saul, J. (2008). Bridging the gap between prevention research and practice: The interactive systems framework for dissemination and implementation. *American Journal of Community Psychology, 41,* 171–181.

Wolfe, S. M., Fleischer, M., Morrell, J. A., & Eveland, J. D. (1990). Decision processes in technological innovation. In L. G. Tornatzky & M. Fleischer (Eds.), *The processes of technological innovation.* Lexington, MA: Lexington Books.

Yin, R. K. (1981). The case study as a serious research strategy. *Science Communication, 3*(1), 97–114.

Community Psychology Education and Practice Careers in the 21st Century

Susan D. McMahon, Tiffeny R. Jimenez, Meg A. Bond, Susan M. Wolfe, and Allen W. Ratcliffe*

Note: Susan D. McMahon, Tiffeny R. Jimenez, and Meg A. Bond were the lead authors on the education portion of this chapter, while Susan M. Wolfe and Allen W. Ratcliff were the lead authors on the career portion.

EDUCATION FOR COMMUNITY PSYCHOLOGY PRACTICE

Community psychologists go beyond an individual focus and integrate social, cultural, economic, political, environmental, and international influences to promote health and empowerment at individual and systemic levels. We engage in action-oriented research to promote social justice and action, influence public policy, and work toward empowerment. We are driven by egalitarian values, celebrate culture and diversity, and support individual and community strengths. We strive to understand behavior in context, reduce oppression, prevent harm, and promote well-being through multidisciplinary scientific inquiry and collaboration. We aspire to ensure that views consistent with community psychology, such as recognizing the importance of environment, culture, and context, become woven into the fabric of our society. As a field, we need to be focused and purposeful in how we prepare community psychologists for a broad range of roles that are anchored in these values. We also need to be explicit regarding the preparation students receive in various types of educational programs, how this training is linked with career opportunities, and how students can promote their skills and engage in meaningful careers in community psychology.

In this chapter, we explore multiple types of educational programs and comment on the goals and challenges we face at each level—undergraduate, master's and doctoral. We examine the practice competencies that programs are fostering and how we, as a field, can enhance education of community psychology practice competencies. Then we turn to an exploration of the wide variety of settings in which community psychologists can and do work, such as academic, healthcare and health promotion, nonprofit and community-based organizations, education, government, community planning and economic development, criminal justice, foundations, community development, research and evaluation, consulting, and business. Strategies for seeking and applying for positions are reviewed and resources are provided. Finally, we offer suggestions for future directions and opportunities to enhance educational opportunities and promote greater visibility of our field. Unfortunately, there is a dearth of research that focuses on education and/or career opportunities; thus, in addition to a review of existing literature, we have drawn upon our personal knowledge and experience.

WHAT TYPES OF COMMUNITY PSYCHOLOGY EDUCATIONAL PROGRAMS EXIST?

There are a variety of educational degree programs in community psychology. While most are founded upon a recognition that we need to prepare students to engage in a variety of careers and settings, the programs vary widely in the extent to which they emphasize practice competencies. Most community psychology programs are at the master's or doctoral levels and include some level of training in community practice competencies; however, undergraduate education in community psychology also provides an important venue for students to learn about the field and develop practice competencies that can be useful to community-based organizations.

Undergraduate Education

Although community psychology has a lot to offer undergraduate students in terms of values, empirical research, and competencies, relatively few universities have undergraduate courses in community psychology. For those that do, there is typically a single course within the broader psychology curriculum. There are a handful of colleges and universities that incorporate more in-depth coverage by either having a multi-course concentration in community psychology or providing more intensive study resulting in an undergraduate degree that is explicitly in community psychology (see http://www.scra27.org/what-we-do/education/academic-programs). Having a degree or concentration in community psychology typically allows students to apply knowledge and skills learned through a sequence of courses during a fieldwork experience that spans more than one term. These supervised applied experiences foster marketable competencies that can be useful in preparing for graduate school and for obtaining jobs, particularly with community-based organizations.

In addition to practical benefits for students, expanding coverage in the undergraduate curriculum can advance college and university missions by yielding students who are better prepared to be effective contributors within the workforce. In a survey of 160 leaders of 4-year colleges and universities, most (91%) indicated that their highest priorities for students were to prepare them to be successful in the global and local economy and to be knowledgeable, effective citizens more generally (Association of American Colleges and Universities [AACU], 2011). Further, in a survey of 305 employers and 510 recent college graduates, the large majority of both groups believe that more emphasis is needed to help students develop the ability to apply knowledge and skills to real-world settings through internships or other hands-on experiences (AACU, 2006). When evaluating potential new hires, employers place the most emphasis on teamwork skills and the ability to collaborate with others in a diverse group, critical thinking and analytical reasoning skills, and the ability to effectively communicate orally and in writing (AACU, 2006). Community psychology education incorporates all of these competencies, and associated fieldwork provides opportunities to practice the skills in real-world settings with diverse groups of people.

The types of fieldwork experiences that many community psychologists have incorporated into their courses since the inception of the field are now receiving more attention in the context of "service learning" (Campus Compact, 2012). The principles that guide service learning coincide well with core values and competencies of community psychology, such as respect for diversity, ecological analyses, social action goals, and collaboration (Reeb, 2010). The service learning movement emphasizes the ways in which experiences in the community can provide students with the opportunity to develop skills (e.g., Olney, Livingston, Fisch, & Talamantes, 2006) and to learn about the myriad ways that local agencies address social problems (Bringle & Steinberg, 2010). Engagement in community psychology service learning, in particular, has been found to foster students identifying more closely with their own heritage, observing positive community responses, becoming more involved in community activities in low-income neighborhoods, presenting at conferences, and applying to graduate school in community psychology and related areas (Davidson, Jimenez, Onifadee, & Hankins, 2010; Keys, Horner-Johnson, Weslock, Hernandez, & Vasiliauskas, 1999).

Thus, the development of community psychology undergraduate concentrations and programs can be a compelling way to meet student, university, and employer needs in an increasingly diverse society and global economy. In addition, there are benefits for our field of focusing advocacy efforts on expanding coverage at the undergraduate level, including growing awareness through better coverage in textbooks and building opportunities across a wide spectrum of community settings.

Master's Degree Programs

The master's programs in community research and action are variably framed as community psychology, community social psychology, clinical-community/counseling, and interdisciplinary programs in community research and action. There are about 45 master's programs in various countries around the world, including the United States, Puerto Rico, Canada, Mexico, Peru, Argentina, Chile, Venezuela, El Salvador, Australia, New Zealand, United Kingdom, Italy, Spain, Portugal, Greece, Egypt, Palestine, South Africa, Japan, and Malaysia (http://www.scra27.org/what-we-do/education/academic-programs/ for more information). Master's programs strive to include more intensive theory-practice integration than undergraduate programs, and many include a significant practice focus and intensive practicum experiences. While there is often curricular emphasis on action research, the main difference between master's and doctoral offerings is that the doctoral programs tend to cover more advanced data analysis and research methods (Dziadkowiec & Jimenez, 2009). Master's programs vary in terms of whether or not there is a master's thesis research requirement, but most place much less emphasis than doctoral programs on conducting independent research (i.e., dissertations).

While master's level education has often been seen as the lesser cousin to the doctoral degree (even the oppressed minority within psychology associations; Hayes-Thomas, 2012), in many countries, master's programs represent the most typical type of postgraduate programs. There is much about master's level training that is in particular sync with the values of community psychology, especially a clear emphasis on theory-practice integration. While some master's students enter such programs with a long-term goal of pursuing a doctorate, most are preparing for practice careers in community psychology. The focus on practice is reinforced by pressure within some universities for master's degrees to be competence-based and distinguished from doctoral programs with respect to the latter's emphasis on theory and the "production of new knowledge."

Several intersecting trends enable master's programs to be particularly well grounded in the community, another critical priority for community psychology training. Master's programs tend to draw diverse students from surrounding communities, particularly in public universities. Some of this local appeal may also be connected to the finding that master's students in general are less likely than doctoral students to enroll full time; only 32 % of master's students in most fields carry a full course load each year compared to 60 % of doctoral students (R. Brown, 2011). Many of those part-time students are employed full time (approximately 70 % of master's compared to 43 % of doctoral students), and thus many are already anchored in local community organizations. Additionally, master's programs place more graduates locally after graduation. Since the majority of students graduating from these programs are looking for applied positions, they may be less likely than those with academic aspirations to be engaged in national job searches. These dynamics combine to enhance opportunities for current students to link with local organizational leaders who have a deeper understanding of and appreciation for a degree in community psychology.

Doctoral Programs

Doctoral programs in community psychology tend to include advanced theory, practice, and comprehensive research competencies, and they prepare students for many career options, including academia, public policy, consultation, and other practice-oriented careers. There are about 46 community research and action doctoral programs that are community, clinical-community, or interdisciplinary, and span a variety of countries, such as the United States, Puerto Rico, Canada, Australia, New Zealand, and Malaysia (http://www.scra27.org/what-we-do/education/academic-programs). Most of these doctoral programs are in the United States and have a primary focus on research, but programs worldwide vary in the extent to which practice competencies are emphasized. We would argue that practice competencies are important for all programs and students, even for students who intend to go into academia.

The tradition of doctoral education has historically emphasized the discovery and production of new knowledge through field-specific, and often mentor-based, research opportunities (Austin & McDaniels, 2006). While the competencies emphasized in more traditional doctoral programs are well suited for preparing future professional academics (e.g., research, writing, statistics, community-based participatory methods), these competencies are transferrable to various community-based career types where writing and critical analysis skills are important (e.g., executive director of an organization, grant writer, evaluation consultant). However, doctoral education more broadly has received a fair amount of scrutiny over the last decade regarding the extent to which there is alignment between student goals, doctoral training, and skills needed for actual careers (Golde &

Dore, 2001; Walker, Golde, Jones, Conklin Bueschnel, & Hutchings, 2008). In an effort to address these issues, initiatives such as the *Carnegie Initiative on the Doctorate* have been designed to enhance the experience of doctoral education to be more supportive of student career needs and interests, such as developing a professional identity within a discipline (see http://gallery.carnegiefoundation.org/cid/).

Doctoral education in community psychology research and action is no exception to this phenomenon and has also undergone some level of scrutiny within the field. Some of the newer doctoral programs are focusing on action research and local impact to address the varied practice-based career goals of students and needs of local communities. These programs are seeking innovative ways to connect students to practice-based mentors and learning experiences outside of the institution. Nonetheless, the extent to which certain methodological tools are valued by and taught by doctoral programs varies depending on the academic values of the program's institution and the expertise of the faculty members who maintain the program (Braxton, Luckey, & Helland, 2002).

Practice competencies have value across many community psychology careers, and those in academia may be preparing students with a range of interests across multiple levels of training (e.g., undergraduate, master's, doctoral). In sum, there are a range of educational opportunities provided by programs at the undergraduate, master's, and doctoral levels. These programs vary by locale, and the competencies provided may vary by the country, institution, level, values, and expertise of those involved in training.

WHAT APPLIED COMPETENCIES ARE COMMUNITY PSYCHOLOGY PROGRAMS CURRENTLY FOSTERING?

As we consider all levels of education in community psychology, and the unique identity of a community psychologist across multiple career contexts, several questions arise: What educational opportunities are being provided to prepare students for careers that utilize community psychology practice competencies? How well are we doing as a field, in fostering the competencies that students need in order to obtain employment and become effective and successful community psychology practitioners? In this section, we review findings from surveys collected from education programs over the last decade to answer these questions.

Past surveys vary in their approach to assessing education in community psychology practice, yet all have contributed to a comprehensive understanding of graduate education in our field. A 2005 exploratory survey of program directors revealed four priority areas for education in community psychology practice emphasizing: (1) community-based intervention, (2) ecological or community/systems perspective, (3) work with diverse communities, and (4) community-based research (Gatlin, Rushenberg & Hazel, 2009). A few years later, a 2008 survey of master's and doctoral program directors assessed the extent to which programs emphasized practice competencies and identified 13 core competencies (Dziadkowiec & Jimenez, 2009). In 2011, Neigher and Ratcliffe assessed community psychologists' perceptions of graduate training and proficiency in certain skill sets; they found curricula tended to focus on community-based applied research, assessment, and evaluation; ecological systems theory; interventions; and program planning and development (endorsed by 80%–90% of survey respondents; Neigher & Ratcliffe, 2010; Ratcliffe, 2011). The results of these studies coalesce to suggest that community psychology training is geared toward fostering a diverse set of unique skills and proficiencies that prepare students for a variety of career options. Further, many community psychology graduate programs are more inclined to focus on community interventions and research and provide fewer opportunities for learning other methods of social and community change. However, it is important to be cautious about generalizing from these surveys to all higher educational programs in community psychology for several reasons, one of which is that most respondents were from programs based in the United States. Further, the fact that results were not tallied separately for master's and doctoral level training and that there were more respondents from doctoral versus master's programs further complicates interpretation.

In an effort to address some of the limitations of previous surveys, a recent survey attempted to capture a more nuanced and in-depth understanding of practice competencies in graduate education from the perspective of graduate students across master's and doctoral programs (K. Brown, Cardazone, Glantsman, Johnson-Hakim, & Lemke, 2014). Using the five competency domains and 18 core competencies of community psychology practice summarized by Dalton and Wolfe (2012), the 2014 report looked at how graduate students' perceptions of *actually receiving* education in the core competencies compared to the extent to which they *preferred to receive* such training. Overall, findings suggest students are interested in gaining more education in practice competencies than what they currently receive, and these gaps vary by program type.

More specifically, results indicated that students in master's programs perceive that they are receiving just slightly less than they preferred to receive in each of the 18 core competency areas, whereas doctoral students' expectations were far higher than their actual experiences. Among these ratings, both master's and doctoral students preferred their education to include curriculum on participatory action research, program development, and program evaluation; master's students, in particular, also expressed strong interest in coverage of empowerment-related topics. Students rated coverage of competencies on a 4-point scale: (1) not at all, (2) exposure, (3) experience, and (4) expertise. Overall, students from both types of programs perceived their programs to be providing education at the *exposure* level across all 18 core competencies. While both program types emphasize program evaluation, some differences between experiences of master's students and doctoral students included greater emphasis on ethical reflective practice and ecological perspectives within master's programs. Doctoral programs were described as providing more focus than master's programs on research/data focused competencies, such as participatory action research. Students at both levels expressed the desire to have more than *exposure* (i.e., actual *experience*) on all of the core competencies. It also appears that the longer students have been in their program, the lower their ratings of their program's actual coverage of many of the core competencies—indicating perhaps their disappointment and/or their increased desire for more intensive training as they move toward graduation.

These survey data provide a glimpse into some of the gaps that we can address to ensure early career community psychologists are prepared for the variety of careers they seek. For instance, the 2014 survey data suggest that alternative options for gaining experiences in competencies not commonly covered in graduate education opportunities may be needed. Some of the students' unmet learning goals included competencies such as resource development, consultation and organizational development, community development, prevention and promotion, as well as small and large group processes. Additionally, while we may be able to provide exposure to these various competency areas, it should be noted that it takes a significant amount of time and effort to gain in-depth experiences or become an expert in these skill sets, and it is not possible in any graduate education program to provide expertise across all competencies.

HOW CAN WE AS A FIELD ENHANCE EDUCATIONAL OPPORTUNITIES TO DEVELOP COMMUNITY PRACTICE COMPETENCIES?

There are two main ways that the field of community psychology can promote the preparedness of community psychologists to participate in addressing current real-world social issues: (1) education programs across levels can enhance their coverage of core competencies through innovative strategies, and (2) SCRA (Society for Community Research and Action) can expand awareness of our field through enhanced articulation, dissemination, outreach, and collaboration. With these two frames in mind, we provide several ideas for both goals.

Program Strategies

Community psychology programs may benefit from taking a multi-pronged approach to fostering the range of practice skills that students need. First, both graduate and undergraduate faculty could further examine the core competencies developed by the Community Psychology Practice Council (http://www.scra27.org/what-we-do/practice), reflect upon the competencies their program currently provides based on student and faculty input, prioritize what areas are the best fit for their specific program, and then build upon strengths and address weaknesses. They should then clearly communicate what they can provide to potential students.

Second, programs can intensify their field-based learning opportunities; there is no substitute for practical experience to develop competencies for work in real-world settings. Providing enhanced opportunities for supervised fieldwork, shadowing people engaged in practice, and developing community partnerships can augment currently existing student training and development. Ideally, these experiences should extend beyond a one quarter or one semester course to promote long-term engagement and an understanding of a system's history, trajectory, and relationship to other community entities as well as of the constituencies and/or populations served. Time and structured mechanisms allowing for reflection also need to be built into the experience.

Third, graduate programs may consider creating a practice track or individualized educational experiences tailored for placement into particular career positions. These approaches could involve directing students to available classes and experiences outside of the psychology department as well as to community-based or government-based opportunities.

Fourth, educational programs may build stronger bridges to local community psychology practitioners. Through allowing students to partner with practitioner colleagues (through volunteer work, fieldwork/practica, internships, or postdoctoral positions), we can augment existing opportunities for students to learn from seasoned professional practitioners in the field. Students can also serve as resources for practitioners through assisting with various tasks (e.g., literature reviews, data analysis, project leadership), depending on the skill levels, time commitments, and needs. These varied models all provide mutual learning opportunities that could help address some of the barriers for practitioners in applied careers (Jenkins, 2010), while also providing important linkages for students.

Fifth, from a practice-based career lens, community psychology programs can consider settings where community psychologists may not be such an obvious fit but where their perspectives and skill sets can be valuable in promoting healthy community development and social justice. Programs could partner with industry to explore how community psychology competencies can help organizations compete in the global market. For example, there are various companies interested in being more socially conscious, and a community psychologist would be a nice fit with that aim (see Bond, 2007, for an example of community psychology work in a manufacturing firm). Programs can also consider the local (and not so local) connections they can make with other types of for-profit organizations as well as with community-based organizations that may not immediately come to mind since they are not explicitly human service oriented (such as libraries, museums, and state and national parks). Intentional partnerships with a wide variety of organizations can lead to creative opportunities for our students and graduates. Given increasing globalization, linkages with our international counterparts and creation of fieldwork experiences in other countries—as well as in international organizations—can also enhance student experiences and development of core practice competencies.

One of the potential advantages of higher education in community psychology—whether at the master's or doctoral level—is the ability to pursue a variety of career options, and yet students still express concern about what they will do with a degree in community psychology. Faculty and staff within training programs need to do a better job of fostering, communicating, and marketing the competencies that students need to be effective in the workplace, confident about their career options, and marketable to employers. The increasingly relevant demands to engage in translational, interdisciplinary research that addresses real-world problems are complemented by the values in our field, our interest in effecting positive change at multiple levels, and our practice competencies. Some educational programs may provide specialized training experiences (Sarkisian & Jimenez, 2011); not all programs need to do all things, but programs should be clear about what they provide. All programs could benefit from reflecting upon the extent to which practice competencies are taught in their programs and how their graduate training prepares future community psychologists for various practice roles.

Strategies for Our Field

SCRA is working on several strategies to promote practice in education, and there is room for additional efforts. For example, the survey results discussed above have led to the identification of needs and compared them to what community psychology educational programs are currently providing. To address the gaps, we need to further articulate the competencies or principles that make our field distinctive. Disseminating information and increasing recognition of these core competencies can aid efforts toward communicating what is distinctive about community psychology. If we are more purposeful about what we do and what competencies we foster, students can become more informed consumers of their education and target their choices based upon the specific competencies they hope to develop.

We can enhance the understanding and awareness of community psychology among students, employers, and the public more broadly through several strategies: (1) create more programs at the undergraduate, master's and doctoral levels; (2) increase outreach efforts to local and national organizations to increase awareness of our competencies and the fit with their work; (3) use technology and social media more effectively to increase visibility of good work in the field, such as through videos that illustrate exemplary projects, public discourse on social issues, search engines that prioritize community psychology information, and online courses; (4) create more linkages with other organizations—both within psychology and in related fields—that have similar values; and (5) look for opportunities to introduce ourselves as community psychologists and provide brief bullet points about the field and what we do. These types of efforts may contribute to growing and strengthening our educational programs and outreach and building opportunities for our graduates.

SCRA also needs to continue to identify effective ways to include and address the needs of practitioners in community psychology publications, meetings, and within the professional organization (Jenkins, 2010). Once people who are trained in community psychology become full-time practitioners, it is somewhat more difficult—but nonetheless important—to find meaningful ways to stay connected to the field as a whole. The field risks losing the tremendous applied wisdom that can further enhance our understanding of how best to promote community change.

A unique collaboration between the SCRA Council of Education Programs (CEP) and the SCRA Community Psychology Practice Council is designed to address the dual goals of attending to core competencies and of linking educational programs with skilled community practitioners. For example, a Joint Task Group established in 2012 secured SCRA funding so that community psychology practitioners could consult with relatively new graduate programs at The American University of Cairo and Pacifica Graduate Institute. The goals of the consultation were to help the educational programs with assessment and planning and with paying particular attention to community psychology competencies as they developed their programs. These types of efforts can support the thoughtful and creative integration of practice competencies into new programs.

Another example of innovative efforts within SCRA to promote practice education is the recently established Professional Development Committee. The committee's mission is to support and promote professional development for all SCRA members. The Professional Development Committee recently adopted five goals: (1) to plan and implement the SCRA Summer Institute that will serve as pre-conference workshops for Biennial conferences and stand-alone opportunities in years when there is no Biennial; (2) to plan and implement online learning opportunities; (3) to plan and implement a mentoring program that will serve students, early career, mid-career and late-career SCRA members; (4) to provide quality programming each year at the American Psychological Association conference; and (5) to identify and publicize professional development opportunities by SCRA and other sources. These strategies can provide valuable information and linkages for education and employment.

PRACTICE-ORIENTED COMMUNITY PSYCHOLOGY CAREERS

Students who are not inclined toward academic careers or who are not sure about their career paths often ask, "What kind of job can I get with a degree in community psychology?" In this section of the chapter we provide a description of the types of jobs that community psychologists have held and the competencies required for each. As discussed in the first part of this chapter, introduction to community psychology and relevant competencies may begin at the undergraduate, master's, or doctoral level, as students create their educational experience with advisors and begin to position themselves for the career of interest. We now turn to helping aspiring and current community psychologists see the range of applied career options that are available and providing information about the competencies tapped in a variety of settings. We also identify some steps community psychologists can take to prepare for the types of jobs that interest them, prepare for the job search, find jobs that fit their interests and competencies, and apply for and land the job. See McMahon & Wolfe (in press) for more information on community psychology careers.

Employment ads in community-based settings rarely say "Seeking a Community Psychologist." During job interviews, a question often asked by employers is "What is community psychology?" However, a closer look at the skills sought in many job postings reveals that many employers are, in fact, seeking a person with community psychology competencies; they just don't know it. Yet, there is increasing recognition among employers of the importance of taking a comprehensive, preventative, ecological, or systems approach to planning, implementing, and evaluating policies and programs. Implementation skills are needed to put theory, research, and policy priorities into action in challenging and divergent settings. Hiring individuals with a community psychology skill set adds value and is cost-effective across a wide employment spectrum, especially if the applicant also has experience collaborating with other professions and citizens to accomplish results.

The *Community Psychology Value Proposition* developed by Ratcliffe and Neigher (2010) is one tool for introducing community psychology to a potential employer. It describes a number of qualities and competencies that community psychologists may possess that would be of value to employers in numerous industries and highlights the most frequent competencies presented by community psychologists. Chapter 2 in this volume provides more details and examples of value propositions. Community psychologists seeking jobs can use these documents as tools to help them to frame their presentation of competencies in cover letters, resumes, and job interviews. In other words, it can be helpful for preparing the answer to the "What is community psychology?" question.

SETTINGS WHERE COMMUNITY PSYCHOLOGY PRACTITIONERS WORK

The first step in preparing for a practice career is to gain some idea of what type of job might be a good fit with the community psychology (CP) practitioner's interests and competencies. CP practitioners work across a wide range of settings; Table 14.1 provides an initial list of some of the most common opportunities. The list, however, is by no means exhaustive since there is an endless number of applied settings where CP competencies are useful. Further, with the consistently changing economic, technological, and global landscapes, new settings will inevitably arise.

Health Care and Public Health

Community psychologists can find employment in medical centers, health insurance companies, or other health-care related organizations. Recognition of the need to adopt more collaborative approaches to health-care delivery along with the passage of the Affordable Care Act are two forces that suggest that there will be a growing need for CP practice competencies within such settings. Adoption of an ecological perspective is tremendously useful in efforts to promote optimal health and disease prevention. Most large medical centers have population medicine departments that provide statistics for grants, strategic planning, and monitoring of the community and environment.

Health-care institutions, including hospitals and community-based clinics, often rely on grants to fund needed services, research, and demonstration programs; so, they need skilled grant writers who understand the broader community context and the needs of multiple stakeholders. When projects are funded, they rely on individuals to implement, manage, and evaluate them. Medical centers that engage in teaching and research need individuals with good research and collaboration skills to assist the medical faculty and residents with design, data collection, and analysis. Health insurance companies employ analysts who can apply research and statistical expertise to make sense out of the large volume of data they gather. Public health departments are another option for people with community psychology–related skills. Positions in planning, project management, grants management, community outreach, service coordination, prevention and control units, and evaluation may all be fitting for CP practitioners.

Health-care related jobs can be found through networking with individuals who work in these settings, employment ads posted on the Internet by the individual institutions, professional association websites (e.g., American Public Health Association), and through listserv messages. Many health-care institutions offer internship opportunities for students, which is another way to get valuable experience as well as a foot in the door. CP competencies that may be useful or necessary are program development, implementation, and management; prevention and health promotion; resource development (especially grant writing); leadership and mentoring; consultation and organizational development; collaboration and coalition development; and community education, information dissemination, and building of public awareness—depending upon the position and setting. Courses in public health, epidemiology, and health policy may also be helpful. Schools of Public Health sometimes offer certificate programs with a specific focus, such as community health or maternal child health.

Table 14.1   Settings, Competencies, and Skills[1]

Setting	Community Psychology Practice Competencies		Other Training/Skills[4]
	Primary[2]	Secondary[3]	
Health Care/ Public Health	• Community research methods • Program development • Program implementation • Prevention/health promotion • Resource development • Grant writing	• Leadership/mentoring • Collaboration • Coalition development • Community education • Information dissemination	• Public health • Epidemiology • Health policy • Certification from School of Public Health • Strategic planning
Nonprofit Agencies and Community-Based Organizations	• Program evaluation • Needs/resource assessment • Resource development • Grant writing • Program development • Program implementation • Program management • Organizational development • Collaboration	• Coalition building • Community education • Information dissemination • Community leadership • Small/large-group process	• Internships • Volunteer work • Budgeting • Financial management • People management • Reporting • Strategic planning
Educational Settings	• Community research methods • Grant writing • Program development • Program implementation • Program evaluation • Needs/resource assessment	• Organizational capacity building • Information dissemination • Collaboration • Policy analysis • Resource development • Organizational development	• Statistics • Educational policy • Curriculum development • Administration • Strategic planning
Government	• Community research methods • Needs/resource assessment • Program evaluation • Program implementation • Program development • Policy analysis • Sustainability/ dissemination	• Information dissemination • Organizational capacity building • Grant writing	• Public health • Epidemiology • Social work • Public administration • Political science

(Continued)

Table 14.1 (Continued)

| Setting | Community Psychology Practice Competencies | | Other Training/Skills[4] |
	Primary[2]	Secondary[3]	
Criminal Justice Agencies	• Program evaluation • Policy analysis • Organizational capacity building • Coalition development • Program implementation • Program development	• Information dissemination • Prevention • Community education • Resource development • Grant writing • Consultation • Community development	• Criminal justice • Law
Foundations	• Program evaluation • Program development • Program implementation • Grant writing • Community leadership	• Prevention and health promotion • Community and organizational capacity building • Community development	• Budgeting • Financial management • Philanthropy
Community Development, Environmental and International Organizations	• Program evaluation • Grant writing • Organizational and community capacity building • Coalition development • Dissemination/ sustainability • Needs/resource assessment • Program development • Program implementation • Resource development • Policy analysis	• Small/large-group process • Information dissemination • Prevention and health promotion • Community development • Community leadership	• Environmental issues • International development • Languages • Public administration • Political science • Peace Corps or other international
Research and Evaluation Firms	• Community research methods • Grant writing • Program evaluation • Needs/resource assessment • Policy analysis	• Information dissemination • Consultation • Information dissemination	• Advanced statistics • Data management • Database development • Project management

| Setting | Community Psychology Practice Competencies | | Other Training/Skills[4] |
	Primary[2]	Secondary[3]	
Consulting	• Community research methods • Program evaluation • Grant writing • Organizational and community capacity building • Needs/resource assessment • Dissemination/ sustainability	• Community development • Policy analysis • Coalition development • Small/large-group process • Information dissemination • Collaboration	• Budgeting • Financial management • Business acumen • Advanced statistics • Data management • Database development • Project management • Reporting • Tolerance for ambiguity
Business, Technology, Entrepreneurship	• Community research methods • Program evaluation • Organizational capacity building • Needs/resource assessment • Small/large-group process • Information dissemination • Collaboration	• Community development • Policy analysis • Prevention and health promotion	• Organizational psychology • Master's in Business Administration • Entrepreneurship • Content/product specific knowledge
Academic, Nonfaculty	• Community research methods • Needs/resource assessment • Program evaluation • Grant writing • Program development • Program implementation	• Policy analysis • Program management • Community education • Information dissemination • Community leadership • Small/large-group process • Resource development • Consultation • Organizational development	• Project management • Budgeting • Financial management • People management • Reporting

[1]Understanding ecological systems, sociocultural competence, and professional judgment and ethics are required competencies for all of these settings. They are the hallmark combination of competencies for community psychology practitioners.

[2]These are the other training and skills an individual might consider cultivating to work in the chosen field.

[3]These are the skills an individual must develop when considering a career in this arena.

[4]These are the skills that will enhance and expand an individual's opportunities in the chosen field.

The Summer 2010 issue of *The Community Psychologist* features three CP practitioners who currently hold positions in health-care settings: (1) Rebecca Lee conducts research on ecological determinants of health at the University of Houston Medical Center; (2) David

Lounsbury works at Sloan Kettering Institute in New York where he conducts research on cancer prevention and control; and (3) William Neigher is Director of Strategic Planning for Atlantic Health in New Jersey (Neigher, Lounsbury, & Lee, 2010). Other CP practitioners engaged in health-care settings include D. Kay Taylor, who is currently the Director of the Hurley Research Center in Flint, Michigan. Her duties include designing, implementing, and evaluating community-based health programs. Susan Wolfe previously worked at Parkland Health and Hospital System as a program manager. In this role she oversaw a program serving pregnant adolescents, a program serving substance abusing pregnant women, and the county rape crisis center. She also developed and implemented a random-ized control trial design study assessing the comparative effectiveness of two different home visiting models with new parents.

Nonprofit Agencies and Community-Based Organizations

Nonprofit agencies and community-based organizations (CBOs) offer community psy-chologists opportunities to work directly in the community and to exercise a range of competencies. Such organizations most often provide services to youth, families, and other individuals. Examples include large, well-known organizations with local affiliates such as Girls, Inc., and Boys and Girls Clubs, as well as small, local organizations such as domestic violence shelters or food pantries. Most CBOs rely on grants or foundations for part or all of their funding and need people who can write grants and evaluate programs. For most CBOs, grant funding and working effectively to serve their consumers/constituents requires collaboration with other CBOs, consumers, and other interested parties. Most CBOs have an executive director who oversees the whole organization and takes on a range of other duties that depend on the size and organizational complexity of the specific CBO. In addi-tion to the top executive position, community psychologists have filled roles that include intern, program manager, community organizer, advocate, program evaluator, and grant writer for nonprofit institutions.

The applicability of CP competences depends on the mission and purpose of the orga-nization. All of the CP competencies are potentially relevant, with the specifics dependent upon such factors as the size, type, history, and position within the network of other com-munity- based organizations, as well as upon the specific the role of the community psy-chologist. Individuals working in CBOs often wear more than one hat, so it is advisable to develop multiple competencies to prepare for work in such organizations. CP practitioners may be hired to do a program evaluation, and then find there is a need for their other com-petencies, such as coalition building, resource development, or program design. Program evaluation in CBOs generally requires a solid understanding of program development, implementation and management, and dissemination. Finally, CP's ecological perspective includes understanding community needs and community networking to sustain the valu-able elements of a grant-funded program beyond the grant's expiration.

Developing competencies for working in nonprofits begins with academic coursework, but are further developed through exposure and experiences in the field. Internships and volunteer opportunities during undergraduate and graduate education and early career are beneficial. Such opportunities provide students and volunteers with exposure to the nonprofit sector and the specifics of a CBO setting so they can see firsthand which competencies are utilized, how they are applied, and what options there may be for gainful employment. Community psychologists who are already working in such settings can be a tremendous resource for those who want to learn what it takes to work with a nonprofit or CBO. In a 2012 issue of *The Community Psychologist,* Geraldine L. Palmer shared information about her experience as an executive director for a nonprofit. In addition to leadership skills required of such a high-level position, she also draws on competencies in community engagement, policy, and advocacy, and the ability to identify, select, and implement evidence-based models that are appropriate for the particular setting and community. Over his many years of experience in nonprofit settings, Chris Corbett (2012) has served as an intern, researcher, advocate, evaluator, and grant writer. Dawn Henderson (2012) used her evaluation skills as a volunteer in a nonprofit setting. As these examples demonstrate, there are a variety of roles a CP practitioner can fill in nonprofit organizations.

Work in international nonprofit organizations will likely require competence in speaking and writing a foreign language. Gaining employment in international organizations generally requires experience and exposure. There are often cultural and political sensitivities involved when engaging with nongovernmental organizations (NGOs), and many organizations have spent years gaining meaningful entry and cultivating trust and relationships. Many community psychologists have gained valuable experience by serving in the Peace Corp or by volunteering with relief organizations. Two community psychologists who were Peace Corp volunteers were Gloria Levin and Sharon Johnson-Hakim. The CDC and large research organizations sometimes offer opportunities for international work. Finding mentors and networking with others working overseas may also be an avenue for entry. The American Evaluation Association has an International and Cross Cultural Evaluation Topical Interest Group with over 950 members distributed worldwide. The American Public Health Association (APHA) has an International Health Section whose membership is comprised of public health professionals with international health interests; it is presented in the resource section of this chapter.

Education

Schools play a key role in children's development and are the one setting with which nearly all families in a community will connect. In fulfilling their role in service to the community, many schools develop programs and seek grants for prevention and intervention programs. Many schools work to involve parents and reach out to other local community members, and much of their funding requires evaluation. Most school districts rely on people with statistical backgrounds to help them make sense of the large volumes of data they gather (e.g., test scores, grades, surveys from teachers, parents, and students, attendance).

Over the past few years, educators have been drawn to more sophisticated statistical analyses to get the most from their data sets, such as value-added models (Sanders & Horn, 1998). These analyses require high level statistical understanding and analytic skills. Obtaining grants to develop more evidence-based education and social programming requires competencies, such as program development, grant writing, program implementation, and program evaluation. School districts need people with community organization and coalition competencies to develop initiatives to engage the community and parents. Additional skills and competencies that are useful are ecological systems thinking, unique methodological research tools (e.g., social network analysis), and organizational capacity building.

Community psychologists have worked in school districts as analysts in research and evaluation departments where they have had the opportunity to engage in a variety of projects, including evaluation of school reform, new initiatives, and programs for homeless students. Susan Ryerson-Espino worked in the research department of the Chicago Public Schools and Susan Wolfe worked in the evaluation department of the Fort Worth Independent School District. Others have worked in departments such as strategy and planning, parent engagement, and student services.

Government

There are many opportunities to utilize CP practice competencies at various levels of government—city, county, state, federal. At the federal level, CP practitioners have found employment with agencies that include the Government Accountability Office (GAO); the Department of Health and Human Services (DHHS), including the Office of the Inspector General's (OIG) Office of Evaluation and Inspections (OEI); the Centers for Disease Control and Prevention (CDC); the Department of Agriculture (USDA); the National Institutes of Health (NIH); and the National Institute on Drug Abuse (NIDA), There are many other possibilities as well.

State governments have departments of health and human services, departments of aging services, public safety departments, and departments of education to name a few. Cities and counties also have departments such as those in public health and social services that can benefit from the competencies CP practitioners possess. One CP practitioner, Debi Starnes, was elected to and served on the Atlanta City Council for 12 years and also served as policy advisor to Atlanta's mayor (Starnes, 2004).

Many government-related positions draw upon CP practice competencies. Federal opportunities are often positions such as "Health Scientist Administrator," "Grants Specialist," "Program Specialist," or "Program Analyst." Research and program evaluation competence is key; however, these positions also require competence in developing and implementing evidence-based prevention and intervention programs, policy analysis and development, an understanding of how to plan for sustainability, and information dissemination. At the state and local levels, the CP competencies most frequently needed vary widely as well. The focus is on meeting the needs of the local context, therefore, in many cases, taking a transdisciplinary approach is key. For example, it may be necessary to pull information and resources from other disciplines to identify the most appropriate tools for the job, such as public health (e.g., epidemiology, biostatistics), social work, business management, or public administration.

One avenue to gaining federal employment is to seek out internships during graduate school. There are year-round opportunities available for those living near Washington, D.C., or one of the cities where there is a regional office (Boston, New York, Philadelphia, Atlanta, Chicago, Dallas, Denver, Kansas City, San Francisco, or Seattle). States, cities, and counties may also offer local internship opportunities that will provide exposure and experience, and when they are not offered, there may be ways graduate program advisors can take an engaged scholar approach to assist in creating opportunities that provide a win-win for all involved in a mutually beneficial collaborative endeavor. Another avenue is to network with individuals who hold positions with government entities and peruse employment ads on relevant job sites (e.g., www.usajobs.gov). A number of community psychologists have held or currently hold positions with government entities. Some examples include Richard Jenkins (CDC and NIDA), Gloria Levin (NIH), Kelly Kinneson (USDA), Theresa Armstead (CDC), Carolyn Feis (GAO), and Susan Wolfe (DHHS OIG).

Community Planning and Development Organizations

Community planning and development can be viewed as "macro community psychology," ripe with opportunities to influence the health, safety, and quality of relationships among community citizens. Locally, opportunities can encompass city planning, architecture, and property development. At the state level, community psychologists may work in departments of community and/or economic development, ecology, and legislative affairs. Content knowledge and skills in policy planning and development can open doors for applicants.

Community planning and development was introduced to community psychology in the 1960s by Don Klein—a founder of what became SCRA—when he co-hosted a workshop at the new planned community of Columbia, Maryland, with its developer, James Rouse. Rouse described in detail the planning, design, and transitional governance process that would evolve as Columbia grew. Only a dozen or so community psychologists were present, and relatively little has been heard among community psychologists about formal employment in community planning and development organizations since then.

Yet, community planning and development offers fertile ground for application of community psychology competencies and for collaboration with planning and development professions, because so much information about the relationship between urban design, characteristics of settings, and human dignity and functioning now exists (see, for example, Montgomery, 2013). Several community psychology competencies are compatible within this domain: ecological perspectives, cultural and cross-cultural competencies, and community inclusion and partnership can add value to community planning and development. Elements of urban planning and health prevention and promotion can contribute to environmental impact assessment and mitigation. All of the community and organizational capacity-building competencies may apply to community input generation under specific circumstances, as do most of the community and social change competencies. Participatory and demographic community research results can help to undergird (or refute) proposed development plans. That said, awareness of, and comfort in, political processes is also very helpful.

A recent SCRA listserv query identified only four examples of formal work done on community planning projects. Al Ratcliffe consulted with an architectural firm and conducted a major demographic needs assessment as one element of the comprehensive Human Services Facilities Plan for the city, county, and the local United Way. Allegra Williams graduated from the University of Massachusetts–Lowell community psychology program and subsequently was employed by the city of Lowell as a Neighborhood Planner. Andrew Williams has done some collaboration recently with a landscape architect, and has been involved as an advocate protesting against a plan by his local public housing authority to construct public housing on a FEMA designated flood plain. Michael Lemke completed an internship with the Wichita–Sedgwick County Metropolitan Area Planning Department, Advanced Plans Division, working on bicycle and pedestrian issues. His work tasks have involved a number of different types of projects, including grant writing, annual reports, collaborative projects between other departments (including police, engineering, and parks and recreation), and helping with community engagement efforts. David Chavis's firm, Community Science, employs an urban planner in its Boston office. Currently, Vanderbilt University offers a master's degree in Community Development and Action. Other universities may have similar offerings.

Criminal Justice Agencies

Law enforcement and corrections organizations are interested in finding solutions that will help them better protect and serve their communities. They are especially interested in forming more effective partnerships with neighborhoods to prevent crime, and in finding effective alternatives to incarceration. Foundational community psychology values including an ecological (systems) perspective, sociocultural and cross-cultural competencies, and community inclusion/partnerships are critically relevant to current law enforcement thinking as leaders seek solutions to chronic and vexing challenges.

Law enforcement and corrections officials realize the importance of coalition building, reciprocal mentoring, and identification of shared goals in order to accomplish positive results. They are interested in finding research and developing best practices that can contribute to positive solutions, and in having that research presented in ways meaningful to both first responders and community citizens. They value training and consultation, data gathering and interpretation, applications of demographic data for preventive patrol, targeted interventions with neighborhoods, timely feedback, outcome evaluation, and training skills that strengthen solutions.

For those interested in working with law enforcement and corrections, it is important to start by learning about and understanding the cultures that exist within law enforcement agencies. There are clear cultural differences across various organizations, and law enforcement agencies are unique in that working in law enforcement and corrections takes some time and credibility, as well as trust-building, on both sides. Because the values of law enforcement and corrections institutions may not be in full alignment with community psychology values, people looking to work in this arena should be prepared to experience this shift, figure out if this is a good fit for them, and learn to navigate it while staying true to their values. Participating in several "ride alongs," seeking out key planners within the department, and getting acquainted with command staff will introduce issues of concern. Students may ask about internship opportunities and present a proposal to be accomplished during internship, and faculty may invite speakers to community psychology classes. Both law enforcement and corrections personnel are "solution oriented" and open to considering collaborations to improve results.

Foundations

Having expertise in competencies such as ecological perspectives; empowerment; socio-cultural and cross-cultural competence; ethical, reflective practice; program development, implementation, and management; prevention and health promotion; community and organizational capacity building, including community leadership and mentoring; resource development; program evaluation; community development; and community education, information dissemination, and building public awareness are all skills that would benefit foundations.

The basic function of a foundation is to use resources to promote the public good and improve the quality of life in communities (Meyers, 2011). Community psychologists have found positions such as program officer, president, and CEO. They describe benefits such as the ability to mobilize money and expertise and try out new ideas to champion social change, and to work on prevention-oriented systems change across domains (Meyers, 2011; Usher & Meissen, 2011). Annette Rickel worked for a large foundation as a program officer, and then moved on to establish her own foundation to provide funding and mentoring to support students working toward becoming math and science teachers (Rickel, 2011).

Community psychologists interested in working for foundations might look for internships during graduate school. Many large foundations offer fellowships and other post-doc and early career opportunities. Job openings and their associated descriptions may be found on the Chronicle of Philanthropy and the Council on Foundation websites. Perusing such ads to see the range of opportunities and competencies required can be helpful to guide skill development.

Research and Evaluation Firms

Community psychologists who wish to focus their careers on research and evaluation may find employment with a research or evaluation firm. There are several large companies that have substantial contracts with the federal government and hire individuals as analysts, statisticians, survey specialists, project managers, and researchers working on health, human services, social and economic policy, education, and other projects. Competencies in statistics and research methods, project management, understanding policy, and being able to translate research findings for policymakers are all necessary.

Some firms offer internships for graduate students, which is an avenue for gaining experience. Because of their size, they also have entry-level positions and training; experience gained during graduate school (e.g., working on large research projects) is sufficient to get a foot in the door. Many jobs require a master's degree or less, and content knowledge may be helpful. For example, if they have a division that works primarily on health-care issues, having experience specific to the field would provide an advantage.

Consulting: Working Independently or Forming a Consulting Company

Consulting is another option for community psychologists. While some have opted to work independently, others have ventured out and formed larger companies. Community Science, founded by David Chavis and Kien Lee, provides research and evaluation; evaluation capacity building and learning systems; community initiative support and system design and implementation; conferences and workshops; and other services based in community psychology values and principles. EMSTAR, founded by Jim Emshoff and Debi Starnes, provides program evaluation, data analysis, evaluation and research training, needs assessment, and grant writing services. The organization has provided services to a long list of government, nonprofit, health-care, higher education, and faith-based organizations.

Other community psychologists have opted to remain independent, focusing their practices on their particular strengths and interests, or offering a full array of services consistent with the CP competencies. Tom Wolff & Associates focuses on collaborative system development and maintenance. He provides technical expertise and workshops, keynote addresses and customized presentations, and tools and resources that he has developed. Susan Ryerson Espino's practice focuses on program evaluation and capacity development work. Susan Wolfe's practice includes evaluation, capacity building, strategic planning, and coaching clients on how to use the data they collect to improve their performance.

In addition to developing specific CP practice competencies relevant to interests through coursework and other means, the first step in preparing to be a consultant is to work in other organizations. Experience is perhaps one of the best teachers, and having some kind of background and track record is essential for building credibility as a consultant. Having experience with communities and organizations, especially the politics and unwritten, norms is essential. Graduate students considering a consulting career may want to work with their advisors to arrange consulting opportunities with local organizations to gain necessary experience under a mentorship. Also, working in other organizations and communities provides opportunities to connect with mentors, observe more experienced professionals, and see what works, and (more important) what does not work. Managing projects, supervising people, engaging in the community, writing grants and reports, and gaining whatever experience possible before hanging up a shingle may make the difference between a practice that thrives and one that merely limps along and gets by.

There are also practical and personal qualities to cultivate. Owning a business or being self-employed requires a level of being able to live with uncertainty and comfort with a variable income. It also requires a certain level of business knowledge. Legal and accounting services cost money, and if there is not enough money to hire such expertise, then it is necessary to be able to read and fully understand the language in contracts, understand self-employment taxes, and have a grasp of the different possible business structures (e.g., sole proprietorship, limited liability corporation, partnership) and the legal and financial implications of each. In addition to being able to write good proposals, a certain level of social savvy is helpful. Building a practice sometimes requires networking with other professionals and being able to market oneself to organizations. See Viola and McMahon's (2010) helpful guidebook on what it takes to get started, be successful, and thrive in the consulting world.

Business, Technology, and Entrepreneurship

Few community psychologists have developed careers in the private sector, leaving this potentially fruitful arena for community psychology careers relatively untapped.

There are an increasing number of for-profit companies that promote social responsibility (e.g., Whole Foods, Tom's), and most major and midsize corporations have community outreach departments and provide grant funding. Some community psychologists work, or have worked, at companies providing consulting and research services to organizations undergoing technological and/or organizational change (e.g., Mitchell Fleischer and David Roitman, both graduates of the Michigan State Ecological-Community Psychology program).

Another example of the application of community psychology to a workplace is provided in Meg Bond's (2007) book *Workplace Chemistry: Promoting Diversity Through Organizational Change*. In this book, Bond illustrates how community psychologists add value to organizations. She describes a collaboration between a team of community psychologists and a manufacturing firm to address diversity. The community psychologists' roles included researcher, consultant, and trainer. Their work was guided by a social ecological perspective based on principles that included multilevel analyses, person-environment adaptation, phenomenological attitude, and attention to interdependencies. The work required assessment and engagement, designing and delivering training, working with teams, and institutionalizing change, all competencies described in earlier chapters in this book.

Community psychologists may also use their knowledge to supplement entrepreneurial endeavors. Businesses such as "philanthropubs" have been springing up in some urban areas whereby diners may donate a portion of their meal price to a specific charity. Although the values of community psychology may seem to be in conflict with those required for product development and marketing, even community psychologists must earn a living, and doing so by developing products that promote and support the community psychology mission and vision would offer the public an alternative to many of the currently available products.

Working in the business, technology, and entrepreneurship realms requires a skill set and personal qualities similar to those used for consulting. The competencies developed in community psychology can be supplemented by classes in business schools, a Master of Business Administration or Master of Public Administration degree, or coursework in entrepreneurship.

Academic Settings

Universities, medical schools, and community colleges offer positions other than tenure-track faculty or lecturer positions. Many of the positions are grant funded and thus contingent upon the continuation of the current grant or receipt of new funding. However, there are also permanent positions, often on the administrative side of the college or university, such as within sponsored programs and institutional research offices. Such jobs are usually found through professional networks (e.g., listservs, ads posted at conferences, word of mouth) or they are posted on the university website under employment openings.

For students who have not yet decided whether they want a primarily teaching and research-oriented career, staying within an academic setting in some sort of role has distinct advantages, particularly if they continue to do some research. It is always possible to move from an academic setting to other types of positions, but it can be much more difficult to move into academia following positions that do not involve research. Practice jobs outside of academic settings rarely provide the time and support required to publish in peer-reviewed journals and/or to apply for research grants, two activities that academic institutions value highly among applicants for full-time faculty positions. However, there can be other ways community psychologists contribute to scholarship, such as reflecting on their work by presenting at conferences and working with students.

Some of the CP competencies useful for nonfaculty careers in academic settings are also research related, and include participatory community research, program evaluation, and grant writing. Other community psychology–related competencies that are often useful for jobs in colleges and universities include skills for: program development, implementation and management; community leadership and mentoring; small and large group processes; resource development; consultation and organizational development; policy analysis; and community education and information dissemination. Research project director and/or other administrative positions in sponsored programs or institutional research require research and analytic skills, resource development, and report-writing for universities and funders. Training and experience with writing successful grant applications to a variety of funding agencies that include federal, state, local and foundation grants is necessary. Additional competencies that help to qualify people for a wide variety of administrative positions as well as positions within student services are project management skills, budgeting and financial management, leadership and people management skills, as well as in-depth understanding of organizational dynamics because there may be internal and/or community level politics to navigate.

FINDING WORK AS A COMMUNITY PSYCHOLOGIST

Preparing for a Job Search

Preparing for a job search should begin long before graduation. Students who are unsure about what they could do will need to engage in some intense exploration. Here are some tips on how to prepare for the job search while in school, or when making a transition from one job to another.

1. Build your networks—networking is a key strategy for seeking employment. Networking can be defined as "the process of forming linkages, making connections, expanding resources, and bringing people and ideas together in a reciprocal manner for mutual benefit" (Knauth, Viola, & Cowgill, 2010, p. 74; see this chapter for exercises that help one assess and strengthen one's relationships). Assess your strengths, weaknesses, needs, and goals as well as identify those in your network who may assist you. Evaluate your existing personal, social, and professional acquaintances, and target your efforts to connect with others who may facilitate your job search and help you learn the landscape of the field. Consider, for example, your skill sets, and those in your personal and professional networks and ask for leads and introductions to their acquaintances who

might be able to help you. Attend conferences relevant to your interests, approach more experienced professionals, and ask questions. You might offer to buy them coffee or tea if they will talk with you for a half hour. An alternative is to contact people at organizations of interest and ask to schedule a meeting at their place of work.

2. In addition to networking within the field, get acquainted and make friendships with students and professionals of other community-focused disciplines who can give useful information about future collaboration and/or consultation opportunities. Networking "outside the community psychology box" while in graduate school can lead to later collaborations in both job search and community practice, particularly when you are able to communicate with others how your approach to the work is an additional asset that complements the strengths of others. Learn some of the basic professional language used in other professions of interest, and compare how community issues and processes are conceptualized in those professions.

3. Identify occupational domains or settings that are compatible with your talents, and that you may want to explore in more depth through informational interviews in community settings. This strategy will help you meet potential employers, learn more about different settings, and identify competencies to develop expertise in. Be prepared with questions and keep the session to the time requested, unless the individual being interviewed suggests otherwise.

4. Visit the job ads in areas of interest and begin reading the competencies potential employers are seeking. Examining job ads may help you find relevant internships or decide on courses to take that will facilitate your preparation for the positions of interest once you know the required competencies. The ads will rarely be posted on sites or publications for the general public (e.g., peruse ads in professional publications, sign up for email blasts from relevant organizations, get to know where jobs are posted for the types of work you are interested in pursuing). For example, community psychologists interested in pursuing a career in evaluation might subscribe to the American Evaluation Association's email notifications, attend the annual conference, examine the job opening board, and subscribe to their listserv, EvalTalk. If you are interested in working for the federal government, all openings are posted on www.USAJobs.gov. You may also peruse openings with the Centers for Disease Control and Prevention and your state and local health departments. Look through the various openings, read the descriptions of skills sought, and make note of the relevant agencies and job titles.

5. Join professional organizations. Of course, SCRA is a perfect fit for community psychologists, but other organizations may also be helpful. For example, community psychologists interested in public health might join the American Public Health Association. The American Evaluation Association, the Association for Community Organization and Social Administration, and the Society for the Psychological Study of Social Issues may also be of interest. Students can take advantage of student rates and further explore opportunities, present at conferences, and network with people in the field who are engaged in work that fits with their interests.

6. Join the Practice Council of SCRA. This group has monthly conference calls where members with various jobs share practice-based tools, experiences, and challenges, so you can learn, connect with people, and ask questions. This group collaborates to present at SCRA Biennial conferences and many members participate in mentoring sessions.

7. Begin marketing your personal and professional brand/interests. It is never too early for you as an aspiring community psychologists to begin marketing yourself, and the Internet is a great place to do so, through tools such as Facebook, Twitter, LinkedIn, Sitepoint, and other social media networking sites (see Resources). These sites have become a resource for organizations in identifying talent, creating pools of potential job candidates, and filling positions.

Applying for and Landing Jobs

Whether the application requires a short resume or a curriculum vitae, highlighting skills and experience is important. It is helpful to keep a log or inventory of the different

Photo 14.1 Dr. Susan McMahon and doctoral students (Elizabeth McConnell, Chrystal Coker, Samantha Reaves, and Linda Ruiz) in clinical-community and community programs at DePaul University reflect upon and discuss community psychology competencies.

Source: Susan D. McMahon.

experiences and skills you have as a reference when you are applying for jobs. For example, if you had an internship that required you learn to use different software packages, write down the name of the software and describe how you used it. Track grant applications you worked on, the role you played, and whether they were funded. Keeping track of these details will be useful when you are writing cover letters and resumes and need to highlight specific experiences relevant to the job that you are applying for.

Potential employers will likely be unaware of the range of competencies community psychologists receive training in, so these competencies will need to be clearly spelled out. Cover letters are an excellent way to highlight how training and experience fit with what the employer is seeking. Each resume and letter should be customized for each application to highlight how the individual applying best fits this specific organization and position. Use example resumes and cover letters from others who work in the positions that interest you. The CP competencies that make up the foundational principles—ecological perspectives; empowerment; sociocultural and cross-cultural competence; community inclusion and partnership; and ethical, reflective practice—contribute to the uniqueness that community psychologists possess, and should be at the core of competencies developed for any of the career settings described.

Applicants should anticipate that employers will likely ask what community psychology is. Community psychologists should all have a 5-second elevator speech memorized and rehearsed so that it comes out naturally. Think through your speech carefully and try it out on some friends to determine what they think about when they hear it. Interview preparation should include reading about the organization and the position and being prepared to demonstrate your value-added. Go to the organization's website, review its mission, financial information, read staff bios, see what services or products they offer, and think about how your skills and expertise will contribute not only to the position that you are interviewing for, but the organization overall. Learn what you can about the person who will be interviewing you if that is possible too.

Resumes and job search strategies and customs evolve and change over time. Look at resources on websites such as LinkedIn and other job-focused sites to update your search skills and knowledge and get tips about resumes, search strategies, and interviewing. Some sites will offer job search and networking opportunities, so explore them to determine whether there are costs associated, and whether what they offer is relevant to the type of job you are seeking.

CONCLUSION

The range of educational and career opportunities for students interested in gaining and applying knowledge and skills in community psychology are both exciting and challenging. We have provided some examples of the types of competencies that students acquire at the undergraduate, master's, and doctoral levels, as well as various career opportunities, yet there is a full array of possibilities. Students and new graduates seeking to develop and engage in various community psychology practice competencies may also keep in mind several strategies as they plan for their future, including:

- Researching educational programs to decide what program is going to be the best fit

- Clarifying interests and values when exploring possibilities

- Seeking out courses, experiences, and academic and professional mentors to obtain a solid foundation in core competencies that are closely aligned with interests

- Networking widely and across relevant professions

- Looking outside the "silos" that come to mind when considering psychology work settings

- Sharing information and learning from others.

Remember that community psychology is a profession well suited to collaboration with others in community and with relevant professions in order to accomplish positive results. As careers advance, we hope that students, new graduates, and community psychologists in a range of settings will maintain their links and participate in the activities of SCRA to encourage and benefit those who will follow. Enhancing educational opportunities, clarifying and honing competencies that community psychologists need, and doing our good work in a variety of settings will facilitate advancement and growth of our field and the positive impacts that we seek to make.

RESOURCES

Educational Programs

- SCRA Education. This feature on the SCRA website includes links to community psychology undergraduate and graduate programs: http://www.scra27.org/what-we-do/education/academic-programs

Career Exploration and Networking

- American Public Health Association International Health Section. This section of APHA includes over 1,500 public health professionals who work in international settings: http://www.apha.org/membergroups/sections/aphasections/intlhealth/

- JobFit.org helps to match career talents and abilities with current occupations. It was created by WorkForce development networks and is a free self-inventory to help people relate their aptitudes, interests, and abilities to relevant occupational categories.

- Onetonline.org provides occupational profiles that include worker characteristics, requirements for skills and knowledge, experience requirements, occupation requirements, occupation specific information, outlook and earnings, and related occupations.

- LinkedIn.com is an especially useful tool for informing other professionals about one's competencies and achievements, even while a student or in early career.

- Sitepoint.com introduces professionals to 20 business-related social networking sites, and searching online for "professional networks" will provide pages of listings, some of which will be relevant.

Job Postings

- American Evaluation Association Career Center. This site presents job postings for currently available positions in the evaluation field: http://www.eval.org/p/cm/ld/fid = 87

- Usajobs.gov. This site is where all federal jobs are posted: http://www.usajobs.gov

- Idealist.org. This site includes listings for jobs and internships in nonprofit settings worldwide: http://www.idealist.org

- Indeed.com is a general site, but may have relevant local postings: http://www.indeed.com.

Community Psychology Consulting and Consulting Firms

- Community Science: http://www.communityscience.com
- EMSTAR: http://www.emstarresearch.com
- Tom Wolff and Associates: http://www.tomwolff.com
- Community Evaluation Solutions: http://www.communityevaluationsolutions.com

REFERENCES

Association of American Colleges and Universities. (2006). *How should colleges prepare students to succeed in today's global economy.* Retrieved from http://www.aacu.org/leap/public_opinion_research.cfm

Association of American Colleges and Universities. (2011). *The completion agenda: Post-secondary education leaders' perspectives on issues of/strategies for increasing completion rates.* Retrieved from http://www.aacu.org/leap/public_opinion_research.cfm

Austin, A. E., & McDaniels, M. (2006). Using doctoral education to prepare faculty to work within Boyer's four domains of scholarship. In J. Braxton (Ed.), Delving further into Boyer's perspective on scholarship [Special issue]. *New Directions for Institutional Research, 129.*

Bond, M. A. (2007). *Workplace chemistry: Promoting diversity through organizational change.* Hanover, NH: University Press of New England.

Braxton, J. M., Luckey, W., & Helland, P. (2002). Institutionalizing a broader view of scholarship through Boyer's four domains. *ASHE-ERIC Higher Education Report, 29*(2), i–xv.

Bringle, R. G., & Steinberg, K. (2010). Educating for informed community involvement. *American Journal of Community Psychology, 46,* 428–441.

Brody, S. M., & Wright, S. C. (2004). Expanding the self through service-learning. *Michigan Journal of Community Service Learning, 11,* 14–24.

Brown, K., Cardazone, G., Glantsman, O., Johnson-Hakim, S., & Lemke, M. (2014). Examining the guiding competencies in community psychology practice from students' perspectives. *The Community Psychologist, 47*(1), 3–9.

Brown, R. (2011). As graduate-student population grows, so does its reliance on financial aid. *Chronicle of Higher Education.* Retrieved from http://chronicle.com/article/As-Graduate-Student-Population/128402/

Campus Compact. (2012). *Indiana Campus Compact annual report 2011–2012.* Retrieved from http://www.indianacampuscompact.org/images/final_10_31_1_-_single_pages_for_web.pdf

Corbett, C. (2012). Applying community psychology knowledge in nonprofit settings. *The Community Psychologist, 45*(3), 10–11.

Dalton, J., & Wolfe, S. (Eds.). (2012). Education connection and the community practitioner. *The Community Psychologist, 45*(4), 7–13.

Davidson, W., Jimenez, T., Onifadee, E., & Hankins, S. (2010). Student experiences of the Adolescent Diversion Project: A community-based exemplar in the pedagogy of service-learning. *American Journal of Community Psychology, 46*(3–4), 442–458.

Dziadkowiec, O., & Jimenez, T. (2009). Educating community psychologists for community practice: A survey of graduate training programs. *The Community Psychologist, 42*(4), 10–17.

Gatlin, E., Rushenberg, J., & Hazel, K. L. (2009). What's up with graduate training? Results of the 2005 graduate program survey. *The Community Psychologist, 42*(2), 13–19.

Golde, C. M., & Dore, T. M. (2001). *At cross purposes: What the experiences of doctoral students reveal about doctoral education.* Philadelphia, PA: Pew Charitable Trusts.

Hayes-Thomas, R. (2012). The delusion of exclusion: Masters psychology as minority. *Psychologist-Manager Journal, 15,* 164–173.

Henderson, D. (2012). A Lorax metaphor: How community psychology values guide work with non-profits. *The Community Psychologist, 45*(3), 9–10.

Jenkins, R. A. (2010). Applied roles and the future of community psychology. *American Journal of Community Psychology, 45,* 68–72.

Keys, C. B., Horner-Johnson, A., Weslock, K., Hernandez, B., & Vasiliauskas, L. (1999). Learning science for social good. *Journal of Prevention & Intervention in the Community, 18,* 141–156.

Knauth, S., Viola, J., & Cowgill, C. (2010). Finding work. In J. Viola & S. D. McMahon (Eds.), *Consulting and evaluation with nonprofit and community-based organizations* (pp. 69–87). Sudbury, MA: Jones & Bartlett.

McMahon, S. D., & Wolfe, S. M. (in press). Career opportunities in community psychology. In M. Bond, I. Serrano-García, & C. Keys (Eds). Handbook of community psychology: Volume II. Washington D.C.: American Psychological Association.

Meyers, J. C. (2011). A community psychologist in the world of philanthropy. *The Community Psychologist, 44*(3), 10–11.

Montgomery, C. (2013). *Happy city: Transforming our lives through urban design.* Toronto, ON: Doubleday Canada.

Neigher, W. D., Lounsbury, D. W., & Lee, R. E. (2010). Community psychology practice in health care. *The Community Psychologist, 43*(3), 10–12.

Neigher, W. D., & Ratcliffe, A. W. (2011). Back to the future, part III. *The Community Psychologist, 44*(1), 13–15.

Olney, C. A., Livingston, J. E., Fisch, S. I., & Talamantes, M. A. (2006). Becoming better health care providers: Outcomes of a primary care service-learning project in medical school. *Journal of Prevention & Intervention in the Community, 32*(1–2), 133–147.

Palmer, G. L. (2012). Community psychology: A new paradigm in leading nonprofits. *The Community Psychologist, 45*(3), 8–9.

Ratcliffe, A. W. (2011). Corrected findings: Back to the future, part III. *The Community Psychologist, 44*(2), 16–17.

Ratcliffe, A., & Neigher, W. (2010, June 29). *Introducing community psychology*. Retrieved from http://www.scra27.org/files/4513/9007/7333/Evidence_based_CP_Value_Proposition__Final_20110829.pdf

Reeb, R. N. (2010). Service-learning in community action research: Introduction to the special section. *American Journal of Community Psychology, 46*, 413–417.

Rickel, A. (2011). Engaging a foundation in community partnerships. *The Community Psychologist, 44*(3), 10.

Sanders, W. L., & Horn, S. P. (1998). Research findings from the Tennessee Value-Added Assessment System (TVAAS) database: Implications for educational evaluation and research. *Journal of Personnel Evaluation in Education, 12*(3), 247–256.

Sarkisian, G., & Jimenez, T. R. (2011). Guiding principles for education in community psychology research and action. *The Community Psychologist, 44*(4), 7–8.

Serrano-García, I., Pérez-Jiménez, D. & Rodríguez-Medina, S. (in press). Educating community psychologists in a changing world. In M. Bond, I. Serrano-García, & C. Keys (Eds). Handbook of community psychology: Volume II. Washington D.C.: American Psychological Association.

Starnes, D. M. (2004). Community psychologists—Get in the arena!! *American Journal of Community Psychology, 33*(1/2), 3–6.

Usher, J., & Meissen, G. (2011). Community psychologist as grant maker. *The Community Psychologist, 44*(3), 11–12.

Viola, J., & McMahon, S. D. (2010). *Consulting and evaluation with nonprofit and community-based organizations.* Sudbury, MA: Jones & Bartlett.

Walker, G. E., Golde, C., Jones, L., Conklin Bueschel, A., & Hutchings. P. (2008). *The formation of scholars: Rethinking doctoral education for the twenty-first century.* San Francisco, CA: Jossey-Bass.

CHAPTER 15

A Vision for Community Psychology Practice

Bill Berkowitz and Victoria C. Scott

A VISION

"How I came to be ten years into the future, I'm still not sure. Maybe it was a dream, or a hallucination, or a waking fantasy I had while dozing off. Maybe there are more exotic explanations, or even simpler ones, for we all know memory can play tricks. But it all seemed so vivid and real, as real as the shoes on my feet. So let me tell you what I saw. Then tell me what you make of it."

* * *

The first thing I noticed when I found myself back in my hometown ten years from now was how similar it looked to the community I'd left behind. The houses looked pretty much the same. The layout of the streets was like how I remembered it. Drivers went by in what were certainly cars, even if they were smaller and quieter. Kids were crossing the same crosswalk on their way to the same school, and yes, there was the same crossing guard; I remember her face, even if she looked a bit older.

But I didn't quite trust my senses. Had time really stood that still? The best way to find out was to take a walk around.

So I began to walk through my old community, where I'd spent many happy times, and as it happens one of the first places I came to was the Town Hall. I walked into the lobby, and there I did see something different. Three large computer screens were displayed near the main entrance. Above one of them was the title "What's going on today?" This turned out to be a long list of activities happening around town, not just today but up to a few weeks ahead, and not just in government but throughout the community.

There was also a separate screen headed "What's needed today?" I scrolled down and saw items that both government and individual residents had listed, divided both by category and by length of time involved. The Senior Center needed someone to give rides; a resident wanted a house-sitter; could someone translate a form into English? And then there was a third screen titled "What do you think?" where you could express your opinion on a variety of policy questions the town was reviewing or offer an idea or suggestion of your own.

Of course, many could get the same access on their mobile devices if they wanted to, and I learned that many townspeople did; but there was something symbolic, as well as inclusive, about seeing this information in the main building in town—it set a tone; it seemed to embody the town's participatory values; and it spoke to what the community was and what it wanted to be.

After sending a few electronic opinions, I went into the mayor's office. I introduced myself as a town resident from years ago, and she was kind enough to invite me in. She had a few minutes, so she told me a story:

"Maybe you remember when we had that major budget crisis, a few years ago—when all of our local services were not just cut, but ripped to shreds, and almost obliterated. No question that our community quality of life was going downhill fast. Truth be told, our community as we knew it was on the verge of collapse. That was our wake-up call.

"It was obvious that we had fewer public resources to go around, in the traditional sense. But then we took a step back and asked ourselves what we really meant by 'resources.' We had to broaden the definition. And when we did that, we realized that we actually had many more resources than we'd thought, a great many more; they were called 'residents.' Of course, we knew intellectually that our residents were the ones who shaped the quality of life in our community. Our diversity here was a strength. But we really didn't get it deep down. And we didn't realize how underutilized they were.

"We surveyed the community, and found that large percentages of our residents were not involved in the town at all. They didn't join anything, they didn't volunteer, they didn't attend events, they didn't participate in the community in any way. So we thought, what if we could double the percentage that was involved? And maybe we could actually do it, if we went about it properly.

"Now that's when we began to utilize something we'd never heard of before; it was called 'community psychology.' We didn't know then that it would transform our community."

As a community psychologist myself back where I came from, that caught my attention.

"And if it's okay with you, let me walk you down the hall and introduce you to the head of our Community Psychology Department."

That was fine with me. And after being welcomed into that new office, here's what I heard:

"We clearly needed more participation from all groups in our community life. And as you know, that's exactly what community psychologists study. So we started a campaign. When someone moved into the community—we found that out from real estate and rental agents, sometimes from word of mouth—we learned their name and something about them. Then we made sure they got a personal visit from someone in town. We greeted them with a bouquet of flowers, plus a small food basket from local merchants, which I personally felt was a lovely thing to do. It was unusual, it was pleasing, and as it turned out, it paid off later in terms of the response we got. Do you remember the principles of novelty and reciprocity? We simply applied them.

"A while after we started these resident visits, we teamed up with the local neighborhood associations, and soon they took over the visits themselves—which made things more personal, more effective, and certainly easier for us. Neighborhood groups have become our partners in running the community. This has expanded the availability of community resources and reduced costs for the town.

"On our new resident visits, we also brought some basic information about the town, with activities that people could participate in. This was available in several languages.

And we chatted with the newcomers, to learn more about their interests and ideas. The basic message we tried to convey was that all of us are not just people living in the same zip code, but rather a real community; that we're all joined together by some common goals; and that we depend on each other for our quality of life.

"We said that as their government leaders, we will support and meet their needs as best we can, for we are genuinely concerned with and want to promote everyone's well-being; but there's also an expectation that they will participate in the life of the community and give something back to it, whatever they choose.

"After a while, we followed up with a survey asking about their interests and any particular skills they would enjoy sharing—playing an instrument, gardening, job coaching, caring for pets. Later on, we extended these surveys to everyone. Then we gave out contact information and also routed the interest and involvement feedback to appropriate contact persons for each activity, who could then get in touch on their own.

"Did residents respond well to all of this? The majority did. Based on our research, it turns out that a great many were genuinely pleased by our outreach efforts. Another group was generally accepting. True, some others were skeptical. And a relative few saw us as intrusive or even potentially threatening, and wanted no part of us at all. We understand and respect the differences in opinion and have always tried to invite open expression of ideas in community meetings. We've found that ongoing dialogue has helped our community to grow and resolve differences.

"So by now we have a voluntary database of most people in the community, listed by neighborhood and interest area. For example, if we want to know how many people in neighborhood X have an interest in helping the elderly, or in youth sports, or in cooking on a budget, we can easily find out."

I asked if it didn't seem strange for a community psychologist to be directly employed by town government and working in town hall.

"No, not at all. We figured out pretty early on that if we were going to get past our budget crisis, and to develop and utilize all the resources of our community, then all of our diverse community sectors would need to contribute. We found that community psychologists had the skills to bring people together and help make this happen.

"And that's because our values in government are much the same as those in community psychology. They believe in participation; so do we. They believe in including everyone; we do too, as both a moral and a practical matter. They believe in making decisions based on data; that's exactly what we do. They believe communities should foster expression of personal capacities; we're absolutely on board with that. And they believe psychological and community well-being are linked; we live out that belief every day. Really, how can you govern without being something of a community practitioner?[1]

"To put it in a nutshell, we see the job of government as not just to administer the dollar resources we have and place them into effective services. It's also to identify and catalyze all of the other resources in our community—especially our own residents—to encourage their full expression and to guide those resources toward where they are most needed.

"All of this is consistent with community psychology values, as well as being pragmatically effective. And I want to stress that there's nothing coercive in what we do. It's totally voluntary. Nobody will pressure you; at least we in government won't. It's more of an expectation of being part of our community, a new cultural norm. We believe that people want to do meaningful civic work, and so we provide them with opportunities to do it.

"One last thing, though. If any of this sounds too fanciful, I need to tell you that it takes a *lot* of time and energy to govern this way. You've got to work hard to make it happen; that part hasn't changed."

* * *

I had to admit, these were new ways for me to think about government and about community practice. But it was time to continue my walk. After a while, I found myself drawn toward the elementary school I remember going to when I was a kid. I was glad it was still there, and like much else I saw, from the outside it didn't seem to have changed that much. That wasn't entirely true, though.

When I got there, they verified that I was an alum doing research, and buzzed me in. I was lucky to find one of my old teachers, who I was very pleased to learn remembered me. She had a few minutes during her break, so we sat down to talk:

"Actually, we teach them much of the same stuff as we did when you went here. If you sat in class now, you'd probably do okay. Words are still spelled the same way. Reading is reading, and grammar is grammar. One thing that's different, though, is that we teach them about community life, starting in the first grade. We spend a lot of time with the kids right in the community, and meeting many of the different people who live and work here—the mayor, the police chief, and the park director, but also the bank teller, the construction worker, the guy who runs the pizza shop, and some of our new immigrants. We visit hospitals, churches, and cemeteries; we go to high school games, and performances in the evening. At least once a week, either we go out or somebody comes in to visit.

"We talk with them. The kids get to ask them about what they do in the community. By doing so, the kids learn lots of things about community life, such as how to open a bank account, what it takes to run a business, how to plant a tree, how new immigrants got here, and why they wanted to get here in the first place.

"But there's more to it. We have the older kids mentor new kids coming into the school. And we bring a lot of parents into class—parents are resources too, right?—for we found that many parents, and grandparents, would gladly meet with our kids if only we asked them. Before, we never did. One of our most popular examples of this is '60s

Day,' when some of the older folks come in, tell their stories, and answer questions. ('What music did you listen to? Did you protest? Did you do drugs?')

"All these community members are a core part of our curriculum. Why? Because these interactions build connections to our community and relationships within it. Those relationships pay off later in life. Some of our local community psychologists— have you met them?—did studies and found that when children learn more about their community, they grow up to care more about their community. Not surprisingly, that translates into fewer youth disturbances in adolescence, less petty vandalism, less crime in general. If you're connected to your community and the people in it, you're less motivated to mess it up and foul your own nest. Doesn't that stand to reason?

"Actually, you're more likely to want to help your community. And in fact we've learned that early community education does seem to result in more community participation as adults, and to what some of us are now calling 'sense of community.' That's a term with a nice ring to it."

* * *

Before we said goodbye, the teacher suggested that I look into the health clinic, a few blocks away. Good advice, I thought; but since it was a nice day, I wanted to walk around some more. As I did, I couldn't help noticing that the streets seemed to be more than the collection of isolated buildings, the bland and barren streetscape I'd grown up with, but were instead full of unexpected discoveries.

At one four-way intersection, a giant sunflower, maybe 25 feet in diameter, had been painted on the pavement right in the middle of the street. The design was not only beautiful in itself, but I learned later on that it helped to slow down traffic at what had been an accident-prone location.[2]

Farther down, a wooden post stood in front of one of the houses, a Plexiglas compartment attached in front, the kind of structure that holds flyers when a house is for sale. But no real estate flyers were inside; instead there were poems—sometimes well-known poems, sometimes written by a neighbor. Passersby were invited to take a poem or download a copy by tapping their phone on an electronic data box. They could also submit requests for future poems or send poems of their own to the poetry coordinator for that neighborhood. In this community, people could and did grab a poem as well as a cup of coffee on their way to work.[3]

On another block, large animal sculptures, very striking in their way, sat in the front yards of most of the houses. I was told they'd been made by a neighborhood sculptor from recycled metal, then painted in bright colors. He had put one of his creations out in his own yard, and to his considerable surprise found that his neighbors wanted one for themselves. I'd never seen a residential street with a ten-foot-high yard sculpture, let alone what seemed like 20 of them. But a resident told me of the strong community feelings that this shared art created.[4]

It was clear that in this community art was not only encouraged, but that outdoor art in particular played a major role in community life. Town leaders already liked art not just because it allowed for expression of individual capacities and boosted the local economy, but they also came to recognize that that art was a community builder; it brought people together. Public art, especially outdoor art, got community members out and about. Then, when art was outside, people would stop to observe, and when they did they would talk to the artist or to neighbors who were there for similar reasons. This built relationships. No wonder the town sponsored a public art prize competition every year, and that art was a key part of most neighborhood festivals. I had never thought that the public artists were actually community practitioners; now I saw they were.

* * *

The health center was busy, and I had to wait a while before I could talk to somebody. But eventually the director got free, and spoke to me about the health-care changes that had taken place.

"You could say there are four main things we do here. One of them is to provide routine health care—for sprains, burns, splinters, cuts, things like that. We also do preventive care, such as vaccinations and wellness exams. This is what most folks think of as basic medical practice.

"But most of what actually goes on is talk; that's the second part. We'll give advice when we're asked, and sometimes when we're not. We give out plenty of health information; but more than that, we have real conversations with our visitors, about their health questions, concerns, and problems, and about their life situation if they're open to it. We've come to understand the importance of listening empathetically and reflectively, rather than prescribing and telling our patients what to do. We've worked hard at becoming culturally competent. And so we spend a lot of time building good trusting relationships with our patients, so that they are comfortable sharing information about themselves and working with us to be healthier.

"We send our staff into schools and workplaces to do basically the same thing. And for those who don't want to visit us, or can't, we have nurse practitioners or other health providers who answer questions online and by phone several hours a day and chat online live weekly. We'll also link to podcasts and the best sources of more detailed health information.

"Then, we run an ongoing array of classes—on exercise, on child care, on fitness and healthy eating. We have walking clubs, cooking classes, t'ai chi and yoga, a long list of support groups. A lot of them meet in the evening, after many people get home from their jobs. We have a community garden, that's part of our work. Specialists sometimes come in to consult; so do midwives, personal trainers, and stress reduction teachers. The aim of these activities is to promote holistic health, or wellness of the body, mind, and spirit. We continue to explore creative ways to meet the needs of our community members and to collect data to learn what benefits their health, and how and why.

"Yet maybe what's most important is that we know who our community members are, and they know us. Our practice is a *community* practice; that's what health care ought to be. We practice health care just as I think you practice community work, with dialogue, participation, relationship building, cultural sensitivity, competence boosting, empowerment, and trust. How else would you want to do it?

"Oh, then there's the last part. You'll also find that many of our visitors are also neighborhood caregivers, who help out for a small stipend we've been able to give them since we lowered our costs. As an example, we train others to become community health workers on their own block, modeling this after the successful block nurse program in St. Paul.[5] That way, people can get a basic health consultation from a neighbor right on their street, and even though we're only a few minutes away for the great majority, some people prefer it that way, and that is fine. We like to call it community practice without borders.

Photo 15.1 Cultivating individual and community wellness through community gardening.

Source: iStockphoto.com/HeroImages.

"You see, our practice is in the community, and for the community, but it is also *by* the community. Our training work is really very simple, and it's been done by others before. Have you heard how they did it in Cincinnati? Listen to this:

"They divided the neighborhood into 31 blocks. Each block had a block council, which then elected a block worker to represent and serve them. The block workers were trained, and paid a small stipend. Then comes the good part. Let me read to you:

> The first project, a child health care center, succeeded remarkably. The nursing staff and block workers made some 5,388 visits to 576 babies, of whom over two thirds received full medical examinations. . . . [A year later] in response to the demand for increased services, the [organization] was sponsoring prenatal care, medical examinations for preschool children, bedside nursing, supervision of local tubercular cases, epidemic disease prevention, and postnatal examinations. In two short years the Cincinnati Social Unit Organization had established one of the most comprehensive, effective, and cooperative public health programs in the nation. (Fisher, 1984, pp. 24–25)

"I never heard of this program," I said. "Did it just start up?"

"No," the director replied. "It began in 1919. Draw your own conclusions."

* * *

While all my visits were illuminating, it was by spending time in the neighborhood that I came to realize my community now was really a different place from the one I'd left behind. It wasn't just the art; more people were out on the street than I ever remembered. Maybe this was because there were more things for them to do outside, which in turn gave them more reasons to enjoy each other's company. The differences came from a lot of little things, so here are some vignettes:

. . . On one street corner was a large wooden cabinet stocked with various household goods, goods freely given by neighbors and freely taken. This corner was now known as Share-It Square and had become widely replicated around town (cf. Walljasper, 2007, p. 22).

. . . Part of it too may have been the thoughtful environmental design—the shade trees, the signage, the little alcoves tucked right into the street with benches at right angles so that people could sit and talk. Many of those benches were at school bus stops, where parents could wait for the bus to bring their little kids to and from school. I could see them talking at the bus stops, and at least once I saw a parent come out with a coffee thermos and cups for the other moms and dads.

. . . Another pleasing observation was that all playgrounds and parks had small bulletin boards. This was surprising, in that you would think many would be attending to their mobiles, and those were certainly prominent; but I saw that people also liked to look at low-tech bulletin boards when they were attractive and well kept up. They became a focal point, one that prompted interaction.

. . . A different note also caught my eye; someone had used a Sharpie pen to write and post his opinion on a local topic, and left the pen attached to the board for others to join in. And they did. It was fun to see this non-virtual neighborhood thread, so simple yet compelling in its way.[6]

I had learned before that when people are outside, they will meet and talk, often in unplanned ways. But also that those small unplanned encounters, those micro-transactions, have cumulative impact over time and help build relationships and community. I suspect someone or some group first needs to facilitate these encounters; but once they begin to happen, they will develop on their own. Once street life starts to grow, it can feed on itself.

But there was something else in the neighborhood I'd never seen before. Near the park entrance, and in some other neighborhood places, there were kiosks with freely available computer terminals, similar in some ways to those I'd seen at Town Hall. But these, I soon learned, were devoted entirely to neighborhood affairs.

Anyone could link onto a variety of different neighborhood and community content, each with its own section. There was "What's going on today?," but this time just for neighborhood events. Items for free or for sale. Neighbors seeking and giving recommendations. Neighbors needing help of some kind—child care, pet care, yard work—and neighbors offering it. Job leads. A lost and found. Those looking to start one activity or another. Specialized discussion threads. Some parts of this resembled a neighborhood Craigslist, but more personal and friendlier, since users knew many of those who were posting.

But other parts were more unique: A number of blogs, written by neighbors with different perspectives, with very lively comment sections. Photos and videos of recent neighborhood events. Who's moving in and who's moving out. Ideas for improving neighborhood life. Quotes of the day. And a lively one-page summary of neighborhood news, posted five days a week. I learned that a small group of volunteer editors got together every weekday evening to assemble and publish the news. I met up with one of them, who told me:

"When we started, our philosophy was very straightforward: Let's build connections. Let's open up communications to everyone, by anyone. Let's strengthen our small community, one message at a time. And once we got fully off the ground, we found that many neighbors would no more miss the neighborhood news in the morning than skip brushing their teeth. If you give them a chance, people want to stay connected (cf. Hampton & Wellman, 2003; McKibben, 2010).[7]

"You know, all this electronic networking and posting turned out to be a lot simpler than it sounded. It wasn't very complicated at all. Fortunately, in this community, almost everyone has one or more computers, and the majority have some kind of mobile device. A few motivated and moderately tech-savvy neighbors came together to plan out the system. They also learned and borrowed from other neighborhoods that had begun this work earlier. Then they got feedback from the rest of the neighborhood, and used it. After that, once the hardware was set up, we were ready to go. How much did it cost? Little or nothing. Very little human maintenance, either.

"True, not everybody was excited about neighborhood electronic technology at the beginning, and some stayed away from it out of indifference or inertia. But we stayed with it, kept reaching out, allowed our successes to be our selling point, and encouraged everyone to link up if and when they wanted to. Over time, most did.

"We felt, and we demonstrated, that a community could be more than bricks and mortar—not simply a collection of houses on a street, but a group of people who could really appreciate each other and enjoy living their lives together. Many of us have become friends in the process, and that feels good. It doesn't cost much. It's not that hard to do. Any neighborhood or any community could do it. I think some just don't know how to get started. . . ."

* * *

"Now that I'm back in the present, what did I learn from my visit into the future? I'm more convinced that envisioning the future benefits today's work. In our professional jobs, we get bogged down in the day-to-day. Who has the time to look ahead? But we could do with more community visioning and imagining in our world.

"And now that I've seen what could be, and how more engagement lifts quality of life, why should we settle for anything less? As I look ahead, we can't afford to. I need to act in the present; but I also need to imagine a more enriching future, based on my values, unapologetically ideal, and draw upon it to guide my actions now."

A CRITIQUE

This is our vision for community life, and an example of the impact of community psychology practice in action. By "our vision," we emphasize the spirit rather than the letter. The vision details offered are incomplete and modifiable for communities of varied types and compositions. But the spirit behind it—with an emphasis on participation, on inclusiveness, on relationships, on competence building, on the full use of community resources (tangible and intangible), and on sense of community—is what we want to highlight here. We don't claim that the spirit of this vision is distinctively original or unique—it is not—but we think it is particularly well suited to our present times, to the foreseeable future, and to our disciplinary strengths.

We are believers in community visioning, as both an aspirational and a motivating force for action. Yet as equally strong believers in community participation, we want to reach out to you as readers of this chapter and ask how our vision compares with your own. What is your vision for your own community? And how could you bring it about?

Important as a vision is, a primary concern in this chapter is how to turn vision into reality. Still, as a prelude to implementation, we must first ask and answer some key questions that apply to visions in general—to ours, to yours, and we think to any other. We then offer some thoughts for creating and implementing a community's vision toward the end of this chapter.

1. Is this vision *desirable?* Does it best reflect the type of community we would want for others—and, to personalize it, that we would want to live in ourselves?

2. Is this a vision that is *relevant* to community psychology and, more specifically, to community psychology *practice?* This is because we are seeking a vision to guide our professional lives and also a vision where our community psychology practice skills will be integral to bringing it about in reality.

3. And if this vision is desirable and relevant for our field, is the vision *feasible* and *achievable*—if not completely, at least in good measure? For our ultimate goal is to generate actual real-world accomplishments that benefit people.

If the answers to all three of these questions are positive, or sufficiently positive, then we can turn our attention to how we might implement our vision, and perhaps your vision, in actual practice.

Is This Vision Desirable?

Visions of ideal community life date back to earliest human history (Manuel & Manuel, 1979). Attempting even to summarize thousands of years of ideal community descriptions is clearly beyond our scope. But we can distill common themes of what most humans have sought in communities across centuries and cultures: satisfaction of biological needs; security; self-sufficiency; fair treatment; expression of one's abilities and capacities; caring and supportive relationships with others. Such commonalities do exist (e.g., Pinker, 2002; Schwartz, 1994).

These commonalities also match up well with community psychology values, as described in SCRA's vision, mission, and goal statements: for example, enhancing well-being, promoting social justice, fostering collaboration, empowerment, preventing harmful outcomes, equal opportunity, non-exploitation, participation, inclusion, respect for all cultures.[8] This is not surprising, since the values of our field have been influenced by an extensive historical and intellectual legacy, mostly Western and primarily American.

More proximately, our disciplinary values have been shaped by domestic historical forces prominent after World War II, including though not limited to the burst of empirical research in social psychology and the social sciences; renewed attempts to reduce poverty in the midst of postwar prosperity; the struggles for racial and gender equality; and the then-prevailing belief that personal defects were primarily due to environmental rather than biological causes. (See Chapter 1 for more on the history of community psychology.)

All these forces, all these expressions of human desire, were in play at the same time, when community psychology was born. They are the antecedent events of community psychology itself. We are the inheritors of those intellectual traditions and that historical vision, and we are now charged with implementing them through our community practice, though now under changed social and economic circumstances.

And so our vision, based upon history and upon community psychology values, is one that emphasizes participation of everyone in community life, because of the belief that everyone has something valuable to offer and that the community is strengthened when talents and resources are shared. It's a vision of social justice, which entails equitable resource distribution. It's a vision of serving and integrating the disenfranchised, because they, together with all members of society, bear the consequences of inequitable distribution (Wilkinson & Pickett, 2009). And it's a vision that is accompanied by a strong sense of community, which is a positive feeling in itself, but which is also linked to both physical and psychological well-being.

These are familiar value elements, not just among community psychologists, but among populations in general (Pinker, 2002; Schwartz, 1994; United Nations, 2000).[9] Adoption of these values will not necessarily lead to the same vision as ours, and opinions on the specific aspects of an ideal community may still vary. Our interpretation, furthermore, does not validate the desirability of our vision in an absolute moral sense, if that were possible; but it does show consistency and continuity with visions of the past, and of our own founding. And it is a vision many of whose elements remain to be implemented in today's society.

But one other aspect of the vision set forth here, and it is an essential one, is that it is focused on the community level. It rests on the belief that the *community* is the locus for much of what is most important in life and also where what is most important can be attained, a belief borne out through most of human history (see, for example, Keller, 2003).

And it further assumes that the community psychology values linked with our vision can best get operationalized and made manifest on a community level—that is, on a relatively small scale, where participation can more easily take place, where relationships are more easily formed, where well-being develops through those relationships, where multiple and accessible outlets for expression of personal competence are present, where one can exert more personal control over life circumstances, and where strong feelings of interdependence exist. We elaborate on these points in the next section.

Is This Vision Relevant to Community Practice?

We think so. For us, it is not enough that a vision simply be desirable and be concerned with community life. There needs to be a connection between the vision and the work we do as community psychologists and community practitioners. In this case, the connection is easily drawn, for a commonly accepted definition of community practice, first proposed with the revival of community practice interests about a decade ago, is

> to strengthen the capacity of communities to meet the needs of constituents and help them to realize their dreams in order to promote well-being, social justice, economic equity and self-determination through systems, organizational and/or individual change. (Julian, 2006, p. 68)

This foundational statement supports our vision's relevance to practice. But on a more concrete level, implementing the spirit of our vision, or your own, will require use of the practice skills that should be part of our training and of our professional work. Skills that include identifying community needs and assets; planning to reach common goals; motivating community members to join together; facilitating group processes; developing cultural competence; providing proper incentives for action; using persuasive techniques to publicize events; applying empirical data to make decisions; resolving conflicts; training others for leadership roles; and evaluating results. By virtue of our training and experience, these are practitioner skills and competencies we should possess in greater degree than the average community resident or the typical human service professional.

The spirit of our vision is also relevant because we believe it is well suited to deal with the social and economic conditions of our national and planetary future. Social predictions are always risky, but at least in the United States, and in the near term, it seems likely that relatively fewer public dollars will be available to maintain established health and social services. The maintenance of community quality of life will then depend more on residents coming together to provide that quality of life for themselves.

If so, in years ahead life satisfaction is likely to depend less on material possessions and more on relationships, including the satisfactions one gets from being with neighbors in a community setting (cf. McKnight & Block, 2010). In the value orientation we have described, those relationships will promote healthier personal and community outcomes. Those outcomes will have the additional advantages of being available, accessible, renewable, and mostly free of charge.

Throughout human history, and until the beginning of the 21st century, most humans lived in village settings, which despite their economic and cultural limitations offered compensating psychological and social rewards. Although traditional village life has been receding, given our psychological knowledge we may be well positioned to promote small, cohesive, relationship-based, village-like, and sustainable community settings that maximize personal benefits while minimizing personal costs.

These prospective communities of the future may become more prominent through natural adaptation and without our involvement, but they will be more likely to occur with community practitioners providing vision, guidance, and training, as participants, as leaders, and as moral exemplars. These are high-minded words. But is our vision really achievable?

Is This Vision Achievable?

We believe both the spirit and the substance of the vision set forth here are feasible and achievable, largely because parts of it have already been achieved in multiple corners of our nation and world. Those looking for examples of participatory, close-knit, relationship-focused, and highly satisfying communities, at least as perceived by their residents, need not look very far.

One might start, for instance, with compilations of best places to live, often published or updated on a regular basis. One illustration is *MONEY* magazine's annual compilation of "the Best Places to Live in America," places judged to have "the optimal combination of economic strength, job growth, affordability, good schools, diversity, health care, a strong sense of community, and more" ("MONEY Reveals the 2013 List," 2013). Alternatively, Livability.com's rankings of the "Top 100 Best Places to Live" are based in part upon ratings of social and civic capital (Livability.com, 2014). And one global study purported to research and find the happiest places on Earth; it concluded that San Luis Obispo, California, is "arguably the happiest and healthiest city in America" (Buettner, 2010, p. 200).

There are certainly cautions, because these and similar sources are sometimes based upon limited community indicators, because those aspects are not typically integrated into a larger overall vision, and because sources often need independent verification by objective investigators not tied to a particular community nor to commercial profit.

But the good news is that if we can cite positive examples of our vision in real life, then they can occur in other places under proper conditions, which we can help create. The better news is that the majority of these examples may still be little known, since many are not publicized beyond their home community borders. Yet some even more promising news is that, at least in the United States, these positive instances tend to happen independently, without governmental push. The strengthening of local community life is not yet on national or state political agendas. If it were, if there were some national leadership behind it, we would surely see more positive developments.

The examples we have cited to date, and the building of strong neighborhoods and communities more generally, have rarely been initiated by community psychologists. More often, someone or some group takes the lead; others follow; new norms become established. But as community psychology practitioners, we can add distinctive value here. We can find out where these examples exist. We can find out why they exist—the factors behind their success. And we can foster the development of model examples and promote them elsewhere.

We are as well placed as anyone to do the needed data gathering, the analysis, and the replication, because those who live in model neighborhoods or communities themselves would not typically place a priority on any of these tasks. They are less likely to have the same broader vision, or the research skills, or the basic motivation, or the time. Making a happy life for oneself is a full-time job. On the other hand, we as a group should have the vision, the skills, and the interest; we nominally have some professional time or can carve it out; and we have some professional prestige attached to our positions that will help influence other communities, perhaps policymakers as well.

Our vision is achievable. But if we truly want it to be a template for how community life should be lived in the future, we have a lot of work to do.

BASIC STEPS IN THE VISIONING PROCESS

Our interest in this chapter goes beyond offering our own vision for community practice. We also want to encourage readers to create and implement their own vision, for their own community. This book on community practice is meant to be *used* in community practice. We believe that the questions and issues discussed above apply to most community visions and that the major elements of our vision will lead to an array of desirable community outcomes. Yet we well realize that each community is different, that community settings do vary, and that specific vision elements will properly differ from place to place.

How, then, to create and implement a community vision? Many sources give step-by-step operational detail (e.g., National Civic League, 2000).[10] But we provide here some more general thoughts based on our experience, corresponding roughly to "before," during," and "after."

Before Visioning: The Role of Desire

We hope it will not be too surprising if we argue that crafting the actual vision is in many ways the easiest part of the process. The harder part is often internal, for we believe that vision creation, and most intentional community change, starts with desire. Someone needs to want something to happen, not just as a vague cognitive goal ("It would be nice"), but rather with emotional energy, with fervor, behind that wish ("This is something we definitely need to do, and I'm going to make sure we do it"). Unless someone or some group feels real urgency for the vision, and also feels ready to champion it, it's less likely to occur.

Although scripture says "Without vision, the people perish" (Proverbs 29:18), the practical truth is that without a vision people will get along as they always have, even though their lives could be better. No one's day is ruined because his or her community does not have a vision. So someone needs to set the visioning process in motion; and if no leader in one's community has so far stepped up, that leaves an opening for readers such as you.

Crafting the Actual Vision

Once enough desire has been generated, the usual next step is to bring together a group to shape the actual vision content. This group is frequently composed of leaders and major stakeholders in the community. The group may determine how the actual vision will be crafted (how many meetings, who will lead them) and usually reach out to broader constituencies and to the general public for input, typically in the form of public meetings, hearings, surveys, focus groups, print articles, flyers, online postings, or some combination of these. Some smaller group is often charged with writing the first draft of the vision itself. Multiple drafts, comment periods, and revisions are the norm.

Some while ago, the first author served on a steering committee that formed a vision for his own community and followed the steps above. We took the additional first-time step of hiring an outside consultant to facilitate our visioning, and spent mid-five-figure public dollars to secure his services. To develop the actual vision took about a year of monthly meetings, in both full groups and subcommittees, including an overnight retreat at a nearby hotel. Our regular meetings were intensive, and they were not short. At the end, our town's vision, called Vision 2020, was approved by our full town government; it remains essentially unchanged more than 20 years after its creation.

Other community visions may be part of a comprehensive planning process, or master planning process, for a community. These tend to follow the same basic procedures, some with more outreach and participation than others. In Lowell, Massachusetts, where one of us works, the most recent master planning process included not only five public visioning sessions, but also an in-depth 800-person multilingual household telephone survey; a photo contest to capture desired images of the city; a city-wide Sustainability Week with a full-scale spectrum of events (the plan's focus was on sustainability); and the utilization of a computer game (Community PlanIt) to capture opinions from those who would not normally attend community meetings.

After Visioning: Implementation and Sustainability

But as suggested earlier, the creation of vision and action plan content, time-consuming as it may be, may ultimately be the least difficult part of the overall task. We should know how to collect data, to plan, to work in groups, and to write. More often than not, the most formidable part is to translate the vision into everyday practice. Once the vision content is created, there's a natural tendency to rest, to feel satisfied, and to think "We've done our job." But that's not so. The vision needs to do work in the real world. In more operational terms, someone has to take charge of the vision and convert it into deliverables.

This can be hard to do, because (1) daily work demands will surface and take priority; because (2) a translated vision suggests that someone would now be accountable for results and thus become open to criticism (when there was no vision, there was no such accountability); but also because (3) no one may actually be responsible for implementing the vision—meaning to generate observable actions felt on the streets. Without implementation, the vision will surely perish, or at best be relegated to a filing cabinet somewhere in the back room.

The original vision of the first author's community's is still the official vision of the town. The actual content can be found on the town's website.[11] There's still an active Vision 2020 Committee, with several equally active task groups. Every year, the Committee mails out a detailed survey to all households on some aspect of town life, which typically yields several thousand returns; these are compiled into an annual report that is made available to government leaders and the public. For all the visioning effort made, has it produced measurable benefits for the townspeople? Very possibly, though that might be hard to demonstrate unequivocally. Is the town itself better off? It very likely is, though that's hard to prove for sure.

Lowell's recent plan, called Sustainable Lowell 2025, is a nearly 200-page document, written in four languages, with not only eight goal areas, but also multiple objectives for each area, multiple action steps per objective, detailed maps, interconnecting flow charts, and a chapter on how the plan is to be implemented.[12] More than most such plans, it emphasizes community building, perhaps because it was in fact primarily written by a community psychologist. What has been its effect in practice? Since the plan was created, there have been managerial changes at the planning office. The daily responsibilities for implementation are not entirely clear. No systematic follow-up assessments of the plan's effects have yet been made. But at this writing, it's too early make a judgment.

To implement a vision calls upon many of the attributes identified earlier, and a few additional ones. Just as at the beginning, it will take desire to do it and, now that it's created, an equivalent implementation commitment. It will take leadership, most naturally from those involved in original vision formation; if government originally took the lead, then that's the likely locus.

More specifically, though, there will need to be a well-defined and written structure through which implementation responsibilities are assigned, along with people who have specific implementation tasks to perform. There will need to be clear and well-communicated procedures for ongoing vision monitoring and review, together with pre-established indicators of success that are regularly measured. Implementation will also mean vision updating, based upon evaluation data and other feedback received, and also taking current developments into account. Rarely will all feedback be glowing. Implementers must be able to accept and act upon less-than-wonderful results openly, nondefensively, and effectively.

Finally, there will need to be mechanisms for communicating and connecting the vision, and whatever planned actions derive from it, with the people in the community. The community's vision may be known to community leaders, but ordinary residents may never have heard of it. To them a "community vision" may seem strange and foreign, far removed from their everyday lives. But if those effects have not somehow percolated down to people where they live, if by virtue of the vision people don't feel a stronger connection to the larger community, then the vision becomes an accomplishment for the governors, but not for the governed.

In other words, a vision must be woven into the fabric of daily community life. How can this be done? By, just for example, State of the Community addresses; community celebration days; piggybacking feedback forms onto routine town mailings; scorecards of progress posted in public places; participatory planning and budgeting; online community forums. There are many ways to do the weaving.

Implementation that incorporates all these aspects won't be easy, and it will be labor intensive, but that is the nature of community practice even when done well. The visioning process may be engaging and rewarding, yet someone will need to do consistent and persistent work. The payoffs may be many, but the shortcuts are few.

SOME IMPLICATIONS FOR COMMUNITY PRACTICE

If we believe in the value of this type of vision for community practice, and see it for the most part as feasible, what will it take to bring it about? That's our next, and last, question of this chapter.

This question is important—it is crucial—because we believe that in the future we *will* need to bring it about. And the short answer is, it will be challenging. It will call upon all the assets we can bring to bear, as professionals and as human beings. It will draw upon our full humanity. We can divide the main attributes needed into those of the head and the heart—or, more precisely, of skill and will.

Skill: Knowledge and Its Applications

It will take considerable and wide-ranging skills to put our vision into place. The more so, since it's not going to be community psychologists doing all or even most of the work directly, simply because there are not nearly enough of us to go around. Community members themselves will need to possess and utilize the skills required to implement our vision.

In particular, it will be those on the front lines—leaders in government, school, nonprofit, health and human service, local media, and business sectors, together with clergy, coaches, grassroots activists—who will need to take primary responsibility.

These are the community's first-line responders; and they are the ones who will need to know how to develop interventions and create desired change successfully in their communities, most often beyond their current skill levels. They will need to know how to assess, plan, design, find members, lead groups, resolve conflicts, publicize, evaluate—to possess all those skills we are supposed to have been trained in as community practitioners, and, hopefully, now utilize in our community worlds.

Some community leaders already have those skills; they've been using them all their adult lives; they may be more proficient than we are. The skill levels of others may be more marginal, or minimal, or less. But if community practice skills are lacking, someone—either ourselves or those we train—will need to teach them. We'll need to use our community skills not simply to engage in practice itself, but to help design systems for teaching those who need to be taught.

All of this has multiple implications for community practice. We start by emphasizing the fundamental skill of knowing the community setting one is working in.

Knowing the community. A vision takes place in a social and environmental context, which means that those creating a community's vision must take that context into account. Just as in persuasion situations, it's essential to know one's audience, in community situations it's essential to know the nature of one's community. "Knowing the community" takes in a lot of territory, but the practical visionary must be a skilled surveyor—of the geography, the history, the demographics, the economics, the politics, the community's resources and access to them. What is the local culture, and what is its belief system? Who are the stakeholders and the potential participants? Who are your potential allies and your potential opponents? Who are the decision makers, and how do they make decisions? What vision goals are realistic and feasible?

All this is necessary groundwork. You probably wouldn't develop the same vision content in a lower-income city as in a higher-toned suburb; the resources and the preferences would very likely differ. Either way, you'd want to know as much as you could before you begin. Being a native will help; native or not, informants and confidants will help too. And you'd want also to develop a sense of what might be happening in the future. What social or environmental factors might augur change—in local officeholders, in funding patterns, in the business climate, in laws and regulations, in national trends? What new threats or opportunities might be waiting in the wings?

One further consideration is the community's readiness for a vision. If a community is in the midst of a crisis, or on the precipice, or if there's a major issue or threat that must now be dealt with, that is not the time for community visioning. Or if a community is just emerging from difficulty, it may need to catch its breath. When things have returned to an even keel, that's likely to be a better time to start a vision process. And then other skills and personal qualities will need to come into play.

But that emphasis on skill development also suggests changes in how we train professionals and educate those in the community.

Training professionals. We need to establish accepted guidelines for community psychology graduate training, to help ensure that essential practice skills are taught, learned, and demonstrated, This training may best take the form of basic competencies and a competency-based curriculum. Students ought to graduate with a practical skill set of competencies, both broad and deep, both empirically grounded and community tested, with sufficient fieldwork opportunities to sharpen skill acquisition. These students—and professionals—need to know how to use those competencies effectively in practice, and in fact to use them in their community settings (see Chapter 14 for more on the topic of community psychology graduate training).

Recent work by SCRA's Council on Education Programs and others has highlighted the value of and need for uniform community psychology competencies (Dalton & Wolfe, 2012). At this writing, an important next step will be to secure widespread adoption and instruction in these competencies in community psychology graduate programs everywhere. Such adoption need not and should not mean that all training programs will be alike. Graduate programs can and should vary, building upon their own unique strengths and contexts. There are considerable gradations between an inflexible curriculum that must be followed to the letter by everyone and no training uniformity at all.

We take a middle ground here, arguing for common general guidelines—or "standards," if one prefers—that graduate program directors can agree upon and abide by. As those guidelines are implemented, and as they evolve over time, they should result in greater community effectiveness and increased likelihood of achieving one's vision, whether it be ours or someone else's. And we should add that much training can of course also be provided in undergraduate community psychology classes, for all college majors, as both prelude and enticement to graduate higher education.

Educating the community. Agreement on basic community competencies and skills should also make it easier to deliver effective community training to diverse community audiences. Along these lines, we can move toward generating and field-testing common skill training curricula, with modular units, adaptable and modifiable for different community settings. Prototypes of such curricula already exist, as in the Training Curriculum of the Community Tool Box (http://ctb.ku.edu/en/training-curriculum); as we proceed, we can refine and improve upon them.

We need to deliver more competency-based community skills training to a wide variety of community groups, for reasons stated earlier in this section. Such delivery will enable us to leverage and maximize our impact. Perhaps more than any other profession, we should know how to do this both in theory and in practice. Fortunately, there are multiple venues where skills training can be delivered. Some examples: college classes in related disciplines; continuing education courses; new civic education curricula in public schools—secondary, but also primary; community adult education centers; neighborhood groups; citizen's academies; and citizen training programs.

There are also plentiful models for such training. For instance, prospective citizen leaders where one of us works can apply for an intensive and competitive year-long leadership training program, with those accepted paying a four-figure fee. But in a different model, university staff have given one-day mini-courses in neighborhood settings ("The University of the Neighborhoods"). And in another, small groups of residents have signed up for a short leadership course together, on completion of which they receive a small cash award to start a community project of their choice. This kind of community training, adapted and refined, can be embedded on an ongoing basis in community life. Every resident ought to learn some basic community skills, just as every resident should learn CPR.

Online training and education. We need more online training opportunities. To bring about our vision, face-to-face training will often be preferred when feasible, but online training can certainly play a positive and powerful role. It's indisputable by now that the impact of online education has been profound and shows no signs of abating. But as we write, we've not fully capitalized on its potential within community psychology (e.g., Berkowitz, 2013).

Online sites such as the Community Tool Box (http://ctb.ku.edu) do teach community-building skills, but surely there is much room for expansion. For example, we can create our own online community-building courses, delivering them for credit through arrangements with other universities. We can develop videos, webinars, and MOOCs. We can add attractive graphics and convert instructional modules into game format.[13] We can mash up our content with the related sites of others. We can greatly enlarge our social media footprint.

And we can extend our online presence beyond formal and institutional settings, opening it to anyone who wants to learn. Much of the untapped potential for community building and community practice lies outside the world's developed countries, where the percentages of those having Internet access are also growing most rapidly. A major part of our disciplinary mission, and of our disciplinary responsibility, should be to give people anywhere in the world the necessary community practice skills so that they can develop and achieve their own community vision.

A marketplace for community ideas. We need to be a marketplace for the exchange of community information and ideas. Training, both direct and indirect, is needed for vision realization. But skill development involves another complementary aspect, which has to do with the exchange of ideas and information.

In communities everywhere, new ideas and new techniques for strengthening community life are always emerging. Many are small in scale, low in cost, simple to apply, effective in practice, and freely adaptable. Many of these ideas also blend well into our community practice vision. Individually they may be fragmentary and unpublicized, but collectively they could bring any community closer to an overarching vision of what community life should be.

Before the Internet, there were few if any ways for these ideas to be known beyond their community boundaries. Now they can be, and many are. Yet still the locations of these ideas, and information about new community initiatives, remain scattered in different domains of cyberspace. What's needed is to bring them together into an integrated site, a one-stop location where any community members could get ideas and information about what's going on in their particular area of interest. It's surprising that this doesn't exist already.[14]

To make that happen would not be extraordinarily difficult. Our current content knowledge gives us a good start. Beyond that, the needed skills would involve the basic competencies already discussed, such as interpersonal skills to build relationships with content providers, publicity skills, and organizational ability, plus a modest amount of technical know-how—coupled, of course, with the vision and the desire to do it. Community psychologists should be leaders in providing this type of community service. And what a contribution to community practice that would be.

Will: Personal Qualities

No matter how much skill we have, or how much we can impart to others, success in realizing our vision will ultimately also rest upon the personal qualities we have within ourselves—qualities not of the head but of the heart, or qualities of will. At the core, and as we've noted, success in almost any enterprise stems first from desire, from the simple but powerful wanting to make something happen, followed by both energy and skill to convert desire into action. Community practice depends upon us as full human beings, upon our affective and moral as well as cognitive selves. Or, in the words of one classic book on human service, "The basic social institution is the individual human heart" (Dass & Gorman, 1985, pp. 164–165).

That truth about personal qualities—for us, a fundamental truth—is too often un- or under-appreciated by community psychologists (and others); it's rarely taught in our community psychology courses. In other disciplines, though, that's not always the case. It is striking to note, for example, that a best-selling management book, written by a Harvard Business School professor, asks corporate managers first to appeal to emotion and feeling rather than logic and fact, and argues that the change process begins with creating a sense of urgency. Readers who want change are advised to "forget trying to persuade them; light their pants on fire" (Kotter & Cohen, 2002, p. 27).

The question then becomes one of where the desire, the urgency, the energy, the personal qualities are going to come from, and that takes us into territory not usually explored by community psychologists, nor by human service professionals of any stripe. There are at least two types of answers to that question, with very different content and consequences.

A possibly easier and possibly true answer is that the needed inner qualities arise from a well-rounded and balanced lifestyle, "balanced" in this case meaning proper attention to nutrition, exercise, sleep, family, friends, and relationships, as well as to work. To these some would add other elements, such as emotional or spiritual grounding, but all of those elements resting on the premises that the community takes on the collective qualities of its members and leaders and that effective community work, at least in the longer run, calls for effective and healthy community workers.

A different answer would instead stress the role of passion, of total emotional engagement and unyielding commitment to the work being done, a stance encapsulated by popular phrases such as "come hell or high water," " leave it all on the playing field," or "give 110% of what you've got." Passion can have multiple sources: Often it stems from anger, even outrage, aroused by a perceived injustice. But in any case the argument is that deep-seated passion, over and above simple motivation, is necessary if not sufficient to do effective work. To move the work down the road may require an alert and careful driver, but also the combustible fuel that passion provides.

One caution about passion is that it needs to be sharply concentrated on the problem, to avoid it being diffused into the atmosphere. But another is that full-bore passionate intensity can pull the practitioner out of balance, causing physical health to be neglected and relationships to be compromised. As the iconic organizer Saul Alinsky (1971) once remarked, "The marriage record of organizers is with rare exception disastrous" (p. 65), and while there is no proven connection between community organizing and marital breakup, the risk is there, and the general point taken. Still, it may be that distinctive, as contrasted with everyday, community practice may in fact mean being pulled out of alignment in the service of the work, and that may be a necessary cost that must be borne.

Which of these viewpoints is correct? If we want to realize our community practice vision, and if will and its associated personal qualities are essential parts of its realization, we would like to know how best to summon, nurture, and sustain them. We hope readers will forgive us if we do not offer a definitive answer—and that is only because we are not entirely sure what the answer is, nor in fact whether there is a single answer generally applicable for all people. Full evidence here is lacking. But to bring this chapter to a provisional summary and conclusion, what we can suggest is this:

LOOKING AHEAD . . .

Effective community practice is important for communities and nations, and will become even more important in coming years. More practitioners, with better developed community competencies, will be needed from both inside and outside community psychology. A vision for community practice is highly desirable, if not absolutely necessary, to stimulate practice development and guide the work. The spirit of the vision we have offered in this chapter is consistent with both community psychology and universal human values, adaptable for different community settings, and well aligned with our projected social and economic future.

That vision is also achievable, in both spirit and substance, in large part if not in whole, since parts of it have already been achieved. To achieve it requires a particular set of community competencies, or skill, as we have described, but also will. Will can be generated in multiple ways. It can be taught by parents, modeled by teachers and community leaders, and honed by successful practice encounters, all of these building on one's natural supply.

How best to generate and mobilize will we must leave for now as an individual matter. While considering this matter, though, we would propose that effective community practice can be, and we believe should be, an activity lasting throughout one's full lifetime. Many readers of this chapter will be of student age, perhaps in their 20s, which means that they could have another 50 years or more of practice work ahead of them. And it's likely there will be no shortage of meaningful work to do 50 years from now.

If you share our attraction and commitment to community practice, and if your own vision bears resemblance to ours, we invite you to join with us in thinking about the long haul. Common questions are then likely to arise: How can one best maintain both productivity and intensity, with both proper balance and undimmed passion, throughout the decades to come? How can community contributions best be maximized? How can one's work best be sustained across a full lifespan, through adulthood and into old age? For any community practitioner, with any community vision, these will be challenges worth reflecting upon and acting upon long after this book is closed.

NOTES

1. One real-life example comes from a survey of citizen well-being conducted by Somerville, Massachusetts, in what has been called the Happiness Project. According to Somerville's mayor: "It may seem odd for a city government to ask people how happy they are. . . . Yet what is the purpose of government if not to enhance the well-being of the public?" See www.somervillema.gov/departments/somerstat/report-on-well-being.

2. See, for example, a street sunflower in Portland, Oregon, described in http://grist.org/cities/2011-12-02-coloring-inside-the-lanes-art-community.

3. For more on actual Poetry Posts, again in Portland, see http://poetrybox.info.

4. Similar sculptures can be found on a residential block in Sebastopol, California; see www-sacbee.com/2013/05/05/5391057/discoveries-on-a-sebastopol-street.html.

5. Some basic background is at www.sapaseniors.org and also www.elderberyy.org/model/asp http://www.elderberry.org/model/asp.

6. A trial attempt in a park in my hometown of Arlington, Massachusetts, (BB) resulted in many interesting commentaries.

7. Many websites offer electronic networking options specifically designed for neighborhoods. In addition to Front Page Forum, described in the McKibben article cited (www.frontpageforum.com), examples include I-Neighbors (www.i-neighbors.org). Neighbortree (www.neighbortree.com), and Nextdoor (www.nextdoor.com). The same goals can also be achieved through more general sites such as Facebook and Google +.

8. SCRA's vision, mission, and goal statements are at http://www.scra27.org/who-we-are/.

9. From the United Nations Millennium Declaration: "We consider certain fundamental values to be essential to international relations in the twenty-first century. These include [summarizing from more detailed descriptions under each value] Freedom, Equality, Solidarity, Tolerance, Respect for nature, and Shared responsibility" (Part I, paragraph 6). See www.un.org/millennium/declaration/ares552e.htm.

10. For a short bibliography on visioning, see www-mrsc.org/subjects/governance/comvision.aspx.

11. Details on Arlington Vision 2020 can be found at www-town.arlingon.ma.us/public_documents/ArtlingtonMA_Vision/index.

12. The current Master Plan for Lowell, Sustainable Lowell 2025, is at www.lowellma.gov/dpd/Documents/Sustainable%20Lowell%202025.pdf.

13. One interesting example of a community-psychology-related game is the Community Organizing Toolkit at http://organizinggame.org.

14. A general compilation of websites that solicit ideas from the public can be found at ideaconnection.com; see www.ideaconnection.com/ideasites. Two sites that solicit ideas of all types are How It Could Be Different (a "Wikipedia for ideas"), at www.howitcouldbedifferent.org, and IdeaStormz, at www.ideastormz.com. But we are not aware of an updatable source that is specifically devoted to ideas for community improvement.

REFERENCES

Alinsky, S. D. (1971). *Rules for radicals: A pragmatic primer for realistic radicals.* New York, NY: Vintage Books.

Berkowitz, B. (Ed.). (2013). Expanding online learning in community psychology: A dialogue. *The Community Psychologist, 46*(2), 16–24.

Buettner, D. (2010). *Thrive: Finding happiness the blue zones way.* Washington, DC: National Geographic Society.

Dalton, J., & Wolfe, S. (2012). Competencies for community psychology practice. *The Community Psychologist, 45*(4), 8–14.

Dass, R., & Gorman, P. (1985). *How can I help Stories and reflections on service.* New York, NY: Knopf.

Fisher, R. (1984). *Let the people decide: Neighborhood organizing in America.* Boston, MA: Twayne.

Hampton, K. N., & Wellman, B. (2003). Neighboring in Netville: How the Internet supports community and social capital in a wired suburb. *City and Community, 2*(3), 277–311.

Julian, D. (2006). Defining community psychology practice: Meeting the needs and realizing the dreams of the community. *The Community Psychologist, 39*(4), 66–69.

Keller, S. (2003). *Community: Pursuing the dream, living the reality.* Princeton, NJ: Princeton University Press.

Kotter, J. P., & Cohen, D. S. (2002). *The heart of change: Real-life stories of how people change their organizations.* Boston, MA: Harvard Business School Press.

Livability.com. (2014). *2014 top 100 best places to live.* Retrieved from http://livability.com/top-100-best-places-to-live

Manuel, F. E., & Manuel, F. P. (1979). *Utopian thought in the Western world.* Cambridge, MA: Belknap Press.

McKibben, B. (2010). Making good neighbors. *Yankee, 74*(2), 86–89.

McKnight, J., & Block, P. (2010). *The abundant community: Awakening the power of families and neighborhoods.* San Francisco, CA: Berrett-Koehler.

MONEY reveals the 2013 list of MONEY's best places to live in America. (2013). *MONEY.* Retrieved from http://www.magazine.org/node/26485

National Civic League. (2000). *The community visioning and strategic planning handbook.* Denver, CO: Author.

Pinker, S. (2002). *The blank slate: The modern denial of human nature.* New York, NY: Viking.

Schwartz, S. H. (1994). Are there universal aspects in the structure and contents of human values? *Journal of Social Issues, 50*(4) 19–45.

United Nations. (2000). *United Nations millennium declaration.* Retrieved May 8, 2014 from http://www.un.org/millennium/declaration/ares552e.htm

Walljasper, J. (2007). *The great neighborhood book: A do-it-yourself guide to placemaking.* Gabriola Island, British Columbia, Canada: New Society.

Wilkinson, R., & Pickett, K. (2009). *The spirit level: Why greater equality makes societies stronger.* New York, NY: Bloomsbury Press.

Author Index

Aarons, G. A., 372
Aase, D. M., 280, 281
Abdul-Adil, J., 276
Aber, M. S., 140
Adams-Leavitt, W., 199
Adeky, S., 201
Ajzen, I., 309
Albee, G., 5, 9
Alexander, J. A., 293, 295, 308, 312
Alinsky, Saul, 224, 274, 432
Allen, A. J., 201
Allen, K. E., 66, 77, 79, 80
Allen, N., 200
Allen, N. A., 305, 306
Allred, S. B., 68
Altman, B. E., 67–68, 70, 84, 96
Alvarez, J., 280, 281
American Evaluation Association
    (AEA), 136, 150
American Heritage Dictionary, 119
American Psychological Association,
    8, 41, 141, 142
Anderson, A. A., 353
Anderson, L., 8
Anderson, P., 244
Anderson-Carpenter, Kaston D., 157
Andrew, M. E., 309
Anoka County Healthy Start, 93
Armenakis, A. A., 244
Arnold, M. S., 265, 266, 267
Aron, D. C., 293, 295, 308, 312
Arthur, M., 160, 161, 166
Asgary-Eden, V., 312
Ashton, M. C., 81
Aspen Institute, 197, 198
Association of American Colleges and
    Universities (AACU), 381
Astin, A. W., 77
Astin, H. S., 77

Auspos, P., 201–202
Austin, A. E., 383
Avellar, J. W., 367
Ayman, R., 80
Azelton, E. E., 76

Backer, T. E., 193, 194, 195, 196, 203
Baird, B. M., 81
Baker, D., 139, 140
Ball, S. A., 81, 272
Ball, V., 270, 271, 274, 275
Bandura, A., 309
Bangi, A., 29, 276
Banks, B., 182
Barker, Roger, 67, 98, 229
Barkhouse, K., 193, 195
Barreiro, T. D., 96
Barton, S., 70
Bateson, G., 70
Becenti-Fundark, T., 140
Becker, A. B., 161
Beebe, J., 302
Beehler, S., 68–69, 75, 76, 83, 101
Behrens, T. R., 70
Bell, E., 273
Bell, R. A., 160
Bellman, G. M., 244
Belza, B., 308
Bennett, C., 8, 40
Benson, E., 70
Berg, M. J., 147
Berkowitz, B., 26, 136, 137, 201, 430
Berkowitz, S. L., 305, 306
Bernhardt, J. M., 354
Bertalanffy, Ludwin von, 65–66
Bierman, K., 317
Biglan, A., 300, 302, 304
Birman, D., 68, 115, 119, 124
Blakely, C. H., 371

Subject Index

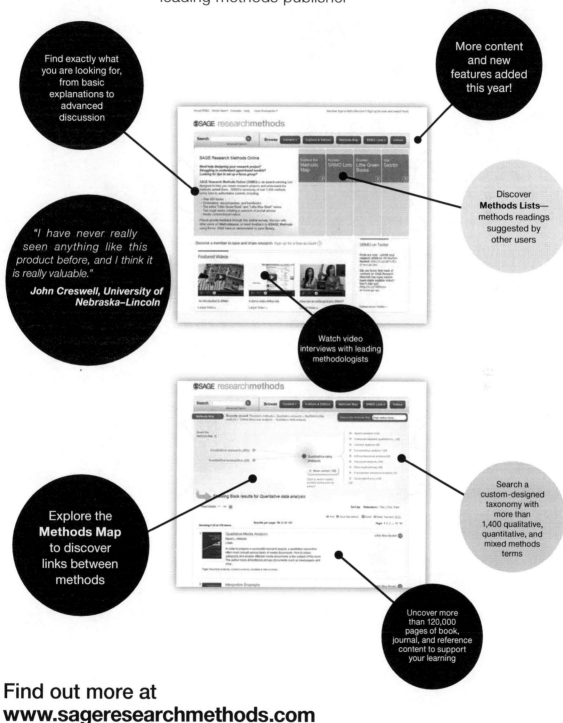

ⓢSAGE research**methods**

The essential online tool for researchers from the world's leading methods publisher

Find exactly what you are looking for, from basic explanations to advanced discussion

More content and new features added this year!

Discover **Methods Lists**— methods readings suggested by other users

"I have never really seen anything like this product before, and I think it is really valuable."

John Creswell, University of Nebraska–Lincoln

Watch video interviews with leading methodologists

Explore the **Methods Map** to discover links between methods

Search a custom-designed taxonomy with more than 1,400 qualitative, quantitative, and mixed methods terms

Uncover more than 120,000 pages of book, journal, and reference content to support your learning

Find out more at
www.sageresearchmethods.com